Lecture Notes in Computer Science   1024

Edited by G. Goos, J. Hartmanis and J. van Leeuwen

Springer
*Berlin
Heidelberg
New York
Barcelona
Budapest
Hong Kong
London
Milan
Paris
Santa Clara
Singapore
Tokyo*

Roland T. Chin   Horace H.S. Ip
Avi C. Naiman   Ting-Chuen Pong (Eds.)

Image Analysis
Applications and
Computer Graphics

Third International Computer Science Conference
ICSC '95
Hong Kong, December 11-13, 1995
Proceedings

 Springer

Series Editors

Gerhard Goos, Karlsruhe University, Germany

Juris Hartmanis, Cornell University, NY, USA

Jan van Leeuwen, Utrecht University, The Netherlands

Volume Editors

Roland T. Chin
Ting-Chuen Pong
Avi C. Naiman
Department of Computer Science
Hong Kong University of Science and Technology
Clear Water Bay, Kowloon, Hong Kong

Horace H.S. Ip
Department of Computer Science, City University of Hong Kong
83 Tat Chee Avenue, Kowloon Tong, Kowloon, Hong Kong

Cataloging-in-Publication data applied for

Die Deutsche Bibliothek - CIP-Einheitsaufnahme

Image analysis applications and computer graphics :
proceedings / Third International Computer Science
Conference, ICSC '95, Hong Kong, December 1995. Roland T.
Chin (ed.). - Berlin ; Heidelberg ; New York ; Barcelona ;
Budapest ; Hong Kong ; London ; Milan ; Paris ; Santa Clara ;
Singapore ; Tokyo : Springer, 1995
  (Lecture notes in computer science ; Vol. 1024)
  ISBN 3-540-60697-1
NE: Chin, Roland T. [Hrsg.]; International Computer Science
  Conference <3, 1995, Hong Kong>; GT

CR Subject Classification (1991): I.3, I.4, I.5, J. 3

ISBN 3-540-60697-1 Springer-Verlag Berlin Heidelberg New York

© Springer-Verlag Berlin Heidelberg 1995
Printed in Germany

Typesetting: Camera-ready by author
SPIN 10512342   06/3142 – 5 4 3 2 1 0   Printed on acid-free paper

Preface

We are very pleased to have the opportunity to organize the 3rd International Computer Science Conference (ICSC'95). The conference is organized and sponsored by IEEE Hong Kong Section, Computer Chapter, in cooperation with the IEEE Computer Society and the International Association of Pattern Recognition. We are also grateful to our sponsors, namely, Silicon Graphics Ltd., Sun Microsystems of California Ltd., Hong Kong Television Broadcasts Ltd., and Motorola Semiconductors Hong Kong Ltd. The technical programme of ICSC'95 focuses on two related areas of visual data processing – Image Analysis Applications and Computer Graphics. We hope that all of you will have a rewarding and pleasant time during the three-day conference in Hong Kong.

We received 155 submissions of full papers from 25 countries in April 1995. This number was larger than we had expected. In order to provide a quality conference and quality proceedings, the Program Committee selected and accepted 76 papers after the review process. Among them, 30 full papers and 21 poster papers are in image analysis applications and 25 full papers are in computer graphics. We must add that the Program Committee and the reviewers have done an excellent job within a tight schedule and we are very pleased with the quality of the papers.

Three eminent invited speakers, Professors Thomas Huang and Narendra Ahuja of University of Illinois, and John Lasseter of Pixar, have contributed to the conference. We are grateful to them. In addition, we would like to express our gratitude to all the contributors, reviewers, Program Committee and Organizing Committee members, and sponsors, without whom the conference would not have been possible.

Finally, we hope that you will benefit from these proceedings.

December 1995

Roland T. Chin
Horace H.S. Ip
Avi C. Naiman
Ting-Chuen Pong

Conference Chair:
Horace H.S. Ip (City U. of Hong Kong)

Program Chair:
Roland Chin (U. of Wisconsin and Hong Kong U. of Science & Technology)

Program Committee:
Image Analysis Co-chair:
Ting-Chuen Pong (Hong Kong U. of Science & Technology)

Computer Graphics Co-chair:
Avi C. Naiman (Hong Kong U. of Science & Technology)

Image Analysis Program Committee:
Jake Aggarwal (U. of Texas)
Narendra Ahuja (U. of Illinois)
Terry Caelli (Curtin U. of Technology)
Chorkin Chan (The U. of Hong Kong)
Francis Chan (The U. of Hong Kong)
Francis Chin (The U. of Hong Kong)
Andrew Choi (The U. of Hong Kong)
Ronald Chung (The Chinese U. of Hong Kong)
Charles Dyer (U. of Wisconsin)
Robert Haralick (U. of Washington)
Thomas Huang (U. of Illinois)
Horace Ip (City U. of Hong Kong)
Anil Jain (Michigan State U.)
Josef Kittler (U. of Surrey)
C.M. Lee (Hong Kong U. of Science & Technology)
Tong Lee (The Chinese U. of Hong Kong)
Zhaoping Li (Hong Kong U. of Science & Technology)
Andrew Luk (City U. of Hong Kong)
Song De Ma (Inst. of Automation, Beijing)
W.Y. Ng (The Chinese U. of Hong Kong)
Linda Shapiro (U. of Washington)
Helen Shen (Hong Kong U. of Science & Technology)
Yoshiaki Shirai (Osaka U.)
Ching Y. Suen (Concordia U.)
Peter Tam (Hong Kong Polytechnic U.)
Demetri Terzopoulos (U. of Toronto)
Peter Tsang (City U. of Hong Kong)
H.T. Tsui (The Chinese U. of Hong Kong)
Saburo Tsuji (Osaka U.)
Andrew Wong (U. of Waterloo)
Guang-You Xu (Tsinghua U.)

Organising Committee:
Secretary: Andrew Layfield (City U. of Hong Kong)
Treasurer: H F Ting (The U. of Hong Kong)
Registration: Joseph Ng (Hong Kong Baptist U.)
Andrew Luk (City U. of Hong Kong)
Publicity: Ronald Chung (The Chinese U. of HK)
H T Tsui (The Chinese U. of Hong Kong)
Tong Lee (The Chinese U. of Hong Kong)
Publications: John C M Lee (Hong Kong U. of Science & Technology)
Local Arragements: Karl Leung (Hong Kong Polytechnic U.)
IEEE (HK) representatives: Richard Chen, L W Chan
ACM (HK) representative: Vincent Wong

Organized and Sponsored by
IEEE Hong Kong Section, Computer Chapter

In cooperation with
IEEE Computer Society
International Association for Pattern Recognition
ACM (HK)

Co-sponsoring organisations:
City University of Hong Kong
Hong Kong Baptist University
Hong Kong Computer Society
Hong Kong Institution of Engineers
Hong Kong Polytechnic University
Hong Kong University of Science and Technology
Hong Kong Society for Multimedia and Image Computing
The Chinese University of Hong Kong
The University of Hong Kong

Sponsored by
Silicon Graphics Ltd.
SUN Microsystems of California Ltd.
Hong Kong Television Broadcasts Ltd.
Motorola Semiconductors Hong Kong Ltd.

Contents

Invited talk

Session IA1a -- Robot Navigation & Tracking

Session CG1a -- Scientific Visualization

Session IA1b -- Feature Matching & Detection

Session CG1b -- Geometric Modeling

Session IA1c -- Document Processing & Character Recognition

Session CG1c -- Rendering

Session IA2a -- 3-D Image Analysis

Session CG2a -- Image Synthesis

Invited Talk

Session IA2b -- Biomedical Imaging

Session CG2b -- Simulation & Animation

Invited Talk

Session CG3a -- Curves & Surfaces

Session IA3b -- Application Systems

Session CG3b -- Human Models

Poster Session

3D Model-based Video Coding:
Computer Vision Meets Computer Graphics

Thomas S. Huang   Li-an Tang

Beckman Institute and Coordinated Science Laboratory
University of Illinois at Urbana-Champaign
405 N. Mathews Avenue, Urbana, IL 61801, U.S.A

Abstract. This paper describes the model-based video coding scheme which combines computer vision and computer graphics techniques. Human face modeling system is used as an example. In this system, a generic 3D face model is used for both facial motion analysis and expression synthesis. The motion trajectories of the feature points are derived using computer vision techniques and computer graphics techniques are used to reconstruct the original motions using the 3D face model and the motion parameters. The potential application of this system in model-based video compression is also discussed in this paper. Some preliminary experimental results show promising future of this approach.

1 Introduction

For many years, computer vision and computer graphics seem to be two isolated areas. Researchers in computer vision have been concentrated in various analysis techniques without paying much attention to how the results could be used for synthesis while people in computer graphics assume known parameters for synthesis and don't care about how the data could be obtained from real world.

In recent years, as researchers seek for collaborations in both areas, analysis-based synthesis and synthesis-based analysis schemes have drawn much attention. More and more researchers have been doing research in combining human facial expression analysis and synthesis [6]. One of many interesting approaches falls into model-based coding technique where an explicit 3D face model is used to analyze and synthesize facial expressions.

Since its first appearance in 1983 by Forchheimer *et al.* [7], the model-based coding method has received much attention because it has also actuated a variety of applications in visual telecommunications [3],[4],[8],[11],[18]. The main idea of this method is to use a 3D face model and derive the facial motion parameters associated with the model structure, then the original facial expressions could be approximately reconstructed using the face model and the motion parameters. It is obvious that these three parts — the face model, facial motion analysis and expression synthesis, constitute a complete model-based coding system. Much significant work has been done for each of these modules.

Face Modeling Many researchers in computer graphics contributed to the construction of 3D human face models. The Parke model [13] was probably the first parameterized face model used for computer animation. Some other face models, such as the physics-based models by Terzopoulos *et al.* [18], the anatomy-based models by Platt and Badler [14] and Waters [20], were built thereafter.

According to the Facial Action Coding System (FACS) developed by the psychologists Ekman and Friesen [5], every facial motion could be defined as a linear combination of several independent basic facial muscle movements called "Action Units"(AUs). The Candide-model designed by Rydfalk [15] was the simplest geometric model which could quantitatively perform almost all AUs. It has been widely used in model-based image coding and some extended versions of this model have been developed [11],[21].

Facial Motion Analysis This is a widely addressed problem in computer vision. There are many algorithms [2] which may be adopted to human facial motions. Basically, the algorithms available for facial motion analysis can be divided into optical flow-based algorithms (*e.g.*, [10],[12]), Feature-based algorithms (*e.g.*, [9],[18]) and Stereo-based algorithms (*e.g.*, [1]).

Facial Expression Synthesis This issue has been studied by many researchers in computer graphics. There are several techniques developed for facial expression animation [19], such as key framing, using FACS parameters and speech driven animation.

We have been developing a complete human face modeling system and trying to solve general problems related to it. We are also seeking potential applications of this system in telecommunications, such as videophone and teleconferencing; in multimedia database management, such as video compression; in security systems, such as face recognition. In the following sections, we shall describe the human face modeling system and its application in model-based very low bit-rate video compression.

2 The Human Face Modeling System

2.1 Fitting the Generic Face Model to Specific Person's Faces

The generic 3D face model is a parameterized wire-frame geometric model. The face surface is approximated by a number of triangular meshes. Currently it consists of 353 vertices and 578 triangles. An interactive human face modeling system has also been developed to build a 3D face model for a particular person. This is done by fitting the generic 3D face model to 2D face images of given person, for example, the front and side profile views. First, a number of key feature points are aligned between the model and the face images. Then a set of interpolation functions are used to locate the remaining vertices to complete the face model. Finally the 2D image intensities are added to the model by texture mapping. Fig. 1 shows the generic face model and the fitting procedure.

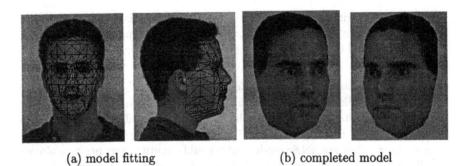

(a) model fitting   (b) completed model

Fig. 1. The modeling procedure

2.2 Obtaining the Motion Parameters

The facial motions in video sequences are represented by motion trajectories of the model vertices. Unlike FACS-based systems, our system will directly use these motion parameters to synthesize facial expressions instead of converting them into combinations of several facial action units(AUs). The latter seems impractical at the moment since it is not quite clear how a specific facial expression can be represented by a combination of several AUs. The motion trajectory of each vertex is estimated using a feature tracking algorithm [16] which uses a motion-based template matching strategy to find the motion of a chosen feature point. The motion trajectories are further linearized into several line segments. Fig. 2 shows a smiling sequence and estimated motion trajectories of the model vertices.

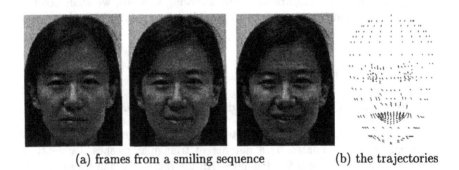

(a) frames from a smiling sequence   (b) the trajectories

Fig. 2. Obtaining motion parameters

2.3 Synthesizing Facial Expressions

We now have both the 3D face model and the facial motion parameters. We are ready to reconstruct the original facial expressions on the face model. The main idea of facial expression synthesis is to dynamically deform the 3D face model based on estimated motion parameters using linear interpolations. There are two kinds of applications where the facial expression synthesis will be required:

- Model-based video compression for videophone/teleconferencing

- Computer animation

For the former, we are actually applying the facial motions to the same person's own face model. We may directly map the motion parameters to the face model to reconstruct original sequences. However, for the latter, since we are usually applying somebody's facial motions to another person's face model, we have to consider different face shapes and scales we used when the images are taken. In other words, directly applying the original motion parameters would possibly result in unexpected effects on synthesized sequences. A local non-rigid mapping algorithm [17] can be used to obtain feasible motion parameters.

In addition, according to different applications, the information needed for interpolation might not be all available. For example, in computer animation, we only have the motion parameters to drive the face model but we do not have the new image intensities matching to the changing models. That is to say, we can only interpolate the motions on the face model but not the image intensities. However, for video compression, both the facial motions and texture information are available so that we can synthesize sequences with facial motions and changing intensities.

3 Application to video compression

3.1 Methodology

As pointed before, one potential application of the human face modeling system is very low bit-rate video compression. We designed an experiment in video compression by frame interpolation. The 3D face model of the person appearing in the scene is built first. The model is then mapped to the person's face in the video and the movements of all vertices of the model are tracked and separated into segments so that the motion trajectories are linearized into motion vectors. The first frame in each segment is also recorded. Linear interpolation technique is then used to create all in-between frames for each segment using the two end frames and the motion vectors. A very low bit-rate video compression system can be constructed in this way.

3.2 Experiments

Sequence synthesis: We collected a real smiling sequence of 20 frames as shown in Fig. 3(a). Every frame had size of 352×288 pixels and each pixel had 8 bits. The total data volume of the original sequence was 1.98 megabytes. The facial motions were nearly linear and uniform during the whole sequence.

Frames 1 and 20 were used as two end frames. Using these two frames and the motion vectors, a sequence shown in Fig. 3(b) was synthesized by interpolating both the motion and intensity changes for each vertex.

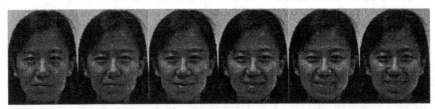

(a) Original smiling sequence (frames 1, 5, 9, 11, 15, 20)

(b) Smiling sequence using model-based codec (frames 1, 5, 9, 11, 15, 20)

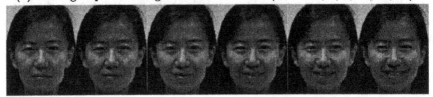

(c) Smiling sequence using H.261 codec (frames 1, 5, 9, 11, 15, 20)

Fig. 3. The original sequence vs. coded sequences

Compression factor: The two end images were encoded using JPEG which gave data volume of 5,551 bytes and 5,622 bytes respectively. Including the face model and the motion trajectories, the total data used to restore the original sequence was 12,705 bytes which resulted in a compression factor of 159.6.

Comparing with H.261: As a comparison, we also encoded this sequence using CCITT H.261 Videoconferencing Coding Standards, as shown in Fig. 3(c), which gave a total compressed data volume of 24,591 bytes. Thus the compression factor of H.261 was 82.4. The compression factor of the model-based coding system was 93.7% larger than that of H.261's.

Error measurement: To see how accurately the original sequence was reconstructed, we calculated mean-squared error per frame between the two sequences. The MSE of two corresponding frames were computed and shown in Fig. 4. The MSE of H.261 encoded sequence is also shown in this figure.

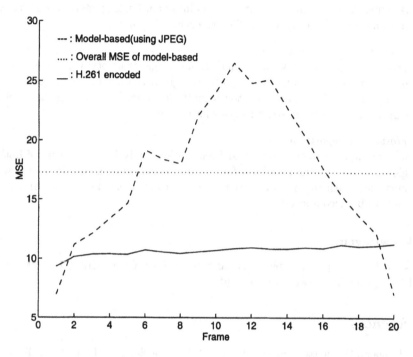

Fig. 4. MSE per frame between the original sequence and encoded sequences

We emphasize that although the model-based results had higher MSE than the H.261 results, subjectively the visual qualities of the two sequences were virtually identical, as we could see from Fig. 3.

4 Conclusion

We have described a human face modeling system and its potential applications. Although much progress has been made in this area, the face modeling system is still in its infancy. Several challenging problems remains.

1. *Better face models*:
   3D modeling of human face is a most important issue. Existing models are either too complex for facial motion analysis or too simple for expression synthesis. A hierarchical face model may be needed to better cope with the face modeling problem.

2. *Automated face model fitting:*
   This is an essential requirement for many applications. It is interesting to see how automatically a generic face model can be fitted to any specific person's face images if certain constraints are maintained. Further effort can be made to remove these constraints while preserving the automation.

3. *Accuracy of face modeling:*
   From the experiments we have made so far, large errors occur in areas where no feature points can be located from the given views, *e.g.*, the cheek areas. One possible solution to this is to use multiple views. The shape of the cheeks can be modified using some intermediate views.

4. *Motion decomposition:*
   The motion parameters obtained from motion analysis may consist of both global head motions and local facial expressions. In some applications, we must deal with the motions separately. That means the motion parameters have to be decomposed.

Acknowledgements

This work was supported by National Science Foundation Grant IRI-8908255 and by a grant from Texas Instruments.

References

1. H. Agawa, G. Xu, etc. "Image Analysis for Face Modelling and Facial Image Reconstruction," *SPIE: Visual Communications and image Processing*, Vol. 1360, 1990, pp. 1184-1197.
2. J. K. Aggarwal and N. Nandhakumar, "On the computation of motion from sequences of images – A review," in *Proceedings IEEE*, August, 1988, pp. 917-935.
3. K. Aizawa and H. Harashima, "Model-based Analysis Synthesis Image Coding System for a Person's Face," *Signal Processing: Image Communication*, Vol. 1, No. 2, 1989, pp. 139-152.
4. K. Aizawa and T. S. Huang, "Model-based image Coding: Advanced Video Coding Techniques for Very Low Bit-rate Applications," *Proceedings of the IEEE*, Vol. 83, No. 2, February 1995, pp. 259-271.
5. P. Ekman and W. V. Friesen, *Facial Action Coding System*, Consulting Psychologists Press, Inc., Palo Alto, California, 1978.
6. P. Ekman, T.S. Huang, T.J. Sejnowski, and J.C. Hager(Eds), "Final Report to NSF of the Planning Workshop on Facial Expression Understanding," Human Interaction Laboratory, University of California, San Francisco, March, 1993.
7. R. Forchheimer and O. Fahlander, "Low Bit-rate Coding Through Animation," in *Proceedings of Picture Coding Symposium*, March 1983, pp. 113-114.
8. M. Kaneko, A. Koike and Y. Hatori, "Coding of Facial Image Sequence Based on a 3D Model of the Head and Motion Detection," *Journal of Visual Communication and Image Representation*, Vol. 2, No. 1, March 1991, pp. 39-54.
9. M. Kass, A. Witkin and D. Terzopoulos, "Snakes: Active Contour models," in *Proceedings of International Conference on Computer Vision*, 1987, pp. 259-269.

10. R. Koch, "Dynamic 3-D Scene Analysis through Synthesis Feedback Control," *IEEE Transactions on Pattern Analysis and Machine Intelligence*, Vol. 15, No. 6, June 1993, pp. 556-568.

11. H. Li, P. Roivainen and R. Forchheimer, "3-D Motion Estimation in Model-Based Facial Image Coding," *IEEE Transactions on Pattern Analysis and Machine Intelligence*, Vol. 15, No. 6, June 1993, pp. 545-555.

12. K. Mase, "Recognition of Facial Expression from Optical Flow," *IEICE Transactions*, Vol. E74, No. 10, October 1991, pp. 3474-3482.

13. F. I. Parke, "Parameterized Models for Facial Animation," *IEEE Computer Graphics and Applications*, Vol. 12, November 1982, pp. 61-68.

14. S. M. Platt and N. I. Badler, "Animating Facial Expressions," *Computer Graphics*, Vol. 15, No. 3, 1981, pp. 245-252.

15. M. Rydfalk, "CANDIDE: A parameterized Face," Technical Report LiTH-ISY-I-0866, Department of Electrical Engineering, Linköping University, Sweden, October 1987.

16. L. Tang, L. S. Chen, Y. Kong, T. S. Huang and C. R. Lansing, "Performance Evaluation of a Facial Feature Tracking Algorithm," in *Proceedings of NSF/ARPA Workshop: Performance vs. Methodology in Computer Vision*, Seattle, Washington, June 1994, pp. 218-226.

17. L. Tang and T. S. Huang, "Analysis-based Facial Expression Synthesis," in *Proceedings of IEEE International Conference on Image Processing*, Vol. III, Austin, Texas, November 1994, pp. 98-102.

18. D. Terzopoulos and K. Waters, "Analysis and Synthesis of Facial Image Sequences Using Physical and Anatomical Models," *IEEE Transactions on Pattern Analysis and Machine Intelligence*, Vol. 15, No. 6, June 1993, pp. 569-579.

19. F. I. Parke, "Techniques for Facial Animation," in *New Trends in Animation and Visualization*, Eds. N. M. Thalmann and D. Thalmann, John Wiley & Sons Inc., 1991, pp. 229-241.

20. K. Waters, "A Muscle Model for Animating Three-Dimensional Facial Expression," *Computer Graphics*, Vol. 21, No. 4, July 1987, pp. 17-24.

21. W. J. Welsh, "Model-based Coding of Images," Ph.D. dissertation, British Telecom Research Laboratories, January 1991.

Autonomous Mobile Robot Navigation Using Fish-Eye Lenses

Shishir Shah and J. K. Aggarwal

Computer and Vision Research Center
Department of Electrical and Computer Engineering
The University of Texas at Austin
Austin, Texas 78712-1084, U.S.A.

Abstract. We present an autonomous mobile robot navigation system using stereo fish-eye lenses for navigation in indoor structured environments. The system estimates the three-dimensional (3D) position of significant features in the environment, and by estimating its relative position, navigates through narrow passages and makes turns at the end of corridors . Fish-eye lenses are used to provide a large field of view, which helps in imaging objects close to the robot. The system is implemented and tested in a structured environment at our laboratory. Results from the robot navigation in real environments are presented.

1 Introduction

The autonomous navigation of mobile robots without human intervention has attracted a number of computer vision researchers over the years. A wide variety of approaches and algorithms have been proposed to tackle this complex problem. The uses of such an autonomous agent range from providing access to hazardous industrial environments to battlefield surveillance vehicles. A number of issues must be addressed in the design of an autonomous mobile robot, from basic scientific issues to state-of-the-art engineering techniques [2]. Complex tasks for navigation cannot be completely programmed *a priori*, thus sensing becomes important in monitoring both the environment and the robot's own internal system. For a review of various techniques the reader is referred to [7].

In this paper, we present a system for autonomous navigation based on binocular stereo using a pair of fish-eye lenses. No *a priori* model is assumed, but the navigation is restricted to an indoor structured environment. Navigating in indoor environments can be very challenging when the environment is narrow and has turns or dead ends which require sharp manuevers of the robot. Conventional visual sensors do not provide enough information to make precise measurements close to the robot and fail to sense areas which exhibit sharp turns in the motion direction. This difference in information is shown by the two images in Figure 1. The system is implemented for a robot (*RoboTex*) that navigates through narrow

* This research was supported by ARO DAAH-04-94-G-0417 and Joint Services Electronics Program Contract F49620-92-C-0027.

passages and makes transitions in motion direction at sharp bends in a structured environment. The lenses are calibrated and distortion corrected before further processing. A specialized line detector is used to extract line segments in three significant 3D orientations. An accurate estimate of the robot's egomotion is obtained from the odometry, corrected by a vision based algorithm which uses vanishing points of the detected lines to accurately estimate the robot's heading, roll, and pitch. Correspondence between the extracted features is established based on an iterative hypothesis estimation and verification procedure to recover depth information [6].

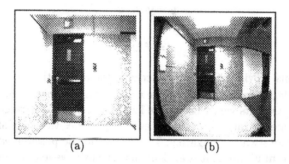

(a) (b)

Fig. 1. (a) Image taken by a wide-angle lens at corridor end. (b) Fish-eye lens image taken from the same position. Note that (b) contains more information about the corridor.

The rest of the paper is organized as follows: Section 2 describes the stereo setup and characteristics of the fish-eye lens and its advantage over conventional lenses. Section 3 discusses the navigation environment. The segmentation approach is described and the representation of the environment using 3D line segments is discussed. Section 4 describes the process of 3D sensing and navigation based on stereo. Experimental results are described in Section 5. Finally, conclusions are presented in Section 6.

2 Visual Sensor

The mobile robot is equipped with two fish-eye lenses configured in a parallel stereo geometry. The sensors are placed so as to maintain a maximum overlap of the viewed images to establish correspondence. The stereo pair used has a calculated focal length of $3.8mm$ and a baseline distance of $398mm$. Using the parallel axis geometry, a disparity value, d, is determined for each matched feature as the difference in their positions on the same horizontal scan line. Any detected two-dimensional (2D) feature in an image is the perspective projection of a 3D feature in the scene. Any number of 3D points can project onto the same 2D point, which results in the loss of depth information. To recover this depth, two images taken from different perspectives are used to establish the transformation relationship between the scene and its projection in the left and right images. As shown in Figure 2, a point P, defined by coordinates (x, y, z) in 3D will project in 2D with coordinates (x_l, y_l) and (x_r, y_r) for left and right images respectively. Knowing the baseline distance, D, which separates the two cameras, and the focal length f, we can define the perspective projections by simple algebra. Considering O to be the origin coinciding with the image center in the left camera:

$$x = x_l.D/d \tag{1}$$

$$y = y_l.D/d \tag{2}$$

$$z = f.D/d \tag{3}$$

These equations provide the basis for deriving the 3D depth from stereo images.

A fish-eye lens provides a field of view which approximates 180° in the diagonal direction. Objects very close to the lens can be imaged with good accuracy. At the same time the large horizontal view also provides valuable information for rotational motions while navigating. This would not be possible using a normal lens. As seen from Figure 1, it is evident that the fish-eye lens senses more information. At the same time, the fish-eye lens image exhibits significant distortion of the information. To make precise quantitative measurements, it is of utmost importance that the lens be properly calibrated and that both the extrinsic and intrinsic parameters be defined. The procedures for calibration are described in [1, 5].

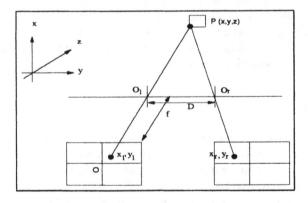

Fig. 2. Stereo system.

3 Robot navigation

The robot navigates in indoor structured environments such as corridors, hallways, etc., based on the 3D information derived by stereo fish-eye lenses along with the robot heading values computed using a vision based algorithm. Visual navigation in indoor structured environments results in the representation of many interesting objects and features by planar patches bounded by linear edges. The 3D orientation of thoses edges often fall in a discrete set of possible orientations. The particular orientations in 3D considered in our approach are the vertical and two horizontal orientations perpendicular to each other. Under the perspective projection geometry, each 3D orientation corresponds to one vanishing point in the image plane. This is the point (possibly at infinity) where all the lines seem to originate from. To segment the images and extract line segments, we employ a specialized line detector which uses the *a priori* knowledge of the locations of the vanishing points [3]. This process can assign the closest 3D orientation to each detected segment. The fish-eye, undistorted, and segmented images are shown in Figure 3. Line segments detected in three orientations are grouped according to their most likely 3D orienatation and are considered for the correspondence problem.

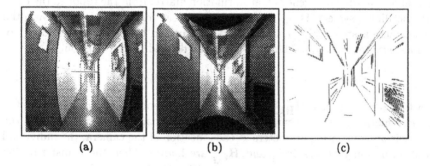

(a)   (b)   (c)

Fig. 3. (a) Fish-eye image. (b) The corrected image. (c) 2D lines extracted in three semantically significant 3D orientations. The dot at the center is the location of the vanishing point of the horizontal lines going into the image plane.

The fish-eye lenses are mounted on the robot, thus the motion of the robot has to be defined with respect to the robot system, as well as the camera system. In order to use quantitative information, the relationship between the robot and camera coordinate systems must be known. Figure 4 shows the world and the robot coordinate systems. The camera is mounted at two positions on the robot. It is assumed that the camera is rigidly attached to the robot. The z-axis is the optical axis of the camera. **W** represents the world coordinate system with a vertical z-axis, $\mathbf{R}$ the robot coordinate system, $\mathbf{C}$ the camera coordinate system, and $\mathbf{P}$ the image coordinate system. If the heading, roll, and pitch of the robot are given by h, r, and p, then the homogenous transformation from the world to the camera coordinate system is given by:

$$H_{WC} = H_{WR}H_{RC} \qquad (4)$$

where $\mathbf{H_{WR}}$ is given by:

$$H_{WR} = T_r \cdot \begin{bmatrix} 1 & 0 & 0 & 0 \\ 0 & \cos p & \sin p & 0 \\ 0 & -\sin p & \cos p & 0 \\ 0 & 0 & 0 & 1 \end{bmatrix} \cdot \begin{bmatrix} \cos h & \sin h & 0 & 0 \\ -\sin h & \cos h & 0 & 0 \\ 0 & 0 & 1 & 0 \\ 0 & 0 & 0 & 1 \end{bmatrix} \cdot \begin{bmatrix} 1 & 0 & 0 & -x \\ 0 & 1 & 0 & -y \\ 0 & 0 & 1 & -z \\ 0 & 0 & 0 & 1 \end{bmatrix}, \qquad (5)$$

where T_r represents the transformation matrix associated with the roll of the camera mount, and x, y and z represent the relative position of the camera mount with respect to the world. For the relationship between the robot and the camera coordinate sytem, given the rotation matrix $\mathbf{M}$ and the translation vector $\mathbf{T}$, the homogenous transformation matrix, $\mathbf{H}$, is given by:

$$H = \begin{bmatrix} M & T \\ 0 \ 0 \ 0 & 1 \end{bmatrix} \qquad (6)$$

To determine the homogenous transformation matrix from the robot to the camera coordinate system, $\mathbf{H_{CR}}$, we need to know the transformations between the two camera systems, $\mathbf{H_{CP}}$, and the transformation between the two robot coordinate systems, $\mathbf{H_{RC}}$. Then $\mathbf{H_{CR}}$ can be defined by the relation:

$$H_{CR}H_{RC} = H_{CP}H_{CR} \qquad (7)$$

For the above equation, $\mathbf{H_{RC}}$ is known from the robot odometry, and $\mathbf{H_{CP}}$, the camera motion, is to be computed from the two images. Having computed the intrinsic and extrinsic parameters at each location of the camera, the individual transformation matrices $\mathbf{H_{Ci}}$ and $\mathbf{H_{Cj}}$ are known. Then the transformation between the two camera systems can be easily calculated.

To accurately determine the robot orientation, we rely both on the odometry and the 3D position estimated by stereo correspondence. The odometers are placed on the left and right wheels of the robot and the average of their reading is taken. Due to slippage, the odometers drift without bounds over long distances and become unreliable measures. This drift is corrected periodically by a vision based algorithm. Although the path of the robot is calculated at each step using both the 3D depth estimate and robot pose from vanishing point, the initial estimate of motion direction is based on the estimated depth. When the depth estimate falls below a threshold, the robot must make a change in its navigating direction. This change in direction is based on the horizontal depth estimate. After making an initial rotation, the robot pose is once again estimated and corrected to move towards the vanishing point.

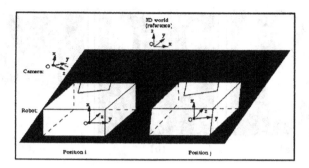

Fig. 4. Coordinate Systems.

4 3D sensing

The mobile robot navigates based on extracted 2D features from the image scene. The features in the stereo images are matched using an iterative hypothesis verification algorithm [6]. From the line correspondences and the predetermined camera parameters, an inverse perspective geometry is used to recover the 3D information. The robot then integrates the information with its pose information and calculates the motion step. Having grouped the extracted line segments into their most likely 3D orientation, the stereo matching problem is greatly simplified. We consider only the lines oriented in the vertical and horizontal direction. The other horizontal direction going into the image plane is ignored, as no definite starting and ending points are known, and thus it will give inaccurate 3D information. The procedure for correspondence is detailed in [6].

A simple process of triangulation can be used to recover the depth information given the corresponding line matches. The projected line in the 2D images represents a plane in 3D. We consider the two end points of each matched line, and determine its 3D location. Each 3D point is represented by a vector $(x, y, z)^T$ and a covariance matrix $cov(x, y, z)$. Representing a 3D line in the parametric form with parameters (a, b, c), the 3D plane can then be represented by:

$$ax + by + cz = d \tag{8}$$

where the uncertainity is captured by $cov(a, b, c)$ and $var(d)$. Thus a plane is defined by each end point of a matched 2D line. Two planes corresponding to the respective end point are represented according to equation 8. Figure 5 shows the 3D depth estimated from a pair of stereo images.

5 Experimental Results

The system has been implemented on *RoboTex*, a TRC Labmate based mobile robot [4]. The robot is 1.5 meters (59.5 inches) tall, 0.65 meters (26 inches)

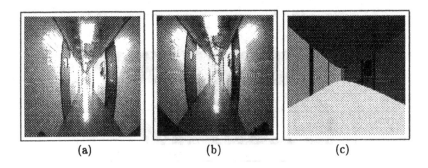

(a)   (b)   (c)

Fig. 5. (a), (b) A stereo pair imaged by fish-eye lenses in a corridor scene. (c) The 3D depth map as estimated.

wide, and weighs about 150 kg. The robot uses Panasonic WV-CD 50 cameras mounted with fish-eye lenses from Toyo Optics that have an effective focal length of 3.8mm. The captured image size is 512 by 480. Numerous runs were made to qualitatively estimate the accuracy of the navigation algorithm. *RoboTex* was able to navigate through narrow passages and make rotations at corridor ends. Figure 6 shows three frames from a typical scene of a real corridor which is approximately 1814.4mm (72 inches) in width, and has been narrowed to 882mm (35 inches). These images are as seen by the robot during navigation. Figure 7 shows three frames as seen by the robot during navigation around the corridor bend. These images show qualitatively the effectiveness of the algorithm. The accuracy of the calculated 3D estimates can be found in [6].

Fig. 6. Three successive images from a typical sequence while navigating through a narrow passage.

Fig. 7. Five successive images from a typical sequence while navigating and turning at a corridor end.

6 Conclusion

In this paper we have presented a system for autonomous mobile robot navigation based on a stereo pair of fish-eye lenses that is capable of navigating through narrow corridors and making rotations at corridor ends. The system has been implemented for navigation in a man-made environment where no *a priori* map is available. Using fish-eye lenses, we are able to estimate 3D information at close range to the robot and to sense the environment in more detail than is possible by using conventional lenses. The system is implemented and the robot successfully navigates through passages with clearance of 4 inches on either side. The robot also makes rotations at 90° corridor turns.

References

1. Y. Chang, X. Lebègue, and J. K. Aggarwal. Calibrating a mobile camera's parameters. *Pattern Recognition*, 26(1):75–88, 1993.
2. I. J. Cox and G. T. Wilfong. *Autonomous Robot Vehicles*. Springer–Verlag, New York, 1990.
3. X. Lebègue and J. K. Aggarwal. Detecting 3-D parallel lines for perceptual organization. In *Proc. Second European Conf. on Computer Vision*, pages 720–724, Santa Margherita Ligure, Italy, May 1992. Springer-Verlag.
4. X. Lebègue and J. K. Aggarwal. Robotex: An autonomous mobile robot for precise surveying. In *Proc. Int. Conf. Intelligent Autonomous Systems*, pages 460–469, Pittsburgh, Pennsylvania, February 1993.
5. S. Shah and J. K. Aggarwal. A simple calibration procedure for fish-eye (high distortion) lens camera. In *Proc. of Int. Conf. on Robotics and Automation*, pages 3422–3427, San Diego, California, 1994.
6. S. Shah and J. K. Aggarwal. Depth estimation using stereo fish-eye lenses. In *Proc. of Int. Conf. on Image Processing*, pages 740–744, Austin, Texas, 1995.
7. S. Shah and J. K. Aggarwal Modelling structured environments using robot vision: A review. To appear in *Proc. Third Int. Computer Science Conf.*, Singapore, 1995.

High-Performance Tracking System

Jiantao Huang

Yale University
New Haven, CT 06520
USA

Jian-zhao Wang

Polytechnic University
Brooklyn, NY 11201
USA

Abstract. In this paper, we describe how reliable SSD feature selection, feature tracking and feature monitoring can be realized and interleaved into a high-performance system with no special-purpose hardware. We consider image brightness and contrast changes in the tracking system which haven't been treated before. We find the decoupled system outperforms the usual coupled system. We perform this calculation at multiple levels of resolution, leading to an adaptive algorithm for tracking both slow and fast motions. A new interpretation of feature selection is based on the trade off between noise resistance and linearization error. The overcorrectness problem in feature monitoring is addressed.

1 Introduction

The central question in visual tracking is the temporal correspondence problem: how to relate two regions of an image taken at two closely-spaced time instants. A popular means for performing temporal correlation on unstructured images is to minimize the sum-of-square differences, often referred to as SSD tracking. The advantage of SSD tracking is its simplicity and versatility. In particular, since it is a correlation-based scheme, it can track both image regions which have gross structure (*e.g.* corners) as well as image regions which are pure textures.

We have addressed the following issues:

- *Feature tracking*: The tracker must operate in real time using minimal hardware support and tolerate to some extent of feature changes.
- *Feature selection*: It must be possible to quickly choose the n most robust trackable features in an image, and the appropriate tracker configuration for tracking them.
- *Feature monitoring*: It must be possible to determine that the accuracy of tracking for a given feature is degrading.

2 SSD Tracking

SSD tracking relies on the *image constancy assumption* which states that two images separated by a brief time instant differ only by a geometric distortion. It is well-known that the geometric distortions of an image are well-approximated locally by an affine transformation [1].

We use a continuous optimization approach, however, different from Shi and Tomasi's method[2], we integrate interframe changes over time so that we are constantly computing the match between the initial and the current frame.

2.1 SSD Tracking for Mobile Systems

Consider the image distortions that occur in a series of frames from a mobile system moving on a level surface with the camera nearly parallel to the surface. If we consider a small region of the image corresponding to a locally planar patch of the world, it is easy to show that the major components of image distortion are: translation, scaling in the x,y direction and the possible brightness or contrast changes. Rotation is not present, and scaling in non-orthogonal directions is inconsequential over the field of view of the camera.

Thus our image constancy constraint is

$$J(\mathbf{S}\mathbf{x} + \mathbf{x}_c) = cI(\mathbf{x} - \mathbf{d} + \mathbf{x}_c) + b + N(\mathbf{x}) \tag{1}$$

where

$I(\mathbf{x}) \stackrel{df}{=} I(\mathbf{x},t)$ and $J(\mathbf{x}) \stackrel{df}{=} I(\mathbf{x},t+\tau)$, $\tau > 0$.

$\mathbf{S}$ is a diagonal matrix with entries $\mathbf{s} = (s_x, s_y)^T$ which are the scale coefficients in the x and y directions, respectively.

$\mathbf{x} = (x, y)^T$ is the image coordinates.

$\mathbf{x}_c = (x_c, y_c)^T$ is the center of the identified region.

$\mathbf{d} = (dx, dy)^T$ is the translation.

b is the brightness variable and c is the contrast variable.

N is a noise process indexed by pixel coordinates.

Given a spatial extent represented as set of image locations, $\mathcal{W}$, our question becomes, at an image location $\mathbf{x}_c$, to find $\mathbf{d}, \mathbf{S}, b$ and c which minimize

$$O(\mathbf{d}, \mathbf{S}, b, c) = \sum_{\mathbf{x} \in \mathcal{W}} [cI(\mathbf{x} - \mathbf{d} + \mathbf{x}_c) + b - J(\mathbf{S}\mathbf{x} + \mathbf{x}_c)]^2 w(\mathbf{x}). \tag{2}$$

where $w(\cdot)$ is a weighting function over the image region.

Usually s_x and s_y are close to one. Define the *biased scale coefficients* $s'_x \stackrel{df}{=} s_x - 1$, $s'_y \stackrel{df}{=} s_y - 1$ and let $\mathbf{S}'$ denote a diagonal matrix with entries $\mathbf{s}' = (s'_x, s'_y)^T$. Similarly, c is also close to one and define the *biased contrast variable* $c' \stackrel{df}{=} c - 1$. Let $b = b^- + \Delta b$, where b^- is the brightness variable integrated until last tracking cycle, and Δb is the increase in current tracking cycle.

Because $\mathbf{d}, \mathbf{s}', \Delta b$ and c' are close to zero, we expand I and J in a Taylor series truncated to the linear order and rearranging yields

$$O(\mathbf{d}, \mathbf{s}', \Delta b, c') = \sum_{\mathbf{x} \in \mathcal{W}} [h(\mathbf{x}) + b^- - \mathbf{g}(\mathbf{x}) \cdot \mathbf{d} - \mathbf{f}(\mathbf{x}) \cdot \mathbf{s}' + \Delta b + c'I]^2 w \tag{3}$$

where,

$$h(\mathbf{x}) = I(\mathbf{x} + \mathbf{x}_c) - J(\mathbf{x} + \mathbf{x}_c)$$

$$\mathbf{g}(\mathbf{x}) = \begin{bmatrix} g_x(\mathbf{x}) \\ g_y(\mathbf{x}) \end{bmatrix} = \left.\frac{\partial I}{\partial \mathbf{x}}\right|_{\mathbf{x}+\mathbf{x}_c}$$

$$\mathbf{f}(\mathbf{x}) = \begin{bmatrix} g_x(\mathbf{x})x \\ g_y(\mathbf{x})y \end{bmatrix}.$$

In the sequel, let $\overline{\zeta} \stackrel{df}{=} \sum_{\mathbf{x} \in \mathcal{W}} \zeta(\mathbf{x})w(\mathbf{x})$ for an arbitrary function ζ of image locations.

Coupled System Taking derivatives and rearranging, we arrive at a linear 6 × 6 *system* of the form

$$
\begin{bmatrix}
\overline{\mathbf{gg}^T} & \overline{\mathbf{gf}^T} & -\overline{\mathbf{g}} & -\overline{I\mathbf{g}} \\
\overline{\mathbf{fg}^T} & \overline{\mathbf{f}\,\mathbf{f}^T} & -\overline{\mathbf{f}} & -\overline{I} \\
-\overline{\mathbf{g}^T} & -\overline{\mathbf{f}^T} & \overline{xy} & \overline{I} \\
-\overline{I\mathbf{g}^T} & -\overline{I^T} & \overline{I} & \overline{I^2}
\end{bmatrix}
\begin{bmatrix}
\mathbf{d} \\ s' \\ \Delta b \\ c'
\end{bmatrix}
=
\begin{bmatrix}
\overline{(h+b)\mathbf{g}} \\ \overline{(h+b)\mathbf{f}} \\ -\overline{(h+b)} \\ -\overline{(h+b)I}
\end{bmatrix}
\tag{4}
$$

Similarly, if we ignored the contrast variation, we obtained a linear 5 × 5 *system* of the form

$$
\begin{bmatrix}
\overline{\mathbf{gg}^T} & \overline{\mathbf{gf}^T} & -\overline{\mathbf{g}} \\
\overline{\mathbf{fg}^T} & \overline{\mathbf{f}\,\mathbf{f}^T} & -\overline{\mathbf{f}} \\
-\overline{\mathbf{g}^T} & -\overline{\mathbf{f}^T} & \overline{xy}
\end{bmatrix}
\begin{bmatrix}
\mathbf{d} \\ s' \\ \Delta b
\end{bmatrix}
=
\begin{bmatrix}
\overline{(h+b)\mathbf{g}} \\ \overline{(h+b)\mathbf{f}} \\ -\overline{(h+b)}
\end{bmatrix}
\tag{5}
$$

Or if the image is scaled with constant aspect ratio, the s' is degraded to a single scale parameter s'. A linear 5 × 5 *system* results

$$
\begin{bmatrix}
\overline{\mathbf{gg}^T} & \overline{v\mathbf{g}} & -\overline{\mathbf{g}} & -\overline{I\mathbf{g}} \\
\overline{v\mathbf{g}^T} & \overline{v^2} & -\overline{v} & -\overline{Iv} \\
-\overline{\mathbf{g}^T} & -\overline{v} & \overline{xy} & \overline{I} \\
-\overline{I\mathbf{g}^T} & -\overline{Iv} & \overline{I} & \overline{I^2}
\end{bmatrix}
\begin{bmatrix}
\mathbf{d} \\ s' \\ \Delta b \\ c'
\end{bmatrix}
=
\begin{bmatrix}
\overline{(h+b)\mathbf{g}} \\ \overline{(h+b)v} \\ -\overline{(h+b)} \\ -\overline{(h+b)I}
\end{bmatrix}
\tag{6}
$$

where $v(\mathbf{x}) = g_x(\mathbf{x})x + g_y(\mathbf{x})y$.

If we ignored both Δb and c', we obtained a 4 × 4 *system*

$$
\begin{bmatrix}
\overline{\mathbf{gg}^T} & \overline{\mathbf{gf}^T} \\
\overline{\mathbf{fg}^T} & \overline{\mathbf{f}\,\mathbf{f}^T}
\end{bmatrix}
\begin{bmatrix}
\mathbf{d} \\ s'
\end{bmatrix}
=
\begin{bmatrix}
\overline{h\mathbf{g}} \\ \overline{h\mathbf{f}}
\end{bmatrix}
\tag{7}
$$

which can be simply represented by

$$
\mathbf{TD} = \mathbf{H}
\tag{8}
$$

where

$\mathbf{T}$ is a 4 × 4 symmetrical matrix. Note that $\mathbf{T}$ can be written in the form

$$
\mathbf{T} =
\begin{bmatrix}
\mathbf{G} & \mathbf{V} \\
\mathbf{V}^T & \mathbf{F}
\end{bmatrix}
\tag{9}
$$

$\mathbf{D}$ is the column vector of shifts and scale coefficients we seek, and
$\mathbf{H}$ is a column vector related to the difference between two regions.

Decoupled System The direct solution to the above systems requires the inversion of a 6 × 6 or 5 × 5 or 4 × 4 matrix and is time consuming. In many cases the image structure may not fully constrain the complete set of parameters, leading to a singular system of equations. A pseudo-inverse can be used to approximately invert the system when it's not full rank, however this is extremely time-consuming, and may lead to unwanted parameter choices.

To overcome those difficulties, we observe that changes in the scale, brightness and contrast of the image are generally much smaller than the translations of the image. This suggests that, locally, scale, brightness or contrast have little effect on the values computed for image translation. Conversely, given two image regions which have been registered via translation, scale, brightness and contrast can be accurately computed. We take advantage of this observation to decouple (7), by sequentially solving the following two linear systems

$$\mathbf{Gd} = \overline{\mathbf{gg}^T}\mathbf{d} = \overline{h\mathbf{g}} = \mathbf{H}_G \tag{10}$$

$$\mathbf{Fs}' = \overline{\mathbf{f}\,\mathbf{f}^T}\mathbf{s}' = \overline{(h - \mathbf{g} \cdot \mathbf{d})\mathbf{f}} = \mathbf{H}_F \tag{11}$$

This can be viewed as a coordinate descent algorithm which optimizes along the translation subspace to register the image, and then optimizes along the scale subspace to accommodate any other image deformations. In the sequel, we refer to (10) and (11) as the *decoupled* system, and (4),(5),(6),(8) as the *coupled* system.

If only a single scale parameter and the translation are computed, the coupled system is:

$$\mathbf{U}\begin{bmatrix} \mathbf{d} \\ s \end{bmatrix} = \begin{bmatrix} \mathbf{G} & \overline{\mathbf{g}v} \\ \overline{\mathbf{g}^T v} & \overline{v^2} \end{bmatrix}\begin{bmatrix} \mathbf{d} \\ s \end{bmatrix} = \begin{bmatrix} \overline{h\mathbf{g}} \\ \overline{hv} \end{bmatrix} \tag{12}$$

where v has the same definition as that in (6).

The corresponding decoupled equations are:

$$\mathbf{Gd} = \overline{\mathbf{gg}^T}\mathbf{d} = \overline{h\mathbf{g}} \tag{13}$$

$$\overline{v^2}s = \overline{(h - \mathbf{g} \cdot \mathbf{d})v} \tag{14}$$

Computationally, the decoupled systems are clearly more efficient than the coupled systems. Furthermore, by separating the computations and computing translation first, translation is allowed to dominate the calculation. Hence, even when the coupled system is singular, the decoupled system will compute a consistent translation. Finally, even when the system is nonsingular, the conditioning of the coupled system is likely to be bad due to the large discrepancy between the effect of translation and scaling on the image. Separating the calculations clusters calculations which have similar conditioning.

By experiments, we know that all decoupled approaches are faster than the corresponding coupled systems, and both appear to be nearly with the same accuracy, so there is a clear advantage to decouple the calculations.

2.2 Hierarchical Tracking

One of the drawbacks of the continuous optimization approach is that it is only guaranteed to work for motions of smaller than a pixel. Furthermore, the linear approximation introduces errors in the calculation of shift and scale. These drawbacks can be obviated by using a hierarchical tracking in which an image pyramid is constructed. Level n is the pyramid computed by increasing the resolution of the image at level $n - 1$ by a factor of two. Tracking begins on a low resolution image (the top of the pyramid) and proceeds toward higher resolutions. If, at any level n, the magnitudes of both dx and dy is smaller than some threshold, tracking terminates at that level. In the next tracking cycle, processing begins at level $n + 1$ (one level lower in the pyramid) and again proceeds downward. This approach ensures that the tracking is performed on the highest possible resolution image, acceleration is accounted for, and the number of SSD computations is minimized.

We note that, it is always possible to process the entire pyramid by using the offsets computed at one resolution to register the two images for processing at the next higher level of resolution. However, a large offset computed at a low resolution indicates fast motion. The computation of SSD at low resolution is faster than at high resolution, so this algorithm has the advantage that it adapts tracking speed and resolution to the magnitude of feature motion automatically.

If scaling information is also needed, once the highest possible resolution image is processed and the offsets are found, the biased scale coefficients are computed on that image using (11) or (14) as appropriate.

2.3 A Control System Point of View

SSD tracking is easily implemented using a window management system that supports acquisition of image regions given location and size. The shift computed above are integrated, and the integrated values are used to predict the new location of the region. This prediction can be augmented with a dynamic model, if appropriate. Figure 1 shows the system for pure translation (10).

We have included an amplifying coefficient λ in the tracking loop. By adjusting this gain, the reactivity and noise sensitivity of the tracker can be adjusted.

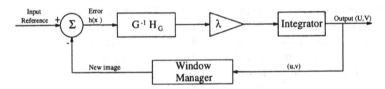

Fig. 1. Closed-loop control diagram of visual tracking.

3 A Framework for Feature Selection

The goal of our feature selection framework is to choose the best n features in an image which have specific scaling properties, *e.g.* scale invariance.

3.1 Basic Theory and Observations

The goal of feature selection is to find features which are resistant to a variety of disturbing influences including image noise. At the same time, feature tracking is subject to errors due to linearization. We express the error between the computed image offset $\mathbf{d}$ and the real offset $\hat{\mathbf{d}}$ as the sum of two terms—a linearization bias $\mathbf{b}$ and a stochastic error $\mathbf{v}$:

$$e_d = \mathbf{d} - \hat{\mathbf{d}} = \mathbf{b} + \mathbf{v} \qquad (15)$$

To understand the effect of image noise, let us assume that there is no motion, and that image noise is zero mean and spatially and temporally uncorrelated with a variance of σ_h^2. From (10), it is easy to show that the covariance matrix of $\mathbf{v}$ is:

$$\Lambda_d = 2\sigma_h{}^2\mathbf{G}^{-1} \tag{16}$$

To understand how this error varies for different types of images, first note that a linearly varying image (in which the gradients are constant), leads to a singular system $\mathbf{G}$. Hence, images which are near linear will be extremely sensitive to noise. Conversely, since these images are nearly linear, the Taylor series approximation will introduce less error, so $\mathbf{b}$ will be relatively small.

Conversely, consider tracking a 32 by 32 black and white image of a corner covering one fourth of the reference image with a gray value standard deviation of 1% of the full dynamic range, we compute the eigenvalues of the covariance matrix Λ_d. The results are between 3.94×10^{-6} and 61.04×10^{-6} from the highest to the lowest resolution and roughly doubles for each halving of image resolution. We see that the variance is extremely low.

To summarize the discussion, it seems that the features which are best at noise resistance are sharp edges and corners. However, these features introduce the largest estimation bias in linear approximation, while the features which minimize estimation bias are most sensitive to noise. By using the hierarchical calculation, we largely mitigate the effect of estimation bias at the expense of a slight increase in noise sensitivity.

This leads us to define a ranking function for feature selection which emphasizes the reduction of noise sensitivity. Assume that image noise is constant throughout the image. For an image region i, let $\mathbf{G}_i$ be the matrix computed in (10) from the image at the lowest allowed tracking resolution. Let λ_i be the minimum eigenvalue of $\mathbf{G}_i$. For an image with N candidate regions, define π_k to be the kth order statistic of the sequence $\lambda_1, \lambda_2, \ldots \lambda_N$. Then , we choose all regions $i_1, i_2, \ldots i_n$, $n \leq N$ such that $\lambda_{i_k} \geq \pi_{N-n}, 1 \leq k \leq n$. Under the assumption that image noise variables are independent and identically distributed, this will choose regions with the largest minor eigenvalue of the matrix $\mathbf{G}_i$. If image noise is not identically distributed, the calculation should also include σ_h^2 for that region. Also, note that the same ordering scheme will work for $\mathbf{U}$ or $\mathbf{T}$ if scaling must be taken into account.

3.2 Accounting for Scaling

In most cases, the ideal feature to track is one which is scale-invariant. An image region at a particular resolution is scale-invariant when the $\mathbf{T}$ and $\mathbf{G}$ for that region and resolution both have rank two.

Occasionally, it is useful to be able to monitor the scale changes of features. In particular, changes in scale provide information about changes in distance. If $\mathbf{T}$ has rank 3 and $\mathbf{G}$ has rank 2, then the corresponding image region has a single scale parameter. Similarly, if $\mathbf{T}$ is full rank, then both position and scale can and must be computed while tracking.

These scaling notions can be incorporated into the feature selection process as a hard constraint. For example, if the goal is to choose features which are scale invariant, then the objective is to choose an image region which maximizes the minimum eigenvalue of **G** and for which **T** is of rank two. If the objective is to choose features with a single scale parameter, then image regions can be first ranked by the minimum eigenvalue of **U**. This list is traversed to choose the first n candidates for which the smallest eigenvalue of **T** is smaller than a threshold τ. If all four parameters are desired, then image regions are ranked using the minimum eigenvalue of **T**.

4 Feature Monitoring

The goal of feature monitoring is to maintain an estimate of the "trackability" of a feature as the image undergoes substantial changes. Since SSD value describes the difference between the reference feature and the current feature, it's a reliable value to monitor the degeneration. To have a reliable feature monitoring, the brightness and contrast issues must be considered in the residue calculation. It's more accurate to use the optimized SSD value for this purpose. After computing the set of desired parameters **d**,s',Δb and c', the optimized SSD value is computed by (3).

If this value is above a threshold, the feature is rejected as a bad match. Occurrences which cause a bad match include: shading changes in the region, partial occlusion, mistracking, or serious distortion in nonorthogonal directions.

The *overcorrectness* problem is observed in which two unmatched features are associated by a very small residual SSD value because of some strange sets of parameters. For instance, any region can be matched with a constant 255 region by applying $c = 0$ (contrast) and $b = 255$ (brightness compensation) in (1). This drawback is obviated by our feature monitoring system.

5 Tracking System

As noted at the outset, we have produced a system which can perform feature selection, tracking and monitoring simultaneously and without pause. When performing feature selection while the system is moving, it is not enough to simply evaluate a set of image regions and select the best. Since the image is changing, these regions move over time and must be tracked while the selection process is being performed.

Our feature selection scheme always maintains a list of the most promising features found so far. This list of features is constantly tracked, and further evaluation of image regions is interleaved with the tracking process. If an image region which is better than any on the current list is found or one active tracked feature becomes obviously bad, the "worst" feature is dropped, and the candidate region is added as a feature. After the entire image is traversed, all currently tracked features (both those just found and any other actively tracked features) are evaluated, and the overall winners are retained. In this way, the system constantly maintains a list of the most trackable features without needing to pause and perform an explicit feature selection step.

In Figure 2, images in time sequences are shown. In the left image, six good features were chosen automatically by the system. Then the system kept tracking and monitoring them. A book was pushed in to occlude the features gradually. As soon as one or more features were occluded, the feature monitoring triggered the system to drop those bad features and adopt the top features in the current waiting list.

Fig. 2. Architecture of interleaving feature selection, tracking and monitoring together.

6 Conclusions

We have implemented a system for performing selection, tracking and monitoring of arbitrary features. Our system is fast and reliable in real-time experiment on a standard workstation. We are continuing to develop this system in a number of ways, such as the automatical choice of window size.

7 Bibliography

References

1. A. Blake, R. Curwen, and A. Zisserman. Affine-invariant contour tracking with automatic control of spatiotemporal scale. In *Proc. Internal Conf. on Computer Vision*, pages 421–430. IEEE Computer Society Press, 1993.
2. J. Shi and C. Tomasi. Good features to track. In *Proc. IEEE Conf. Comp. Vision and Patt. Recog.*, pages 593–600. IEEE Computer Society Press, 1994.
3. C. Tomasi and T. Kanade. Shape and motion from image streams: a factorization method, full report on the orthographic case. CMU-CS 92-104, CMU, 1992.
4. P. Anandan. A computational framework and an algorithm for the measurement of structure from motion. *Int. Journal of Computer Vision*, 2:283–310, 1989.
5. B. D. Lucas and T. Kanade. An iterative image registration technique with an application to stereo vision. In *Proc. Int. Joint Conf. Artificial Intelligence*, pages 674–679. 1981.
6. N. Papanikolopoulos, P. Khosla, and T. Kanade. Visual tracking of a moving target by a camera mounted on a robot: A combination of control and vision. *IEEE Trans. on Robotics and Automation*, 9(1), 1993.

A 3D Predictive Visual Tracker for Tracking Multiple Moving Objects with a Stereo Vision System

Yi-Ping Hung[1], Cheng-Yuan Tang[2], Sheng-Wen Shih[3],
Zen Chen[2], Wei-Song Lin[3]

[1]Institute of Information Science, Academia Sinica, Taipei, Taiwan

[2]Institute of Computer Science & Information Engineering,
National Chiao Tung University, Hsinchu, Taiwan

[3]Institute of Electrical Engineering, National Taiwan University, Taipei, Taiwan

Email: hung@iis.sinica.edu.tw

Abstract. This paper presents a 3D feature-based visual tracker for tracking multiple moving objects by using a predictor that first partitions 3D features into different common-motion clusters and then predicts the motion of each cluster with Kalman filters. The 3D features are computed from a sequence of stereo images by combining two 2D temporal matching modules and one stereo correspondence module. To partition the 3D features into different common-motion clusters, we propose a RANSAC-based clustering method by using *rigid body consensus* which assumes that all the extracted 3D features on a rigid body have the same 3D motion. By using the motion estimates obtained with the RANSAC-based method as the measurements, we are able to use *linear* Kalman filters to predict the motion of each cluster, and then, to predict the next position of each 3D feature. Preliminary experiments showed that the proposed 3D predictive visual tracker can serve as a robust 3D feature tracker for an active stereo vision system.

1 Introduction

Active vision is becoming an important field in computer vision. Due to the availability and popularity of the experimental equipments, active vision can be expected to receive more attention in the field of computer vision and robotics. There are many interesting and important problems in active vision, including gaze control, attention shift, hand-eye coordination, and object tracking. In this paper, we present a new 3D feature-based predictive visual tracker for tracking multiple moving objects in a cluttered environment with a computer-controlled binocular head.

The work closest in spirit to ours is the recent work by Cheng and Kitchen [2]. They also used the rigid body constraint in motion clustering and estimation. However, their motion estimation method was nonlinear and their motion clustering algorithm was quite primitive, which made their results sensitive to noise and initial guesses. Furthermore, the initial stereo correspondences were selected manually in their system, and the motion model they used could not even describe a constant angular velocity motion, not to say long term motion behavior.

Another related work is the tracking system built by Zhang and Faugeras [10], which used line-based features instead of point features. Although line segments are useful features for tracking, there are usually more point features than line features in a natural scene, and it would be better to use all the information available in order to get better results. Using only line segments may limit its applications to classes of images where line features are prevalent [7]. Although we deal only with point features in this paper, our approach can be easily extended to using both point features and line features.

The use of the Kalman filters (KF) or the extended Kalman filters (EKF) has now become popular for visual tracking. Zhang and Faugeras [10] derived some closed-form solutions for some 3D motion models, and used them to formulate an EKF to deal with nonlinear measurement equations. In this paper, we formulate a *linear* Kalman filter for motion tracking by using the motion estimates as the measurements for the Kalman filter. In order to track multiple moving objects with multiple Kalman filters, the system has to partition the 3D feature points into several common-motion clusters before applying Kalman filtering. In this paper, we propose a RANSAC-based clustering method for solving the 3D motion clustering and estimation problem by using the *rigid body consensus* principle. This clustering method is an extension of the RANSAC (RANdom SAmple Consensus) algorithm proposed by Fischler and Bolles [3].

The next section gives an overview of our 3D predictive visual tracker. Section 3 introduces the RANSAC-based method for motion clustering and estimation. Section 4 describes the *linear* Kalman filter for predicting the 3D cluster motion. Section 5 shows the experimental results and section 6 gives some conclusions.

2 Overview of the Predictive Visual Tracker

The 3D predictive visual tracker operates in two phases: an initialization phase and a tracking phase (Figure 1 shows the system block diagram for the tracking phase). Initially, the stereo cameras are calibrated, in an automatic way, to get a 3D measurement accuracy of 1 millimeter [8]. The calibration parameters of the stereo cameras are used in the subsequent binocular visual tracking. In the initialization phase, salient features are extracted from the first stereo image pair and initial stereo correspondences are determined by using both the epipolar line constraint and the mutually-supported consistency constraint [4].

In the tracking phase, the 2D temporal matching modules use the prediction from the previous images to locate possible 2D feature positions in the new images. Based on the possible 2D corresponding features in the stereo image pair, the stereo correspondence module uses the epipolar line constraint and the mutually-supported consistency constraint to reduce the possibility of having ambiguous or incorrect matches. Once the stereo correspondences are obtained, we compute, by stereo triangulation, the corresponding 3D feature positions at the current time instant. Given the set of all 3D feature correspondences between two image pairs, we then apply the RANSAC-based clustering method to solve the motion clustering and estimation problem simultaneously. By using the motion estimates obtained from the RANSAC-based clustering module as the measurements for the Kalman filter, we can predict the 3D positions of the features at the next time instant, which are then projected onto the 2D image planes to provide the information required by the 2D temporal matching module. At the next time instant, the 2D temporal matching module will use this information to determine the search region for the best match.

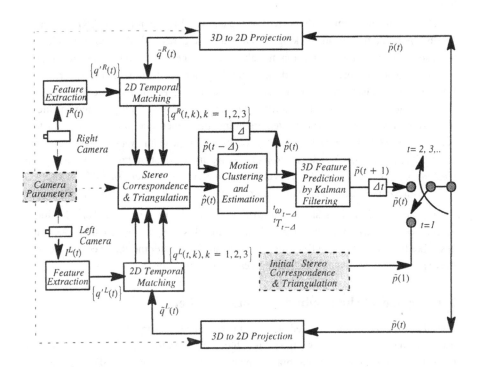

Figure 1. The system block diagram of the tracking phase ($t = 1, 2, ...$). The notation used is described below: $\hat{p}(t)$ is the estimate of the 3D coordinates of a 3D feature point P under tracking at time t. $'\omega_{t-\Delta}$ and $'T_{t-\Delta}$ are the estimates of the rotational and translational motion of the rigid body to which P belongs. $\bar{p}(t + 1)$ is the 3D prediction of P at time $t + 1$, obtained by using the motion estimates from the Kalman filter. $\bar{q}^L(t)$ and $\bar{q}^R(t)$ are the 2D projections of the 3D predicted feature $\bar{p}(t)$, in the left and right images, respectively. $\{q'^L(t)\}$ and $\{q'^R(t)\}$ are the sets of 2D features extracted with a lower threshold. $\{q^L(t, k), k = 1, 2, 3\}$ and $\{q^R(t, k), k = 1, 2, 3\}$ are the candidate sets of temporal correspondence in the left and right images, respectively. $\hat{p}(t)$ is the estimate of the coordinates of the 3D feature point P at time t, using the current image pair.

3 Motion Clustering and Estimation

To track multiple rigid objects, our system partitions 3D feature points into several clusters, each having a common 3D motion. Once the clustering is done, for each cluster of

3D feature points, a motion model can be applied to predict the locations of the 3D features at the next time instant.

Let $\hat{p}_i(t), i = 1, 2, ..., N$, be the position estimates of the ith 3D feature obtained by the stereo correspondence module at time t. Suppose we have a set of N 3D feature correspondences between time $t - \Delta$ and time t, denoted by:

$$S = \left\{ \left(\hat{p}_i(t - \Delta), \ \hat{p}_i(t) \right) \middle| \ i = 1, 2, ..., N \right\}. \tag{1}$$

Our goal is to partition the 3D feature points into different common-motion clusters by using the information contained in S. Here, we propose a RANSAC-based clustering method which can solve the motion clustering and segmentation problem simultaneously and robustly.

A 3D rigid body motion can be uniquely characterized by a rotation matrix R and a 3D translation vector T. For any three non-collinear 3D feature points, their 3D correspondences over time can be used to compute a least square solution to the motion parameters, R and T, by using the Arun method [1]. If there are enough number of 3D feature points having *similar motion with respect to this R and T*, then all of these 3D feature points (including the three non-initiating 3D feature points) form a common-motion cluster. Here, a 3D feature P_i with 3D correspondence $\left(\hat{p}_i(t - \Delta), \ \hat{p}_i(t) \right)$ is said to have *similar motion with respect to cluster j having motion* ${}^{r}R^{j}_{t-\Delta}$ *and* ${}^{r}T^{j}_{t-\Delta}$ if

$$\left\| \hat{p}_i(t) - {}^{r}R^{j}_{t-\Delta} \, \hat{p}_i(t - \Delta) - {}^{t}T^{j}_{t-\Delta} \right\| < Tolerance \ . \tag{2}$$

The strategy we used for clustering 3D feature points in the initial clustering stage is different from that in the cluster maintenance stage. In the initial clustering stage, 3D feature points are partitioned into common-motion clusters by the *Initial Clustering Algorithm* [4]. In the cluster maintenance stage, points having inconsistent 3D motion will be removed from the existing clusters and merged into an un-clustered set S^0. If the number of un-clustered points in S^0 exceeds the minimum size required for a consensus set, then the system will try to form a new common-motion cluster from the un-clustered set S^0, which indicates the appearance of a new moving object (or cluster). Splitting and merging of clusters are also considered with our cluster maintenance algorithm. Details of the algorithm are described in [4].

4 Motion Prediction by Kalman Filters

The motion estimate for each common-motion cluster, obtained with the motion clustering module, can be used as the new measurement for the Kalman filter to predict the next motion of the common-motion cluster. The predicted 3D motion will then be used to predict the 3D feature locations at the next time instant. *Linear* Kalman filters, instead of EKFs, can be applied by formulating the problem in the following way.

As shown in [4], the state vector s_t at time t can be chosen to be a 15×1 vector

$$s_t \equiv [\omega(t)^T, \ \mu(t)^T, \ b(t)^T, \ v(t)^T, \ a(t)^T]^T, \tag{3}$$

where $\omega(t)$, $\mu(t)$, $b(t)$, $v(t)$ and $a(t)$ are 3×1 vectors representing the angular velocity, the angular acceleration, the position of the rotation center, the translational velocity and the translational acceleration, respectively, at time t.

In this paper, we assume constant acceleration, i.e., $a(t) = a(t - 1)$ and $\mu(t) = \mu(t - 1)$. Then, the state equation can be written as (see [4])

$$s_{t+1} = H s_t + n_t , \qquad (4)$$

where the state transition matrix H is

$$H = \begin{bmatrix} I_3 & I_3 & 0 & 0 & 0 \\ 0 & I_3 & 0 & 0 & 0 \\ 0 & 0 & I_3 & I_3 & \frac{1}{2}I_3 \\ 0 & 0 & 0 & I_3 & I_3 \\ 0 & 0 & 0 & 0 & I_3 \end{bmatrix}, \qquad (5)$$

and the random disturbance n_t is white with covariance matrix Q_t.

An important step in applying *linear* Kalman filtering to the motion prediction problem is, instead of predicting the 3D motion of the individual 3D feature directly, we first predict the 3D motion of a common-motion cluster and then use this motion prediction to compute the 3D position prediction of each 3D feature within this common-motion cluster. Our next step is to establish a linear relation between the cluster motion estimates (i.e., measurements) and the system state, s_t. Here, the measurement vector is defined as

$$x(t) \equiv \begin{bmatrix} {}^t\omega_{t-\Delta} \\ {}^tT_{t-\Delta} \end{bmatrix}, \qquad (6)$$

where the angular velocity ${}^t\omega_{t-\Delta}$ can be computed from the estimate ${}^tR_{t-\Delta}$ by using the Rodrigues formula [5]. By using the motion kinematics described in [4], the measurement equation can be written as

$$x(t) = F_t s_t + \eta_t , \qquad (7)$$

where

$$F_t = \begin{bmatrix} I_3 & I_3 & 0 & 0 & 0 \\ 0 & 0 & I_3 - {}^tR_{t-\Delta} & {}^tR_{t-\Delta} & -\frac{1}{2}{}^tR_{t-\Delta} \end{bmatrix}, \qquad (8)$$

and the measurement noise η_t is white with covariance matrix Λ_t.

5 Experimental Results

In our experiments, the camera parameters and the kinematic parameters of the binocular head were calibrated [8][9] in advance such that the binocular head could be controlled to fixate on any given 3D points. For our stereo vision system, the error for 3D point measurements, due to calibration inaccuracy and 2D feature detection error, is less than 2 millimeters in general.

This section presents the results of the tracking experiments on three motion sequences, each of them having 30 stereo image pairs. In the first image sequence, a cola can was moving from right to left on a conveyor belt while the observer and the background objects were stationary. In the second image sequence, the cola can was moved from right to left as in the first image sequence, and the binocular head was panning (0.2° per frame) from right to left while the background was stationary. In the last image sequence, the background was still stationary, but the moving cola can was fixated by the active binocular head such that the cola can was roughly held at the center of the image. In all the above three image sequences, the cola can moved approximately 7 millimeters per frame.

Figures 2, 4 and 6 show the initial stereo correspondences of each image sequence, respectively. The image size is 512 by 512 pixels, and the corner features are marked by 5x5 squares. The initial stereo correspondences obtained with our automatic matching algorithm are quite reliable, which gives a good foundation for the subsequent tracking. Figures 3, 5 and 7 show the trajectories of the tracked 3D features plotted on the last stereo image pair. Notice that most feature points are still under tracking after 30 image frames, and objects having different 3D motions were successfully clustered and segmented by using our algorithm.

Figure 2. (Image sequence 1) Initial stereo correspondence feature pairs superimposed on the first left and right images.

Figure 3. (Image sequence 1) Trajectories of the tracked feature points superimposed on the last left and right image.

Figure 4. (Image sequence 2) Initial stereo correspondence feature pairs superimposed on the first left and right images.

Figure 5. (Image sequence 2) Trajectories of the tracked feature points superimposed on the last left and right image

Figure 6. (Image sequence 3) Initial stereo correspondence feature pairs superimposed on the first left and right images.

Figure 7. (Image sequence 3) Trajectories of the tracked feature points superimposed on the last left and right image.

6 Conclusions

This paper has presented a 3D predictive visual tracker capable of tracking multiple moving objects even when the stereo cameras are moving. Therefore, it can be used to control the binocular head (a robot manipulator for moving the cameras around) to fixate its cameras on the object it is interested in. This tracker is completely autonomous in the sense that it requires no initial correspondence of any kinds, either temporal or stereo correspondence. Any 3D rigid objects, or any articulated objects such as robot manipulators, can be tracked with our visual tracker as long as there are some features on each moving component. We are currently working on extending this system to track slightly non-rigid object by adaptively adjusting the tolerance for testing motion similarity and by considering the spatial relationship between the 3D features. If at some tracking stage, the object is recognized (or hypothesized) to be a known object with some parametric model, then techniques used by Koller, Daniilidis and Nagel [6] can be applied in the 2D template matching module to enhance the performance of our tracker.

The performance of our 3D predictive visual tracker is mainly based on the following factors: (i) A RANSAC-based motion clustering and estimation algorithm using the rigid body consensus is proposed for grouping features into common-motion clusters and estimating their 3D motion simultaneously. This clustering method provides a systematic way for managing splitting, merging, new appearance and disappearance of multiple moving rigid objects. (ii) *Linear* Kalman filters are used to predict the next movements of common-motion clusters, which can then be used to provide better prediction for tracking 3D features (i.e., finding temporal correspondence). (iii) Two parallel 2D temporal modules are utilized to make full use of the temporal information contained in the image sequence. (iv) The constraint of mutually-supported consistency is used to eliminate incorrect stereo correspondences. (v) Calibration is done automatically and accurately to assure the accuracy of 3D inference. Preliminary experiments have shown that our tracking system does give good results and can serve as a robust 3D feature tracker for our stereo vision system.

Acknowledgements

We would like to thank Dr. Leslie Kitchen and Dr. Lin-Guo Liou for their helps and useful discussions. This work was supported in part by the National Science Council, Taiwan, under grants NSC 83–0408–E–001–010 and NSC 84–0408–E–001–004.

References

[1] K. S. Arun, T. S. Huang, and S.D. Blostein, "Least–Square Fitting of Two 3–D Point Sets," *IEEE Trans. on Pattern Analysis and Machine Intelligence*, Vol. 9, NO. 5, pp. 698–700, 1987.

[2] T. K. Cheng and L. Kitchen, "Preliminary Results on Real-Time 3D Feature-Based Tracker," *DICTA-93 Conf.*, Australian Pattern Recognition Society, Sydney, Dec. 1993.

[3] M. A. Fischler and R. C. Bolles, "Random Sample Consensus: A Paradigm for Model Fitting with Applications to Image Analysis and Automated Cartography," *Communications of the ACM*, Jun. 1981, pp. 381–395.

[4] Y. P. Hung, C. Y. Tang, S. W. Shih, Z. Chen and W. S. Lin, "A 3D Feature-Based Tracker for Tracking Multiple Moving Objects with a Controlled Binocular Head," Technique Report TR-IIS-95-004, Institute of Information Science, Academia Sinica, Taiwan, 1995.

[5] K. Kanatani, *Group-Theoretical Methods in Image Understanding*. Springer-Verlag 1990.

[6] D. Koller, K. Daniilidis and H. H. Nagel, "Model-Based Object Tracking in Monocular Image Sequences of Road Traffic Scenes," *Int. J. Computer Vision*, Vol. 10, No. 3, 1993, pp.257–281.

[7] M. S. Lew, T. S. Huang, and K. Wong, "Learning and Feature Selection in Stereo Matching," *IEEE Trans. on Pattern Analysis and Machine Intelligence*, Vol. 16, No. 9, Sep. 1994, pp. 869–881.

[8] S. W. Shih, Y. P. Hung and W. S. Lin. "Accurate Linear Techniques for Camera Calibration Considering Lens Distortion by Solving an Eigenvalue Problem," *Optical Engineering*, vol. 32, No. 1, 1993, pp. 138–149.

[9] S. W. Shih, Y. P. Hung and W. S. Lin, "Kinematic Parameter Identification of a Binocular Head Using Stereo Measurements of a Single Calibration Point," Proceedings IEEE International Conference on Robotics and Automation, May 1995, pp. 1796-1801.

[10] Z. Zhang and O. Faugeras, *3D Dynamic Scene Analysis: A Stereo Based Approach*. Springer-Verlag 1992.

Vision Guided Circumnavigating Autonomous Robots *

Nick Barnes and Zhi-Qiang Liu

Computer Vision and Machine Intelligence Lab, Department of Computer Science
The University of Melbourne, Parkville, Victoria, 3052, AUSTRALIA
nmb@cs.mu.OZ.AU

Abstract. In this paper, we propose a system for vision guided autonomous circumnavigation, allowing robots to navigate around objects of arbitrary pose. The system performs knowledge-based object recognition from an intensity image using a canonical viewer-centred model. A path planned from a geometric model then guides the robot in circumnavigating the object. This system can be used in many applications where robots have to recognize and manipulate objects of unknown pose and placement. Such applications occur in a variety of contexts such as factory automation, underwater and space exploration, and nuclear power station maintenance. We also define a canonical-view graph to model objects, which is a viewer-centred representation.

1 Introduction

In this paper we describe an autonomous robot system which is able to navigate around a given object. This circumnavigating system provides greater flexibility for robots that need to interact with objects, because only a model of the object is required, not of the environment, or position relative to the environment.

Our system identifies both the object and the view using a viewer-centred object representation. The inverse perspective transform of the object is then calculated, allowing the robot to geometrically generate a safe path around the object from the object model. The robot follows the path to the required relative location using odometry. It checks that each new view is expected given its belief about the object's position and its own relative position and motion. This increases the robustness of identification and prevents accumulation of the uncertainty inherent in navigation and odometry.

There are some difficulties in navigating around an object, for instance, background objects that are similar to the object concerned may confuse the robot resulting in moving to the wrong object, or wandering in an entirely wrong direction. Object recognition allows our system to discriminate similar objects. If the robot is required to navigate around one of several identical objects, our method is able to guide the robot by constantly updating its expectation about its position. Furthermore, deep, narrow concavities in the object can create difficulties for following the object's surface. A concavity that is marginally wider

---

* This work is supported in part by an Australian Research Council (ARC) large grant.

than the robot could cause a naive system to get stuck. However, a knowledge-based system should be able to reason about the size of the concavity relative to itself and determine how far it can safely move into such a concavity.

Our current system navigates around 3D objects with the robot moving on the ground plane. Camera elevation may be varied as long as the absolute height is known. As a result there are only three degrees of freedom (one rotational and two translational) for calculating the respective locations of robot and object. We assume that the robot is close enough to the object for recognition.

Our system is novel in the following ways:

1. There is no need to model the environment, or the object's position in the environment. Robot navigation systems such as those proposed in [6] and [8] require a fix on object location within the world frame.
2. If the object is rotated, occluding the required surface, our system can navigate around it to find the required location. Arkin and MacKenzie [1] do not model the environment, but require that a specific object surface be visible.

2 System Architecture

Figure 2 shows the system architecture. There are four basic parts: pre-processing; view recognition; determination of the inverse perspective transform; and model-based geometric path-planning. Pre-processing takes a raw image and returns the required features, for instance, edge segments. View recognition matches the features to views in a *canonical-view* model, identifying the view in an image and correspondence between the image and model. Image-to-model correspondences are used to calculate the 3 degree of freedom inverse perspective transform using a direct algebraic solution. From a relative fix on object location the robot can plan a path around the object to attain its goal, then execute the movement of the planned path. Details of pre-processing and a derivation of the inverse perspective transform are available in [2].

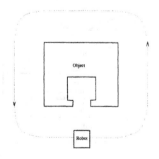

Fig. 1. Expected path for an object with a hole too narrow for safe robot access.

2.1 Object Recognition Using Canonical-Views

Our object recognition system recognises both the object and the view in the image. We use a viewer-centred, model-based technique, similar to the aspect graph representation. Viewer-centred representations require only a 2D-2D match, significantly reducing the computational cost of evaluating candidate views.

Aspect graphs enumerate every possible *characteristic view* of an object, where a characteristic view is a continuous region of views, for which all visible edges and vertices, together with their connectivity relationships are the same [7]. Such changes in visible feature topology are called *visual events*.

Aspect graphs have problems of practicality [4]. A single surface may be redundantly represented in many separate views, which are differentiated only by visual events that may not be observable in practice. Also, there is no adequate indexing mechanism for these views. In the context of robot navigation, we may eliminate many views by applying the following observations:

1. Real cameras are not point but have finite size.
2. Objects have features that contribute little to recognition.
3. Robots are not generally expected to recognise objects at very close range.
4. Camera images are discrete, thus for a particular viewing range, features below a certain size are not distinguishable.
5. Causality present in mobile robots plays an important role in recognition.

Definition 1 *A canonical-view is a set of neighbouring characteristic views: which are differentiated only by visual events involving features of size s for which $\frac{s}{l} \leq k$, where l is the size of the largest surface in the view, and k is constant; and which models only features that make a significant contribution to recognition.*

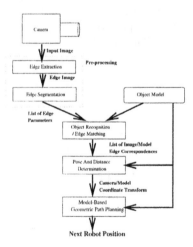

Fig. 2. System Architecture

Note that k is set empirically to incorporate visual events such as the change from the front view to a side view of a wheel into a single view. The rule for the view allows recognition with either feature visible.

Definition 2 *A canonical-view graph has a node for each canonical-view of an object that is not a subset of the surfaces modeled for any other view; and has an edge between all view nodes that are neighbouring in the path of the robot.*

An aspect graph for the visible portion of the cube shown in Figure 3 would consist of 7 views. One possible canonical-view graph is derived by recognising that all views are subsets of view 7, and so only view 7 is represented. A matching scheme for such a representation would have to give a true match if any of the seven views occur. A second possible canonical-view graph would have nodes for views 1, 3, and 5. Here an image of view 7 would match all three canonical-views.

Figure 4 shows the form of the canonical-view graph for the model car pictured in the centre. The four views represent the adjacent car surfaces, and view ranges overlap at the corners of the car. Feature value ranges (discussed in the next section) were derived from segmented edge images of these views, with variance estimated using the perspective equations.

Causal Image Matching The system initially must check the image against every view in the model to find the best match, as object pose is unknown. However, once the first match is made and a move performed, the next view is *causally* defined by the previous position and the movement. Each subgoal point, where the system will visually check its position, is linked to the canonical-view that the system expects to see. Thus, the system will generally only need to match one view for each move. Note that the combination of evidence from matching several *causally related* views greatly increases the certainty of identification.

Our canonical-view graph represents the causal relation between object views defined by the robot navigation problem described here, i.e. canonical-view graphs are indexed by order of appearance.

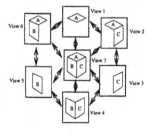

Fig. 3. The partial aspect graph for three neighbouring faces of a cube.

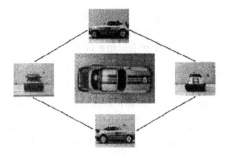

Fig. 4. The four canonical views of the model car used in our second experiment.

Features A canonical-view represents a range of actual views, therefore must allow a range for features. We use features similar to those discussed by Burns et. al. [3] for our canonical-view model: relative length of edges (Continuous range); orientation of edges (Continuous range); coincidental end-points of edges ([True, False]); and relative location of edges ([Above, Below], [Left-of, Right-of]).

We use edge orientation, η, relative to the image y-axis as there is only rotation about the Z axis, see Figure 5. Perspective variance of η is proportional to the angle, α, of the edge to the image plane, and the relative displacement, Δd, of the line end-points from the camera focal centre. Also, as α increases, foreshortening of the horizontal component of the edge, may η decrease.

The relative length of two edges varies when there is a greater change in the length of one edge between view angles. Edge length decreases proportionally to the distance from the camera, and proportionally to α.

End-points of two image edges are labeled coincidental if the ratio of the distance, d, between the nearest end-points and the length, l of the shorter of the edges is less than a constant c, for the range of the canonical-view: $\frac{d}{l} < c$.

Relative edge location can be used as a feature due to the restricted rotation. A pair of edges is labeled if every point on one edge is above/below/left-of/right-of every point of the other, for every viewing angle. If a pair of edges has a left-of

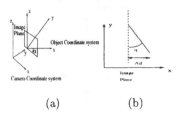

(a)   (b)

Fig. 5. (a) The camera to object transform. (b) The image plane.

or right-of relation in one view it will be true for all views. This occurs except for cases where one edge is on a limb which is above the surface of the other edge, see Figure 6(a) and (b). Above/Below relations are affected by perspective. Parallel lines, coplanar in Z, will not cross, but, non-parallel edges or edges at varying depths may, (Figure 6(c) and (d)). The perspective effects vary with displacement from the image centre in x, and with α.

Feature ranges for canonical-views can be estimated by considering perspective projection of views which maximise variation. This can be empirically derived for each feature from images at extreme views, or estimated using the perspective equations for this restricted case, [2].

2.2 Model-Based Path Planning

To circumnavigate an object, the robot moves around the object in a single direction, following its surface, and remaining a safe distance away. The distance the robot must maintain from the object is problematic. Generally, it must be large enough for most of the object to fit into the view frame for recognition, but small enough for object points to be well spread in the image, allowing accurate pose and distance determination.

The robot generally moves to the next occluding boundary of the closest visible surface. Each move is performed as a view-based local navigation problem. The robot determines the closest object point and the closest occluding corner point, in the direction of motion. If the corner is less than a threshold distance from the closest point to the robot, and the robot is approximately at the required distance from the object, then the robot is at the corner. The robot is guided by the surface normal and whether it is at a corner, as follows:

1. If not at a corner, move to be at the required distance from the object along the surface normal at the nearest corner in the direction of motion. See the path from Initial Position to (1), (Figure 7).
2. If at a corner, at the leading edge of a surface in the direction of motion, move at the required distance from the surface along the surface normal to the next occluding boundary. For example, the path from (2) to (3).

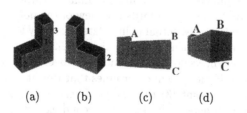

(a)　　　(b)　　　(c)　　　(d)

Fig. 6. Relative spatial relations between edges (a) edge 1 is right-of edge 2, (b) edge 1 is left-of edge 3. Edge 1 is left-of edge 3 whenever both are visible, (c) Edge B and C are parallel and at the same depth, edge A is at a different depth, A is above B, (d) B is above A. B is always above C.

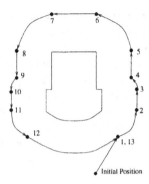

Fig. 7. Circumnavigation path derived for the terminal in the first experiment.

3. If at the corner, at the end of a surface in the direction of motion, move around the corner. This is done by subtending an arc with a radius of the required distance, and centred at the corner, finishing at the same corner on the next surface. For example, the path from (5) to (6).

Note that if a concavity is encountered, the path remains at least the required distance from all surfaces. From (3) to (4) (Figure 7) the robot does not move around to be perpendicular to the small surface behind the screen as that would bring it too close to the adjoining edge. Path generation is described in [2].

3 Experimental Results

We have conducted experiments using: a simulated image of a computer terminal, see Figure 8; and camera images of a model car, see Figure 9. The simulated images were generated using the POV ray tracing package.

3.1 Simulated Circumnavigation

The task is to circumnavigate a computer terminal, returning to the first surface encountered. Figure 8(a) shows a birds-eye view of the points where the system was expected to move, verses actual points determined by the system. Tabulated results for both our experiments are available in [2].

Note, Figure 8(a) shows no actual points for expected points between (3) and (4), and (7) and (8). If the system determines that it is at a corner, it progresses to the next corner. At point (3) the system determines that it is close enough to both the nearest corners, so it skips the second expected point entirely, and moves directly to point (4). Similarly at point (7).

This simulation demonstrates circumnavigation of an object. The system recognises the terminal, and generates a safe path around it, maintaining knowledge of its approximate relative pose and position.

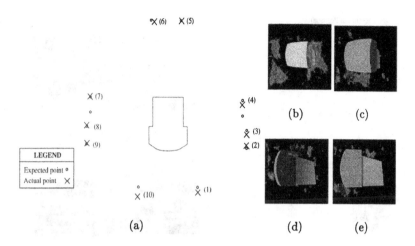

Fig. 8. (a)Expected and actual positions for the second experiment, (b) Initial view, (b) First view chosen, (c) Second view chosen, (d) Third view chosen.

3.2 Docking With a Model Car

Our second series of experiments uses a model car to demonstrate an application in an industrial automation setting. The robot is required to identify the car and navigate around it to the driver's side door (for Australian cars), where it is to move in close to the door's back edge for final docking. In doing this, it should determine the shortest path (clockwise or anti-clockwise) around the object, and pick the required car out of the two cars in the first image. The canonical-view model used for this experiment is shown in Figure 4.

Figures 9(b)-(e) show the camera views determined by the system. From 9(b) the system determines the number of points to be visited in either direction around the object: three moving clockwise; or seven anti-clockwise. Thus, clockwise is chosen, demonstrating high-level reasoning. As can be seen from Figure 9(a) the system was able to generate a safe path around the car, and arrive close to the required docking position.

4   Conclusion

We have implemented a vision system to guide an autonomous robot in circum-navigating objects of arbitrary pose. By applying 3D object/view recognition and pose determination the system was able to plan a path around the object, based on a geometric model, allowing the robot to navigate safely around a known object. The technique handles errors in position estimation and odometry by frequently visually checking its position relative to the object, and by restricting the distance moved based on any single estimate, relative to the robot's distance

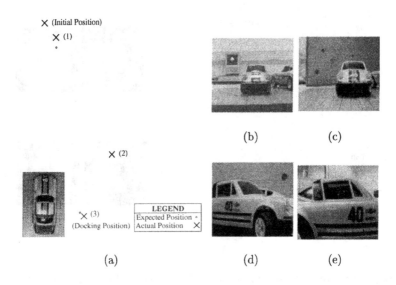

Fig. 9. (a) Expected and actual positions for the second experiment, (b) Initial view, (c) First view chosen, (d) Second view chosen, (e) Final docking position.

from the object. We also defined a canonical-view model for object recognition suited to mobile robots.

Our subsequent experiments include background objects blocking the robot's path. Further experiments will determine partial shape-from-shading to discriminate between objects with similar wire-frames, and allow partial modeling, so that the path can be planned based on the robot's determination of shape. Also, fixation techniques [5] need to be added to allow the system to fixate on a single object when there are similar or identical objects in the background.

References

1. R. C. Arkin and D. MacKenzie, Temporal coordination of perceptual algorithms for mobile robot navigation, *IEEE Trans on Robotics and Automation,* **10**(3) (1994).
2. N. M. Barnes and Z. Q. Liu, Model-based circumnavigating autonomous robots, Technical report, Dept. of Computer Science, Univ. of Melbourne. (1995).
3. J. B. Burns, R. S. Weiss, and E. M. Riseman, View variation of point-set and line-segment features, *IEEE Trans. on Pattern Analysis and Machine Intelligence,* **15**(1) (1993).
4. O. Faugeras, J. Mundy, N. Ahuja, C. Dyer, A. Pentland, R. Jain, and K. Ikeuchi, Why aspect graphs are not (yet) practical for computer vision, in *Workshop on Directions in Automated CAD-Based Vision,* 97–104 (1991).
5. D. Raviv and M. Herman, A unified approach to camera fixation and vision based road following, *IEEE Trans. on Systems, Man and Cybernetics,* **24**(8) (1994).

6. U. Rembold, The karlsruhe autonomous mobile assembly robot, in S. S. Iyengar and A. Elfes, editors, *Autonomous mobile robots*, IEEE Computer Society Press: California, **2**, 375–380 (1991).

7. N. A. Watts, Calculating the principle views of a polyhedron, in *9th International Conference on Pattern Recognition*, 316–322 (1988).

8. C. R. Weisbin, G. de Saussure, J. R. Einstein, F. G. Pin, and E. Heer, Autonomous mobile robot navigation and learning, *IEEE Computer*, **22**(6) (1989).

Force-Driven Optimization
for Correspondence Establishment

W. H. Wong and Horace H.S. Ip,

**Image Computing Group, Department of Computer Science,
City University of Hong Kong.
Tat Chee Ave., Kowloon, Hong Kong**

Abstract. Correspondence establishment has been a difficult problem in machine vision. In this paper, we present an optimization technique for the task. The geometric constraints to the solution are formulated as forces, which are combined to provide clue for mapping between two sets of points such that the geometric constraints are best satisfied. The strong point of this method is that it is easy to integrate several sources of information to obtain a solution while keeping the decision simple, and does not suffer from the uncontrollable flexibility as in active contour models. We illustrate the method with the problem of establishing correspondence between parallel curves.

1. Introduction

In this paper, we introduce an optimization technique which is particularly suited to correspondence establishment, where both soft and hard constraints are involved. Very often, soft constraints are classified as criteria because it is not a must to have them satisfied. In the proposed technique, we formulate the set of constraints into forces and perform optimization by finding the equilibrium amongst these forces. Traditional approaches to optimization can be broadly subdivided into three main categories, namely, calculus-based techniques, enumerative techniques and guided random search techniques [4]. Calculus-based techniques use necessary and sufficient conditions to be satisfied by the solutions of an optimization problem. Active contour model [5] formulated by Kass *et al* is an example of that category. There are several drawbacks associated with these techniques. Firstly, they are applicable only to well-behaved problems. Secondly, they fail to work with hard constraints[1]. Thirdly, they suffer from numerical instability when applied in digital computers. Enumerative techniques do not suffer from any of these drawbacks but they are computationally expensive, as they need to search every point in the domain space of the objective function. Obviously, they cannot be applied on problems with large domain space. Dynamic programming is an example of this category.

Guided random search techniques overcome the complexity problem of the enumerative techniques by using additional information to guide the search. They are quite general in scope and can solve every complex problems. Simulated annealing [6] is an example of this category, with annealing interpreted as an optimization procedure, the thermodynamic evolution process is adopted to guide the search. Better known techniques in the category are the evolutionary algorithms, which are based on natural-selection principles, with search evolves at the most promising solutions in each generation. Two common techniques are evolutionary strategies [7] and genetic algorithm [4]. Force-driven optimization we introduce in this paper stands somewhere in between these categories. The idea of equilibrium stems from calculus-based techniques, where we want the values of certain functionals to be zero. Gradient information is required also to determine the direction of forces. However, unlike the calculus-based methods, we do not solve for the values of the variables in the functionals, rather we measure the values of these functionals, similar to the enumerative techniques. The searching direction is prompted by the resultant force, resembling the guided random search approaches.

2. The force-driven model

Denote the constraints by $Q_i(x)$ conforming to the format

$$Q_i(x) \equiv q_i(x) = 0 \qquad (2\text{-}1)$$

where x can be a vector and $q_i(x)$ representing the corresponding function of the constraint. In establishing correspondence, these constraints are usually due to geometry measurements. We can easily set up $q_i(x)$ such that the function values indicate the degree of deviation from geometric requirements. Therefore function values vanish to zero when the geometric requirements are satisfied and increase as deviation from expectancy enlarges.

The importance of these constraints are reflected from the weights being assigned to them, we denote these weights w_i. To favour hard constraints, we assign relatively larger weights to them. But instead of a simple summation of function values, when $q_i(x)$ is nonzero, we measure the gradient $g_i(x)$, then the two are combined to create a force vector $v_i(x)$, with direction $-g_i(x)$ and magnitude $w_i q_i(x)$. These vectors are added together to give the net resultant force $v(x)$ at x. Following the steepest-descent-based optimization methods, the force direction of $v(x)$ is the direction of search where we can hopefully find the optimal solution. As with all other steepest-descent-based methods, the force-driven mechanism is an iterative algorithm.

Once the searching direction is determined, any line search method can then be applied to the searching for the optimal solution. The line search method we adopt is the golden section search with which the best solution could be obtained in $O(\log_r \ell)$ time, where r is 1/golden-ratio and is approximately 1.618, and ℓ is number of points in the search space. Another merit of the golden section search method is that the solution is insensitive to the absolute values of the weights w_i, only their relative ratios are important.

For correspondence establishment, usually we have to define the mapping between two series of points or features. Let's denote these points by x_m and y_n. To simplify discussions, we study the single direction mapping from x_m to y_n. The inverse mapping can be done in exactly the same manner except that their roles are interchanged. Under this situation, often it is necessary to have constraints that describe the interrelationships among the established correspondences (all constraints except the first in our example in section 3 are of this type). This looks very much like the need for the internal energy term in active contour models, only we do not distinguish them from any other constraints. We are then looking for a mapping scheme f that maps a continuous sequence of x_m to a continuous sequence of y_n such that the constraints are best satisfied. That is, we want to minimize

$$\sum_m \sum_i w_i q_i \left(f(x_m) \right) \tag{2-2}$$

But instead of finding the global optimal solution, we break this into a series of local optimization using the mechanism we described earlier. When the corresponding local objective functions at each individual x_m are minimized, the global objective function is minimized implicitly. Notice also that by formulating the mapping scheme f in this manner, we can handle occlusion.

3. An Example: Correspondence Between Two Parallel Curves

Let a curve C_q be represented in a parametric form as

$$C_q(s) = \left(x_q(s), y_q(s) \right)$$

where $0 \leq s \leq curveLength(C_q)$. We represented tangent measures using direction-dependent tangents (DDT) [9] because concavity information is incorporated into the representation. The compatibility measure between DDT's takes both orientation and concavity into consideration. Let's denote $\varphi_q(s) \in [0, 2\pi)$ the unit tangent vectors at $C_q(s)$, and $\psi_q(s) \in [0, 4\pi)$ the corresponding DDT vector,

$$\psi_q(s) = \begin{cases} \varphi_q(s) + 2\pi & if \Gamma\left(\varphi_q(s), \varphi_q(s + \Delta s) \right) \\ \varphi_q(s) & otherwise \end{cases} \tag{3-1}$$

where the relation $\Gamma(<a>, <b>)$ is defined to mean two *unit* vectors with orientations a, b are positively oriented [2]. In mathematical terms,

$$\Gamma(\langle a \rangle, \langle b \rangle) \Leftrightarrow \begin{vmatrix} cos(a) & cos(b) \\ sin(a) & sin(b) \end{vmatrix} \geq 0 \tag{3-2}$$

Notice that we use the notation $<\theta>$ to denote the unit vector with orientation θ. Since DDT's in concave regions and convex regions are represented in different ranges. We need an operator $Left(.)$ such that we can check for their equivalency,

$$Left(\psi) = \begin{cases} \psi & if \psi < 2\pi \\ (\psi - \pi) \, mod \, 2\pi & if \psi \geq 2\pi \end{cases} \tag{3-3}$$

Equivalency between two DDT's, denoted by $\psi_1 \hat{=} \psi_2$, is defined as

$$\psi_1 \hat{=} \psi_2 \Leftrightarrow Left(\psi_1) = Left(\psi_2) \tag{3-4}$$

3.1 Constraints for correspondence between parallel curves

Having presented the representations, we now concentrate on the perceptual characteristics of parallel curves. We identified four perceptual characteristics which can be employed to guide the correspondence establishment process. They are discussed one by one below.

Tangent alignment criterion: corresponding points between two parallel curves C_x and C_y should have compatible tangents (i.e., equivalent DDT's). Hence we expect the angular difference between them to be zero. This can be tested from dot product

$$\langle Left(\psi_x(m))\rangle \bullet \langle Left(\psi_y(f(m)))\rangle = 0 \qquad (3\text{-}5)$$

Similarity criterion: to reduce computation, it is more efficient to approximate one of the curves by its salient points [3] and establish the correspondences for these salient points only, with the rest done by simple linear interpolation. If the two curves are parallel, it is natural to expect the corresponding points $f(m)$'s should also approximate the other curve. The fitness of approximation can be measured by the area bound by the curve segment and the chord joining two successive $f(m)$'s or the biggest distance of points along the curve segment from the same chord (see Figure 1). We take distance measures because it is simpler to implement. Denote $d_y(f(m))$ the greatest distance in between $f(m)$ and $f(m+1)$, it is easy to see that we are looking for

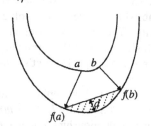

Figure 1. Fitness of approximation. Let a and b be successive salient points with their correspondences established at $f(a)$ and $f(b)$. The fitness of approximation can be measured from either the size of the shaded area or the distance measured from the point the furthest away from the chord (marked d in the figure).

$$d_y(f(m)) = 0 \qquad (3\text{-}6)$$

When $d_y(f(m))>0$, there is a force that act tangentially at $f(m)$ to push it towards $f(m+1)$ and also a force of the same magnitude acting tangentially at $f(m+1)$ to push $f(m+1)$ towards $f(m)$. Note, however, that neighbourhood information is required for satisfying this criterion. In the force-driven model, whenever neighbourhood information is required, we need to consider all immediate neighbours. In this case, for $f(m)$ we need to consider both $f(m-1)$ and $f(m+1)$. If $d(f(m-1))>0$, there is a force at $f(m)$ to push it towards $f(m-1)$. Similarly, if $d_y(f(m-1))>0$, there is a force at $f(m)$ to push it towards $f(m+1)$. Since both forces act tangentially at $f(m)$ but at opposite direction, we are interested in the net remaining force. Hence, we modify our criterion function as

$$d_y(f(m)) - d_y(f(m-1)) = 0 \qquad (3\text{-}7)$$

Elasticity criterion: imagine that we are stretching or compressing an elastic object into another shape, we expect the force to be even distributed within the object itself. This property leads us to the uniform distribution of stretching or lengthening of curve segments. Again, when lengthening or shortening is measured, we need information about all immediate neighbourhood information. Formally, we have

$$\frac{arcLength_y(f(m-1), f(m))}{arcLength_x(m-1, m)} - \frac{arcLength_y(f(m), f(m+1))}{arcLength_x(m, m+1)} = 0 \qquad (3\text{-}8)$$

If the result is greater than zero, there is a force to drive $f(m)$ towards $f(m-1)$ so as to shrink the first term while at the same time to enlarge the second term, and vice-versa.

Sleepers criterion: based on the study described in [8], lines joining corresponding points between two parallel curves (which were named *sleepers*) are expected to be either parallel or intersecting at the vanishing point. But before corresponding establishment, we cannot solve for the vanishing points. Therefore, we compare the orientation of each sleeper with their immediate neighbours to align them properly. Let's look at the geometry involved.

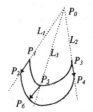

Figure 2. Geometry of expected orientation of correspondence.

In Figure 2 we replaced $C_x(m-1)$ by P_1, $C_x(m+1)$ by P_3, $C_x(m)$ by P_5, $C_y(f(m-1))$ by P_2, $C_y(f(m+1))$ by P_4, $C_y(f(m))$ by P_6, and P_0 the intersection of L_1 and L_2. The geometric relationships among them are

$$L_1 = P_1 + t_1(P_2 - P_1)$$
$$L_2 = P_3 + t_2(P_4 - P_3) \qquad (3\text{-}9)$$
$$L_3 = P_5 + t_3(P_0 - P_5)$$

In our 2D case, the values t_1 and t_2 can be solved from the equations for L_1 and L_2. Solve t_1 by

$$t_1 = \frac{(P_3(x) - P_1(x))(P_4(y) - P_3(y)) - (P_3(y) - P_1(y))(P_4(x) - P_3(x))}{(P_2(x) - P_1(x))(P_4(y) - P_3(y)) - (P_2(y) - P_1(y))(P_4(x) - P_3(x))} \qquad (3\text{-}10)$$

then, we can solve for P_0 with

$$P_0 = P_1 + t_1(P_2 - P_1) \qquad (3\text{-}11)$$

The expected orientation of L_3 is described by $(P_5\text{-} P_0)$. Hence, this is what we want to have

$$\langle (P_5 - P_0) \rangle \bullet \langle (P_6 - P_5) \rangle = 0 \qquad (3\text{-}12)$$

Notice also that t_1 cannot be solved when the denominator is approaching zero, which implies L_1 and L_2 are almost parallel, then we expect the orientation of L_3 to be identical to that for L_1, which is $(P_2\text{-} P_1)$.

Summarizing we have these four competing constraints:

$$Q_1(f(m)) \equiv \langle Left(\psi_x(m)) \rangle \bullet \langle Left(\psi_y(f(m))) \rangle = 0$$

$$Q_2(f(m)) \equiv d_y(f(m)) - d_y(f(m-1)) = 0$$

$$Q_3(f(m)) \equiv \frac{arcLength_y(f(m-1), f(m))}{arcLength_x(m-1, m)} - \frac{arcLength_y(f(m), f(m+1))}{arcLength_x(m, m+1)} = 0 \quad (3\text{-}13)$$

$$Q_4(f(m)) \equiv \begin{cases} \langle (P_5 - P_0) \rangle \bullet \langle (P_6 - P_5) \rangle = 0 & \text{if } \langle (P_2 - P_1) \rangle \bullet \langle (P_4 - P_3) \rangle > 0 \\ \langle (P_2 - P_1) \rangle \bullet \langle (P_6 - P_5) \rangle = 0 & \text{otherwise} \end{cases}$$

where P_i are assigned as defined previously. Notice that they are all conforming to the format specified in (2-1) but their nature is so different. Next we need to determine the weights and to initialize the iterative process.

3.2 The only hard constraint: global consistency

We have mentioned earlier that heavier weights should be assigned to hard constraints, but indeed all four constraints we have discussed are only soft constraints, they should be satisfied but are not mandatory. The setting of weights then becomes a trial-and-error process. From experiment, we found that these settings give very good results: $w_1=7$, $w_2=1$, $w_3=1$ and $w_4=4$. This agrees well with our intuition that tangent equivalency is the most important criterion in parallelism. The only hard constraint is implicit, which is the requirement for global consistency. This can be satisfied if and only if the mapping scheme $f(.)$ is either increasing or decreasing monotonically. This is enforced by limiting the range of line search along the net resultant force direction in each iteration and by filtering impossible mappings in the initialization process.

Concerning initialization, we can select one of the constraints that does not depend on neighbourhood information and apply the constraint to locate for each salient point on one curve the nearest neighbour on the other curve. In our case, the only constraint that does not depend on neighbourhood information is the tangent alignment criterion. Therefore, we map for each salient point the nearest point on the other curve with equivalent DDT. However, since this process is done independently without reference to neighbourhood results, the global consistency requirement is not guaranteed. We need to filter out mappings that crossed out each other and remove multiple matches.

For example, in Figure 3 we approximated the lower curve with its salient points and we initialized the force-driven correspondence establishment process by locating for each salient points the nearest point on the upper curve with compatible DDT. Two of the coupling

Figure 3. Initialization (see text).

results are crossing each other (marked with dotted arrows in the middle) and we remove the coupled results at these two salient points. Instead, based on the bounding good initial fittings we apply linear interpolation to map these salient points to the other curve as marked by grey arrows. Also, the two salient points at the left-hand end are both coupled to the left-hand end point at the other curve. Based on proximity, the mapping which has the shortest distance is retained, all others are uncoupled. Thus the mapping at the left most salient point is uncoupled, as indicated by the dotted arrow. This completes the discussion on initialization.

The global consistency constraint must also be satisfied during the force-driven optimization process. The simplest way to achieve this is to restrict the searching range to only one-third of the points to the nearest coupled point in the searching direction. For example, at a particular iteration, $C_x(m-1)$ is mapped to $C_y(f(m-1))$, $C_x(m)$ to $C_y(f(m))$ and $C_x(m+1)$ to $C_y(f(m+1))$, after all four constraints are checked against as described in section 2, we get a net resultant vector $v(f(m))$ at $C_y(f(m))$. If the vector direction points us towards $C_y(f(m+1))$, then the searching range for the golden section search is

$$\left(f(m), f(m) + \frac{1}{3}\big(f(m+1) - f(m)\big) \right) \tag{3-14}$$

This precaution is necessary to prevent successive correspondence results from running across each other and violate the global consistency constraint requesting the mapping scheme $f(.)$ to be either increasing or decreasing monotonically. Once the search space is delimited, we can bring in the golden search algorithm to look for the point where, assuming that $f(m-1)$ and $f(m+1)$ remain unchanged, the net resultant force generated from the four constraints would be at the minimum possible magnitude. We then map $C_x(m)$ to this optimal point by updating the value of $f(m)$. The iterative optimization process terminates when there is no update to this mapping scheme within an iteration.

4. Experiment Results

Two examples are shown in detail in Figure 4. As mentioned in section 3.2, in all our experiments, we assigned $w_1=7$, $w_2=1$, $w_3=1$ and $w_4=4$. The example on the left shows a pair of parallel curves undergone perspective projection. Parallelism is disrupted but the correspondence is correctly established by the algorithm. Observe the way force-driven mechanism moves the inaccurate initial guess in (a) to arrive at the solution in (c). The example on the right demonstrates the value of the approach applied to the case with partial matches. It can be seen that the way initialization helps in arriving at the right solution efficiently.

5. Conclusion

Correspondence is a difficult problem is machine vision. In this paper, we proposed a new optimization scheme by formulating various constraints as forces to guide the searching for the optimal solution that minimises the total deviations as measured by these criteria. We illustrated the algorithm to establish correspondence between parallel curves. The strong point of this optimisation mechanism is that it is easy to integrate several sources of information to obtain a solution while keeping the decision simple, and does not suffer from the uncontrollable flexibility as in active contour models. The only drawback of the approach is that we need to try out the weights to the underlying constraints. For further development, we shall evaluate the technique for stereo correspondence and temporal correspondence problems.

References:

[1] A.A.Amini, S. Tehrani and T.E. Weymouth, "Using dynamic programming for minimizing the energy of active contours in the presence of hard constraints," *Proceedings, 2nd International Conference on Computer Vision*, pp. 95-99, 1988.
[2] T. Banchoff and J. Wermer, *Linear Algebra through Geometry*, 2nd Ed., Springer-Verlag, New York, 1992.
[3] R. Duda and P. Hart, *Pattern classification and scene analysis*, Wiley, New York, 1973.
[4] D. Goldberg, *Genetic algorithms in Search, Optimization and Machine Learning*, Addison-Wesley, Reading, Mass., 1989.
[5] M. Kass, A. Witkin and D. Terzopoulos, "Snakes: Active Contour Models," *International Journal of Computer Vision*, pp. 321-331, 1988.
[6] S. Kirkpatrick, C. Gelatt and M. Vecchi, "Optimization by simulated annealing," *Science*, volume 220, number 4598, pp. 671-681, 1983.

[7] I. Rechenberg, *Evolutionstrategie: Optimierung technischer Systeme nach Prinzipien der biologischen evolution* (Evolution strategy: optimization of technical systems according to the principles of biological evolution), Frommann-Holzboog Verlag, Germany, 1973.

[8] W.H. Wong and H.S. Ip, "On detecting parallel curves: models and representations," to be published in *International Journal of Pattern Recognition and Artificial Intelligence.*

[9] W.H. Wong and H.S. Ip, "Direction-dependent tangent: a new tangent representation," *Proceedings, Image and Video Processing III*, SPIE-2421, pp. 203-207, 1995.

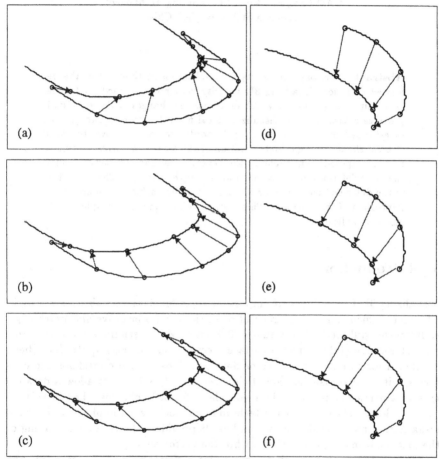

Figure 4. *Left*: an example of parallel curves on perspective projection. (a) shows the salient points and initial mapping. (b) shows the mapping after three iterations. (c) shows the correspondence established after seven iterations. *Right*: an example of correspondence establishment with partial matches. (d) shows the salient points and initial mapping. (e) shows the mapping after one iteration. (f) shows the correspondence established after two iterations.

The Deformed Cube: A Visualization Technique for 3D Velocity Vector Field [*]

Xundong Liang, Bin Li, Shenquan Liu

CAD Lab., Institute of Computing Technology
Academia Sinica, Beijing, China

Abstract. This paper presents a visualization method called the deformed cube for visualizing 3D velocity vector field. Based on the decomposition of the tensor which describes the changes of the velocity, it provides a technique for visualizing local flow. A deformed cube,a cube transformed by a tensor in a local coordinate frame, shows the local stretch ,shear and rigid body rotation of the local flow corresponding to the decomposed component of the tensor. User can interactively view the local deformation or any component of the changes. The animation of the deformed cube moving along a streamline achieves a more global impression of the flow field. This method is intended as a complement to global visualization methods.

1 Introduction

Visualizing 3D flow fields is an important topic for data visualization research. The main difficulty is a fundamental one : there is no intuitive and psychologically meaningful method to visualize 3D flows. Many techniques such as arrow plot, streamline [1,2,3], stream surface, vector field topology[4] etc. have been developed for visualizing 3D vector data[5,6]. Most of these methods are concerned with global visualization of the vector field, but do not allow a detailed look at a particular point in the field. The deformed cube described in this article is a local field visualization technique intended as a complement to global visualization methods such as streamline. It provides a better understanding of the local deformation that exists within the vector field.

The existed methods such as arrow plot and streamline can only show the magnitude, direction and global structure of the velocity field. But in some applications , the changes in velocity vector are of interest. These changes can be represented by a second order tensor. Thus the velocity field can be visualized by vectors(velocity) and tensors(local change).

In [8,9], a second order tensor field visualization method called hyperstreamline is described. They sweep a geometric primitive of finite size sweeping along one of eignvector field. The trajectory is not the streamline of velocity , but a

---

[*] This work is supported by National Natural Science Foundation of China and State Key Lab of Scientific and Engineering Computing

stress trajectory. A probe[10] and stream polygon[11] are two other methods to visualize 3D flow fields by using tensor representation.

In this paper,we use a deformed cube to visualize the local changes of a point in velocity field. Based on the tensor decomposition theorem, the deformed cube provides 3D view of the local stretch, shear, and rigid body rotation. In section 2, the velocity tensor decomposition method and its physical meaning are given. In section 3, we describe our deformed cube . In section 4, we explain how to calculate the tensor in structured grids. The implementation is described in section 5.

2 Vector Field and Tensor Representation

Before our method is described, it is necessary to study the characteristics of vector field. Here we are interested in the local decomposition of the velocity vector and its physical meaning.

2.1 Local Decomposition

Consider a velocity vector field D consisting of the local vectors V=(u,v,w). We decompose the velocity near a given point M_0 and show that the velocity vector is the sum of three meaningful components. Let the velocity vector at $M_0(x,y,z)$ be V_0, and velocity vector at $M(x + \delta x, y + \delta y, z + \delta z)$ in the infinitesimal fluid element be V . The first order Taylor's series expansion of V about M is

$$V = V_0 + \frac{\partial V}{\partial x}\delta x + \frac{\partial V}{\partial y}\delta y + \frac{\partial V}{\partial z}\delta z$$

or

$$v_i = v_{0i} + \frac{\partial v_i}{\partial x_j}\delta x_j \tag{1}$$

Here,$\frac{\partial v_i}{\partial x_j}$, represented by second order tensor, is the velocity derivatives or Jacobian matrix of the velocity

$$T = \frac{\partial v_i}{\partial x_j} = \begin{bmatrix} \frac{\partial u}{\partial x} & \frac{\partial u}{\partial y} & \frac{\partial u}{\partial z} \\ \frac{\partial v}{\partial x} & \frac{\partial v}{\partial y} & \frac{\partial v}{\partial z} \\ \frac{\partial w}{\partial x} & \frac{\partial w}{\partial y} & \frac{\partial w}{\partial z} \end{bmatrix} \tag{2}$$

According to the tensor decomposition theorem, the second order tensor T can be decomposed into a antisymmetric tensor A and a symmetric tensor S.

$$T = \frac{1}{2}\left(\frac{\partial v_i}{\partial x_j} - \frac{\partial v_j}{\partial x_i}\right) + \frac{1}{2}\left(\frac{\partial v_i}{\partial x_j} + \frac{\partial v_j}{\partial x_i}\right) = a_{ij} + s_{ij} = A + S$$

where,

$$S = S_{ij} = \begin{bmatrix} \frac{\partial u}{\partial x} & \frac{1}{2}\left(\frac{\partial v}{\partial x} + \frac{\partial u}{\partial y}\right) & \frac{1}{2}\left(\frac{\partial u}{\partial z} + \frac{\partial w}{\partial x}\right) \\ \frac{1}{2}\left(\frac{\partial v}{\partial x} + \frac{\partial u}{\partial y}\right) & \frac{\partial v}{\partial y} & \frac{1}{2}\left(\frac{\partial w}{\partial y} + \frac{\partial v}{\partial z}\right) \\ \frac{1}{2}\left(\frac{\partial u}{\partial z} + \frac{\partial w}{\partial x}\right) & \frac{1}{2}\left(\frac{\partial w}{\partial y} + \frac{\partial v}{\partial z}\right) & \frac{\partial w}{\partial z} \end{bmatrix} = \begin{bmatrix} \varepsilon_1 & \frac{1}{2}\theta_3 & \frac{1}{2}\theta_2 \\ \frac{1}{2}\theta_3 & \varepsilon_2 & \frac{1}{2}\theta_1 \\ \frac{1}{2}\theta_2 & \frac{1}{2}\theta_1 & \varepsilon_3 \end{bmatrix} \tag{3}$$

and
$$\varepsilon_1 = \frac{\partial u}{\partial x}, \varepsilon_2 = \frac{\partial v}{\partial y}, \varepsilon_3 = \frac{\partial w}{\partial z}, \theta_1 = \frac{\partial w}{\partial y} + \frac{\partial v}{\partial z}, \theta_2 = \frac{\partial u}{\partial z} + \frac{\partial w}{\partial x}, \theta_3 = \frac{\partial v}{\partial x} + \frac{\partial u}{\partial y}$$

$$A = \begin{bmatrix} 0 & -\frac{1}{2}\left(\frac{\partial v}{\partial x} - \frac{\partial u}{\partial y}\right) & \frac{1}{2}\left(\frac{\partial u}{\partial z} - \frac{\partial w}{\partial x}\right) \\ \frac{1}{2}\left(\frac{\partial v}{\partial x} - \frac{\partial u}{\partial y}\right) & 0 & -\frac{1}{2}\left(\frac{\partial w}{\partial y} - \frac{\partial v}{\partial z}\right) \\ -\frac{1}{2}\left(\frac{\partial u}{\partial z} - \frac{\partial w}{\partial x}\right) & \frac{1}{2}\left(\frac{\partial w}{\partial y} - \frac{\partial v}{\partial z}\right) & 0 \end{bmatrix} = \begin{bmatrix} 0 & -\omega_3 & \omega_2 \\ \omega_3 & 0 & -\omega_1 \\ -\omega_2 & \omega_1 & 0 \end{bmatrix}$$

(4)

$$\omega = [\omega_1, \omega_2, \omega_3] = \frac{1}{2} rotV \tag{5}$$

From equation 1,3,5, we have
$$v_i = v_{0i} + a_{ij}\delta x_j + s_{ij}\delta x_j$$

That is
$$V = V_1 + V_2 + V_3 = V_0 + \frac{1}{2} rotV \times \delta r + S \cdot \delta r$$

So, the velocity vector V is decomposed into the following three parts

- Local translation (motion in the direction of the local velocity vector) $V_1 = V_0$
- Deformation rate $V_3 = S \cdot dr$, which is the local strain rate given by the local strain tensor S.
- Rotation rate $V_2 = \frac{1}{2} rotV \times \delta r$, which is the local rigid body rotation given by the rotation tensor A.

2.2 Strain Tensor

The deformation rate V_3 is

$$\begin{bmatrix} u_3 \\ v_3 \\ w_3 \end{bmatrix} = \begin{bmatrix} \varepsilon_1 & \frac{1}{2}\theta_3 & \frac{1}{2}\theta_2 \\ \frac{1}{2}\theta_3 & \varepsilon_2 & \frac{1}{2}\theta_1 \\ \frac{1}{2}\theta_2 & \frac{1}{2}\theta_1 & \varepsilon_3 \end{bmatrix} \begin{bmatrix} \delta x \\ \delta y \\ \delta z \end{bmatrix} \tag{6}$$

Consider $\varepsilon_1 \neq 0$, $\varepsilon_2 = \varepsilon_3 = \theta_1 = \theta_2 = \theta_3 = 0$, equation 6 becomes

$$u_3 = \varepsilon_1 \delta x, v_3 = w_3 = 0$$

It is clear that ε_1 describes the relative stretch rate in the direction of x-axis. Similarly, $\varepsilon_2, \varepsilon_3$ gives the relative stretch rates in y-axis and z-axis respectively.

Let $\theta_3 \neq 0$, $\varepsilon_1 = \varepsilon_2 = \varepsilon_3 = \theta_1 = \theta_2 = 0$, equation 6 becomes

$$u_3 = \frac{1}{2}\theta_3 \delta y, v_3 = \frac{1}{2}\theta_3 \delta x, w_3 = 0$$

That is
$$\frac{u_3}{\delta y} = \frac{v_3}{\delta x} = \alpha = \frac{1}{2}\theta_3$$

Thus θ_3 describes the shear rate of the angle between x-axis and y-axis. Similarly, θ_1 is the shear rate of the angle between y-axis and z-axis. θ_2 is the shear rate of the angle between z-axis and x-axis.

2.3 Rotation Tensor

The rotation tensor A given by equation 4 describes the local rigid body rotation. The rotation tates around x-axis, y-axis, and z-axis are ω_1, ω_2, and ω_3 respectively.

3 The Deformed Cube

To visualize local flow, meaningful visual representation must be used. As described in section 2, a velocity vector can be represented by velocity V_0, rotation rate $\frac{1}{2} rotV \times \delta r$ and deformation rate $S \cdot \delta r$. We use a transformed cube to visualize the local rotation and deformation.

3.1 Local coordinate frame

To visualize the local flow clearly, a Frenet frame is applied. The origin of this frame is the point where the tensor is calculated. The x-axis of the frame is parallel with the velocity vector V and the y-axis is parallel with the curvature vector at this point(Fig.1).

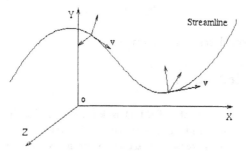

Figure1. Local coordinate frame

In order to define a Frenet coordinate frame, the curvature of the streamline through the origin has to be calculated. The curvature vector C of a curve P(s) through the origin is given by

$$C = \frac{d^2 p}{ds^2}$$

where s is the parameter of path length. It can be shown that the curvature vector at a given point in the flow is given by

$$C = \frac{TV(V \cdot V) - V(V \cdot TV)}{\|V\|^4} \tag{7}$$

With curvature vector C and velocity vector V the Frenet frame can then be constructed. The base of the frame consists of the normalized velocity vector, the normalized curvature vector, and the cross product of these two vectors

$$\left(\frac{V}{\|V\|}, \frac{C}{\|V\|}, \frac{V \times C}{\|V \times C\|} \right) = (N_0, N_1, N_2) \tag{8}$$

3.2 The Deformed Cube

To visualize the local flow, place a cube at the point we are interested in and apply the transformations given by strain tensor A and rotation tensor S. Then the deformed cube shows the 3D view of local relative stretch , shear , and rigid body rotation at that point.

The center of the cube is the point where the tensor is calculated. In Frenet frame, the eight point $P_i (i = 0, 1, \cdots, 7)$ of the cube is determined by the unit vectors (N_0, N_1, N_2)

$$P_0 = N_0 + N_1 + N_2$$
$$P_1 = N_0 + N_1 - N_2$$
$$P_2 = N_0 - N_1 + N_2$$
$$P_3 = N_0 - N_1 - N_2$$
$$P_4 = -N_0 + N_1 + N_2$$
$$P_5 = -N_0 + N_1 - N_2$$
$$P_6 = -N_0 - N_1 + N_2$$
$$P_7 = -N_0 - N_1 - N_2$$

The eight points $P_i' (i = 0, 1, \cdots, 7)$ of the deformed cube are

$$P_i' = M \cdot P_i \tag{9}$$

where M is a tensor described in section 2.

4 Tensor Calculation

In most applications the vector field D is known only at discrete grid points. The grid may be structured or unstructured, regular or irregular. If the grid is rectilinear, the velocity vector at arbitrary point $X = (x, y, z)$ can be calculated using trilinear interpolation. The derivatives can be calculated by centered differences. If the grids are structured or irregular meshes, a more complex numerical evaluation of the derivatives of the Jacobian matrix T is required. Here we limite ourselves to structured grids.

The grid in domain D is defined as

$$G = \{(x_i, y_j, z_k) \mid i = 0, 1, ..., i_{max}; \ j = 0, 1, ..., j_{max}; \ k = 0, 1, ..., k_{max}\}$$

where (x_i, y_j, z_k) is the physical coordinate of grid point (i, j, k). A cell is determined by the eight grid points $(i, j, k), (i, j, k + 1), (i, j + 1, k), (i, j + 1, k + 1), (i + 1, j, k), (i + 1, j, k + 1), (i + 1, j + 1, k), (i + 1, j + 1, k + 1)$. We denote it by $cell(i, j, k)$. The velocity vector V at grid point (i, j, k) is denoted as

$$V(i, j, k) = \{(u(i, j, k), v(i, j, k), w(i, j, k)) \mid (x_i, y_j, z_k) \in G\}$$

To calculate the derivatives of the Jacobian matrix, we transform the irregular geometry to a regular one called the "computational space". Equation 10 describes how to compute physical coordinates of a arbitrary point $X = (x, y, z)$ of a cell if the computational coordinates $\Xi = (\xi, \eta, \varsigma)$ are known:

$$\mathbf{X} = \sum_{i=1}^{8} \psi_i(\xi, \eta, \varsigma)\mathbf{X}_i \qquad (10)$$

ψ_i is so-called shape function[7] and X_i are the physical coordinates of the eight nodes of the cell. For an iso-parametric cell type, the shape function ψ_i are the same as that of the geometry. The velocity vector $V = (u, v, w)$ inside a cell in physical space can be computed as

$$V = \sum_{i=1}^{8} \psi_i(\xi, \eta, \varsigma)V_i \qquad (11)$$

The shape functions ψ_i for our hexahedron cell are given in terms of the computational coordinates ξ, η, and ς

$$\psi_1 = \tfrac{1}{8}(1 + \xi)(1 + \eta)(1 - \varsigma)$$
$$\psi_2 = \tfrac{1}{8}(1 + \xi)(1 + \eta)(1 + \varsigma)$$
$$\psi_3 = \tfrac{1}{8}(1 + \xi)(1 - \eta)(1 + \varsigma)$$
$$\psi_4 = \tfrac{1}{8}(1 + \xi)(1 - \eta)(1 - \varsigma)$$
$$\psi_5 = \tfrac{1}{8}(1 - \xi)(1 + \eta)(1 - \varsigma)$$
$$\psi_6 = \tfrac{1}{8}(1 - \xi)(1 + \eta)(1 + \varsigma)$$
$$\psi_7 = \tfrac{1}{8}(1 - \xi)(1 - \eta)(1 + \varsigma)$$
$$\psi_8 = \tfrac{1}{8}(1 - \xi)(1 - \eta)(1 - \varsigma)$$

with $\xi, \eta, \varsigma = \pm 1$ at the eight nodes of the cell, and $-1 < \xi, \eta, \varsigma < 1$ inside the cell. Obviously , at node i ,$\psi_i = 1$ and $\psi_j = 0 (j \neq i)$. The relationship between physical and computational coordinates can be expressed with $(\Delta\xi, \Delta\eta, \Delta\varsigma)$ as computational and $(\Delta x, \Delta y, \Delta z)$ as physical coordinates relatively to the center of gravity by

$$\begin{bmatrix} \Delta x \\ \Delta y \\ \Delta z \end{bmatrix} = \begin{bmatrix} \frac{\partial x}{\partial \xi} & \frac{\partial x}{\partial \eta} & \frac{\partial x}{\partial \varsigma} \\ \frac{\partial y}{\partial \xi} & \frac{\partial y}{\partial \eta} & \frac{\partial y}{\partial \varsigma} \\ \frac{\partial z}{\partial \xi} & \frac{\partial z}{\partial \eta} & \frac{\partial z}{\partial \varsigma} \end{bmatrix} \begin{bmatrix} \Delta \xi \\ \Delta \eta \\ \Delta \varsigma \end{bmatrix} = J \begin{bmatrix} \Delta \xi \\ \Delta \eta \\ \Delta \varsigma \end{bmatrix}$$

hence

$$\begin{bmatrix} \Delta \xi \\ \Delta \eta \\ \Delta \varsigma \end{bmatrix} = J^{-1} \begin{bmatrix} \Delta x \\ \Delta y \\ \Delta z \end{bmatrix} \qquad (12)$$

Using an iteration method , e.g., Newton-Raphson, the computational coordinates $\Xi = (\xi, \eta, \varsigma)$ corresponding physical coordinates $X = (x, y, z)$ are calculated by equation 12.

The derivatives of vector V in computational space is given by

$$\frac{\partial V}{\partial \Xi} = \begin{bmatrix} \frac{\partial V}{\partial \xi} \\ \frac{\partial V}{\partial \eta} \\ \frac{\partial V}{\partial \varsigma} \end{bmatrix} = J^T \begin{bmatrix} \frac{\partial V}{\partial x} \\ \frac{\partial V}{\partial y} \\ \frac{\partial V}{\partial z} \end{bmatrix}$$

and

$$\begin{bmatrix} \frac{\partial V}{\partial \xi} \\ \frac{\partial V}{\partial \eta} \\ \frac{\partial V}{\partial \varsigma} \end{bmatrix} = \begin{bmatrix} \sum \frac{\partial \psi_i}{\partial \xi} V_i \\ \sum \frac{\partial \psi_i}{\partial \eta} V_i \\ \sum \frac{\partial \psi_i}{\partial \varsigma} V_i \end{bmatrix}$$

Hence, the local derivatives $T = \frac{\partial v_i}{\partial x_j}$ in equation 2 can be computed by

$$\begin{bmatrix} \frac{\partial V}{\partial x} \\ \frac{\partial V}{\partial y} \\ \frac{\partial V}{\partial z} \end{bmatrix} = \left(J^T \right)^{-1} \begin{bmatrix} \frac{\partial V}{\partial \xi} \\ \frac{\partial V}{\partial \eta} \\ \frac{\partial V}{\partial \varsigma} \end{bmatrix} \tag{13}$$

5   Interactive Visualization

The local flow visualization method described in this article has been implemented on SGI $INDIGO^2$ workstation. The application is based on our previous work in fluid field visualization[3]. The streamline and stream surface in the work can reveal the global structure of the flow field, while the deformed cube described here displays the local information of a given point.

The application provides users with a friendly interface. The user can zoom in or out to view the global and local flow structure. Animations of the deformed cube moving along a streamline can also be generated in real time. Users can select a position in the flow and start the animation of the cube. The path of the cube is shown during the animation. Thus a more global impression of the flow field can be achieved.

The effects of stretch, shear, and rotation of the local flow can be viewed separately. Consider the second order tensor S determined by equation 3 and 13. If the terms off the diagonal of the tensor are set to zero,

$$M = \begin{bmatrix} s_{00} & 0 & 0 \\ 0 & s_{11} & 0 \\ 0 & 0 & s_{22} \end{bmatrix}$$

as described in section 2.2, the deformed cube transformed by equation 9 shows the local stretch rate of that point.

If the tensor is

$$M = \begin{bmatrix} 0 & s_{01} & s_{02} \\ s_{10} & 0 & s_{12} \\ s_{20} & s_{21} & 0 \end{bmatrix}$$

the deformed cube shows the local shear rate of point.

Similarly, the rigid body rotation can be shown by setting

$$M = A$$

The total deformation can be represented by setting

$$M = \frac{\partial u_i}{\partial x_j} = A + S$$

in equation 9.

6 Conclusion

The visualization method described in this paper is based on tensor decomposition. It provides a powerful local flow visualization tool. There are some other tensor decomposition methods such as polar decomposition that may provide other cues for visualizing local flow. This is our future work.

Acknowlegements

We wish to thank Dr. Hua Li for many helpful discussions on Tensor Theory and Computational Fluid Dynamics. We thank Professor Huamo Wu and Yuansheng Chen, who work at State Key Lab. of Scientific and Engineering Computing, for providing interesting data sets.

References

1. A. Sadarjoen, T. van Walsum, A. J. S. Hin: Particle Tracing Algorithms for 3D Curvilinear Grids. Fifth Eurographics Workshop on Visualization in Scientific Computing, Rostock, Germany, May 1994.
2. K. Koyamada: Visualization of Simulated Airflow in a Clean Room. IEEE Proceedings of Visualization '92, Los Alamitos, Calif., (1992) pp.156-163.
3. X.D. Liang, B. Li, S. Q. Liu: Visualization of Three Dimensional Flow Fields. Proceedings of The International Conference for Young Computer Scientists, Beijing (1995).
4. J. L. Helman, L. Hesselink: Visualizing Vector Field Topology in Fluid Flows. IEEE Computer Graphics and Applications, May, (1991) pp.36-46.
5. J.J van Wijk, A. J. S. Hin, etc.: Three Ways to Show 3D Fluid Flows. IEEE Computer Graphics and Applications, Sept. (1994) pp.33-39.
6. L.Hesselink, F.H.Post: Research Issues in Vector and Tensor Field Visualization. IEEE Computer Graphics and Applications, March (1994) pp.76-79
7. O. C. Zienkiewize: Finite Elements and Approximation. John Wiley & Sons, (1983)
8. T. Delmarcelle, L. Hesselink: Visualizing Second Order Tensor Fields with Hyperstreamlines. IEEE Computer Graphics and Applications, (July, 1993) pp.25-33
9. T. Delmarcelle, L. Hesselink: Visualization of Second Order Tensor Fields and Matrix Data. IEEE Proceedings of Visualization '92, Los Alamitos, Calif., (1992)
10. W. C. de Leeuw, J.J van Wijk: A Probe for Local Flow Field Visualization. IEEE Proceedings of Visualization '93, Los Alamitos, Calif., (1993)
11. W. J. Schroeder, C. R. Volpe, W. E. Lorensen: The Stream Polygon: A Technique for 3D Vector Field Visualization. IEEE Proceedings of Visualization '92, (1992)

Interactive Particle Tracing Algorithm for Unstructured Grids *

Jicheng Ren, Guangzhou Zeng and Shenquan Liu

CAD Lab., Institute of Computing Technology
Academia Sinica, P. O. Box 2704, Beijing 100080, P. R. China

Abstract. Particle tracing algorithms are used to investigate complex data set from Computational Fluid Dynamics(CFD). But few methods exist for particle tracing on unstructured grids. This paper present a particle tracing algorithm to address this problem. The new algorithm, based on tetrahedral cells, use an efficient heuristic searching method to find the cell which contains the moving particle's new position. By using this efficient searching method, the presented algorithm allow an interactive investigation of complex vector data sets organized on unstructured grids.

1 Introduction

Computational Fluid Dynamics(CFD) is concerned with modeling fluid flows. Unexpected phenomena may be hidden in CFD results, because little information about the flow field can be obtained in advance. Through the effective visualization method, scientists and engineers can clarify the knowledge about these physical phenomena.

Several techniques have been developed for visualizing vector fields, and some of them are described in [1, 3, 11, 13]. Most of these techniques are particle-based flow visualization techniques, such as streamlines[5], streaklines[8], stream surfaces[4] and stream polygons[10]. Most of the particle-based techniques require particle tracing, which involves releasing particles into a flow and calculating their positions at specific times.

In general, CFD simulation provide a velocity field defined on a discrete grid. The simplest grids are Cartesian grids. Particle tracing algorithm for such grids are investigated in [6, 14]. Other grids are often boundary-fitted curvilinear grids, with the purpose of solving flows in complex geometries. Sadarjoen and Van Valsum have discussed this in detail[9]. More and more often, CFD data is computed on unstructured Finite Element grids, which makes particle tracing difficult. One approach might be to resample the grids to a regular one for visualization purposes. But this would either cause a great loss of accuracy, or result in a grid too huge to handle. On the other hand, resampling require exact the same operation but much more computation than particle tracing[2].

---

* This work was supported by National Natural Science Foundation of China.

Unfortunately, few methods exist for particle tracing algorithm on unstructured grids. This paper present an efficient particle tracing algorithm based on tetrahedral cells to address this problem. The new algorithm can locate the cell which contains the succeeding point quickly by using a heuristic searching approach, when integrating in unstructured grids. The algorithm can allow an interactive visualization of vector data in unstructured volumes. For reasons of simplicity, this paper consider the flow field to be time-independent(steady). It is easy to adapt it to time-dependent(unsteady) flow dynamics.

2 Fundamentals

The computation of a particle path is based on a numerical integration of the ordinary differential equation:

$$\frac{dx}{dt} = v(x) \tag{1}$$

where t denotes time, x the position of the particle and v(x) the velocity. The starting position x_0 provide the initial condition:

$$x(t_0) = x_0 \tag{2}$$

The solution is a sequence of particle positions $(x(t_0), x(t_1), ...)$.

A particle tracing algorithm must perform the following steps:

- A search is performed to find the cell which contains the position of the particle.
- The velocities in the cell corners are interpolated to determine the velocity in this point.
- An integration step calculates the next position of the particle.

The process of point location, interpolation and integration must be repeated until the particle leaves the volume or other terminative conditions are fitted.

Point location in a Cartesian grid is as simple as division and truncating[9]. The standard interpolation way in such grid is trilinear interpolation. In particle tracing in a curvilinear or unstructured grid, similar problems arise. Especially point location and interpolation become more complex. While some algorithms transform grids in the physical domain to Cartesian grids in computational domain[2, 12], Koyamada described an alternative particle tracing algorithm in physical domain[7]. The algorithm presented in this paper is a physical domain algorithm.

3 Algorithm

3.1 Definitions

For visualization of an unstructured volume, our algorithm is based on tetrahedral cells. However, an unstructured volume cell is not necessary a tetrahedral cell. If a visualized volume contains cells other than tetrahedral cells, we can subdivide those cells into a number of tetrahedral cells in pre-process.

On the assumption that four nodes of a tetrahedral cell is p_0, p_1, p_2 and p_3, an edge and face number is defined in each cell by the following edge-node and face-node relations:

Definition 1. $edge_{ij}$ of a cell is the edge which two nodes are p_i and p_j, where $i, j = 0, 1, 2, 3; i \neq j$.

Definition 2. $face_i$ of a cell is the face which three nodes are p_k, p_l and p_m, where $i, k, l, m = 0, 1, 2, 3; i \neq k; i \neq l; i \neq m; k \neq l; k \neq m; l \neq m$.

For convenience, the adjacent cells of a specific cell are divided into three types which are defined as follow:

Definition 3. $face_i$-adjacent-cell of a specific cell is the cell which shares the specific cell's $face_i$ with it.

Definition 4. $edge_{ij}$-adjacent-cell of a specific cell is the cells which share the specific cell's $edge_{ij}$, but have no shared face with it.

Definition 5. $node_i$-adjacent-cell of a specific cell is the cells which share the specific cell's node, p_i, but have no shared face and no shared edge with it.

3.2 Point Location

During the process of particle tracing of the new algorithm, a current cell which contains the current point is kept. Point location algorithm is used to find the cell which contains the next point. The next point is either in the current cell or out of it.

On the assumption that the next point is p_{next} and four nodes of the current cell are p_0, p_1, p_2 and p_3, whether the p_{next} is in the current cell can be determined by using its barycentric coordinates($\mathbf{a} = (a[0], a[1], a[2], a[3]); a[0] + a[1] + a[2] + a[3] = 1$) in the current cell, which can be used as weighting values for interpolation. p_{next} can be expressed as:

$$p_{next} = \sum_{i=0}^{3} a[i] * p_i \qquad (3)$$

we can solve $\mathbf{a}$ as following simultaneous equations:

$$\begin{cases} p_{next} = \sum_{i=0}^{3} a[i] * p_i \\ \sum_{i=0}^{3} a[i] = 1 \end{cases} \qquad (4)$$

If the resulting coordinates satisfy $0 \leq a[0] \leq 1, 0 \leq a[1] \leq 1, 0 \leq a[2] \leq 1$ and $0 \leq a[3] \leq 1$, p_{next} is in the current cell. Otherwise, p_{next} is out of the cell. A searching algorithm must be performed to find the cell which contains p_{next}. By using barycentric coordinates, we can determine not only whether p_{next} is in the current cell, but also which cells p_{next} is probably in.

If you extend four faces of a tetrahedral cell, the whole volume can be divided into 15 sub-volumes, include the cell itself. For an arbitrary point, the sign of four components of its barycentric coordinates can indicate which sub-volume it is in. The principle is demonstrated in 2D in Figure 1, where the equivalent of tetrahedral volume is triangular area and the equivalent of barycentric coordinates is area coordinates. The area that contains the point is marked by an asterisk(There is no probability that all components of coordinates are less then zero, because the sum of them is equal to one).

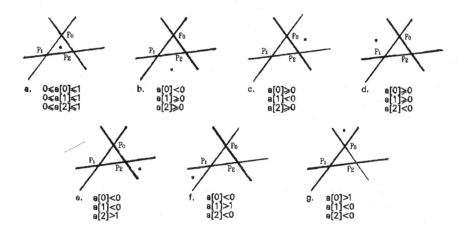

Fig. 1. Principle of which area contains the point

If p_{next} is not in the current cell, the current cell is changed to one of its adjacent cells which p_{next} is probably in, according to which sub-volume p_{next} is in. The operations described above are repeated until the cell that contains p_{next} is found or p_{next} is out of the volume. The principles for changing current cell in 3D unstructured volume are:

- If only one coordinates component is less than zero, i.e. $a[i] < 0 (i = 0, 1, 2, 3)$, take the current cell's face$_i$-*adjacent-cell* as new current cell.
- If two coordinates components are less than zero, i.e. $a[i], a[j] < 0 (i, j = 0, 1, 2, 3; i \neq j)$, take one of the current cell's edge$_{km}$-*adjacent-cells* $(k, m = 0, 1, 2, 3; k \neq m, k \neq i, k \neq j, m \neq i, m \neq j)$ as new current cell. If there is no edge$_{km}$-*adjacent-cell*, take face$_i$-*adjacent-cell* or face$_j$-*adjacent-cell* as new current cell.

– If three coordinates components are less than zero, i.e. $a[i], a[j], a[k] <$ $0 (i, j, k = 0, 1, 2, 3; i \neq j, i \neq k, j \neq k)$, take one of the current cell's node$_m$-adjacent-cells $(m = 0, 1, 2, 3; m \neq i, m \neq j, m \neq k)$ as new current cell. If there is no node$_m$-adjacent-cell, take face$_i$-adjacent-cell, face$_i$-adjacent-cell or face$_i$-adjacent-cell as new current cell.

3.3 Interpolation

When the cell that contains $\mathbf{p}_{next}$ is determined, the barycentric coordinates of $\mathbf{p}_{next}$ in that cell are also calculated. On assumption that the velocities of four nodes of the cell are $\mathbf{v}_0, \mathbf{v}_1, \mathbf{v}_2$ and $\mathbf{v}_3$, the barycentric coordinates can be used as weighting values for interpolation:

$$\mathbf{v}_{next} = \sum_{i=0}^{3} a[i] * \mathbf{v}_i \tag{5}$$

3.4 Integration

Many integration methods are known in the literature. Starting from position $\mathbf{p}_n$ at time $t = t_n$, you can choose any integration method to calculate next position $\mathbf{p}_{n+1}$ at time $t = t_{n+1}$. The simple, but less accurate, one is first-order Euler Scheme:

$$\mathbf{p}_{n+1} = \mathbf{p}_n + \Delta t * \mathbf{v}(\mathbf{p}_n) \tag{6}$$

A well known and more accurate second-order method is Heun's Scheme, also known as a second-order Runge-Kutta Scheme. In this scheme, the next position $\mathbf{p}_{n+1}$ is calculated in two steps:

$$\mathbf{p}_{n+1}^* = \mathbf{p}_n + \Delta t * \mathbf{v}(\mathbf{p}_n) \tag{7}$$

$$\mathbf{p}_{n+1} = \mathbf{p}_n + \Delta t * \frac{1}{2}\{\mathbf{v}(\mathbf{p}_n) + \mathbf{v}(\mathbf{p}_{n+1}^*)\} \tag{8}$$

3.5 Probing

Probing is a technique for visualizing at arbitrary point. A probing technique should efficiently search for a seed cell that involves a specified point(seed point), and efficiently interpolate data at that point. For particle tracing algorithm, a probing technique should allow user to specify an arbitrary point as the starting point for particle tracing. The algorithm present in this paper can satisfy the two requirements.

Section 3.2 has described an point location algorithm during the particle tracing. In the algorithm, if the next point is not in the current cell, a searching algorithm is performed to find the cell that involves it. By using barycentric coordinates, we have the knowledge about which cells the seed point is probably in. So we can traverse cells directly toward the object point. It is an efficient heuristic searching algorithm.

When point location algorithm is used for probing, an arbitrary boundary cell is taken as the current cell at beginning. The algorithm is performed to search the seed cell. The algorithm can efficiently search for the seed cell because of traversing cells directly toward the seed point, even though the seed point may be far from the current cell at beginning. For a convex volume, a single traverse is enough to find the seed cell. For a nonconvex volume, if a simple brute-force algorithm is used, a seed point is found to be outside the volume only after all the boundary cells have been checked.

After the seed cell is found, the barycentric coordinates of the seed point can be used as weighting values for interpolation as equation(5).

4 Conclusion

Particle tracing techniques are widely used in visualization of complex data fields form Computational Fluid Dynamics(CFD). This paper presented a particle tracing algorithm for unstructured grids. The algorithm is based on tetrahedral cells and perform particle tracing in physical space. It allow a truly interactive investigation of vector fields. The proposed algorithm has been implemented as a part work of our Data Fields Visualization System(DVS).

5 Acknowledgments

This work was supported by National Natural Science Foundation of China and State Key Laboratory of Scientific and Engineering Computing. The authors would like to thank Professor Huamo Wu and Yuansheng Chen for providing interesting data sets and for many discussions on fluid dynamics. Thanks are also given to Weiqing Tang Ph.D. for his help in system development.

References

1. Crawfis, R. and Max, N.: Direct Volume Visualization of Three-Dimensional Vector Fields. in: A. Kaufman and W. Lorensen(eds.): 1992 Workshop on Volume Visualization. Boston, Massachusetts, October 1992, pp. 55–60
2. Frühauf, T.: Interactive Visualization of Vector Data in Unstructured Volumes. Comput. & Graphics. 18, 73–80 (1994)
3. Helman, J. and Hesselink, L.: Visualizing Vector Field Topology in Fluid Flows. IEEE Computer Graphics & Applications. 11, 36–46 (1991)
4. Hultquist, J.: Constructing Stream Surfaces in Steady 3D Vector Fields. in: A. Kaufman and G. Nielson(eds.): Proceedings of Visualization'92. Boston, Massachusetts, October 1992, pp. 171–178
5. Kenwright, D.N. and Mallinson, G.D.: A 3D Streamline Tracking Algorithm Using Dual Stream Functions. in: A. Kaufman and G. Nielson(eds.): Proceedings of Visualization '92. Boston, Massachusetts. October 1992, pp. 62–68

6. Kontomaris, K. and Hanratty, T.J.: An Algorithm for Tracking Fluid Particles in a Spectral Simulation of Turbulent Channel Flow. Journal of Computational Physics. **103**, 231–242 (1992)

7. Koyomada, K.: Visualization of Simulated Airflow in a Clean Room. in: B. Shriver, G. Nielson and L. Rosenblum(eds.): Proceedings of Visualization '90, 1990, pp. 156–163

8. Lane, D.A.: Visualization of Time-Dependent Flow Fields. in: G. Nielson and D. Bergern(eds.): Proceedings of Visualization '93. San Jose, California, 1993, pp. 32–38

9. Sadarjoen, A., Van Walsum, T. and Hin, A.J.S.: Particle Tracing Algorithm for 3D Curvilinear Grids. Fifth Eurographics Workshop on Visualization in Scientific Computing. Rostock, Germany, May 1994

10. Schroeder, W., Volpe, C. and Loresen, W.: The Stream Polygon: A Technique for 3D Vector Field Visualization. in: G. Nielson and L. Rosenblum(eds.): Proceedings of Visualization '91. San Diego, California, October 1991, pp. 126–132

11. Shirayama, S.: Visualization of Vector Fields in Flow Analysis I. 29th AIAA Aerospace Sciences Meeting and Exhibit. Reno, Nevada, January 1991, AIAA 91-0801

12. Shirayama, S.: Processing of Computed Vector Fields for Visualization. Journal of Computational Physics. **106**, 30–41 (1993)

13. Van Wijk, J.J., Hin, A.J.S., De Leeuw, W.C. and Post, F.H.: Three Ways to Show 3D Fluid Flow. IEEE Computer Graphics & Application. **14**, 33–39 (1994)

14. Yeung, P.K. and Pope, S.B.: An Algorithm for Tracking Fluid Particles in Numerical Simulations of Homogeneous Turbulence. Journal of Computational Physics. **79**, 373–416 (1988)

Fast Resampling Using Vector Quantization

Patrick C. Teo[*] and Chase D. Garfinkle[†]

*Department of Computer Science
Stanford University, Stanford, CA 94305
†Silicon Graphics Computer Systems
Mountain View, CA 94043

Abstract. We present a fast resampling scheme using vector quantization. Our method differs from prior work applying vector quantization to speeding up image and volume processing in two essential aspects. First, our method uses blocks with overlapping rather than disjoint extents. Second, we present a means of trading off smaller block sizes for additional computation. These two innovations allow vector quantization to be used in performing a broader class of operations. We demonstrate the performance of our method in warping both images and volumes, and have also implemented a ray-traced volume renderer utilizing this technique. Experiments demonstrate a speed up of 2-3 times over conventional resampling with minimal errors.

1 Introduction

Resampling, the process of extracting values from gridded data, is a ubiquitous operation in image processing and computer graphics. Most applications which use data in the form of a stored image or volume must perform this operation many times, and computation time is often dominated by this cost. Such applications include many types of image and volume warping, filtering, texture mapping and volume rendering. In general, the locations at which data is to be sampled may be non-integral, or subpixel. Because there is no explicit representation of the data at these locations, resampling consists of interpolating the data at nearby grid points. The set of weights used to combine these points is known as the resampling kernel. Performing a single resampling operation consists of the following steps:

1. Load from memory all data which contribute to the computation of the interpolated value. For example, linear interpolation requires the nearest four samples in an image and eight in a volume.
2. Compute the weights for each of the samples. These weights are often the cartesian product of one-dimensional filters in each dimension of the data. For a linear interpolant, these functions are simple linear ramps
3. Multiply each sample value by the corresponding weight and sum to compute the interpolated value.

We can see that there are two fundamental costs in resampling: memory accesses to retrieve stored data, and floating-point operations to interpolate from these samples. In conventional resampling, these costs are proportional to the size of the resampling kernel. In this paper, we present a method based on Vector Quantization (VQ) which allows the resampling operation to be performed with fewer memory access and no run-time computation of the weights. The rest of the paper is organized as follows. In section 2, we present background on VQ and prior work using VQ in conjunction with image and volume processing operations. In section 3, we describe our technique for fast resampling. Section 4 gives the results of using our method in several applications. Finally, we conclude in section 5 with suggestions for extensions and future applications.

2 Background

Vector Quantization. Vector Quantization is a lossy data compression scheme, which can be understood as a generalization of scalar quantization. In scalar quantization, a range of possible values is mapped onto a smaller discrete set of representative values. This mapping operation might consist of an operation such as "rounding to the nearest multiple of four". In general, no restriction needs to be placed on the possible set of quantized values; they may be unevenly spaced, or even be non-integers. When this set is explicitly enumerated, it is commonly referred to as a *codebook* and its elements are called *codewords*. The process of choosing the codewords of a codebook is known as codebook design. Once the codebook has been designed, each input value is mapped to one of the codewords via some encoding rule (typically, the nearest neighbor rule).

Unlike scalar quantization, vector quantization quantizes sets of numbers (or *vectors*) as a group, rather than each value individually. As in scalar quantization, VQ codebook design involves producing a set of vectors which can be used to represent some collection of input vectors with the minimum possible error, or distortion. Various metrics can be used to measure distortion; squared error is the most common, and we have used it in this work. To design codebooks, we have used the pairwise nearest neighbor (PNN) algorithm[4], which operates by grouping the input vectors into clusters, and then choosing one representative vector for each cluster.

Codebook Design. The PNN algorithm works by first organizing the set of input vectors into a *k-d tree*[1], a data structure which spatially partitions data along axis-aligned planes to form a balanced binary tree. We form the tree by recursively subdividing the data until each leaf of the tree contains fewer than some fixed number of vectors. We choose the axis along which to subdivide each node to be the one in which the vectors have the maximum variance. We then choose the median location of the vectors along this axis as the plane with which to subdivide the node.

Once we have constructed the initial tree, the clustering proceeds as follows. We first consider each vector to be a cluster of size one, and then repeat the following process until the total number of clusters is reduced to the desired number of codewords.

1. Select from each leaf of the k-d tree a candidate pair of clusters such that combining them, and representing the aggregate by its centroid, will yield the smallest distortion over all pairs in that node.

2. For a fixed percentile of the candidate pairs, ranked by distortion, combine the clusters.
3. Rebalance the k-d tree.

Once the number of clusters is reduced to the number of desired codewords, the centroids of the remaining clusters are used as the codewords of the codebook. Algorithms that generate optimal codebooks are computationally expensive[5]. As a result, codebooks are commonly designed for use across a large number of data sets. This avoids the need to design a new codebook for each data set. While the PNN method is not guaranteed to generate the optimal codebook for a given set of input vectors, it generates good codebooks in practice, and is sufficiently fast that we are able to compute a new codebook for each data set. *Prior Work.* A number of authors have previously explored the use of VQ to accelerate image or volume processing operations. The general technique has been to encode the data, perform the desired operation on the vectors of the codebook, and then use this processed codebook in the decoding stage. For example, in [2] and [3], the authors describe performing histogram equalization on VQ encoded images. In the case of global equalization, each codeword is equalized using a histogram for each image. Adaptive equalization is achieved by computing a number of versions of each codeword, each equalized for a different region of the image, and interpolating between these copies during decoding. Another interesting example is the use of VQ in volume rendering, presented in [6]. The author presents an orthographic ray-tracing volume renderer which operates in two stages. First, each codeword is individually rendered into a pixmap using conventional volume ray-tracing. The rendering of the entire volume is then produced by stepping from block to block within the volume along the projection direction and compositing the pixmaps for the codewords encountered.

Our method differs from prior work in two essential aspects. First, in prior work the vectors have encoded non-overlapping blocks in the input data. In this work, however, we allow the blocks to overlap. This makes a larger class of operations amenable to such a VQ approach. In our particular application, overlapping blocks are necessary to guarantee that all the data required to interpolate a sample is contained in a single block. Second, we present a means of trading off smaller block sizes for additional computation. Typically, the size of the block is determined by the spatial extent of the input region of the operation. Hence, when the input region is large, the size of the block may become prohibitively large for such a VQ scheme. By decomposing the operation appropriately, we can use smaller blocks at the cost of a moderate increase in computation.

3 Methods

3.1 Preprocessing

Our method involves three preprocessing steps: (1) designing the VQ codebook, (2) computing the extended codebook, and (3) encoding the input data. During codebook design, the input data is decomposed into overlapping blocks, each of which is usually the size of the resampling kernel. For example, when resampling image data with a bilinear interpolant, a 2×2 block is used (as shown in Figure 1). The use of overlapping blocks is a crucial difference from standard VQ

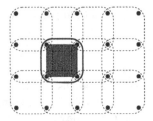

Fig. 1. Decomposition into overlapping blocks of an image which is to be resampled using a bilinear interpolant. Filled circles denote locations of image pixels. Resampling of the image at any location within the shaded region will be computed from the extended VQ codebook entry of the enclosing block (see Section 3.2.

methods. If the input data were encoded as disjoint blocks, the computation of a new sample value might require samples which reside in several different blocks. By using overlapping blocks, we can guarantee that all the data necessary to compute a sample will reside in a single block.

A small set of representatives is then derived from the blocked data to form the initial VQ codebook (as described in Section 2). Next, the extended codebook is generated by resampling each codeword in the initial VQ codebook at some finite number of subpixel locations. Lastly, each overlapping block in the input data is encoded with the index of its best representative from the codebook.

The extended VQ codebook contains the same number of entries as the original VQ codebook. However, unlike the entries in the original codebook which are blocks of values from the original data, each entry in the extended codebook is a small table of resampled values computed at a fixed number of subpixel locations within the block. Hence, we can index these resampled values by the concatenation of the original codebook index and an index designating the discretized subpixel location.

When resampling image data with a bilinear interpolant, for example, each entry in the original codebook is a 2×2 block of pixel values. If the subpixel displacements are discretized onto a 4×4 grid, then each entry of the extended codebook is made up of 16 values computed by resampling the corresponding block in the original codebook at each subpixel location on the grid. Typically, codebooks of 256 entries are used for 8-bit gray-level images. As a result, the index into this extended codebook would be 12 bits wide, consisting of 8 bits for the original codebook index and 4 bits to encode the discrete subpixel location. Figure 2 shows a typical entry in an original VQ codebook along with its corresponding extended VQ codebook entry.

3.2 Resampling using the Extended VQ Codebook

After preprocessing, the input data can be efficiently resampled such that only two memory accesses are required, one to the encoded data, and one to the codebook. First, the integral grid location is computed and the codebook index

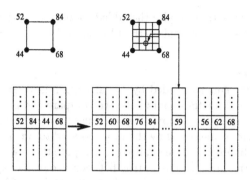

Fig. 2. Original and extended VQ codebook entries for image resampling using a bilinear interpolant. (a) One entry in the original VQ codebook. This entry corresponds to a 2 × 2 block of image pixels. (b) Corresponding entry in the extended VQ codebook. This entry contains a 4 × 4 table of image pixel values resampled at the corresponding subpixel locations.

for this location is retrieved from the encoded input data. For example, if we want to draw a sample at location $(53.3, 28.7)$ in an image, we would retrieve the codebook entry whose index is stored at location $(53, 28)$. Second, the fractional displacement of the new location from this grid point is used to retrieve the precomputed, resampled value from the codebook. If we have resampled the codebook on a 4 × 4 grid, we would quantize the offset in our example to $(\frac{1}{4}, \frac{3}{4})$, and so retrieve the value at position $[1, 3]$ within the codeword.

In comparison to these two memory accesses, bilinear interpolation of scalar image data requires four memory accesses and three linear interpolations. Trilinear interpolation of scalar volume data requires eight memory accesses and seven linear interpolations.

3.3 Trading off block size for computation.

Using the method described so far, interpolants with larger kernels require larger block sizes. For example, a bicubic interpolant for images would require blocks that are 4 × 4 pixels wide and a tricubic interpolant for volumes would require blocks that are 4 × 4 × 4 in size. In order to keep the average quantization error low, larger block sizes must be accompanied by larger codebooks. Unfortunately, VQ becomes unmanageable as codebooks become too large. On the other hand, if the codebook size is kept fixed, the average quantization error introduced increases with the use of larger blocks.

Our solution is to adopt a hybrid method in which smaller block sizes are traded off for additional computation. For interpolations that can be decomposed into a sequence of operations with smaller supports, the size of each block only needs to be the size of these smaller support regions. For example, when resampling an image with a bicubic interpolant, a 4 × 1 pixel block could be used. Resampling now requires looking up the codebook entries associated with four contiguous blocks and combining them using a one-dimensional cubic interpolant. Section 4 shows that despite the added computation, the hybrid method still outperforms the conventional method by more than a factor of two.

4 Results

4.1 Performance

We assess the improvement afforded by our algorithm in resampling image and volume data. For each of these data sets, we compare the performance of our method against conventional resampling when used with linear and cubic interpolants. Performance is measured by the time required to warp and resample the entire data set, including the time required to compute the new sample locations. We also compute the mean squared error between the results generated by our method and by conventional resampling. Implementations of both our method and the conventional method were optimized for speed. All running times reported are for an implementation on a Sun Microsystems Sparc10 workstation with 32 Mb of main memory.

Image Resampling. Figure 3 shows two versions of a 512 × 512, 8-bit gray-level image, resampled using a bilinear interpolant. The image on the left was resampled using the conventional method while the image on the right was resampled with our method. The codebook contained 512 entries, and subpixel locations were discretized onto an 8 × 8 grid, yielding a 32Kb extended codebook.

Table 1 reports the average times taken by our method and the conventional method to rotate the image over a range of 2π radians in 256 uniform steps, using both bilinear and bicubic interpolants. Note that the last four rows of the table report results for the hybrid method.

Volume Resampling. Table 2 reports the times taken by our method and the conventional method to perform an affine warp on a 200 × 200 × 200, 8-bit volume, using trilinear interpolation. Note again that the last two rows of the table report results using the hybrid method.

4.2 Application (Volume Rendering)

Figure 4 shows ray-traced volume renderings of a 200 × 200 × 200, 8-bit volume data set. Trilinear interpolation was used to resample the volume. The image

	Block Size	Codebook Size	VQ Resampling (sec)	Conventional (sec)	MSE
Bilinear	2 × 2	256	0.62	1.45	7.30
Bilinear	2 × 2	512	0.63	1.45	5.37
Bicubic	4 × 4	2048	0.72	2.48	18.01
Bicubic	4 × 4	4096	0.73	2.48	14.65
Bicubic	4 × 2	512	0.89	2.48	17.32
Bicubic	4 × 2	1024	0.95	2.48	14.42
Bicubic	4 × 1	256	1.00	2.48	8.14
Bicubic	4 × 1	512	1.01	2.48	5.57

Table 1. Times required to resample a 512 × 512 image of 8-bit data and their associated mean squared errors (MSE).

	Block Size	Codebook Size	VQ Resampling (sec)	Conventional (sec)	MSE
Trilinear	$2 \times 2 \times 2$	1024	35	76	6.75
Trilinear	$2 \times 2 \times 2$	2048	35	76	5.13
Trilinear	$2 \times 2 \times 1$	256	41	76	4.04
Trilinear	$2 \times 2 \times 1$	512	41	76	2.66

Table 2. Times required to resample a $200 \times 200 \times 200$ volume of 8-bit data and their associated mean squared errors (MSE).

on the left was rendered using the conventional resampling method. The image on the right was rendered using our method with a codebook size of 2048 and a block size of $2 \times 2 \times 2$. In rendering the image on the right, the codebook was used to precompute gradients needed to shade the volume. The image rendered using the conventional resampling method took 200 seconds while the image rendered using our method took 94 seconds on a 150 MHz Silicon Graphics Indigo2 with 64 Mb of main memory.

5 Conclusions

We have presented a fast resampling scheme using vector quantization. Our method differs from prior work in two essential aspects. First, our method uses blocks with overlapping extents. Second, we present a means of trading off smaller block sizes for additional computation. Experiments using our method to resample images and volumes demonstrate a speed up of 2-3 times over conventional resampling with only small errors. In general, the use of overlapping blocks allows vector quantization to be applied in image/volume processing applications where disjoint blocks do not provide sufficient information. Our fast resampling method can also be used on non-rectangular grids.

References

1. J. L. Bentley and J. H. Friedman. Data structures for range searching. *ACM Computing Surveys*, 11(4):397–409, December 1979.
2. P. Cosman, K. Oehler, E. Riskin, and R. Gray. Combined vector quantization and adaptive histogram equalization. In *SPIE Proc. Medical Imaging VI*, 1992.
3. P. Cosman, K. Oehler, E. Riskin, and R. Gray. Combining vector quantization and histogram equalization. *Information Processing Management*, 28(6):681–686, 1992.
4. W. Equitz. A new vector quantization clustering algorithm. *IEEE Trans. on Acoustics, Speech and Signal Processing*, 37(10):1568–1575, 1989.
5. Y. Linde, A. Buzo, and R. Gray. An algorithm for vector quantizer design. *IEEE Trans. on Communications*, 28:84–95, 1980.
6. P. Ning. Applications of data compression to 3-d scalar field visualization. Technical report, Stanford University, 1993. PhD Dissertation.

Fig. 3. Both images are bilinearly resampled versions of the original 512 × 512, 8-bit gray-level image. The image on the left was resampled using the conventional method while the image on the right was resampled using our method.

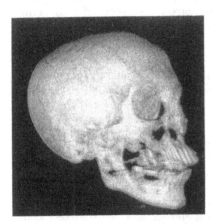 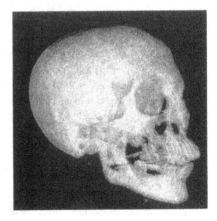

Fig. 4. Both images are ray-traced volume renderings of a 200 × 200 × 200, 8-bit volume data set. Trilinear interpolation was used to resample the volume. The image on the left was rendered using the conventional resampling method. The image on the right was rendered using our method with a codebook size of 2048 and a block size of 2 × 2 × 2.

A B-spline Surface Interpolation Technique for [*] Reconstructing 3D Objects from Serial Arbitrary Shaped Planar Contours

Meihe Xu   Zesheng Tang   Junhui Deng

CAD Center, Dept. of Computer Science and Technology, Tsinghua University, Beijing, 100084, China

E'mail: dcstzs@tsinghua.edu.cn

Abstract A new method is presented to the B-spline surface presentation of an object defined by a set of parallel slices. For the application of B-spline inversion procedure, the methods about the data points generated are mainly introduced. The mesh of the data points is generated from interpolation curves of the vertex of the contour, which enable the interpolating surface to approximate the original object. It has the advantage that the reconstructed surface keep the smoothness in total longitudinal direction. The proposed method is also capable of handling the branching problem. Several experimental results corroborate the theory. The results show the image with high fidelity and the rendering speed are satisfactory and pleasing.

1. Introduction

In many scientific and technical applications, an object or a set of objects are known by a sequence of cross sections. These cross-sections may be obtained by intersecting the three dimensional object with a collection of parallel planes. For example, in section anatomy, the thin sections are obtained by moving a paralleled scalper. And in medical diagnosis and therapy, cross-section images are obtained by moving an CT apparatus or a MR apparatus. So, the problem for reconstructing a 3D surface from a set of sectional contours is an important problem in many applications.

The main task in 3D surface reconstruction usually consists of extracting the contours of the interesting region in all the cross-sectional images and forming surface and volume between the contours of successive slices. Since the information provided for recovering a 3D object is serial sections only, the smoothness of the reconstructed surface is a major concerned. A number of triangulation-based technique for reconstructing surface of an object are presented[1][2][3]. The triangulation process produces local bounding patches between every pair of consecutive contours. It uses the triangular faces of the mesh as the surface. Unless the contours sample the original surface very finely, this piecewise planar approximation will not be very good. Currently, there are a number of methods for solving the problem of fitting a smooth surface to the triangular mesh in three dimensional space. The general

---

[*] This project is supported by National Natural Science Foundation of China

method is to use a series of parametric surface patches in which the vertices of the mesh are the control points of the surface patches, and the topology of the mesh determines which vertices are used in each patch[4]). But, no one scheme has proven to be perfect[1].

A scheme about the dynamic elastic surface interpolation, which reconstructs 3D objects in volumetric representation, has been proposed in [5]. The approach provides a mechanism to generate iteratively a series of intermediate contours for filling the gaps between the start and the goal contour. The 3D object is reconstructed by stacking up the start, intermediate, and goal contours. Since the object is also formed by stacking up the contours together, even with a fine interpolation the resulting surface might be coarse if the degree of dissimilarity among these contours is high. An improvement on the smoothness of surface about this approach is made by Wei[6]. It combines the elastic interpolation algorithm and the spline theory, it may produce a good result if it is used to small data set. When it applies to a large data field, this method may be time consuming and even unpractical. Shinagawa[7] used a homotopy model to generate smooth parametric surface connecting consecutive contours. But, as far as total longitudinal direction is concerned, the reconstructing surface is not smooth yet. In[9], a lofting technique which utilizes one family of parametric curves for surface representation was presented. The approach can't tackle the branching problem and the reconstructed surface may look unnatural or unrealistic.

In this paper, the B-spline surface interpolation technique[8] is applied to reconstructing 3D object from a serial contours. Section 2 and section 3 deal with the generation of the array of interpolated points. Section 4 includes the method for surface fitting. Section 5 and section 6 are respectively the experiment results and conclusion.

2. The generation of the mesh of the data points about single branching problem

2.1 The generation of the array of the data points from the convex contours

Let $P_{k,0}$, $P_{k,1}$, ...,P_{k,m_k} be the sequence of the points defining the planar closed contour $C_k(k=0,1,...n)$, ordered in the clockwise direction. For the B-spline interpolation of the points set$\{P_{k,j}|j=0,1,\cdots,m_k;\ k=0,\cdots n\}$, the sequence of the points $\{P_{k,j}|j=0,1,\cdots,m_k\}$ on k-th slice are first interpolated with a non-uniform B-spline curve of l-th order. i.e.:

$$Q_k(u)=\sum_{j=0}^{M_k} V_{k,j} B_{j,l}(u) \qquad (1)$$

$$u \in [u_0, u_{m_k}],\ M_k=m_k+l-2$$

where the vectors $V_{k,j}(j=0,1\cdots,M_k)$ are the control points of the curve. $B_{j,l}(u)$ is the basic function of the B-spline. And

$$Q_k(u_j)=P_{k,j} \qquad (j=0.1,\cdots m_k) \qquad (2)$$

By solving the inversion procedure eq(2), the sequence of the points $\{V_{k,j}|j=0,1,\cdots,M_k\}$ are obtained. Because the number of points on each slice are different, the number of $V_{k,j}$ for each slice are also different.

In order to apply the uniform B-spline surface to the interpolation of non-rectangular ordered data points $\{P_{k,j}|\ j=0,1,\cdots,m_k;\ k=0,1,\cdots,n\}$, a rectangular array of the data points(i.e. the interpolated points) $\{S_{k,j}|j=0,1,\ \cdots\ ,\ m;\ k=0,1,\cdots,\ n\}$ must be interpolated cross-sectionally, with a non-uniform B-spline curve for each of the j values. For this purpose, the local polar coordinate system of the each contour must first be set up. Assume that the pole of the local polar coordinate system of the current contour is the centroid of the convex contour polygon. i.e.:

$$o_{k,x}=\frac{1}{m_k+1}\sum_{i=0}^{m_k}x_{k,i} \qquad o_{k,y}=\frac{1}{m_k+1}\sum_{i=0}^{m_k}y_{k,i}$$

where $(x_{k,i},y_{k,i})$ $(i=0,1,\cdots,m_k)$ are the vertexes of the k-th contour polygon. $(o_{k,x},o_{k,y})$ is the coordinate of the centroid of this contour. Then, the polar angle of each vertex of the contour is defined as follows:

$$\alpha_{k,i} = \begin{cases} \arcsin\dfrac{y_{k,i}-o_{k,y}}{\sqrt{(x_{k,i}-o_{k,x})^2+(y_{k,i}-o_{k,y})^2}}(x_{k,i}\geq o_{k,x},y_{k,i}\geq o_{k,y}) \\[4mm] \pi+\arcsin\dfrac{y_{k,i}-o_{k,y}}{\sqrt{(x_{k,i}-o_{k,x})^2+(y_{k,i}-o_{k,y})^2}}(x_{k,i}<o_{k,x}) \\[4mm] 2\pi+\arcsin\dfrac{y_{k,i}-o_{k,y}}{\sqrt{(x_{k,i}-o_{k,x})^2+(y_{k,i}-o_{k,y})^2}}(x_{k,i}\geq o_{k,x},y_{k,i}<o_{k,y}) \end{cases}$$

$$(3)$$

$$(i=0,1,\cdots,m_k;\ k=0,1,\cdots,n)$$

With the local polar coordinate system of each contour, a criterion for producing the data points from B-spline interpolation curve of the current contour is given. i.e., the same column data points, which have the same u-value and lie on each sectional contour, have the equal polar angle in the respective local polar coordinate system(Fig.1).

An equal division of the angle intervals $[0,2\pi]$ is uniformly given for each local polar coordinate system:

$$0=\theta_0<\theta_1<\cdots<\theta_m<\theta_{m+1}=2\pi$$

and

$$\theta_j - \theta_{j-1} = \frac{2\pi}{m}$$

The data point $S_{k,j}$ is determined by the angle θ_j. Its parameter value on the k-th B-spline curve is $u'_{k,j}$.

For k-th slice, we assume

$$\alpha_{k,i} \leqslant \theta_j \leqslant \alpha_{k,i+1}$$

where $\alpha_{k,i}$ and $\alpha_{k,i+1}$ are respectively the polar angle of the vertexes $P_{k,i}$ and $P_{k,i+1}$, and are defined by eq(3). $\{\alpha_{k,i}\}$ (i=0,1,$\cdots$,m_k) are monotonous because the polygon $\{P_{k,i}\}$ is convex.

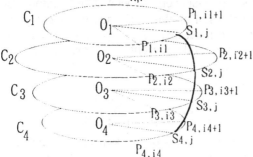

Fig.1 The same column data points, which have the same u value and lie on each contour, have the equal polar angle

The parameter values $\{u_{k,i}\}$(i=0,1, $\cdots$,m_k) can be calculated from the vertexes $\{P_{k,i}\}$(i=0,1, $\cdots$,m_k) according to the data points parametrization method[10] of non-uniform B-spline curve. Let the vertexes $P_{k,i}$ and $P_{k,i+1}$ be respectively corresponding to the parameter value $u_{k,i}$ and $u_{k,i+1}$. When the central angles are relatively small, we may assume that the central angles are proportional to the length of the chords:

$$\frac{u'_{k,j} - u_{k,i}}{u_{k,i+1} - u_{k,i}} = \frac{\theta_j - \alpha_{k,i}}{\alpha_{k,i+1} - \alpha_{k,i}}$$

then

$$u'_{k,j} = u_{k,i} + \frac{\theta_j - \alpha_{k,i}}{\alpha_{k,i+1} - \alpha_{k,i}}(u_{k,i+1} - u_{k,i})$$

According to eq(1), then

$$S_{k,j} = Q_k(u'_{k,j})$$

Thus, a mesh of the data points has been obtained.

2.2 The generation of the array of the data points from the concave contours

For the generation of the mesh of the data points from the concave contours, a mapping method, which maps each vertex of the contour onto its convex hull, is first introduced. It is defined as follows.

Let $\{P_i|i=1,2,3,\cdots\}$ be the vertexes of the contour. Each point $P_i(x_i,y_i)$ of the concavity $P_sP_iP_t$ (Fig.2) is transformed to the line segment joining the points P_s to P_t. The coordinate (x_i',y_i') of P_i', the projection of the point $P_i(x_i,y_i)$, is given by

$$x_i'=x_s+T_i(x_t - x_s)$$
$$y_i'=y_s+T_i(x_t - x_s)$$

where T_i is a weighing factor which is given as follows.

$$T_i = \sum_{j=s}^{i} l_j \bigg/ \sum_{j=s}^{i} l_j$$

and

$$l_j=|P_j-P_{j-1}|$$

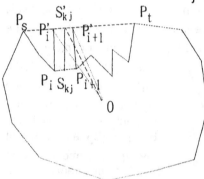

Fig.2 The transformation from the points of the concavity to its convex hull

then, the polar angle of the vertex on concavity is substituted by the polar angle of its projecting point on the convex hull, which is given by eq.(3). The parameter value $u'_{k,j}$, which correspond to the given angle θ_j, can be found according to the method described in previous section. It is used to be as the parameter value of the interpolating point $S_{k,j}$.

Thus, for the concave contour the parameter value $u'_{k,j}$ of the interpolating point $S_{k,j}$ can be obtained by the polar angles of the points $P'_{k,i}$ and $P'_{k,i+1}$ which are the projections of interpolated points $P_{k,i}$ and $P_{k,i+1}$. So, a mesh of the data points has been obtained. With the array of the data points, a skinning surface for the arbitrary sectional contour is obtained by B-spline interpolation technique. The major procedures include the following four steps:

(1) The B-spline curve interpolation from the vertexes of each sectional contour is made.

(2) The projection each vertex of the contours to their convex hull is performed in order to obtain the parameter value of the interpolating points according to the linear relation between the polar angles and chords of the vertexes on the contour.

(3) The array of the data points(or interpolating points) is generated.

(4)The B-spline surface interpolation is performed according to the surface interpolation technique.

3. The generation of the data points in mesh for multiple-branching problem

In dealing with the situation of branching(i.e., one contour splits into several contours or several contours merge into a single one), the B-spline surface interpolation procedure is divided into two phases: First, the multiple-branching problem is transformed into a single branching problem; Then, the B-spline surface interpolation is performed according to the skinning technique of the single branching problem.

The multiple-branching problem is sovled by decomposing it into a set of single-branching problems. Assume that the lower contour consists of one loop C_{k-1} and upper contour consists of several loops. For this purpose, the loop in the lower contour is divided into as many loops as that of the upper contour.

As shown in Fig.3, the dividing methods are described as follows. Without loss of generality, we suppose that there are three loops in the upper contour and B_1, B_2, B_3 are the centroids of loops in the upper contour respectively. A_0 is the centroid of the lower contour. We first compute the centroid B_0 (i.e. arithmetic mean) of the centroids B_1, B_2 and B_3 in the upper contour .

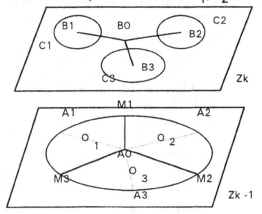

Then, the radius A_0A_1, A_0A_2 and A_0A_3 are connected which are respectively parallel to B_0B_1, B_0B_2 and B_0B_3 of the upper contour. Next, we find such radius that it divide the central angle $\angle A_1A_0A_2$ into two parts at the rate of perimeters of loop C_1 and C_2. The radius A_0M_2, A_0M_3 are found by the same method. Finally, the mid-points O_1, O_2 and O_3 of A_0A_1, A_0A_2 and A_0A_3 are

Fig.3 Dividing the contour which has only one loop into three parts corresponding to each loop on the upper contour

found, which correspond to B_1, B_2 and B_3 respectively. So, the tri-branching problem is transformed into three of single-branching problem. i.e. the loop C_1 corresponds to the loop $M_1A_0M_3A_1M_1$, the loop C_2 corresponds to $M_2A_0M_1A_2M_2$ and the loop C_3 corresponds to $M_3A_0M_2A_3M_3$.

Thus, the multiple-branching problem is decomposed into n "single start contour to single goal contour" surface interpolation subproblem. The method described in the above section can be respectively applied to each of the subproblem. Each one of them can be solved in the same manner. In other word, the rectangular data point mesh of the interpolation surface can be generated according to the above method. As shown in Fig.4, two interpolating surface are respectively fitted to the data points of each branch in the upper part and one interpolating surface is fitted to the data points of one branch in the lower part.

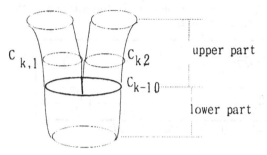

$C_{k,1}$ C_{k2} upper part

C_{k-10}

lower part

Fig.4 The branching problem is decomposed into the single branch subproblem

4. Surface Fitting

After the rectangular data points mesh for the B-spline surface interpolation is obtained, the control mesh for the interpolating surface is obtained by the B-spline surface inversion procedure. So, a smooth surface, which go through the mesh of the data points and approximate a family of sectional contours, is generated. Then, the intersecting curve between two surface must be found in order to keep the position continuity of the interpolating surface at the merging contour. Finally the smoothing surface may be rendered based on the parametric surface rendering approach.

5. Results and Conclusion

The algorithm for the generation of the B-spline from the sectional contours, has been successfully implemented. It is applied to reconstruction of surface from a set of three-dimensional anatomical thin sections of the human head. There are fifty sections of the sellar region of the human brain. The thickness of each section is 1.2 mm and the distance between adjacent sections is 0.3 mm. The anatomical structure in 3D, such as the running of vessels and nerves, the branching of vessels and nerves, and the geometry of pituary in sellar region and so on, are shown in the 3D image. Displaying artery and base of brain, skull bone and vein, nerve and pituary together shows the position relationships of various organs in the human brain(Fig.5, Fig.6). By comparing with the triangulation-based method[11], we find that the method presented in this paper has advantage in the fidelity such as the smoothness of the surface. By rotating the image, the structure may be viewed from a different direction(Fig.7). Table 1 sums up the experimental results. The CPU times(in milli-second) have measured on a SGI Indigo2/XZ workstation .

Our experiments show that the running time of the above approach is nearly proportional to the number of points. The speed of the surface interpolation is much faster than that of rendering.

In this paper,a new method is presented to the surface approximation of an object defined by a set of parallel slices and several experimental results corroborate the theory. The proposed technique for surface generation from interpolation curves of the vertex of the contour enable the interpolating surface to approximate the original object. It adapts to the representation of the objects with complex shape, which is often encountered in reconstructing blood vessels or neuron networks. The problem of complex branching problem is perfectly solved except the case of n-branching (n ⩾ 3) if the centroids of the n loops are collinear. The smoothness of the surface at the merging contour entails a lot of further research.

	skull	brain base	artery	nerve	vein
Number of points on all contours	34716	22479	3757	3516	232
Interpolating time	62	43	9	8	2
Rendering time	482	374	65	63	11

Table 1. Experiment result about the interpolation surface

6. References

1. David Meyers and Shelley Skinner Surface from contours. ACM Trans. on Graphics vol.11, No.3, 1992
2. Ekoule,A.B., Peyrin,F.C. and Odet,C.L. A triangulation algorithm from arbitrary shaped multiple planar contours. ACM Trans. on Graphics vol.10, No.2,1991
3. Boissonnat,J.D., Shape reconstruction from planar cross-sections. Computer vision, Graphics, Image process ing Vol.44, No.1(1988)
4. Lounsbery, M., Loop,C., A testbed for the comparison of parametric surface methods. In SPIE Symposium on Electronic Imaging science and technology. 1990
5. C. C. liang, Dynamic Elastic Interpolation for 3D object Reconstruction from serial cross-sectional Images. IEEE Trans. Med. Imaging No.3, 1988
6. W. C. Lin and S. Y. Chen A new surface interpolation technique for reconstructing 3D objects from serial cross-sections. Comp. vision, Graphics & Image Processing 48(1989)
7. Y. Shinagawa and T. L. Kunii A generalized model for smooth surface generation from cross-sectional data. Visual Computer 7(1991)
8. C. D. Woodward Skinning techniques for interactive B-spline surface interpolation. Computer-aided design Vol.20, No.8,1988
9. S. Wu, J. F. Abel and D.P.Greenber, An interactive computer graphics approach to surface representation, commum. ACM,20, No.10 1977, P703-712
10. Lee E t y. Choosing nodes in parametric curve interpolation. CAD, vol.21, No.6, 1989
11. Meihe Xu, Zesheng Tang and Junhui Deng A New Algorithm for Contours-Connection CAD/CG' 95 Wuhan, China, 1995

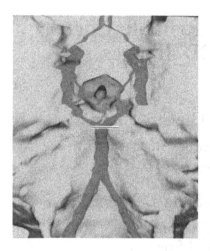

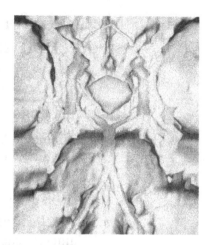

Fig.5 The superior view of the skull (the white is the skull bone, the brown yellow is the pituitar, the blue is the vein and the red is the artery)

Fig.6 The inforior view of the brain base (the golden yellow is the nerve, the red is the artery and the brown yellow is the brain base and the pituitar.)

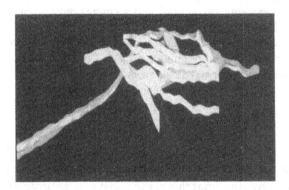

Fig.7 The rendering result by using the proposed method, the left lateral view of the nerve, artery and pituitary (the golden yellow is the nerve, the red is the artery and the brown yellow is the pituitar.)

Two Methods for a Reliable Corner Detection in 2D Images

Richard Lengagne, Olivier Monga

INRIA, Domaine de Voluceau - Rocquencourt
BP. 105, 78153 Le Chesnay Cedex, France

Cong Ge, Ma Song De

NLPR, Institute of Automation
Chinese Academy of Sciences
Zhong Guan Cun P.O.Box 2728, Beijing 100080, China
e-mail: Richard.Lengagne@inria.fr

Abstract

In this paper, we apply successively two methods for corner detection in two-dimensional images, i.e. a differential geometry-based approach relying on multi-scale curvature computation and curvature extrema extraction, and a connexionist approach based on neural networks. We point out the limits of each method and we investigate the way to combine those two strategies in order to get more accurate and more reliable results.
This methodology is tested on an indoor scene.

1   Introduction

Corner detection in 2D images is a quite important problem in computer vision, which can be directly applied to pattern recognition, geometrical modelling, stereovision, matching, etc... Several approaches have already been used to try to solve that keypoint. Some of them focus on the design of a corner operator, e.g. a function, the maximum of which, or the zero-crossings of which must be obtained at the corner location [6]. Other ones try to find a model for the corner pattern and derive operators to detect the corners [2], [3].
In this paper, we propose two different approaches for corner extraction;

the first one is based on differential geometry: once we have extracted the egdes of the image, we compute at each edge point the curvature and the derivative of the curvature and detect the zero-crossings of this derivative in order to get the curvature extrema. The corners can be defined as the maxima of the curvature in an indoor scene mostly composed of polyhedral objects. To refine this method, we apply a multi-scale detection, according to the width of the filter used to compute the partial derivatives of the image.

The second approach uses neural networks; different kinds of inputs can be given to the network, such as the edge map, the grey level of the pixels surrounding the candidate pixel, or a functional of this grey level (partial derivatives, curvature, ...). The output gives an estimation of the probability that the candidate point is a corner.

Better results can be achieved if we combine the two methods: a "blind" detection of the curvature extrema using a multi-scale approach is followed by a learning-based extraction applying the neural network theory. We give finally some experimental results on an indoor scene.

2   A multi-scale approach for corner detection

This approach uses the differential properties of the objects in the image, computed with filtering techniques from the grey level image. We use here the scheme presented in [4], [5], i.e.:

- we use isotropic smoothing filters to compute the partial derivatives of the image signal $I(x, y)$. If s is the smoothing filter, the partial derivative $\frac{\partial^n I}{\partial x^m \partial y^p}$, $n = m + p$ is computed as $I(x, y) * \frac{\partial^n s}{\partial x^m \partial y^p}$.
  If s is isotropic, i.e. the response $I * s$ is the same when applied to a point M and to the image of M by a rigid motion, then the partial derivatives of I will also be invariant under rigid motion (see [5] for the proof). Otherwise, some features, like the norm of the gradient, the curvature, will depend on the orientation of the pattern in the image. Thus we decide to use the Gaussian filter $g(x) = e^{-x^2/2\sigma^2}$ as a smoothing filter. Each partial derivative is computed using separable filtering.

- we approximate with Prony's method the Gaussian filter and all its derivatives by a function $h(x) = (a_0 \cos(\omega_0 \frac{x}{\sigma}) + a_1 sin(\omega_0 \frac{x}{\sigma})) e^{-\frac{b_0}{\sigma} x} + (c_0 \cos(\omega_1 \frac{x}{\sigma}) + c_1 sin(\omega_1 \frac{x}{\sigma})) e^{-\frac{b_1}{\sigma} x}$ so that it can be implemented recursively (see [1]).

- we normalize the filters to ensure an appropriate response to given polynomial inputs, so that:

  - $\sum_{i=-\infty}^{+\infty} f_0(i) = 1$ and $\sum_{i=-\infty}^{+\infty} i f_1(i) = 1$.
  - $\sum_{i=-\infty}^{+\infty} f_2(i) = 0$ and $\sum_{i=-\infty}^{+\infty} \frac{i^2}{2} f_2(i) = 1$.
  - $\sum_{i=-\infty}^{+\infty} i f_3(i) = 0$ and $\sum_{i=-\infty}^{+\infty} \frac{i^3}{6} f_3(i) = 1$.

where f_0, f_1, f_2, f_3 denote respectively the smoothing filter, and the first, second and third order derivative filters.

The numerical values for each filter are given in [5].

We first perform edge detection with the non-maxima (of the gradient) suppression or the extraction of the zero-crossings of the Laplacian, both methods using the previously described filters. The indoor scenes we want to test the algorithm on are mostly composed of polyhedral objects. Thus a corner can be defined as a local maximum of the curvature along the edge. Since there is a smoothing step in the derivative computation, the gradient is also defined at the corner location.

We thus calculate, on each edge point and for a given value of σ, the curvature k and the derivative of the curvature with respect to the arc length s, with the formulas:

$$k = \frac{-t^T H t}{\|\vec{g}\|}, \text{ where } H \text{ is the Hessian of the grey level function } I(x,y):$$

$$H = \begin{bmatrix} I_{xx} & I_{xy} \\ I_{xy} & I_{yy} \end{bmatrix} \text{ and } \vec{t} \text{ is the unit tangent vector to (C) at point } m:$$

$$\vec{t} = \frac{(-I_y, I_x)^t}{\sqrt{I_x^2 + I_y^2}}.$$

The curvature derivative, that we call the "extremality criterion", is given by:

$$k'(s) = \frac{3\,(t^T H t)(g^T H t) - \|\vec{g}\|^2\, t^T \begin{pmatrix} t^T H_x t \\ t^T H_y t \end{pmatrix}}{\|\vec{g}\|^3} \text{ where } H_x = \begin{bmatrix} I_{xxx} & I_{xxy} \\ I_{xxy} & I_{xyy} \end{bmatrix}$$

and $H_y = \begin{bmatrix} I_{xxy} & I_{xyy} \\ I_{xyy} & I_{yyy} \end{bmatrix}$.

We then detect the edge points which are zero-crossings of the extremality criterion, which correspond to the maxima and the minima of the curvature. We have to discriminate the maxima from the minima using the curvature values in the neighbourhood of the current point. This distinction can induce many errors: a flat, but not exactly horizontal nor vertical edge, can be composed of several steps due to the digitization effect. On the step location, the point can be considered as a maximum of curvature, though it is obviously not a corner. This algorithm can be applied to any value of σ. Figure 1 shows the curvature maxima detection for the scale $\sigma = 2$.

It is quite impossible to know which value of σ (scale) really suits to the image. One given scale can be appropriate for one area of the image, but not for another area. We thus apply a multi-scale approach for curvature extrema detection, similarly to the extraction of the zero-crossings of the Laplacian ([7]). We run the previous algorithm for different scales $\{\sigma_1, ..., \sigma_n\}$ and track the extrema from the coarsest scale (the largest one) to the finest one. A large scale can prevent from extracting too many spurious points, which could be due to noise, digitization effect, etc... Figure 1 shows that the choice of a too fine scale implies the detection of many extra points. But on the other hand, the accurate localization of a zero-crossing must be done at a fine scale. Stable points will thus be found at large scales but tracked down to the smallest one to find their precise location. Each edge point is given an output value according to the number of scales where it has been detected as a zero-crossing of the curvature derivative. The larger this output value is, the more stable this extremum is. We can also distinguish the maxima from the minima in the multi-scale case. Figure 2 shows the curvature maxima which appear at at least 2 scales out of 4, after running the multi-scale algorithm for the scales 2, 4, 6 and 8. The multi-scale approach, though it gives theoretically more significant results than the mono-scale one, is still not satisfying. Is is quite efficient to estimate the stability of a curvature extremum, but the discrimination between maxima and minima is still hard and not convincing.

3   Corner detection with neural networks

A "blind" method as the one previously described is quite powerful to extract some features which have an analytical meaning based on differential geometry, but fails to detect successfully some more subjective features such as corners. Therefore, a learning-based method can then appear as a good way of refining the previous method and help detect more subtle characteristics. A neural network can be a quite simple and efficient way of achieving this goal.

We have implemented a 3-layer (one hidden layer) feed-forward neural network, trained with the back-propagation algorithm.

The input layer nodes can be the grey level, the edge map, and/or the curvature values of the neighbours of each edge pixel inside a 5*5 window. The curvature values are computed with the formula and the filters given in the previous section. The output value ranges from 0 to 1, and gives an estimation of the probability that the center of the window is a corner. We have trained the network with several points selected from the indoor image and tested it on all the edge points.

Figure 3 shows the corner detection when giving the grey level image and the edge map as the input of the network with 200 training points (75 corners and 125 "non-corners") and taking into account the invariance under rotation of the edge. We cover the neighbourhood of the candidate point in a circular way from the closest neighbours to the furthest ones; the first neighbour is determined by the gradient direction at the candidate point; we thus create a new grid and we resample the image according to that grid. This ensures that the neighbourhood will be covered in the same way whatever the rotation applied to the pattern. The threshold for the output of the network has been set to 0.8.

Though the geometry of the edge is probably the most important feature for corner detection, it seems that a network given the edge map as the only input does not yield good results, because of the digitization effect we have already mentioned before.

We thus have to add other kinds of input: the grey level, and also some features computed from the partial derivatives, such as the curvature. These features are computed from the partial derivatives of the image with the algorithm presented in Section 2, but they depend on the scale σ chosen for the filters. This leads us to another approach combining the multi-scale "blind" detection and the neural networks.

4 Combining the two approaches

The approach based on differential geometry fails to distinguish very precisely the maxima (or the minima) of the curvature, but it can be efficient if we just want to extract the extrema of the curvature. Moreover the multi-scale approach gives some information about the stability of these extrema. We can thus consider the output of the approach described in Section 2 as an estimation of the probability that the current point is considered as a curvature extremum.

If M has been detected as a curvature extremum at m scales out of n, we can thus write:

$\tilde{P}$(M is considered as a curvature extremum) $= m/n$, where $\tilde{P}$ denotes an estimation of P.

Since we are interested in $\tilde{P}$(M is a corner), we can write:

$\tilde{P}$(M is a corner)$=\tilde{P}$(M is a corner/M is considered as a curvature extremum)$\tilde{P}$(M is considered as a curvature extremum) $+$ $\tilde{P}$(M is a corner/M is not considered as a curvature extremum)$\tilde{P}$(M is not considered as a curvature extremum) $= p1 + p2$

We know:

$\tilde{P}$(M is considered as a curvature extremum)$=m/n$ and
$\tilde{P}$(M is not considered as a curvature extremum)$=1-m/n$.

$\tilde{P}$(M is a corner/M is considered as a curvature extremum) depends on the scales where M has really been detected as an extremum by the method of Section 2. Since the neural network is trained to detect corners, if we apply it to an extremum of curvature at a given scale σ_i, its output is in fact:

$\tilde{P}$(M is a corner/M is considered as a curvature extremum and $\sigma = \sigma_i$).

Therefore:

$\tilde{P}$(M is a corner/M is considered as a curvature extremum)$=\sum_{i \in S}\tilde{P}$(M is a corner/M is considered

as a curvature extremum and $\sigma = \sigma_i$)$\tilde{P}(\sigma = \sigma_i)$,

where $S = \{i \in \{1, ..., n\}$/M is detected as a curvature extremum by the first method at scale $\sigma = \sigma_i\}$. We can set: $\tilde{P}(\sigma = \sigma_i)= 1/n$.

Similarly, we can compute p2.

We have tested this method with the grey level, the edge map and the curvature computed at a given scale as inputs of the network, for every point around the candidate point inside a 5*5 window. This leads to 5*5*3=75 nodes in the first layer of the network. There are 150 hidden nodes and 1 output node which gives an estimation of $\tilde{P}$(M is a corner). A thresholding can then enable to select the most probable corners.

Figure 4 shows the result, which is better than the mere use of neural networks without the first multi-scale "blind" detection: the corners are located more accurately. Moreover, the discrimination between corners and "non-corners" is quite successful and we do not need set a very high threshold to get the desired points.

5   Conclusion

In this paper, we have shown that the use of a learning-based method can be a quite powerful tool to detect features like corners and help compensate the drawbacks of a "blind" method; we first use the results given by a differential geometry-based method which does not use any a priori knowledge about the corner pattern nor any corner model, and then apply the neural network-based approach to detect accurately the corners. The combination of those two powerful approaches seems very promising and could be succesfully applied on more complex data, such as crest points or crest lines in 3D volumic images.

References

[1]   Rachid Deriche. Recursively implementing the gaussian and its derivatives. *INRIA Research report*, 1993.

[2]   Rachid Deriche and Gérard Giraudon. Accurate Corner Detection: an analytical study. *ICCV*, 1990.

[3]   Rachid Deriche and Gérard Giraudon. On corner and vertex detection *CVPR*, 1993.

[4]   Olivier Monga, Serge Benayoun, and Olivier D. Faugeras. Using third order derivatives to extract ridge lines in 3d images. In *IEEE Conference on Vision and Pattern Recognition*, Urbana Champaign, June 1992.

[5]   Olivier Monga, Richard Lengagne, and Rachid Deriche. Extraction of the zero-crossings of the curvature derivative in volumic 3D medical images: a multi-scale approach. *INRIA Research report*, 1994.

[6]   J. Alison Noble. Finding corners. *Image and Vision Computing, vol 6, May 1988, pp 121-128*.

[7]   A. Witkin. A multi-scale approach to extract zero-crossings of the laplacian. In *Proceedings of International Joint Conference on Artificial Intelligence*, 1982.

Fig.1 (left): maxima of curvature extraction at scale $\sigma = 2$
Fig.2 (right): maxima of curvature extraction: multi-scale approach.

Fig.3 (left): corner extraction with neural networks: input=grey level and edge map.
Fig.4 (right): corner extraction: combination of the two methods.

On the Deletability of Points in 3D Thinning

R. Watzel[1], K. Braun[2], A. Hess[2], H. Scheich[2], W. Zuschratter[2]

[1] Department of Digital Technology, Technical University of Darmstadt, Germany
e-mail: row@dtro.e-technik.th-darmstadt.de
[2] Federal Intitute for Neurobiology, P. O. Box 1860, 39008 Magdeburg, Germany

Abstract. An appropriate description of the shape of objects is essential for image analysis and understanding. A well known approach to this is the concept of skeleton. This paper considers a parallel thinning algorithm to compute the skeleton in 3D and proposes a new deletability criterion which retains points whose deletion depends on the deletion of their neighbors. The criterion is incorporated by filling components in a 3x3x3 window.

1 Introduction

A useful approach to shape description is the skeleton which is known as a set of thin arcs and curves. Other terms such as medial axis transform, grassfire transform or thinned image have been used to denote familiar concepts [LLS92],[JP92], [LL92]. Here we denote the process as thinning and the result as skeleton. We are interested in skeletons that are thin, central to the objects and topology preserving.

We consider binary images that are defined in a 3D cubic grid [KRR92]. A point $p = (x, y, z)$ is assigned to 1, if it belongs to an object, and we say p is *black*. Otherwise, p is assigned to 0, and we say p is *white*. We use 26-adjacency for black points and 6-adjacency for white points. Let $N(p)$ denote the local 3x3x3 window around p. Following [SC94], we define

- a point 6-adjacent to p is called an *s-point*.
- a point $q \neq p$ that is 6-adjacent to two s-points is called an *e-point*.
- a point in $N(p)$ that is neither an s- nor an e-point is called a *v-point*.
- if x is an s-point and S' is the set of all 6-neighbors of x in $N(p) \setminus \{p\}$ and S'' is the set of v-points 6-adjacent to any point in S', the set $S = S' \cup S''$ is called $x - surface(p)$.
- each s-point x is assigned to a direction r such that r is a vector $x - p$. Then $x - surface(p)$ is also called $r - surface(p)$.
- a point whose 6-neighbor in direction r is white is called *r-free*.

2 The Thinning Algorithm

Thinning algorithms erode the surface of an object while preserving topology, until a thin skeleton is left. They are classified as sequential and parallel algorithms[LS91]. A sequential algorithm examines the points in a predetermined order and deletion of a point depends on the current state of progress. On the other hand, parallel algorithms consider an unordered set of border points in one iteration and decide on the deletion of these in parallel, i.e. based only on the result of the preceding iteration.

Our thinning algorithm works as follows.

Algorithm A:

1. Define an ordered set of directions $R = \{r_0, \ldots r_5\}$ that lie in the cubic grid. Select r_0. Set $i = 0$.
2. Let B denote the set of all black points. Determine the set $M \subseteq B$ of all r–free black points.
3. Determine the set of points $D \subseteq M$ of deletable points (for deletability, see section 3).
4. If $D = 0$, terminate.
5. Replace B by $B \setminus D$, set $i = (i+1) \mod 6$ and select direction r_i. Continue with step 2.

Parallel algorithms like this base the decision on the deletion of some point p on the assumption that in the local neighborhood $N(p)$ no other point will be deleted. Actually, there is dependency among adjacent points [TF81]. Section 3 gives a criterion that says when a point is deletable in $N(p)$. Section 4 solves the problem of dependency.

3 Determining the Deletability

One of the essential problems of thinning is the question whether a point is simple or not. From [KR89] we have the following theorem:

Theorem 1: Let p be a black point in a digital picture $P = (Z^3, 26, 6, B)$. Let $B' = B \setminus \{p\}$. Then p is simple iff the following conditions hold:

1. p is 26-adjacent to just one black component of $N(p) \cap B'$.
2. p is 6-adjacent to just one white component of $N(p) \setminus B$.
3. $\Delta\chi = \chi((Z^3, 26, 6, B \cap N(p))) - \chi((Z^3, 26, 6, B' \cap N(p))) = 0$.

where $\chi(P)$ is the genus of a digital picture P. As also stated in [KR89], $\chi(P)$ equals the number of white components minus the number of tunnels plus the number of black components in a digital picture P. These numbers are known as the Betti numbers b_0, b_1, b_2, respectively, see e.g. [Cro78], [LP91]. An example of a tunnel is illustrated in figure 1. Deletion of the center will keep b_0 and b_2 constant while a tunnel is created. We call condition 1, 2 and 3 BDC (Black Deletability Criterion), WDC (White Deletability Criterion), and GDC (Genus Deletability Criterion), respectively, and the combination of all these DC. WDC is coverd by BDC and GDC for our choice of adjacency. This can be seen easily by observing that deletion of p can only increase b_0, decrease b_1 and increase b_2, but b_2 is constant due to BDC. So $\Delta b_0 - \Delta b_1 \leq -1$ if WDC is violated.

According to the Euler-Poincare theorem [Cro78], $\Delta\chi$ can be computed easily by

$$\Delta\chi = \Delta v - \Delta e + \Delta f - \Delta q \qquad (1)$$

where v is the number of white points, e the number of white edges (6-adjacency), f the number of white square faces and q the number of whit elementary cubes.

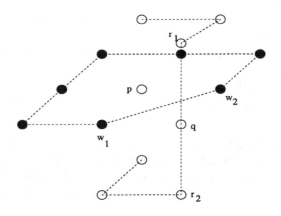

Fig. 1. Example of a tunnel.

First we describe an algorithm to determine whether BDC holds. We define the neighborhood vector x as a binary vector with components $x_0 \ldots x_{26}$ assigned to the values of the points in $N(p)$. Adjacency relations can be defined by an adjacency matrix A such that $A_{i,j} = 1$ if there is an adjacency between some x_i and x_j, and $A_{i,j} = 0$ otherwise. Then the product $y = A \cdot x$ is defined by

$$y_i = \bigvee_{j=0}^{26} A_{i,j} \wedge x_j \qquad 0 \le i < 27 \qquad (2)$$

where point y_i will be set iff x_i has a neighbor in x defined by A. Matrices A_6 and A_{26} denote 6– and 26–adjacency, respectively.

Algorithm B determines if BDC holds for a given neighborhood vector x. It searches some point in a black component and fills this component in variable y by adding to y all neighbors of the component filled so far. It terminates when no change occurs and the component is filled completely. If the component was the only one, $y = x$ and the algorithm will return 1. Algorithm B will terminate after at most 9 iterations and after 2 or 3 iterations in most cases.

Algorithm B:

Input: neighborhood vector x.

Output: 1, if BDC holds.

0, if BDC is violated.

Algorithm: clear p in x

if $(x = 0)$ return 0

determine any position k such that $x_k = 1$

(check s–points first, then e–points and then v–points)

if (k corresponds to a v–point)

if (no other v–point is set in x) return 0 else return 1

$y = 2^k$

do $y' = y$

$y = (y \vee A_{26} \cdot y) \wedge x$

while $(y' \neq y)$

if $(y = x)$ return 1 else return 0

In addition to topology preservation we require that a point must not be deleted if it is an end point (which has only one neighbor) or a point of high curvature. Here we define that high curvature is observed if three mutually adjacent surfaces in $N(p)$ are white. We call this the curvature condition (CC).

4 The problem of dependency

In algorithm A the points in the set D are deleted in parallel, i.e. assuming that none of their neighbors is deleted at the same time. But actually this may happen. Some approaches modify the deletability criterion to avoid this [TF81], but no proof is given that all dependencies will be covered. If attention is restricted to the 3x3x3 window, they result in a skeleton that is not thin which requires some postprocessing. We give a new deletability criterion that will cover such dependencies. We show that dependency can only be implied by BDC but not by WDC or GDC, resulting in a simplified test which can be performed by algorithm B.

First we consider WDC. We argue by contradiction. Let p and q be points deletable alone due to DC. Let p and q have white 6–neighbors p' and q' in the same direction, respectively, as guaranteed in step 2 in algorithm A. Dependency can be implied by WDC only if p is 6–adjacent to some white component c and q is 6–adjacent to some white component d, but c and d are not identical, as illustrated in figure 2a. Dependency also requires that p and q are 6–connected by some white 6–path π, or they are 6–adjacent. From the deletability of p and q WDC yields:

- $p' \in c$ and $q' \in d$
- if π exists, π is 6–adjacent to c
- if π exists, π is 6–adjacent to d
- if π does not exist, p' and q' are 6–neighbors as are p and q.

From the 2nd and 3rd conclusions it follows that c and d must be 6–adjacent and thus are identical, because otherwise they were no components. This is a contradiction. QED.

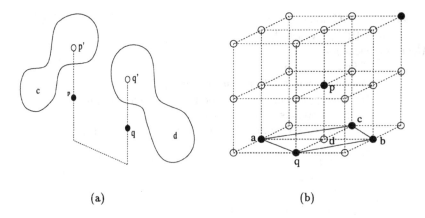

Fig. 2. Examples illustrating (a) dependancy of white points and (b) dependency of black points.

Now consider GDC. Since we know that WDC is not affected by dependency, we have to show that the number of tunnels, b_1, is not affected, too. Let p and q be defined as above. From the deletability of p we know that no tunnel is created. Now, if q is also deleted and if this creates a tunnel, deletion of p alone will change b_0. In this case p is not deletable regardless whether q is deleted or not.

Detection of dependencies can be included in BDC. Before checking BDC by algorithm B, we make a copy of $N(p)$ and call it N. According to step 2 in the thinning algorithm we assume that all points to be deleted are r–free. To determine the deletability of some point p, we identify all such points in N and delete them in N if the conditions in the following proposition apply. We refer to the operation of removing all the points specified in the proposition as *reduction*.

Proposition: Let $N(p)$ be the neighborhood of some point p and let N be a copy of $N(p)$. Remove all points q_i from N that satisfy the following conditions:

- q_i is r–free or is in $r - surface(p)$.
- p and q_i have at least two 26–neighbors in common that are not 26–adjacent to each other.

(i) If N satisfies BDC and $N(p)$ satisfies WDC, $N(p)$ also satisfies BDC.
(ii) If $N(p)$ does not satisfy BDC, N will not satisfy BDC or $N(p)$ will violate WDC.

Proof: First we prove (i). Assume one point q satisfies the conditions above. According to the condition q has two 26–neighbors a and b that are not 26–adjacent to each other. N satisfies BDC implies that a and b are 26–connected and they belong to the only black component in $N(p) \setminus \{p\}$. Thus q belongs to the same component in $N(p)$, and $N(p)$ satisfies BDC.

On the other hand, it is possible that a will be deleted from N due to the second condition, too. It must be shown that if $N(p) \setminus \{q, a\}$ satisfies BDC, $N(p) \setminus \{q\}$ also satisfies BDC. Because of the second condition, a has a 26–neighbor c that is not 26–adjacent to q. First assume that c is not 26–adjacent to b. Since $N(p) \setminus \{q, a\}$ satisfies BDC, c must be 26–connected to q. Thus c and q belong to the same component in $N(p)$, and $N(p)$ satisfies BDC. This discussion can be continued until a point is reached that does not satisfy the second condition. Now assume a point, say c, is reached that is 26–adjacent to b but not to q, see figure 2b. Then there is a closed 26–path π of points all of which are deleted in N. Now, if N satisfies BDC and π was a component in $N(p)$ and there is another component in $N(p)$, $N(p)$ will not satisfy BDC. It remains to show that in this case $N(p)$ will violate WDC. All points in π are r–free. Thus the s–point d in the opposite direction of r seen from p will not belong to π, nor will p or its neighbor p' in direction r. Two cases are possible: (1) At least one point in π is 26–adjacent to d. Then d must be white since π comprises a component, and since p' is white, too, WDC does not apply to $N(p)$. (2) All points in π are in $r - surface(p)$. Since π is a component, p must be 6–adjacent to at least one white point other than p', and p' will not be 6–connected to this point. Thus WDC will not apply to $N(p)$.

Now we prove (ii). Assume that deletion of all q_i from N does not remove a complete component. Then p is adjacent to as many components in $N(p) \setminus \{p\}$ as in $N \setminus \{p\}$. Thus BDC gives the same result for $N(p)$ and N. If a component was deleted from N completely, $N(p)$ will violate WDC as shown in case (i). QED.

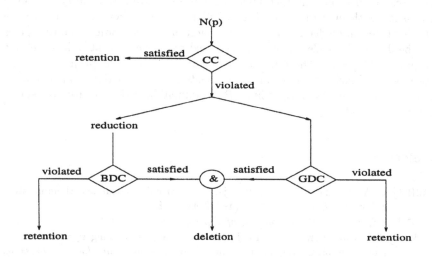

Fig. 3. Overview about the overall deletability criterion DC.

5 Discussion

Since for our choice of adjecency (which is very common) the Euler characteristic is not sufficient to indicate changes in 3D topology, we incorporated its invariance into the criterion that the number of black and white components be invariant. Besides topological considerations the problem of mutual dependency is an essential issue in parallel 3D thinning algorithms. Our approach (computing deletability after deletion of all other points that could possibly affect deletability) seems rather conservative, but it is reliable and can be easily incorporated into WDC. As we observed, retention can only be implied by dependency if the object is already eroded to an almost thin skeleton (at most 2 points wide) or if the point under consideration lies in a medial face. So it does only cause slight anisotropies near the object center. We also observed that near the end of the thinning process the dependency will slow down the thinning process considerably, because only few points will be deleted in each iteration. Therefore, we recommend to change the algorithm at this stage of progress and dismiss the reduction in DC while checking for DC a second time for each point immediatly before deletion. In the latter stage a thin (one point wide) skeleton is obtained while dependency will in some cases prevent the skeleton from being thin in the first stage. Inclusion of the dependency criterion will prevent medial faces from erosion. After the change in the algorithm, these faces will be eroded, too, resulting in a line skeleton.

We successfully apply the line skeletons constructed by the above algorithm to detect dendritic spines in 3D grayscale images. The left side of figure 4 shows a dendrite with some spines attached to it. The image was taken by a confocal laser scan microscope and then binarised. Our objective is to identify the spines and separate them from the dendrite in order to analyse their morphology. Since the dendrite can be determined by the longest path in the object and the spines can be defined by skeleton subtrees attached to it, the concept of line skeleton is quite appropriate. The right side of Figure 4 shows a 2d-projection of the corresponding skeleton. Here, all line segments between junctions and end points have been replaced by straight lines. By examination of the skeleton, the spines can be identified.

References

[AdB85] C. Arcelli and G. Sanniti di Baja. A width independent fast thinning algorithm. *IEEE Trans: PAMI*, 7(4):463–474, 1985.

[Cro78] F.C. Croom. *Basic Concepts of Topology*. Springer, 1978.

[CWS87] R.T. Chin, H.K. Wan and D.L. Stover. A one-pass thinning algorithm and its parallel implementation. *Computer Vision, Grphics and Image Processing*, 40:30–40, 1987.

[JC92] Ben K. Jang and Roland T. Chin. *One-Pass Parallel Thinning: Analysis, Properties, and Quantitative Evaluation. IEEE Trans: PAMI*, 11:1129–1140, 1992.

98

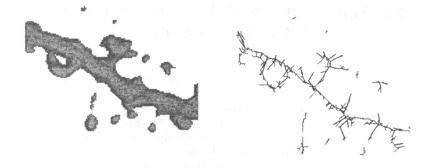

Fig. 4. A dendrite with spines and a 2d–projection of the corresponding skeleton.

[JP92] Liang Ji and Jim Piper. *Fast Homotopy-Preserving Skeletons Using Mathematical Morphology. IEEE: PAMI*, 14(6):653–664, 1992.

[KR89] T.Y. Kong and A. Rosenfeld. *Digital Topology: Introduction and Survey. Computer Vision, Graphics and Image Processing*, 48:357–393, 1989.

[KRR92] T.Y. Kong, W. Roscoe and A. Rosenfeld. *Concepts of digital topology. Topology and its Applications*, 46:219–262, 1992.

[LL92] Frederic Leymarie and Martin D. Levine. *Simulating the Grassfire Transform Using an Active Contour Model. IEEE Trans: PAMI*, 14(1):56–75, 1992.

[LLS92] Louisa Lam, Seong-Whan Lee and Ching Y. Suen. *Thinning Methodologies - A Comprehensive Survey. IEEE Trans: PAMI*, 9:869–885, 1992.

[LP91] Chung-Nim Lee and Timothy Poston. Winding and euler numbers for 2d and 3d digital images. *CVGIP: Graphical Models and Image Processing*, 53(6):522–537, November 1991.

[LPR93] Chung-Nim Lee, Timothy Poston and Azriel Rosenfeld. Holes and genus of 2d and 3d digital images. *CVGIP: Graphical Models and Image Processing*, 55(1):20–47, 1993.

[LS91] Louisa Lam and Ching Y. Suen. *A Dynamic Shape Preserving Thinning Algorithm. Signal Processing*, 22:199–208, 1991.

[SC94] P. K. Saha and B. B. Chaudhuri. *Detection of 3-D Simple Points for Topology Preserving Transformations with Application to Thinning. IEEE Trans: PAMI*, 16(10):1028–1031, 1994.

[TF81] Y.F. Tsao and K.S. Fu. *A Parallel Thinning Algorithm for 3D Pictures. Computer Graphics and Image Processing*, 17:315–331, 1981.

This work has been supported by DFG under the registration number INK 15/A1.

Real-Time Textured Object Recognition on Distributed Systems

J. You[1], W.P. Zhu[1], H.A. Cohen[2] and E. Pissaloux[3]

[1] School of Computer and Information Sciences
University of South Australia, The Levels, Australia 5095
[2] Department of Computer Science and Computer Engineering
La Trobe University, Bundoora, Victoria, Australia, 3083
[3] Institut d'Electronique Fondamentale
Université Paris XI, 91405, Orsay, Cedex, France

Abstract. This paper presents the development of a real-time system for recognition of textured objects. In contrast to current approaches which mostly rely on specialized multiprocessor architectures for fast processing, we use a distributed network architecture to support parallelism and attain real-time performance. In this paper, a new approach to image matching is proposed as the basis of object localization and positioning, which involves dynamic texture feature extraction and hierarchical image matching. A mask based stochastic method is introduced to extract feature points for matching. Our experimental results demonstrate that the combination of texture feature extraction and interesting point detection provides a better solution to the search of the best matching between two textured images. Furthermore, such an algorithm is implemented on a low cost heterogeneous PVM (Parallel Virtual Machine) network to speed up the processing without specific hardware requirements.

Key words: object recognition, image matching, feature extraction, interesting points, distance transform, parallel processing, distributed systems.

1 Introduction

Object detection and recognition have played an important role in image analysis and computer vision. In the past, many recognition systems have been developed for particular applications by applying different techniques of image matching [1],[2],[3]. However, they are restricted to various conditions and cannot be applied to a general task. A simple but effective and efficient matching approach is highly desirable to measure the degree of similarity between two image sets that are superimposed on one another. When edge points are selected as image features, the existing matching algorithms include Chamfer matching[1], hierarchical Chamfer matching[2] and Hausdorff matching[3]. In order to characterize image with fewer feature points without losing information for distance transform, in our previous work, we proposed to replace edge points with interesting points by means of a dynamic thresholding selection procedure[4].

However, the conventional interesting point detection techniques based on detection of discontinuities in pixel properties are not suitable for distinguishing boundaries between differently textured regions because texture is characterized by its local features over some neighbourhood rather than in pixel gray scale. In this paper we describe a new approach to recognize and localize objects in textured images, which involves dynamic texture feature extraction and parallel implementation of hierarchical image matching. Section 2 summarised a mask based stochastic method to dynamically extract texture features and Section 3 highlights the detection of texture interesting points to guide the searching for the best matching between two images. The hierarchical image matching scheme is outlined in Section 4 and the parallel implementation of the recognition system on a low cost heterogeneous PVM (Parallel Virtual Machine) network is detailed in Section 5. Finally the experimental results and conclusion are presented in Section 6 and Section 7 respectively.

2 Texture Feature Extraction Over Mask Tuning

Texture is essentially a neighborhood property which provides a higher-order description of the local image content and has been used as an aid in segmentation and in the interpretation of scenes. Structural and statistical approaches can be both applied to extract texture features[7]. The statistical approach to texture classification and segmentation pioneered by Laws is notable for its computational simplicity[5]. He introduced the concept of a single parameter, the local 'texture energy'(TE) defined at each pixel location (i,j) in the convolved image over a large window size 15*15 or 31*31 as the measure of texture features in the spatial domain. The objective of the mask tuning scheme is to increase the classification accuracy by replacing the constants of Laws' masks with variables. The mask coefficients are therefore adjusted on the training samples by optimizing a given performance index, which is an extension of both Laws' concept[5] and Benke et al's method[6]. The mask is assumed 5*5 size with zero sum in each row. Thus there are 20 mask coefficients to be determined during the training session. In our approach the local variance after convolution is well-approximated the sum of squared values of convolved image within the test window, which is expressed as below:

$$TE(i,j) = \frac{\sum_{W_x} \sum_{W_y} (I * A)^2_{rs}}{P^2 W_x W_y}$$

where the rs sum is over all pixels within a square window W of size $W_x * W_y$ centered on the pixel at i,j, A is a zero sum 'tuned' $5 * 5$ convolution mask and P is the parameter normalizer $P^2 = \sum_{i,j} (A_{i,j})^2$.

When such a tuned mask is determined, the original textured image will be converted in terms of the texture energy measurement $TE(i,j)$. The detection of interesting points is then applied to this feature image named texture energy image to capture texture feature points for image matching.

3 Detection of Interesting Points

The detection of interesting points is based on the measure of how interesting a point is. Unlike the traditional methods in which interesting point detector is directly applied to the original gray scale image, the detection procedure in our test is performed on the texture energy image E obtained in the previous stage. From the simplicity point of view, Moravec operator[9] is used for testing. It is noted that the traditional selection of interesting points on the basis of Moravec operator depends on the pre-defined threshold value. We further introduce a dynamic thresholding procedure based on the histogram. Figure 1 shows the comparison of textural image feature pixels represented by edge points, texture energy, interesting points and texture interesting points respectively. Clearly, texture interesting points best represent the original image with less points.

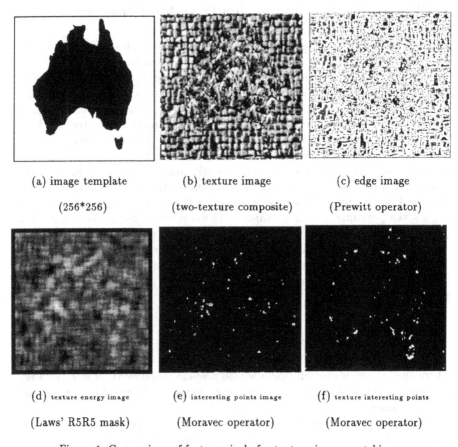

(a) image template
(256*256)

(b) texture image
(two-texture composite)

(c) edge image
(Prewitt operator)

(d) texture energy image
(Laws' R5R5 mask)

(e) interesting points image
(Moravec operator)

(f) texture interesting points
(Moravec operator)

Figure 1. Comparison of feature pixels for texture image matching

4   Hierarchical Image Matching Scheme

In order to avoid the blind searching for the best fit between the given patterns, a guided search strategy is essential to reduce computation burden. In this section we introduce a hierarchical matching scheme guided by the dynamic detection of interesting points for the search for the optimal matching. In contrast to the traditional concept of edge distance for matching measurement, we replace edge points with interesting points to calculate the interesting point distance as the matching measurement, which improves the efficiency and reliability of the testing results. The hierarchical matching presented here is performed on the interesting points pyramid from coarse level to fine level by minimizing the matching criterion. The image pyramid used in our test is built up based on the number of interesting points used for matching. The matching starts from the coarse level in the pyramid with less interesting points. A limited number of areas corresponding to relatively low value of the root mean square average are marked as possible candidates for further precise matching. Then the matching process is moved to the upper level with more interesting points considered and the searching for the best matching is focused on those areas which are marked in the previous level and the same marking process will be repeated in search for the global minimum root mean square average.

5   The Parallel Implementation On PVM

Vision computing involves the execution of a large number of operations on large sets of structured data. The need for very high speed processing in real-time image processing means parallel solutions have to be explored. Image matching based on image feature pixels involves heavily iterated computation and repeated memory access, thus both data parallelism and functional parallelism are applicable to the detection of interesting points, the distance transform, the creation of interesting points pyramid and the search for the best fit in our hierarchical matching scheme to reduce the execution time. In contrast to the conventional parallel implementation where either the dedicated hardware or the software are required, the parallel implementation of our hierarchical matching scheme is on a low cost heterogeneous PVM (Parallel Virtual Machine) network. Our investigation indicates that the distributed memory multicomputer can best meet the high computational and memory access demands in image processing.

PVM is viewed as a general and flexible parallel computing resource which enables the implementation of parallel processing on loosely coupled network. Such a network contains various computers as processing elements and supports a message passing model for communication between the processing elements. In our initial test, a four node PVM network, including 4 SPARC ELC stations, is used for the parallel implementation of our hierarchical matching scheme. The system structure is shown in Figure 2.

103

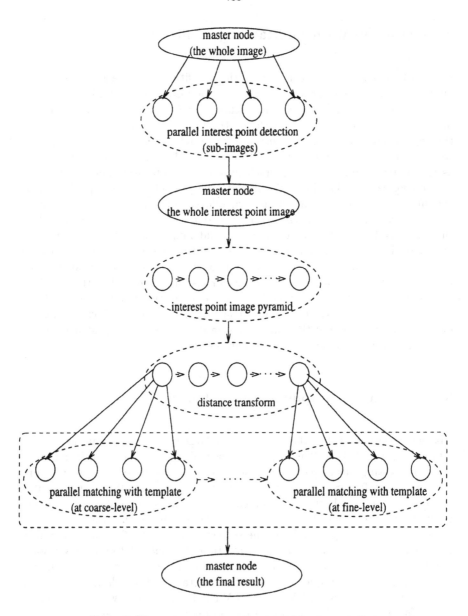

Figure 2. The system structure for parallel implementation

6 Experimental Results

The texture used in this study were selected from Brodatz's well-known compilation. In order to show the advantages of the mask tuning scheme in capturing the common texture feature invariant of rotation and scale effects on real textures, Figure 3 provides examples of multi-scale and orientation image segmentation by pixel labeling in terms of its texture energy extracted by the tuned mask. It is noted that convolution operation plays a key role during mask tuning, the speed-up of the calculation will benefit the overall performance. On the average the sequential execution time for each convolution with 5*5 mask on 256*256 image implemented on Classic SPARC workstation is about 5.8 sec. while the parallel computation with 4 processes increases the processing speed by 15% to 4.96 sec. for each convolution. The processes involved are executed on four different SPARC workstations which are connected by an Ethernet. The higher speed is expected when high speed network, such as ATM , is used and more processes are invoked for parallel implementation.

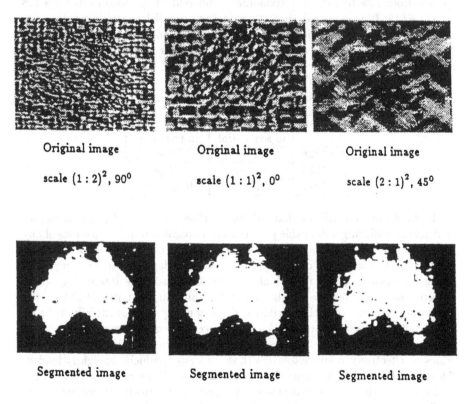

Original image	Original image	Original image
scale $(1:2)^2$, 90^0	scale $(1:1)^2$, 0^0	scale $(2:1)^2$, 45^0

| Segmented image | Segmented image | Segmented image |

Figure 3. Textured image segmentation using 'tuned' mask

The advantages and potentials of a general distributed system for parallel image processing is further demonstrated by the parallel detection of interesting points for image matching. The parallel performance improvement is measured by the following ratio:

$$\gamma = \frac{T_s - T_p}{T_s}$$

where T_s refers to the sequential execution time and T_p refers to the parallel execution time. Table 1 lists the average execution time for the detection of interesting points on different images with various sizes. In our test, Morevec operator was applied to images ranging from 128*128 to 512*512. The sequential processing is performed on a single SPARC ELC station while the parallel implementation is on a 4-node structure using SPARC ELC stations. These experimental results indicate that in general the parallel implementation is faster than the sequential one even for a simple operation on a small size image (*e.g.* Moravec operation on a 128*128 image). The advantage of parallelism becomes more obvious when the test image size grows larger and the adopted algorithm gets more complicated. For the Moravec operation, the speed improvement ratio γ is from 26% to 28% corresponding to different image sizes from $128 * 128$ to $512 * 512$. It is expected that the gain from parallel processing will be increased with the increment of the test image size and the complexity of the task. Moreover, the overall performance will be further improved by introducing appropriate granularity for parallel processing.

Table 1: The comparison of execution time in parallel and sequential

image size	execution time (in sequential)	execution time (in parallel)
128*128	3.3 sec.	1.79 sec.
256*256	15.7 sec.	7.07 sec.
512*512	140.7 sec.	46.62 sec.

It should be pointed out that the distribution of workload plays an important role in achieving a desirable performance in parallel implementations of any computational tasks. During the parallel experiment of our hierarchical matching system, the workload of each processor heavily depends on the complexity of each subtask and the related algorithms. Obviously the interesting points detected as image feature pixels cannot be uniformly distributed. Thus, the processing elements of each distributed processor may have drastically different computational loads. In order to keep all processors equally busy at each stage of the computation, a load balancing procedure is essential which will direct processes to effectively migrate towards those processors which are lightly loaded. Therefore, the execution time of a particular task will be reduced by dynamic resource allocation. In our future work, we concern with the improvement of parallelism by developing a workload allocator which can determine and evaluate the effect of a nonuniform workload distribution on performance and guide the allocation of resources for balanced processing by moving load from heavily to lightly loaded processors via task scheduling.

7 Conclusion

Image matching plays an important role in pattern recognition, image analysis and computer vision. We propose a guided matching scheme by developing a hierarchical matching algorithm based on the detection of interesting points. We conclude that interesting points reduce the number of pixels essential for distance transformation in image matching and the detection of texture interesting points following texture feature extraction provides an efficient method for object recognition in textured images. The algorithm is easy to implement and provides satisfactory results. Such a hierarchical scheme is further extended by parallelism on a low cost heterogeneous PVM (Parallel Virtual Machine) network on the basis of a divide-and-conquer policy. Our investigation confirms that distributed memory multicomputer can meet the high computational and memory access demands in image processing and the parallel implementation on a general distributed system can be widely applied in practice for better performance without specific hardware requirements.

References

1. H.G. Barrow, J.M. Tenenbaum, R.C. Bolles and H.C. Wolf, "Parametric correspondence and chamfer matching: Two new techniques for image matching", *Proc. 5th Int. Joint Conf. Artificial Intelligence*, Cambridge, MA, pp. 659-663, 1977.
2. G. Borgefors, "Hierarchical chamfer matching: a parametric edge matching algorithm", *IEEE Trans. Patt. Anal. Machine Intell.*, Vol. PAMI-10, pp. 849-865, 1988.
3. D.P. Huttenlocher, G.A. Klanderman and W.J. Rucklidge, "Comparing images using the Hausdorff distance", *IEEE Trans. Patt. Anal. Machine Intell.*, Vol. PAMI-15, pp. 850-863, 1993.
4. J. You, E. Pissaloux, J.L. Hellec and P. Bonnin, "A guided image matching approach using Hausdorff distance with interesting points detection" *Proc. of 1st IEEE international conference on image processing*, Austin, USA, November 13-16, 1994, pp. 968-972.
5. K.I. Laws, "Textured image segmentation", *Ph.D thesis*, University of Southern California, January, 1980.
6. K.K. Benke, D.R. Skinner and C.J. Woodruff, "Convolution operators as a basis for objective correllates for texture perception", *IEEE Trans. Syst., Man, Cybern.*, Vol. SMC-18, pp. 158-163, 1988.
7. R.M. Haralick, "Statistical and structural approaches to texture", *Proc. IEEE*, Vol.67, pp. 786-804, 1979.
8. T.M. Caelli and D. Reye, "On the classification of image regions by colour, texture and shape", *Pattern Recognition*, Vol. 26, No. 4, April, pp. 461-470, 1993.
9. H.P. Moravec, "Towards automatic visual obstacle avoidance", *Proc. 5th Int. Joint Conf. Artificial Intelligence*, Cambridge, MA, pp. 584, 1977.
10. P. Brodatz, *Textures: A Photographic Album for Artists and Designers*, Dover, New York, 1966.
11. T.S. Huang, (ed.), *Image Sequence Processing and Dynamic Scene Analysis*, Springer-Verlag, New York, 1983.

Off-Line Signature Verification Without Requiring Random Forgeries for Training

Nabeel A. Murshed[‡], Flávio Bortolozzi[†] and Robert Sabourin[††]
[‡†]Centro Federal de Educação Tecnológica do Paraná (CEFET-PR) -
Pontifícia Universidade Católica do Paraná (PUC-PR)
Av. Sete de Setembro 3165, Curitiba - Paraná 80230-901, Brasil.
[‡†]email: murshed@dainf.cefetpr.br[1]
[††]École de Technologie Supérieure
4750 rue Henri-Julien, Montréal QC, H2T 2C8, Canada.
e-mail: sabourin@gpa.etsmtl.ca

Abstract. This paper presents an Off-line Signature Verification System for the elimination of random forgeries. Compared with the proposed systems thus far, our system is trained with genuine signatures only. This eliminates many of the problems existent in the current systems. The proposed system is evaluated with a data base of 200 signatures.

1 Introduction

With the advancement of computer technologies, various researches in the field of document image processing and analyses have come to existence. These researches have two principle objectives: understanding the contextual meaning of a document, by recognizing the handwritten characters or digits, or verifying its validity by verifying the handwritten signatures. A common feature distinguishes these two fields of researches, is the high degree of variations in the handwritten data which makes the task in hand a difficult and a challenging one.

In the field of signature verification, two types of systems exist: *on-line* and *off-line* systems, depending on the type of features being examined. In on-line systems, dynamic features such as the writing velocity and pressure are being examined. Whereas, in off-line systems graphic features such as shape, length and orientation of the whole signature or of its constituents, are being examined. In both systems, the functional structure is similar to that of a standard pattern recognition system; and the objective is to decide upon the claimed identity of some writer i by *making a one-to-one comparison* between an unknown signature S_j and a set of reference ones R_i of this writer [7]. In this regard, five types of forgeries may exist: random, simple, traced, servile, skilled and disguised. Random forgeries are characterized by having complete different graphic shape and semantic constituents, with respect to the genuine signatures of an individual writer i. The definition of the other types of forgeries can be found in [7]. System performance is evaluated in terms of the percent-

---

[1]Author to whom correspondence should sent to.

age of genuine signatures rejected as being forgeries (False Rejection Rate, *FRR*) and in terms of the percentage of false signatures accepted as being genuine (False Acceptance Rate, *FAR*). The research presented in this paper is concerned with Off-line Handwritten Signature Verification *(OHSV)* system for the elimination of random forgeries aimed at banking application[2]. In such application, it is not necessary that the OHSV system must decide upon the type of forgery being rejected or identify its writer.

In the last two decades, various systems have been proposed for off-line verification of handwritten signatures [1, 2, 5, 8]. In those systems signature verification has been considered as being a *two-class problem*: the class of genuine signatures, ω_1, and the class of forgeries, ω_2, for each writer i. Consequently, the process by which the OHSV system acquires a knowledge of the genuine signatures of an individual writer, is performed by *training* the system with *genuine signatures of this writer as well as with forgeries*. Therefore, the classification protocol, during the training phase, will attempt to classify, through the use of a decision threshold, the genuine signatures into class ω_1 and the forgeries into class ω_2. Based on this approach, it is valid to assume that for each writer i the OHSV system acquires a knowledge of the genuine signatures of this writer as well as of the forgeries.

Plamondon and Lorette [7] have pointed out some of the problems that must be solved before any OHSV system can be put into practice, and have suggested that these problems can be solved by increasing our knowledge of the writing process itself and of the forgery process. These problems are: How to cope with the difficulty of obtaining signature forgeries for training? What is the best classification protocol for a two-class problem with one class unknown? How to choose the optimum decision threshold to perform the training process?. Indeed, as suggested by Plamondon and Lorette[7], these problems, among others, must be solved before any OHSV system can be put in a practical environment. In our opinion, the cause of these problems lies in the approach itself.

To cope with the difficulty of obtaining signature forgeries, researchers have used the genuine signatures of other writers. For example to train the classifier of some writer i, a set of genuine signatures taken from other writers in the system are selected as being the signature forgeries with respect to this writer. By definition, these types of signatures are considered random forgeries. But the use of random forgeries for training requires a careful selection. Cardot et al [5] have observed that different types of random forgeries resulted in different system performance, with respect to an individual writer. To overcome this problem, the authors have performed a pre-classification process to select only the random forgeries that are *similar* to the genuine ones of each writer i. Another problem with this approach is that the FAR error rates are artificially reduced, during the evaluation of system performance. When training and testing the system with random forgeries of the same writers, the system will use its knowledge of those signatures, acquired during training, and will most probably succeed in rejecting them. In our opinion the reported values of the FAR errors, based on this experimental protocol, are not realistic. The actual

---

[2]Random forgeries occur in almost 95% of bank checks fraud.

performance may not be the same if the system is presented with signatures of different writers that it did not learn about during the training phase. In this regard, we suggest that a separate set of random forgeries, belonging to writers whose signatures are not learned during the training, should be used for the evaluation.

To solve the above problems, we propose to consider signature verification as a one-class problem in the sense that the system need not to be trained with signature forgeries. This is identical to the process adopted by the expert examiner of signatures, in which a priori knowledge of the class of forgeries is not required in order to perform the verification task. Based on this approach, we present an OHSV system, using the Fuzzy ARTMAP neural network at the classification stage. The cognitive information learning processing of the Fuzzy ARTMAP makes it ideal for implementing the proposed approach. A complete description of the Fuzzy ARTMAP neural networks can be found in Carpenter et al [3].

The next section of this paper presents the architecture of the proposed OHSV system. Section 3.0 describes the numerical experiments and the obtained results.

2 Architecture of the Proposed OHSV System

The functional structure of the proposed OHSV system is depicted in figure 1. The system has two inputs S_j and i and one output $D(S_{ij})$. They indicate, respectively, the input gray image signature, the writer identification code and the decision of the system with respect to the authenticity of the input signature in comparison with the genuine signatures of writer i. The purpose of the identity grid is to divide the input signature, after being preprocessed, into regions so as to perform the verification process on a region-by-region basis, and to give the final decision based on the results of each verification. The data base contains information about the genuine signatures of each writer and their identity grid, as explained bellow. The dimensionality reduction and comparison stages consist, respectively, of a Backpropagation and Fuzzy ARTMAP neural networks.

For the sake of clarity, we'll present first a description of the identity grid. Description of other components is given next.

2.1 Definition of The Identity Grid

The identity grid reflects the global shape of the writer's reference signatures as well as the spatial locations of the graphical segments in those signatures. An example of such identity grid is shown in figure 2a. The identity grid is formed by first building a rectangle, at the center of the 512x128-pixel area, with width and height equal to the length and height, respectively, of the first reference signature plus some margins such that, the final length and height is a multiple of 32 and 16 pixels, respectively. The extra margin is necessary to account for possible variations within the genuine specimens. The rectangle is then divided into k subrectangles equal

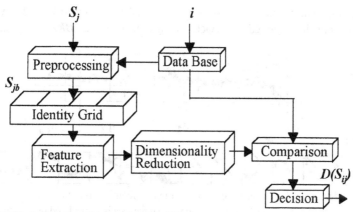

Fig. 1. Block diagram of the proposed Off-line Signature Verification System. All stages are used during learning and evaluation, except the decision stage which is used during evaluation only.

twice the number of words in the reference signature, with the aid of an interactive graphic program. Furthermore, each subrectangle is divided into two equal regions. The geometrical dimensions of the resulting structure are then saved. Based on this structure, an input image when centralized on the image area it becomes also centralized on the identity grid and, consequently, becomes divided into m regions ($m = 2k$). To build into the system a knowledge of the spatial locations of the graphical segments in the reference signatures, for each writer i, the resulting structure is then divided into squares of size 16x16 pixels. This is done by superposing a set of reference signatures on the center of the image area, and then trimming the resulting structure to produce the final form of the identity grid (Fig. 2a). The xy-coordinates of the 16-pixel squares in each region as well as the minimum and maximum numbers, min_i^p, max_i^p ($p=1,2,...,m$) of graphical segments found in each region of the identity grid are then saved in the data base.

2.2 Overall Process Description

At the first stage, the signature is segmented from the background, using Ostu's algorithm [6], and then centralized onto the image area (512x128) by translating the center of gravity of the binary image S_{jb} to the center of the image area which then becomes divide into m regions. As a consequence of this division criteria, the subsequent processes are carried out in a region-by-region basis. An illustration of these processes is shown in figure 3. From each region, a set of graphical segments of size 16x16 pixels with 50% overlapping in the x and y directions are extracted and fed to the dimensionality reduction stage. With this extraction criteria, the input signature is represented by a set of graphical segments of size 32x32 pixels (Fig. 2b). Each extracted graphical segment (pattern **X** in fig. 3) is then scanned by a 2x2 window (pattern **Y**) and then applied to a Back-propagation network *(BKP)*. The output of

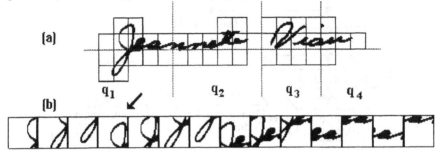

Fig. 2. Identity grid and signature representation. a) Identity grid of a writer whose signature is composed of two words ($m=4$). When the signatures is centralized on the image area it also becomes centralized on the identity grid and becomes divided into m regions. b) Signature representation. The segments are extracted from the first region.

the middle layer is then formed into a vector of size 24x32 (pattern **Z**). The reduced pattern is then applied to the comparison stage (a Fuzzy ARTMAP neural network) for learning/verification. Finally, the decision stage *analyzes* the results produced by each Fuzzy ARTMAP and gives the decision of the system with respect to the authenticity of the unknown signature.

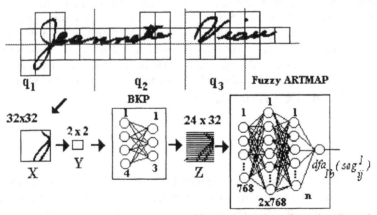

Fig. 3. Visual representation of the processes of feature extraction, dimensionality reduction and comparison.

2.3 Structure of the BKP Network for Dimensionality Reduction

Cottrell et al have introduced the use of 3-layers BKP network for the purpose of gray image compression [4]. The network is trained in its autoassociative mode to reconstruct the same input pattern at the output layer. After training has been successfully terminated, the network produces at its middle layer a compressed representation of the input pattern. As demonstrated by Cottrell et al, the quality of reconstruction is inversely proportional to the degree of compression. In our research we have developed a 3-layer BKP for binary image compression with a good reconstruction quality. The network contains four neurons in the input and output layers and three neurons in the middle layer. This gives a reduction of 1/3. To obtain good generalization for all signatures in the database, i.e., good image reconstruction quality, the network was trained with all the possible binary patterns (0000, 0001, ..., 1111) using the Quickpro learning rule, and was terminated when the network error reached a value of 0.2. The network was then tested to reconstruct each one of the 200 binary signatures in the database. The results of the reconstruction are shown in table 1.

Writer's Name	E1	Et
a	3	24
b	2	14
c	7	119
d	4	10
e	3	19

Table 1. Test results for the BKP network. E1 and Et indicate, respectively, the highest number of misclassified pixels occurred in a single signature, and the total number of miscalssified pixels ocuured in all the signatures of an individual writer.

2.4 The Role of the Fuzzy ARTMAPs in the Verification Process

According to the definition of the identity grid of each writer i, there will be a set of m Fuzzy ARTMAPs, each of which will focus on one region. During the training process, each Fuzzy ARTMAP will learn the characteristics of the genuine signatures, of this writer, situated in the respective region. After training has been completed, the Fuzzy ARTMAPs would have had a knowledge of the overall characteristics of the genuine signatures of the writer i. During verification when the system is required to verify the authenticity of an unknown signature with respect to the genuine signatures of some writer i, each Fuzzy ARTMAP will compare the characteristics of the unknown signature, situated in its region of focus to those of the writer i encoded into its memory and will give its answer accordingly.

2.5 The Decision Stage

The decision of the system with respect to the authenticity of an unknown signature is made by analyzing the decision of each Fuzzy ARTMAP network, according to the following two *majority decision rules*:

1. Consider the region of the signature, situated in one of the m regions of the identity grid of writer i as genuine, if the number of graphical segments l extracted from this region, is within the expected range $[min_i^p, max_i^p]$ and, if **half or more than half** of these segments are classified correctly by the respective Fuzzy ARTMAP, or as false otherwise. In mathematical form, this decision rule is written as follow:

$$D(s_{mj}^i) = \begin{cases} 1, & \text{if } min_i^m \leq l \leq max_i^m \text{ and } \left(\sum_{o=1}^{n} dfa_{im}(seg_{oj}) \right) \geq \dfrac{l}{2} \\ 0, & \text{otherwise} \end{cases} \qquad (1.0)$$

2. Consider the signature S_j as genuine with respect to the writer i reference signatures, if **half or more than half** of the m regions of this signatures are considered genuine by the first rule, or as false otherwise. In mathematical form, the second rule is represented as follow:

$$D(S_j^i) = \begin{cases} 1, & \text{if } \left(\sum_{p=1}^{m} D(s_{pj}^i) \right) \geq \dfrac{m}{2} \\ 0, & \text{otherwise} \end{cases} \qquad (2.0)$$

where the digits '1' and '0' indicates, respectively, genuine and forgery. The decision criteria **half or more than half** is represented by the second inequality in equation 1.0 and the inequality in equation 2.0.

3 Simulation and Results

The performance of the system was evaluated, in the context of random forgeries, using a database of 200 signatures taken from five writers (40 signatures/writer). Six experiments were performed using different training sets. All experiments were performed with the Neural Works simulator running on an IBM DX2/66MHZ Compatible PC .

3.1 Experimental Protocol

For each writer, the total signatures were divided into two sets: training and evaluation sets. Each set contained, respectively, 18 and 22 signatures. The training set was further divided into six sets, each of which contained a number of signatures equal to $3J$ ($J = 1, 2, ..., 6$). Based on this data division, for each writer the system was trained with each training set, *of this writer only*, and then was tested with the test signature of this writer as well as with the signatures of all other writers (160 signatures). Training of the Fuzzy ARTMAP is simple and straight forward. The network parameters were: $\rho = 0.75$, $\alpha = 0.001$, $\beta = 1.0$. The results of the experiments with respect to the FRR and FAR errors are shown in table 2 for various combinations of the decision criteria. Each combination is denoted in the table by the decision pair (**d**n, **d**n) where n = 1 or 2. The first decision applies to equation 1 and the second one to equation 2. The digits 1 and 2 indicates, respectively, *half or more than half* and *more than half*.

# Sig.	Decision Pares							
	(d1,d1)		(d2,d1)		(d1,d2)		(d2,d2)	
	FRR	FAR	FRR	FAR	FRR	FAR	FRR	FAR
3	17.27	6.25	23.64	4.63	54.55	0.125	62.73	0.13
6	7.27	22.63	8.18	16.38	30.91	3.75	38.18	2.13
9	11.82	6.13	16.36	4.0	38.18	0.5	45.45	0.13
12	4.54	14.5	6.36	12.13	21.82	3.25	28.18	2.13
15	9.09	11.38	11.82	8.3	31.82	1.75	40.91	1.13
18	7.27	11.00	9.09	7.63	23.64	0.38	28.18	0.25

Table 2. Performance of the system in terms of FRR and FAR errors. All values are in percentage.

Training Set.	% Increase in FRR	% Decrease in FAR
3	4.4	50
6	5.25	10.6
9	3.84	49
12	6.2	6.82
15	4.5	10.12
18	3.88	44

Table 3. Effect of increasing the decision criteria on the FRR and FAR errors.

Authors	FRR	FAR
Mighell et al [1]	1	4
	3	14
Cardot et al [5]	5	2
McCormack et al [2]	13.8	10.6
Sabourin et al [8]	0.2	(mean)
The OHSV Proposed in this paper	7.27	11.00

Table 4. Comparison of the results obtained in this work to those of other authors.

3.2 Comments on the results

As it can be observed from the table 2, the error rates are acceptably good, though are not as good as it should be. The best performance is obtained with the training set of 18 signatures. The rather high rate of false rejection FRR , was mainly due to the variations in the handwritten signatures of an individual writer, and to the sensitivity of neural networks to this variations. The cause of the FAR error rates could be related to the recoding characteristic and to the matching criteria of the Fuzzy ARTMAP. This hypotheses is currently under verification.

The FRR and FAR errors can be reduced, respectively, by rendering the Fuzzy ARTMAP insensitive to the variations in the signatures and by increasing the decision criteria, as demonstrated in table 2. The effect of increasing the decision criteria will not have a great effect on increasing the FRR errors as it will have on decreasing the FAR errors, as can be observed from table 3.

As it can be seen from the table 4, our results compare favorably to those of the other authors based on the two-class problem. A major difference, however, is that the FAR errors based on the one-class problem reflect the real performance of the system. Whereas those based on the two-class problem do not, for the reasons mentioned in section 1. In general, it is difficult to judge which system performs best. This is due to the fact that the experimental data base, the division criteria and the experimental protocol are different from one system to another. For example, the results reported by Mighell et al [1] are for one writer only which are not realistic.

4 Conclusion

In this paper we have presented an Off-line Signature Verification System for the elimination of random forgeries aimed at banking application. For each writer, the approach to the verification is based on training the system with genuine signatures of this writer only. This is similar to the approach adopted by the expert examiner of signatures. We believe that this approach may provide an efficient solution to unresolved and very difficult problems in the field of signature verification. Our initial results are very promising. However, we are very well aware that we have evaluated the performance of the system with a small data base. Our next step is to evaluate the performance of the system on a large data base and to overcome the problem of signature variations.

References

1. D. A. Mighell, T. S. Wilkinson and J. W. Goodman. Backpropagation and its application to handwritten signature verification. Tourtzkey, D. (Ed), **Advances in Neural Information Processing Systems 1,** pp. 341-347, Morgan Kaufman, 1989.
2. D. K. R. McCormack and B. M. Brown. Handwritten signature verification using the Backpropagation neural network. **In Neural Computing Research and Applications: Part Two,** pp. 243-251, Queen's University of Belfast, N. Ireland, 1992.
3. G. A. Carpenter, S. Grossberg, N. Markuzon, and J. H. Reynolds. Fuzzy ARTMAP: A neural network architecture for incremental supervised learning of analog multidimensional maps. **IEEE Tran. Neural Networks.** Vol. 3, No. 5, 698-713, 1992.
4. G. W. Cottrell, P. Munro, and D. Zipser. Image Compression by back propagation: an example of extensional programming. **Advances in Cognitive Sciences, 3**, Sharkey, N.E. (Ed), Norwood, NJ, 1989.
5. H. Cardot, M. Revenu, B. Victorri, and M. Revillet. An artificial neural network   a rchi tecture for handwritten signature authentication, SEPT, 42 rue des Coutures, 14000 Caen, France, 1992.
6. N. Ostu. A threshold selection method from gray-level histograms. **IEEE Trans. Syst. Man. Cybernetics,** Vol. SMC-9, NO. 1, 62-66, 1979.
7. R. Plamondon and G. Lorette. Automatic Signature Verification and Writer Identification: The State of The Art. **Pattern Recognition,** Vol. 22. No. 2, 107-131, 1989.
8. R. Sabourin, M. Cheriet and G. Genest.   An Extended-Shadow-Code Based Approach For Off-Line Signature Verification. **Proc. 2nd. Int. Conf.   Doc. Ananlysis and Recognition.,** pp. 1-6, Tsukuba science city, Japan, October 20-22, 1993.

Noisy Subsequence Recognition Using Constrained String Editing Involving Substitutions, Insertions, Deletions and Generalized Transpositions[1]

B. J. Oommen and R. K. S. Loke
School of Computer Science
Carleton University
Ottawa ; CANADA : K1S 5B6

Abstract. We consider a problem which can greatly enhance the areas of cursive script recognition and the recognition of printed character sequences. This problem involves recognizing words/strings by processing their noisy subsequences. Let X^* be any unknown word from a finite dictionary **H**. Let U be any arbitrary *subsequence* of X^*. We study the problem of estimating X^* by processing Y, a noisy version of U. Y contains substitution, insertion, deletion and *generalized transposition* errors -- the latter occurring when transposed characters are themselves subsequently substituted. We solve the *noisy subsequence recognition problem* by defining and using the constrained edit distance between $X \in$ **H** and Y subject to any arbitrary edit constraint involving the number and type of edit operations to be performed. An algorithm to compute this constrained edit distance has been presented. Using these algorithms we present a syntactic Pattern Recognition (PR) scheme which corrects noisy text containing all these types of errors. Experimental results which involve strings of lengths between 40 and 80 with an average of 30.24 deleted characters and an overall average noise of 68.69 % demonstrate the superiority of our system over existing methods.

1 Introduction

A common problem in syntactic pattern recogniton is that of correcting errors in a string. A package solving this problem is typically used in the recognition of printed character sequences and cursive script (and more recently, even closed boundaries [3]) after the individual symbols of the "alphabet" have been hypothesized using statistical methods. Such a scheme would permit us to recognize strings and sequences by using only noisy partial (occluded) information.

In this paper we consider a far more general problem. To pose it in its generality, let us assume that a sender intends to transmit a string $X^* \in$ H. However, rather than send the entire string X^* he chooses to (randomly or otherwise) delete characters from it, and merely transmit U, one of its *subsequences*. U is transmitted through a noisy channel and is further subjected to substitution, deletion, insertion and *generalized transposition* errors. The receiver receives Y, the garbled form of U. We intend to recognize X^* by merely processing Y. The reader will be able to comprehend the difficulty in the PR problem if he observes that any substring

---

[1]Partially supported by the Natural Sciences and Engineering Research Council of Canada.

consisting of the consecutive characters of U, need not be a contiguous substring of X^*, and that whereas there are $O(N^2)$ contiguous substrings for a string X of length N, there are $O(2^N)$ subsequences.

Clearly, a syntactic package which achieves this will greatly enhance the power of OCR systems which recognize printed character sequences and cursive script. Indeed, we will then be able to recognize strings and sequences, by merely having as an input a noisy versiuon of *any* of its subsequences. This could permit the recognition of strings and sequences which have been "occluded" at multiple junctures, and thus permit far more noisy environments.

To achieve this we present the first reported solution to the analytic problem of editing (or more precisely, aligning) one string to another using these four edit operations subject to any arbitrary constraint involving the number and type of these operations. Using these algorithms we present a syntactic PR scheme which corrects the noisy subsequences containing all these types of errors.

The relationship between our present work and the work that has been done in noisy string processing is found in [8]. The paper [8] also gives references to the longest common subsequence problem and sequence correction using the GLD as a criterion for strings, substrings, dictionaries treated as generalized tries and for grammars. Also, although some work has been done to extend the traditional set of SID operations to include adjacent transpositions [5, 9, 10] our work tackles the unsolved problem for constrained editing for "Generalized" Transposition (GT) errors.

1.1 Notation

A is a finite alphabet, and A^* is the set of strings over A. θ is the null symbol, where $\theta \notin A$, and is distinct from μ the empty string. Let $\tilde{A} = A \cup \{\theta\}$. A string $X \in A^*$ of the form $X = x_1...x_N$, where each $x_i \in A$, and is said to be of length $|X| = N$. Its prefix of length i will be written as X_i, for $1 \leq i \leq N$. Uppercase symbols represent strings, and lower case symbols, elements of the alphabet.

Let Z' be any element in $\tilde{A}^*$, the set of strings over $\tilde{A}$. The *Compression Operator* $\mathbb{C}$ is a mapping from $\tilde{A}^*$ to A^* : $\mathbb{C}(Z')$ is Z' with all occurrences of the symbol θ removed from Z'. Note that $\mathbb{C}$ preserves the order of the non-θ symbols in Z'. For example, if $Z' = f\theta o\theta r$, $\mathbb{C}(Z') = for$.

We now define the costs associated with the individual edit operations. If R^+ is the set of nonnegative real numbers, we define the elementary edit distances using four elementary functions $d_s(.,.), d_i(.), d_e(.), d_t(.,.)$ defined as follows : (i) $d_s(.,.)$ is a map from $A \times A \to R^+$ and is the Substitution Map. $d_s(a,b)$ is the distance associated with substituting b for a, $a,b \in A$; (ii) $d_i(.)$ is a map from $A \to R^+$ and is called the Insertion Map. The quantity $d_i(a)$ is the distance associated with inserting the symbol $a \in A$; (iii) $d_e(.)$ is a map from $A \to R^+$ and is called the Deletion or Erasure Map. The quantity $d_e(a)$ is the distance associated with deleting (erasing) the symbol $a \in A$, and (iv) $d_t(.,.)$ is a map from $A^2 \times A^2 \to R^+$ called the Transposition Map. The quantity $d_t(ab,cd)$ is the distance associated with transposing the string "ab" into "cd". A formal expression for $D(X,Y)$ in terms of these elementary edit distances and the set of ways by which X can be edited to Y, $\Gamma_{X,Y}$ is given in [8].

2 Permissible and Feasible Edit Constraints

Consider the problem of editing X to Y, where $|X| = N$ and $|Y| = M$. Suppose we edit a prefix of X into a prefix of Y, using exactly i insertions, e deletions (or erasures), s substitution and t GTs. Since the numbers of edit operations are specified, this corresponds to editing $X_{e+s+2t} = x_1...x_{e+s+2t}$ the prefix of X of length $e+s+2t$, into $Y_{i+s+2t} = y_1...y_{i+s+2t}$, the prefix of Y of length $i+s+2t$.

To obtain bounds on the magnitude of the variables i, e, s and t, we observe that they are constrained by the lengths of the strings X and Y. Thus, if $r = e + s + 2t$, $q = i + s + 2t$ and $R = \text{Min } [M, N]$, these variables will have to obey the following obvious constraints:

$$0 \le t \le \text{Min}\left[\left\lfloor\tfrac{N}{2}\right\rfloor,\left\lfloor\tfrac{M}{2}\right\rfloor\right] ; \quad \text{Max}[0, M\text{-}N] \le i \le q \le M ;$$

$$0 \le e \le r \le N ; \qquad 0 \le s \le \text{Min}[N, M].$$

Quadruples (i, e, s, t) which satisfy these constraints are termed *feasible*. Let

$$H_t = \{ j \mid 0 \le j \le \text{Min}\left[\left\lfloor\tfrac{N}{2}\right\rfloor,\left\lfloor\tfrac{M}{2}\right\rfloor\right]\}; \quad H_i = \{ j \mid \text{Max}[0, M\text{-}N] \le j \le M \} ;$$

$$H_e = \{ j \mid 0 \le j \le N \} ; \qquad H_s = \{ j \mid 0 \le j \le \text{Min}[N, M] \} \qquad (1)$$

H_t, H_i, H_e and H_s are called the set of *permissible* values of i, e, s and t. A quadruple (i, e, s, t) is feasible if apart from $t \in H_t$, $i \in H_i$, $e \in H_e$ and $s \in H_s$, the inequalities $\{i + s + 2t \le M ; e + s + 2t \le N \}$ are also satisfied.

Theorem 1 specifies the permitted forms of the feasible quadruples encountered in editing X_r, the prefix of X of length r, to Y_q, the prefix of Y of length q.

Theorem 1   To edit X_r, the prefix of X of length r, to Y_q, the prefix of Y of length q, the set of feasible quadruples is given by

$$\{ (i, r\text{-}q+i, q\text{-}i\text{-}2t, t) \mid \text{Max}[0, q\text{-}r] \le i \le q\text{-}2t \} \qquad (2)$$

Proof.   The proof is included in the unabridged paper [8].   ◆◆◆

An edit constraint is specified in terms of the number and type of edit operations that are required in the process of transforming X to Y. It is expressed by formulating the number and type of edit operations in terms of four sets Q_t, Q_i, Q_e and Q_s, which are subsets of the sets H_t, H_i, H_e and H_s defined in (1). For every value of t in the set Q_t, we define the sets Q_i^t, Q_e^t and Q_s^t as :

$$Q_i^t = \{ i \mid i \le M\text{-}2t \} \cap Q_i ; \qquad Q_e^t = \{ e \mid e \le N\text{-}2t \} \cap Q_e ;$$

and $Q_s^t = \{ s \mid s \le \text{Min}[N\text{-}2t, M\text{-}2t]\} \cap Q_s.$

These sets represent the number of edit operations given that t GTs had occurred.

Theorem 2   Given a value of t, every edit constraint specified for the process of editing X to Y can be written as a unique subset of H_i.

Proof.   The proof is given in the unabridged paper [8] and involves computing subsets of H_i for the various subsets Q_i^t, Q_e^t and Q_s^t.   ◆◆◆

The set (the subset of H_i) referred to above, which describes the constraint given a value of t will be written as T_t. A detailed example of how these sets are created is found in the main paper. Also, we shall refer to the edit distance subject to the constraint T_t as $D_t(X,Y)$. By definition, if $T_t = \varnothing$, then $D_t(X,Y) = \infty$. The distance for the optimal edit transformations is denoted by $D_c(X,Y)$ which is the minimum of all $D_t(X,Y)$.

3 W: The Array Of Constrained Edit Distances

Let $W(i,e,s,t)$ be the constrained edit distance associated with editing X_{e+s+2t} to Y_{i+s+2t} subject to the constraint that exactly i insertions, e deletions, s substitutions and t GTs are performed in the process of editing. As before, let $r = e+s+2t$ and $q = i+s+2t$. Using the notation in [8], let $\Gamma_{i,e,s,t}(X,Y)$ be the subset of the pairs in Γ_{X_r,Y_q} in which every pair corresponds to i insertions, e deletions, s substitutions and t transpositions. Since we shall always be referring to the strings X and Y, we refer to this set as $\Gamma_{i,e,s,t}$. Assuming (i,e,s,t) is feasible for the problem, $W(i,e,s,t)$ has the expression

$$W(i, e, s, t) = \underset{(X_r',Y_q')\in \Gamma_{i,e,s,t}}{\text{Min}} \sum_{j=1}^{|X'|} d(X_{rj}', Y_{qj}') \tag{3}$$

We shall derive the recursively computable properties of the array $W(i, e, s, t)$.

Theorem 3   Let $W(i, e, s, t)$ be as defined in (3) for strings X and Y. Then,

$$W(i, e, s, t) = \text{Min}\ \big[\ \{W(i\text{-}1, e, s, t) + d(\theta, y_{i+s+2t})\},$$
$$\{W(i, e\text{-}1, s, t) + d(x_{e+s+2t}, \theta)\},$$
$$\{W(i, e, s\text{-}1, t) + d(x_{e+s+2t}, y_{i+s+2t})\},$$
$$\{W(i, e, s, t\text{-}1) + d(x_{e+s+2t\text{-}1}x_{e+s+2t}, y_{i+s+2t\text{-}1}y_{i+s+2t})\}\big]$$

for all feasible quadruples (i, e, s, t).
Proof.   The proof is involved and can be found in the unabridged paper [8]. ◆ ◆ ◆

The computation of the distance $D_t(X,Y)$ from the array $W(i, e, s, t)$ only involves combining the appropriate elements of the array using T_t. This is proved in the following theorems whence we derive a computational scheme for $D_c(X,Y)$.

Theorem 4   The quantity $D_t(X,Y)$ is related to the elements of the array $W(i, e, s, t)$ as follows:

$$D_t(X,Y) = \underset{i \in T_t}{\text{Min}}\ W(i, N\text{-}M+i, M\text{-}i\text{-}2t, t)$$

Proof.   The theorem follows from Theorem 1 by setting $r = N$ and $q = M$. ◆ ◆ ◆

Theorem 5   The distance $D_c(X,Y)$, is obtained as follows:

$$D_c(X,Y) = \underset{k \in Q_t}{\text{Min}} \ D_k(X,Y)$$

Sketch of Proof. Consider the individual $D_t(X,Y)$ quantities. Each is the minimum edit distance associated with transforming X to Y with a feasible set of operations, given that there are t transpositions. The minimum of these would be the minimum edit distance for the optimal edit transformations.   ◆◆◆

4 The Computation Of The W-Array And $D_c(X,Y)$

To compute $D_c(X,Y)$, we make use of the fact that although this index does not itself seem to have any recursive properties, the index $W(.,.,.,.)$, which is closely related to it, has the interesting properties proved in Theorem 3. The evaluation of the array $W(.,.,.,.)$ has to be done in a systematic manner, so that any quantity $W(i,e,s,t)$ must be evaluated before its value is required in any further evaluation. This is easily done by considering a four-dimensional coordinate system whose axes are i, e, s and t respectively. Initially, the value associated with the origin, $W(0,0,0,0)$ is assigned the value zero, and the contributions with the vertices, axes, planes and cubes are evaluated sequentially in an intelligent manner. Finally, $D_c(X,Y)$ is evaluated by minimizing over the relevant contributions of $W(.,.,.,.)$ associated with the points that lie on the four-dimensional line given by the parametric equation :

i = i;   e = N - M + i;   s = M - i - 2t;   t = t

Rather than use this traditional method for traversing the W-array, we shall develop a compact version of it using a pair of three dimensional arrays instead of a four-dimensional array. To do this, we shall take advantage of the following fact. For a particular value of t, in order to compute W(i, e, s, t) for all permissible values of i, e and s, it is sufficient to store only the values of W (i, e, s, t-1) for all the corresponding permissible values of i, e and s. Consider the four-dimensional trellis described above. We shall successively evaluate the array Wc (for current W-array) in cubes *hyper-parallel* to the cube t = 0. Two arrays are maintained, namely,

(i) Wp: the cube *hyper-parallel* to t = 0, for the previous value of t, and,

(ii) Wc: the cube *hyper-parallel* to t = 1 maintained for the current value of t.

The algorithm, given as *Algorithm Gen_Constrained_Distance* below, evaluates these two arrays in a systematic manner. Initially, the quantities associated with the individual axes are evaluated. The lines, planes and cubes of the Wc array are initialized and traversed as described above. Also, prior to updating Wp, its pertinent component required in the computation of $D_c(X,Y)$, is used to update the latter. It is clear that given X and Y, $D_c(X,Y)$ is computed with $O(|X| \cdot |Y| \cdot \text{Min}(|X|,|Y|))$ space and in $O(R \cdot |X| \cdot |Y| \cdot \text{Min}(|X|,|Y|))$ time, where $0 \leq R \leq \text{Min}\left[\left\lfloor \frac{|X|}{2} \right\rfloor, \left\lfloor \frac{|Y|}{2} \right\rfloor\right]$.

ALGORITHM GEN_CONSTRAINED_DISTANCE

Input: The strings $X = x_1 x_2 ... x_N$, $Y = y_1 y_2 ... y_M$, the edit distances and the constraint sets T_t . Let R be the largest integer in the set Q_t.

Output: The constrained distance $D_c(X,Y)$.

Notation: Values at negative indices of Wc and Wp are set to infinity.

Method :
  For $t \leftarrow 0$ **to** R **Do**
    For $i \leftarrow 0$ **to** M-2t **Do**
      For $e \leftarrow 0$ **to** N-2t **Do**
        For $s \leftarrow 0$ **to Min** [M-i-2t,N-e-2t] **Do**
          Wc(i, e, s) $\leftarrow$ **Min** [Wc(i-1, e, s) + $d_i(y_{i+s+2t})$,
                           Wc(i, e-1, s) + $d_e(x_{e+s+2t})$,
                           Wc(i, e, s-1) + $d_s(x_{e+s+2t}, y_{i+s+2t})$,
                           Wp(i,e,s) + cost],
                where cost = $d_t(x_{e+s+2t-1} x_{e+s+2t} y_{i+s+2t-1} y_{i+s+2t})$
         If i,e,s,t are all equal to zero then Wc(i,e,s) = 0
        EndFor
      EndFor
      If $i \in T_t$, then $D_c(X,Y) \leftarrow$ **Min**[$D_c(X,Y)$, Wc(i, N-M+i, M-i-2t)]
    EndFor
    For $i \leftarrow 0$ **to** M-2t **Do**
      For $e \leftarrow 0$ **to** N-2t **Do**
        For $s \leftarrow 0$ **to Min**[M-i-2t,N-e-2t] **Do**
          Wp(i, e, s) $\leftarrow$ Wc(i, e, s)
        EndFor
      EndFor
    EndFor
  EndFor
END ALGORITHM GEN_CONSTRAINED_DISTANCE

5 Noisy Subsequence Recognition and Experimental Results

Let us assume the characteristic of the noisy channel are known, and further, let L_i be the expected number of insertions introduced in the process of transmitting U. This figure can be estimated although the actual number of symbols inserted in any particular transmission is unknown. Since U can be any arbitrary *subsequence* of X^*, and since the words of the dictionary can be of completely different lengths, it is obviously meaningless to compare Y with every $X \in H$ using the GLD. Thus, before we compare Y with the individual words of the dictionary, we have to use the additional information obtainable from the noisy channel.

    Since the number of insertions introduced in any transmission is unknown, it is reasonable to compare $X \in H$ and Y subject to the constraint that the number of insertions that actually took place is its *best estimate*. Of course, in the absence of any other information, the best estimate of the number of insertions that could have taken place is indeed its expected value, which we have referred to as L_i. However, if L_i is not a feasible value for the number of insertions, then the closest feasible value is used to compare $X \in H$ and Y. An identical argument can be given for the reason why L_t, the expected number of GTs that take place per transmission, is used as the best estimate for the number of GTs that took place in yielding Y. Thus, the procedure to estimate X^* is as follows : If L_t and L_i are feasible values, the constraint set T_t is set with respect to L_t and L_i. Otherwise, the constraint set T_t is set with as the feasible integers closest to L_t and L_j. The distance $D_c(X,Y)$ is computed using Algorithm Gen_Constrained_Distance, for every $X \in \mathbf{H}$. X^+, the estimate of X^*, is obtained as the string which minimizes $D_c(X,Y)$. The formal algorithm is in [8].

To investigate the power of our new measure (and its computation) and to demonstrate the accuracy of our new scheme in the original PR problem various experiments were conducted. The results obtained were remarkable. The algorithm was compared with PR results obtained if (i) only SID errors were assumed and corrected using Wagner & Fischer [11] algorithm, (ii) SID and traditional transposition errors were assumed and corrected using Lowrance and Wagner [5,10] algorithm and (iii) SID and generalized transposition errors were assumed and corrected using a recent unconstrained editing algorithm for all the four operations [7].

The dictionary, $\mathbf{H}$, used consisted of a hundred strings taken from the classical book on pattern recognition by Duda and Hart and were randomly truncated so that the length of the words in $\mathbf{H}$ was uniformly distributed in the interval [40, 80]. Using random deletions as in [6] a set of 500 subsequences were generated. The resultant subsequence U had an average of 30.24 characters deleted from the original strings. Each subsequence U was further subjected to insertion, deletion, substitution and transposition errors using a technique similar to the one described in [8]. A typical example of a noisy subsequence corrected is given below :

X^*: theoriginationofpartiofthisbookisprimarilystatisticalchaptertwostatesthecla

U : theorigiofpartisbookistachartwost

Y : theoriyiopratribdooksitacahrtowst

In this case, the number of errors is 51. The error statistics associated with the set of noisy subsequences used is given in Table 1. Notice that even though the number of errors associated with each Y is large, it would be even larger from the perspective of the set of *standard* operations where a GT is a combination of two substitution errors.

The four algorithms were tested with the 500 noisy subsequences. In the case of our algorithm, rather than have the constraint set use only a single feasible integer for the number of insertions and transpositions, the algorithm was marginally modified to include a small range of integers. The details of the individual inter-symbol edit distance and the distance assignments used are given in [8]. The results obtained in terms of accuracy are tabulated in Table 2. Note that our scheme far outperforms the traditional string correction algorithm (94.0 % instead of 64.2 %). It also outperforms the Lowrance and Wagner algorithm (which had an accuracy of 75.6 %). Our recent unconstrained distance criterion for all the four errors [7] yielded an accuracy of 74.6 %. The power of the strategy in PR is obvious !!

6   Conclusions

In this paper we have considered the problem of recognizing strings by processing their noisy subsequences. The solution which we propose is the only known solution in the literature when the noisy subsequences contain substitution, insertion, deletion and generalized transposition errors. Given a noisy subsequence Y of an unknown string $X^* \in \mathbf{H}$, the technique we propose estimates X^* by computing the constrained edit distance between every $X \in \mathbf{H}$ and Y. Experimental results using strings of length between 40 and 80 and with a high percentage of noise, demonstrate the power of the strategy in pattern recognition.

References

1. P. A. V. Hall and G. R. Dowling, Approximate string matching, Comput. Surveys, 12:381-402 (1980).
2. R. L. Kashyap and B. J. Oommen, An effective algorithm for string correction using generalized edit distances -I. Description of the algorithm and its optimality, Inform. Sci., 23(2):123-142 (1981).
3. A. Marzal and E. Vidal, Computation of normalized edit distance and applications, IEEE Trans. on Pat. Anal. and Mach. Intel., PAMI-15:926-932 (1993).
4. A. Levenshtein, Binary codes capable of correcting deletions, insertions and reversals, Soviet Phys. Dokl., 10:707-710 (1966).
5. R. Lowrance and R. A. Wagner, An extension of the string to string correction problem, J. Assoc. Comput. Mach., 22:177-183 (1975).
6. B. J. Oommen, Recognition of noisy subsequences using constrained edit distances, IEEE Trans. on Pat. Anal. and Mach. Intel., PAMI-9:676-685 (1987).
7. B. J. Oommen and R. K. S. Loke, Pattern recognition of strings with substitutions, insertions, deletions and generalized transpositions. Unabridged Paper. Available as a Carleton University technical report (1994).
8. B. J. Oommen and R. K. S. Loke, Noisy subsequence recognition using constrained string editing involving substitutions, insertions, deletions and generalized transpositions. Unabridged Paper. Available as a Carleton University technical report (1994).
9. J. L. Peterson, Computer programs for detecting and correcting spelling errors, Comm. Assoc. Comput. Mach., 23:676-687 (1980).
10. D. Sankoff and J. B. Kruskal, Time Warps,String Edits and Macromolecules: The Theory and practice of Sequence Comparison, Addison-Wesley (1983).
11. R. A. Wagner and M. J. Fischer, The string to string correction problem, J. Assoc. Comput. Mach., 21:168-173 (1974).

	Average Errors in Y
Number of insertions	2.142
Number of deletions	30.442
Number of substitutions	3.220
Number of transpositions	5.410
Total number of errors	41.214
Percentage error	68.69%

Table 1. A table showing the average error statistics in the noisy strings.

Algorithm	Accuracy
WF	64.20%
LW	75.60%
SID_GT	74.60%
Const_SID_GT	94.00%

Table 2. The recognition accuracies of the various algorithms tested. The details of the algorithms used are found in the text.

GEOFF – A Geometrical Editor for Fold Formation

Hing N. Ng and Richard L. Grimsdale

Centre for VLSI and Computer Graphics, School of Engineering
University of Sussex, Falmer, Brighton, BN1 9QT, UK
E-mail: {H.N.Ng I R.L.Grimsdale}@sussex.ac.uk

Abstract. A new technique for modelling clothing is described in which the cloth layer is closely associated with the shape of the underlying flesh layer. The position of fold lines are determined on the basis of the distances between the layers. Folds are generated along the fold lines using a modified sinusoidal function. In contrast with techniques which are based on the physical properties of the material, the technique is fast and yet produces visually acceptable results. The technique has been incorporated within the GEOFF interactive editor which allows the user considerable control over fold generation.

1 Introduction

Realistic display of cloth is important in the modelling of animated figures. This has been an active subject of research in computer graphics since the 80s and a growth in interest has been evident in recent times. Many models of cloth have been developed which produce good results. However, these models are not widely used in computer animation, due to the fact that many require large amounts of computation. In particular there is a requirement to model the shape of a garment when worn by a human. The present paper takes a sleeve worn on an arm as an example, but the method is applicable to all parts of a garment.

A new geometrical model is presented in which the sleeve and the arm on which it is worn are represented as a connected layered structure. The sleeve and arm are thereby closely integrated within the model. The main goal has been to develop a technique for generating folds in the cloth requiring minimal computational power. There is an emphasis on the production of visually acceptable results, rather than on solutions based on complex physical modelling. Moreover, previous techniques have not always provided the user with adequate provision to influence the results; accordingly an interactive editor has been incorporated to allow users to make adjustments to the results.

2 Related Work

The modelling of cloth has been categorised into three types: the *geometrical approach*, the *physical approach* and the *hybrid approach*. In the geometrical approaches, the models are based solely on geometry considerations. Curve fitting technique is used in [24] and [9] uses surface fitting technique.

In the physical approach, the physical properties of the cloth are used, which typically include the elasticity, strain constant and density. Energy minimisation is used in [8,16] to predict the garment shapes. A deformable model [20,21] is used by Thalmann's research team [5,12,14,15,25,26,27]. The conecpt of a *particle system* [17] is used in [3,4] to model cloth. Li *et al.* [13] have simulated a cloth sample in an air flow using aerodynamic theory. Aono [2] utilised the equilibrium equation of elasticity theory and D'Alembert's principle to simulate wrinkles in his model.

The physical approach requires extensive numerical processing and the time required to yield a result is greater than that of the geometrical approach. The hybrid approaches [7,11,18,19,22] are the combinations of geometrical and physical techniques.

3 The Model

3.1 A New Layered Structure

Most of the previous work has treated the cloth and the underlying object as separate entities, with the subsequent collision detection requiring considerable computational time. A layered concept has already been used successfully in many areas [6,10,23]. In this paper, we propose a new layered strucutre to facilitate the simulation of cloth.

The structure used in the method presented here is shown in Fig. 1. The cloth layer and flesh layer are represented by two hollow polygonal cylinders. The flesh layer surrounds the skeleton which is here represented by a thin rod. The shapes of the cylinders are defined by cross sections which can assume elliptical form, the eccentricity of which is under user control. In the examples to be described, cross sections which are initially circular have been employed for simplicity, but without loss of generality. The shape of a cross section is specified by vertices around its circumference. The two layers have identical numbers of vertices and for each vertex on one cylinder there is a matching vertex on the other. The structure shown in Fig. 1 can be taken to represent a section of an arm or leg.

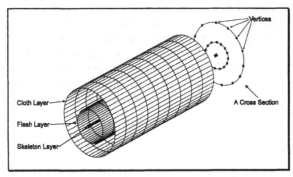

Fig. 1. Layered structure.

In Fig. 2, the cloth and grid layer can be represented as a 2D rectangular grid. The vertices on the grid can therefore be easily accessed as a 2D array in the C language.

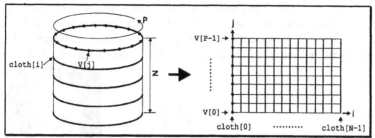

Fig. 2. Cloth or flesh layer as grid.

3.2 Production of the Folds in the Cloth

Folds are positioned along fold lines. The fold lines occur along the contours of maximum slackness; that is where the separation between the two layers is the greatest. The fold lines do not coincide exactly with the contours of maximum separation, but are deflected by random amounts. From observation, the shape of a fold perpendicular to a fold line appears to be sinusoidal [9,11]. In this simulation the $sinc^2(x)$ function has been used to define the shape of the folds, as shown in Fig. 3.

In Fig. 4, the cloth layer has been cut and flattened to form a rectangle. A fold line is shown between the points A and B. The *fold function*— $sinc^2(x)$ is mapped along the fold line. Since the height of a real fold changes along its path, a *profile function* is introduced to control the amplitude variation along the fold line. A parabola has been selected as a suitable candidate for this function (see Fig. 5). The maximum amplitude of the profile function is normalised to unity.

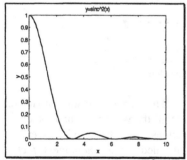

Fig. 3. The fold function $sinc^2(x)$.

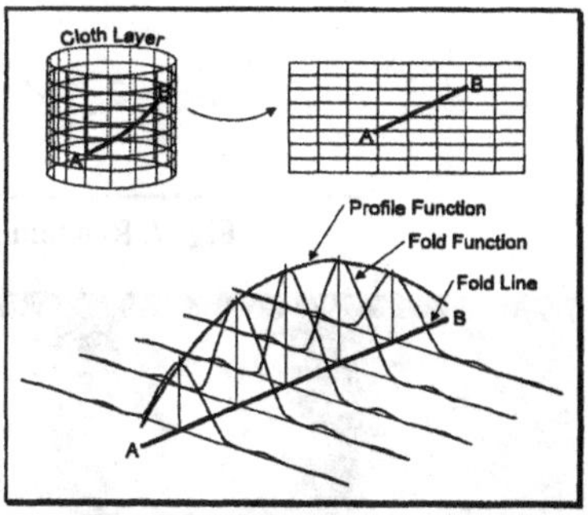

Fig. 4. The mapping process.

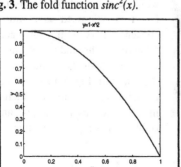

Fig. 5. The profile function $y=1-x^2$.

The production of folds along fold lines is illustrated in Fig. 6. In Fig. 6a, the five fold lines have been positioned on the cloth grid. After the generation of folds, the resulting wire-frame is shown in Fig. 6b and a rendered version is shown in Fig. 6c. Refinements to this technique will be described in the following sections of this paper.

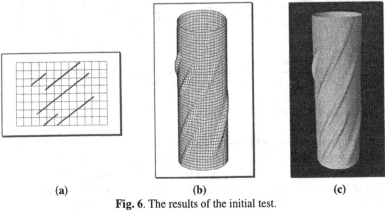

(a)   (b)   (c)

Fig. 6. The results of the initial test.

3.3 Perturbation of the Initial Cloth Layer

The surface of the cloth will not be entirely flat, but will possess a certain degree of randomness. Random perturbations are now introduced into the initial model of the cloth layer (Fig. 7).

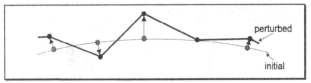

Fig. 7. Random perturbation of the cloth layer.

Fig. 8. Three different smoothness factors.

The random displacement of each of the vertices around the cross sections of the cloth layer is controlled by a *smoothness factor* which can be set by the user. This factor is expressed as a ratio of a chosen maximum displacement relative to the radius of the cloth layer. The effects of the factor are illustrated in Fig. 8 in which the left cylinder has the smallest factor, the middle one has the largest and the right one has a medium value.

3.4 Determination of the Positions of the Fold Lines

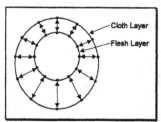

Fig. 9. Gaps between two layers.

The concept of fold lines has been introduced in Section 3.2. From observations of real cloth samples, it seems appropriate to locate folds in the cloth layer where there is the largest amount of slackness. Locating the positions of maximum slackness between the cloth layer and the underlying object (flesh layer) is facilitated by the layered structure. The gaps between the two layers can be found simply by calculating the distance between the corresponding points as shown in Fig. 9.

The following algorithm is used to generate the starting and ending points of fold lines.

1. The gaps, are sorted in descending order, and recorded in a list.
2. The end regions of the cloth layer are chosen by the user, for example end regions have been selected as $RS \{i=0..4\}$ and $RE \{i=N-1...N-5\}$.
3. Vertices with the largest gap value in the regions RS and RE are selected as the starting and ending points respectively, for the first fold line; these selected gap values are deleted from the sorted list.
4. The positions of the starting and ending points are perturbed by a random amounts. The maximum perturbation is user definable.
5. The above sequence is repeated until the number of fold lines (defined by the user) has been reached.

3.5 The Editor GEOFF

GEOFF has been developed to allow the user to interact with the model, and in particular to influence the locations of the folds. The distribution of the gap between the cloth and flesh layers, which have been unfolded, is depicted on a two dimensional grid (Fig. 10a). Larger gaps are shown in lighter colour. This effectively shows the slackness between the cloth and flesh layers. The display also shows positions of fold lines which have been suggested by the algorithm. The user can modify these positions and introduce further fold lines and delete unwanted ones. When the user has accepted the fold lines, the result is displayed in two new windows, one showing a wire-frame version (Fig. 10b) and the other its shaded form (Fig. 10c). The production of the fold lines is fast and the wire-frame is produced almost instantaneously when using a personal computer with an Intel 486™.

4 Simulation Results

Cylinders have been used to represent the layers in both examples. The axes of the cylinders are parallel, but have been separated to introduce a degree of slackness between them.

4.1 First Example

Fig. 10a shows the Gap Display of GEOFF and the lines shown are the fold lines suggested by the algorithm. Fig. 10b is the wire-frame output after generating folds along those lines, and the rendered version is shown in Fig. 10c.

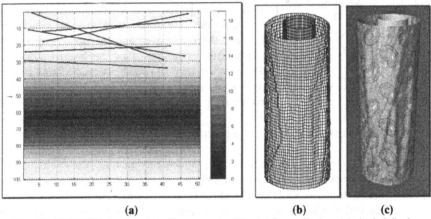

(a)   (b)   (c)

Fig. 10. (a) GEOFF display of the first example, (b) wire-frame display, (c) shaded display.

4.2 Second Example

This example (Fig. 11a) is essentially the same as the first, except that some fold lines (shown in lighter colour) have been generated by the user. The fold line shown in darker colour is one generated in the first example. The wire-frame and the rendered version are shown in Fig. 11b and 11c respectively.

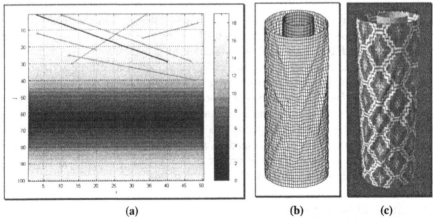

(a)   (b)   (c)

Fig. 11. (a) GEOFF display of the second example, (b) wire-frame display, (c) shaded display.

5 Conclusion and Future Developments

A new geometrical approach for modelling cloth has been presented. In this, a layered structure for linking the cloth to the underlying object has been proposed. Rules have been designed to generate folds and with the aid of the GEOFF editor, users can influence the positions of the folds. Although this work is still in its early stage, the results are quite encouraging. The technique is based on simple concepts and has the advantages of versatility and speed of execution. Future work to develop the technique is as follows:

- The algorithms used to generate fold lines are rule-based. The rule base will be argumented to include further rules associating folds with the geometrical structure of the underlying body.
- The system will be extended to include some physical properties. The classical spring-mass-dashpot model between the cloth and the flesh layer will be incorporated so that the large-scale deformation can be generated automatically and external forces can be taken into account.
- The editor GEOFF will be provided with features to enable the user to describe complex patterns of fold lines with a range of high-level commands. This will provide the user with a simple means to generate a rich variety of fold patterns. Facilities for animating the fold patterns will be incorporated.
- Attribute will be associated with the fold lines to specify a greater variety in the shapes of the folds.

References

1. G. Anderson: A Particle-based Model of the Draping Behaviour of Woven Cloth. Internal Report, Edinburgh Parallel Computer Centre, University of Edinburgh, September 1993.
2. M. Aono: A Wrinkle Propagation Model for Cloth. In: T.S. Chua, T.L. Kunii (eds.): CG International 90, Springer-Verlag, pp. 95-115, 1990.
3. D.E. Breen, D.H. House, P.H. Getto: A Physically-based Particle Model of Woven Cloth. The Visual Computer, Vol 8, pp. 264-277, 1992.
4. D.E. Breen, D.H. House, M.J. Wozny: Predicting the Drape of Woven Cloth Using Interacting Particles. Proc. of SIGGRAPH 94, pp. 365-372, 1994.
5. M. Carignan, Y. Yang, N. M-Thalmann, D. Thalmann: Dressing Animated Synthesis Actors with Complex Deformable Clothes. Proc. of SIGGRAPH 92, pp. 99-104, 1992.
6. J.E. Chadwick, D.R. Haumann, R.E. Parent: Layered Construction for Deformable Animated Characters. Proc. of SIGGRAPH 89, pp. 243-252, 1989.
7. S.G. Dhande, P.V.M. Rao, S. Tavakkoli, C.L. Moore: Geometric Modelling of Draped Fabric Surfaces. Proc. of the IFIP International Conf. on Computer Graphics ICCG 93, Elsevier Science Publishers B.V., pp. 349-356, 1993.
8. C.R. Feynman: Modelling the Appearance of Cloth. MSc Thesis, MIT, 1986.
9. B.K. Hinds, J. McCartney: Interactive Garment Design. The Visual Computer, Vol 6, pp. 53-61, 1990.

10. P. Kalra, A. Mangili, N. M-Thalmann, D. Thalmann: SMILE: A Multilayered Facial Animation System. In: T.L. Kunii (ed.): Modeling in Computer Graphics, Springer-Verlag, pp. 189-198, 1991.

11. T.L. Kunii, H. Gotoda: Singularity Theoretical Modelling and Animation of Garment Wrinkle Formation Processes. The Visual Computer, Vol 6, pp. 326-336, 1990.

12. B. Lafleur, N. M-Thalmann, D. Thalmann: Cloth Animation with Self-Collision Detection. In: Kunii T L (ed.): Modelling in Computer Graphics, Springer-Verlag Tokyo, pp. 179-187, 1991.

13. L. Li, M. Damodaran, R.K.L. Gay: A Quasi-Steady Force Model for Animating Cloth Motion. Proc. of the IFIP International Conf. on Computer Graphics ICCG 93, Elsevier-Science Publishers B.V., pp. 357-363, 1993.

14. N. M-Thalmann, Y. Yang: Techniques for Cloth Animation. In: N. M-Thalmann, D. Thalmann (eds.): New Trends in Animation and Visualisation, John Wiley and Sons, UK, pp. 243-256, 1991.

15. N. M-Thalmann: Tailoring Clothes for Virtual Actors. In: L. MacDonald, J. Vince (eds.): Interacting with Virtual Environments, John Wiley and Sons, UK, pp. 205-216, 1994.

16. H. Okabe, H. Imaoka, T. Tomiha, H. Niwaya: Three Dimensional Apparel CAD System. Proc. of SIGGRAPH 92, pp. 105-110, 1992.

17. W.T. Reeves: Particle Systems – A Technique for Modeling a Class of Fuzzy Objects. Proc. of SIGGRAPH 83, pp. 91-108, 1983.

18. I.J. Rudomin: Simulating Cloth Using a Mixed Geometric-Physical Method, PhD Thesis, University of Pennsylvania, 1990.

19. F. Taillefer: Mixed Modelling. Proc. of CompuGraphics 91, pp. 467-478, 1991.

20. D. Terzopoulos, J. Platt, A. Barr, K. Fleischer: Elastically Deformable Models. Proc. of SIGGRAPH 87, Vol 24, No 4, pp. 205-214, 1987.

21. D. Terzopoulos, K. Fleischer: Deformable Models. The Visual Computer, Vol 4, pp. 306-331, 1988.

22. N. Tsopelas: Animating the Crumpling Behaviour of Garments. Proc. of Eurographics Workshop on Animation and Simulation 91, pp. 11-24, 1991.

23. K. Waters, D. Terzopoulos: A Physical Model of Facial Tissue and Muscle Articulation. Proc. of the 1st Conf. on Visualisation in Biomedical Computing, pp. 77-82, 1990.

24. J. Weil: The Synthesis of Cloth Objects. Proc. of SIGGRAPH 86, pp. 49-54, 1986.

25. H.M. Werner, N. M-Thalmann, D. Thalmann: User Interface for Fashion Design. Proc. of the IFIP International Conference on Computer Graphics ICCG 93, Elsevier-Science Publishers B.V., pp. 197-204, 1993.

26. Y. Yang, N. M-Thalmann, D. Thalmann: Three-dimensional Garment Design and Animation – A New Design Tool for the Garment Industry. Computers in Industry, Vol 19, pp. 185-191, 1992.

27. Y. Yang, N. M-Thalmann: An Improved Algorithm for Collision Detection in Cloth Animation with Human Body. Proc. of Pacific Graphics 93, pp. 237-251, 1993.

Simplification of Polygonal Surface with Attributes

Eihachiro Nakamae[1], Jianyun Chai[2], Hiroyuki Inuyama[3] and Fujiwa Kato[4]

[1] Hiroshima Prefectural University, Shoubara 727, Japan
[2] Tsinghua University, Beijing 100084, China
[3] Sanei Giken Co., Ltd, Hiroshima 730, Japan
[4] Tokyo Electric Power Co., Yokohama 230, Japan

Abstract. Hierarchical modeling obtained from reducing detailed polygonal meshes to simple ones has been approved to be an effective alternative for fast rendering. In this paper, we address two important problems remained in simplification of polygonal surface: (1) reducing a meshed surface with attributes; (2) dealing with geometric and nongeometric feature lines on the surface; A concept of semicircle criteria is proposed, that takes not only geometric features but attributes of the polygonal surfaces into account. Comparing with previous work, our method is more general, practical and flexible to complex objects. Several examples are demonstrated.

1 Introduction

Polygonal surfaces with certain attributes have been widely used for modeling various objects. By attributes, such as material properties and groups, one can distinguish different parts of the surface(e.g. on a human face), and render them correctly. A detailed model may come from a design or measurement, which usually contains large amount of patches. It is not practical to render objects always by their detailed models, because of wasteful computing time. Hierarchical models were proposed [1-3] to save rendering time, where several models with different resolutions are pre-produced and stored, and the one with proper level of details is chosen for rendering. These models reduced detailed polygonal surfaces to desired levels, however, no surface attribute was included.That brings two problems in practical use. First, the surface regions with different attributes have to be simplified individually, otherwise the borders among different regions may mingle with each other in the simplified models. Although some of previous algorithms can be simply modified to tag vertices on borders as permanent, it will lead to that the patches connected to these vertices can not be properly simplified. Second, because of diversity of objects, it is inadequate to obtain satisfied results only by using the existed geometric criteria, since they lack of the operations for dealing with geometrical or nongeometric feature lines on the meshed surface, e.g. crease lines and high light lines or regions.

The algorithms for simplifying polygonal surface can be classified into two categories, namely global reconstruction and local simplification.The former covers mesh simplification and mesh subdivision.The typical algorithms used for mesh simplification include surface fitting methods[4],[5], re-tiling surface method

[6], and mesh optimization method[7]. The most advantage of these algorithms is that the error in distance of the simplified models can be easily controlled in a given bound. On the other hand, they usually take much CPU time. The latter modifies polygonal surfaces locally; that iteratively removes vertices and their related patches from the surface, and re-triangulates the resulted holes. Because of making use of local topological information, the local simplification algorithms are much faster than global ones. The typical local simplification algorithms are proposed by Schroeder[8], Hamann[9] and Schroder[10]. The major differences among them may be in choosing criteria. [8] defined its criterion of the distance from a vertex to its average plane or to its boundary edge. While [9] and [10] developed the criteria based on surface local curvatures and local normal directions, respectively. But they lack of operations for feature edges.

All the algorithms mentioned above neglected away surface attributes.The aim of this paper is to develop a general and fast approach, which can deal with polygonal surface with attributes, and provide the operations for feature lines. Our method bases on the local simplification. We develop a concept of semicircle criteria and their associated operations considering not only geometric features but attributes of the polygonal surfaces. Two benefits are obtained from the semicircle criteria. First, the borders between the regions with different attributes are automatically extracted and simplified. Second, directionality of the surface curvature can be examined, so that some important segments and lines with geometric features, e.g. ridge and valley lines, can be properly simplified and retained in the simplified models. To keep some important surface features that are not easy to be measured by the geometric criteria, e.g. highlights lines, some additional attributes can be imposed on the related polygons.The paper begins with discussing the new criteria and triangulation. Considerations about data structures and accelerating method are given in the followed sections. Several examples are demonstrated and compared with those of previous ones.

2 Semicircle Criteria

In the local simplification algorithms, simplifying a polygonal surface can be considered as a procedure of removing redundant vertices and relatively unimportant vertices iteratively. The criteria are used to measure the importance of each vertex. Let's investigate what kind of vertices can be removed.

2.1 Redundant Vertices

Redundant vertices refer the following vertices, which do not change any geometric shape if they are removed from a polygon mesh: (1) the vertex surrounded by several triangles composing one plane. (2) the vertex on a straight crease line which divides all related patches around it into two parts, and in each part the patches are located on one plane. (3) the vertex on a straight boundary line and all patches related to it are located on one plane. See Fig.1(a),(b) and (c).

2.2 Regular and Irregular Vertices

In principle, any vertex on a polygonal surface without any attribute is removable except some single point connection vertices (see Fig. 1(d)). However, when

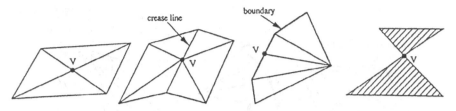

(a) interior redundant vertex   (b) redundant vertex on crease line   (c) boundary redundant vertex   (d) single point connection

Fig. 1. Examples of redundant vertices and single point connection

a surface has some attributes, the borders between different regions lead to additional constraints for vertex removal. The following vertices are defined as *irregular* and should not be removed from the surface: (1) the vertex belongs to both a boundary edge and a border edge, see Fig.2(a). (2)the vertex is surrounded by several triangles belonging to more than two regions of different attributes, see Fig.2(b), or even if the number of regions equals two, but they are separated as shown in Fig.2(c). All vertices except the vertices mentioned above are *regular* vertices that become candidates of removal.

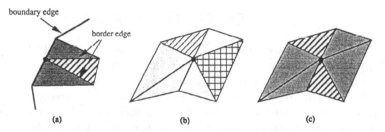

Fig. 2. Irregular vertices that should not be deleted

2.3 Semicircle Criteria

Removable vertices mentioned above can be divided into three types: (1) the interior vertex, surrounded by triangles with same attributes. (2) the boundary vertex, all patches connected to it are of same attributes. (3) the border vertex, surrounded by triangles which can be divided into two successive parts by their attributes.(see Fig. 3). The first two types are similar to those in a polygonal surface without any attribute. For type (1), we adopt the flatness criterion. Supposing patches $P_i (i = 1, 2, \ldots, k)$ linking to the vertex V form a closed patch circle $C\{P_1, P_2, \ldots, P_k\}$, average normal vector $\mathbf{N}_{av}$ at vertex V can be calculated and the circle flatness is defined by the following equation;

$$\mathbf{N}_{av} = \sum_{i=1}^{k} \mathbf{N}_i / |\sum_{i=1}^{k} \mathbf{N}_i|, \tag{1}$$

$$f_c = 1 - \max\{\mathbf{N}_i \cdot \mathbf{N}_{av}\}, \quad i = 1, 2, \ldots k, \tag{2}$$

here, $\mathbf{N}_i$ is the unit normal vector of patch P_i. If f_c equals zero, the patches in patch circle C lie on a plane. The smaller the value of f_c, the flatter the patches surrounding the vertex.

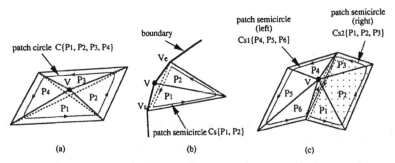

Fig. 3. Three types of removable vertices

For type (2), *semicircle criterion* is employed which consists of two sub-criteria: a flatness criterion and a straightness criterion. Supposing that successive patches $P_i(i = 1, 2, \ldots, k)$ connected to vertex V form a patch semicircle $C_s\{P_1, P_2, \ldots, P_k\}$, and start and end vertices are termed V_e and V_e, respectively, the definition of semicircle flatness, f_s, has the same form as that of circle flatness, while the semicircle straightness, l_s, is defined by the dot product of the unit direction vectors of boundary segments $\overline{V_eV}$ and $\overline{VV_s}$:

$$l_s = 1 - (\overline{\mathbf{V_eV}} \cdot \overline{\mathbf{VV_s}})/(|\overline{\mathbf{V_eV}}| \cdot |\overline{\mathbf{VV_s}}|), \tag{3}$$

when l_s equals zero, two segments $\overline{V_eV}$ and $\overline{VV_s}$ lie on a straight line. The smaller value of l_s corresponds to the straighter broken line V_sVV_e.

For type (3), we expand the semicircle criterion to *double-side semicircle criterion*, that measures f_s and l_s of the two successive parts separately by the semicircle criterion, and takes the larger ones in them as final criterion values. Let the values of semicircle criteria of the two parts, C_{s1} and C_{s2}, be f_{s1}, l_{s1}, and f_{s2}, l_{s2} (Fig.4(c)), the values of the double-side semicircle criterion will be:

$$\begin{aligned} f_{st} &= \max(f_{s1}, f_{s2}) \\ l_{st} &= \max(l_{s1}, l_{s2}) \end{aligned} \tag{4}$$

The double-side semicircle criterion is also available for type (1), if in patch circle C, two edges linked to vertex V with enough small straightness exist. In this case C is divided by the edges into two semicircles. This concept is helpful to treat the vertices at which curvatures significantly vary with the direction, e.g., ridge and valley lines.

3 Triangulation

Once a vertex is removed from a polygonal surface, all patches in its patch circle or semicircles are deleted, and the resulted hole or holes(for the double-side semicircle criterion) must be re-triangulated. In [8], a loop splitting procedure was introduced to triangulate the holes directly in a 3D space because the boundaries of the hole or holes is less constrained by the distance criteria. In our method, however, always the vertex on a locally flattest place is chosen as the removal candidate, thus it is possible to triangulate the holes on 2D planes. The boundary loop of the hole is projected onto a plane oriented by the average normal direction of the vertex , and the projected polygon on the plane is triangulated by a recursively loop splitting Delaunay procedure, the resulted patches are then returned to the original 3D space. The proposed process is rather efficient and robust, most failures occuring during triangulation(e.g. in [7]) are avoided.

4 Implementation

Since the algorithm based on the semicircle criteria provides a tool to simplify polygonal surfaces with attributes, some very convenient options can be realized. For example, we can simplify only some regions of a polygonal surface by giving their material or group codes. The three types of removable vertices, interior, boundary and border vertices(or crease line vertices) can be deleted together or separately. The following options can be taken as input data: the threshold values of criteria, the desired number of patches or vertices, material or group codes of the regions to be simplified, and the operation codes for the vertex types.

When vertices are removed from a polygonal surface iteratively, always the vertex with the minimum criteria values is deleted in every step, that leads to an optimal result in the simplified meshes. It avoids adopting dual criteria at vertices as in [10]. To reduce the time of searching removal candidates or re-ordering vertices, the removable vertices are grouped into several blocks, in each block the number of vertices is less than a fixed number determined by the square root of the total vertex number. The removal candidate then can be selected only from the top order vertices in every blocks, and the re-ordering procedure is needed only for the blocks that are related to the patch circle of the removed vertex.

The following data structure represents polygonal surfaces; two main lists are used for vertices and patches, and one auxiliary list is used for vertex blocks. The patch circle or patch semicircles and block number are taken as members of the vertex structure to record the local topology for removable vertices.

5 Examples

Three examples coming from the creature, natural and industrial product objects are used to verify the quality of the new algorithm. In each example, four detail levels of 100%(up left), 50%(up right), 25%(low left), and 12.5%(low right) are displayed.

Fig. 4 shows a human head consisting of several parts with different attributes, e.g. hair, face, mouth, eyebrow, sclera, iris, etc.(table 1). The borders of every part, i.e., mouth and eyebrows, are simplified and clearly remained even in the 12.5% simplified model.

Model Level	100%	50%	25%	12.5%
Number of Triangles	21,103	10,551	5,275	2,639
Number of Vertices	10,614	5,337	2,699	1,372

Table 1. Models of a human head

Fig. 5 shows the automatic extraction of the ridge and valley lines by our semicircle criteria. The skeleton of the mountain faithfully appears in the simplified models, Table 2 listed the data of the mountain models.

Model Level	100%	50%	25%	12.5%
Number of Triangles	3,227	1,609	813	401
Number of Vertices	1,680	851	453	247

Table 2. Models of a mountain

In Fig. 6 and Fig. 7, models of a car body(table 3) show how a curved and smooth surface can be simplified, the key point is to preserve the feature lines, e.g. highlight curves on the surface. Thanks to the option of attributes, we kept these features easily.

Model Level	100%	50%	25%	12.5%
Number of Triangles	19,590	9,756	4,901	2,448
Number of Vertices	12,875	7,835	5,220	3,967

Table 3. Models of a car body

To measure the executing speed of our algorithm, a set of terrain model data with 234,374 triangles and 135,709 vertices was simplified to the 45% details(105,468 triangles and 71,254 vertices). It took 223.1 seconds processing time on a SGI Indy with one R4600 100Mhz processor, in which 51.79 seconds for pre-procession(reading disk and setting data list in the memory), 161.98 seconds for removing vertices and triangulating and 9.29 seconds for outputting result. The speed is at least three times faster than that given in [10] for a similar data set(12 CPU minutes for reducing a DTM data set with 230,000 triangles and 120,000 vertices to 45% details on a SGI Indigo2 with one R4400 150Mhz processor).

6 Conclusions

We have developed a new method for simplifying polygonal surface. Unlike previous methods, it directly deals with the polygonal surface with attributes. A more important merit is that provides user more chances to control the mesh reduction. The results obtained so far are satisfied; the algorithm is flexible, robust and fast.

References

1. James H. : Clark. Hierarchical geometric models for visible surface algorithms. CACM, 19(10) : (Oct.1976)547–554
2. John S. Falby, Michael J. Zyda, David R. Pratt, and Randy L. Mackey, NPSNET: Hierarchical data structure for real-time three-dimensional visual simulation. Comput. Graphics, **17**,1(1993)65–69
3. Paul S. Heckbert and Michael Garland.: Multiresolution modeling for fast rendering. Graphics Interface '94, (May 1994)43–50
4. F. J. M. Schmitt, B. A. Barsky, and Du Wen-hui: An adptive subdivision method for surface-fitting from sampled data, Comput. Graphics, **20**,4(1986)179–188

138

5. Michael J. Dehaemer, and Michael J. Zyda, Simplification of objects rendered by polygonal approximations, Comput. Graphics, **15**, 2(1991)175–184
6. Greg Turk: Re-tiling polygonal surfaces, Computer Graphics, **26**, 2(SIG-GRAPH'92) 55–64
7. H. Hoppe, T. DeRose, T. Duchamp, J. McDonald, and W. Stuetzle: Mesh Optimization, Computer Graphics, (SIGGRAPH'92)19–26
8. William J. Schroeder, Jonathan A. Zarge, and William E. Lorensen: Decimation of triangle meshes, Computer Graphics, **26**, 2(SIGGRAPH'92)65–70
9. Bernd Hamann, A data reduction scheme for trianglulated surfaces, Computer Aided Geometric Design, No.11 (1994)197–214
10. Florian Schroder and Patrick Robbach: Managing the complexity of digital terrain models, Comput. Graphics **18**, 6(1994)775–783

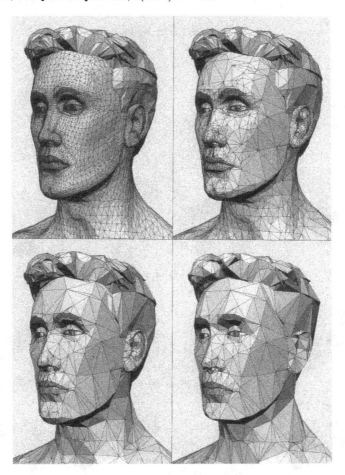

Fig. 4. Four level models of a human head.

Fig. 5. Four level models of a mountain.

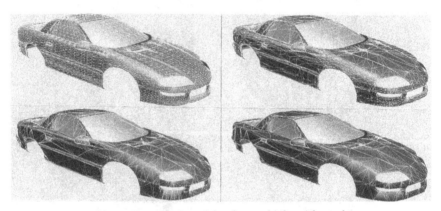

Fig. 6. Four level models of a car body with mesh.

Fig. 7. Four level models of a car body (smooth shaded).

Reducing Polygonal Data by Structural Grouping Algorithm

Daisuke NISHIOKA

and

Mikio NAGASAWA

Ultra-high Speed Network and Computer Technology Laboratories (UNCL)
Central Research Laboratory, HITACHI Ltd.
Higashi-Koigakubo, Kokubunji, Tokyo 185 Japan

Abstract. In the field of computer graphics, polygonal representations are used for modeling three-dimensional geometrical objects. When recognizing structural characteristics, however, they often have much redundancy. Large numbers of polygons are difficult to render on graphic workstations or transfer over the network. To allow remote handling of polygonal data in virtual reality environments, the rational reduction of polygonal data is required. This paper describes a new algorithm which reduces the number of such polygonal primitives without losing the detailed structures of an object. This method is a kind of grouping algorithm and is effective for reducing structural redundancy. In the reducing process, we merge adjoining polygons, which satisfy a given coplanar criterion, into one plane. This grouping method is designed not to destroy the object structural patterns. The geometrical data are divided into groups satisfying the condition of required accuracy. The local reduction rule of polygons is applied to each classified group. We test this reducing method with geometric models representing human faces. The effectiveness for reducing polygon numbers and keeping the 3-D rendered image quality is investigated.

1. Introduction

Polygonal representation is used for special effects in the movies, computer graphical animations, and scientific visualizations. Recently, the transfer of massive geometrical data has become possible using computer networks, especially high-speed Local Area Networks. Users also want to work with virtual 3-D space over the Wide Area Network. Multimedia communications and realtime visualization of scientific data output from supercomputers are considered to be realistic. Although high-speed networks are prevailing, such geometrical data

---

e-mail: nisioka@crl.hitachi.co.jp, m-nagasa@crl.hitachi.co.jp

are still gigantic to transfer, sharing the network bandwidth. Thus, it is important not only to gain a wider communication bandwidth, but also to reduce the transfer data. To increase the efficiency of 3-D data transmission, we extract the redundancies included in polygonal data and reduce them.

In general, there are four kinds of redundancies :

(1) Statistical Redundancy

A reducing method using statistical redundancy extracts correlations between data and bunches a series of data like the Run-Length algorithm.

(1) Structural Redundancy

This reducing method uses structural redundancy to divide data into structural parts. Their structures are stored compactly.

(2) Visual Redundancy

For example, a reducing method using visual redundancy omits the hidden invisible part of the objects for rendering and transmission [1].

(3) Intellectual Redundancy

A reducing method for intellectual redundancy classifies the patterns of geometrical structures, describes their characteristics, and recognizes them.

JPEG and MPEG have become standards for reducing the statistical and visual redundancies of the 2-D images or motion pictures. However, data compression methods for 3-D data are still open to investigation because of their wide variety of applications such as entertainment, medical, geophysical or engineering applications, and so on. The data structures cannot be handled in a unified manner for such a vast variety of data. In this paper, we concentrate on polygonal data and describe how geometrical objects can be compressed without losing the detailed information. We apply the grouping method for reducing the statistical, structural, and visual redundancy of polygonal representations of geometrical objects.

2.   Conventional Method

There are two major methods for polygonal data reduction [2]. One is to omit vertices at regular intervals. This method can be applied to polygonal data whose vertex positions are arranged regularly, such as a surface measured by a laser scanner device. Laser-scanned data usually consist of over 100,000 polygons, and it is hard to treat them in realtime simulations. Because of the regular arrangement of vertices, one can reduce the number of polygons efficiently by omitting vertices at arbitrary intervals. We show the general idea of the omitting vertices method in Fig. 1. However, there are not many data whose results with this method are of satisfactory quality. The Adaptive Subdivision method is a good method for such case [3]. However, these method can be applied only to regular vertex polygonal data, so they are not so general as the comparison method as shown in next paragraph [4].

Another method is the comparison of normal vectors between neighboring polygons. This comparison method is applied not only to laser-scanned data but also to more general polygonal data. In this method, there are four steps. First, the normal vectors of polygonal surfaces are calculated. Next, the group for merging polygons is selected as shown in Fig. 2(a). The third step is to judge the criterion between the normal vectors of the base polygon and those of adjoining polygons as shown in Fig. 2(b). In this example, we merge the polygon B to the base polygon if the directional angle difference between their normal vectors is less than a given threshold angle. The threshold angle can be defined by the user. In Fig. 2(a), polygon C does not adjoin the base polygon, so we do not need to compare the normal vectors of the base polygon with those of polygon C. Figure 2(c) shows the result of this merging process. There are some other methods based on this [5].

These two methods mentioned above, can reduce the total number of polygons. However, they apply the criterion so equally in a uniform and global manner that important structural information could be lost with the same frequency as less important structures. In these methods, the significance of the local structure of the geometrical data is not considered. Even an important part of the data could be reduced with some aliases in the course of the reduction process. The users cannot choose the threshold angle so that the result has a required quality and conserves the characteristics of the initial polygonal data. We notice that a single threshold angle is not enough for a satisfactory reduced image.

For example, a polygonal object, which represents a human face, has some characteristic parts such as *"eyes"* or *"mouth"*. These parts of the data should keep their identity without destroying their boundary structure. It is true that some parts of the face such as *"hair"* or *"cheeks"* can be reduced uniformly. The problem is caused by the neglect of the structural redundancy of initial polygonal data. Both the omitting vertices method and the normal vector comparison method are mainly designed to reduce statistical redundancy.

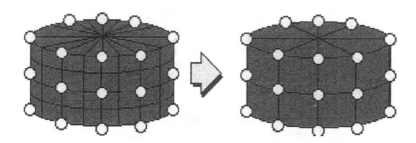

Fig. 1. Omitting Vertices Method. Because of regular arrangement of vertices, one can reduce the number of polygons by coarse-graining the vertices.

3. Structural Grouping of Polygons

As a whole, the uniform reduction of polygonal data has this problem mentioned in the preceding section. A solution to this problem is to divide initial polygons into groups which have independent requirements for accuracy. This grouping process could make the polygonal data structured before starting the ordinary reduction process. Then, a conventional method of reduction, such as the normal vector comparison method, is applied after the grouping procedure.

The reduction procedure with the grouping option is as follows :

(1) Divide initial polygonal data into structural groups.

(2) Specify the threshold angle for every polygonal group.

(3) Merge the nearly coplanar polygons in each group using the normal vector comparison method with each given threshold, respectively.

In this grouping method, we have to chose some principles to divide initial polygons into appropriate groups. For this purpose, we report an interactive

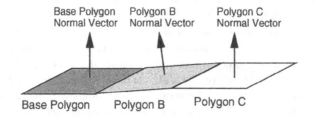

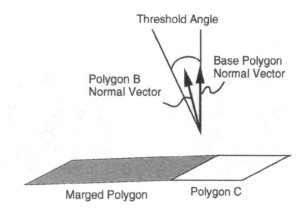

Fig. 2. (a) Left: Polygons and their normal vectors for merging criteria. (b) Center: Comparison of angle difference between normal vectors of the neighboring polygons. (c) Right: Reduced polygons as result of this merging operation.

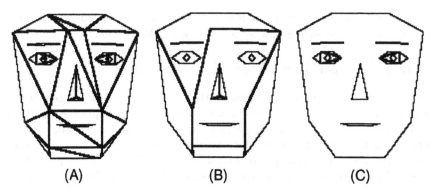

(A)   (B)   (C)

Fig. 3. Simple example of structural polygon reduction. Model (A) is initial polygonal data of human face. Model (B) is result of conventional normal vector comparison method without grouping option. Model (C) is result of reduction with our grouping algorithm. Models (B) and (C) have same number of polygons(15).

system for the selection of polygon groups. We developed a system in which the threshold angles of respective groups can be specified by user interaction. We are also developing an automatic algorithm for polygon grouping, which will be reported soon elsewhere.

We can demonstrate the effect of this grouping option in the reduction processes. A schematic example of this reduction effect is shown in Fig. 3. Model (A) is the original polygons of human face data. This polygonal object consists of 47 polygons and 3 groups. The specified groups are *"eyes"*, *"nose and mouth"*, and *"other"*. Model (B) is the result of the conventional normal vector comparison method without the grouping option. While model (C) is the result of reduction with our grouping algorithm. The threshold angle of *"eyes"* is set to zero in this model. Models (B) and (C) have different appearances, but both data consist of the same number of polygons, 15. From this example of reduction with the grouping option, we notice the following four advantages :

(1) It conserves the outlines of groups. Because reduction is performed in every group independently, boundary polygons of each group should not merge with the polygons of different group.

(2) The reduction is more efficient than the other conventional method. We can optimize the threshold angle to get a high reduction rate for certain polygonal groups of less importance.

(3) Very fast sorting is possible. In order to compare the normal vector difference, we have to chose pairs of adjoining polygons. The pre-conditioned grouping process gives us small numbers of polygonal data. The searching procedure finishes much more easily than conventional methods, because the number of possible adjoining polygon candidates is far fewer than with global searching.

(4) The reduction process can run faster on parallel computers. Since the re-

duction process in each group is independent from other group reductions, we can process each group reduction in a parallel fashion.

4. Implementation of Reduction Algorithm

We describe here our implementation of the polygon reduction system with grouping options. Polygonal data reduction with the grouping option consists of two procedures, that is, a grouping process and a reducing process. First of all, in order to get output data with a high reduction rate, we have to specify the groups of polygons in an appropriate way. Then, the reduction program receives the sets of grouped polygons and starts to reduce them effectively.

4.1 Polygonal Grouping Editor

The basic geometrical object data consist of vertices and polygons. Each vertex has an assigned number and position coordinates information. Polygonal element information links the vertex numbers. If we use a kind of text editor, it is possible to edit such data structures and specify groups of polygonal data. However, this is a tedious and troublesome task. Real polygonal data is often too large for the users to edit in the source text.

In order to sophisticate this grouping procedure and free users from such troublesome work, we developed a polygon grouping editor which has a graphical user interface and interactive tools for editing polygons. Figure 4 shows a sample GUI of our polygon grouping editor.

The way to use this polygon editing system is as follows:

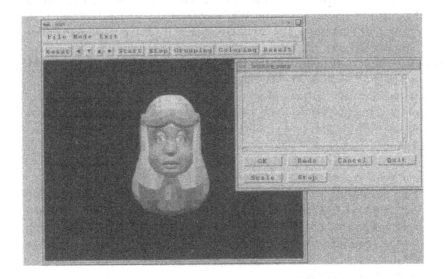

Fig. 4. Sample screen window of polygon grouping editor.

First, the polygonal data are loaded on the working screen window. The user can recognize the characteristic groups in this preview stage. Then one can determine a rough group boundary by dragging a pointing cursor to certain components of a polygonal object. These roughly selected polygons are highlighted with a special color to distinguish them from other polygons. At this stage, unnecessary polygons happen to be included in this specified group or important polygons may not be picked up. Thus, after the rough grouping stage, a more strict editing process should take place. When the user picks up a polygon from the roughly grouped area, the condition flag of the polygon will be toggled resulting in a different color state. In this way, grouped polygons are displayed using a different color from the other groups. The user can recognize his selection of groups by the color distinction of each polygonal component.

4.2 Reducing Criterions

Once the structural polygon groups are specified, we start coplanar reduction by applying the normal vector comparison method to each group. First in the coplanar reduction process, we read all the geometrical object data, *i.e.* (a) vertex data of coordinate position, (b) polygon data of vertex connection list, and (c) grouping information. After loading such information, we divide the geometrical data arrays into groups and apply the normal vector comparison method, as in Fig. 2 , to merge the coplanar polygon pair into one polygon. At the end of this reduction process, we display the resultant polygonal data.

The coplanar reduction process has four components :

    (1) Input module to read all the initial data.

    (2) User interface module to set the merging threshold angles.

    (3) Merging module which reconnects the new vertices for coplanar polygons.

    (4) Output module to write the resultant polygonal data structure.

The input module routine is very simple. First, this module reads all the data that consist of vertices, groups, and polygons. Then, the polygonal data are divided into each group. For each polygonal surface, the normal vectors are calculated.

In the user interface module, the threshold angles for each polygonal group are specified interactively. We choose a certain polygonal group, and set a threshold angle for this group. Then we perform a similar operation for the other polygonal groups, optimizing the threshold angle interactively, *e.g.* 0.5 degree in group A, 1.2 degree in group B, and so on.

In general, the merging module routine is somewhat complex [6]. This routine has to be invoked for every group. First of all, in this subroutine, a certain polygon is selected as a base polygon of the group. Then, the adjoining polygons are listed up with reference to that selected base polygon.

We identify the adjoining polygons by the condition that they should have more than two common vertices and a corresponding ridge. Figure 5 shows a sample of such adjoining polygon configuration. Polygon A is the base polygon and polygons B and D are adjoining polygons. While, polygon C is not an adjoining polygon because it has only one common vertex and no contact ridge. When

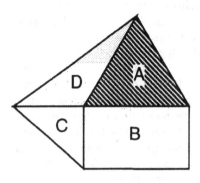

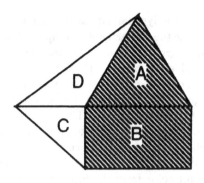

Fig. 5. Adjoining polygons. In this polygonal group, the base polygon is polygon A. The adjoining polygons, for example, polygons B and D are shown.

Fig. 6. Merged polygons. If the normal vector of polygon B is almost coplanar within a criterion of angle difference, it is merged with the base polygon A to reduce the numbers of polygons.

the adjoining polygons of a given base polygon are listed, their normal vectors are compared with that of the base polygon as shown in Fig. 2. If the angle between a normal vector of the base polygon and that of an adjoining polygon is less than the threshold angle of its group, the adjoining polygon is merged into the base polygon. Such a merged polygon configuration is shown in Fig. 6. This shows the case that polygons A and B in Fig. 5 are almost coplanar and so are merged within the criterion for this polygon group.

After the merging operation, the base polygon has combined with the merged polygons and becomes larger. The polygon that has merged with a base polygon should be marked with a flag of *"removed"* to prevent a duplicated operation.

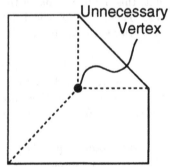

Fig. 7. Unnecessary vertex after merging operation. In order to reduce the total data size, we have to remove the garbage vertices from the polygonal data structure.

When the merging procedure for each group is finished, we have to remove the unnecessary garbage vertices before saving the resultant data. Such an unnecessary garbage vertex is shown in Fig. 7. In this example, three polygons are merged into a single pentagonal polygon, a merged polygon. The vertex at the center is no longer needed. The output module processes this garbage-collection operation by re-configuring the resultant polygonal data structure. After removing unnecessary vertices, the reduced polygonal data could be stored as an archive or transmitted over the computer network.

5. Results and Efficiency

In this section, we present the results of reduction by the normal vector comparison method with grouping options. We apply this method to two geometrical model data: One is general geometrical data whose vertices are not arranged regularly. The other is the relatively uniform polygonal data scanned by a laser measuring device.

5.1 General Geometric Data

As a first example, we try to reduce the general geometrical data which represent a little girl's face. These polygonal data are taken from the sample data provided by Viewpoint Data Labs International, USA.

In a familiar way, these polygonal data are divided into nine groups tagged as follows : *"Hair"*, *"Brow"*, *"Eyelash"*, *"Iris"* *"White eyes"*, *"Pupil rim"* *"Cheek and nose"*, *"Upper lip"*, and *"Lower lip"*.

The original geometrical data are shown in the left part of Fig. 8(a). When we apply the simple normal vector comparison method without the grouping option, a poor result as in Fig. 8(b) is reduced. There are many aliases caused by the ignorance of structural boundary. While, the result with our grouping method can reduce the original data and keep a good quality of output image as shown in Fig. 8(c).

The precise reduction numbers of polygons and their ratios of data size reduction are listed in Table 1. Judging the results of the two methods, the reduced data by the conventional method without the grouping option has some artificial defects, for instance, a part of *"chin"* and the right *"eye"* are coagulated with the *"cheek"* group boundary. On the other hand, the result of the method

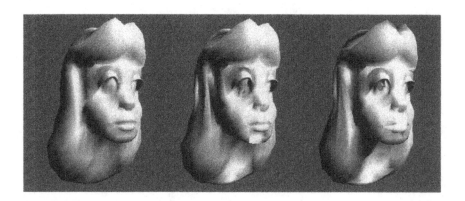

Fig. 8. (a) Left: Original geometrical polygonal data. (b) Center: Reduced polygons by conventional normal vector comparison method. (c) Right: Reduced polygons by normal vector comparison method with grouping option described in text.

Table 1. Reduction of Geometrical Polygonal Data.

Data	Method	Vertices	Polygons	Data size	Image quality
	Raw	948	962	100%	Redundant
Girl-M-Head	Uniform Merge	932	688	28.5%	Poor
	Structural Group	928	632	34.3%	Good
	Omission	10086	19759	100%	Redundant
Laser-Scan	Uniform Merge	8492	15799	80.0%	Fair
	Structural Group	8101	15454	78.2%	Good

with the grouping option maintains the detail of the structures, because there is no interference between independent respective groups. The resultant reduction rate by the grouping method is also better than that of the conventional case without grouping.

5.2 Laser-Scanned Uniform Data

We also apply the grouping method to laser-scanned data representing a girl's face. The data consist of $512^2 = 262144$ vertices. There are so many vertices that we need a lot of computational time to reduce the polygonal data structure. Thus, as a preprocessing operation, we reduce the original data by the omitting vertices method first. The omission of vertices at every four intervals makes the data as compact as 16,384 vertices. We notice that the scanned data include some invalid vertex data, which manifests as a lack of polygons at the top of

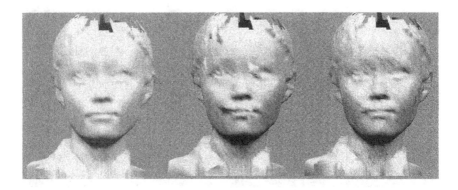

Fig. 9. (a) Left: Preprocessed Laser-Scanned Head data using constant vertex omission method. (b) Center: Reduced polygons of Laser-Scanned Head by conventional normal vector comparison method. (c) Right: Reduced polygons of Laser-Scanned Head by normal vector comparison method with grouping option described in text.

the head in Fig. 9, due to the ill setting of the input device hardware. After correction for these defects, the available vertices were 10,086 and there are 19,759 polygons for this model.

Starting from this omitted version of initial laser-scanned data as in Fig. 9(a), we apply the normal vector comparison method both with and without grouping to compare the efficiency of the grouping operation. Applied to preprocessed data such as Fig. 9(a), the result of the conventional method and that of the grouping method are shown in Fig. 9(b) and Fig. 9(c), respectively.

In Table 1, we list the actual numbers of polygons and the data reduction rate. Since the starting data was already reduced by means of the omitting vertices method, these two results have little difference with respect to the compression rate. However, as for the quality of output image, we can easily see the great difference between the two results. The reduced polygonal data (Fig. 9(c)) with the grouping option has less aliases than the case without grouping (Fig. 9(b)).

6. Conclusions

In this paper, we presented a method for reducing polygonal data. The polygonal data reduction algorithm with the grouping option enables us to reduce the amount of polygonal data efficiently. We investigated an advantage of this grouping method, by comparing the results of both methods applied to girl's face data. We also applied this grouping method to another kind of large laser-scanned data. Choosing an appropriate merging criterion for each polygonal group, it is possible to get a better polygonal reduction rate than with the conventional normal vector comparison method without grouping options.

The reduction methods with grouping options can improve the ratio of polygon reduction. However, there are some problems to solve in the future. One of the most important problems is to further develop the method for automatic grouping of polygonal data. We have started developing such an automatic grouping method using the quantization of normal vectors. Even in the interactive specification of polygonal groups, this would be helpful for the user to determine the group boundaries.

The proposed algorithm is related to the statistical and structural redundancies. We are trying to proceed to the quantitative treatment of other redundancies of polygonal data, such as a visual redundancy concerned with human recognition.

References

1. T. Ohshima, S. Uchiyama, H. Yamamoto and H. Tamura, *3-D Image Conference '94 (Japan)* 201-206 (1994)
2. D. Salesin and F. Tampieri, *Graphics Gems* **III**, 225-230 (1992)
3. M. J. DeHaemer and M. J. Zyda, *Computer & Graphics* **14**, 175-184 (1992)
4. G. Turk, *Computer Graphics* **26**, 55-63 (1992)
5. W. J. Schroeder, J. A. Zarge, and W. E. Lorensen, *Computer Graphics* **26**, 65-70 (1992)
6. P. Hinker and C. Hansen, *Proc. of Visualization 93* (ed. Nielson and Bergeron, IEEE CS Press) 189-195 (1993)

Daisuke Nishioka is a researcher at the Ultra-high Speed Network and Computer Technology Laboratories, Tokyo. His research interests include computer graphics, character animation systems, and computer music. Nishioka received a Bachelor of Information Science degree in 1990, and a Master of Information Science degree in 1992 from Tokyo University of Agriculture and Technology. He is a member of the Information Processing Society of Japan.

Mikio Nagasawa is a senior researcher at the Ultra-high Speed Network and Computer Technology Laboratories, Tokyo. His research interests include Computational Fluid Dynamics, scientific visualization of volume data, and system integration of heterogeneous supercomputing environments. He is now working on the effective transfer of scientific volume data for remote simulations. Nagasawa received a Bachelor of Science degree in 1982, a Master of Science in Physics in 1984, and a Ph.D. in Astrophysics in 1987 from Kyoto University. He is a member of the Japan Society of Fluid Mechanics, the Astronomical Society of Japan, the Information Processing Society of Japan, and IEEE Computer Society.

Address: UNCL, Central Research Laboratory, Hitachi Ltd., 1-280 Higashi-Koigakubo, Kokubunji, Tokyo 185 Japan. (`nisioka@crl.hitachi.co.jp`, `m-nagasa@crl.hitachi.co.jp`)

An Object-Oriented Architecture for Chinese Character Composition

Ivan S.B. Wong and Avi C. Naiman

Department of Computer Science
The Hong Kong University of Science and Technology
Clear Water Bay, Kowloon, Hong Kong

Abstract. In the process of digitizing Chinese characters, approaches which are quite different from those used for European characters can reduce the storage required for the glyphs and, at the same time, improve the efficiency of digitization. However, these approaches often induce some other subprocesses and intermediate arguments which require a lot of human effort and knowledge. We illustrate an *object-oriented approach* to digitization of Chinese character glyphs (which we have implemented in Postscript), in which all intermediate subprocesses and arguments are hidden from the user, generating the characters in a black-box process.

1 Introduction

Along with the rapid expansion of the desktop publishing industry, there has been an increase in the demand for high-quality digital fonts. In the process of producing digitized characters for Chinese fonts (Japanese and Korean are other examples), unique difficulties are often encountered. For example, because of the huge character set size — thousands, rather than the hundreds of characters found in Latin alphabets — and the complicated character shapes, more resources (e.g., time and effort in building the *glyphs*[1], storage space for the glyphs, etc.) have to be expended in digitizing the characters. Moreover, most Chinese characters remain unavailable in industrial digital standards: although more than 60,000 Chinese characters exist, only 6,763 characters are available in GB2312-80 [4] and only 13,053 in Big5; even in Unicode [7], all the characters in the world will not be codable in the 2-byte (i.e., 65,536-entry) format.

Several methods exist for creating digital characters [6]. One approach is for designers to digitize each glyph from scratch, storing them individually. Although this human approach provides great control over the quality of character shapes, the human effort and storage space required are often too great a price to pay. Another approach for creating digital glyphs that is particularly useful for Chinese fonts is the use of hierarchical structures with which complex characters can be constructed from simpler components. For example, 森 can be constructed from 木 and 林, while 林, in turn, is composed of 2 other instances of 木. Build-

---

[1] A glyph is the graphical description of a character.

ing characters through the composition of other characters or strokes[2] can save time, effort and storage space. However, design experience is essential in obtaining quality results and much time is often needed to fine-tune the parameters — location, scaling and distortions — involved in the composition process [8].

Traditionally, each occurrence of a glyph is (intended to be) identical. The concept of *Dynamic Fonts* [5] has been introduced to increase the flexibility in printed characters, by allowing different instances of a character to be rendered in different ways. For example, by incorporating a random number into a character's parametric description, successive invocations of a single character definition can result in modifications to the resultant shape, without any intervention by a user (see Figure 1). This concept can be extended to allow characters to communicate with each other, thereby enabling the possibility for a character's rendition to take into consideration its neighboring characters.

Fig. 1. 5 A's are drawn from the same Dynamic Font

We propose, here, to combine the two approaches of hierarchical glyph composition and Dynamic Fonts in order to improve the Chinese font creation process. This approach is implemented using *object-oriented* programming techniques, so that all intermediate subprocesses and parameters induced during the composition are stored inside each character (i.e., object) and, thereby, hidden from the user. We believe that this approach will lead to significant reductions in the resources — time, effort and storage space — needed to generate Chinese character fonts.

2 Traditional Approach in Character Composition

In the traditional approach, we can create a *composite character* with reference to a hierarchical structure of subcomponents. If the subcomponents are also whole characters, we call them *base characters* when they are used as subcomponents. For example, 森 can be composed of 3 木, scaled and placed in appropriate positions. In Postscript [1], this can be accomplished with the following commands:

```
gsave 0 500 translate 1.0 0.5 scale  木 grestore
gsave 0   0 translate 0.5 0.5 scale  木 grestore
gsave 500 0 translate 0.5 0.5 scale  木 grestore
```

---

[2] Some systems use radicals as their basic building blocks, while others employ the 8 basic strokes used in writing Chinese characters.

where '木' represents the glyph drawing routine for the character 木, the character size is 1000 × 1000, and the character anchor point is at the lower-left corner.

Although character composition is, conceptually, quite straight forward, achieving high-quality results requires attention to detail. Parameterized subprocesses are often introduced to deal with three distinct problems : *visual corrections, stroke distortions* and *anchor points*.

2.1 Visual Corrections

If base characters are scaled uniformly, the composite character often suffers from visual irregularity [2]. The strokes in the scaled-down base characters will often be perceived as too thin and the composite character will often appear inconsistent in visual size or font style when presented along with the original base characters (see Figure 2a).

In order to preserve visual regularity, non-linear scaling functions must be applied to each base character as it is scaled. These scaling functions may differ from font to font, from character to character within a font, or even from stroke to stroke within a character. Figure 2b presents visually-corrected versions of the characters from Figure 2a. Note that the thicknesses of strokes in the scaled-down base characters have not been reduced as much as the base characters themselves.

(a) with uniform scaling

(b) with visual corrections

(c) with visual corrections and stroke distortions

Fig. 2. Composite characters

2.2 Stroke Distortions

In the lower half of the character 森, the character 林 is composed of 2 instances of the base character 木. In fact, the base character 木 on the left should be a little bit different from the one on the right in their right oblique strokes (Figure 2c). Writing rules [3] tell us that many stroke distortions of this kind are needed inside a base character when it serves as a subcomponent in a composite character. The traditional approach has been to store each version of the base character in a different glyph, referencing the appropriate one as needed. For example, there would be one glyph for the left 木 and another one for the right 木 in 林.

Rather than storing complete glyphs, another approach is to store the individual strokes and create a glyph by combining relevant strokes, after appropriate scaling and positioning. This approach might improve the storage requirement because, for example, the two versions of 木 could share the same horizontal, vertical and left oblique strokes. Only 2 versions of the right oblique would have to be created and stored. However, this approach require more parameters than designing complete glyph, and it can be quite time consuming to set all the parameters correctly.

2.3 Anchor Points

Even after base characters (or their strokes) have been scaled, visually-corrected, and had their strokes properly modified, in order to achieve high-quality composite characters, anchor points must be used to position the subcomponents carefully. Many trials — involving experimentation with the spacing between strokes and/or base characters, alignment amongst subcomponents, etc. — are often needed to obtain satisfactory results.

2.4 Evaluation and Iterative Design

In addition to the problems addressed so far, the designer must ensure that characters have proper symmetry and blackness (i.e., density), both in isolation and in the context of the other characters in the font. To accomplish this, the parameters used in the subprocesses above need to be refined iteratively. Because some of these parameters are interdependent — e.g., scaling ratios and anchor points — the whole design process can require quite a few iterations before satisfactory results are achieved.

3 Object-Oriented Model in Character Composition

We have seen that, in the traditional approach to Chinese character glyph production, a great deal of time, human effort, and storage are needed. Because the subprocesses and parameters involved in creating each character are interdependent, much design time is required to achieve good results iteratively. It would be quite beneficial if resource duplication could be avoided by, for example, reusing strokes, glyphs and subprocess parameters when possible. Toward this end, we propose an object-oriented approach to managing Chinese font design resources.

3.1 Base Characters as Objects

In object-oriented environments, the *object* is the basic data structure. Each object contains not only its data, but also its own internal procedure: other objects cannot access its data or procedure directly (this is known as *data encapsulation/hiding*). Objects can, however, *communicate* with each other and may thereby request and grant information. In our approach to Chinese character glyph production, we define each base character as an object, the subprocess parameters (e.g., the scaling function, stroke distortions and the anchor point locations) as the private data inside an object, and the glyph description (i.e., the method for drawing a character's shape) as the internal procedure. In addition, communication routines are defined for each object, to allow sharing of information between base characters as they are combined into a composite glyph. The base character is drawn when a *message* is received by its communication

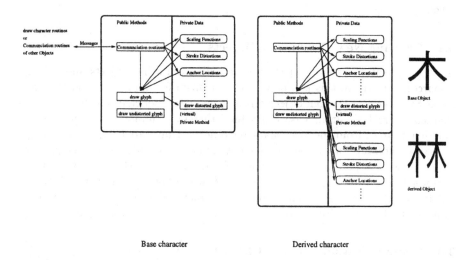

Base character   Derived character

Fig. 3. Character objects

routine from a draw character routine or from the communication routines of other objects (i.e., other base characters in the composite character). From the information in the messages received, the communication routine configures the parameters for rendering the base character and invokes the draw glyph routine.

Recall that the same stroke may sometimes have one appearance in a base character, and sometimes another (refer Figure 2). In the traditional approach, entire different glyphs are invoked for the two versions. In the object-oriented model, we distinguish between strokes that vary across instances and strokes that never vary, by providing two stroke categories: varying and non-varying. The base character object always invokes the same non-varying stroke routines, regardless of stroke variation parameters. However, for each of the strokes that vary, the glyph routine must dynamically choose from amongst a set of candidate stroke routines, based on the stroke variation parameters communicated in the received messages.

For example, in the base character 木, the vertical, horizontal and left oblique strokes are non-varying, while the right oblique stroke varies. In this case, two different right oblique routines are defined in the base character object 木: one for when it is drawn as the left base character in 林 and one for when it is drawn on the right. As is normal in object-oriented systems, the two routines share the same name (i.e., right oblique), but only one of them is invoked each time a base character is rendered.

The final step for rendering the base character is to place it in its proper location, as determined by the anchor point parameters in the object. The object then sends a message to the next base character to be rendered, communicating relevant information about its position, stroke variation, etc., from which the next base character can determine which of its own varying stroke routines to invoke.

3.2 Creating New Characters/Objects

In object-oriented system, objects can be built from other objects and *inherit* resources from them: this is a powerful mechanism for data reduction through reuse. Such is the case in our object-oriented character model, in which composite characters are built from base characters, thereby defining new objects that inherit resources from the base character objects. Duplicated resources — e.g., the same glyph routines — can be shared within the new object while the private data — e.g., the parameters — cannot. For example, the character 林 can be composed from 2 instances of the character 木 with only one shared set of glyphs but two copies of the parameters, and the character 森 can also be constructed to form another new object with one set of glyphs and 3 copies of parameters.

3.3 Communication Between Characters/Objects

To facilitate the inter-dependency and self-modifiability of object parameters, there must be a channel for the objects to communicate with the outside, either with other objects or with the draw character routine. To preserve the data/parameter encapsulation, message passing should be free of intermediate parameters and be simple enough for the naive user to initiate. In our object-oriented approach, messages contain information only about structural shape, position and size. The following list shows some of the elementary structural shapes available, along with some example characters corresponding to each shape [3].

When the character/object 森 is created by composing 木 and 林 in structural shape ⊟, an additional data field is stored in object 森 indicating the structural shape. When the draw character 森 routine is called, the location and size of the character's bounding box — i.e., the structural shape ☐ along with location and size — is passed into 森's communication routine as messages. 森 then configures its internal parameters — e.g., visual corrections, stroke variations and anchor points — and sends outgoing messages to the objects that are its sub-characters (i.e., 林 and 木). When a sub-character receives a message containing structural

Structural shape	Example Characters
☐	金 日
⊞	林 汨
⊟	昌 晶
⊞	樹 倒
⊟	亮 會
⌐	可 武
☐	固 圖
⊔	凶

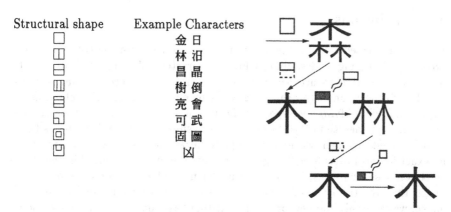

Table 1. Some elementary structural shapes and their example characters

Fig. 4. Message passing in the hierarchy

shape, position and size from 森, it will, in turn, configure its own parameters and further propagate messages to its sub-characters until no more sub-characters remain, i.e., until the sub-character is a base character. For example, at the top of Figure 4, 森 receives a message from the draw character routine with the location and size for drawing. 森 first checks its internal data, which is the structural shape ⊟, as well as the corresponding sub-characters, 木 and 林 in this case. Object 森 then sends a message to object 木 to render itself as the upper part of ⊟. 木 then checks its own internal structural information; since it is a ☐ base character, it starts to render using the position and size received from 森 , configuring its parameters, rendering the base character and then determining the outgoing messages for 林. Object 林 is asked to render itself in the lower part of ⊟, which has been positioned and sized by the above-rendered 木. Since 林 is also an object composed from 2 instances of 木 in structure ⊞, it sends a message to the first (i.e., left) 木 of structure ⊞ with the location and size it received. This second instance of 木 will also configure its internal parameters for rendering. However, in this instance, because 木 is on the left side of a ⊞, the visual result will be different in the right oblique stroke. This second instance of 木 then sends a message to a third instance of 木 to render itself on the right side of ⊞, using a specified position and size. Once this final 木 has drawn itself, the whole character 森 is complete.

To build up a font in this way, the developer needs to specify the intelligence and details only once in defining each base character/object, of which there are several hundred. Whenever a new character is to be composed, only the sub-characters and the structural shapes in which they are combined need to be specified. The composite character only takes on definitive shape at the time the draw character routine is called. If character objects are built with sufficient internal information for serving as sub-characters in any of the possible structural shapes, even naive users would be able to compose their own user-defined characters in a straightforward manner.

4 Conclusions

We have addressed some of the design problems inherent in the traditional approach to digitizing or describing Chinese characters. We proposed an object-oriented model that reduces the required resources by resource sharing in a hierarchy of objects and eases the design task by encapsulating parameters inside objects and simplifying messages by the use of structural shape. A prototype has been implemented in Postscript and the feasibility of this approach has been demonstrated. Though, without a complete library of base characters, we have no exact figures in terms of storage and resource reduction involved in the character composition process, we believe this scheme will lead to a more economical model than the traditional one. Moreover, from the perspective of font maintenance, we can easily add new or modify existing base characters/objects without any alteration to other objects, with the whole font library being re-configured dynamically on demand.

In the process of character porting from font to font, our approach also provides a convenient architecture by merely replacing the glyph routines in each base character object. In addition, if the characters are defined only at rendering time, we can shift the whole process of character generation to an output device — e.g., a laser printer — and the transportation size for each character between terminal and printer can be largely reduced by communicating to the printer only the relevant base object IDs and messages for starting up the character composition, instead of sending the whole rendered glyph to the printer. In this case, we only need to store a small number of character objects — i.e., several hundred — on the printer, but the capacity of printing extends to the whole character set — i.e., more than 60,000 characters.

5 Acknowledgments

We are grateful to Dr. Scott Deerwester for his help in sparking the interest and the ideas in creating fonts in Postscript, and to Mr. Torsten Buck of Fontworks Limited for his generosity in providing us with relevant materials during the development of these ideas.

References

1. Adobe Systems, *Postscript Language Reference Manual.* Addison Wesley, 1990.
2. Bridget Lynn Johnson, *"A Model for Automatic Optical Scaling of Type Designs for Conventional and Digital Technology,"* Masters Thesis, School of Printing, Rochester Institute of Technology, May 1987.
3. 吳佑壽, 丁曉青, 漢字識別 — 原理. 方法與實現. 高等教育出版社, 中國, 1992.
4. *Codes of Chinese Graphic Characters for Information Interchange, Primary Set (GB2312-80).* National Standards Bureau of China, Beijing, 1980.
5. Jacques Andre and Bruno Borghi, "Dynamic fonts," in *Raster Imaging and Digital Typography* (J. Andre and R. D. Hersch, eds.), pp. 198–204, Cambridge University Press, 1989.

6. Peter Karow, *Font Technology Description and Tools*. Springer-Verlag, 1994.
7. Unicode Consortium, *The Unicode Standard: Worldwide Character Encoding*, vol. 1 and 2. Addison-Wesley, 1991.
8. Y. S. Moon and T. Y. Shin, "Chinese fonts and their digitization," in *Proceedings of the International Conference on Electronic Publishing, Document Manipulation & Typography*, pp. 235–248, 1990.

Fig. 5. Characters created of different structural shapes

Bank Check Reading: Recognizing the Courtesy Amount

Valeri Anisimov[1], Nikolai Gorski[1,2], David Price[2], Olivier Baret[2], Stefan Knerr[2]

[1] SPIIRAS, 39
14th Line
199178 St. Petersburg, Russia

[2] A2iA
Tour CIT, BP 59
75749 Paris Cedex 15, France
email: a2ia@dialup.francenet.fr

Abstract. We developed a check reading system which recognizes both the legal amount and the courtesy amount on bank checks. It addresses the problem of French, omni-scriptor, cursive handwriting recognition, and is designed to meet industrial requirements, such as high processing speed, robustness, and extremely low error rates.

Our system is based on several key ideas: (1) *hierarchical* organization; starting out with pixel images, the system elaborates intermediate representations, such as strokes, letters, and words, which are grouped to form objects in higher levels. (2) The objects of any hierarchical level are described in terms of *soft decisions* (probabilities). Hard decisions are only taken in the final amount recognition process. (3) Use of *prior* information when available. (4) Wherever possible, our system makes use of several *complementary* algorithms to accomplish a given task.

This paper deals particularly with the recognition of the courtesy (numeral) amount. Results obtained on a large data base of French bank checks are presented.

1   Introduction

With recent advances in character recognition techniques, automatic reading of bank checks involving cursive handwriting (courtesy amount and legal amount) is within reach. A2iA has developed such a system. It addresses the omni-scriptor check reading task for French bank checks, and is designed to meet real-world requirements, such as processing speed, robustness, and extremely low error rates. Recognition performances appear to be highly encouraging, and industrial implementations are on their way.

The complete recognition system is too complex to be presented here in detail. Therefore, we briefly outline the overall system, and then focus on the recognition of the courtesy (numeral) amount of bank checks. The part of our system dealing with the literal amount recognition has been presented elsewhere recently [1, 5]. Figure 1 shows the general organization of our recognition system.

The task of automatic bank check reading is extremely difficult due to several reasons:
1. Most bank checks are handwritten, and thus more difficult to read automatically than machine printed checks.

2. The automatic check reading system has to deal with many different scriptors, using different pens, often in a disturbing environment (e.g. in a supermarket).
3. In most languages, a given amount may be written in several ways, e.g. "one thousand two hundred francs" or "twelve hundred Frs".
4. There is still no standard for check forms. Therefore, a successful system has to deal with various formats for bank checks, colored background, drawings, and printed text, making the extraction of the amounts extremely difficult.

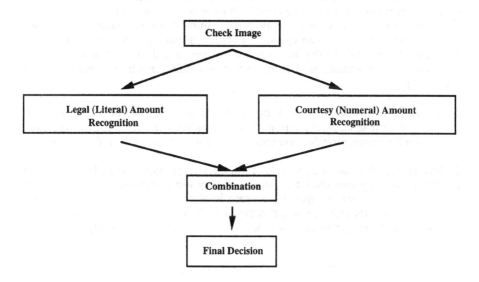

Figure 1: Organization of our check reading system, including legal amount recognition and courtesy amount recognition.

On the other hand, bank checks show a perfect redundancy of information between the courtesy amount and the legal amount. In order to profit from this redundancy, our check recognition system consist of two main parts. The first deals with recognizing the numeral (courtesy) amount, while the second is responsible for recognizing the literal (legal) amount. The results of both parts are used to reach a final decision as to the amount displayed on the check. Figure 2 displays a typical French check.

We start from some fundamental ideas which form the basis of our system and which are valid for both parts:
1. The system is *hierarchically organized*: starting out with a pixel image, a first level is concerned with finding simple features describing the lines in the image. In a second level, these features are grouped in order to form strokes, and in the third level these strokes are again grouped to graphemes. Cursive letters and numerals, the fourth hierarchical level in our system, can be composed of one to three graphemes. Therefore, letter hypothesis are formed using several different combinations of the graphemes. Letter candidates are then submitted to several character recognition algorithms. The most probable word candidates, the fifth level in the hierarchy, are found using dynamic programming techniques. Finally, a semantic analysis is carried

out in order to find the most probable sentence among all the word hypothesis. This hierarchy is described in detail in [1].

2. *Segmentation and recognition* are carried out simultaneously. Handwriting is first (over)-segmented into objects of the size of characters or smaller. Then, the best segmentation option is identified as the one which optimizes the recognition results.

3. The objects of any hierarchical level are described in terms of *probabilities*. Probabilities provide what is often called *soft decisions* (as opposed to hard decisions, which are still commonly used in pattern recognition systems). Thereby, it becomes possible to recover from sub-optimal or wrong decisions in lower levels of the hierarchy. Probabilities are the "language" of our system, and information is transferred from one level to another in terms of lists of possible candidates along with their probabilities.

4. In any given hierarchical level, our system uses two types of information: (i) *bottom-up* information, resulting from observations and computation at a lower level, (ii) *prior* information, providing expectations available at the given or higher levels.

5. Several algorithms are used to accomplish a given recognition task. Typically, they are based on *complementary* techniques, or they use complementary data or data representations (see for example [6]). At each level, the results of these algorithms are combined, using for instance neural network techniques. As a consequence of this complementarity, recognition performances of our system could be greatly improved.

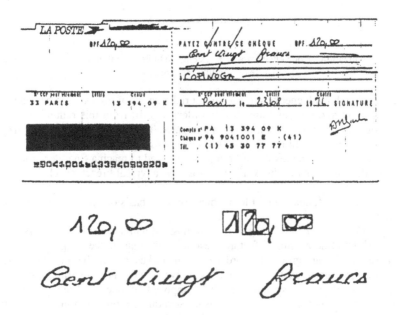

Figure 2: Example of a French handwritten bank check with extracted courtesy and legal amount.

The present paper describes the numeral amount recognition system, see figure 3, and is organized as follows: Section 2 presents the extraction of the courtesy amount from the check image; section 3 is devoted to the segmentation of the amount image into characters; Section 4 presents the algorithms used for character recognition; a description of the amount recognition level is given in section 5. Section 6 presents some specifications concerning an ongoing industrial implementation.

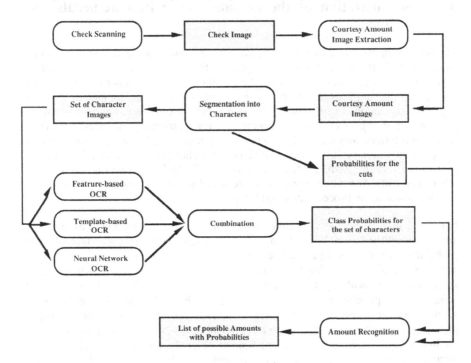

Figure 3: Organization of the courtesy amount recognition system.

2 Extraction of the courtesy amount image

The original check is scanned and thresholded using a locally adapted threshold. The results reported later in this paper were obtained with check images having a resolution of 260 dpi. The extraction of the numeral amount subimage proceeds in three steps.

In the first step, the local average orientation of the contours, as well as the average skew of depicted writing is estimated for the upper-right part of the check image [7]. Note that all French checks display the numeral amount in this part of the check. These informations, together with histograms characterizing the vertical and horizontal pixel densities in this part of the image appear to be sufficient in order to estimate the position of the numeral amount. The numeral amount subimage is then extracted, possibly still containing horizontal lines and/or a surrounding rectangular box.

In the second step, a filter detects and removes horizontal and (if present) vertical printed lines from the extracted subimage. The result of this step is an image of the numeral amount, but possibly with some noise and/or printed characters.

In the third step, all connected components of the extracted subimage are detected and analyzed. Several characteristics, such as length, thickness, perimeter, square, etc. are computed for each component. Based on these characteristics, some components are interpreted as noise and eliminated.

3 Segmentation of the amount image into numerals and letters

The basic idea we use throughout our system for segmenting complex objects into simpler ones is to handle the segmentation task the same way as a recognition task: first, several segmentation options for the complex object are generated, then, class conditional probabilities for the resulting (simpler) objects are computed. The true segmentation option is recognized as the one which maximizes the probability of the resulting set of objects [1]. This concept is used for segmenting sentences into words, words into letters, and numeral amounts into numerals and letters. In the courtesy amount recognition system, we consider 20 distinct classes of characters: digits from 0 to 9, comma, point, dash, 6 letters, such as "F", "f", "R", "S", and one class for all other characters. We now describe in more detail the segmentation of the courtesy amount, which again proceeds in several steps.

In the first step, all connected components resulting from the extraction of the courtesy amount image (section 2) are analyzed. Using several geometrical features, the probability of representing a single character is computed for each of the connected components. If this probability is higher than a predefined value, the image of the connected component is put into a set L_0. In the same spirit, all neighboring pairs of connected components are considered, and again, the probability of representing a single character is computed. The merged object is put into L_0, if this probability is higher than a predefined value. The two neighboring components are associated with the intention of merging, usually small, objects which do not represent a character by themselves. Finally, large connected components are split along a straight line which is positioned according to a set of criteria, including the number of intersections of the splitting line with the connected component, upper and lower profile of the object, and others. The inclination of the splitting line is set to the average slant in the amount image. If the probabilities of the parts resulting from the split operation are high enough, these parts are also incorporated into L_0.

Thus, the result of the first segmentation step is a set of objects with a high probability of being a single character. Note, that parts of the amount image can appear in several objects.

In the second step, all possible options to segment the amount image into a set of objects from L_0 are analyzed, and their probabilities are computed. Each segmentation option covers the complete amount image, not allowing for objects to overlap. The result of the second segmentation step is a list L_1 of segmentation options of the amount image along with their probabilities.

In the third step, all objects which have pixels below the baseline in the amount image are analyzed to whether they contain a comma. The position of the comma is used later for the final interpretation of the courtesy amount. The comma itself is eliminated from the object image in order to facilitate its recognition.

Finally, the 16 best segmentation options from L_1 make up the result of the segmentation level. This list of candidate options along with their probabilities is transferred to the character- and amount recognition levels.

Experimental test results for the segmentation of the courtesy amount into numerals are presented in table 1. The training set comprises numeral amount images from 1000 checks which have been segmented manually. Another set of 1000 checks was used as test data.

K	1	2	4	8	16	AV.POS
REC(K) (%)	71.0	85.9	93.9	95.8	96.7	1.95

Table 1: Segmentation of the courtesy amount into numerals. REC(K) gives the percentage of cases for which the true option is in the list of K best segmentation options, and AV.POS is the average position of the correct answer in the candidate list.

As it can be seen from table 1, the full list of 16 segmentation options covers the true segmentation in 96.7% of the cases. However, the other 3.3% do not necessarely result in a wrong recognition of the courtesy amount, because higher levels in the recognition system often compensate for segmentation errors and correctly recognize the amount even when the true segmentation was not found. Note, that the performances in table 1 should be considered with caution since they rely on the opinion of a human supervisor who determined the "true" segmentation option.

4   Character recognition

As described, for each of the segmentation options, the courtesy amount was split into a number of character hypothesis. The images of these hypothetical characters are input to several character recognition algorithms. It should be noted that any given character hypothesis usually appears in several segmentation options. Thus, the number of images to be recognized is much smaller than the total number of objects in all segmentation options. The average number of different character images to be recognized is 14.5 per check, while the average number of segmentation options in the candidate list L_1 is 8.9, and the average number of hypothesis in one segmentation option is about 6.5 (which amounts to an average of 57.9 character images per check).

Our system uses four recognition algorithms. Two of them process the pixel image directly, whereas the two others use features extracted from the raw image. In the following, we present the four recognition algorithms in more detail.

4.1   Feature-based recognizer

Nine operators, using a total of 80 integer valued features, are used to estimate the probabilities for the 20 character classes. In the following, we give a brief description of the operators and their feature inputs.

Operator 1 (1 feature):	height of character.
Operator 2 (1 feature):	the ratio of height to width of the character.
Operator 3 (20 features):	characteristics of the left, right, upper, and lower profiles.
Operator 4 (36 features):	the reduced binary image of the character (6x6 pixel matrix).
Operator 5 (12 features):	describes "breaks" in the left, right, upper, and lower profiles.
Operator 6 (1 feature):	number of loops in the character image.
Operator 7 (6 features):	indicates the number of intersections of 3 horizontal and 3 vertical lines with the character.
Operator 8 (2 features):	character position in the amount image.
Operator 9 (1 feature):	number of connections of the given character candidate with neighboring character candidates.

Training of the feature based operators involves the evaluation of discrete probability densities p(feature value | class) for all features of a given operator and all classes. In practice, this evaluation results in 20 histograms, one for each class, with as many bins as the feature has values. Using Bayes rule, the posterior class probabilities for each feature can be computed based on the density estimations.

For the operators using several features, the posterior probabilities for all features are multiplied, assuming mutual independence. It should be noted that this assumption is usually not realistic. As a result, the obtained class probabilities tend to be overly close to the extreme values, i.e. high probabilities are too close to 1, and small probabilities are closer to 0 than they should be. In order to compensate for this effect, the class probabilities of each operator are corrected: P(class | feature value) is powered in order to provide the minimum of the average value of -log(P(true class | feature value)) which is computed on a validation set (different from the training set) [8]. The resulting scores are normalized to obtain class probabilities which sum to 1. Our experiments show that the thereby corrected class probabilities are more realistic.

The final result of the feature-based recognizer is obtained by multiplying the class probabilities of the 9 operators for each class. The resulting scores are again normalized in order to sum to 1. Experimental results of the feature based character recognizer are presented in table 2 (see Section 4.4).

4.2   Template-based OCR

Simple (structural) features are extracted from the characters after some low-level processing resulting in a graph: strokes in four directions (0, +45, -45, 90), loops, ascenders/descenders, singularities etc. For each character class six 5x5 pixel templates are constructed, each coding for the position of one feature type. The templates are learned by simple accumulation of a large number of 5x5 pixel maps for each class. The result is a set of under-sampled smoothed templates containing the average position of characteristic features of the characters. During recognition by simple correlation matching, each of the six matches gives a score which is normalized. The six normalized scores are then multiplied assuming mutual independence. The template-based recognition algorithm is discussed in more detail in [1] and [6].

Experimental results of the template based recognizer are presented in table 2.

4.3 Neural network recognizers

Two of the four character recognition algorithms are based on a neural network architecture which was described in detail in [9]. Each neural network uses one of two different data representations as input which we assume to be independent. Therefore, we expect the character recognition algorithms to be complementary.

The architecture of our neural networks relies on the decomposition of a K class problem into K*(K-1)/2 two class problems. Each of the two class problems can be efficiently solved by a simple neural network: in the case of a high dimensional data representation, a single neuron (defining a hyperplane in the input space) is sufficient in order to separate the two character classes. Therefore, the final network comprises K*(K-1)/2 neurons, each separating a given class ω_i from another class ω_j. The two-class probabilities Pr_{ij} based on the (sigmoidal) outputs of these neurons are transformed into posterior class probabilities by use of the following simple relation which is explained in more detail in [10]:

$$Pr(\omega_i|\mathbf{x}) = \frac{1}{\sum_{j=1, j \neq i}^{K} \frac{1}{Pr_{ij}} - (K-2)}$$

We chose this architecture for two reasons: the first reason is that training is an order of magnitude faster than for Multilayer Perceptrons trained by the backpropagation algorithm (the most commonly used neural network for pattern recognition tasks). This increase in training speed allowed for the testing of several different data representations, different numbers of character classes, and various data bases during the design phase of our complete recognition system. The second reason is that the recognition performances turned out to be comparable to those of Multilayer Perceptrons using the Softmax output function and an entropy cost function [8]. Many of our experiments in character recognition have shown that the latter neural network type usually gives the best recognition performances when compared to other neural network algorithms and traditional classification algorithms such as k-nearest neighbors [10].

We used the following two data representations as input to the neural networks:

The first is obtained by performing edge detection: the original image is convoluted with 4 pairs of Kirsch edge operators, resulting in 4 graded feature maps, coding for the presence of horizontal, vertical, and diagonal edges. The 4 maps are normalized in size to an 8x8 format using a linear transformation which preserves the aspect ratio of the pattern. The four maps are finally concatenated, thereby losing the two-dimensional topology of the image, which results in a 256 dimensional vector.

The second data representation consists of the 80 dimensional feature vector already described in section 4.1. Each feature value is normalized in order to fit into the interval [-1, +1].

The performances of the neural network character recognizers are presented in table 2 in the next section.

4.4 Combining the results of the four character recognition algorithms

The probabilistic outputs of the four character recognizers are combined using the same technique already described in Section 4.1: Bayesian estimation of character probabilities under the assumption of mutual independence of the four recognition algorithms. More recently, we also used a method for the combination of several classifiers which is based on neural network techniques. The latter results in comparable performances, but has the advantage of being completely automatic.

Recog. Algorithm	R(1)	R(2)	R(4)	R(8)	AV.pos	-AV.log
Feature based	91.6	96.3	98.7	99.9	1.2	0.28
Template based	85.7	93.3	98.1	99.9	1.3	0.45
Neural Net (image)	87.1	93.2	96.9	99.7	1.3	0.50
Neural Net (features)	93.9	97.4	99.4	99.9	1.1	0.20
Combination	95.7	98.4	99.6	100.0	1.1	0.14

Table 2: Recognition performances of the character recognition algorithms and their combination.

Table 2 presents the recognition performances for the ten digit classes ("0"-"9") for the individual character recognition algorithms as well as for their combination. The results in table 2 give the percentage $R(K)$ of well recognized digits in the list of the best K candidates. Av.pos gives the average position of the correct answer in the candidate list. Av.log gives the average value of the entropy of the candidate list. The test set consists of 3950 correctly segmented digits extracted from 1000 checks.

At this point, we can draw two conclusions from the results of table 2: firstly, the performance of the feature based algorithms is superior to the ones using the raw image as input. Secondly, simple combination of several techniques improves greatly the recognition results.

5 Amount recognition

The result of the segmentation level is a list of segmentation options for the courtesy amount (section 3). Each segmentation option consists of a number of character candidates. For each character candidate, 20 class probabilities have been computed by the character recognition algorithms (section 4). At the amount recognition level, the most probable segmentation option along with the corresponding amount is identified.

For each segmentation option of length n (n character candidates), there are 20^n different possible paths through the 2 dimensional diagram spanned by the character candidates and the character classes. Most of these paths do not correspond to semantically meaningful amounts: for example, "23R07f" or "-f200rs00". In the following, only meaningful amount candidates are considered. This is performed by stochastic generation of amount candidates, using the most probable character candidates first. The average number of meaningful amount candidates is 190 per check.

Then the probability of each path is computed as the product of (i) the character probabilities given the position of the character, and (ii) the transition probabilities for subsequent characters of the path. Some of the candidate amounts generated may be semantically identical, such as "200,00" and "200 Fr". Probabilities for such identical amount candidates are summed, thereby reducing the list of amount candidates to about 60 candidates.

When the amount candidate lists are obtained for all segmentation options, the probabilities of candidates with semantically identical amounts are again summed. The 16 most probable candidates of the resulting list make up for the result of the amount recognition level.

Table 3 presents experimental results at the amount recognition level for a data base of postal checks. These results were obtained on a test set of 1000 numeral amount images extracted from French Postal checks. The average number of characters in the courtesy amount is about 6.5. Therefore, we expect a recognition performance of about 75% (= $95.7^{6.5}$). The difference between the expected recognition performance and the 72.7% we obtained is mainly due to segmentation and extraction errors. Table 4 gives experimental results for a data base comprising checks of various French banks.

K	1	2	4	8	16	AV.POS
REC(K) (%)	72.7	83.0	89.4	92.5	95.0	2.5

Table 3. Recognition performances at the courtesy amount recognition level for a postal check data base (percentage of correctly recognized amounts among the K best candidates).

K	1	2	4	8	16	AV.POS
REC(K) (%)	70.8	77.0	80.9	83.3	84.8	3.3

Table 4: Recognition performances at the courtesy amount recognition level for an omni-bank check data base (percentage of correctly recognized amounts among the K best candidates).

As described in the outline of our complete recognition system, the result of the courtesy amount recognition is combined with the result of the legal amount recognition system. Using both informations, we obtained on the postal check data base a recognition performance of about 80% for less than 1 error per 1000 checks.

6　Industrial Application

A2iA is currently developing an industrial software package for off-line bank check recognition which uses the complete system we have just described. In addition to the image of a check, a document (called "coupon") associated with the check is supplied which gives informations about the amount to be paid. This information consists of a list of three amounts. Statistics on a large set of checks supplied by a customer, a personal loan company, revealed that approximately 80% of the true check amounts were equal to one of the amounts given on the coupons, and 90% of the checks had an amount in the boundaries defined by the minimum and maximum of the three coupon amounts. Using the coupon information (no amount out of the minimum/maximum interval defined by the coupon list is excepted), the final result of our recognition system is either the most probable amount according to the results of the courtesy amount recognition system and the legal amount recognition system (usually, but not necessarily, corresponding to one of the coupon amounts), or the rejection of the check. In the latter case, the check is processed manually by a human operator. Recognition performances of the courtesy amount recognition system are: 65 % correct decision, 35 % rejection, and less than 1/1000 confusion. The complete system, including the legal amount recognition part, obtains on a test set of about 200 000 checks: 70 % correct decisions, 30 % rejection, and of the order of 1/10000 confusion. Our system proceeds in batch mode: first, all checks and coupons are scanned and the images stored. Later, the images are analyzed automatically and those rejected by the system are transferred to a human operator for recognition. Batch mode is necessary for practical reasons, such as the need to process more than 50.000 checks per day, and the fact that our system has very different recognition times depending on the difficulties of a given image. The average processing time is about 2.7s per check on an IBM UNIX work station using a 66 MHz PowerPC processor. Processing the checks in a batch mode has the advantage of allowing for simple parallelization: the computational load can be easily distributed among several machines, where the number of machines can be increased when needed.

7   Conclusions

We have presented a system for the recognition of amounts on French checks. Both, the recognition system for the courtesy amount as the one for the legal amount are based on the following key ideas:
- hierarchical organization,
- soft decisions at any level in the system,
- use of bottom-up information flow and prior knowledge where available,
- use of complementary processing techniques.
Amount images are first extracted from the check image, then segmented into recognizable entities. The most probable amount is finally found by analyzing the segmentation options based on the character- and transition- probabilities of each option.
Recognition performances on large data bases proofed to be interesting enough to encourage industrial applications. A complete off-line system making use of additional informations concerning the true amount is currently installed in a French personal loan company. Performance comparisons to other check recognition systems are difficult for paractical reasons: common data bases of real world check images are not available, in general because data is confidential; only few industrial systems exist, and their performances are often estimated on too small, statistically insignificant data bases. However, conservative comparisons show that our system is among the best systems today.

Acknowledgments

The authors wish to thank J.-C. Simon for many stimulating discussions, and the French Postal Service (S.R.T.P., Nantes) for providing a check data base.

References

1. Baret O., Gorsky N., Simon J.-C., A system for recognition of handwritten literal amounts of checks. *Proc. of the Workshop Document Analysis Systems*, Kaiserslautern, 1994.
2. Gilloux M., Leroux M., Recognition of cursive script amounts on postal cheques. *JET POST'93, Proc. of the 1st European Conf. on Postal Technologies*, Nantes, pp. 705-712, 1993.
3. Dimauro G., Grattagliano M.R., Impedovo S., Pirlo G., A system for bankcheck processing. *Proc.of the second ICDAR*, Tsucuba, pp. 454-459, 1993.
4. Moreau J.V., A new system for automatic reading of postal checks. In: *From Pixels to Features III. Frontiers in Handwriting Recognition*, S. Impedovo and J.-C.Simon, eds., North-Holland, 1992.
5. Simon J.-C., Baret O., Gorsky N., Reconnaissance d'ecriture manuscrite. *C. R. Acad. Sci Paris*, t.318, Serie II, pp.745-752, 1994.
6. Simon J.-C., Off-line cursive word recognition. *Proc. of the IEEE*, Vol.80, No.7, pp.1150-1161, 1992.
7. Kimura F., Shridar M., Chen. Z., Improvements of a lexicon directed algorithm for recognition of unconstrained handwritten words. *Proc. of the second ICDAR*, Tsucuba, pp. 18-22, 1993.
8. Bridle J.S., Probabilistic Interpretation of Feedforward Classification Network Outputs with Relationships to Statistical Pattern Recognition. In *Neurocomputing: Algorithms, Architectures and Applications*, F. Fogelman-Soulie and J. Herault (eds.), NATO ASI Series, Springer, 1990.
9. Knerr S., Personnaz L., Dreyfus G., Handwritten digit recognition by neural networks with single-layer training. *IEEE Transactions on Neural Networks*, Vol. 3, No. 6, 1992.
10. Price D., Knerr S., Personnaz L., Dreyfus G., Pairwise neural network classifiers with probabilistic outputs. *Proc. of Neural Information Processing Systems7*, Denver, 1994.

An Automatic Extraction Approach of Road Information on the Basis of Recognition of Character Regions

Masakazu NISHIJIMA and Toyohide WATANABE

Department of Information Engineering,
Graduate School of Engineering, Nagoya University
Furo-cho, Chikusa-ku Nagoya 464-01, JAPAN

Abstract. The subjects about the automatic extraction of road information from maps have been recognized as effectual means to construct GIS(Geographic Information Systems) and support the services of various kinds of information, the managements of our life-lines, the planning of city projects and so on. Many researches were reported with respect to this subject. However, it is not always easy to accomplish this subject successfully because roads are, in general, overlapped and interrelated with other map components complicatedly. In this paper, we propose an experimental approach to extract road information from urban maps. The characteristic in our approach is not to extract roads directly like many traditional approaches, but to distinguish individual roads cooperatively on the basis of recognition of character regions. We do not only mention the recognition method in our approach, but also discuss the recognition results through some experiments.

1   Introduction

The issue about map recognition is one of important subjects to compose the basic resource data in constructing GIS(Geographical Information System) and various types of information systems. Until today, many approaches/methods[8,9] have been proposed, concerning this issue. For example, the skip-scan method[1], the method using negative images[2], the method based on Voronoi graphs[3] and so on were typically developed. However, since these methods were based on only the bottom-up approaches, which interpret map images directly, the processing capabilities are limited.

On the other hand, the methods based on the top-down approaches also were proposed: method based on the combination of bottom-up and top-down processings[4], method based on the cooperative paradigm among bottom-up and top-down processings[5]. In the combination method, the bottom-up processing is first applied to urban map images in order to extract the road information and then the top-down processing is used to refine the locally extracted road information globally. While, the cooperative method is developed as an enhanced version of the combination method from a viewpoint of cooperative processing.

However, it is not easy to distinguish the road information from urban map images completely even if these advanced methods were applied. This is partly because different types of data such as roads, rivers, buildings, street names, building names, characteristic symbols and so on are overlapped or intersected on one sheet, and partly because individual data can not be well defined from a viewpoint of the formal description. In this paper, we address an experimental approach to extract road information. Our approach is based on the paradigm which first identifies character regions and then extracts the road information with help of identified character regions. Namely, though the traditional approaches focused on the direct and simple extraction problem of only the road information, our approach concentrates on the cooperative recognition method interrelated between road information and character information.

2 Approach

It is not easy, in general, to extract the road information automatically from urban map images because various kinds of map components are mutually overlapped or interconnected. Additionally, these map components are not always effectively defined by means of formal descriptions. Our objective is to recognize the road information from urban map images, and then construct the road network as a topological feature of road information. With a view to attaining to this objective, we adopt an experimental approach, which makes use of the relationships between other map components and road fragments complementarily. Fig.1 illustrates our processing flow instinctively. Our approach, which refines the extracted road fragments complementarily on the basis of recognition of character regions, is very different from many currently proposed approaches, which concentrated only on the direct extraction subject of road information.

Since the roads are interfered or overlapped by other map components such as characters and symbols, it is difficult to extract roads exactly. If we can identify the map components overlaid on roads and infer the connectivity among mutually cut-off road fragments, these separated roads are interrelated by means of the recognition of character regions. Here, we define the road as the basic recognition object, and also the road network as our target results briefly.

〖Definition:Road〗   The road(or road fragment) is defined as a pair of two
parallel line segments.   □

〖Definition:Road network〗   The road network is a topological graph for
expressing road information, and is composed of nodes and edges. Nodes are
characteristic points in roads: intersections, connection points among neighboring roads and terminal points in road sequences. While, edges represent
the connective relationships among neighboring nodes.   □

3 Extraction Process of Primitive Elements

3.1 Extraction of Character Regions

It is not necessarily easy to extract character regions from urban maps automatically because the map components are mutually interfered or overlaid under the complementary relationships. Our method is an enhanced version of MF(Merlin Farber Hough Transformation) method[7]. MF method[6] is useful to identify arbitrary line-drawn objects from the original images. In our method, plane-based objects must be identified since character regions are regarded as rectangular

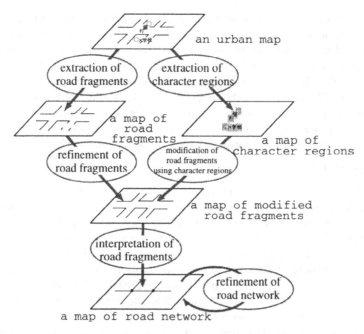

Fig. 1. Processing flow in our approach

blocks. Our extraction process based on MF method is composed of the following two steps: (1)voting and (2)selection of center points.

(1) Voting: The square-form template, whose size is almost equal to that of estimated characters, is applied with a view to finding out character areas. Also the critical point which corresponds to the center point of this templete is attached to it. The voting procedure allocates the critical point to all black pixels in the map images one by one, and assigns the number of black pixels included in this template to each corresponded black pixel, as the score. Namely, this voted score is the density of each black pixel for the character region.

(2) Selection of center point: This phase selects the center points of character regions from the points which have higher voted values, using two distinctive features:

   1. The voted values are limited by thresholds as follows: $\alpha_{min} < \alpha < \alpha_{max}$, where α is the density of focussed point, α_{min} is the minimum value, and α_{max} is the maximum value.

   2. The numbers of black pixels spreading over the rectangles of character regions are few.

3.2 Extraction of Road Fragments

The road is a pair of parallel line segments. In order to recognize roads in urban maps, we must extract line segments, first of all. Thus, the extraction process of roads(or road fragments) is composed of (1)preprocessing, (2)selection of line segments and (3)identification of parallel line segments.

(1) Preprocessing: The preprocessing is a necessary task as the first process for analyzing urban map images interpretatively. This process is divided into three steps: binalization, thinning and vectorization.

(2) Selection of line segments: All of various line segments in urban maps, which were approximated by the preprocessing, do not always correspond to the line segments of practical roads. Thus, some line segments, which satisfy the following condition, must be selected as candidates: $l \geq l_0$, where l is the length of line segment, and l_0 is the threshold value. Generally, this judgement is dependent on the assumption that line segments corresponding to the components of roads are relatively longer than those of other components.

(3) Identification of parallel line segments: This phase distinguishes candidate roads as pairs of parallel line segments which represent roads as defined in the previous section.

4 Composition Process of Road Network

This process composes the road network, which represents a topological information of the map, on the basis of recognized results such as character regions and roads. This construction process consists of three phases: (1)recognition of intersections, (2)composition of road network and (3)refinement of road network.

4.1 Recognition of Intersections

Intersections are characteristic points in which two or more roads are connected mutually. In order to recognize intersections, we identify the corners configurated by two different line segments, first: intersections are composed of two or more corners. The extraction procedure is divided into two steps.

1. First step of corner extraction
   If a pair of two different line segments l_1 and l_2 satisfies the following conditions, they are regarded as a set of line segments for the corner.
   [Definition:Corner] The angle between l_1 and l_2 is θ: $\theta_1 < \theta < \theta_2$. The distance between l_1 and l_2 is d: in case of $d_0 < d < d_1$, a set of l_1 and l_2 is an element of the corner when a sequence of short line segments exists between l_1 and l_2; and in case of $d \leq d_0$, a set of l_1 and l_2 is an element of the corner. □
   Here, θ_1, θ_2, d_0 and d_1 are predefined constants.

2. Second step of corner extraction
   It is difficult to extract the corner in the case that some intersection is overlaid by a character in the first step. The second step is successful to solve this problem. The processing algorithm is as follows:
   (a) Search character regions from terminal points of all line segments, which have not been identified as composite line segments of corners, toward the extensible directions of individual line segments. In this case, every extracted character region in the urban map must be checked up. The search range is the maximum length of character regions.
   (b) Compose a set of candidate line segments which were found out in (a).
   (c) Select a pair of candidate line segments l_i and l_j from the set, and check

up the first condition in the first step: $\theta_1 < \theta < \theta_2$ (θ is the angle between l_i and l_j).

(d) Extract the corner with respect to two line segments, which were selected appropriately in (c). If two or more line segments, which can satisfy the condition in (c), are found out, then extract the corner for the line segment which makes the distance with d shortest.

After these corner extraction steps, we can identify intersections. The procedure is effective under the following conditions.

【Definition:Intersection】 The distance among corners is d: $d_2 < d < d_3$. The same line segment is not shared with other line segments(see Fig.2(a)). The geometric shapes constructed by a pair of parallel line segments and their corners are not one of shapes as illustrated in Fig.2(b)-(e). □

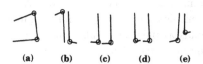

(a)　(b)　(c)　(d)　(e)

Fig.2. Examples of wrong intersections

Here, d_2 and d_3 are predefined constants. We show the processing results in Fig.3, with respect to the recognition procedures of intersections.

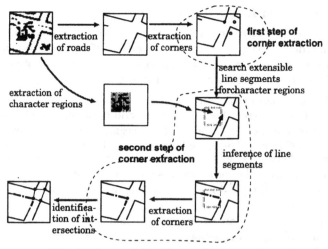

Fig. 3. Recognition phase of intersections

4.2 Composition of Road Network

The road network is a graph whose nodes are intersections, and whose edges are roads. Since a continuous road is looked upon as a sequence of pairs of parallel line segments, two different pairs of parallel line segments are connected as the same road if they have connective relationships, when one pair of parallel line segments has already been recognized as the road. In this case, we select intersections as the first road-searching points because the intersection is the most confident object for distinguishing roads.

【Definition:Connection of two neighboring roads】 The distance between

178

mutual parallel line segments is d: $d < d_4$. The difference between widths of mutual parallel line segments is dw: $dw < dw_0$. The angle between mutual parallel line segments is θ: $\theta < \theta_3$. □

Here, d_4, dw_0 and θ_3 are threshold values.

This composition procedure works from the intersection toward the directions of connectable roads continuously until all connectable roads are checked up direction by direction. Also, this procedure is applied to all intersections.

4.3 Refinement of Road Network

The road network composed in the previous phase does not always represent the practical road map sufficiently because the following difficulty is imposed in our processing strategy.

- The directions to search connectable pairs of parallel line segments are not clearly determined since various road structures are observed in practice.
- Only pairs of parallel line segments, which were distinguished explicitly as the processing objects, are used by the successive processes, and extraction-failure objects(or its fragments) are not absolutely recognized by the following procedures.
- The distance to search connectable pairs of parallel line segments is not always defined uniformly since different kinds of map components are included and they disturb roads and the connection relationships.

It is necessary to refine the existing road network for these drawbacks of processing strategies with respect to some heuristics. Thus, we introduce an inference mechanism which interprets first the road network topologically and logically, then finds out inferable relationships on the road network, thirdly checks up the intermediately extracted objects step by step, and finally modifies the road network itself if possible. The main inferable relationships between nodes or edges in the road network are follows:

- In the case that the terminal nodes correspond to points of T-junctions or corners, the terminal nodes must be inferred on maps of pairs of parallel line segments, maps of line segments or binalized maps. The typical examples are shown in Fig.4(a-1) and (a-2).
- In the case that a line segment is found among two neighboring terminal nodes, whose direction is almost similar to these of pairs of parallel line segments, these terminal nodes are merged into a common node. The typical example is shown in Fig.4(b).
- In the case that two neighboring

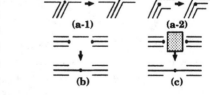

Fig.4. Inference of road network

terminal nodes are possibly interraped by character regions, these terminal nodes are merged into a common node. The typical example is shown in Fig.4(c).

5 Experiments

Here, we show the effects of our approach through some experiments. The original urban map of scale 1:10000 is digitalized by the image scanner with 200 dpi and 256 gray levels. Fig.5 is a binary urban map image(400x400 pixels). Fig.6 shows the extracted character regions. In this case, two types of templates such as 14x14 pixels and 22x22 pixels are used. 14x14-pixels template is applied to extract small characters in Fig.5 and 22x22-pixels template is to distinguish large characters. In comparison with Fig.5, these templates in Fig.6 could not extract some characters: the extraction ratio of 14x14-pixels template is 0.75(=9/12), and that of 22x22-pixels template is 0.77(=17/22). Next, Fig.7 and Fig.8 show the identified intersections. Fig.7 is the result with the information of extracted character regions; and Fig.8 is the result without the information. When we compare Fig.7 with Fig.8, we can find the difference for three marked points "A". The identification procedure, associated with character regions, is superior. Moreover, Fig.9 and Fig.10 show the final road networks. Fig.9 is the result with the refinement procedure, based on the character regions((c) in Fig.4); and Fig.10 is the result modified without the character-regions-based refinement process. Of course, these results are generated from intersections identified in Fig.7. In comparing Fig.9 with Fig.10, the distinction between these processing strategies is clear. In Fig.9 , three marked points "B" are refined though these could not be found in Fig.10. If we apply the refinement procedure without character-regions-based method, the road network has less road information than that in Fig.9.

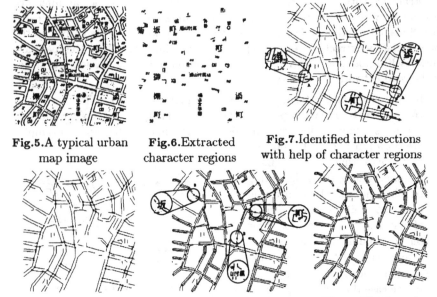

Fig.5.A typical urban map image

Fig.6. Extracted character regions

Fig.7. Identified intersections with help of character regions

Fig.8. Identified intersections without help of character regions

Fig.9. Final road network

Fig.10. Final road network without character regions

6 Conclusion

In this paper, we proposed an experimental approach to recognize the road information from urban map images. Our approach is successful to attain to this objective in comparison with many traditional approaches. The approach, which makes use of the positional information about character regions in urban maps with a view to extracting the road information effectively, is powerful to recognize maps with ill-defined drawing symbols. The effects, which were reported through experiments, made our approach valid. However, the recognized result shown in this paper does not always refer that our approach is perfect. We must refine the algorithms of individual recognition/extraction processes, and also investigate more advanced method such as knowledge-based inference mechanism, generation/verification mechanism of hypotheses and so on. These issues are located sooner as our next steps.

Acknowledgements

We are very grateful to Prof. T. Fukumura of Chukyo University, and Prof. Y. Inagaki and Prof. J. Toriwaki of Nagoya University for their perspective remarks, and also wish to thank our research members for their many discussions.

References

1. T.Nago, T.Agui and M.Nakajima:"Automatic Extraction of Roads Denoted by Parallel Lines from 1/25,000 Scaled Maps Utilizing Skip-scan Method", Trans.on IEICE, Vol.J72-D-II, No.10, pp.1627-1634(1989) [in Japanese].
2. S.Katsuno and I.Yamasaki:"Extraction of Parallel Elements from Urban Maps by Using Negation Images", Trans.on IEICE, Vol.J74-D-II, No.3, pp.340-347(1991) [in Japanese].
3. M.Ilg and R.Dgniewicz:"Knowledge-based Interpretation of Roads Maps, Based on Symmetrical Skeltons", Proc.of MVA'90, pp.161-164.
4. T.Hayakawa, T.Watanabe, Y.Yoshida and K.Kawaguchi:"Recognition of Roads in an Urban Map by Using the Topological Road-network", Proc.of MVA'90, pp.215-218.
5. T.Watanabe, T.Hayakawa and N.Sugie:"A Cooperative Integration Approach of Bottom-up and Top-down Methods for Road Extraction of Urban Maps", Proc.of ICARCV'92, pp.61-65.
6. Merilin,P.M.et al.:"A Parallel Mechanism for Detecting Curves in Pictures", IEEE Trans. on Comput., C-24, pp.96-98(1975).
7. O.Shiku, M.Anekawa, C.Nakamura and A.Nakamura:"Extraction of Characters from Maps", Trans.on IPSJ, Vol.34, No.2, pp.273-280(1994) [in Japanese].
8. W.kim, T.Furukawa, Y.Hirai and R.Tokunaga:"Extraction and Reconstruction of Road Segments by Spatial Filters", Proc.of MVA'92, pp.515-518.
9. R.Janssen, R.Duin and A.Vossepoel:"Evaluation Method for an Automatic Map Interpretation System for Cadastral Maps", Proc.of ICDAR'93, pp.125-128.

Interpreting Music Manuscripts: A Logic-Based, Object-Oriented Approach*

W. Brent Seales and Arcot Rajasekar

Computer Science Department, University of Kentucky,
Lexington, Kentucky 40506, USA

Abstract. This paper presents a complete framework for recognizing classes of machine-printed musical manuscripts. Our framework is designed around the decomposition of a manuscript into objects such as staves and bars which are processed with a knowledge base module that encodes rules in Prolog. Object decomposition focuses the recognition problem, and the rule base provides a powerful and flexible way to encode the rules of a particular manuscript class. Our rule-base registers notes and stems, eliminates false-positives and correctly labels notes according to their position on the staff. We present results that show 99% accuracy at detecting note-heads and 95% accuracy in finding stems.

1 Introduction

The goal of music manuscript analysis is to obtain a complete representation of a musical document given only a digital image. The form of this recovered internal representation is chosen so that the music can be reproduced with a typesetter, manipulated with an editor, or played via a sound tool. Approaches that hope to recover a representation that is close to complete clearly cannot rely on image processing techniques alone. Bottom-up techniques cannot overcome the ambiguities and noise that are present in the input image, and robust solutions to the Optical Music Recognition (OMR) problem must employ high-level, model-centered feedback based on semantic information about musical notation and manuscript structure.

In this work we describe a multi-level framework for recovering complete music manuscript semantics. This framework offers two characteristics that we believe are very powerful. First, the fundamental structures in a music manuscript such as staves, measures, and notes induce an object-oriented representation of the manuscript that naturally encodes its semantics. This representational construct is very useful in the incremental process of building an interpretation of the manuscript from the image data. It also allows flexibility and context-sensitive functionality by associating image processing functions (methods) to certain objects and contexts.

The second unique aspect of this work is the logic-based rule set associated with detected manuscript primitives. These rules fire based on a knowledge base

---

* An expanded version of this paper is available via the World Wide Web at
  http://www.dcs.uky.edu/~seales

of initial information, which is obtained by user-selected image processing functions. A human editor can design rules based on the syntax that governs the meaning and placement of symbols in a particular manuscript class. New rules are easily inserted or modified given this structure. This rule-based framework allows a simple mechanism for employing a feedback step in order to robustly handle noise in the image and encode semantic information embedded in the manuscript structure. Rules can also invoke special-purpose, highly-localized image operations that are too costly to apply across the entire image.

This paper describes our approach to the OMR problem, giving results from a prototype system that can recognizes staves, bars, notes, and beams. Section 2 gives some context. Section 3 describes the system design. Section 4 describes the rule forms, Section 5 shows results, and Section 6 summarizes the contribution of this work.

2 Background

The problem of optical music recognition (OMR) has generated a fair amount of attention and there have been many efforts toward a robust solution. Even within the domain of machine-printed manuscripts, the lack of a standard type by the music publishing community makes the OMR problem challenging [1].

Processing to recognize individual symbols and to detect and remove staff lines are clearly central low-level problems, and much recent work is concentrated in these areas [1, 2]. But most agree that solving OMR using low-level detection alone has several major drawbacks. First, staff line removal creates breaks in other symbols that must be repaired. Some work has been done using component post-processing to repair these breaks [11]. Second, symbol regions often overlap and interfere with one another. Correct decomposition is necessary for successful classification. Finally, many symbols have a similar appearance and it simply is not possible to reliably extract them all as a primitive image processing step.

Our framework is layered and attempts to improve the overall success and robustness of OMR by using a flexible knowledge representation hierarchy that can encode the context-sensitive structure of music manuscripts. This idea of layered processing that brings manuscript semantics to bear on the OMR task is not new. However, we believe that the framework we have obtained, which uses an object-oriented manuscript class together with logic-based rule sets, is a powerful, flexible and robust way to achieve it.

We make use of image processing techniques such as projection [4, 3] and mathematical morphology [9], which are also used by other systems. Projection methods work well on isolated shapes that have only small variations from their prototype model. Others have shown projection to be an efficient means for performing initial classification, but the projection method alone is insufficient for robust OMR since it is rotation-sensitive and fails if the image or the symbol in question is not oriented properly. The key difference in our approach is that we use projection together with rule-based semantics to improve performance.

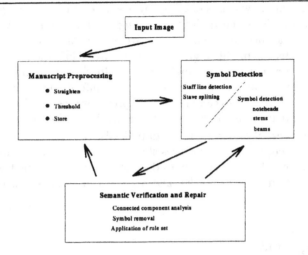

Fig. 1. The layers of processing shown above are driven by the knowledge base module and the object-oriented components of the reconstructed manuscript.

The shape-based approach described by Modayur et al. [9] lends itself well to analyzing and subsequently recognizing music scores that are rich in well-defined musical symbols. Mathematical morphology also forms a set of basic operations in our approach toward OMR. We combine these low-level operators with an object-oriented design and a logic-based knowledge base to obtain a flexible design and a more reliable result.

3   System Design

The layers of processing shown in Fig. 1 are driven by the initial division of the manuscript into *staves*. Each stave is processed as a separate object, which inherits all the semantics of the *stave* class. The processing components shown in Fig. 1 are all connected to a global knowledge base that contains both rules that fire and the object-oriented representation of the manuscript interpretation, which is incrementally refined as symbols are detected and combined.

The manuscript pre-processing layer is responsible for converting the input image into a binary image that is registered. Registration means that the staff lines are made to be horizontal. Most manuscripts that are scanned are close to horizontal and need only to be adjusted slightly. We rotate the image based on a horizontal pixel projection measure to register the manuscript image. Manual selection of rotation parameters is also possible in the pre-processing stage. The manuscript is converted to a binary image using adaptive thresholding, briefly described in a later section.

Once the manuscript is prepared for initial processing, the *symbol detection* layer detects the first features and measures to begin the processing. These features are staff-lines, a staff-line spacing measure, staves and a stave spacing measure. The result of this initial symbol detection phase is the identification of the location of all staff-lines and staves, and the division of the large image into individual staves that are members of the stave class. The staff-line spacing and stave spacing measure helps to calibrate the later image processing processes according to the type of the particular manuscript. For example, staff-line spacing determines the note-head template size. The individual stave objects are subsequently processed separately.

The semantic verification and repair layer obtains staves from the symbol detection layer and begins verification and processing. Through a combination of image processing primitives such as morphological operations, initial hypothesis are formed as to the location of basic symbols like note-heads, stems and beams. These hypotheses, formed in the semantic layer based on stave information, invoke the knowledge base module. The knowledge base module attempts to register and validate hypotheses based on correct semantics, consistency and further support under renewed scrutiny in the symbol detection layer. Section 4 gives a more complete description of the specifics of the rules in the knowledge base module.

We have employed several different image processing techniques as the low-level primitives for the system. The musical symbols are extracted using the operations described below.

1. **Thresholding**: we use adaptive thresholding to obtain a binary image of the music manuscript.
2. **Mathematical morphology operations** [5, 8]: we use combinations of dilation, erosion, opening and closing. Structuring elements are chosen based on the symbol being detected. For example, a disk is used for note-head detection.
3. **Projection methods**: horizontal and vertical pixel projections are used to detect staff lines, staff line spacings, and inter-stave spacing.

4   Knowledge Base

The knowledge base module (KBM) forms an integral part of the music recognition system. The KBM contains domain-specific rules that can be used to aid the symbol recognition process, and performs two inter-related tasks:

Identify higher-level symbols: The KBM integrates primitive symbols into higher level symbols (e.g., note-heads and stems make a note/stem pair) that can be given a semantic meaning such as scale, rhythm and tempo based on musical notation. Knowledge-bases systems encode information in the form of rules and make them available to other functions that perform aggregation operations [10, 6].

Repair mis-registered symbols: The KBM also tries to repair errors caused by noise in the primitive symbol recognition stage. For example, when two note-heads appear to share a stem, the KBM can determine which note-head belongs with the stem and which note-head is possibly a mis-classified symbol. It may be that the note-heads do share the same stem legally, or that there are two stems but one was not detected because the image processor module recognized them as a single stem. It repairs this mis-registration. If the KBM is unable to account for a particular anomaly, it flags the image region for the image processing (IP) layers to check with refined detection parameters.

The KBM is written as a Prolog program. It contains rules and data with information about symbol integration, repairs, domain-specific data, etc. The main task of the KBM is to integrate the primitive structures recognized by the IP layers into notes and combination of notes. The musical notation follows a grammar, and although this grammar is not context-free, it can be easily encoded as Prolog rules. For example, we encode rules such as:

$$quarter\_note \leftarrow filled\_note\_head, stem$$
$$filled\_note\_head \leftarrow filled\_circle$$
$$stem \leftarrow short\_vertical\_line$$
$$staff \leftarrow staff\_line(5)$$
$$staff\_line \leftarrow long\_horizontal\_line$$

Such semantic information can be coded as rules so that the whole underlying structure can be represented as one musical-object in the representation, along with its parameters. In this sense, the KBM acts as an expert system in music recognition and performance. The flexibility offered by the integration of a knowledge base module and an object-oriented database makes the system adaptable and robust for OMR.

Next we describe some of the specific rules that have been implemented in the knowledge base system.

Rule R1: match each note to an appropriate stem to form a (semantic) note/stem pair; check the position of the note on the stave and label it with its symbol from the musical-scale.

Rule R2: repair any unattached note-heads, which arise from double-notes (sharing the same stem), bad image processing response due to noise, or mis-registered notes from an adjacent stave.

Rule R3: repair unattached stems, which are caused by noise and registration errors.

Rule R4: This rule tries to resolve the issue of stem-sharing by finding which is the best possible note-stem combination. This is done by checking adjacent notes, their stem directions and positions. In the case the rule is unable to resolve the ownership of the stem with respect to the competing note-heads, the rule flags the region as a 'bad region' and asks the image processor to perform analysis with finer techniques.

Rule R5: This rule is a counterpart to rule R4 and resolves the problem of shared note-heads. This is caused by additional stem-shaped objects recognized by the image-processor. Again, the rule tries to resolve the ambiguity and flags appropriate message for the image-processor.

These five rules pertain specifically to note-head and stem detection, registration and repair. The rules either combine information from several symbols

Fig. 2. Every other stave is from the original manuscript. The interleaved staves show the result of our system in detecting notes, beams and stems.

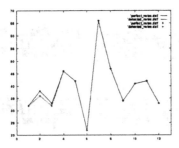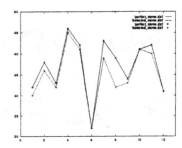

Fig. 3. The graph on the left compares the number of detected note-heads to the correct number of note-heads for each of 12 staves of the sonata. The graph on the right shows the same comparison for stems.

or send a very specific sub-region of the image back to the IP layer for further processing. The next section shows results from using these rules in the object-oriented knowledge base together with the image processing operations.

5 Results

Our system implements the basic design features described in the sections above. Images are obtained from a 300 dpi flatbed scanner. For the purposes of performance evaluation we have obtained (by hand) the correct count of notes and stems that occur in each stave of a test manuscript. We compare our results to these correct values.

Figure 2 shows staves 4 through 8 of the first (12-stave) page of a violin sonata. Interleaved with each stave of the original scanned image is the result of the detection process. The figure shows the performance of the system at detecting the following features: global staff-line orientation, stave segmentation, stave separation, staff-line separation, note-head, stem and beam detection. The regions where errors in the detection occur are marked on the output staves with boxes.

One of the primary errors that occurs is missing stems. The knowledge base module flags these cases where a note-head cannot be matched with a stem, and a small image subregion is identified for further processing by the image processing layer. Likewise, stems that are not matched with note-heads trigger a localized search.

Overall, detection of stems is 95% and note-heads is 99%. Furthermore, every missing stem was correctly flagged and the proper image region was tagged for further image processing. The graphs in Fig. 3 show plots of the results. On the left is a plot of the number of detected note-heads compared to the correct number of note-heads. The graph on the right is a plot of the number of detected stems compared to the correct number of stems.

6 Summary

This paper has presented an object-oriented, rule-based approach to the problem of optical music recognition (OMR). Our framework is robust, extendable and has demonstrated encouraging potential on real images of manuscripts. There are two central distinctives of our approach. First, we represent the manuscript as an object, divided into sub-objects like staves and bars. Second, we encode higher-level semantic rule information using a Prolog knowledge base module that operates on the manuscript objects. This framework has produced promising results; the Prolog-based rules can be very specific and descriptive, and the system is easily modified and manipulated.

References

1. Dorothea Blostein and Henry S. Baird. A critical survey of music image analysis. In H. S. Baird, H. Bunke, and K. Yamamoto, editors, *Structured Document Image Analysis*. Springer, 1992.
2. Nicholas P. Carter and Richard A. Bacon. Automatic recognition of printed music. Dept. of Physics, University of Surrey, GB., 1992.
3. Ichiro Fujinaga. Optical music recognition using projections. Master's thesis, McGill University, Montreal, CA, 1988.
4. Ichiro Fujinaga, B. Alphonce, B. Pennycook, and G. Diener. Interactive optical music recognition. In *Proceedings of the International Computer Music Conference*, pages 117–120, San Jose, 1992.
5. Ichiro Fujinaga, Bo Alphonce, and Bruce Pennycook. Issues in the design of an optical music recognition system. In *Proceedings of the International Computer Music Conference*, pages 113–116, Ohio State University, November 1989.
6. T. Gaasterland, J. Minker, and A. Rajasekar. Deductive Database Systems and Knowledge Base System. In *Proceedings of VIA 90*, Barcelona, Spain, 1990.
7. G.Cook. *Teaching Percussion*. Schirmer Books, Collier Macmillan Publishers, New York, 1988.
8. Gonzales and Woods. *Digital Image Processing*. Addison-Wesley, 1993.
9. Bharath R. Modayur, Visvanathan Ramesh, Robert M. Haralick, and Linda G. Shapiro. Muser - a prototype musical score recognition system using mathematical morphology. Intelligent Systems Laboratory, EE Dept, FT-10, University of Washington, Seattle WA 98195, June 1992.
10. T. Moko-Oka. Challenge For Knowledge Information Processing Systems (Preliminary Report on Fifth Generation Computer Systems). In *Proc. International Conference on Fifth Generation Computer Systems*, pages 1–85, 1981.
11. Martin Roth. OMR - optical music recognition. diploma thesis, Swiss Federal Institute of Technology, Institute for theoretical computer science, ETH Zürich, CH-8092 Zürich, Switzerland, October 1992.

On-Line Chinese Character Recognition with Attributed Relational Graph Matching

Jianzhuang Liu†, W. K. Cham† and Michael M. Y. Chang‡

†Department of Electronic Engineering, The Chinese University of Hong Kong
‡Department of Information Engineering, The Chinese University of Hong Kong

Abstract. A structural method for on-line recognition of Chinese characters is proposed, which is stroke order free and allows variations in stroke type and stroke number. Both input characters and the model characters are represented with complete attributed relational graphs (ARGs). An optimal matching measure between two ARGs is defined. Classification of an input character can be implemented by inexactly matching its ARG against every ARG of the model base. The matching procedure is formulated as a search problem of finding the minimum cost path in a state space tree, using the A* algorithm. In order to speed up the search of the A*, besides a heuristic estimate, a novel strategy that utilizes the geometric position information of strokes of Chinese characters to prune the tree is employed. The efficience of our method is demonstrated by the promising experimental results.

1 Introduction

Although great progress has been made in on-line Chinese character recognition (OLCCR) since the 1970's [1], a number of researchers are still involved in this topic for achieving better performance of OLCCR. Recognition of handwritten Chinese characters is considered as a very hard problem because of large categories, complex structure, and widely variable and many similar shapes of Chinese characters. Researchers hope to develop efficient algorithms which are stroke order and stroke number free, and can run on general computers (e.g. PCs) within an acceptable computation time. Commercial OLCCR systems are available now but their performance still needs to be improved.

Both statistic and structural methods can be used for recognition of Chinese characters [2]. Intuitively, human beings classify Chinese characters by making use of their local structural information instead of their global statistic features. An attributed relational graph (ARG) is a powerful tool for the representation of relational structure of a pattern [3]. Recognition of an input candidate is carried out by matching its ARG with all the ARGs of models. In this paper, we represent both the characters of our model base and the input candidates with *complete* ARGs, whose nodes describe strokes of characters and arcs the relations between any two strokes. In order to speed up the recognition procedure, matching between two ARGs is formulated as a problem of search in a state space tree, and the A* algorithm is used to perform the heuristic search. As the A* has exponential complexity in many cases, acceptable recognition time cannot obtained if heuristic functions good enough are not available. For further saving CPU time, we propose an efficient tree pruning strategy which uses the geometric position information of Chinese characters to assist the search of A*.

2 Complete ARGs of Chinese Characters

In our complete ARG representation, nodes of an ARG describe stroke types. A stroke is defined as the writing from pen down to pen up when one writes on a digitizer with a stylus pen. On-line devices can capture the temporal information of the writing, such as the number and order of strokes as well as the direction change of each stroke. Table 1 defines 14 types of primitive strokes. The types and approximate direction changes of these strokes are stored in a stroke base. For an unknown input stroke, we use straight lines to represent the stroke. A simple piecewise linear curve fitting procedure called the iterated endpoint fit [4] is suitable for our application. Recognition of an input stroke can be implemented by compairing the direcion changes of its fitting lines with those of strokes in the stroke base. For a stroke having more than three fitting lines, a method similar to dynamic programming [5] is used to get the optimal matching between the stroke and the primitive strokes. Fitting strokes with straight lines has the advantages of (1) reducing noise (many preprocessing algorithms such as smoothing, filtering, dehooking, stroke connection, and so on [1] are not needed.), and (2) easily extracting geometric position information of strokes which will be discussed in Section 4.

Table 1. Primitive strokes

Type	Strokes	Type	Strokes
1	→	8	↙
2	│	9	⌄
3	╱	10	└
4	╲	11	⌐ ⌄ ⌐
5	╱	12	⌁
6	⟨ ∠ ╲ └	13	⌁
7	→ ⌐ ⌐	14	⌁ ⌁ ⌁

ARGs were first used to represent the structural information of patterns in [3]. Recognizing the structure of a given unknown pattern may be performed by transforming this pattern into an ARG and then matching the ARG with those which represent the structures of model patterns. Below we begin with Definition 1 for ARGs that is defined in [3].

Let V_N and V_A be sets of node lables and arc labels, respectively. Each element belonging to V_N or V_A is of the form (u, v), where u is a syntactic symbol denoting the structure of (u, v) and $v = (v_1, v_2, ..., v_m)$ is a semantic vector denoting m numerical and/or logical attributes of (u, v).

Definition 1. An attributed relational graph over $V = V_N \cup V_A$ is a 4-tuple $\omega = (N, A, \mu, \varepsilon)$, where N is a finite nonempty set of nodes; $A \subset N \times N$ is a set of distinct ordered pairs of distinct elements in N called arcs; $\mu : N \rightarrow V_N$ is a function called node interpreter; $\varepsilon : A \rightarrow V_A$ is a function called arc interpreter.

To represent the complexe structure of a Chinese character with an ARG, perhaps it is the most straighforward way that the nodes of the ARG describe the strokes of the character and the arcs the relations between any two different strokes. Considering the computation rate and wide stroke variations, we use only simple but relatively stable stroke relation features of Chinese characters. The complete ARG representation is given as follows.

(1) Nodes of an ARG—The syntactic symbol of a node has one of the 14 stroke types as shown in Table 1. The semantic vector of a node is a binary value '1' or '0', where '1' denotes the stroke is a long one and '0' a short one. A short stroke in a handwritten Chinese character is a relatively unstable stroke which may be written as one of the first 4 types in Table 1.

(2) Relations of an ARG—The syntactic symbol of a relation, r_{ij}, between stroke i and stroke j is represented as a vector $r_{ij} = (a_{ij}^1, a_{ij}^2, a_{ij}^3)$, where a_{ij}^1, a_{ij}^2 and $a_{ij}^3 \in \{0, 1, 2\}$. Let c_i and c_j be the geometric centers of stroke i and stroke j, respectively. Then $a_{ij}^1 = 0, 1$, or 2 denotes c_i being 'below', 'above', or 'below or above' c_j. Also, $a_{ij}^2 = 0, 1$, or 2 denotes c_i being on the 'right of', 'left of', or 'right of or left of' c_j. $a_{ij}^3 = 0, 1$ or 2 denotes that stroke i 'crosses', 'uncrosses' or 'crosses or uncrosses' stroke j. The sematic attributs of the relations are not used.

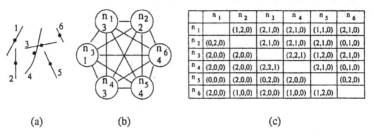

	n_1	n_2	n_3	n_4	n_5	n_6
n_1		(1,2,0)	(2,1,0)	(2,1,0)	(1,1,0)	(2,1,0)
n_2	(0,2,0)		(2,1,0)	(2,1,0)	(2,1,0)	(0,1,0)
n_3	(2,0,0)	(2,0,0)		(2,2,1)	(1,2,0)	(2,1,0)
n_4	(2,0,0)	(2,0,0)	(2,2,1)		(2,1,0)	(0,1,0)
n_5	(0,0,0)	(2,0,0)	(0,2,0)	(2,0,0)		(0,2,0)
n_6	(2,0,0)	(1,0,0)	(2,0,0)	(1,0,0)	(1,2,0)	

| (a) | (b) | (c) |

Fig. 1. (a) Chinese character '伏'; (b) complete ARG of Fig. 1(a); (c) relation matrix of Fig. 1(b).

Fig. 1 shows an example of the complete ARG representation for the model character '伏'. The points on or near the strokes in Fig. 1(a) are their geometric centers. Fig. 1(b) is the ARG of '伏', where nodes n_{1-6} describe 6 strokes and their types. The relations of the graph are represented by a generalized matrix $R = [r_{ij}]_{6 \times 6}$ shown in Fig. 1(c). Here $r_{ii}(i = 1, 2, ...6)$ have no definition. Note that there is some kind of symmetry between the elements $r_{ij} = (a_{ij}^1, a_{ij}^2, a_{ij}^3)$ and $r_{ji} = (a_{ji}^1, a_{ji}^2, a_{ji}^3)$. In order to tolerate daily handwriting variations, the relation matrix of a Chinese character must be designed carefully. For example, '伏' may be written as '伏', '伏' or '伏'. Therefore, the relation 'above' or 'below' between the geometric centers of stroke 1 and stroke 4 is uncertain, and so a_{14}^1 is set to 2. In addition, stroke 6 belongs to a short unstable one, so its attribute value is equal to 0.

3 ARG Matching via State Space Search

3.1 Definitions of Costs and Matchings

Determining whether two Chinese characters are similar or not can be formulated as a graph matching problem. In the matching procedure there are costs with respect to node mappings and arc mappings. We use function $C_1(i, s_1; k, s_2)$ to denote the cost of mapping node i with stroke type s_1 in ARG1 to node k with stroke type s_2 in ARG2. Because of variations in handwriting, different stroke type mappings may have different cost values.

Let i and j be nodes in an ARG, then ordered pair (i, j) is called a (directed) arc of the ARG. The cost of mapping arc (i, j) in ARG1 to arc (k, l) in ARG2 is defined as

$$C_2(i, j; k, l) = \sum_{m=1}^{3} w_m d_m(a_{ij}^m, a_{kl}^m),$$

(1)

where w_{1-3} are weighting factors, and

$$d_m(a_{ij}^m, a_{kl}^m) = \left\{ \begin{array}{ll} 0, & \text{if } (a_{ij}^m = a_{kl}^m) \text{ or if } (a_{ij}^m \text{ or } a_{kl}^m = 2), \\ 1, & \text{otherwise,} \end{array} \right\} m = 1, 2, 3.$$

In natural Chinese character handwriting, several primitive strokes are often written in the form of one stroke and one primitive stroke is sometimes written in the form of two strokes. To deal with these, we use inexact graph matching, which allows matching between two ARGs with different numbers of nodes. Therefore, we introduce a cost $C_3(k, s; t)$ with which node k with stroke type s in the graph having more nodes is mapped to a *null* node in the other graph, where t is the stroke number of the graph with fewer nodes. If we regard all mappings between any type of stroke and a null stroke as the same, then $C_3(k, s; t)$ may be written as $C_3(k; t)$.

Definition 2. Let $|N|$ be the cardinal of a set N and $NULL$ the set of null nodes. Also let $\omega_1 = (N_1, A_1, \mu_1, \varepsilon_1)$ and $\omega_2 = (N_2, A_2, \mu_2, \varepsilon_2)$ be two ARGs, with $|N_1| \leq |N_2|$. An inexact matching between ω_1 and ω_2 is defined as the function $f : N_1 \cup NULL \to N_2$, where $|N_1| + |NULL| = |N_2|$ (in the case of $|N_1| = |N_2|$, $NULL = \emptyset$), if the following condition is satisfied:

$$n \neq m \Rightarrow f(n) \neq f(m), \forall n, m \in N_1 \cup NULL \text{ and } f(n), f(m) \in N_2.$$

Definition 3. Let ω_1 and ω_2 be two ARGs and $f : N_1 \cup NULL \to N_2$ be an inexact matching. The cost of the matching, $cost(f, \omega_1, \omega_2)$, is defined as

$$cost(f, \omega_1, \omega_2) = \sum_{\substack{f(i)=k \\ i \in N_1}} C_1(i, s_1; k, s_2) + \sum_{\substack{f(i)=k \\ f(j)=l \\ i,j \in N_1, i \neq j}} C_2(i, j; k, l) + \sum_{\substack{f(i)=k \\ i \in NULL}} C_3(k, s; t).$$

(2)

Definition 4. The optimal matching between ω_1 and ω_2, with $|N_1| \leq |N_2|$, is a mapping function $f^* \in M(f)$ such that

$$cost(f^*, \omega_1, \omega_2) = \min_{f \in M(f)} \{cost(f, \omega_1, \omega_2)\}, \tag{3}$$

where $M(f)$ is the set of all possible mappings.

Definition 5. Let $\omega = (N, A, \mu, \varepsilon)$ be the ARG of a candidate and $W = \{\omega_1, \omega_2, ..., \omega_p\}$ be the ARG set of p models. Partition W into two subsets W_1 and W_2 such that $W = W_1 \cup W_2$, $W_1 \cap W_2 = \emptyset$, $\omega_i = (N_i, A_i, \mu_i, \varepsilon_i) \in W_1$ with $|N_i| \leq |N|$, and $\omega_j = (N_j, A_j, \mu_j, \varepsilon_j) \in W_2$ with $|N_j| > |N|$. Define

$$cost(f_k^*, \omega_k, \omega) = \min_{\omega_i \in W_1} \{cost(f_i^*, \omega_i, \omega)\} \tag{4}$$

and

$$cost(f_l^*, \omega, \omega_l) = \min_{\omega_j \in W_2} \{cost(f_j^*, \omega, \omega_j)\}. \tag{5}$$

If $cost(f_k^*, \omega_k, \omega) \leq cost(f_l^*, \omega, \omega_l)$ and $cost(f_k^*, \omega_k, \omega) < T$, the candidate is called most similar to model k; if $cost(f_l^*, \omega, \omega_l) \leq cost(f_k^*, \omega_k, \omega)$, and $cost(f_l^*, \omega, \omega_l) < T$, the candidate most similar to model l; otherwise the candidate not similar to any model. T is a pre-defined upper limit which may vary with the node number of ω.

Exhaustive search for obtaining $cost(f^*, \omega_1, \omega_2)$ is very time-comsuming. The computational complexity of that search is $O(|N_1|!)$ when $|N_1| = |N_2|$. Therefore, it is necessary to find some fast search strategies.

3.2 State Space Search with A* Algorithm

The optimal ARG matching may be modelled as a search problem of finding the minimum cost path from the initial state to the goal state in a state space tree. In this paper, a state, represented as a node of the state space tree, means a mapping (matching) between ω_1' and ω_2', where ω_1' and ω_2' are the subgraphs of ω_1 and ω_2 (two ARGs to be matched), respectively. From the initial state (null mapping) to that state, the path cost similar to (2), i.e., the cost of matching between the two subgraphs is defined. When a search reaches a goal node, a matching is completed. The minimum cost path from the initial node to a goal node corresponds to the optimal matching between two ARGs.

A* algorithm is a best-first search approach. It can utilize certain domain-dependent information to focus the search to the minimum cost path, and is expected to expand fewer nodes in the state space tree [6,7]. A so-called evaluation function is employed to estimate the costs of the nodes in the tree. At node n of the tree, the evaluation function $g(n) = g_1(n) + g_2(n)$, where $g_1(n)$ is the path cost from the initial node to node n, and $g_2(n)$ is an estimate of cost from node n to a goal node using any available heuristic information. If $g_2(n) \leq g_2^*(n)$ holds for any node n, $g_2(n)$ is called a *consistent lower bounded estimate* of $g_2^*(n)$, where $g_2^*(n)$ is the cost of an optimal path from node n to a goal node. In this case, A* always guarantees to find a minimum cost path and expands fewer nodes than other exhaustive search algorithms [7]. In our application, $g_1(n)$ is equal to the cost of matching between two subgraphs ω_1' and ω_2'. For the calculation of $g_2(n)$, the cheapest cost of node mappings between the two remaining subgraphs, $\omega_1 - \omega_1'$ and $\omega_2 - \omega_2'$, is used to estimate $g_2^*(n)$.

The efficiency of the A^* search depends critically on how precise the estimate for $g_2^*(n)$ is. Although efforts have been made for finding good heuristic functions [3,7,8], in general, precise estimates of $g_2^*(n)$ are still quite difficult. In next section, we propose to make use of the geometric position information of Chinese characters to prune the state space tree. Our strategy expands much fewer nodes in the tree and so results in significant improvement of the search efficiency of A^*.

4 A Pruning Strategy

In on-line recognition, a Chinese character as a whole can be regarded as no rotation variety. Hence a lot of information about the geometric positions of strokes in the character may be used to assist A^* algorithm's search for the minimum cost path.

Fig. 2(a) shows the Chinese character '秌' and a smallest rectangle $ABCD$ that surrounds it. Intuitively, strokes 1, 2 and 5 are written near the upper-left corner, the left side, and the lower-right corner of $ABCD$, respectively; strokes 3 and 4 in the middle; stroke 6 near the upper-right corner or the right side. In the following we formulated these character-dependant features by using a set of stroke geometric position features.

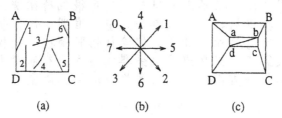

(a)　　　　　　(b)　　　　　　(c)

Fig. 2. (a) Character '秌' and rectangle $ABCD$; (b) 8 directions; (c) geometric illustration of $D_{0-3}(i)$.

Let $abcd$ be a smallest rectangle that surrounds stroke i. Eight directions in Fig. 2(b), are used to denote the directions of eight distances $D_{0-7}(i)$, where $D_{0-3}(i)$ are distances form a to A, b to B, c to C, and d to D, respectively, as shown in Fig. 2(c), and $D_{4-7}(i)$ are distances from the geometric center of $abcd$ to the respective four sides of $ABCD$. Besides, a function $od(D_q(i))$, $q \in \{0, 1, ..., 7\}$, is used to denote the order of $D_q(i)$. For example, consider the case where a Chinese character has s strokes. $od(D_q(i)) = 1$ denotes that the distance $D_q(i)$ of stroke i is the smallest among $\{D_q(1), D_q(2), ..., D_q(s)\}$, and $od(D_q(i)) = m$ denotes that there are $m - 1$ distances among $\{D_q(1), D_q(2), ..., D_q(s)\}$ which are smaller than $D_q(i)$.

Definition 6. The set of stroke geometric position features of a model Chinese character with s strokes is defined as a set of s 3-tuples

$$GPF = \{(d_i, x_i, y_i)|i = 1, 2, ..., s\}, \tag{6}$$

where $d_i \in \{0, 1, ..., 7\}$, $x_i \leq od(D_{d_i}(i)) \leq y_i$, and $x_i, y_i \in \{1, 2, ..., s\}$.

When searching the state space tree for the optimal matching between ARG1 of the candidate and ARG2 of a model, A* algorithm runs with a pruning procedure inserted. The generation of a node in the tree means that a stroke (say, stroke i) in ARG1 is mapped to a stroke (say, stroke k) in ARG2. Let the kth elements of GPF of the model be (d_k, x_k, y_k). If $x_k \leq od(D_{d_k}(i)) \leq y_k$, the newly-generated node will be put in the open list of the A* algorithm; otherwise, the node is pruned out.

5 Experimental Results and Conclusions

The approaches presented in the previous sections have been implemented in C on a PC/486. For the time being, 102 frequently used Chinese characters (see Fig. 3) each with stroke number between 9 and 11 are selected for testing the performance of our method. We choose the weighting factors w_1, w_2 and w_3 in (1) to be 7,7 and 3, respectively, and the cost $C_3(k, s; t)$ to be 7. As some strokes of many Chinese characters are easily written to cross each other while they are not supposed to do so in standard writing, so w_3 is assigned a smaller value.

冠冒便侯侵信咱奏契峙帮度庭彦很徊待律恍恰拱
指拾按挺拷拴政故段毒亭帝重要准凋兼倚借哲哭
容宵宴屑展峭峨峰差座健徐徒悟耻悄捕捉捐挨捆
捎效氧消浙鬼乘班高偏奢婴偿宿寄屠崔崩崎崇液
彬淋彩得徘惜情惟患悠悉挽救虚毫辆商堂

Fig. 3. 102 models.

冠律侵帮庭彦恍 冠冒奏信咱契度要
拱按挺段毒亭重准 很拱拾拴政帝凋
哭兼宵倚屑悄峨健 故哲展差悟挨捕
徒悄捉挨效氧鬼班 捎消消乘班高偏
偏婴寄崔崇淋彩 奢屠崩得惟悠液
徘情患悉挽毫商奢 徊帮毒崎徊兼乘

(a)   (b)

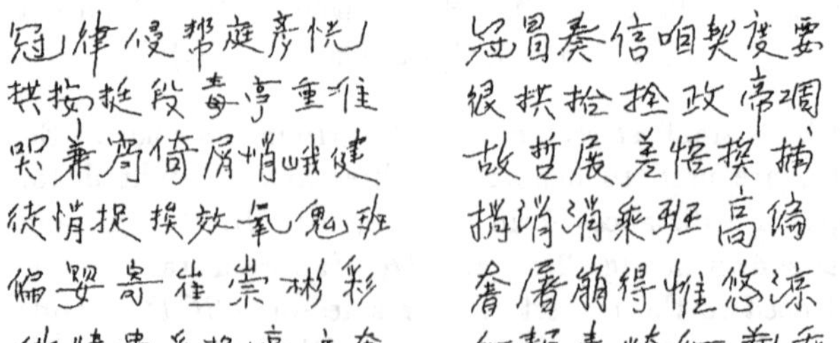

Fig. 4. (a) Some test data having correct stroke number;
(b) some test data having stroke number variations.

Two experiments were carried out and more than 2000 Chinese characters written by 6 people were used as test data. The first experiment consists of the characters that have correct stroke number, and the second consists of those that have one or two connected or split strokes. Both are stroke order free and may have stroke type variations. The correct recognition rates of the two experiments are about 98% and 94%, respectively. The recognition time of a character is less than 1 sceond. Fig. 4 shows some of the experiment data. The tentative results obtained are satisfactory. Our method can be used in the fine classsification for Chinese characters.

In this paper, a structural method for on-line recognition of Chinese characters has been proposed, which is stroke order free and allows variations in stroke type and stroke number. Both candidates and models are represented as complete ARGs. The recognition of a candidate is implemented by matching its ARG with those of the model base, and the matching is formulated as the search for the minimum cost path in a state space tree, using A^* algorithm. In order to speed up the search procedure of A^*, a novel strategy that utilizes the geometric position information of strokes in a Chinese character is employed for pruning the nodes in the tree. The experimental results obtained are very promising. This may be due to the fact that a lot of structural information of Chinese characters are used. To further improve the performance of our method, future research efforts may include the study and development of (1) more precise but computation-simple heuristic functions, (2) auto- or semiauto-approach for generating ARGs of the model base, (3) the influence on recognition rate with other weighting factors, and (4) the use of other geometric features of Chinese characters.

Acknowledgment

We are thankful for the financial support provided by the Hong Kong Earmarked Research Grant CUHK67/92E.

References

1. C. C. Tappet, C. Y. Suen, and T. Wakahara, The state of the art in on-line handwriting recognition, *IEEE Trans. PAMI* 12, 1990, pp.787–808
2. V. K. Govindan and A. P. Shivaprasad, Character recognition— a review, *Pattern Recognition* 23, 1990, pp.671–683
3. W. H. Tsai and K. S. Fu, Error-correcting isomorphisms of attributed relational graphs for pattern analysis, *IEEE Trans. SMC* 9, 1979, pp.757–768
4. R. O. Duda and P. E. Hart, *Pattern Classification and Scene Analysis*, Wiley-Interscience, New York, 1973
5. F. S. Hillier and G. J. Lieberman, *Introduction to Operations Research*, McGraw-Hill, New York, 1990
6. C. Thornton and B. D. Boulay, *Artificial Intelligence through Search*, Kluwer Academic Publishers, The Netherlands, 1992
7. J. Pearl, *Heuristics: intelligent search strategies for computer problem solving*, Addison-Wesley, Reading, MA, 1984
8. A. K. C. Wong, M. You, and S. C. Chan, An algorithm for graph optimal monomorphism, *IEEE Trans. SMC* 20, 1990, pp.628–636

On-Line Handwritten Alphanumeric Character Recognition Using Feature Sequences

Xiaolin Li and Dit-Yan Yeung

Department of Computer Science
Hong Kong University of Science and Technology
Clear Water Bay, Kowloon, HONG KONG
Internet: {xiaolin,dyyeung}@cs.ust.hk Fax: +852-2358-1477

Abstract. In this paper we present an approach in which an on-line handwritten character is characterized by a sequence of dominant points in strokes and a sequence of writing directions between consecutive dominant points. The directional information is used for character preclassification and the positional information is used for fine classification. Both preclassification and fine classification are based on dynamic programming matching. A recognition experiment has been conducted with 62 character classes of different writing styles and 21 people as data contributors. The recognition rate of this experiment is 91%, with 7.9% substitution rate and 1.1% rejection rate. The average processing time is 0.35 second per character on a 486 50MHz personal computer.

1 Introduction

With the development of digitizing tablets and microcomputers, on-line handwriting recognition has become an area of active research since the 1960s [3]. One reason for this is that on-line handwriting recognition promises to provide a dynamic means of communication with computers through a pen-like stylus, not just a keyboard. This seems to be a more natural way of entering data into computers.

The problem of on-line handwriting recognition can be defined in various ways. Variables in the problem definition include character set, writing style, and desired recognition rate. In general, each problem definition lends itself to different algorithmic approaches, which in turn make use of different features for classification [1, 2, 3, 4].

In this paper, we present an approach to on-line handwritten alphanumeric character recognition based on sequential features. In particular, points in strokes corresponding to local extrema of curvature are detected. These points correspond to the minima of curvilinear velocity of the pen-tip movement in the delta log-normal theory [6]. In addition, the mid-point between two consecutive points that correspond to curvature extrema or pen-down/pen-up locations is also used to represent a local minimum of angular velocity. We refer to all these points as dominant points in strokes.

In our system, an on-line handwritten character is characterized by a sequence of dominant points in strokes and a sequence of writing directions between consecutive dominant points. The directional information of the dominant points is used for character preclassification and the positional information is used for fine classification. Both preclassification and fine classification are based on dynamic programming matching using the idea of band-limited time warping.

Our recognition process consists of several stages: 1) data preprocessing, 2) feature extraction, and 3) character classification. Details of these stages are discussed in the following sections.

2 Data Preprocessing and Feature Extraction

2.1 Data Preprocessing

In the current context, a handwritten stroke refers to the locus of the pen tip from its pen-down to the next pen-up position. It can therefore be described as a sequence of consecutive points on the $x-y$ plane: $S = p_1 p_2 \cdots p_L$, where p_1 and p_L are the pen-down and pen-up points, respectively. Based on this representation, a handwritten character can then be described as a sequence of strokes $C = S_1 S_2 \cdots S_N$.

Since handwritten characters often have large variations in size and position, it is necessary to normalize the input data to facilitate subsequent processing. In our system, data normalization is performed by scaling each character both horizontally and vertically such that it is tightly bounded by a $W \times H$ box with the top-left corner of the box at the origin $o(0,0)$. Following this normalization step, stroke smoothing and linear interpolation are performed so that each stroke can be represented by a chain code sequence $D = d_1 d_2 \cdots d_{L-1}$. Figure 1(a) and (b) illustrate these ideas.

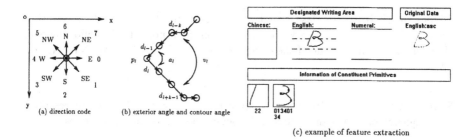

(c) example of feature extraction

Fig. 1. Data preprocessing and feature extraction

2.2 Feature Extraction

Feature Types The stroke-based features used in our system are dominant points in strokes and direction primitives between dominant points.

Dominant points refer to points of the following types: (a) pen-down and pen-up points; (b) points corresponding to local extrema of curvature; and (c) mid-points between two consecutive points of type (a) or (b).

A direction primitive refers to one of the eight chain-code directions: E, SE, S, SW, W, NW, N, and NE (see Figure 1(a)). It represents the writing direction from a dominant point to the next one.

Dominant Points Based on the chain coding scheme, consecutive *exterior angles* and *contour angles* formed by pairs of arrows along the stroke can be defined as shown in Figure 1(b). In Figure 1(b), the exterior angle a_l at point p_l is formed by the pair of arrows d_{l-1} and d_l, and is located on the left-hand side of the arrows. The value of a_l can be obtained easily by table lookup. Denoting the sequence of exterior angles in a stroke as $A = a_2 a_3 \cdots a_{L-1}$ and performing low-pass filtering on A, one can segment the stroke into a sequence of convex/concave/plain regions.

The contour angle v_l at p_l is defined within a support region and its value is estimated by averaging angles a_{lk}, where for $k = 1, 2, \ldots, K$, a_{lk} is formed by the pair of arrows d_{l-k} and d_{l+k-1}. Denoting the sequence of contour angles in the stroke as $V = v_2 v_3 \cdots v_{L-1}$, one can easily obtain the maximum within a convex region and the minimum within a concave region. All such maxima and minima constitute the local extrema of curvature along a stroke. More details of the above technique can be found in [5].

After detecting the extreme points, a mid-point between two consecutive points of type (a) or (b) along a stroke is then located to approximate the point of local minimum in angular velocity. The pen-down and pen-up points, the local extrema of curvature and these mid-points together then constitute the dominant points in a stroke.

Direction Primitives Based on the dominant points extracted, a direction primitive can be defined as a vector from a dominant point to the following one, after quantization into one of the eight directions E, SE, S, SW, W, NW, N, and NE.

Feature Sequences After feature extraction, a character C can be represented as a sequence of dominant points and a sequence of direction primitives.

2.3 Other Considerations

There are a few other special considerations in our system design. First, different writing areas are designated for different character sets (Chinese, English, and numerals). Second, ledger regions are used for English ascender-descender judgement. Third, if a large portion of a stroke is part of a circle or a very smooth arc (i.e. no curvature extreme in that portion), we identify the mid-point of that region as a pseudo extreme of curvature.

2.4 An Example

Figure 1(c) shows an example of the letter 'B'. The original handwriting is located in the designated writing area with its discrete data sampled by the digitizing tablet displayed in the top-right region. In the lower region, the two preprocessed strokes are displayed, with the local extrema of curvature marked. Each stroke is also characterized by a sequence of direction primitives. The first stroke has three dominant points (no curvature extrema) with sequence '22'. The second stroke has nine dominant points (three extreme points) with sequence '01340134'. Since this character is written in the area designated for (lowercase or uppercase) English letters, and the upper portion of the first stroke is above the mid-level of the top ledger region, it is therefore categorized as an English letter with ascender.

3 Character Classification

3.1 Dynamic Programming for Elastic Matching

Band-limited Time Warping Time warping is a useful technique for finding the correspondence between two strings (sequences). Given two strings, many time warps are possible. A cost (or gain) function can be defined to evaluate each warp. If we assume that there is only local variation and deformation, we can limit the extent of possible positional shift of each symbol. This results in a reduction in the number of possible warps that need to be investigated using dynamic programming.

Dynamic Programming Algorithm Dynamic programming is a useful technique for finding the optimal path from one node to another in a graph. Suppose G is a matching graph with nodes in N levels (such as the graph in Figure 2(b)) and each node in the graph is associated with an index and a cost value. Let v_1 be the source and v_T be the sink. Starting from the source there are a number of paths leading to the sink, with each path associated with a total cost value. Denoting the cost value of node v_i as c_{v_i} and the minimum partial cost (over all possible partial paths) from node v_i to the sink v_T as p_{v_i}, the minimum total cost from the source to the sink can then be determined as follows:

1. Initialization step:

$$p_{v_T} = c_{v_T} \tag{1}$$

2. Induction step:

$$p_{v_i} = c_{v_i} + \min_{\langle v_i, v_j \rangle \in G} \{p_{v_j}\} \tag{2}$$

where $\langle v_i, v_j \rangle$ denotes a directed edge in G.

The algorithm for dynamic programming based on a gain measure can be derived in a similar manner.

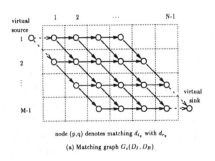

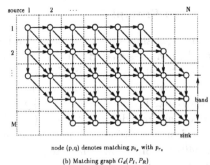

node (p,q) denotes matching d_{i_p} with d_{r_q}

(a) Matching graph $G_s(D_I, D_R)$

node (p,q) denotes matching p_{i_p} with p_{r_q}

(b) Matching graph $G_d(P_I, P_R)$

Fig. 2. Matching graphs

3.2 Preclassification

Similarity Between Two Sequences Let D_I and D_R be the sequences of direction primitives of an input character C_I and a reference character C_R, respectively:

$$D_I = d_{i_1} d_{i_2} \cdots d_{i_{M-1}} \tag{3}$$

$$D_R = d_{r_1} d_{r_2} \cdots d_{r_{N-1}} \tag{4}$$

Without loss of generality, assume that $M \leq N$. Using the idea of band-limited time warping, one can construct a matching graph $G_s(D_I, D_R)$ with nodes in $N+1$ levels, as shown in Figure 2(a).

As shown in the figure, a direction primitive in D_R is allowed to have only one match in D_I, but a direction primitive in D_I may have multiple matches in D_R. Furthermore, virtual source and sink nodes are introduced so that matching of the two ends is not enforced. The gain at a node (p, q) can be interpreted as the similarity between d_{i_p} and d_{r_q}, which is determined as (see Figure 1(a))

$$s(d_{i_p}, d_{r_q}) = \begin{cases} 1 & d_{i_p} = d_{r_q} \\ 0.6 & |d_{i_p} - d_{r_q}| = 1 \text{ or } 7 \\ 0 & \text{otherwise} \end{cases} \tag{5}$$

The gains at the source and the sink are set to zero.

The maximum total gain G_{max} from the source to the sink can be found by dynamic programming as discussed above. The similarity between D_I and D_R is then defined as

$$S(D_I, D_R) = \frac{G_{max}}{N - 1} \tag{6}$$

Candidate Classes Suppose C_I and C_R belong to the same character set, and they have the same ascender-descender property if the character set is the set of English letters. C_R is said to be a candidate class for C_I if

$$S(D_I, D_R) \geq T_S \tag{7}$$

where T_S is a threshold.

3.3 Fine Classification

Distance Between Two Sequences Let P_I and P_R be the sequences of dominant points of the input character C_I and a reference character C_R, respectively:

$$P_I = p_{i_1} p_{i_2} \cdots p_{i_M} \tag{8}$$

$$P_R = p_{r_1} p_{r_2} \cdots p_{r_N} \tag{9}$$

Using the idea of band-limited time warping, a matching graph $G_d(P_I, P_R)$ with nodes in N levels can be constructed as shown in Figure 2(b).

Unlike in the matching graph $G_s(D_I, D_R)$, a dominant point in either sequence may have multiple matches in the other sequence. The cost at a node (p, q) is defined as the Euclidean distance between dominant points p_{i_p} and p_{r_q}. The minimum total cost C_{min} from the source to the sink can be found by dynamic programming. With this cost, the distance (or dissimilarity) between P_I and P_R is defined as

$$D(P_I, P_R) = \frac{C_{min}}{N} \tag{10}$$

Character Classification Let $\{P_R\}$ be the set of dominant point sequences corresponding to the set of candidate classes $\{C_R\}$ obtained from the preclassification step. The input character C_I is classified as $C_R^* \in \{C_R\}$ if P_R^* corresponding to C_R^* satisfies

$$P_R^* = \arg \min_{P_R} \{D(P_I, P_R)\} \tag{11}$$

and

$$D(P_I, P_R^*) \leq T_D \tag{12}$$

where T_D is a threshold. Otherwise, the input character will be rejected.

4 Recognition Experiment

Our system has been implemented on a 486 50MHz personal computer running Microsoft Windows 3.1, with a WACOM digitizing tablet as input device. The width and height of each normalized character are set to $W = 108$ and $H = 128$, and the thresholds for preclassification and fine classification are set to $T_S = 0.6$ and $T_D = 32$.

Character Classes and Writing Styles We use 62 character classes with different writing styles in our experiment, i.e., numerals 0-9, uppercase letters A-Z, and lowercase letters a-z. Our writing templates are derived from the Italian manuscript style and some other writing styles.

Data Collection and Reference Set In order to evaluate the performance of our system, 21 participants were invited to contribute handwriting data for our recognition experiment. The data for each participant are stored in three data files, one each for numerals, uppercase and lowercase letters written in Italian manuscript style and some other styles. The first file contains 20 numeral instances (0-9, 0-9). The second files contains 52 uppercase letters (A-Z, A-Z). The third files contains 52 lowercase letters (a-z, a-z). Figure 3 shows two examples of such data files.

Data from shirley, 5 July 1995   Data from james, 15 June 1995

Fig. 3. Uppercase and lowercase letters written by participants

All the 124 characters written by the first participant were used as reference patterns to form the initial reference set. Reference set evolution was then performed by using the data from five randomly chosen participants. After running this procedure, 56 new reference patterns were selected to give a total of 180 patterns in the reference set. This reference set was then used in the recognition of the characters written by the other 15 participants.

Recognition Results To collect more statistics about the performance, the data from 15 participants were tested. The recognition results are summarized in Table 1. From the table, one can see that the recognition rate for numerals is the highest while that for lowercase letters is the lowest. The overall recognition rate is 91.0%, with 7.9% substitution rate and 1.1% rejection rate. If we consider the three best candidates, the hit rate is 97.1%.

The average time for processing one data file of 20 numerals is about 6 seconds, while that for 52 English letters is about 18 seconds. Thus, the average processing time is estimated to be about 0.35 second per character on a 486 50MHz personal computer.

5 Conclusion and Remarks

In this paper, we have presented an approach to on-line handwritten alphanumeric character recognition. In our approach, an on-line handwritten character

	Numeral		Uppercase		Lowercase		Overall	
Total	300	100%	780	100%	780	100%	1860	100%
1st	289	96.3%	725	92.9%	679	87.1%	1693	91.0%
2nd	8	2.7%	31	4.0%	61	7.8%	100	5.4%
3rd	0	0.0%	1	0.1%	13	1.7%	14	0.7%
Others	1	0.3%	10	1.3%	22	2.8%	33	1.8%
Rejected	2	0.7%	13	1.7%	5	0.6%	20	1.1%

Table 1. Recognition results

is represented by a sequence of dominant points in strokes and a sequence of writing directions between consecutive dominant points, which form the basis for character classification. An advantage of this approach over other methods comes from the fact that our character matching processes are elastic and hence can tolerate local variation and deformation. Besides, dominant points are quite easy to extract using the technique described in [5]. Moreover, our approach can handle large alphabets (such as Chinese characters) due to its fast preclassification. However, since our approach is based on sequential handwriting signals, it is intrinsically stroke-order dependent.

Acknowledgement

The research work reported in this paper has been supported by a Sino Software Research Centre (SSRC) Research Award (SSRC 94/95.EG11) and a Research Infrastructure Grant (RI 92/93.EG08) of the Hong Kong University of Science and Technology.

References

1. D.D. Kerrick and A.C. Bovik. Microprocessor-based recognition of handprinted characters from a tablet input. *Pattern Recognition*, vol.21, no.5, pp.525–537, 1988.
2. M.S. El-Wakil and A.A. Shoukry. On-line recognition of handwritten isolated Arabic characters. *Pattern Recognition*, vol.22, no.2, pp.97–105, 1989.
3. C.C. Tappert, C.Y. Suen and T. Wakahara. The state of the art in on-line handwriting recognition. *IEEE Transactions on Pattern Analysis and Machine Intelligence*, vol.12, no.8, pp.787–808, 1990.
4. C.K. Lin, K.C. Fan and F.T. Lee. On-line recognition by deviation-expansion model and dynamic programming matching. *Pattern Recognition*, vol.26, no.2, pp.259–268, 1993.
5. X. Li and N.S. Hall. Corner detection and shape classification of on-line handprinted Kanji strokes. *Pattern Recognition*, vol.26, no.9, pp.1315–1334, 1993.
6. R. Plamondon. Handwriting generation: the delta lognormal theory. *Proceedings of the Fourth International Workshop on Frontiers in Handwriting Recognition*, pp.1–10, 1994.

An Adaptive Supersampling Method

Rynson W. H. Lau

Computer Graphics and Media Laboratory, Department of Computing,
Hong Kong Polytechnic University, Hong Kong

Abstract. Original z-buffer method is a very efficient method for image generation. The limitation is that it introduces aliases into the output image. Although many different kinds of methods have been published to address this problem. most of them suffer from requiring a large memory space, demanding for high computational power, or having some other limitations. In this paper, we propose a simple anti-aliased method based on the supersampling method. However, instead of supersampling every pixel, we supersample edge pixels only. This method has the advantages of requiring less memory and less processing time than the traditional supersampling method. It is also less problematic than some other rendering methods in handling intersecting surfaces.

1 Introduction

Image generation based on the original z-buffer algorithm [5] requires only the colour value and the depth value of the closest object at each pixel. However, having these two values alone produces aliased images. This aliasing is the result of the point sampling nature of the z-buffer method. To solve this problem means that we need to solve the visibility problem in subpixel level. This requires the calculation of the visible area of each polygon at each pixel.

Existing hidden surface removal methods that calculate subpixel visibility can roughly be classified into *fixed-sized buffering (FSB) methods* in which the buffer used for image generation has a fixed memory size, and *variable-sized buffering (VSB) methods* in which the buffer does not have a fixed memory size.

Examples of FSB methods include supersampling z-buffer method [7] in which the scene is supersampled and then filtered down into the output resolution. The problems of this method are that it requires a lot of memory to store the supersampled image and a lot of processing time. The advantages, however, are that it is a simple extension of the z-buffer method and hence it can be implemented into hardware without too much addition effort [2, 11]. The RealityEngine [3] is also an hardware implementation of this kind although colour and depth are only sampled once per pixel to improve performance. To reduce memory usage, the RealityEngine uses the sparse mask method to reduce the number of samples per pixel. Four, eight or sixteen sample locations are chosen from an 8×8 coverage mask for anti-aliasing. Other FSB methods include [1] in which all polygons are required to clip against each other to produce a list of visible polygons before the scan-conversion process and [8] in which the scene is sampled multiple times at different subpixel positions to produce multiple images which are combined to produce an output image. Both of these methods require less memory but considerable amount of processing time.

VSB methods can be further divided into *the span buffering methods* [6, 12, 14], which break polygons into horizontal spans and store in the buffer, and *the pixel buffering methods* [4, 10], which break polygons into pixel fragments and store in the buffer. A common feature of these methods is that they accumulate information of all visible objects in the buffer for hidden surface removal and anti-aliasing. In all these methods, memory usage depends on the complexity of the scene and there is no theoretical upper limit to it. Hence, they normally require run-time memory allocation. As such, real-time image generation using VSB methods is difficult. Hardware implementation of these methods are usually complex. [9] and [13] describe two rare hardware implementations of a span buffering method and of a pixel buffering method respectively.

In this paper, we describe a new scan-conversion method called the adaptive supersampling method. Although it is based on the supersampling method, it uses a variable-sized buffer called the adaptive supersampling buffer for adaptive supersampling. The new method tries to make a compromise between the supersampling method, which is easy to implement in hardware and can solve the surface intersection problem correctly but demands for a lot of memory and computation time, and the A-buffer method, which uses less memory and demands for less computation time but is difficult to implement into hardware and cannot solve the surface intersection problem correctly.

The outline of the paper is as follows. Section 2 describes the adaptive supersampling buffer. Section 3 discusses two implementation issues regarding to finding the depth increments and allocating run-time memory. Section 4 compares the strengths and limitations of the new method with three other major scan-conversion methods in terms of memory usage, performance and handling of surface intersection. Finally, Section 5 draws a conclusion of the paper.

2 Adaptive Supersampling Buffer

In the traditional supersampling method, memory is allocated to store the depth and colour values of each subpixel. Hence a lot of memory is needed and the actual memory usage is directly proportional to the subpixel resolution.

We have noticed that during the image generation process, there may be a lot of edge pixels created temporarily. These edge pixels may represent an edge of a polygon. However, when the connecting polygon is processed, an edge fragment from the former polygon may be merged with the edge fragment from the latter polygon and together they cover the whole pixel. Thus the edge pixel will become a non-edge pixel. In our experience, the maximum number of edge pixels for most of the complex images during the image generation process does not excess 20% the total number of pixels.

Because edge pixels contribute to only a small percentage of the total number of pixels in an image, our idea here is to supersample a polygon only when we need to. This may result in a considerable amount of saving in both memory and processing time compared to the supersampling method.

To achieve this, when scan-converting a polygon, if the polygon covers the whole pixel, we sample the polygon once only. However, if the polygon partially covers the pixel, we perform a supersampling of the polygon within the pixel region. This demands for a buffer that can handle the information generated from either of the two sampling resolutions. Here, we apply a technique similar to the one used in the A-buffer [4]. A standard 2D buffer is used for normal z-buffer scan-conversion (one sample per pixel). When a polygon edge is encountered, a larger memory block is allocated to the pixel for storing the high resolution samples. However, unlike the A-buffer method, there is at most one memory block allocated to a pixel no matter how many polygon edges found in the pixel. In the A-buffer, there are two dimensions of uncertainty. The first one is the number of edge pixels in an image and the second one is the number of fragments in each edge pixels. The new method reduces it to one dimension – the number of edge pixels in an image. Because there is no need to traverse through a possible long list of fragments as in the A-buffer method, the new method greatly simplifies the algorithm and makes it easier to be implemented into hardware. In addition, the new method, like the supersampling method, can resolve surface intersection in subpixel level while the A-buffer method deals with the problem with an approximation method.

The new buffer uses two data structures as follows:

```
typedef struct {
    unsigned char r, g, b;
    unsigned char zflag;
    union {
        int z;
        PixelBlock *pblock;
    } zORpblock;
    short deltazx;  /* change of z in x axis */
    short deltazy;  /* change of z in y axis */
} Pixel;

typedef struct {
    int r[SUBPIXELS_Y][SUBPIXELS_X];
    int g[SUBPIXELS_Y][SUBPIXELS_X];
    int b[SUBPIXELS_Y][SUBPIXELS_X];
    int z[SUBPIXELS_Y][SUBPIXELS_X];
} PixelBlock;
```

Pixel is the basic element of a 2D pixel buffer. If a polygon completely covers a pixel, the **Pixel** element is used in a way similar to the traditional z-buffer method. However, when a polygon partially covers the pixel, the memory location for storing **z** is used as a pointer instead. The flag **zflag** is set to false to indicate such a situation. **deltazx** and **deltazy** are used to store the the depth increments in the x and y directions respectively. These two values are calculated once for each polygon and are used to generate the depth values for each subpixel so that hidden surface removal may be performed in a subpixel level. **PixelBlock** is a run-time allocated memory block used to store the supersampled polygon information inside the pixel.

At start, the pixel buffer is initialised so that the contents of all **rgb** fields store the background colour. All **zflag**'s are set to true to indicate that **zORpblock** contains a depth value and all **z**'s are initialised with the maximum depth value. All **deltazx**'s and **deltazy**'s are set to zero.

Polygons are processed at random order and before scan-converting a polygon, we calculate its depth increments both in x and in y directions. When scan-converting the polygon, if a pixel is fully covered by it, the contents of **rgb** and **z** in the **Pixel** element are updated provided that the depth of the polygon at the pixel position is smaller than **z**. The pre-calculated depth increments of the polygon in the x and y directions are then stored to **deltazx** and **deltazy** respectively. If, instead, the pixel is partially covered by the polygon, a **PixelBlock** is requested and is linked to the corresponding **Pixel** element by setting **pblock** to point to the **PixelBlock**. **zflag** is then set to false to indicate that **zORpblock** is a pointer. All the **rgb** fields in the **PixelBlock** are initialised with the **rgb** values stored in the **Pixel** element and the **z**'s are initialised by interpolating the value of **z** stored in **Pixel** with **deltazx** and **deltazy**. Then the polygon fragment is supersampled to update the contents of **PixelBlock** based on the z-buffer method.

If a pixel with a **PixelBlock** is found fully covered by a polygon fragment with a smaller depth value, the information from the polygon is stored into the **Pixel** element and the **PixelBlock** is returned to the memory pool. However, if the pixel is partially covered by the polygon fragment, the polygon fragment is supersampled to update the contents of **PixelBlock** already stored in the pixel.

3 Implementation Issues

In this section, we discuss two implementation issues regarding to the calculation of the depth increments to be stored in **deltazx** and **deltazy** and the allocation of the **PixelBlock** memory.

3.1 Calculation of the Depth Increments

The depth increments, **deltazx** and **deltazy**, are the increments of **z** in x and in y directions respectively within the pixel region. From Figure 1, **deltazx** can be calculated as

$$\mathbf{deltazx} = \frac{Zx_{inc}}{X_{inc}} .$$

However, in a three dimensional world, the polygon can have any orientation and calculating X_{inc}, Zx_{inc} and likewise Y_{inc}, Zy_{inc} are not straightforward.

Hence, instead, we calculate the depth increments from the polygon normal vector. After a polygon has been perspectively transformed, we calculate the unit normal vector of the transformed polygon as $\mathbf{N} = (dx, dy, dz)$. (This unit normal vector may already be available in some implementations of the rendering process. They are used for detecting back-surfaces.) With this normal vector, the depth increments can be calculated as

$$\mathbf{deltazx} = \frac{dx}{-dz} \quad and \quad \mathbf{deltazy} = \frac{dy}{-dz} \; .$$

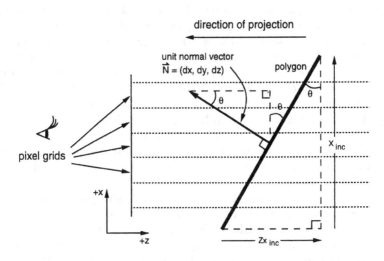

Fig. 1. Example of a perspective transformed polygon.

3.2 PixelBlock Memory

In order to reduce the frequency of calling the dynamic memory allocator provided by the compiler, which is usually not very efficient and tends to use up extra memory, we choose to pre-allocate a one dimensional array of **PixelBlock**'s in advance. Each **PixelBlock** in the array is made to point to the next, using one of the z's, to form a list of free **PixelBlock**'s. When there is a request, the first **PixelBlock** in the list is returned and is put back to the head of the list when it is no longer needed. If the list is empty, we may then request the system for a new **PixelBlock** array.

4 Results and Comparisons

In this section, we compare our method with three other scan-conversion methods, the z-buffer method, the supersampling method and the A-buffer method, in terms of memory usage, processing time, and accuracy of determining surface intersection.

4.1 Memory Usage

Figure 2 compares the memory usage of the four scan-conversion methods against the number of polygon edges appearing in a pixel. The sizes of the data structures used in the calculation are based on our implementation of the methods — they are the minimum memory sizes needed to implement the methods. Except for the z-buffer method, the subpixel resolution of all the methods are 4×4. Each pixel of the z-buffer requires 8 bytes. Each pixel of the A-buffer requires 12 bytes but each fragment created will need 24 bytes of memory. (This calculation includes 4 extra bytes to store the second depth value for surface intersection detection.) However, the first polygon edge encountered will cause two fragments to be created, one for the polygon edge and the other for the background. Each pixel of the adaptive supersampling buffer requires 12 bytes but each **PixelBlock** created will need 112 bytes of memory. The supersampling z-buffer method, on the other hand, will need 112 bytes of memory for every pixel of the image.

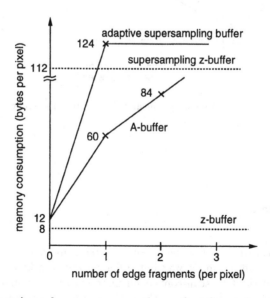

Fig. 2. Comparison of memory consumption against the number of edge fragments per pixel.

Figure 3 compares the memory usage of the four methods against the scene complexity. The size of the image used for the tests is 512×512 in resolution and the subpixel resolution is again 4×4. The scene complexity is proportional to both the total number of edge pixels and the total number of overlapping polygon edges in the image. The memory consumptions of the z-buffer method and the supersampling method are independent of the scene complexity. The memory consumption of the A-buffer method increases in a close to linear manner. Perviously, we mentioned that the maximum number of edge pixels for most of the complex images during the image generation process does not excess 20% of the total number of pixels. This is because as the scene complexity increases, more and more polygons tend to overlap each others. Hence, the memory consumption of our method will approach to a constant value as the complexity increases. This corresponds to a total memory size of 8.6M bytes.

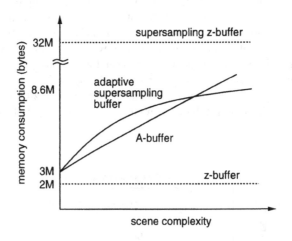

Fig. 3. Comparison of memory consumption against the scene complexity.

4.2 Performance

In our implementation of the four scan-conversion methods, all programs are written in C and in a similar way but differ only in the final scan-conversion parts. We tested the four scan-conversion methods with the image as shown in Figure 5. The following table shows the performance comparison of the methods and the results were taken on an SGI Indigo^2 machine with a 200MHz R4400 CPU. (The graphics accelerator in the machine was not used in the experiments.)

Rendering Methods	Times
Z-buffer method	1.74 sec.
Supersampling method	8.82 sec.
A-buffer method	2.05 sec.
Adaptive Supersampling method	1.96 sec.

From the results, the z-buffer method is obviously the fastest method of all. The supersampling method increases the rendering time dramatically. The new method has a slightly higher rendering time than the z-buffer method due to the extra computations in the edge pixels. However, it is interesting to see that the new method is also faster than the A-buffer method. After we have experienced with a few images with different complexity, we notice that when the scene complexity is low, the A-buffer method is faster and when the scene complexity is high, the new method becomes faster. The reason is that as the scene becomes more complex, more fragments will need to be processed in the A-buffer method and hence more floating-point operations will need to be executed to blend the colour values of the fragments, while in the new method, the number of edge pixels does not increase linearly with the increase in scene complexity and the merging of colour values within a **PixelBlock** involves only integer calculations.

In terms of memory consumption in rendering Figure 5, the A-buffer method uses a total of 87,075 fragments (equivalent to 2M bytes of memory) while the adaptive supersampling method uses a total of 22,081 **PixelBlock**'s (equivalent to 2.36M bytes of memory).

4.3   Handling of Surface Intersection

When surfaces intersect each other, we need to determine where they intersect in the subpixel level to prevent aliasing appearing along the line of intersection. In the supersampling method, the depth calculation and comparison are performed at each subpixel position. Hence, the surface intersection problem is solved automatically at the subpixel level. In the A-buffer method, the depth value is not available in subpixel level and an approximation method is suggested to detect the occurrence of surface intersection and to calculate where it happens. Two depth values representing the maximum and minimum depths of the fragment are stored for each polygon fragments. If two fragments overlap in depth, surface intersection is assumed to occur. The four depth values from the two fragments are then used to approximate the visibility of each of them. This method is problematic as has already been pointed out by Carpenter. One of the problems is that when two parallel surfaces are very close to each other and overlap each other in depth as shown in Figure 4, the A-buffer method will mistreat them as intersecting surfaces and blend them together. Although polygon B is not supposed to be visible but will appear as behind a somewhat semi-transparent polygon A. Similar to the supersampling method, our method can solve the surface intersection problem correctly in subpixel level.

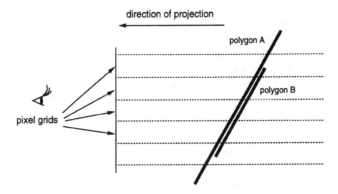

Fig. 4. Two parallel surfaces which are very close to each other.

5   Conclusion

In this paper, we have described a new buffer architecture for scan-conversion called the adaptive supersampling buffer. This method tries to make a compromise between the supersampling method, which is easy to implement in hardware and can solve the surface intersection problem correctly but demands for a lot of memory and computation time, and the A-buffer method, which uses less memory and demands for less computation time but is difficult to implement into hardware and cannot solve the surface intersection problem correctly.

References

1. Abram, G., Westover, L. and Whitted, T: "Efficient Alias-free Rendering Using Bit-masks and Look-up Tables". *Computer Graphics* **19**(3) (July 1985) 53–59.
2. Akeley, K., Jermoluk, T.: "High-Performance Polygon Rendering". *Computer Graphics* **22**(4) (Aug. 1988) 239–246.
3. Akeley, K.: "RealityEngine Graphics". *Computer Graphics* (Aug. 1993) 109–116.
4. Carpenter, L.: "The A-buffer, an Antialiased Hidden Surface Method". *Computer Graphics* **18**(3) (July 1984) 103–108.
5. Catmull, E.: *A Subdivision Algorithm for Computer Display of Curved Surfaces.* Ph.D. Dissertation, Computer Science Department, University of Utah (1974).
6. Catmull, E.: "A Hidden-Surface Algorithm with Anti-Aliasing". *Computer Graphics* **12**(3) (Aug. 1978) 6–11.
7. Crow, F.: "The Aliasing Problem in Computer-Generated Shaded Images". *Communication of the ACM* **20**(11) (Nov. 1977) 799–805.
8. Haeberli, P., Akeley, K.: "The Accumulation Buffer: Hardware Support for High-Quality Rendering". *Computer Graphics* **24**(4) (Aug. 1990) 309–318.
9. Kelley, M., Winner, S., Gould, K.: "A Scalable Hardware Render Accelerator using a Modified Scanline Algorithm". *Computer Graphics* **26**(2) (July 1992) 241–248.

10. Lau, W., Wiseman, N.: "Accurate Image Generation and Interactive Image Editing with the A-buffer". *Conference Proceedings of EuroGraphics '92* **II**(3) (Sept. 1992) 279–288.
11. Molnar, S., Eyles, J., Poulton, J.: "PixelFlow: High-Speed Rendering Using Image Composition". *Computer Graphics* **26**(2) (July 1992) 231–340.
12. Nakamae, E., Ishizaki, T., Nishita, T., Takita, S.: "Compositing 3D Images with Anti-aliasing and Various Shading Effects". *IEEE Computer Graphics & Applications* (Mar. 1989) 21–29.
13. Schilling, A., Straßer, W.: "EXACT: Algorithm and hardware Architecture for an Improved A-Buffer". *Computer Graphics* (Aug. 1993) 85–91.
14. Whitted, T., Weimer, D.: "A Software Test-Bed for the Development of 3-D Raster Graphics Systems". *Computer Graphics* **15**(3) (Aug. 1981) 271–277.

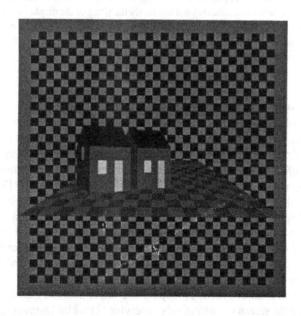

Fig. 5. Image generated using the adaptive supersampling method.

Dynamic Memory Mapping for Window Based Display System

C M Ng
Department of Computing,
The Hong Kong Polytechnic Univeristy, Hung Hom, Hong Kong.

Abstract. The use of a frame buffer that reads the memories in the left-to-right, top-to-bottom raster scan sequence dictates that the frame buffer must contain a pixel-to-pixel map of the whole display image. This is not an efficient or convenient manner to store raster images and update the display screen. A different approach to raster scan image generation is the use of a *dynamic memory mapping* mechanism to fetch the images directly from the various areas of the frame buffer to the display device during the active display time. This paper presents a data structure that is used to specify the tiling of the display screen, and the algorithms used to process the display description list in real time with no inherent limitation on the number of window boundaries per scan line that can be accommodated.

Introduction

The evolution of raster display devices can be described in terms of two general types of architectures. The most common type is *frame buffer display system* [1], in which the display surface reflects the contents of a single contiguous section of graphics memory - the *frame buffer*. A different approach to raster scan image generation is dynamic memory mapping. The origins of this trend can be traced to the *ALTO* [2], which was one of the first displays to include a facility for dynamic mapping, albeit as a means of conserving display memory in text processing applications. Documents were subdivided into smaller bit-maps to eliminate the storage of the white space between paragraphs and in margins. As such, ALTO employed only a limited form of dynamic mapping: each scan line could display the contents of one bit-map and only at pixel boundaries which were divisible by 16.

A different form of dynamic mapping was implemented by the *DEC VT-30* [3] display in which the screen was effectively subdivided into 8 by 8 arrays of pixels (cells), each of which could be set to one of 128 pre-determined patterns. The *VT-80* [4] which was designed and implemented at Independent Television News (ITN) is an outgrowth of the VT-30. The VT-80 picture element is a cell which may range in size from a single pixel to the entire screen. Effectively, each cell represents a one-bit deep pixel pattern which may be set to one of 512 user-defined colours and to one of eight levels of priority. The location of each cell is specified in a doubly buffered display (list) memory which maintains a vertically sorted file of cell specifications. The location of a cell is altered by changing its display specification.

The *Rainbow Display* [5] is an experimental device built to evaluate a method of supporting windows by dynamically mapping memory to video. The *Intel 82786 Graphics Coprocessor* [6,7] implements dynamic mapping in a form which is quite similar to the Rainbow band structure. In both the Rainbow Display and the Intel 82786 all the context information describing the viewport and window structure is stored and processed centrally. This limits the number of boundaries per scanline to the number that can be processed by the display controller. (The limit is 10 for the Rainbow display and 16 for the Intel 82786).

The *Distributed Window-Based Graphics Frame Store* approach [8] is based on a pipelined linear array of common elements called microframe store. The parameters defining the windows and viewports are stored and processed within the individual microframe stores, allowing a distributed approach to be used for the generation of screen images.

The performance of many new multiple frame buffer graphics systems, such as the IBM GXT150L [9] and the Denali graphics subsystem from Kubota [10], can be enhanced by using dynamic memory mapping. With such approach, the partial images stored in the multiple frame buffers can be displayed in the right order without using a refresh buffer that requires tremendous data movement.

The rest of this paper presents a data structure (the *Band Structure*) that is used to specify the tiling of the display surface, and the algorithms used by a processor (the *Display List Processor - DLP*) to process this display list.

The Band Structure

The virtual display map is subdivided into a band structure. Bands can contain blank spaces, corresponding to non-output of pixel data. The virtual space is very large (4096 by 4096 in the evaluation of the system), and only part of it (corresponding to the visible screen) will be mapped to the display screen at a time.

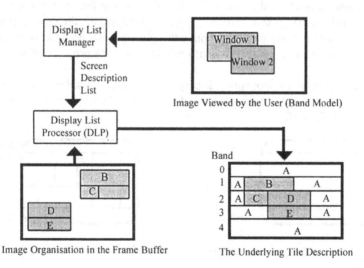

Figure 1 *Dynamic Memory Mapping*
   (e.g: Memory Mapping Mechanism for a Display with Two Overlapping Windows)

The display list is generated by the display list manager but stored in the double buffered description list of the DLP. As both the list computation and data transfer between the lists divert the list manager from other activities, it is crucial to perform this operations in the minimum time possible and to minimise the size of the list. The resolution of both problems lies in the horizontal subdivision of the display screen into bands which contain horizontally adjacent pixels from groups of images that have the same horizontal position in the screen. The information contained in each band is then used for the generation of the display list. A tile representation of a screen with two windows is shown in figure 1.

In figure 1, tiles labelled A represent the background area, and may be of an arbitrary pattern. Data need not be fetched from the frame buffer for these tiles, since the background pattern is stored in a register in the display processor. The areas of tiles B and C map the visible portion of window 1. The display processor fetches data for these tiles from the frame buffer region. Tiles D and E represent the visible portion of window 2. As an example, consider the composition of the first (uppermost) scan line in band 2. This band consists of 4 tiles; labelled A, C, D and A. The corresponding action for the display processor is to generate the background pattern for the area corresponding to tile A; then to read from the frame buffer, at the appropriate place, image data for tiles C and D; and finally to output the background pattern for the remainder of the scan line. If the user puts window 1 on top, the variables specifying the width of tile C, the frame buffer starting address and the width of tile D will be changed, so instructing the display processor to fetch more data for tile C and less for tile D.

Bands

The use of bands arises from the observation that adjacent scan lines on the screen often contain vertical adjacent pixels from the group of images having the same horizontal position in the screen. With the application of this principle, it is possible to divide the screen horizontally into a number of bands within which this property of adjacency holds.

As an example, a screen which displays only the background colour contains a single band. The addition of a first image and then a second one generate the bands as shown in figures 2 and 3.

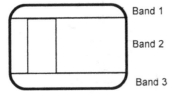

Fig.2 A single image induces three bands   *Fig. 3 Two images induce five bands*

Band specification

The display list is a vertically ordered list of band specifications, corresponding to each band on the virtual display map. Each band specification (Figure 4) contains a band header and the tile specifications.

In order to reduce the time required by the DLP to fetch data from the display list, the data bus between the DLP and the list is 64-bit wide. Therefore, a band header or a tile specification can be retrieved by a single list memory access. The Header stores the height of the band (*BandHeight*) in scan lines and the number of rectangular image portions across the band (*NoofTile*). The *TopY* and *BottomY* are the vertical positions of the top and bottom of the band. These vertical positions can be determined by accumulating the height of the bands above the current one, therefore can be omitted from the header. However, with the provision of these values, the display processor is able to make a rapid determination of which band is currently to be displayed.

	64-bit			
BandHeight	NoofTile	TopY	BottomY	◄— Band Header
XOffset	RowAddr	ColAddr	Width	
XOffset	RowAddr	ColAddr	Width	Description
XOffset	RowAddr	ColAddr	Width	of three tiles
...	...	...	...	

Figure 4 The Band Specification

For each tile in the band, the *XOffset* refers to the X (horizontal) position of the tile in the virtual display space and may be offset to account for placement of the screen anywhere over the virtual space; *RowAddr*, *ColAddr* refer to the physical location (Row address and Column address) of the tile in the frame buffer; the *width* is the horizontal dimension of the tile in pixels, which is used to determine how many pixels should be shifted out from the frame buffer.

Display List Generation

The display viewport is a rectangular portion of the virtual display map corresponging to the display screen, the position of this viewport in the virtual map is specified by the registers *ScreenX* and *ScreenY*. There are two strategies to generate the display list. In the first approach, the two display viewport position registers are stored locally in the display list processor (DLP). Display list update will generate a new display list for the entire band model, and the DLP will process viewport clipping in real time. The second approach performs viewport clipping during display list generation by storing the ScreenX and ScreenY registers within the display list manager, hence the display list contains only those bands and tiles within the display viewport.

The first approach provides a more straightforward way for display list generation. However, the cost of the DLP will be increased as extra hardware circuitry are required to clip the bands and tiles. Moreover, this approach induces two limitations on the system: (i) the number of bands above and (ii) the number of tiles on the left of the display viewport. The DLP needs to find the first tile for the next scan line within the horizontal blanking period and it requires two clock cycles to determine whether a tile is within the display viewport. With a 50 nanoseconds clock cycle, only 118 tiles can be processed within the 11.841 microseconds horizontal blanking period. If there are more than 118 tiles on the left of the display viewport in any display scan line, then the DLP will not able to complete the clipping during the non-active blanking period, and may not be able to control the frame buffer to output the required pixel data for that scan line.

In the second approach, the bands and tiles are clipped against the four boundaries of the display viewport by the display list manager during the display list generation process. This approach is more efficient if a large number of bands are above or below the viewport, or a small number of tiles exist within the viewport. If a band is above the top of the viewport, the whole band will be discarded, and once a band containing the last scan line of the viewport has been found, all bands below do not need to be processed. Similarly, the tiles that are totally outside either the left or the right boundary can also be ignored. The major drawback of this approach is the requirement to regenerate the display list when panning and scrolling the display content. Panning and scrolling can simply be performed by changing the mapping of the display viewport to virtual display without affecting the band model. Therefore, in the first approach, the new viewport position can be downloaded to the DLP registers, and these new viewport boundaries are used to clip the bands and tiles in real time, and avoiding the regeneration of a new display list.

The display list manager, using an Intel i960 processor [11] run at 40MHz with a 64-bit external data bus, allows a band or tile specification of the display list to be generated from the band model within an average of 10 processor cycles of 25 nanoseconds. In a single active interlacing display frame period (0.04 second), 160,000 such specifications can be generated. This number is adequate for most application, since it supports very fine images (2 pixels by 3 pixels) of a 1024 by 1024 display resolution, or up to 2048 by 2048 for an average image size of 4*6 pixels. Any changes to the band model or the position of the display viewport with bands and tiles less than 160,000 can be displayed in the next frame. A higher number will cause a delay in display list generation, and hence delay the display of the required output.

The display management system of the design proposed adopts a combination of these two approaches. It has the advantage of efficient display list generation from the first approach and the advantage of efficient panning and scrolling of the display viewport without the regeneration of the display list offered by the second approach.

During the display list generation process, the size of the display viewport is extended by 50% in all four directions. The band and tile specifications of the band model will clip against these extended viewport boundaries. Therefore, the display list manager need not process the entire band model, and hence the display list generation is more efficient. Since the boundaries of the viewport are extended during the display list generation process, the list generated will not only contain details of the viewport, but also contain the bands and tiles that are around the viewport. Panning and scrolling of the viewport can then be performed by modifying the value of the registers that are specifying the viewport position. The new underlying tile description of the display viewport can be obtained by clipping the specifications of the bands and tiles contained in the display list against the new viewport position in real time. This approach eliminates the need for the regeneration of the display list for panning and scrolling the content of the viewport except when the movement is greater than the extended size.

Generation of the display list starts with the top band in the band model, compares the base scan line number (BottomY) of the band with the top scan line number (ScreenY) of the display viewport, and skips those bands that are totally above the viewport. The viewport is usually only contained in a portion of the full band height of the first band (band 1 in Figure 5). The gap between the first scan line of the band and the top of the viewport is subtracted to form the new height of the clipped band. This gap is also used as an offset to the frame buffer starting row address of the tiles, so that the tiles can start from the clipped vertical location. If the top of the band coincides with the top of the viewport, this algorithm still applies, since the gap will become zero, the band height and the starting row address remain unchanged.

The process continues to generate the display list elements for all bands which would be completely covered by the display viewport (bands 2 and 3). Finally, if the bottom of the viewport is not aligned with the last scan line of a band (band 4), the height of the band in the display list will be set to the height of the viewport contained in the band. The tile elements of each band are generated by clipping the tiles of the band with the left and right boundaries of the viewport. The process starts with the first tile in the band, skips those tiles that are totally on the left of the viewport (tiles 2.1, 3.1), and adjusts the width of the tile clipped by the left boundary (tiles 2.2, 3.2, 4.1).

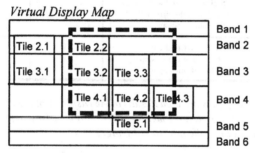

Figure 5   *Virtual Display Map to Viewport Mapping*
(the dotted rectangle is the display viewport)

Performance Evaluation

One way to evaluate the performance of a system is to test the system with different parameters, and apply the same set of parameters to test another system that uses an alternative approach. The results of the tests can then be compared to evaluate the performance of the two systems.

In the evaluation of the performance of the Windowing System that uses dynamic memory mapping techniques, the system used for comparison is one with a traditional display approach - a frame buffer display system. As the aim of this test is to compare the display update performance of the two different display technologies, all images are stored in the local frame buffers before the start of the test.

Five tests were applied to both systems:

Case 1: move a window of 50% of the display screen size to a new position on the screen.

Case 2: display two full screen size transparent windows.
i.e. one window is totally overlapping the other window

Case 3: display four full screen size transparent windows.

Case 4: add a full screen wide window with different height to a display containing a huge number of very small windows.

Case 5: add a full screen tall window with different width to a display containing a huge number of very small windows.

	Display Delay (no. of frames):	
	Refresh Frame Buffer System *	Dynamic Memory Mapping System
Move a half screen size window	2	1
Display two full screen size transparent windows	7	1
Display four full screen size transparent windows	16	1
Add a full screen wide window to a display filled with small windows (Both the additional window and the originally displayed windows are stored in the same bit-map)	1-2	2
Add a full screen wide window to a display filled with small windows (Both the additional window and the originally displayed windows are stored in different bit-maps)	1-2	1
Add a full screen tall window to a display filled with small windows (Both the additional window and the originally displayed windows are stored in the same bit-map)	1-2	1
Add a full screen tall window to a display filled with small windows (The additional window and the originally displayed windows are stored in different bit-maps)	1-2	1

Figure 6   *Summary of the Simulated Results of the Display Update Performance (* The display delay times of the last four cases depend on the height/width of the additional image)*

Figure 6 summarises the display update performance of the Dynamic Memory Mapping System. It can be noticed that except in the extreme case (adding a full screen tall window to a display which is currently displaying a huge number of small windows), the required display can always be output in the next display frame after a display update command is sent to the Display List Manager (DLM). Even for the exceptional case, if the new additional window is not stored together with the other displayed windows in the same bit-map, or the window is copied to another bit-map, then, instead of modifying the complicated display list of the original display, the DLM will generate a new display list which will contain the new window only. The display list processors of the two frame buffer, one responsible for the output of the original display, one for the new window will process the two display lists in parallel, and the required display can also be output in the next display frame.

Conclusion

The traditional approach to frame buffer display, to store the display image in a single contiguous section of graphics memory, is not an efficient or convenient manner to store raster images and update the display screen. A new approach to raster scan image generation is the use of a dynamic memory mapping to organise information on the display. With this approach, the windows are stored in separate and contiguous areas of the graphics memory. On screen, the window format is broken down into a series of horizontal strips (*bands*), each containing a number of rectangular areas (*tiles*).

The tiling description of the display screen (*the band model*) is updated by the Display List Manager, and the updated display list is then downloaded to the Display List Processor. As the tiles are defined by a set of pointers, operations such as panning and scrolling images within a window, or even resizing and moving the window about the screen can be performed simply by manipulating these pointers. Since the windows are read directly from the frame buffer, the changes are always presented to the user in a single frame time without any delay.

This paper has presented the structure of the band model and discussed the display list generation of a hardware supported window display system. The system is capable of supporting real time window display with the following features:

- Each window is independently controlled.
- Each window can have a different number of bits per pixel.
e.g. 1 bit per pixel for a text window, 32 bits per pixel for a full colour image window.
- Real-time dragging of window.
- Real-time roaming of viewport.
- Real-time scrolling and panning of image data within a window.
- Memory and system bandwidth need not be wasted for background areas of the screen.
- Individual window zooming can be achieved by pixel replication.
- Windows may occlude, be superimposed with other windows.
- Output may be merged with an external video source for multi-media applications.

References

1. Newman W., Sproull R. (1973), *Principle of Interactive Computer Graphics*, second edition, McGraw-Hill, New York, 1979.
2. Thacker E., McCreight E., Lampson B., Sproull R., Boggs R., "Alto: A Personal Computer", in Siewiorek O., Bell G. and Newell A. *Computer Structure: Readings and Example*, McGraw-Hill, New York, second edition, 1981.
3. McKee P., Long C., Corbyn T., "VT80: ITN's new Computer Graphics Generator", *Television: the Journal of the Royal Television Society*, January/February 1981, pp. 21-23.
4. Corbyn T.E. (1984), "VT80: ITN's Advanced graphics Generator", *Television: Journal of the Royal Television Society*, January/February 1984, pp. 14-16.
5. Nicholls B. (1987), "Inside the 82786 Graphics Chip", *BYTE*, Aug. 1987, pp. 135-41.
6. Wilkes A.J., Singer D.W., Gibbons J.J., King T.R., Robinson P., Wiseman and N.E. (1984), "The Rainbow Workstation", *The Computer Journal*, **27(2)**, 1984, pp. 112-120.
7. Shires G. (1986), "A New VLSI Graphics Coprocessor - The Intel 82786", *IEEE CG & A*, October 1986, pp. 99-105.
8. Westmore R.J. (1988), "A Window-Based Graphics Frame Store Architecture", *ACM Transaction on Graphics*, **7(4)**, October 1988, pp. 233-248.
9. Machover C., Dill J. (1994), "IBM Graphics Acceleration Speed RISC System 6000s", *IEEE Computer Graphics and Applications*, **14(5)**, Sept. 1994. pp. 90.
10. Burksy D. (1994), "Acceleration Puts The SNAP Inti Graphics", *Electronic Design*, July 1994, pp. 55-74.
11. Intel (1989), *i960 Embedded Processor Product Overview*, Intel Corporation, 1989.

Convert Non-Convex Meshes to Convex Meshes for Depth Sorting in Volume Rendering

Yong Zhou   Zesheng Tang

Department of Computer Science and Technology
Tsinghua University, Beijing 100084, P. R. China
Email:dcstzs@tsinghua.edu.cn

Abstract. Irregular mesh depth sorting plays an important role for volume rendering in scientific visualization. In recent years, some algorithms have been proposed for the depth sorting of irregular convex meshes, but less attention has been devoted to the depth sorting of non-convex meshes. In this paper, two different approaches for converting non-convex meshes into convex meshes are proposed. The first one is to fill original meshes with a set of tetrahedra on the exterior boundaries of meshes. The second one is to take the plane of exterior faces of meshes to divide the space until each subspace includes only one acyclic convex submesh. The subdivision process is represented by a binary tree, Binary Mesh Partitioning tree (BMP tree). Theoretical analysis and experimental results are shown.

1. Introduction

In volume rendering for scientific visualization, in order to show the different substances distributions within an image, we must detect the front-back relation, namely light accumulation order, of substances projected onto the screen pixels. Volume rendering for irregular meshes can be classified into three main categories: Ray Casting, Mesh Scanning and Polyhedra Depth Sorting. Ray Casting scheme collects intensities along rays shooting from a viewpoint and passing through the pixels. It resorts to calculating intersection of meshes with rays[2,4,9]. Mesh Scanning scheme utilizes successfully traditional scan techniques to sort segments generated by scanning [3,10]. These two methods possess high precision, but huge computation cost is required.

In recent years, some work has been done in polyhedra depth sorting with directed graph searching [5,12]. Before rendering, sorting all the polyhedra within meshes, then collect light intensity in front to back or back to front order. The space coherence of meshes is exploited, the computation time is linear. But these methods are only appropriate for convex meshes. P. L. Williams introduced an approximate approach to any non-convex meshes [11]. Unfortunately, the method is not apt to boundaries anomalies. The theoretical alternatives suggested by him is to triangulate the meshes by Delaunay Triangulation algorithm. For researchers on graphics rather than computational geometry, this is not a straightforward work [1]. Furthermore, the boundary and interior faces of new triangulation will not be

---

* This project is supported by the National Natural Science Foundation of China

the same as the original meshes. This results in difficulty in setting up adjacent relations of meshes. A BSP tree [8] can be used to order polyhedra in meshes, regardless of whether the meshes are non-convex or acyclic. This can be done by using each shared face as a splitting plane to generate the BSP tree. But for meshes filled fully by polyhedra, a large amount of polyhedra could be split, resulting in an overwhelming memory requirement. Paterson and Yao [6] pointed out that the performance of the BSP tree could be $O(f^2)$, where f is the number of faces in original mesh.

Up to now, less attention has been devoted to two problems: (1) convert non-convex meshes into convex meshes without destroying original primitive topological adjacent relations and (2) discuss the real feasibility for using BSP tree in meshes sorting.

In this paper, two different approaches for non-convex meshes depth sorting are proposed. Their common purpose is to convert non-convex meshes into convex meshes. The first one is to fill original meshes with a set of tetrahedra on the boundary of the meshes. Filling process maintains invariance of the number of exterior faces and edges and the sequence of the generated exterior boundaries in meshes is convergent to their convex hull. The second one is to take the planes of exterior faces of meshes to divide the space until each subspace includes only one acyclic convex submesh. The subdivision process is represented by a binary tree, namely Binary Mesh Partitioning tree (BMP tree). The result of mesh partitioning is that the leaf nodes of BMP tree correspond to acyclic convex submeshes. The node number of the BMP tree is not more than the number of dihedral angles of less than 180 degrees, formed by the arbitrary adjacent exterior faces in meshes. The storage requirement is acceptable. The first method is called Tetrahedra Mesh Filling method (TMF method) and the second one is called Binary Mesh Partitioning method (BMP method).

This paper is arranged as follows. Section 2 introduces the basic concepts and several properties. Section 3 presents the principles and the implementation of TMF method in detail. Section 4 describes the partitioning process of BMP method. Finally, the experiment results and conclusions are shown in section 5..

2 Preliminary Definitions and Basic Properties

For convenience, several concepts are introduced. A *mesh* is a finite set S of polyhedra (or element), where (1) each polyhedron is convex; and (2) the intersection of any two polyhedra is either empty or a face, edge or vertex of each. Two meshes are disconnected if they do not share any face (Fig. 1). If a face **f** of some element in a mesh S is not shared by any other element in S, then **f** is an *exterior face*. Before sorting, we initialize normals of exterior faces toward outside. The union of all exterior faces of S constitutes the boundary of S. A face that is not an exterior face is an *interior face*. An *exterior polyhedron* has at least one exterior face. The *convex hull* of a mesh S is the smallest convex set containing the polyhedra of S. If the boundary of a mesh S is also that of convex hull of S, S is called a *convex mesh*; otherwise it is called a *non convex mesh*.

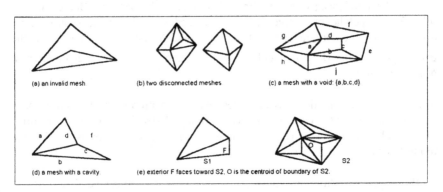

Figure 1

Let S be a non-convex mesh. A polyhedron p, not necessarily convex, which is not a member of S, such that each face of p is shared by some polyhedra in S, is called a *void*. If p is convex, then we call it a *convex void*. A non-convex mesh may have zero or more voids. The union of all face of a void is referred to as the *void boundary*. The union of all faces in the boundary of S that are not faces of a void is the *exterior boundary* of S. The region between the exterior boundary of the non-convex mesh S and its convex hull is referred to as a *cavity*. In fact, all these definitions have been given in [11]. Further, given two disconnected meshes S_1 and S_2, and an exterior face f of S_1. The centroid of exterior boundary of S_2 is denoted by O, if the normal of f and the vector from the center of f to point O makes an angle of less than 90 degrees, then f is called facing toward mesh S_2 (Fig. 1).

In addition, for a given viewpoint VP and two regions V_1 and V_2 in a mesh, if any point belonging to V_1 does not occlude any point belonging to V_2, we call that region V_2 possesses higher visibility priority than region V_1 or region V_1 can not occlude region V_2. For a polyhedron p of mesh S, the number of polyhedra within S occluding and sharing a common face with polyhedron p is referred to as *incident degree* of p. A plane divides the whole 3D space into two parts, the part including viewpoint VP is called *positive half space*. In the following, if no special description, we only discuss acyclic meshes.

On the basis of these concepts, there exist the following three properties.

Property 1: *A set of faces which encompass a region divide the 3D space into two parts. The part which is the intersection of all positive half spaces of the faces has higher visibility priority than the another one..*

Property 2: *Given a viewpoint VP and a mesh.. If the mesh is convex and connected, the polyhedra with incident degree of zero are not occluded by any other polyhedra. But, for a non-convex mesh, it is not true.*
A 2d example is shown in Fig.2(a), triangle EGH with incident degree of zero is not occluded by triangle DCE, because the polyhedra is not convex.

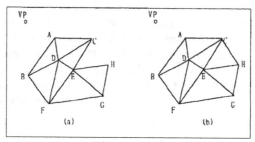

Figure 2

Property 3: *With respect to a given viewpoint, for two arbitrary polyhedra in a convex connected acyclic mesh, if one hides another, then there is a sequence of pairwise adjacent cells connecting them and each polyhedron is in front of the next sharing a common face.*

Properties 2 and 3 actually give a theory and implementation process of convex mesh sorting. The details have been given in [12]. For non-convex mesh, it must be converted to convex one before depth sorting.

3 Tetrahedra Mesh Filling Method

The TMF method is based on the assumption that the mesh is acyclic, connected and the exterior faces are all triangle patches. Because our volume rendering algorithm is based on the construction of iso-surfaces within tetrahedra, the original data cubes have been subdivided into tetrahedra before depth sorting.

3.1 Principle for Filling Meshes

The filling principle is very straightforward and intuitive. If two exterior faces P_1AB and P_2AB share an edge AB, and these two faces form a dihedral angle of less than 180 degrees, it is called a V-form dent of triangle (V-dot), denoted by P_1-AB-P_2. P_1 and p_2 are called a vertex pair. In the boundary of a mesh, V-dots and their edges set up a one to one relation. Here, the normals of exterior faces are taken pointing toward outside. Obviously, if a mesh does not exist any V-dots, it is a convex mesh. Our purpose is to fill all these V-dots.

For this, the boundary of meshes is detected. Once a V-dot, for example, P_1-AB-P_2, is found, it will be processed as follows. The vertex pair P_1 and P_1 are connected and two new exterior faces P_1P_2A and P_1P_2B are generated. Meanwhile, the original two exterior faces ABP_1 and ABP_2 now become interior faces and a new tetrahedron P_1P_2AB is formed. The original V-dot disappears.

The filling process does not increase the number of vertices, exterior faces as well as the edges formed by two adjacent exterior faces. Meanwhile, it could cause new V-dots. But as the filling process continues, the boundary of the mesh will gradually approach the convex hull of the mesh. Suppose the difference between the volume of the convex hull and the mesh itself after filling with tetrahedra for i times is D_i, then the sequence $\{ D_i \}$ decreases monotonously and will be convergent to zero.

Although the tetrahedra filling strategy is straightforward, its implementation is not easy. Not all the V-dots can be filled directly by connecting corresponding vertex pairs. Actually, if the newly generated tetrahedron intersect other tetrahedra of meshes, the filling process fails. Fig.3 is a typical example.

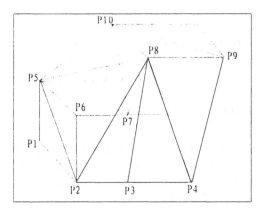

Figure 3. V-dot P_2-P_7P_8-P_5 can not be filled, for tetrahedra $P_2P_5P_8P_7$ intersects existing tetrahedron $P_2P_5P_7P_6$.

The key step for filling tetrahedra meshes is to examine efficiently whether the newly generated tetrahedra intersects other ones. This work can be simplified to judge whether the connecting segment of vertex pair intersects other tetrahedra. For this, we first analyze various geometric configurations of V-dot P_1-AB-P_2. Denote the plane passing through points P_1, P_2 and perpendicular to segment AB by β. The V-dot can be classified into three cases according to the locations of points A and B related to plane β:

(a) Points A and B lie on the different sides of plane β, respectively (Fig.4(a))

(b) A and B lie on the same side of β, the distance of A to plane β is farther than that of B to β. (Fig.4(b))

(c) A and B lie on the same side of β, the distance of B to plane β is farther than that of A to β. (Fig.4(c))

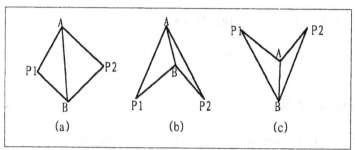

(a)   (b)   (c)

Figure 4 Various cases of V-dots.

According to the geometric configurations of V-dots, the connecting segment does not intersect any tetrahedra in case (a). For case (b), connecting segment P_1P_2 could only intersect the tetrahedra with exterior faces in which B is a vertex, while for case (c), P_1P_2 could only intersect the tetrahedra with exterior faces in which A is a vertex. Once a candidate has been found, it must be tested whether the segment P_1P_2 really intersects the candidate. If the segment indeed intersects a face of the candidate, this V-dot cannot be filled with a tetrahedron. If all the possible tetrahedra do not intersect the segment, the V-dot can be filled.

3.2 Implementation of Filling Process

In order to ensure smoothness of filling process and record the mutual adjacent relation of elements, the data structure is designed as in Fig. 5

Since the filling manipulation always occur in the boundary of meshes, here the edge structures only record the properties of edges generated by intersection of two exterior faces. Besides, it also records the codes of two exterior faces, and a flag indicating whether corresponding V-dot can be filled. Each exterior face corresponds to a exterior face structures, which also record the normals of related faces. Tetrahedron structures also keep their incident degrees and marks describing whether the tetrahedron are original or newly generated.

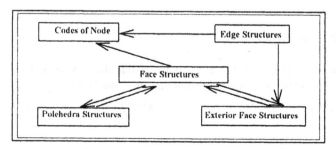

Figure 5. Mutual adjacent relations of vertices, edges, faces and polyhedra.

The implementation process begins with scanning edge structures. If a V-dot P_1-AB-P_2 is found, and it has been confirmed that the corresponding line segment P_1P_2 does not intersect any existing tetrahedra, the vertices P_1 and P_2 are connected, meanwhile the corresponding data strictures are set up and modified.

4. Binary Mesh Partitioning Method

If the assumptions of the TMF method can not be met, the following BMP method can be used.

4.1 Subdivision of Meshes

As well known, it is impractical to resort to a BSP tree for mesh depth sorting entirely. A reasonable suggestion is to combine traditional convex mesh sorting techniques with a BSP tree. This means that the arbitrary irregular meshes are first subdivided into a set of convex submeshes, this process is represented with a BSP tree. Each node corresponds to one or more submeshes. Once a node corresponds to only one convex submesh, subdivision process stops. Then the conventional methods are exploited to sort polyhedra in the new generated convex submeshes. For acyclic meshes, there exist following four cases:

1. meshes of interest consist of several disconnected meshes.
2. meshes of interest consist of a single mesh with voids.
3. meshes of interest consist of a single mesh with cavities, or
4. a convex mesh.

If the exterior boundaries of meshes consist of several disconnected sets of exterior faces, case 1 happens. If there exist more than one disconnected boundaries in one mesh, it must includes voids, *i.e.*, case 2 occurs. If an exterior face and another adjoining exterior face make a dihedral angle of less than 180 degrees, there exists a cavity in the mesh.

Cases 1, 2, and 3 are not convex meshes, they should be converted into a set of convex meshes, respectively. In the BMP method, it is implemented by partitioning all the non-convex meshes into convex submeshes, This process is represented with a BSP tree.

4.2 Selection of Partitioning Planes

The algorithm begins with case 1. Once it is detected that the meshes under consideration consist of several disconnected submeshes, denoted by S_1, S_2, ..., S_m, it should be tested whether one or more submeshes among them are separable from the others along some coordinate axis. If so, the separating plane is taken as a partitioning plane. In this time, it is not necessary to perform partitioning process, but corresponding BMP tree must be set up. Then its left and right subtrees. are processed continuously. If these meshes are not separable along any coordinate axis, select one of the exterior faces as the partitioning plane.

For Case 2, if the void is convex polyhedron, the only thing need to do is to mark it as an imaginary polyhedron, only taking part in depth sorting and not contributing intensity to the final image. If the void is non-convex, it is processed as in case 3. Meanwhile, when the non- convex void is divided into convex subvoids, each subvoid also be regarded as imaginary polyhedra.

As to case 3, it is a common situation. The algorithm only needs to traverse exterior boundaries of the mesh, if two adjacent exterior boundary faces which share an edge make a dihedral angle of less than 180 degrees, there exist a cavity. One of the two faces is taken as partitioning plane to subdivide the corresponding mesh and the related node of BMP tree is set up.. This process continues until all the cavities have been cut. In order to avoid repeating test, the partitioning planes picked should not coincide with the existing ones.

When meshes corresponding to all the leaf nodes of the tree have been changed into convex submeshes, a traversal of the tree starts from the root node and results in a convex submesh depth sorting. Each time a leaf node is met, i.e., case 4 occurs, the traditional convex mesh depth sorting techniques are used to sort polyhedra within each submesh Note that above discussion supposes meshes are acyclic. If a mesh with cycles has been detected, a plane is selected to partition the mesh.

5. Experimental Results and Conclusions

The test data is a finite element result for analysis of temperature over a 200 MW nuclear reactor in Nuclear Energy Institute, Tsinghua University. Here, we only list some experiment results generated by TMF method. Table 1 lists the numbers of tetrahedra and triangles included in Plate 1 to 4 before and after the filling process respectively. Plate 1 and 2 are wireframs, Plate 3 and 4 are the result generated by volume rendering, covered by exterior boundary before and after filling tetrahedra.

Table 1

Before Filling Plate (Tetrahedra, Triangles)	After Filling Plate (Tetrahedra, Triangles)
Plate 1 (40, 594)	Plate 2 (95, 673)
Plate 3 (5000, 10862)	Plate 4 (5965, 12555)

Irregular mesh depth sorting is a bottleneck of volume rendering for meshes. In this paper, we have presented two feasible solutions to convert non-convex meshes to convex meshes: Tetrahedra Meshes Filling method and Binary Mesh Partitioning method. In TMF method, all the manipulations and the modifications of data structure occur on the exterior boundary of meshes. The computation expenses is less than BMP method. But TMF method can not be user to process disconnected and cyclic meshes. Therefore, these two methods can be combined together. BMP method can be used to partition any irregular non-convex meshes at first. If all the nodes of BMP tree are corresponding to the cyclic and connected submeshes, the partition can be stopped and move to the TMF method. After conversion, the depth sorting algorithms for irregular convex meshes can be used for depth sorting

6. References

1) A. M. Day, "The Implementation of An Algorithm to Find the Convex Hull of a Set of 3D Points", ACM Trans. on Graphics, Vol. 9, No. 1, Jan. 1990, pp.105-132.

2) T. Fruhauf, " Raycasting of Nonregularly Structured Volume Data", Computer Graphics Forum (Eurographics'94), Vol. 13, No. 3, 1994.

3) C. Giertsen, "Volume Visualization of Sparse Irregular Meshes," IEEE CG&A, Vol. 12, No. 2, March 1992, pp.40-48.

4) M. Garrity, " Raytracing Irregular Volume Data", Computer Graphics, Vol. 24, No. 5, 1990.

5) N. Max, P. Hanrahan, and R. Crawfis, "Area and Volume Coherence for Efficient Visualization of 3D Scalar Functions," Computer Graphics, Vol. 24, No.5, Nov.1990, pp.27-33.

6) M. S. Paterson and F. F. Yao, "Binary Partitions with Application to Hidden-Surface Removal and Solid Modeling", In Proc. 5th Annual Symposium on Computational Geometry, June 1989, pp.23-32.

7) P. Speray and S. Kennon, "Volume Probe: Interactive Data Exploration on Arbitrary Grids", Computer Graphics, Vol. 24, No. 5, 1990, pp.5-12.

8) W. C. Thibault and B. F. Naylor, "Set Operations on Polyhedra Using Binary Space Partitioning Trees", Computer Graphics, Vol.21, No.4 July 1987, pp.153-162.

9) B. Tabatabai, E. A. Sessarego, and H. F. Mayer, " Volume Rendering on Non-regular Grids", Computer Graphics Forum (Eurographics'94), Vol. 13, No. 3, 1994.

10) J. Wilhelms and A.V. Gelder, "A Coherent Projection Approach to Direct Volume Rendering", Computer Graphics , Vol. 25, No.4, July 1991, pp. 275-284.

11) P. L. Williams, "Visibility Ordering Meshed Polyhedra", ACM Transaction on Graphics, Vol. 11, No. 2, April 1992, pp.103-126.

12) Yong Zhou and Zesheng Tang, "Constructing Isosurfaces in 3D Data Sets Taking Account of Polyhedra Depth Sorting", Journal of Computer Science and Technology, Vol.9, No. 2, April 1994.

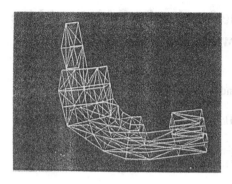

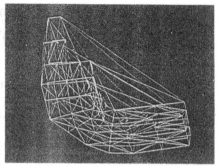

Plate 1

Plate 2

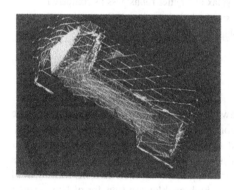

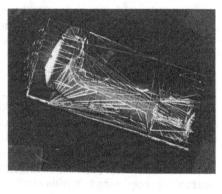

Plate 3

Plate 4

A New Chain Coding Scheme for Cursive Script and Line Drawings

H. Yuen [1] and L. Hanzo [2]

[1] Department of Electronic Engineering, The Hong Kong Polytechnic University, Hong Kong

[2] Department of Electronics and Computer Science, University of Southampton, Southampton, SO17 1BJ, U.K.

Abstract. A new chain coding scheme, called DM-like differential chain coding (DM-DCC) is proposed in this paper for coding, storage and transmission of cursive script and line drawings. Analogous to the traditional delta modulation (DM) for waveform coding, DM-DCC uses one bit which corresponds to two vector links to encode a trace segment. It offers greatly reduced coding rate, smaller encoded file size, simpler data syntax and better robustness as compared to differential chain coding (DCC) and standard chain coding (SCC) while still maintaining comparable subjective graphical qulity.

1 Introduction

On-line handwritten cursive script and drawings can be captured using an electronic writing tablet which produces the x-y coordinate data of pen-tip movement. Such dynamographical image data may be coded for on-line handwriting recognition [1] or stored for later image analysis and processing. Multimedia telecommunication has become increasingly popular with promising applications such as teleworking and telebanking, employing telewriting technique which enables the transfer of handwritten information over the public switched telephone networks. Dynamographical data can also be used to represent information which cannot be covered by the standard ASCII character set, such as signatures, mathematical formulae, non-English languages like Chinese or Japanese, and line drawings. In order to reduce the storage and transmission bandwidth, compressing the inefficient x-y coordinate data is necessary. Chain coding pioneered by Freeman [2] is an efficient data compression source coding for two-dimensional line trajectories, which preserves and reproduces the sequence of differential movements of the pen-tip.

Differential chain coding (DCC) scheme which encoded data into strings of ASCII-compatible bytes had been developed for personal computers with EGA resolution of 640×350 pixels for dynamographical communications over electronic-mail networks [3]. DCC achieves better coding rate efficiency than standard chain coding (SCC) by exploiting the dependence between successive vectors in handwriting and encoding the differential information. It assigns a 2-bit codeword (00, 01 and 10) to the most frequently occurring vector difference (0, +1 and -1) which are referred to as relative vectors, and uses 11 as header bits for the less frequent vectors encoded by SCC, known as absolute vectors. However, DCC codes still have not achieved maximum efficiency due to its use of vectors with different lengths, and the 2-bit header for absolute vector is vulnerable to bit errors [4].

In this paper, we propose a novel chain coding scheme, which we refer to as DM-like differential chain coding (DM-DCC), inspired by the traditional delta modulation for waveform coding. Using only two vector links to encode a trace segment, DM-DCC produces a vector chain of 1-bit codewords. We will show that when compared to DCC and SCC, the proposed DM-DCC offers greatly reduced coding rate, smaller file size, simpler data syntax, and it is more robust against bit errors. By employing adaptive coding technique and postprocessing smoothing, DM-DCC is able to maintain a comparable subjective graphical quality as DCC.

2 DM-like Differential Chain Coding

Real-time handwriting on an electronic writing tablet is sampled based on space coding which provides a fixed amount of samples per unit trace segment. If a trace of handwriting is denoted as $l(s) = [x(s), y(s)]$ that specifies the trace coordinates at any arbitrary point s travelled by the writing stylus, uniform space sampling with a sampling interval D_s converts $l(s)$ into a discrete function given by

$$
l(kD_s) = [x(kD_s), y(kD_s)] = \begin{cases} [x(s), y(s)] & \text{for } s = kD_s \\ 0 & \text{otherwise} \end{cases} \tag{1}
$$

where $k = 0, \pm1, \pm2, \pm3, \dots$ Each trace is then encoded by the DM-DCC scheme into a chain of vectors started with a pen-down byte and ended with a pen-up byte.

A square coding ring is slid in steps along the successive points of a trace from the line graphics. The coding ring has sides of $2n\tau$ and contains $M = 8n$ nodes, where $n = 1, 2, 3, \dots$ is the order of the ring and τ is the spacing of the ring. The first vector displacement along the the trace is the best fitting vector defined by standard chain coding (SCC). The coding ring is then translated along this starting vector to determine the next vector along the trace. A differential approach very similar to traditional delta modulation is employed to encode all the following vectors along the trace. This is essentially a quantizer with first-order of memory. Encoding of next vector link is dependent on the current link. Hence, given the current link, there are two and only two candidates for the next vector link. For a ring of size $M = 8$, the most logical choice for the two vector links are the vectors immediately adjacent to the current vector. Therefore, only 1 bit is used to represent the binary selection, with "0" being the left vector link and "1" being the right vector link in a counterclockwise direction. Fig. 1 illustrates the general coding principles of DM-DCC for a ring of size $M = 8$. It can be seen that the two binary vector links are perpendicular to each other. Hence, the angle between the two vectors is 90°.

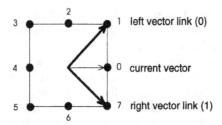

Fig. 1 Coding principles of DM-DCC for a ring of size $M = 8$

The data syntax of the proposed DM-DCC scheme is shown in Fig. 2. A trace starts with a pen-down (PD), followed by a number of vectors and ends with a pen-up (PU). For a VGA resolution of 640×480 pixels, the starting coordinates X_0 and Y_0 of the trace are directly encoded using 10 and 9 bits respectively. The starting vector (SV) is encoded by SCC using $I \lceil \log_2 8n \rceil$ bits, where $I[x]$ denotes the smallest integer equal to or greater than x. All vectors afterwards are the 1-bit delta vectors (DV). The DM-DCC scheme results in a simple and uniform data syntax.

PD	X_0	Y_0	SV	DV	DV	DV		DV	PU

PD	pen-down	(1 byte)
X_0	X-coordinate of trace origin	(10 bits)
Y_0	Y-coordinate of trace origin	(9 bits)
SV	starting vector	($I\lceil \log_2 8n \rceil$ bits)
DV	delta vector	(1 bit)
PU	pen-up	(1 byte)

Fig. 2 Data syntax of DM-DCC

To evaluate the performance of DM-DCC scheme, we adopt the per-length coding rate in [5] as a measure of coding efficiency. Conventionally, coding rate of a chain code is defined as the number of bits produced by the coding scheme per unit length of the curve segment. A low coding rate corresponds to a higher coding efficiency [5, 6]. When a curve is encoded by a chain coding scheme, it is sliced by the coding ring into small segments. Consider a sampled curve segment s. Let v be the corresponding vector link produced by the coding ring of order n. Coding rate of a chain code is given by

$$r = \frac{E[b(s, v)]}{E[l_n(s)]} \tag{2}$$

where $b(s, v)$ is the number of bits used to encode the vector link v, and $l_n(s)$ is the length of curve segment s for a coding ring of order n. $E[x]$ represents the expected value of a random variable x. It has been shown [7] that for the universe of all curves, the product of a segment length, and the probability $p(\alpha)$ that this segment occurs with a direction α remains constant. Thus, the expected length of the curve segment s becomes

$$E\left[l_n(s)\right] = 8 \int_0^{\pi/4} \frac{n\,\tau}{\cos\alpha}\, p(\alpha)\, d\alpha = \frac{\pi\, n\,\tau}{2\sqrt{2}} \tag{3}$$

Using eqn. 2 and 3, the theoretical coding rate of a chain code is

$$r = \frac{2\sqrt{2} \cdot E\left[b(s,\,v)\right]}{\pi\, n\,\tau} \tag{4}$$

where the expected number of bits per vector link for the three chain coding schemes DM-DCC, DCC and SCC, respectively, are

DM-DCC: $\quad E\left[b(s,\,v)\right] = 1$

DCC: $\quad E\left[b(s,\,v)\right] = 2P_{RV} + \left\{2 + I\left[\log_2 8n\right]\right\}\cdot\left(1 - P_{RV}\right)$

SCC: $\quad E\left[b(s,\,v)\right] = I\left[\log_2 8n\right]$

and P_{RV} is the probability of relative vectors.

DM-DCC is more efficient owing to its use of only 1 bit to encode the vector chain, as opposed to DCC which uses 2 bits to encode relative vectors and $2 + I\left[\log_2 8n\right]$ bits for absolute vectors. Therefore, DM-DCC is able to greatly reduce the coding rate. Its data syntax is simpler and more uniform than DCC since the vector chain of DCC is a mixture of relative vectors and absolute vectors, and the header bits for the absolute vectors account for the redundancy that is removed by DM-DCC scheme.

When we choose a particular chain coding scheme, the size of the encoded file is important because the smaller the file size, the less storage space or less transmission bandwidth thus required. The file size of a cursive script or a line drawing in bits encoded by a chain coding scheme can be defined as

$$S = \sum_n \left(PD + X_0 + Y_0 + V_i + PU\right) \tag{5}$$

where n is the number of traces, PD is the number of bits for pen-down, X_0 is the number of bits for x-coordinate of trace origin, Y_0 is the number of bits for y-coordinate of trace origin, V_i is the number of bits for the vector chain in trace i, and PU is the number of bits for pen-up. For a coding ring of size $M = 8n$, number of bits for the vector chain in trace i for the three chain coding schemes are

DM-DCC: $\quad V_i = \left(I\left[\log_2 8n\right] \text{ bits}\right) + m_{DV}\cdot(1\text{ bit})$

DCC: $\qquad V_i = m_{AV} \cdot \left(2 + I\left[\log_2 8n\right] \text{ bits}\right) + m_{RV} \cdot \left(2 \text{ bits}\right)$

SCC: $\qquad V_i = m_{AV} \cdot \left(I\left[\log_2 8n\right] \text{ bits}\right)$

where m_{DV} is the number of delta vectors, m_{AV} is the number of absolute vectors and m_{RV} is the number of relative vectors.

Since DM-DCC uses only two binary vectors to represent the next segment of the trace, distortion may occur when the next trace segment is deviated too much in direction from its present segment (curvature overload noise), or when the next segment is in almost the same direction as the present one (granular noise). However, as we found out, adaptive coding technique and postprocessing smoothing can be applied to reduce these quantisation noises. The curvature mistracking becomes obvious when sequences of more than four consecutive 1's or 0's occur in the coded bit stream. Then the adaptive DM-DCC codec will use binary vector links with larger angle between them, which corresponds to using a larger stpe size in traditonal delta modulation. The high frequency granular noise is detected when an encoded trace tries to follow the original trace in some typical zig-zag patterns, and it can be reduced by replacing these zig-zag vector links by straight

When a dynamographical image is decoded either from storage or transmission channel, it may contain bit errors. Since DM-DCC uses only 1-bit delta vectors, effect of errors on vector bits can only change one delta vector to another, which will have a 90° rotational effect on the remaining trace. For DCC, however, each corrupted relative vector or absolute vector will have rotational, distorted or translational effect on the remaining trace. In addition, errors corruptting the header bits of an absolute vector may cause it to become several relative vectors. Alternatively, errors corrupting a relative vector may cause it to become the pattern of the header bits. Such happenings may corrupt the decoding process until the next trace starts. SCC has fixed-length vector codes similar to the proposed DM-DCC, but since it uses $I\left[\log_2 8n\right]$ bits for each vector, error corruption in the higher order bit will have worse effect than in the lower order bit. Therefore the proposed DM-DCC scheme is more robust against bit errors than DCC and SCC schemes.

3 Simulation and Results

To evaluate the performance of the proposed DM-DCC, different types of cursive script including an English script and a Chinese script, and line drawings such as a map and a mathematical graph were coded using DM-DCC, DCC and SCC, respectively. Table 1 shows the coding rates produced by DM-DCC, DCC and SCC together with the theoretical coding rates. It can be seen that DM-DCC reduces coding rate by more than 50% compared to DCC and its coding rate is less than one-third of SCC's coding rate. The encoded file sizes produced by DM-DCC, DCC and SCC are shown in Table 2. Clearly, DM-DCC produces the smallest encoded file, which represents the highest data compression efficiency. The effect of the adaptive coding and postprocessing smoothing is shown in Fig. 3. It can be seen that the decoded traces are much smoother and therefore give better subjective quality. Fig. 4 shows the decoded dynamo-graphical images of DM-DCC scheme with adaptive coding and postprocessing smoothing, while the corresponding images of DCC scheme are also shown for comparison. It is observed that the proposed DM-DCC scheme achieves comparable subjective graphical quality as DCC.

Table 1 Coding rate comparison for DM-DCC, DCC and SCC with a ring of $M = 8$, $\tau = 1$

	Coding rate (bits per unit length)		
	DM-DCC	DCC	SCC
English script	0.8535	2.02	2.71
Chinese script	0.8532	2.04	2.66
Map	0.8536	2.04	2.71
Drawing	0.8541	1.94	2.74
Theoretical coding rate	0.9	2.03	2.70

Table 2 Encoded file sizes for DM-DCC, DCC and SCC with a $M = 8$ coding ring

	File size (bytes)		
	DM-DCC	DCC	SCC
English script	1554	2873	3612
Chinese script	2970	4590	4891
Map	252	531	621
Drawing	996	1856	2263

4 Conclusion

A novel and efficient chain coding scheme for cursive script and line drawing has been proposed. Similar to the traditional delta modulation for waveform coding, DM-DCC uses only one bit and hence two binary vector links to encode a curve segment. It has been shown that DM-DCC scheme offers greatly reduced coding rate, smaller encoded file size, simpler data syntax and better robustness against bit errors when compared to DCC and SCC schemes. Adaptive coding technique and postprocessing smoothing have been applied to reduce the quantisation noises for better subjective image quality.

References

1. C.C. Tappert, C.Y. Suen, and T. Wakahara, "The state of the art in on-line handwriting recognition," IEEE Trans. Patt. Anal. Mach. Intel., vol. 12, pp. 787-808, Aug. 1990

2. H. Freeman, "On the encoding of arbitrary geometric figures," *IRE Trans. Electron. Comput.*, vol. EC-10, pp. 260-268, June 1961

3. J.C. Arnbak, J.H. Bons, and J.W. Vieveen, "Graphical correspondence in electronic-mail networks using personal computers," *IEEE Journal on Selected Areas in Communications,* vol. 7, pp.257-267, Feb. 1989

4. K. Liu and R. Prasad, "Performance analysis of differential chain coding," *European Transaction on Telecommunications and Related Technology,* vol. 3, pp. 323-330, Jul-Aug. 1992

5. A.B. Johannessen, R. Prasad, N.B.J. Weyland and J.H. Bons, "Coding efficiency of multiring differential chain coding," *IEE Proceedings, Part I,* vol. 139, pp. 224-232, April 1992

6. D.L. Neuhoff and K.G. Castor, "A rate and distortion analysis of chain codes for line drawings," *IEEE Tran. Information Theory,* vol. IT-31, pp. 53-68, Jan. 1985

7. F.C.A. Groen and P.W. Verbeek, "Freeman-code probabilities of object boundary quantized contours," *Comput. Graphics & Image Process.*, vol. 7, pp. 391-402, 1978

(original)

(primitive DM-DCC)

(adaptively coded & smoothed)

Fig. 3 Part of decoded English script

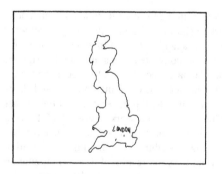

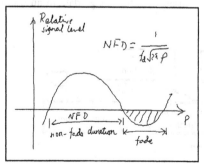

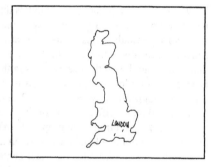

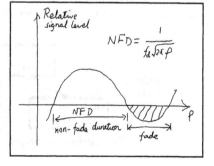

Fig. 4 Decoded dynamographical images of DM-DCC (left) and DCC (right)

Adaptive Hierarchical Indexing and Constrained Localization: Matching Characteristic Views

Gunter Bellaire and Mathias Lübbe

Computer Vision Group, Dep. of Computer Science, Technical University of Berlin
Franklinstr. 28-29, FR 3-11, 10587 Berlin, Germany, email:bellaire@cs.tu-berlin.de

Abstract. This article presents a complete hybrid object recognition system for three-dimensional objects using the characteristic view (ChV) idea. To apply the ChV representation method in a recognition system investigations are needed concerning the processing of large object data bases. First we present two methods to reduce the number of views in the object data base. Second we developed an accumulator (AC)-based matching strategy combined with a localization process. This strategy bases on a hierarchical indexing structure that uses a Gaussian distributed voting. The off-line part of the matching includes a statistical analysis of the object data base and an interface to process results of a sensor configuration analysis. The calculated results support the construction of an adapted layer model suitable for hierarchical indexing. Further an unsupervised learning module is introduced, that investigates the measurement errors and adapts the system online. Results of the matching are verified by a localization tool, which uses an interpretation tree search combined by a shape from angle method and a constrained alignment technique. The article shows results with real greyscale images.

1   Introduction and Background

Viewer-centered approaches use models that represent the visible information from a defined view point. The suggested recognition system shows the computation of distinct view sets under particular constraints. We introduce an adaptive hybrid matching framework and shows results with real data. Image features are converted in a symbolic description, that is compared with the descriptions in the model base, see [3]. Finally a decision taking procedure completes the recognition process. Our method combines model- and data-driven strategies to a hybrid system. The data driven indexing generates hypotheses that are localized and verified by an object driven localization. Our work focuses the following aspects: • 1) computing an appropriate ChV representation • 2) developing a generic data base • 3) developing adaptive data-driven matching procedures • 4) building a localization and verification tool, which is object-centered but uses the results of 3) • 5) realizing an edge based segmentation and an edge linking to transform the image data in an useful form. Aspects' 1-4 are described in this paper.

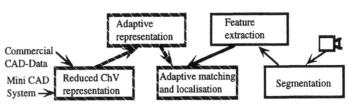

Fig. 1: The modules of the recognition system.

1) Our system generates either ChV sets of arbitrary shaped objects [6] or aspect graphs of planar objects [10, 5]. Vertex, edge and face data specify instances of both models. General problems of ChV models, that are discussed in the paper are:

• the lack of disposable ChVs generating algorithms, especially for curved objects, • the number of views computed by these algorithms, • the missing information about the probability of a certain object view [8] and • the absence of methods to reduce the amount of the original views to get an appropriately reduced ChV set [8]

2) The exact classification of scene objects and the efficient access to complex model data -largely independent from amount of the ChVs- are goals of a recognition system. The use of "a priori" knowledge as the feature distribution in the data base supports the recognition realization. Further an interface to an "a priori" analysis module of the actual sensor configuration is put at the user's disposal.

3) We describe the adaptive hierarchical indexing and its learning module, that adjusts the indexing in dependence of the sensor behavior. In [4] You can find the description of the system's second matching module that uses a local feature for ChV matching.

4) The successive localization and verification module uses an object driven strategy. Each of the candidates of the indexing or hashing candidate list is investigated. First the localization module uses a shape from angle (SfA) method to verify the candidates. If this method fails, an alignment process inspects the candidates. Fig.1 shows a system overview.

2   Related work

Ikeuchi [12] presented a system for the automatic generation of recognition and localization programs. He investigated the linear view changes in ChV-classes by employing reduced sets of ChVs, which correspond to certain sensor configurations. Flynn [9] described the transformation of CAD-object representations to viewer position independent relational graphs, that are appropriate for vision applications. The uniform tessellation method generates 2D views. Dickinson's [7] method searches scenes for a fixed alphabet of generalized cylinders, the so called object primitives. This approach's aim is the independence of the aspect graph from of the object number and complexity. A problem seems to be the processing of occlusions. Lu [14] applied CAD-data to generate a vision model and a recognition strategy. A data structure called relational pyramid manages primitives of different complexity levels. To process inexact matching they have investigated the AC-based matching, that adds votes to views with similar feature constellations. Arman [1] used the initial graphics specification (IGES) to connect their system to commercial CAD systems. They derive a recognition strategy from feature attributes that are extracted from the IGES data of the desired object model.

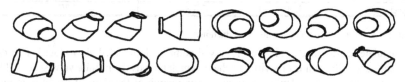

Fig. 2: Bottle representation. 16 ChVs remain from original 80 views.

3   Reduced Characteristic View Sets

We designed an interface to the DXF data format to connect our system to commercial CAD-data. The number of views in ChV sets of complex objects can reach high numbers. In this chapter we report about techniques to reduce ChV sets by the computation of isomorphic views and to calculate the probability of particular ChVs.

3.1   Isomorphic View Sets

Regarding polyhedral objects, similar views caused by symmetry axis may occur. An isomorphy detecting procedure computes these views. We use the isomorphy detecting algorithm to compute classes of similar views of curved objects. The in Bellaire [2] proposed method is adopted, that constructs isomorphic view sets. It is improved concerning its time efficiency. This version uses the whole information of a labeled image structure graph (LISG) [10]. The algorithm works as follows:

- comparing *edge, vertex and face numbers* to detect evidently non similar views
- finding an *isomorphic covering* -the necessary condition of the covering is the identity of the edge- and vertex-attributes of two structures-

Fig. 2 shows the views of the ChVs of a bottle that is generated from originally 80 views.

3.2   Probable View Sets

The probability of a view is determined by the object's functionality or the size of view space in which the view is visible. In our system we use the size of view space to assign probabilities to the particular views. Using the uniform tessellation method the calculation of this size is simple. During the computation of the ChVs an AC summarizes the sizes of the sphere patches, that are combined to equivalence classes. This information is assigned to the representative [2]

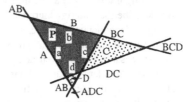

Fig. 3: Probability calculation of ChVs related to the size of the view regions in the perspective case. The set of view regions of the polygon P consists of two bounded (C, D) and eight unlimited, infinite large view regions.

of the built class. Using an analytic method to compute aspects, the exact calculation of the size of the view patches or spaces is more complicated. Concerning the case of orthographic projection, an EEE-event [10] influences the tessellation of the view-cube by intersecting the cube surface with a quadric ruled surface. For the calculation of the exact bounds of the view patches the interaction of several of these quadric ruled surfaces has to be handled. Our system uses a linear approximation of the calculated intersection points in view space to estimate the size of particular patches. In the perspective case additional problems arise: the distinction has to be realized between the size of infinite large view spaces and the comparison between bounded and infinite view spaces. Fig. 3 shows view regions of the analog 2-D case. Tab. 1 shows the reduction factors our algorithms applied on distinct data bases.

Data base	%of isomor-phic views	% of views with min. 2% view space size of the total	% of isomorphic views with min. 2% view space size of the total
uniform tessellation	42, 6%	49,9%	23,7%
aspect graph[*]	33,1%	31,3%	9,2%

Table 1: ChV distribution following distinct reductions

We calculate the distance of the most removed point of all bounded view spaces. This distance influences the radius of a virtual sphere, which bounds the infinite view spaces. This outer bound allows the calculation of an approximation of the sizes of the infinite view spaces. In the following we use a data base generated by the orthographic uniform tessellation method. The data base is reduced on isomorphic views with a view size larger then 2% of the total view space size.

4   Inexact Matching via Hierarchical Indexing

The hierarchical indexing comprehends statistical analysis routines and the inexact matching. Additionaly to the analysis part we put an interface, that combines the results of a sensor analysis tool with the generation of the recognition scheme, at the user's disposal.

---

[*] orthographic projection without EEE-events

The interface offers the possibility to process weight factors w_i for n Sensors, $w \in [0, ..., 1]$, $0 < i < n$, that are initialized by $w = 0.5$. Sensors with a high accuracy capture w_i close to 1.0 and less accurate features capture small w_i. The matching algorithm multiplies the w_i values with the calculated AC votes. This interface allows to control the influence of accurate sensors.

4.1 Statistical Analysis and Extraction of Particular Feature Groups

Distinct object libraries consisting of altered objects demand adapted recognition strategies. The attribute frequency of the features depends on the particular object shapes. E.g. a zero-frequency of a globally observed attributes in the data base reports about the attribute's insignificance for the object distinction. At this time our analysis functions calculate the sum, the mean, the spectrum, the standard deviation, the density, the homogeneity and the correlation coefficient.

The selection of the feature set, which is performed during the recognition process, affects the accuracy and the response time of an reconition system. A small feature attribute spectrum, features with similar attribute distribution and feature distributions with small homogeneity and/or very small standard deviation lack separating power. Each additionally evaluated feature increases the performance time. The objective of an automatic feature selection process is the choice of an object discriminating and a fast feasible feature set. The usage of the reported statistic functions applied on the model base and the analysis of the sensor configuration allows a dismissal of *inappropriate* and *redundant* features. Criteria for the feature *dismissal* are:
• The sum of the attribute value of a feature in all ChV is zero. • The frequency distribution of a feature in all objects is constant or its standard deviation is zero. • The features are correlated in pairs -the size of the correlation coefficient is compared-.

These steps are performed to generate an *adapted* hierarchical indexing structure:
• Computation of correlating features to generate non-correlating feature groups
• Calculation of the variance, the homogeneity and the density

Additionaly a balanced search, with a homogeneous feature attribute distribution in a large feature spectrum is suitable. Our system proposes the feature group of non-correlating features ranked by the best number in homogeneity, density and variance.

4.2 Accumulator-Based Adaptive Indexing

We introduce an inexact matching strategy, that is adapted by the actual object data base, the "a priori" knowledge about the current sensor configuration, see [2], and the measured sensor errors. The CAD-data processing modeling component computes a set of ChVs for each object. The ChV sets of all model objects build the object data base. Feature vectors describe the particular ChVs. One feature vector exists for each ChV. During the matching procedure the scene object is processed by comparing its feature vectors with the complete ChV set feature vectors.

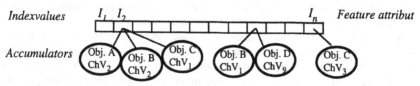

Fig. 4: Index layer connected to various ACs of object views

The indexing process consists of a relation from the area of the scene features into the area of the index space. If a set of n scene features exists, then a vector of g ($g \leq n$) feature attributes determine an index I_s. The values of the index depend on the content of the feature attributes. An index vector specifies exactly a point in the index space. The hierarchical system organizes g features of interest in g index layers. Each feature is represented by certain layer in the layer model, see fig. 5. The model is adapted for the data base and the used sensors. Each layer delineates the index space of a feature. The layer indexes point to ACs of those ChVs, that contain similar feature attributes.

In the case of inexact data a method has to be found, that relates the data to comparative models. The proposed matching strategy increases the ACs of several ChVs by the value $e^{-k^2/2}$, with $k = 0, ..., k_{max}$ denoting the deviation of a model feature to the measured data. That means the AC of an object with a feature value close to the measured data is increased more than an AC of an object view with a less similar feature value. This method is called Gaussian distribution method. In contrast the exact method is denoted as spike distribution method. The particular AC values determine the ranking in a list, that manages best ChVs.

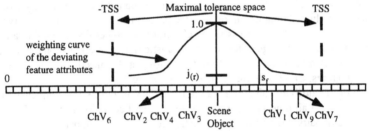

Fig. 5: Indexing layer showing the tolerance space dimension and a Gaussian distributed voting function.

The voting function v(k) for a node with the distance k, $-TSS \leq k \leq TSS$ (tolerance space size), from the scene object feature attribute value is calculated by the following formula. Here k_{max} denotes the size of the maximal tolerated node distance from the concerning scene object feature attribute value. The function values are transformed in a discrete number series v(k), where the Gauss range r scales the range of the function:

$$\varphi(x) = e^{-\frac{x^2}{2}} \quad v(k) = e^{-\frac{1}{2}\left(\frac{k \cdot r}{k_{max}}\right)^2} ; k = 0, 1, ..., k_{max}$$

The max/min votes define the borders of v(k): $v(0) = \varphi(0) = 1.0$ and $v(k_{max}) = \varphi(r)$

A time consuming process in an AC based system is the increase of the affected ACs, followed by the sorting of the best list, that depends on the ACs' weights. The fewer views remain in the system the faster the AC value increase and the sorting runs. The following conditions constrain the indexing, see fig. 5:

- The width of the Gaussian curve -used to calculate the vote- is adapted on the standard deviation of the regarded feature σ_f multiplied by a scale factor s. For $s = 2.0$ it's well known, that 95% of the deviations caused by measuring errors are covered by the curve. Pursuing this, the absolute amount of the deviations remains relatively small.
- A tolerance space, that is larger than $s \cdot \sigma_f$, causes an assignment of the smallest possible vote $v(k) = \varphi(r)$ to nodes outside the Gaussian curve. It follows, that ChV candidates with larger errors in particular features are allowed to concur the matching race.
- The TSS is determined by the "a priori" sensor analysis and the online learning module. A ChV is omitted from searching if a feature value drops out the layer's tolerance space. The initial size of the TSS is 50% of the feature spectrum.

4.3 Unsupervised Learning by Integration of the Measured Sensor Accuracy

A technique to improve the performance of the matching is to adapt the TSS on the feature attribute distribution of the measured data. The system performs an online adaptation by integrating the measured sensor accuracy. The indexing generates a list of the best matching ChVs. The localization function verifies or discards the hypothesis of the indexing procedure. This process operates unsupervisedly. The accuracy is measured by the comparison of the correct result feature vector x_{ChV} and the feature vector calculated from the scene object. The maximal difference between the real and the measured feature value is stored in a learning map for each feature attribute, that is element of the feature vectors. This learning map supervises the mean standard deviation and maximal deviation value max_{dev} of the particular features. After t successfully processed recognition tasks the TSSs and the σ_f' of the index layers adapt. The standard deviation for a feature g after the n+1 recognition task is computed by the following form:

$$\text{var}_{g_{n+1}} = \left(\Delta x_g{}^2 + n \cdot \text{var}_{g_n}\right)/n+1; \; \sigma_{g_n} = \sqrt{\text{var}_{g_n}}; \; \Delta x_g = \left|x_{ChV_g} - x_{SzO_g}\right|$$

The TSS is calculated by the max_{dev} of the features. Since the TSS excludes views from the matching procedure, the learning algorithm allows the expansion of the TSS by adding 0.33 * max_{dev} to max_{dev}. The algorithm decreases the TSS by deleting the current max_{dev} after t recognition tasks and choosing the next smaller $max2_{dev}$ as new

Online adaptation steps	% of the existence of the correct view in the candidate list
0	62,6 %
20	82,2 %
40	85,5 %

Table 2: Correctly proposed real objects in the candidate list of the indexing

max_{dev}. In tab. 2 we demonstrate the learning capability of the system. The results show the increasing performance of the indexing caused by the learning procedure.

5 Verification by Localization

We realized the object localization by two different methods. First we combined Kanatani's SfA technique with an interpretation tree oriented correspondences solving algorithm. Second we used a constraint alignment technique in cases the SfA method fails. The verification module searches the distance between the image points and the corresponding model points. The correspondence between image and model point is determined by the following. The algorithm searches in a circle for the nearest model point. The circle size is 10% of the distance of the transformed model point to the transformation center. E. g. in a 512^2 image the circle size varies between 1 and 36 pixel. 80% of the model points has to be matched by image points to verify a hypothesis.

5.1 Shape From Angle (SfA)

Kanatani [13] described the detection of the orientation of polyhedral objects under the assumption that rectangular corners exist. He showed a method to determine the 3-D orientation of the 2-D image of a rectangular corner. We combined his analysis by an interpretation tree driven constrained search for at least one trihedreal orthogonal corner (TOC) located in the reconstructed line drawing. The vector n_i is the vector starting from the observed corner extending along the i-edge. The angle's θ_i and φ_i are the spherical coordinates of n_i. The angle's φ_i can be observed on the image plane, while the angle's θ_i are computed by the following form:

$$\theta_1 = \arctan \sqrt{\frac{\cos(\varphi 2 - \varphi 3)}{\cos(\varphi 1 - \varphi 2)\cos(\varphi 3 - \varphi 1)}}$$

The vector $\mathbf{n}_i$ is defined by the following:
$$\mathbf{n}_i = (\sin\theta_i\cos\varphi_i, \sin\theta_i\sin\varphi_i, \cos\theta_i)$$

$$\theta_2 = \arctan \sqrt{\frac{\cos(\varphi 3 - \varphi 1)}{\cos(\varphi 2 - \varphi 3)\cos(\varphi 1 - \varphi 2)}}$$

The computation of the 3D orientation of the TOC edges is performed by the following. It holds: if the i-edge directs away to the viewer then $(0 < \theta_i < \pi/2)$, else if one of the i-edges is directed towards the

$$\theta_3 = \arctan \sqrt{\frac{\cos(\varphi 1 - \varphi 2)}{\cos(\varphi 3 - \varphi 1)\cos(\varphi 2 - \varphi 3)}}$$

viewer then the computed angle is replaced by $\pi - \theta_i$. The interpretation tree search has to find the correspondences between the model TOCs and the

candidate trihedreal image corners. During the transformation calculation the system does not know, whether the searched trihedreal image corner is orthogonal or not. All m model TOCs are combined with all n trihedreal image corners. The cost for the correspondence analysis is $m * n * 3$! Our object data base consists of 630 object views. Tab. 3 shows the TOC distribution in the data base views. The percentage relates the TOC number to the total number of object corners. The object label refers to fig. 6. Our test shows that 26.1% is the mean TOC number of the data base views. Due to lack of space the rendering in Fig. 6 contains only the half of the data base objects.

Fig. 6: Shaded example objects of the data base

In the case that TOCs are not available in the model or no trihedreal corner is found in the image the algorithm exceeds. If trihedreal image corners are found and TOCs are available, all possible transformations are computed and verified. During verification all TOCs are applied as centers to process the calculated transformation. The verification procedure decides about the accuracy of the calculated transformation. The following reasons cause the failure of a computed transformation: 1) The searched trihedreal image corner is not the projection of a TOC. 2) The calculated transformation matrix is applied on a not corresponding TOC. 3) The projection of the model TOC in the image is incomplete. The reason is the need for a correct edge length of the edges $\mathbf{n}_i$ of the TOC. If an edge $\mathbf{n}_i$ is partially occluded, the algorithm calculates an incorrect scale factor. 4) The projected angle's φ_i are measured inaccurately. The occurrence of one described point invokes the constraint alignment module. Tab. 4 shows the percentage of the correct verified objects.

object name ‖ label	min TOC percent	max TOC percent	mean TOC % over all views
car 1 ‖ 1	0%	39%	20%
table ‖ 19	23%	57%	40%
cow ‖ 12	16%	54%	29%
heart ‖ 10	0%	53%	19%
data base	0%	67%	**26,1%**

Table 3: TOC distribution of data base views and mean trihedreal corner number of the analyzed images.

ChV set	% of correct transformations	Mean TOC # in the recognized views
Reduced uniform tessellation	48,1	7,9 TOCs

Table 4: Results of a shape from angle experiments

5.2 Constraint Alignment

An alignment procedure uses three corresponding model and image points to calculate the correct transformation. In the worst case the number of possible alignments is $m^3 * n^3$ regarding the unconstrained alignment method. In [11] two real and one virtual point are used two compute the transformation. The virtual point is determined by two orientations stored with the real points. This reduces the worst case on $O(m^2*n^2)$ possible feature comparisons. The verification costs in both versions are n*m comparisons. In a inter-pretation tree method we constrain the correspondence search by the junction types of the investigated image corners. This means only corners that carry the same junction type label are used to calculate the transformation. The list of the image corner is sorted by its junction type. $\uparrow$–junctions show the highest probability of the junction types being extracted correctly. This is caused by the assumption that background segmentation is more feasible as object segmentation. This implies the sorting of the searched model point first by all $\uparrow$–junctions, followed by the Y- and L-junctions.

Under the assumption of 100% correctly extracted image corners, three model points are matched with n image points. The higher the detection probability increases the less features the algorithm has to permute. E. g., a 50% sufficient correctness conditions the permutation of six model points -assumption three have correct corresponding image points- with n image points. In this case it follows the cal-culation of $6*n^3$ transformations as worst case. Each transformation has to be verified. Tab. 5 shows results under distinct assumption about the correctness of detected image points.

Assumed correctness probability	100%	75%	60%	37,5%
Percentage of correct results	29,6%	55,6%	77,8%	81,4%

Table 5: Results of the constraint alignment with distinct correctness probabilities of the extracted image points executed over all data bases (*150 tests*).

6 Conclusion

In this paper we present a complete hybrid object recognition system, that localizes objects as shown in fig 6. in real greyscale images. The peculiarities of the proposed system are the development of a reduced ChV model, the generation of an adaptive hierarchical indexing algorithm with an online learning component and the generation of suitable combination of the SfA method with an interpretation tree search. These algo-rithms compute results, which are published first here. In the future we will research for different types of equivalence criteria to generate processable view sets of more real world objects. Topological equivalence is too power full in combination with the ChV model in respect to the need of the representation of more "real objects". The matching and localisation methods seem to be very suitable to process large data bases with more complicated objects.

7 References

1. F. Arman, J. K. Aggarwal, "CAD-Based Vision: Object Recognition in Cluttered Range Images Using Recogniton Strategies", CVGIP: Image Understanding, Vol. 58, no. 1, July, pp. 33-48, 1993
2. G. Bellaire, "Feature-Based Computation of Hierarchical Aspect-Graphs", Machine GRAPHICS & VISION, Vol. 2, no 2, pp. 105-122, 1993
3. G. Bellaire, K. Schlüns, A. Mitritz, K. Gwinner, "Adaptive Matching Using Object Models Generated From Photometric Stereo Images", to appear in Proc. of 8th ICIAP, San Remo, Italy, 1995
4. G. Bellaire, "Hashing with a Topological Invariant Feature", to appear in Proc. of ACCV´95, Singapore

5. K.W. Bowyer (Org) "Why Aspect Graphs are not (yet) Practikal for Computer Vision", Workshop Panel Report, CVGIP, Vol. 55, no. 2, March, pp. 97-105, 1992

6. I. Chakravarty, H. Freeman, "Characteristic Views as a Basis for 3-D Object Recognition", Proc. Soc. Photo-Optical Instrumentation, Robot Vision, Vol. 336, SPIE Bellingham, WA, pp. 37-45, 1982

7. S. J. Dickinson, A. Pentland, A. Rosenfeld, "3D Shape Recovery Using Distributed Aspect Matching", IEEE Trans. on PAMI, Vol. 14, no. 2, pp. 174-197, 1992

8. D. E. Eggert, K. W. Bowyer, Ch. R. Dyer, H. I. Christensen, D. B. Goldgof, "The Scale Space Aspect Graph", Proc. CVPR, pp. 335-340, 1992

9. P. Flynn, A.K. Jain, "CAD-Based Computer Vision: From CAD Models to Relational Graphs", IEEE Trans. on PAMI, Vol. 13, no. 2, Feb, pp. 114-132, 1991

10. Z. Gigus, J. Malik, "Computing the aspect for line drawings of polyhedral objects, "IEEE Trans. on PAMI, Vol. 12 no. 2, pp. 113-123, 1990

11. D. P. Huttenlocher, S. Ullman, "Recognizing Solid Objects by Alignment with an Image", IJCV, Vol. 5, no. 2, pp. 195-212, 1990

12. K. Ikeuchi, "Determining Linear Shape Change: Toward Automatic Generation of Object Recognition Programs", CVGIP, Vol. 53, pp. 154-170, 1991

13. K. Kanatani, "Group-theoretical Methods in Image Understanding", Springer, Heidelberg, 1990

14. H. Lu, L. G. Shapiro, "Model-Based Vision Using Relational Summaries", SPIE Vol. 1095, Applications of Artificial Intellience VII, pp. 662-675, 1989

Statistical Estimation for Exterior Orientation from Line-to-Line Correspondences

Chung-Nan Lee

Institute of Computer and Information Engineering, National Sun Yat-Sen University
Kaohsiung, Taiwan 80424, ROC

Robert M. Haralick

Intelligent Systems Laboratory, Department of Electrical Engineering • FT-10
University of Washington, Seattle, WA 98195, USA

Abstract. This paper presents a statistical estimation from which a new objective function for exterior orientation from line correspondences is derived. The objective function is based on the assumption that the underlying noise model for the line correspondences is the Fisher distribution. The assumption is appropriate for 3D orientation, is different from the underlying noise models for k pixels positions, and allows us to do a consistent estimation of the unknown parameters. The objective function gives two important facts: its formulation and concept is different for that of previous work, and it automatically estimates six unknown parameters simultaneously. As a result, it provides an optimal solution and better accuracy. We design an experimental protocol to evaluate the performance of the new algorithm. The results of each experiment shows that the new algorithm produces answers whose errors are 10% - 20% less than the competing decoupled least squares algorithm.

1 Introduction

The problem of determining the orientation and position of an object in a 3D world coordinate system relative to a 3D camera coordinate system is equivalent to solving the relation between the 3D object features and their corresponding perspective projection features. It is an important problem both in computer vision and in photogrammetry. Most methods use point features to obtain the transformation function, which is governing the orientation and position of an object[1-4]. Besides point-to-point correspondences, line-to-line correspondences can be used to obtain the transformation function [5-7].

The paper is organized in the following way. We first give a review on a traditional least sqaure approach in Section 2. Section 3 discusses the statistical estimation of unknown parameters of position and orientation of a camera. In Section 4 we design an experimental protocol to carry out the performance characterization of the algorithms. Finally, Section 5 provides the results and discussion.

2 The Decoupled Least Square Approach

The decoupled least sqaure approach is proposed in [7]. It decouples the transformation function into a rotation matrix and a translation vector which are successively determined to reduce the computational complexity. This approach has the advantage of computational efficiency, but sacrifices some numerical accuracy due to not estimating six unknown parameters simultaneously.

Fig. 1 shows the camera coordinate system, the 3D line after transformation, the center of perspective, and the 2D image line. As we can see the center of perspectivity, the 2D image line which is the perspective projection of the 3D line, and 3D line itself are on the same plane which is called the interpretation plane[8]. Let a be a unit normal vector of the interpretation plane. Then a will be perpendicular to the 3D line. It gives

$$a^t(Rp + T) = 0 \quad \& \quad a^t RN = 0 \tag{2.1}$$

where $N = [l \; m \; n]^t$ is the vector of direction cosines of the 3D line before transformation, p is an arbitrary point on the 3D line, R is a 3 by 3 orthonormal rotation matrix, i.e., $RR^t = I$ and T is a translation vector. The superscript t means the transpose and is used through the paper.

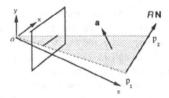

Fig. 1. shows the interpretation plane passing through the the center of perspective, the 2D image line, and the 3D line after transformation.

Estimation of Unknown Parameters

When the observation contains noise, equation (2.1) are no longer satisfied. In order to infer R and T from n noisy observations, the traditional least squares approach makes an assumption that the noisy is the ideal $a_i^t RN_i$ plus additive independent identically distributed Gaussian distribution, then it minimizes the following error function (objective function)

$$F_1 = \epsilon^t \epsilon = \sum_{i=1}^{n} (a_i^{*t} RN_i)^2 \tag{2.2}$$

Equation (2.2) can be solved by a singular value decomposition in the least squares sense. Once the estimated rotation matrix $\hat{R}$ is obtained, we can minimize the following error function to obtain the translation vector

$$F_2 = \epsilon^t \epsilon = \sum_{i=1}^{n} \sum_{j=1}^{2} \{a_i^{*t}(\hat{R}P_i^j + T)\}^2 \tag{2.3}$$

Discussion

Although the estimation procedure mentioned above is commonly used, it has two problems: one is that the underlying noise for the objective function is assumed to come from a Gaussian distribution, but this is not necessarily correct; the other is that the unknown parameters are not estimated simultaneously; in other word, the estimation is not an optimal one, since the error in the rotation matrix calculation is propagated to the translation vector calculation.

3 Statistical Estimation

Statistical estimation to unknown parameters of the exterior orientation involves the posterior distribution and the prior distribution of the unknown parameters and an underlying noise model. In this section we first discuss the underlying noise model. We make the assumption that the underlying noise model is the Fisher distribution [9,10] for the line correspondences based on the observation and characteristics of the line correspondences. Then, we obtain the posterior distribution of the unknown parameters. Finally, we estimate the unknown parameters by the maximum a posterior.

3.1 Noise Model

The Fisher distribution is one kind of spherical distribution. The density function of the Fisher distribution with mean direction along an arbitrary vector (λ, μ, ν) in spherical coordinates is expressed as

$$g(l, m, n) = c(k_c)e^{k_c(l\lambda + m\mu + n\nu)}, \quad k_c > 0 \tag{3.1}$$

where (l, m, n) is defined on the surface of the sphere with unit radius and center at the origin and $c(k_c) = \frac{k_c}{2\pi(2sinhk_c)}$. The parameter k_c is called as the concentration parameter. For large k_c the distribution is clustered around the mean direction. If the vector (λ, μ, ν) is the polar axis we have

$$g(l, m, n) = c(k_c)e^{k_c cos\theta}, \quad 0 < \theta < \pi, 0 < \phi < 2\pi, k_c > 0 \tag{3.2}$$

3.2 Posterior Distribution

In this subsection we derive a posterior distribution for the unknown parameters. Let $\Phi = [\omega \ \phi \ \kappa \ t_x \ t_y \ t_z]^t$ be the unknown parameter vector. Now given the observations ,2D lines $\{a_i^* | i = 1, 2, ..., n\}$ and the 3D lines $\{l_i | i = 1, 2, ..., n\}$. We wish to find the most probable value of Φ,

$$P(\Phi|a_1{}^*, a_2{}^*, ..., a_n{}^*, l_1, l_2, ..., l_n) = \frac{[\prod_i P(a_i{}^*|\Phi, l_i)]P(\Phi)}{P(a_1{}^*, a_2{}^*, ..., a_n{}^*|l_1, l_2, ..., l_n)} \qquad (3.3)$$

Because $a_i{}^*s$ are conditionally independent on Φ and $l'_i s$, and Φ is also conditionally independent on $l'_i s$, we have where $P(\Phi)$ is the prior distribution. Though the calculation of the exact value is very complicated, it is a constant which does not depend on Φ. Thus we may rewrite equation (3.3) as

$$P(\Phi|a_1{}^*, a_2{}^*, ..., a_n{}^*, l_1, l_2, ..., l_n) = c[\prod_i P(a_i{}^*|\Phi, l_i)]P(\Phi)$$

where c is the constant.

3.3 Estimating the Unknown Parameters

After the posterior distribution obtained, we want to choose Φ to maximize the distribution, i.e., maximize a posterior,

$$Maximize \prod_i P(a_i{}^*|\Phi, l_i)P(\Phi), \qquad (3.4)$$

As stated earlier our underlying noise model is the Fisher distribution. Therefore,

$$P(a_i{}^*|\Phi, l_i) = c(k_c)e^{k_c cos \delta\theta_i}, i = 1, 2, ..., n \quad 0 < \delta\theta_i < \pi, 0 < \phi < 2\pi, k_c > 0 \qquad (3.5)$$

Using the relationships of trigonometric functions and let $sin\frac{\delta\theta_i}{2} = \frac{1}{2}||a_i{}^* - a||$ Then, we can rewrite equation (3.3) into

$$\prod_i P(a_i{}^*|\Phi, l_i)P(\Phi) = \prod_i c(k_c)e^{k_c(1-\frac{1}{2}||a_i{}^* - a_i||^2)}P(\Phi) \qquad (3.6)$$

Upon taking logarithms of the above equation there results

$$ln \prod_i P(a_i{}^*|\Phi, l_i) = \sum_{i=1}^{n}\{lnc(k_c) + k_c(1 - \frac{1}{2}||a_i{}^* - a_i||^2)\} + lnP(\Phi) \qquad (3.7)$$

In the exterior orientation problem the domain of unknown parameter vector, Φ is in $[0, 2\pi] \times [0, 2\pi] \times [0, \pi] \times R^3$. Without any preference, Φ should be uniformly distributed over the domain. Hence, we can always assume the prior distribution $P(\Phi)$ is a constant. Thus, maximizing equation (3.7) is equivalent to determining Φ to minimize

$$\sum_{i=1}^{n}\frac{k_c}{2}||a_i{}^* - a_i(\Phi)||^2 \qquad (3.8)$$

Equation (3.8) is quite different from equation (2.2) both in concept and formula. The object function in equation (2.2) minimizes the error of the dot product between the observed unit normal vector and the direction cosines of 3D line. However, the objective function in equation (3.8) is to minimize the norm distance between the observed unit normal vector and the true unit normal vector of the plane by which the 3D line lies.

4 Experimental Protocol

Generation of Simulated Data

In order to evaluate the algorithms we arbitrarily generate the corresponding 3D and 2D line segments by giving segment midpoints, orientations, and lengths uniformly over the image. If the length of each image side is s, the lengths are uniform over the range $[s/50, s/10]$. The orientation is uniform over the range $[0, 2\pi]$.

Each of the line segments backprojects to an infinite triangle in 3D. To determine the corresponding 3D line segment, we backproject the end points of image line segment. We randomly choose a magnitude between 30 and 70. The end point of the 3D line is obtained by multiplying the unit vector that is passing the center of perspectivity and the end point of image line segment by the magnitude. The focal length is taken to be one. Two end points determine the 3D line segment in the camera coordinates. To determine the line segments in the 3D object coordinate system, we generate a random rotation and translation (6 degrees of freedom). The range of Φ is in $[15°, 45°] \times [30°, 60°] \times [45°, 75°] \times [-20, 20] \times [-20, 20] \times [-20, 20]$ for the simulated data. The unit for the translation vector is the same as focal length. Then, we use the Φ to transform the 3D lines from the 3D camera coordinate system to the world coordinate system. The noise is generated by using the transformation method [11] to obtain the Fisher distribution from a uniform distribution in $[0, 1]$.

Performance Characterization

To evaluate the performance of the least squares solution and our algorithm we run one thousand trials based on the two controlled parameters: The number of corresponding line pairs n and The concentration parameter k_c. The larger value of k_c corresponds to the smaller noise level. The initial guess is generated within 20% of the true value. For example, the value of ω is generated from $[15°, 45°]$ and the initial value, for ω_i is generated from a uniform distribution satisfying $|\omega_i - \omega| < 0.2|\omega|$.

Real Image Experiment

We apply the new algorithm to the hallway image obtained from the image library of the VISIONS group at the University of Massachusetts. The image is 512 by 484 with a field of view of 24.0 degree by 23.0 degree. Detailed model parameters are described in [6]. One of the images and its segmentation results is shown in Fig. 2. We take nine line segments for the exterior orientation is shown in Fig. 3.

 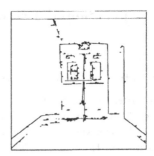

Fig. 2. The hallway image and its segmentation results. The origin of the image plane is assumed to be at (242, 256).

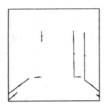

Fig. 3. The line segments used for the exterior orientation

5 Results and Discussions

In the first experiment we study the numerical stability of the new algorithm and the decoupled least squares algorithm by applying both algorithms on the unperturbed observations. The results of the study are shown in Table I. The computation resolution is twelve digits, that means, the error for Φ in the new algorithm and Ψ (three Euler angles) in the decoupled least squares algorithm is less than 10^{-12}. However, the unnoticeable error in the Euler angles is propagated to the translation vector when the decoupled calculation is used. As a result, all three components in the translation vector have an error around 10^{-6}. This explains why we should estimate the six parameters simultaneously in order to obtain the optimal solution.

In the second experiment we study how the number of line correspondences affects the accuracy of the estimation. The number of line correspondences can be 6, 10, 20, and 30. As shown in Fig. 4, the increase of the number of line correspondences surely improves the estimation results for both techniques. The mean absolute error of translation vector is inversely proportional to the number of line correspondences. The mean absolute error of the three Euler angles is improved too.

In the hallway image we list the results in Table II. The results show that the estimation is very close to the ground truth in x and z components and

Table I. The results of unperturbed observation with initial guess within 20% of the true value. The number of correspondences N changes based on 6, 10, 15, and 30.

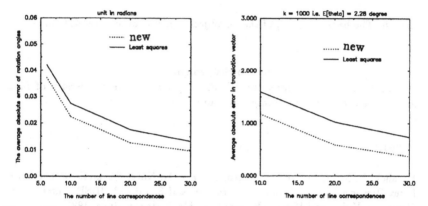

Fig. 4. The study of the number of corresponding lines affects on the estimation. The initial guess is within 20% of the true value and $k_c = 1000$.

about 7% difference in y component. The error in y component may be caused by the bias along the horizontal axis of the image center. Since the true rotation is unknown, we backproject the 3D model lines onto the image in Fig. 2 by the estimated transformation. The result is shown in Fig. 5.

Though the new algorithm is better in accuracy, it pays a price in computing cost due to more complicated derivation of the unit normal vector **a**. However, the number of iterations is about the same for both methods.

Table II. The estimation of six unknown parameters and the ground truth for the hallway image. NA means that data are not available. The translation x direction is parallel to hallway, the y direction is the horizontal direction, and the z-direction is the vertical direction.

Parameter	ω	ϕ	κ	t_x (ft.)	t_y (ft.)	t_z (ft.)
True	NA	NA	NA	34.792	4.033	3.6
Estimation	0.00318	0.01207	-0.01047	34.533	3.740	3.545

Fig. 5. The backprojection of the 3D object model lines onto the 2D image.

Acknowledgements

The authors wish to thank the VISIONS group at the University of Massachusetts for providing the image data and information.

References

1. Haralick, R. M., C. N. Lee, K. Ottenberg, and M. Nölle, "Analysis of The Three Point Perspective Pose Estimation Problem and Solutions", IEEE conference on Computer Vision and Pattern Recognition, Maui, Hawaii, June, 1991.

2. Linnainmaa, S., D. Harwood, and L.S. Davis, "Pose Estimation of a Three-Dimensional Object Using Triangle Pairs," *IEEE Transactions on Pattern Analysis and Machine Intelligence*, Vol.10, No.5, 1988, pp. 634-647.

3. Pope, J.A., "An Advantageous, Alternative Parameterization of Rotations for Analytical Photogrammetry," *ESSA Tech. Rep.*, C and GS 39.

4. Thompson, E.H. "On Exact Linear Solution of the Problem of Absolute Orientation," *Photogrammetria, Vol. 13, No. 4*, 1958, pp. 163-178.

5. Lowe, D. G. *Perceptual Organization and Visual Recognition,* Boston: Kluwer, 1985

6. Kumar, R., and R. Hanson, "Analysis of Different Robust Methods for Pose Estimation," *,IEEE Workshop on Robust Computer Vision*, Seattle, WA, Oct. 1-3, 1990.

7. Liu, Yuncai, Thomas S. Huang, and O. D. Faugeras, " Determination of Camera Location from 2-D to 3-D Line and Point Correspondences," *IEEE Transactions on Pattern Analysis and Machine Intelligence*, Vol.12, No.1, 1990, pp. 28-37.

8. Barnard S. T., "Interpreting Perspective Images," *Artificial Intelligence*, Vol. 21, 1983, pp. 435-462.

9. Fisher, R. A., "Dispersion on a Sphere," Proceedings Royal Society of London, Vol. 217, A., 1953.

10. Mardia, K.V., "Statistics of directional data," New York: Academic Press, 1972.

11. Papoulis, A., "Probability, Random Variables, and Stochastic Process," 1984.

High Level Scene Interpretation using Fuzzy Belief*

Sandy Dance and Zhi-Qiang Liu

Department of Computer Science, University of Melbourne, Parkville, 3052, Australia
sandy@cs.mu.OZ.AU

Abstract. In this paper we present an image understanding system using fuzzy sets. This system is based on a symbolic object-oriented image interpretation system (SOO-PIN) we developed previously. It is known that in many image analysis and understanding applications, objects are not well-defined and are engaged in dynamic activities, which in most cases can only be described vaguely. Using fuzzy sets we are able to capture subtle variations and manage uncertainty properly. We demonstrate the effectiveness of our system with complex traffic scenes.

1 Introduction

In scene understanding and image analysis we often face many uncertain factors. Traditionally uncertainty is handled by probabilistic methods such as Bayesian networks and the Dempster-Shafer paradigm. However, these methods are based on rigid and crisp occurrence of events and in many cases are unable to treat vagueness and subtlety. Furthermore, such methods are not suitable for natural linguistic descriptions.

The SOO-PIN concept is built upon the idea that high-level interpretation is best performed using a network of independent "processes" (called concept-frames), each concerned with an aspect of the interpretation – a concept. They run in parallel, and communicate via message passing. The network is initiated by low level image segmentation and labeling, and the interpretation is generated by high level concept-frames.

2 Fuzzy Belief Measure

In [6] it is pointed out that there are two kinds of evidence: disjunctive, in which the evidence is seen as narrowing the range of possibilities of a variable, and conjunctive, in which the variable takes on a range as its value, as in "John stayed in Paris from 1980 till 1982". Fuzzy set theory handles conjunctive evidence naturally. Also, fuzzy measures (possibility theory) are more tolerant of non independent evidence than Dempster-Shafer (DS) or Bayes, and fuzzy sets are useful when definitions are imprecise [1].

---

* This work is supported by an Australian Research Council (ARC) large grant

In scene understanding, features of objects are extracted by low-level processing, usually resulting in imprecise and incomplete information. For instance, a car in the scene can be segmented as a rectangular blob having what could be described as degrees of "car-ness". We require a measure to attach to statements like "segment A is a car", where "car" can be considered a fuzzy set in the space of all possible segments.

The measure must also be manipulated and combined with other propositions as the interpretation is conveyed through the network. A possibility measure can be defined from fuzzy sets via the mechanism of α-cuts [6] that define a set of "focal elements" in the sense of DS evidence theory, although in this case the focal elements are consonant, ie, the sets are nested. The sets F_α are defined from the fuzzy set F, given by its membership function $\mu_F : \Omega \to [0,1]$, by $F_\alpha = \{\omega|\mu_F(\omega) \geq \alpha\}$. It is shown [6] how a mass assignment can be defined for the consonant focal sets F_α and thus support S and plausibility P can be defined, and that:

$$P(\{\omega\}) = \mu_F(\omega) \tag{1}$$

ie, the plausibility of the proposition "ω is a member of fuzzy set F" is its membership value, where $\{\omega\}$ is a singleton. Plausibility defined from consonant focal sets is called **possibility**. The complement of possibility is called **necessity**.

In [5] we show the derivation of the combination rules for these fuzzy measures, which are in brief

$$P(u \cap v) = \min(P(u), P(v)) \tag{2}$$
$$P(u \cup v) = \max(P(u), P(v)),$$

and we go on to argue that necessity measures in a continuous frame of discernment (such as those used here) are in general zero.

3   Fuzzy Set Processing

In this section we discuss how we use fuzzy sets within our system. Fuzzy sets whose frame of discernment is the real line are a mapping ("compatibility function" [8]) $\mu : \mathcal{R} \Rightarrow [0,1]$, the range being membership values in the fuzzy set.

For simplicity, convex fuzzy sets [3, p47] can be limited to a class defined by 5 numbers [2] (S,B,H1,H2,E) where S is the vertical scale (S = 1 for a normalised fuzzy set), B is where the set becomes nonzero, H1 is where it becomes maximum, H2 is where it leaves the maximum, and E is where the set returns to zero.

To deal with fuzzy sets, we need to implement the implication $I \Rightarrow O$ where I and O are fuzzy sets. Beyond that, given a value in the frame of discernment of I, and a set of fuzzy implication rules from I to O, find the output response in O. These steps are accomplished as follows:

Assuming input value $x \in I$, the membership value of x in I is $\mu_I(x)$. Applying a rule $I \Rightarrow O$ gives fuzzy set O scaled by $\mu_I(x)$ [7]. The crisp output from this set is given by the centroid of the scaled O. More complex scenarios [7] come about when combining fuzzy sets based on different frames of discernment, say,

$X_1 \cap Y_1 \Rightarrow O_1$, $X_2 \cap Y_2 \Rightarrow O_2$, where X_1 and X_2 are in frame of discernment X, Y_1 and Y_2 are in frame of discernment Y, and O_1 and O_2 are in frame of discernment O.

To get a crisp output, the output sets are summed and the centroid is found as in [7]. Thus, the centroid of the fuzzy set (S,B,H1,H2,E) is $(E^2 + H2 * E + H2^2 - H1^2 - H1 * B - B^2)/3(E1 + H2 - H1 - B)$ along the X axis (frame of discernment axis), and $S(E + 2H2 - 2H1 - B)/3(E1 + H2 - H1 - B)$ along the Y axis (scale or membership value of the centroid). The area of the trapezoidal fuzzy set is given by $S(E + H2 - H1 - B)/2$. The centroid of a series of fuzzy sets based upon the same frame of discernment is given by $\sum_i c_i a_i / \sum_i a_i$ where a_i is the area of the ith set and c_i is the X or Y coordinate of the centroid of the ith set, depending on which coordinate is required.

4 Interpretation of Traffic Scenes

We have implemented the SOO-PIN system for a number of scenarios, especially the traffic scenario [4]. Here the system takes images of road intersections (Figure 6(a)), interprets vehicle activities (ie, *vehicle A is turning right from the west*) and produces legal analyses of the scene such as:

- Whether the car is on the wrong side of road or intersection.
- When a car should give way to another.
- Traffic jams (ie, give-way deadlocks).

These concepts have been incorporated in the network shown in Figure 1.

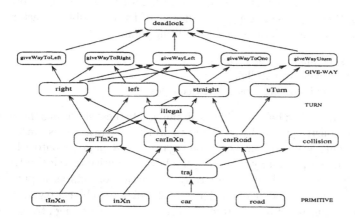

Fig. 1. The traffic scenario network-of-frames. The arrows refer to check or create messages, inquiry and update messages are not shown. inXn refers to "intersection", tInXn to "T-intersection", carInXn to the concept of a car in an intersection, carTInXn refers to a car in a T-intersection, and carRoad to a car in a road.

5   Fuzzy processing in SOO-PIN

In this section we describe some of the fuzzy belief measures input into the SOO-PIN system, and how these measures are used. These inputs come from:

- the detection of a car, as indicated by segmented blobs.
- the determination of velocity.
- car activity, ie, whether it is turning left, right or going straight ahead.

It can be seen that these fuzzy belief generators all occur at numeric–symbolic boundaries, which are characterized by vague information. Fuzzy belief measures and fuzzy linguistic hedges[8] can be used in this case to produce more natural and easily understandable scene interpretations. In [5] we describe the fuzzy processing involved in finding the car segments and car acitivities, here we describe the fuzzy sets processing involved in determing car velocities.

5.1   Fuzzy belief from velocity

In computer vision, velocity, like stereopsis, generally involves the correspondence problem, ie, finding segments in two or more images that are the "same" object in the world. This is possible because in both velocity and stereopsis there are strong constraints imposed upon such matching. Of course, such a matching involves uncertainty, the system must choose the "best" from several possible matches. Fuzzy sets provide a mechanism for dealing with such uncertainty because the dynamical contraints (in our case involving the inertia of the cars) imposed on any possible matches are not in themselves statistical or probabilistic, but rather express concepts like "degree of fit to possible trajectory". The system has to deal with ambiguities resulting from:

- objects moving in close vicinity,
- objects moving in parallel,
- objects moving along crossing trajectories.

The system described below is able to disambiguate these situations through such dynamical constraints, and the degree to which the trajectories are *consistent* with the dynamical constraints can be regarded as a mapping onto a fuzzy set, thus providing a possibility measure. In addition, consistent velocity trajectory (CVT) plays a key role in dynamically interacting objects as it gives causal information about the dynamic behaviour of individual objects (eg, cars). CVT can reinforce our belief in the presence of the object, even though the object can initially have a low plausilility value.

Velocity is found by comparing 3 frames of video 9 or 10 frames apart, or more precisely, matches are found between the two adjacent pairs of frames from the three frame sequence. Finding a matching pair involves optimizing the match on the basis of consistency of velocity and orientation. Below we consider how to attach a confidence to the match between two pairings of cars between three frames, given that we have the following from any given pairing:

- apparent velocity given by the pair,
- rotation of principle axis between the pair.

From these, we calculate for each such match the measures (Figure 2):

- average speed over the three sequential image frames (AV),
- speed difference (ΔV),
- rotation rate difference (ΔR),
- difference between velocity rotation and principle axis rotation (ΔVO).

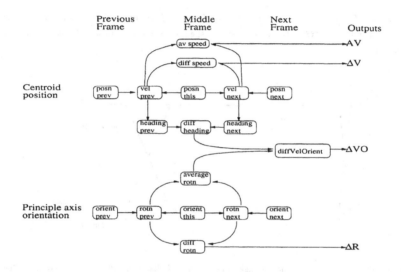

Fig. 2. The data flow involved in calculating the input values to the fuzzy processing. The centroid position and orientation of the cars in the 3 frames are manipulated to produce avSpeed (AV), diffSpeed (ΔV), diffVelOr (ΔVO) and diffRotn (ΔR).

Fuzzy sets are found from the 3 measures above (Figure 3), plus from the average speed of the match (Figure 4). This last is used to distinguish cars that are stopped from moving in order to apply different fuzzy rules, ie, stopped cars should show no orientation rotation, but quite arbitrary velocity headings.

The fuzzy rules used are as follows:

```
      lowDiffSpeed, lowDiffRotn, lowDiffVelOr ⇒ LowDiffOK   (high belief)
       lowAvSpeed, lowDiffSpeed, lowDiffRotn ⇒ LowSpeedOK (med belief)
        okDiffSpeed, okDiffRotn, okdiffVelOr ⇒ MedSpeedOK (med belief)
                       lowAvSpeed, medDiffRotn ⇒ BadRotn    (low belief)
highDiffSpeed ∪ highAvSpeed ∪ highDiffRotn ⇒ OutOB     (low belief)
              medAvSpeed, highdiffVelOr ⇒ OutOB     (low belief)
```

The output fuzzy sets are over a confidence measure, ie, the frame of discernment is the closed interval [0, 1] (Figure 5). For each match, the centroid of

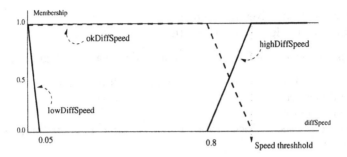

Fig. 3. The fuzzy sets in the speed difference frame of discernment. The sets are `lowDiffSpeed`, `okDiffSpeed` and `highDiffSpeed`. The fuzzy sets in the frames of discernment `diffRotn` and `diffVelOr` are similar.

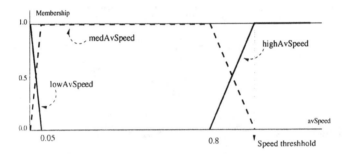

Fig. 4. The fuzzy sets in the average speed frame of discernment. The sets are `lowAvSpeed`, `medAvSpeed` and `highAvSpeed`.

the sum of these sets is found using the procedure described in Section 3. The matching with the highest confidence measure is chosen as the correct match, and is used to create a trajectory instance.

5.2 Fuzzy Linguistic Hedges

The final interpretations have possibility values attached to them which are used to alter the linguistic output using hedges – English words that modify the confidence in statements. We have chosen the following map between possibility values and hedges: *(0.0–0.05)* ⇒ no output, *(0.05–0.3)* ⇒ *conceivably*, *(0.3–0.7)* ⇒ *possibly*, *(0.7–0.95)* ⇒ *probably*, *(0.95–1.0)* ⇒ no hedge.

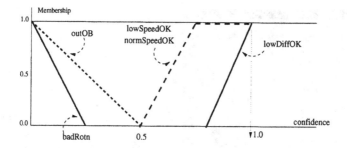

Fig. 5. The fuzzy sets in the confidence frame of discernment. The sets are lowDiffOK, lowSpeedOK, medSpeedOK, badRotn and outOB.

6 Results

Figure 6 shows a typical input image together with an intermediate result showing positions of cars found and their velocities, if any, within the intersection boundary. As an example, the normalised measures for the trajectory calculation for car $c2\_150$ are: AV = 0.33, ΔV=0.13, ΔR=0.26, ΔVO=0.23. These map into: *medAbsSpeed=1, okDiffSpeed=1, lowDiffRotn=0.34, medDiffRotn=0.65, okDiffRotn=1, lowDiffVelO=0.40, medDiffVelO=0.59, okDiffVelO=1*, which in turn sum to a final trajectory belief of 0.75. The interpretation for this scene is:

* *Give Way to left-turner: car $c4\_150$ turning right from west has possibly given way to car $c1\_150$ from east.*
* *Give Way to left-turner: car $c5\_150$ turning right from west has possibly given way to car $c1\_150$ from east.*

In this case every car activity has been correctly identified, and both the interactions in the interpretation are correct. One can see how two cars are speeding through the intersection, and the turners are creeping forward with short but correctly oriented velocity arrows. The linguistic hedge "possibly" has been generated in both these interpretations, reflecting a medium belief.

7 Conclusion

We have presented a new approach for image interpretation using fuzzy belief measures and fuzzy linguistic hedges. Our approach is based on our SOO-PIN system which is an object-oriented network-of-frames introduced in the artificial intelligence literature. The system is implemented in the object oriented concurrent logic programming language PARLOG++.

To demonstrate the effectiveness of our method, we presented the problem of complex traffic scene analysis. In the examples, we discussed in detail the uncertainty present in the determination of vehicle velocity, and proposed several different fuzzy membership functions to cover such uncertainties and vagueness.

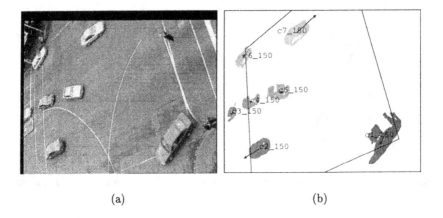

(a) (b)

Fig. 6. Traffic scene, middle image of the triple (a) and processed image (b) with car labels, and velocities shown as arrow lengths. The intersection boundary is input manually, north is up.

Our experiments show that indeed, with the incorporation of fuzzy mechanisms, the system is able to handle diverse uncertain situations and to produce more natural and consistent results.

We are currently refining our system to handle more complicated and subtle cases in traffic interpretation and in medical information analysis.

References

1. J. Baldwin, Support logic programming, in A. Jones et al., editors, *Fuzzy sets - Theory and Applications, Proceedings of NATO Advanced Study Institute*, Reidel Pub. Co., Norwell, MA (1986).
2. M. Cayrol, H. Farreny, and H. Prade, Fuzzy pattern matching, *Kybernetes*, **11**, 103–116 (1982).
3. S.-J. Chen and C.-L. Hwang. *Fuzzy Multiple Attribute Decision Making*, Lecture Notes in Economics and Mathematical Systems. Springer-Verlag, Berlin (1992).
4. S. Dance, T. Caelli, and Z.-Q. Liu. *Picture Interpretation: a Symbolic Approach*, Series in Machine Perception and Artificial Intelligence. World Scientific Publishing Co., Singapore. (1995).
5. S. Dance and Z.-Q. Liu, Fuzzy belief and scene interpretation, in T. Huang and S. Negadharipour, editors, *Proceedings of the 1995 IEEE International Symposium on Computer Vision*, Florida, USA (1995).
6. D. Dubois and H. Prade, A set-theoretic view of belief functions: logical operations and approximations by fuzzy sets, *International Journal of General Systems*, **12**, 193–226 (1986).
7. B. Kosko. *Neural Networks and Fuzzy Systems*. Prentice Hall (1992).
8. L. A. Zadeh, The concept of a linguistic variable and its application to approximate reasoning: Part I, *Information Sciences*, **8**, 199–249 (1975).

Estimating Shape and Reflectance of Surfaces by Color Image Analysis

Yingli Tian   Hungtat Tsui

Department of Electronic Engineering
The Chinese University of Hong Kong

Abstract. Sato and Ikeuchi[4] proposed an interesting method of shape recovery based on color image analysis which requires the object to be enclosed in a spherical diffuser. In this paper, we improve the method to relax this restriction. Like [4], we use the dichromatic-reflection model to separate the specular reflection and the diffuse reflection. In our method, the point light source is enclosed by a diffuser and is moved to different specified locations by a robot arm. This changes the lighting geometry and a new radiance function of the source is derived. On the whole, this is an improvement on the inconvenient set up of [4]. The capability of our method is verified by real experiments. A simulation package is also developed to test the efficacy of our approach for objects of different sizes under various forms of lighting geometry.

1 Introduction

Shape recovery is a classical problem in computer vision. *Local Shape from Specularity* [13][14], *Shape from Shading*[9][11], *Photometric Stereo*[7][12] are examples of techniques that extract three-dimensional shape information from photometric measurements. These methods usually assume the surface reflectance to be either Lambertian or specular. In practice, many surfaces are hybrid, i.e. surfaces which have diffuse and specular reflection. Generally, surface reflection can be classified as one of three groups: diffuse, specular, and hybrid reflection. Fig. 1 shows three reflection components of a surface in relation to the source angle for a fixed viewing direction.

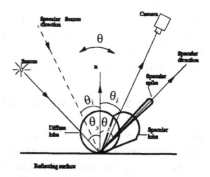

Fig. 1. Three reflection components of surface in relation to the source angles for a fixed viewing direction

Comparing with *Shape from Shading, Photometric Stereo*[12] is a more accurate method with less assumptions. In this approach, different reflectance maps are derived for corresponding light sources at different locations. The light sources are illuminated, one at a time, and a corresponding image is taken. At each light source location, one constraint equation of intensity can be obtained from each image and the corresponding reflectance map. Very often, two constraint equations will yield a unique solution. Sometimes, three constraint equations are required for the purpose. Additional constraints may be used to give more robust estimations on the surface. However, the conventional photometric method works only for Lambertian surfaces.

Recently, the color information had been used to recover surface shape[4][7]. In[4], Sato et. al. use the temporal-color space whose axes are the three color axes R(red), G(green), B(blue) and one temporal axis. Conceptually, the two reflection components of the dichromatic-reflection model: the specular-reflection component and the body-reflection component, form two subspaces in temporal-color space. Specular and diffuse reflections were separated and were used individually to recover the surface shape. A large diffuse spherical lampshade with a diameter of 20 inches is used to provide the required extended lighting. A point light source is moved in steps around and outside the diffuser in its equatorial plane to provide lighting for the image at each step. However the target object must be small and located at the center of this shade. Though it is obviously not very practical and inconvenient, yet it shows a method of shape recovery using color information.

In this paper, we improved the method of Sato and Ikeuchi[4] eliminate the above shortcomings. A new movable extended light source is used to recover the surface shape and reflectance from color image sequences grabbed by a fixed camera. Like [4], we use the dichromatic-reflection model to separate the specular reflection and the body-reflection. In our method, the diffuser is enclosing the point light source which is moved to different specified locations by a robot arm. This is an improvement on the inconvenient set up of [4] which requires the target object to be enclosed by a very large fixed diffuser. The capability of our method is verified by both synthetic and real experiments. From our experiments, we found that interreflection has a detrimental effect on shape recovery and must be reduced to a minimum. Section 2 introduces our light source model. Section 3 gives a brief account of the basic photometric functions. Section 4 gives a brief account of the algorithms of Sato and Ikeuchi used by us for shape recovery from color images. Experimental results are given in section 5.

2 Extended Light Source Model

We generated an extended light source by illuminating a bulb of light-diffusing material with a point light source. The geometry of the extended light source is shown in Fig. 2. The point light source is placed at a distance H from the object and is located at the center of a spherical diffuser of radius r. Let us assume that the diffuser is "ideal", i.e. incident energy is scattered equally in all directions. Then the radiance $L(\theta, \theta_s)$ of the outer surface of the diffuser is proportional to the irradiance $E(\theta, \theta_s)$ of the inner surface of the diffuser[12]:

$$L(\theta, \theta_s) = C E(\theta, \theta_s) \tag{1}$$

where C is a constant of proportionality. The analytic expression for the surface

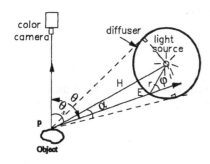

Fig. 2. Geometry of the extended light source

irradiance $E(\theta, \theta_s)$ may be derived from the basics of radiometry as in[12]:

$$E(\theta, \theta_s) = \frac{I \cos\varphi}{r^2} \qquad (2)$$

where I is the radiant intensity of the point light source. The radiance of the extended source can be determined by expressing the variables φ in equation (2) in the terms of the parameters r, H, and θ_s of the illumination geometry:

$$L(\theta, \theta_s) = \frac{CI\sqrt{r^2 - H^2 \sin^2(\theta - \theta_s)}}{r^3}, \qquad (3)$$

$$\theta_s - \alpha < \theta < \theta_s + \alpha$$

The radiance function $L(\theta, \theta_s)$ is symmetric, with respect to the source direction($\theta = \theta_s$), and its magnitude decreases as θ deviates from θ_s. Points on the diffuser that lie in the interval $\theta_s - \alpha < \theta < \theta_s + \alpha$ contribute to the irradiance on the object. The source termination angle α is determined from Fig. 2 as:

$$\alpha = \sin^{-1}\frac{r}{H} \qquad (4)$$

3 Basic Photometric Function

Since image intensity is assumed to be proportional to image irradiance, the basic photometric function is similar to the image irradiance equation. Consider an object illuminated by a point light source, the source direction vector **s**, surface normal vector **n**, and viewing vector **v**, all lie in the same plane. So we can express the two components of image intensity by the zenith angle θ_s and θ_n. The point source emits light in all directions. The intensity at any point in the image of the surface may be expressed as[12]:

$$I = I_B + I_S = A \cos(\theta_s - \theta_n) + B \delta(\theta_s - 2\theta_n) \qquad (5)$$

where I_B and A is the intensity and the reflectance of the Lambertian component respectively. I_S and B is the intensity and the reflectance of the specular component.

An extended source can be thought of as a collection of many point light source. The radiance of each point light source is dependent on its position on the extended source. The irradiance of the object surface can be determined by integrating the light energies reflected from all points on the extended source. Therefore, the modified photometric function $I'(\theta)$ is determined by convolving the basic photometric function $I(\theta)$ with the extended source radiance function $L(\theta, \theta_s)$. For a surface point of orientation θ_n, the lambertian component $I_B{}'(\theta)$ of the modified photometric function is determined using the equations by Nayar et al.[12]:

$$I_B'(\theta) = A \int_{\theta_s - \alpha}^{\theta_s + \alpha} L(\theta, \theta_s) \cos(\theta - \theta_n) \, d\theta \tag{6}$$

The limits of the integral are determined by the width of extended source. Similarly, the specular intensity component $I_S{}'(\theta)$ resulting from the extended source $L(\theta, \theta_s)$ is determined as[12]:

$$I_S'(\theta) = B \int_{\theta_s - \alpha}^{\theta_s + \alpha} L(\theta, \theta_s) \, \delta(\theta - 2\theta_n) \, d\theta \tag{7}$$

From equation (3), we know $L(\theta, \theta_s)$ is symmetric with respect to the source direction θ_s, and the center of mass of the radiance function is in the direction θ_s. The modified photometric function relates image intensity $I'(\theta)$ to extended source direction θ_s is expressed as the sum of the components $I_B{}'(\theta)$ and $I_S{}'(\theta)$. We obtain from our lighting equation as:

$$I'(\theta) = I_B'(\theta) + I_S'(\theta) = \frac{A'}{H r^2} \cos(\theta_s - \theta_n) + \frac{B'}{r^3} \sqrt{r^2 - H^2 \sin^2(\theta_s - 2\theta_n)} \tag{8}$$

where the constant A' and B' represent the same means as A and B.

4 Extracting Shape and Reflectance of Surfaces from Color Images

In this section, a short account of the Sato and Ikeuchi algorithm for extracting shape from the body reflection and specular reflection is given.

4.1 Temporal-color Space Analysis of Reflection

Considering the hybrid reflectance model when there is no interreflection and there is only an extended light source, the pixel intensities in R, G, and B channels obey the following formulas from [4]:

$$I(\theta_s) = \left[I_R(\theta_s), \ I_G(\theta_s), \ I_B(\theta_s) \right]^T = K_L \cos(\theta_s - \theta_n) + K_S L(\theta_s - 2\theta_n) \tag{9}$$

where $L(\theta_s - 2\theta_n)$ is the geometrical term of the incident light. $\mathbf{K_L}$ and $\mathbf{K_S}$ represent the color of the body reflection and specular reflection components in the dichromatic reflectance model[1].

The pixel intensities in the R, G, and B channels with m different light-source directions with a fixed camera are measured at one pixel. For hybrid reflection model, Sato and Ikeuchi[4] represent the intensity values in the R, G, and B channels as:

$$I = [I_R I_G I_B] = [D_L \ D_S] \begin{bmatrix} K_L^T \\ K_S^T \end{bmatrix} = DK, \tag{10}$$

where the two vectors D_L and D_S represent the intensity values of the body reflection and specular reflection components with respect to the light source direction θ_s.

If we know the color matrix K, then we can obtain the two reflection components represented by the geometry matrix D and the two color vectors K_L and K_S[4]:

$$D = IK^* \tag{11}$$

where K^* is a 3 x 2 pseudoinverse matrix of the color matrix K.

Once matrix D has been obtained, the loci of the body-reflection component and the specular-reflection component in the temporal-color space can be extracted as shown in equation (12):

$$I_{body} = D_L K_L^T, \qquad I_{spe} = D_S K_S^T \tag{12}$$

4.2 Estimation of Illuminant Color K_S and the Color Vector of the Body-Reflection Component K_L

Estimation of Illuminant Color Vector K_S. We use the same technique as Sato and Ikeuchi[4] for estimating K_S. According to the dichromatic reflection model [2], the color of reflection from a dielectric object is a linear combination of the body and the specular reflection components. The color of the specular-reflection component is equal to the illumination color.

In our experiment, we use a multi-colored object to calculate the illuminant color K_S[4]. First, several pixels of different colors in the image are manually selected. Then, by plotting the observed reflection color of each pixel in the x-y chromaticity diagram[10] over the image sequence, we obtain several line segments in the x-y chromaticity diagram. The illuminant color can be determined by the intersection of those line segments in the diagram. In our calculation, for getting x-y diagram from the R, G, and B values of the pixel, we change the RGB color space to the XYZ color space and obtain the normalized x, y from X, Y, and Z.

Estimation of the Color Vector of the Body-Reflection Component K_L. If two vectors, $W_i = [W_{Ri} \ W_{Gi} \ W_{Bi}]^T$ ($i = 1, 2$), are sampled on the θ_s axis at an interval greater than 2α, at least one of these vectors is equal to the color vector of the body-reflection component K_L. This vector has no specular-reflection component. Therefore the desired color vector of the body-reflection component K_L is the vector W_i that subtends the largest angle with respect to the vector K_S. The angle between the two color vectors can be calculated using the dot product:

$$\gamma = \cos^{-1} \frac{K_S^T \cdot W_i}{|K_S^T||W_i|} \qquad (13)$$

For purely specular-reflection object, $K_L=0$. For object with body-reflection only, the rank of the matrix W will be one.

4.3 Recover Surface Shape and Reflectance

After we obtained K_L and K_S, the geometry matrix D can be calculated from equation (11), and the body-reflection component and the specular-reflection component can be separated from equation (12). Like Sato & Ikeuchi[4], we use a cosine curve to fit the body-reflection component and a Gaussian curve to fit the specular-reflection component as the approximation of $L(\theta_s - 2\theta_n)$ [Equation (14)]:

$$I_{body} = C_1 \cos(\theta_s - C_2) + C_3, \qquad I_{spe} = D_1 \exp\left[\frac{-(\theta_s - D_2)^2}{D_3^2}\right] \qquad (14)$$

where C_1 and D_1 are the reflectance of the body-reflection and specular reflection components respectively. C_2 and $D_2/2$ are the directions of the surface normal.

5 Experimental System and Results

5.1 Basic Experimental System

The experiment setup is shown in Fig. 3. The distance between the camera and the object is about 32cm. A lampshade with a diameter of 15.3cm enclosing a point light source is used as an extended light source. It is attached to a SCORBOT-ER IX robot arm which moves around the object along a circular path in the plane containing the optical axis of the camera. The distance H between the object and the light source center is 29.4cm. The

Fig. 3. The experiment setup

number of samples is 14 with $\alpha=15°$. We use a CCD color camera to grab images. One image was grabbed in steps of $10°$ from $-90°$ to $+90°$(excluding $-20°$, $-10°$, $0°$, $10°$ and $20°$ where the camera is located). Generally, more accurate results can be obtained when the number of sample is larger. This is especially true for using the specular reflection component to recover surface shape.

5.2 Experimental Results

There Is Interreflection from the Environment. In this experiment, there is interreflection from the robot arm and the rack. For our extended light source model, $K_S=[0.2921, 0.2827, 0.4253]$. $K_L=[0.4720, 0.3106, 0.2174]$. The surface normals obtained by the cosine curve fitting from body-reflection component are shown in the column θ_s1 in Table 1. The results is not too good because of the effects of interreflection.

There Is Little Interreflection from the Environment. In this experiments, we use some black clothes to cover the robot arm and the camera. So there is little interreflection from the environment. The number of samples is the same as before. The surface normals obtained by cosine curve fitting from body-reflection component are shown in the column θ_s2 in Table 1. The results are good. The interreflection has a serious effect on shape recovery.

The Simulation Results. In the simulation, we use a reddish sphere as our object. $K_S=[0.3333, 0.3333, 0.3333]$. $K_L=[0.52, 0.27, 0.21]$. The number of samples is 18 with $\alpha=15°$. One image was grabbed in steps of 5° from 5° to 90°. The surface normals obtained by cosine curve fitting of the body-reflection component and by Gaussian curve fitting of the specular-reflection component are shown as the column of θ_n-*body* and θ_n-*spe* in Table 2 respectively. The results are very good.

Table I The surface normal recovered from body reflection component

θ_n	θ_n1	θ_n2
-90°	-53.60°	-79.59°
-60°	-79.56°	-60.02°
-45°	-84.87°	-45.44°
-30°	-45.98°	-28.23°
0°	-6.67°	-5.91°
30°	27.96°	28.63°
45°	42.67°	41.43°
60°	81.30°	58.49°
90°	83.59°	84.83°

6 Conclusions

In this paper, we improve the method of Sato and Ikeuchi[4] for object shape estimation from color image sequences by using a more convenient lighting arrangement. In our method, a point light source is enclosed by a diffuser which is moved to different specified locations by a robot arm. This is an improvement on the inconvenient set up of [4] which requires the target object to be enclosed by a very large fixed diffuser. We derive a new lighting equation [equation(8)] due to the change in the lighting geometry. Like [4], we use the dichromatic-reflection model to separate the specular reflection and the body-reflection. The capability of our method is verified by both real and simulated experiments. A simulation package is developed to test the efficacy of our approach. The package can also be used to check the practicality of our approach on shape estimation of large objects and on the effect of various form of lighting geometry. From the experiments, we found that interreflection is a serious problem on shape recovery and has to be dealt with carefully.

References

1. G. J. Klinker, S. A. Shafer and T. Kanade "*A Physical Approach to Color Image Understanding,*" IJCV, 4, p7-38, 1990

2. S.A.Shafer *"Using Color to Separate Reflection Components,"* Color Research and Application.10(4):210-218,1985

3. G.J. Klinker, S.A.Shafer and T. Kanade "*Using a Color Reflection Model to Separate Highlights from Object Color,*" Proc. the 1st ICCV, pp.145-150, London, June 1987

4. Y. Sato and K. Ikeuchi," *Temporal-Color Space Analysis of Reflection,*" Proc. of the CVPR, p570-576, 1993

5. S. K. Nayar and Y. Gong," *Colored Interreflections and Shape Recovery,*" Proc. of Image Understanding Workshop, p333-343, DARPA Jan. 1992

Table II The surface normal recovered from body reflection component and specular reflection component

θ_n	θ_n-body	θ_n-spe
0°	0.28°	0.39°
10°	9.80°	9.80°
20°	19.51°	20.00°
30°	30.01°	30.20°
40°	40.01°	38.83°
50°	50.06°	--
60°	59.95°	--
70°	70.33°	--
80°	80.11°	--

6. G. J. Klinker, S. A. Shafer and T. Kanade," *The Measurement of Highlights in Color Images,*" IJCV, 2, p7-32, 1988

7. P. H. Christensen and L. G. Shapiro,*"Three-Dimensional Shape from Color Photometric Stereo,"* IJCV,13:2, p213-227,1994

8. P. Dupuis and J. Oliensis *"Direct Method for Reconstructing Shape from Shading,"* Proc. Image Understanding Workshop, 1992 DAPRA

9. B. Kim and P. Burger,*"Depth and Shape from Shading Using the Photometric Stereo Method,"* CVGIP:Image Understanding,Vol.54,No.3,p416-427,Nov.1991

10. H. C. Lee,*"Method for computing the scene-illuminant chromaticity from specular highlight,"* J. Opt. Soc. Am. A3, p1694-1699,1986

11. B. K. P. Horn and M. J. Brooks, *Shape from Shading,* The MIT Press, 1989

12. S. K. Nayar, K. Ikeuchi and T. Kanade, " Extracting Shape and Reflectance of Hybrid Surfaces by Photometric Sampling ," *Proc. of Image Understanding Workshop,* pp.563-583, 1989

13. Y. L. Tian and H. T. Tsui,"Shape from Specular Reflection using Image Sequence," *Proc. ACCV'93,* pp.97-100, 1993 '

14. G. Healey and T. O. Binford,"Local Shape from Specularity," *CVGIP* 42,pp.62-86,1986

Feature Detection Using Oriented Local Energy for 3D Confocal Microscope Images

Chris Pudney[1], Peter Kovesi[2] and Ben Robbins[2]

[1] Biomedical Confocal Microscopy Research Centre, Department of Pharmacology
[2] Robotics and Vision Research Group, Department of Computer Science
The University of Western Australia, Nedlands, Western Australia, 6907.

Abstract. The ability to detect features within confocal microscope images is important for the interpretation and analysis of such data. Most detectors are gradient-based, and so are sensitive to noise, and fail to accurately locate some feature types that are important in confocal microscopy. The local energy feature detector developed by Morrone and Owens marks locations where there is maximal congruence of phase in the Fourier components of an image. Points of maximal phase congruency occur at all common feature types: step and roof edges, line features and Mach bands. A 3D implementation of the local energy feature detector, suitable for confocal microscope data, is presented. The detector computes local energy by convolving an image with oriented pairs of 3D filters that are 3D versions of Morlet wavelets. To increase the speed of the convolution, the filters are designed in frequency-space and multiplied by the image's Fourier transform. Results are presented for real confocal images and a synthetic 3D image volume. These results are compared with those from a 3D implementation of the Sobel edge detector.

1 Introduction

The extraction of surfaces from volumetric data such as confocal microscope images is an important step in the interpretation and analysis of such data. Extracted surfaces can be used in the 3D reconstruction of the imaged specimen, and for measurement of specific structures within the volume.

The automatic identification of surfaces within 3D image volumes is analogous to the edge detection problem in 2D image processing. As a result most surface detection techniques are 3D extensions of 2D edge detectors, and as most edge detectors are gradient-based, so too are most surface detectors [1, 3, 4, 9]. Gradient-based detectors mark image locations where there is a sharp intensity gradient. Unfortunately they are usually sensitive to image noise and fail to accurately locate line-type features such as would be exhibited by membrane-like structures in confocal microscope images. As a result gradient-based surface detectors are not always suitable for confocal data.

The local energy feature detector developed by Morrone and Owens [6] marks locations where there is maximal congruence of phase in the Fourier components of an image. Points of maximal phase congruency occur at all common feature types: step and roof edges, line features and Mach bands. In this paper the local energy feature detector is extended to 3D and used to detect surfaces within confocal microscope images.

Local energy can be computed in 1D by convolving an image with a quadrature pair of filters. One filter is even-symmetric, and so extends naturally to higher dimensions, while the other is odd-symmetric, and so its extension to higher dimensions has an imposed orientation. To compute local energy in 3D, images are convolved with several pairs of 3D filters having different orientations. The filters used are 3D versions of Morlet wavelets.

The layout of this paper is as follows: Section 2 introduces the phase congruency and local energy models. The use of wavelets to compute local energy is also described. Local energy computation is then extended to 3D in Section 3. Section 4 presents results of the 3D local energy operator on real and synthetic images, and compares them to results from a gradient-based operator. The paper concludes in Section 5 with suggestions for future development of this research.

2   The Local Energy Model

The local energy model of feature detection [6] postulates that features are perceived at points of maximum phase congruency in an image. No assumptions are made about the shape of feature profiles. One is simply looking for points in the image where there is a high degree of order in the Fourier domain. The phase congruency function is developed from the Fourier series expansion of the image, namely

$$F(x) = \sum_{n=0}^{\infty} (A_n \sin(n\omega x + \phi_n)),$$

where ω is a constant (typically 2π) and ϕ_n is the phase offset of the nth component. The phase congruency function is

$$PC(x) = \max_{\theta \in [0,2\pi]} \frac{\sum_n (A_n \cos(n\omega x + \phi_n - \theta))}{\sum_n A_n}.$$

The angle θ that maximises this equation represents the weighted mean phase angle of all the Fourier terms at the point being considered. Taking the cosine of the difference between the actual phase angle of a frequency component and this weighted mean, θ, generates a quantity approximately equal to one minus half this difference squared (the Taylor expansion of $\cos(x) \approx 1 - x^2/2$, for small x). Thus finding where phase congruency is a maximum can be considered to be equivalent to finding where the weighted standard deviation of phase angles is a minimum.

As it stands phase congruency is an awkward quantity to calculate. As an alternative, Venkatesh and Owens [8] showed that points of maximum phase congruency can be located by searching for peaks in the local energy function.

The local energy function is defined for a one-dimensional luminance profile, $F(x)$, as

$$E(x) = \sqrt{F^2(x) + H^2(x)},$$

where $H(x)$ is the Hilbert transform of $F(x)$ (a 90° phase shift of $F(x)$ in the Fourier domain). It can be shown that

$$E(x) = PC(x) \sum_n A_n.$$

Thus the local energy function is directly proportional to the phase congruency function, so peaks in local energy will correspond to peaks in phase congruency.

However, there are some problems with this approach to calculating local energy. While local energy can be calculated via the Fourier transform (the Hilbert transform is a 90° phase shift in the Fourier domain), the Fourier transform is not good for determining local frequency information. Windowing has to be used as the mechanism to control the scale over which local energy is determined. A more effective way of obtaining local frequency information in a signal is to use wavelets.

A measure of local energy can be calculated by convolving the image with a pair of masks in quadrature. The image is first convolved with a mask designed to remove the DC component from the image. This result is saved and the image is then convolved with a second mask that is in quadrature with the first (the Hilbert transform of the first). This gives two images, each being a band passed version of the original, and one being a 90° phase shift of the other. The results of the two convolutions are then squared and summed. Wavelets can be used to form quadrature pairs of masks for computing local energy.

2.1 Calculating Local Energy via Wavelets

Recently the Wavelet Transform has become a method of choice for obtaining local frequency information [5]. This approach involves using a bank of filters to analyse the signal. The filters are all created from rescalings of the one wave shape, each scaling designed to pick out particular frequencies of the signal being analysed. An important feature is that the scales of the filters vary geometrically, giving rise to a logarithmic frequency scale.

The Morlet wavelet is a complex valued wavelet made up of a sine wave (odd) and a cosine wave (even), each modulated by a Gaussian. The two waves in quadrature can be used to calculate the amplitude and phase of the signal at a given frequency and at a given spatial location.

The calculation of local energy requires $F(x)$, the signal with its DC component removed, and $H(x)$, the Hilbert transform. These can be obtained by convolving the signal with a bank of odd and even Morlet wavelets as follows:

$$F(x) = \sum_{f \in Freq} I(x) \otimes M_f^{\text{even}}(x), \text{ and } H(x) = \sum_{f \in Freq} I(x) \otimes M_f^{\text{odd}}(x),$$

where $I(x)$ is the original signal, $M_f^{\text{even/odd}}(x)$ is an even/odd wavelet tuned to frequency f, $Freq$ is the set of frequencies targeted by the wavelets, and $\otimes$ denotes image convolution. Convolution is commutative, so that

$$F(x) = I(x) \otimes \sum_{f \in Freq} M_f^{\text{even}}(x), \text{ and } H(x) = I(x) \otimes \sum_{f \in Freq} M_f^{\text{odd}}(x).$$

The advantages of this approach are that we obtain high spatial localization of the calculation of local energy, and the range of the spectrum over which phase congruency is calculated is easily controlled.

3 3D Implementation

3.1 3D Filters

Thus far we have only considered a 1D signal. Unfortunately, it is not obvious how to generalise the local energy model to higher dimensions because the Hilbert transform is only defined in one dimension. The approach taken in this paper is to compute 1D local energy at several orientations in 3D, and sum the results. The computation of oriented 1D local energy has been used previously to detect features in 2D images. Venkatesh and Owens [8] convolved 1D filters with the rows and columns of 2D images. More recently, Robbins and Owens [7] and Kovesi [2] have developed more general implementations using oriented 2D filters.

The filters are made up of banks of wavelets that are oriented, 3D versions of Morlet wavelets. Each wavelet consists of a 1D sine wave and a 1D cosine wave, oriented to a particular 3D orientation, and modulated by a 3D Gaussian. The even-symmetric wavelet oriented along the unit vector $\hat{\mathbf{v}}$, and tuned for frequency f is given by the following formula:

$$M_{f,\hat{\mathbf{v}}}^{\text{even}}(x, y, z) = \frac{1}{\sqrt{2\pi}\sigma} e^{-\frac{x^2+y^2+z^2}{2\sigma^2}} \gamma^2 \cos(\gamma\beta), \tag{1}$$

where $\sigma = k/f$, $\gamma = 2\pi f$, and $\beta = \hat{\mathbf{v}}.[x \ y \ z]^T$. The ratio between the wavelet's width σ and frequency f is controlled by k. The odd wavelet has a sine in place of the cosine. Rescalings of the wavelet are obtained by scaling f. Note that γ^2 is used in (1) so that at all scales the wavelets have equal amplitude in the Fourier domain.

To compute local energy in 3D, 1D local energy is computed for a set of orientations, $Orient$, and the results summed, that is

$$E(x, y, z) = \sum_{\hat{\mathbf{v}} \in Orient} E_{\hat{\mathbf{v}}}(x, y, z),$$

where

$$E_{\hat{\mathbf{v}}}(x, y, z) = \sqrt{F_{\hat{\mathbf{v}}}^2(x, y, z) + H_{\hat{\mathbf{v}}}^2(x, y, z)},$$

$$F_{\hat{\mathbf{v}}}(x,y,z) = I(x,y,z) \otimes G_{\hat{\mathbf{v}}}^{\text{even}}(x,y,z),$$
$$H_{\hat{\mathbf{v}}}(x,y,z) = I(x,y,z) \otimes G_{\hat{\mathbf{v}}}^{\text{odd}}(x,y,z),$$
$$G_{\hat{\mathbf{v}}}^{\text{even}}(x,y,z) = \sum_{f \in Freq} M_{f,\hat{\mathbf{v}}}^{\text{even}}(x,y,z),$$
$$G_{\hat{\mathbf{v}}}^{\text{odd}}(x,y,z) = \sum_{f \in Freq} M_{f,\hat{\mathbf{v}}}^{\text{odd}}(x,y,z),$$

and $I(x,y,z)$ is the 3D image.

3.2 Fourier Multiplication

For large images such as confocal microscope images, spatial convolution can be performed more rapidly as a Fourier multiplication. Thus, $F_{\hat{\mathbf{v}}}$ and $H_{\hat{\mathbf{v}}}$ can be computed as follows:

$$F_{\hat{\mathbf{v}}}(x,y,z) = InvFT(\mathcal{I}(u,v,w) \times \mathcal{G}_{\hat{\mathbf{v}}}^{\text{even}}(u,v,w)), \text{ and}$$
$$H_{\hat{\mathbf{v}}}(x,y,z) = InvFT(\mathcal{I}(u,v,w) \times \mathcal{G}_{\hat{\mathbf{v}}}^{\text{odd}}(u,v,w)),$$

where $\mathcal{I}$ is the Fourier transform of the image I, and $\mathcal{G}_{\hat{\mathbf{v}}}^{\text{even/odd}}$ is the Fourier transform of the even/odd filter $G_{\hat{\mathbf{v}}}^{\text{even/odd}}$.

If $F_{\hat{\mathbf{v}}}$ and $H_{\hat{\mathbf{v}}}$ are computed separately then two Fourier multiplications and two inverse Fourier transforms are required for each orientation. This can be halved by designing a filter that is the sum of the even filter and odd filter multiplied by i:

$$\mathcal{G}_{\hat{\mathbf{v}}}(u,v,w) = \mathcal{G}_{\hat{\mathbf{v}}}^{\text{even}}(u,v,w) + i\mathcal{G}_{\hat{\mathbf{v}}}^{\text{odd}}(u,v,w).$$

The inverse Fourier transform of this filter is complex, the real part of which corresponds to $\mathcal{G}_{\hat{\mathbf{v}}}^{\text{even}}$ and the imaginary part of which corresponds to $\mathcal{G}_{\hat{\mathbf{v}}}^{\text{odd}}$. Thus, if this filter is multiplied by $\mathcal{I}$ and an inverse Fourier transform applied to the result then $F_{\hat{\mathbf{v}}}$ will be the real part of the result and $H_{\hat{\mathbf{v}}}$ will be the imaginary part. Local energy can then be calculated by computing the magnitude of this complex result:

$$E_{\hat{\mathbf{v}}}(x,y,z) = \|(InvFT(\mathcal{I}(u,v,w) \times \mathcal{G}_{\hat{\mathbf{v}}}(u,v,w))\|.$$

Memory requirements are an important consideration when processing image volumes. It should be noted that due to the opposing symmetries of $\mathcal{G}_{\hat{\mathbf{v}}}^{\text{even}}$ and $\mathcal{G}_{\hat{\mathbf{v}}}^{\text{odd}}$ half of $\mathcal{G}_{\hat{\mathbf{v}}}$ cancels out. This fact is exploited by cropping each filter to a box that bounds only the significant values. This cropping allows filter sizes to be reduced by about 90% without significantly affecting the computed values of local energy.

The cropped filters are pre-computed and stored in files. During the computation of local energy, when an orientation is processed the appropriate filter file is loaded. This is much quicker than computing the filters on-line. Once local energy is computed for a particular orientation, the memory used to store the filter can be freed.

3.3 Post-processing

As mentioned in Section 2, peaks in local energy correspond to peaks in phase congruency. To locate these peaks, non-maximal voxels in the local energy image are suppressed. A voxel is considered to be maximal if its value is greater than those of the voxels either side of it in a particular direction. This direction is given by the orientation of the filter with the strongest response at the voxel. This usually works well but problems can arise when multiple features intersect. In such cases the orientation of the strongest feature is used, possibly resulting in the suppression of valid features nearby. The result of non-maximal suppression is then thresholded, and voxels with values greater than the threshold are labeled as surface voxels. Rather than use non-maximal suppression, we are developing 3D ridge tracing techniques that will handle the intersections of multiple features.

To render the detected surfaces a texture mapping technique is used. A 3D image volume is constructed in which each surface voxel is given the value of the corresponding voxel in the original image, and all other voxels have zero values. An opacity is also associated with each voxel; surface voxels are opaque (opacity = 1), and non-surface voxels are transparent (opacity = 0). The volume is then rendered using ray tracing.

4 Results and Discussion

Figure 1 shows ray-traced volume renderings of three 3D images: a $64 \times 64 \times 64$ synthetic image, a $256 \times 256 \times 128$ confocal microscope image of prostate gland cells, and a $512 \times 256 \times 64$ confocal microscope image of a flea. The voxel values of the images have 8-bit values. The synthetic image consists of three orthogonal planes intersecting a sphere containing a cube. The planes and walls of the cube are one voxel thick, and the cube is solid. The planes, cube and sphere have grey-values of 255, 191 and 127, respectively. The background is a diagonal ramp of grey-values from 0 to 63. All three images are isotropic, that is, the voxels are cubes. Note, however, that possible anisotropy must be considered when constructing filters.

These three images were processed using the local energy detector described in this paper. The number of orientations considered was 13. These orientations correspond to (half of) the directions from a centre voxel to its 26 neighbours. This is a convenient choice as it means that non-maximal suppression can be performed without having to interpolate between voxels. However, the 13 orientations are not evenly spaced. Sets of evenly spaced orientations have also been used. In general the more orientations considered the better the results.

The filters were constructed from wavelets tuned for a set of six frequencies $Freq = \{1/4, 1/(4 \times 1.25), 1/(4 \times 1.25^2), 1/(4 \times 1.25^3), 1/(4 \times 1.25^4), 1/(4 \times 1.25^5)\}$. The ratio of width to frequency was $k = 4$. The more frequencies used and the more closely they are spaced the better the results. Care must be taken when constructing the filters to ensure that they are zero at the origin and Nyquist cutoff frequencies, otherwise a DC component and ringing artifacts can be introduced into the local energy results.

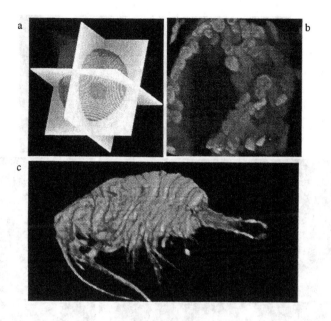

Fig. 1. Volume renderings of (a) a synthetic image, and confocal microscope images of (b) prostate gland cells, and (c) a flea.

For the sake of comparison a 3D implementation of the gradient-based Sobel edge detector was also used [9]. Figure 2 shows the texture mapped (see Section 3.3) surface voxels detected using the local energy feature detector and 3D Sobel detector. The Sobel detector has failed to detect some of the surfaces found using local energy. This is because the Sobel detector, like most gradient-based detectors, is tuned to detect features with step-like profiles, whereas the local energy detector responds to a variety of feature types. For example, in the synthetic image, the planes and sphere, which do not have step-like profiles, have been mislocated by the Sobel detector. The detector has actually responded to voxels either side of these features. This double response problem is common to all gradient-based detectors that have been developed for the detection of step-like edges and surfaces. Some of the problems due to non-maximal suppression are evident in the synthetic image results where the sphere intersects the planes.

The following table lists the processing times of the surface detectors for implementations running on a DEC AlphaStation 4/266.

Detector	Processing Time (*seconds*)		
	Synthetic	Prostate	Flea
3D Sobel	4	137	99
Local Energy	19	1527	1527

These times do not include the pre-processing time taken to build the filters nor

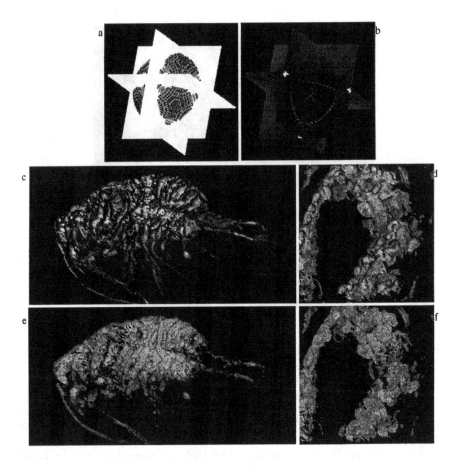

Fig. 2. The texture mapped surface voxels detected in the images using (a), (c) and (e) local energy, and (b), (d) and (f) 3D Sobel.

do they include the post-processing time taken for non-maximal suppression, thresholding and rendering. Clearly, local energy takes longer to compute than does 3D Sobel. This is because local energy is computed over more orientations and scales than the 3D Sobel detector. The Sobel detector could be extended to include more orientations and multiple scales, then it would require similar computation times to local energy. However, this would not solve the problems described above.

5   Conclusion and Future Work

A 3D implementation of the local energy feature detector has been presented. The use of local energy to detect features has some important advantages over the use of gradient-based detectors. Gradient-based detectors are optimised to find step discontinuities. However, volumetric confocal microscope images can contain a wide variety of feature types, including membrane-like surfaces upon which gradient-based detectors perform very poorly. Local energy responds strongly to a wide range of feature types including step, line and roof edges. This ensures that features of interest are more likely to be accurately detected, allowing better measurement, segmentation and visualization of structures in 3D images.

Future work will concentrate on three main areas: developing better methods of performing 3D non-maximal suppression, calculation of phase congruency rather than local energy, and the extraction of higher order image features.

6 Acknowledgements

Many thanks to GSF - Forschungszentrum, Institut of Pathology, Neuherberg, Germany for permission to use the prostate image. Chris Pudney is supported by a Saw Medical Research Fellowship. Ben Robbins is supported by an Australian Postgraduate Research Award.

References

1. M. Bomans, K.-H. Hohne, U. Tiede, and M. Riemer. 3-D segmentation of MR images of the head for 3-D display. *IEEE Transactions on Medical Imaging*, MI-9(2):177–183, June 1990.
2. P. D. Kovesi. Image features from phase congruency. Submitted to *The International Journal of Computer Vision*, May 1995. Also The University of Western Australia, Department of Computer Science Technical Report 95/4, available from ftp.cs.uwa.edu.au:/pub/techreports.
3. O. Monga, R. Deriche, G. Malandain, and J. P. Cocquerez. 3D edge detection by separable recursive filtering and edge closing. In *10th International Conference on Pattern Recognition*, pages 652–654, Atlantic City, NJ, June 1990. IEEE Computer Society Press.
4. D. G. Morgenthaler and A. Rosenfeld. Multidimensional edge detection by hypersurface fitting. *IEEE Transactions on Pattern Analysis and Machine Intelligence*, PAMI-3:482–486, July 1981.
5. J. Morlet, G. Arens, E. Fourgeau, and D. Giard. Wave propagation and sampling theory - Part II: Sampling theory and complex waves. *Geophysics*, 47(2):222–236, February 1982.
6. M. C. Morrone and R. A. Owens. Feature detection from local energy. *Pattern Recognition Letters*, 6:303–313, December 1987.
7. B. Robbins and R. Owens. 2D feature detection via local energy. Submitted to *Image and Vision Computing*, August 1995.
8. S. Venkatesh and R. A. Owens. An energy feature detection scheme. In *IEEE International Conference on Image Processing*, pages 553–557, Singapore, September 1989.
9. S. W. Zucker and R. A. Hummel. A three-dimensional edge operator. *IEEE Transactions on Pattern Analysis*, PAMI-3(3):324–331, May 1981.

Advancing Front Meshing for Radiosity Solutions

George Baciu and Rico K. W. Tsang

The Hong Kong University of Science and Technology,
Clear Water Bay, Kowloon, Hong Kong

Abstract. Radiosity rendering is not only dependent on the computational complexity of balancing the energy rate equation, but also on the speed of generating an acceptable mesh of the environment. The tedious process of mesh refinement consists of region decompositions, conformity at the boundaries, grading and smoothing. Each step may involve numerous proximity node searches, edge selections, additions and deletions. In this context we present two variations of an efficient mesh generation procedure based on the advancing front paradigm. We show where the bottlenecks occur and suggest further improvements.

Keywords: mesh generation, radiosity, rendering

1 Introduction

A large portion of the current research work on radiosity computations is focused on the spatial discretization for accurate sampling of the radiance distribution. Occluders and their projected shadows are amongst the main factors contributing to variations in the global illumination of interior spaces.

In most of the related work on radiosity [1, 25, 24, 11, 9, 10], the meshing of interior spaces is initially based on a regular grid decomposition. While regular grids are easy to generate and refine, in a general setting there will often be features which are more difficult to mesh by regular grids. Some of these features are: (1) conforming to irregular holes, and (2) satisfying irregular boundaries and internal constraints. This becomes more apparent in the generation of discontinuity meshes [18, 19] and shadow boundaries in backpropagation algorithms [10, 26] where internal constraints from the intersection of shaddow volumes with surfaces in the scene generate multiple irregular regions. Meshing these regions is mostly based on applying the Delaunay triangulation on a set of points assumed to form a planar convex set [23, 5, 12].

In this article, we demonstrate the discretization and refinement of polygonal surfaces by an advancing front method that exhibits efficiency, generality and robustness. The efficiency is derived from avoiding some computationally demanding comparisons such as edge–crossing and edge–flipping in the triangulation phase. The algorithm can easily handle both convex and nonconvex regions at no extra cost, as well as variable density regions with internal holes.

[0] Supported by the RGC grant HKUST 598/94E and the HKUST infrastructure funding.

2 Problem domain

The classical radiosity problem for Lambertian diffuse reflection and emission [6, 8] demands a solution function $B(\mathbf{p})$ which balances the energy rates at a point $\mathbf{p}$ on a surface S:

$$B(\mathbf{p})dA = E(\mathbf{p})dA + \rho(\mathbf{p}) \int_S V(\mathbf{p}',\mathbf{p})B(\mathbf{p}')dF_{dA' \to dA}dA' \qquad (1)$$

where B is the radiosity at point $\mathbf{p}$, S is the domain surface, ρ reflectivity at surface point $\mathbf{p}$, dF is the form–factor between $\mathbf{p}$ and $\mathbf{p}$', or the fraction of the energy leaving point $\mathbf{p}'$ and reaching $\mathbf{p}$, and V is the visibility of point $\mathbf{p}$ from $\mathbf{p}$'. The solution to this problem involves the discretization of surfaces into small enough elements $i = 1,..,n$ of area A_i;

In this work, we employ an irregular discretization of the domain S with refinement in regions exhibiting a high gradient in the radiosity function $B(\mathbf{p})$. The meshing procedure is based on the advancing front paradigm proposed by Cavendish [4] and further improved by Lo [20, 21], Bui and Hanh [2].

We propose a further enhancement to the algorithm presented in [2] and apply the advancing front meshing to the global illumination problem.

3 Mesh generation

The general mesh generation procedure for r independent planar regions $R_1, R_2, ..., R_r$, takes the following form:

Input: $C_1, C_2, ..., C_r$ /* *boundary curves of $R_i, i = 1..r$* */
Output: $M_1, M_2, ..., M_r$ /* *meshes of regions $R_i, i = 1..r$* */
Process: 1   **for** i **from** 1 **to** r **do**
        2          $N_B \leftarrow$ *boundaryNodes(C_i)*;
        3          $E_B \leftarrow$ *boundaryEdges(N_B)*;
        4          $N_I \leftarrow$ *interiorNodes(R_i)*;
        5          $N_R \leftarrow N_B \cup N_I$;   /* *all nodes of region R_i* */
        6          $M_i \leftarrow$ *mesh(E_B, N_R)*;   /* *final mesh of region R_i* */
        7          $M_i \leftarrow$ *smooth(M_i)*;
        8 **endfor**

Each region R_i can be a multiply connected domain bounded by a continuous curve C_i. The discretization of the boundaries of R_i results in the set of boundary nodes N_B. These nodes are connected by oriented straight line segments e_j which form the set of boundary edges E_B. An edge segment $e_j \in E_B$ is bounded by the nodes n_a and n_b, Fig. 1. The main differences between the available meshing methods lies in steps **4** and **6**.

The *node generation* in step **4** can be achieved by superimposing a structured grid [13, 4], plane sweep [20], or boundary transformation [2].

The *meshing or triangulation* in step **6** can be obtained by inserting elements either globally or locally. In a *global insertion mechanism*, each node is chosen arbitrarily from the entire set of nodes in the region. Edges are added and removed in the process of forming an element [14]. In a *local element addition*,

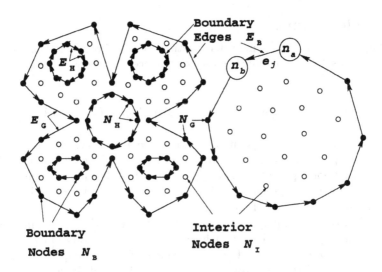

Fig. 1. Boundary edges of the planar regions

a node is selected locally from a close neighborhood of nodes. Edges are only added to form a new element.

4 Advancing front

The advancing front method [4] is a geometrically–based greedy local insertion meshing strategy with significant processing savings. The triangulation phase culminated with an efficient algorithm proposed by Lo [20], which eliminated costly validation tests in the node generation phase and the formation of triangular elements in the meshing phase. However, this left unresolved the costly search for a candidate node. We propose a further improvement of this algorithm with application to radiosity problems.

The basic mechanism constructs a front E_F of connected edges that advances through the interior of the region R until all the nodes are exhausted. At each step a new element is formed by adding one or two edges and removing the previously considered edge from the front. The remaining nodes form the set N_F. The algorithm is shown below:

```
Input:        N_B, N_I, E_B  /* all nodes and boundary edges */
Output:       M  /* constrained mesh */
Initialize: 1 M    ← {}  /* set of mesh elements */
            2 N_F  ← N_B ∪ N_I  /* nodes to be considered */
            3 E_F  ← E_B  /* front edges */
Mesh:       4 while cardinality(E_F) > 0 do
            5     e_s  ← selectEdge(E_F);
            6     n_a  ← tailNode(e_s);
```

```
7          n_b  ← headNode(e_s);
8          n_s  ← selectNode(N_F);
9          if n_s ∈ E_I then
10             e_a  ← edge(n_a, n_s);
11             e_b  ← edge(n_s, n_b);
12             E_S  ← {e_s};    /* selected edges */
13             E_A  ← {e_a, e_b};   /* edges to be added */
14         else
15             e_t  ← edge(n_s, n_a);   /* n_s ∈ N_B */
16             if e_t ∈ E_F then   /* a front edge */
17                 e_b  ← edge(n_s, n_b);
18                 E_A  ← {e_b};
19             else   /* not a front edge */
20                 e_a  ← edge(n_a, n_s);
21                 e_t  ← edge(n_b, n_s);
22                 E_A  ← {e_a};
23             endif
24             E_S  ← {e_t, e_s};
25         endif
26         E_F  ← (E_F − E_S) ∪ E_A    /* remove and add edges */
27         Δ_s  ← triangle(n_a, n_s, n_b);   /* form element */
28         M  ← M ∪ {Δ_s}    /* add element to mesh */
29    endwhile
30         M  ← smooth(M);   /* smooth the final mesh */
```

The cases considered in lines **9, 16** and **19** are illustrated in Fig. 2 as **(a)** an internal node is selected, **(b)** and **(c)** a boundary node selected, respectively. For each case the three steps in the advancing front show the initial front, the edges to be added to the front and the edges removed from the front.

The selection of edges in line **5** is simply implemented as a dequeue operation on a queue of edges E_F. The edge at the front of the queue will always be the next one in the counterclockwise ordering of edges for E_G and clockwise ordering for E_H. The addition of edges is also a simple appending of the currently formed edges to the queue E_F. These edges will be selected after all the edges in front of the queue have been considered.

The bottleneck of the algorithm is line **8**. The selection of a candidate node for forming an element with an edge in E_F involves a distance calculation between the endpoints of edge e_s and each node $n_s \in N_F$. Node n_s is selected so that $|e_a| + |e_b|$ is a minimum over all candidates $n_s \in N_F$. The time complexity resulting from this check is $O(n^2)$ where n is the number of points in N_R that are considered for nodes in the mesh.

For a constrained Delaunay triangulation the set E_F must be split into two sets, a non–Delaunay set E_F' and a Delaunay set E_F''. At initialization, $E_F' \leftarrow E_B$ and $E_F'' \leftarrow \phi$. When a new element is formed, it is checked for the Delaunay property. If it is satisfied, then the new edges are added to E_F'', else they are added to E_F'. This partition of E_F allows the direct selection of non–Delaunay front

Advancing Front Cases

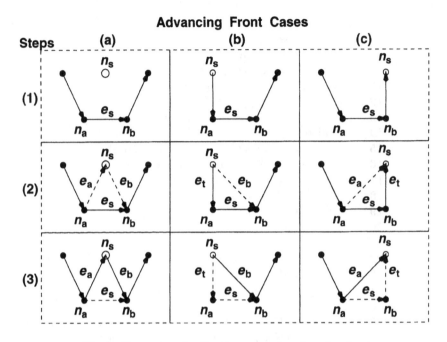

Fig. 2. Three steps for the three cases in advancing front

edges first, before the Delaunay ones. This selection ensures that the constrained elements are done before the unconstrained ones.

5 An improved advancing front

A *layered* node generation scheme is employed so as to maintain the order of nodes relevant to the meshing sequence. The generated internal nodes will conform to the shape of the boundaries. This property can be exploited in the mesh generation phase, especially for strongly convex regions, such as squares and regular n-gons.

A layer is generated from the current boundary. In the meshing phase, the points that need to be checked for the construction of an element are only those from the closest layer to the advancing front since the rest of the points are located on layers further from the front edges.

Since the traversal of the boundary at each step can be oriented in the same direction as the generation of points on each layer, we can consider appending the new points of the current layer into a queue of points. By ensuring that the starting point on each layer is in the proximity of the first point on the next layer, we obtain the same ordering of the points as the order in which we select edges for triangulation from the advancing front. For example, in Fig. 3, the

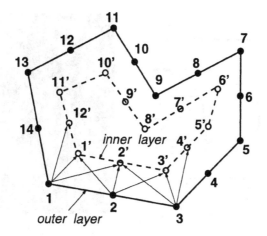

Fig. 3. Ordered layers in the advancing front

points in the proximity of node **1** on the outer layer are **12'**, **1'** and **2'** on the inner layer. Similarly, the points in the proximity of node **2** on the outer layer are **1'**, **2'** and **3'** on the innger layer.

At each stage, the only points that need to be considered for node selection are the points at the beginning or at the end of the queue. The number of distance checks from the endpoints of the current edge in the front can then be restricted to at most three as the distances will increase with the points towards in the middle of the queue. Furthermore, it is not necessary to generate all the points at once. The meshing can be started as soon as we have one layer of internal points. Thus, the meshing and the node generation can be combined in one module. This may be a desirable feature for very large convex regions.

For convex regions, the combination of the layered node generation and a proper ordering of points on the current layer results in $O(1)$ processing time for the node selection in line **8** of the advancing front meshing. This is because a constant number of points need to be checked for triangulation validity at each stage.

6 Examples

The resulting meshes applied to both convex and nonconvex regions with or without holes are illustrated in the following example, Fig. 4. This shows (a) the variable density meshing of the nonconvex umbra and penumbra regions, falling off the edge of a desk in a room with a single area light source; (b) the full radiosity rendering of the room in (a); (c) a different view of the room showing a highly nonconvex polygonal mask hanging on the wall; the mask has multiple interior holes and a star–shaped interior region which serves as a light source; note that all these features are embedded polygonal regions and not overlapping polygons; (d) the full radiosity rendering of the view in (c).

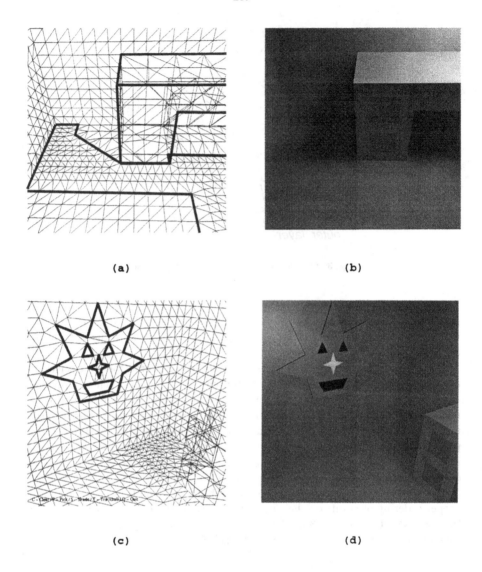

(a)
(b)

(c)
(d)

Fig. 4. Office space meshing and rendering

7 Conclusion

We have investigated the applicability of the advancing front based automatic triangulation to radiosity rendering. The generality of the method makes it suitable for meshing complex nonconvex penumbra regions directly without resorting to the convex–hull decompositions of these regions.

While the processing of the element insertion by the advancing front follows the simplest procedure possible, the main variations are attained in interior node generation and the node proximity search.

The layered node generation has the potential for speeding up the node search since an automatic ordering of nodes based on the geometry of the region yields constant time search for a good candidate in the construction of the new element. Further experimentation with a variety of complex geometrical scenes and comparisons with other available meshing procedures are necessary to fully evaluate the benefits of this strategy. As it can be observed in the examples, the preliminary experiments have yielded encouraging results.

References

1. D. K. Baum, S. Mann, K. P. Smith, and J. M. Winget. "Making Radiosity Usable: Automatic Preprocessing and Meshing Techniques for the Generation of Accurate Radiosity Solutions". *Computer Graphics (Proc. SIGGRAPH 91)*, vol. 25 no. 4, July 1991.

2. T. D. Bui and V. T. N. Hanh. "automatic mesh generation for finite element analysis". *Computing*, vol. 44, pp. 305–329, 1990. advancing front method improvement over Lo85.

3. Campbell, A. T. III and Fussel, D. S. "Adaptive Mesh Generation for Global Illumination". *Computer Graphics (SIGGRAPH'90)*, vol. 24 no. 4, pp. 155–164, July 1990.

4. J. C. Cavendish. "Automatic Triangulation of Arbitrary Planar Domains for the Finite Element Method". *International Journal of Numerical Methods in Engineering*, vol. 8, pp. 679–696, 1974. first advancing front method - node generation is different.

5. L. Chew. "Constrained Delaunay Triangulation". In *3rd Symposium on Computational Geometry*, 1987.

6. M. Cohen and D. P. Greenberg. "The Hemi–Cube: A Radiosity Solution for Complex Environments". *Computer Graphics (SIGGRAPH'85)*, vol. 19 no. 3, pp. 31–40, Aug 1985.

7. M. Cohen, J. R. Wallace, and D. P. Greenberg. "A Progressive Refinement Approach to Fast Radiosity Image Generation". *Computer Graphics (SIGGRAPH'88)*, vol. 22 no. 4, pp. 75–84, Aug 1988.

8. M.F. Cohen and J.R. Wallace, editors. *Radiosity and Realistic Image Synthesis*. Academic Press, 1993.

9. G. Drettakis. "Simplifying the Representation of Radiance from Multiple Emitters". In *Fifth Eurographics Workshop on Rendering*, pages 259–272, Darmstadt, Germany, June 1994.

10. G. Drettakis and E. Fiume. "A Fast Shadow Algorithm for Area Light Sources Using Backprojection". In *Computer Graphics (SIGGRAPH'94)*, pages 223–230. ACM, July 1994.

11. G. Drettakis and E. L. Fiume. "Concrete Computation of Global Illumination Using Structured Sampling". In *Third Eurographics Workshop on Rendering*, Bristol, UK, May 1992.

12. T.P. Fang and L. A. Piegl. "Algorithm for Constrained Delaunay Triangulation". *Visual Computer*, vol. 10, pp. 255–265, 1994. advancing shell; similar to advancing front; no node generation.

13. J. Fukuda and J. Suhara. "Automatic Mesh Generation for Finite Element Analysis". In J. T. Oden, R. W. Cough, and Y. Yamamoto, editors, *Advances in Computational Methods in Structural Mechanics and Designs*. UAH Press, 1972. first automatic meshing.

14. P. L. George. *Automatic Mesh Generation Application to Finite Element Methods*. John Wiley & Sons, 1991.

15. P. S. Heckbert. *Simulating Global Illumination Using Adaptive Meshing*. PhD thesis, Computer Science Department, University of California, Berkeley, June 1991.

16. P. S. Heckbert. "Discontinuity Meshing for Radiosity". In *Third Eurographics Workshop on Rendering*, pages 203–216, May 1992.

17. P. Lalonde. "An Adaptive Discretization Method for Progressive Radiosity". In *Graphics Interfce*, pages 78–86, 1993. recent work on adaptive meshing in radiosity.

18. D. Lischinski, F. Tampieri, and D. P. Greenberg. "Discontinuity Meshing for Accurate Radiosity". *IEEE Computer Graphic and Applications*, vol. 12 no. 6, November 1992.

19. D. Lischinski, F. Tampieri, and D. P. Greenberg. "Combining Hierarchical Radiosity and Discontinuity Meshing". In *Computer Graphics (SIGGRAPH'93)*, pages 199–208. ACM, Aug 1993.

20. S.H. Lo. "A new mesh generation scheme for arbitrary planar domains". *Int. J. for Numerical Methods in Engineering*, vol. 21, 1985.

21. S.H. Lo. "Delaunay triangulation of non-convex planar domains". *Int. J. for Numerical Methods in Engineering*, vol. 28, 1989.

22. R. Lohner. "Three–Dimensional Grid Generation by the Advancing–Front Method". In *Fifth Int. Conf. Num. Meth. in Laminar and Turbulent Flow*, pages 1092–1105, 1987. first 3D advancing front.

23. F. P. Preparata and M. I. Shamos. *Computational geometry: an introduction*. Springer-Verlag, 1985.

24. B. Smits, J. Arvo, and D. P. Greenberg. "A Clustering Algorithm for Radiosity in Complex Environments". In *Computer Graphics (SIGGRAPH'94)*, pages 435–442. ACM, July 1994.

25. B. Smits, J. Arvo, and D. H. Salesin. "An Importance–Driven Radiosity Algorithm". *Computer Graphics (SIGGRAPH'92)*, vol. 26 no. 2, pp. 273–282, July 1992.

26. J. A. Stewart and S. Ghali. "Fast Computation of Shadow Boundaries Using Spatial Coherence and Backprojections". In *Computer Graphics (SIGGRAPH'94)*, pages 231–238. ACM, July 1994.

An Efficient Cluster-Based Hierarchical Progressive Radiosity Algorithm

Karol Myszkowski   Tosiyasu L. Kunii

The University of Aizu, Aizu-Wakamatsu, 965-80 Japan

Abstract. This paper describes a cluster-based hierarchical approach to energy transfer within the framework of a progressive radiosity algorithm. The clustering does not rely on the input geometry, but is performed on the basis of a local position in the scene for a pre-meshed scene model. The locality of the resulting clusters improves the accuracy of form factor calculations, and increases the number of possible high-level energy transfers between clusters within the imposed error bound. Limited refinement of the hierarchy of light interactions is supported without compromising the quality of shading when intermediate images are produced immediately upon user request. The algorithm performs well for complex scenes, and the growth of required data structures is linear with geometric complexity. The results of the experimental validation of the algorithm against measured real-world data show that calculation speed is reasonably traded for accuracy.

1 Introduction

Realistic computer images are widely used in many engineering applications, such as architecture, lighting and interior design. These applications usually require global illumination calculations to secure high quality of images and reliability in reconstructing the appearance of real-world scenes. An important component of global illumination is indirect light, modeling of which involves intensive computations. For complex environments, very high accuracy of the whole lighting simulation is too elaborate to be tractable in practical applications; special attention must be paid to the most important energy transfers, while higher order bounces of the reflected light can be handled in a simplified way. (Since analytic evaluation of such simplifications and interactions between them is generally impractical, the correctness of the algorithm must be checked experimentally by comparison of the simulation results to real-world measurements.) In this paper we are interested in development of practical lighting simulation and rendering algorithms that satisfy the following requirements:

1. Low growth rate of calculation time for increasing complexity of scenes.
2. Low memory requirements.
3. Progressive refinement, i.e., quickly producing approximate, but meaningful results, which converge to an accurate solution.

An important feature of a robust lighting simulation algorithm is low sensitivity to the style of preparation of the geometric model by the user, who should not be forced to adjust his modeling habits to the specific requirements of the algorithm. Also, the possibility of walkthrough animation, which implies view-independent calculations of diffuse interreflections, becomes crucial in many applications.

2 Previous work

Candidate algorithms that satisfy many of the aforementioned requirements are Progressive Radiosity (PR), and more recently developed Hierarchical Radiosity (HR) techniques.

In the PR technique the energy transfers between surfaces in the environment are ordered according to their impact on the scene illumination [2]. The complexity of PR algorithm is $O(n^2)$, which means that calculation load increases quadratically with the number of mesh elements n.

The HR algorithm imposes strict control of energy transfers, introducing links between interacting surfaces and refining these links up to the point when the energy sent through each link falls below a predefined threshold [4]. The complexity of HR algorithm is $O(m^2 + n)$, where m is the number of input surfaces. Since usually $m \ll n$, the HR technique exhibits lower complexity compared to the PR approach. On the other hand, the performance of the HR algorithm depends heavily not only on scene characteristics, but also on the geometric model preparation, which can strongly affect m. Also, the reconstruction of radiosity for display is prone to shading artifacts, because of disproportions between neighboring elements which are imposed by the hierarchy [13], [7], [12]. In order to avoid these problems Smits et al. [13] force finer subdivision than required by the assumed accuracy of the energy transfer for visible part of the scene (their algorithm is view-dependent). Lischinski et al. [7] propose two passes: (1) the global pass which uses HR to compute radiosity solution, and (2) the local pass to refine the radiance distribution locally on each surface. The similar approach was also applied by Smits et al. [12], however, they found it very time consuming and postulated further research of acceleration of the local pass.

The HR technique requires much memory to store data structures, e.g., 239.9 Mb and 1,116.1 Mb for medium complexity scenes composed of 1,418 and 7,054 polygons respectively [14]. Teller et al. [14] solved this problem partitioning radiosity computations for the whole scene into smaller *working sets*, and transferring the related data between disk and memory. However, for complex scenes even the required disc space can raise some problems. The advantage of the storage of links and repeated energy gathering for point light sources (often used in practice) is not obvious, because after the refinement performed in the first iteration, the further refinement is not needed (secondary light cannot contribute to these links). Also, in the case of area primary light sources the contribution of indirect light is usually rather small compared to its direct counterpart.

Another drawback of the HR algorithm is the cost of the initial linking, which is performed before any energy transfer is calculated. The initial linking delays the display of the approximated image and affects the progressivity of the HR algorithm. Timings reported for initial linking are rather discouraging, e.g., 75 minutes for 1,002 polygons [13], and 136 minutes for 1,668 polygons [7]. Recently Holzschuch et al. [5] proposed the lazy initial linking technique, which accelerates this phase to the order of single minutes (for scenes built of 1,000–2,500 polygons), ignoring all links transferring low energy.

Clustering (grouping) techniques accelerate the initial linking phase. Existing algorithms are focused on clustering of small elements of the scene, like leaves of plants or furniture [6], [10], [11], [12]. This approach is very efficient if the clusters are local in the scene. However, in architectural applications we face many sliver-like elements that have significant length with respect to the scene size, but whose contribution to the energy exchange is rather small, which makes them perfect candidates for clustering. Current clustering techniques are limited to the input surfaces of the model (not their portions). In many cases clustering is performed manually by the user [6], [10].

3 Overview

The approach proposed in this paper can be described as an extension of the PR technique that uses a limited hierarchy of interacting surfaces combined with clustering when the solution for secondary light sources is calculated. The elements of the HR technique and clustering introduced into the PR algorithm reduce significantly the cost of the shooting iteration, which originally treats all energy transfers equally, disregarding their impact on the final radiosity solution.

We start lighting simulation by calculating direct illumination at vertices of the initial mesh. Adaptive mesh subdivision is performed to improve the quality of shading and accuracy of energy transfer. The most intensive interaction with the user is during direct lighting calculations. Recalculation of luminance and corresponding update of the mesh is handled exclusively for the lights modified by the user [3]. In many practical cases when light sources have narrow output distributions described by goniometrical diagrams [15], the processing is very fast (the order of seconds).

Indirect lighting calculation is the most expensive part of the whole simulation. Fortunately, changes of secondary illumination over surfaces are usually gradual, so that density of samples (the complexity of the mesh) can be significantly relaxed compared to the direct component. We have two passes of indirect light simulation. At first, secondary lighting is calculated for initial mesh elements (subdivision performed due to primary lights is ignored at this stage), and then, if necessary, the solution is refined using adaptive subdivision of mesh elements exhibiting high gradients of luminance due to indirect light. Usually, the quality of shading is quite good after the first phase, so in practice the second phase is very often omitted, unless subtle shading effects must be produced, e.g., shadows resulting from secondary lights in the regions that are not directly illuminated.

4 Clustering

The clustering of mesh elements and the hierarchical energy transfers constitute an efficient approach to reduction of the quadratic complexity of the PR algorithm with respect to the number of the initial mesh elements. When the interacting surfaces are located far enough apart and the transferred energy is low, then the interaction between clusters offers sufficient accuracy of calculations. Otherwise, interaction between mesh elements must be considered. The question

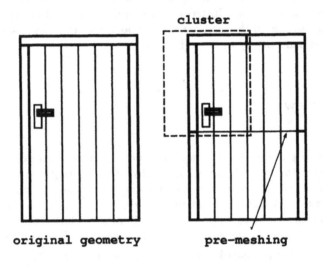

cluster

original geometry   pre-meshing

Fig. 1. Mechanics of clustering

that arises is why should we first subdivide surfaces during initial meshing, and then group them back during clustering? The most important motivation behind this strategy is to make the radiosity solution less sensitive to the original input geometry. The problem of long, thin polygons (common in architecture applications) should be recalled here. Instead of grouping input polygons, which is used by all the aforementioned clustering algorithms, a better locality of clusters can be expected when the slivers are subdivided into better-shaped polygons and then grouped into multiple local clusters (Fig. 1). In such a case, the clustering does not rely on the input geometry, but is performed on the basis of local position in the scene. The locality of clusters thus obtained allows them to be used safely for more energy interactions than the clusters based on input geometry. The better aspect ratio of mesh elements improves the accuracy of form factors calculation, as well as the quality of shading. The mesh constitutes a good basis for displaying images reporting the current status of computation immediately upon user request. Of course, the cost of subdividing the polygons must be amortized by the gains of clustering.

It is worth noting that the proposed approach to clustering combines into a unified framework the clustering of input polygons and the hierarchy of subdivisions performed on input polygons. In traditional techniques, clustering and hierarchical subdivision constitute two independent processes, depending heavily on the input geometry. In our case the hierarchy is not built upon the input geometry, but rather uses the coherence of positioning in the space. This means that a single cluster can be built from:

- original input polygons (as in traditional clustering),
- selected mesh elements belonging to the same input polygon (as in the hierarchical radiosity algorithm),
- selected mesh elements belonging to different input polygons (portions of the input polygons tessellated by mesh).

5 Hierarchy flattening

Having in mind the shading artifacts that appear because of poor grading of the surface size imposed by the hierarchy [13], [7], [12], we decided to flatten our hierarchy. The initial meshing is the first step in this direction. Tessellation of big surfaces into a uniform mesh makes the transferred energy by mesh elements smaller and better balanced. Furthermore, we limit the hierarchy to two levels (clusters and mesh elements) in the course of the radiosity solution for indirect lights. When further subdivision is required because of error bounds imposed on the energy transfer between surfaces, we adaptively increase the accuracy of form factor calculations instead of extending the number of hierarchy levels. (As was already stated, when the radiosity solution for secondary lights is found, an arbitrary level of adaptive mesh subdivision is allowed to enhance shading quality.) The experimental results published in literature justify this decision to a certain extent, e.g., Lischinski et al. [7] report an average depth of hierarchy in the range 1.31–2.04 for scenes they tested; similar results were obtained by Holzbuch et al. [5]. In both cases the hierarchy was built for both primary and secondary light sources. In our approach an even lower depth of hierarchy can be expected, because the input surfaces are pre-meshed, and hierarchical interactions between surfaces involve only secondary lights.

Of course, the flattened hierarchy of light interactions may decrease the algorithm performance for some scenes compared to a fully hierarchical approach. On the other hand, a limited hierarchy offers some advantages, such as better accuracy of shading, immediate image display reporting progress of simulation upon user's request, simplicity of data structures, and fast traversal of hierarchical data structures during calculations.

6 Description of algorithm

In our approach the clustering is performed automatically. A grid of voxels is used to group the mesh elements into clusters. All elements belonging to a cluster are located in the same voxel and have similar orientations in the space within the specified tolerance of the normal vector direction. The tolerance of variation of normal vectors trades the number of clusters for quality of shading (illumination of the cluster is pushed down to the elements ignoring their orientation). In order to avoid assignment to multiple clusters of a single element spanning the border between voxels, the location of the center of gravity is considered. The number of voxels which determines the size of clusters can be defined by the user explicitly, or implicitly as the average number of mesh elements in the cluster.

Data structures storing the record of light interaction in the scene are maintained on the level of clusters and mesh elements. The total Le_i and unshot ΔLe_i luminances stored for the i-th element correspond to the data structures used by the PR algorithm. The unshot luminance of a cluster ΔLc is derived as the area-weighted average of ΔLe_i for all elements k assigned to the cluster:

$$\Delta Lc = \sum_{i=1}^{k} \Delta Le_i \frac{A_i}{A_{tot}} \tag{1}$$

where A_i and A_{tot} are the surface areas of the i-th element and of all elements in the cluster, respectively. This schema corresponds to energy pulling up in the HR algorithm, but involves the unshot energy. The lighting energy exchanged between clusters is stored as illumination Ic, which is pulled down to each cluster's elements as follows:

$$Le_i = Le_i + Ic\frac{\rho_i}{\pi}, \qquad \Delta Le_i = \Delta Le_i + Ic\frac{\rho_i}{\pi}, \qquad Ic = 0, \tag{2}$$

where ρ_i is the diffuse reflection coefficient of the i-th element.

For the non-hierarchical PR algorithm, the total and unshot energy are implicitly updated during lighting calculations, but the hierarchical lighting interaction requires an explicit energy update between the levels of hierarchy (the push-pull procedure). In our algorithm the cluster illumination Ic is pulled down to the elements (2), and then the updated unshot energy of elements is pushed up to ΔLc (1). The cost of traversing our flat hierarchy is relatively small, but performing this procedure for all clusters after every shooter is considered would be impractical. On the other hand, the update of unshot energy cannot be done too lazily, because the progressivity of the algorithm may be affected (the choice of the most important shooter). In our algorithm the push-pull procedure is performed each time as the user-predefined percentage of the unshot energy for the whole scene is processed. Also, the push-pull procedure is executed when the image display is requested by the user, or when the shooting cluster is selected (and its ΔLc must correspond to its analog for the elements ΔLe_i).

Calculations of ΔLc (1) based on direct illumination for every cluster initialize secondary lighting simulation. The iterative solution proceeds within the PR framework until the unshot energy falls below a predefined (by the user) threshold. At every step the most important shooter (a cluster or a mesh element that does not belong to any cluster) is chosen based on its unshot energy ΔLcA_{tot} (candle power). Energy transfer cluster→cluster is allowed when the resulting illumination of a receiver is smaller than a predefined threshold value δI_{max}. The lower bound on the required distance between the clusters is evaluated as

$$R = \sqrt{\frac{\text{Lc} A_{tot}}{\delta I_{max}}} \qquad (3)$$

where the total cluster luminance Lc is derived using equation (1) for Le_i instead of the originally used ΔLe_i (for direct illumination, $\Delta \text{Lc} = \text{Lc}$). The distance R is expressed in terms of voxels r_v (used to define clusters), where $r_v > 1$, to prevent an abrupt degradation of the form factor accuracy for clusters located in neighboring voxels. If (i, j, k) denotes the indices of the voxel where the shooter is located, then the cluster→cluster energy transfer is performed for the voxels (x, y, z) that satisfy the condition

$$\max(|x - i|, |y - j|, |z - k|) \geq r_v. \qquad (4)$$

Otherwise, the energy shooting between the mesh elements is performed. The distance r_v is stored and compared at subsequent iterations with its updated value calculated for current values of $\text{Lc}A_{tot}$. When old and current values of r_v are equal, the unshot energy $\Delta \text{Lc}A_{tot}$ is transferred in the same way as for the last shooting. Otherwise, for voxels which do not satisfy condition (4) for the current r_v but satisfy the condition for the old r_v, the level of hierarchy of interacting surfaces is refined, and the energy transfer cluster→cluster is replaced by the element→element schema. In such a case the full energy transfer $(\text{Lc}A_{tot})$ between polygons must be considered, because the resulting illumination can be higher than δI_{max}. This is done in four steps:

1. Illumination of the receiving cluster Ic_{rec} (the result of the cluster→cluster interaction in the previous iterations) is reconstructed. Our algorithm is deterministic, so we can repeat exactly the form factor calculations which were done previously for the considered pair of clusters. The difference $(\text{Lc} - \Delta \text{Lc})A_{tot}$ is equal to the energy shot by the source cluster at the previous iterations.

2. The total Le_i and unshot ΔLe_i luminances stored for every element of the receiver cluster are decreased by the value $\text{Ic}_{rec}\rho_i/\pi$.

3. Lighting interaction between elements is performed; the total energy $\text{Le}_i A_i$ of the source element i is shot instead of the unshot energy $\Delta \text{Le}A_i$, which is used when the level hierarchy does not require refinement.

4. Push-pull procedure is executed to update ΔLc for the receiver cluster.

The presented schema of refinement is equivalent to the link refinement in the HR algorithm, but steps 1, 2 and 4 are not required in the HR framework, in which all links are stored. The costs of the extra steps are rather small, because the results of shadow feeler calculations (the most time consuming part of the whole simulations) at step 1 are re-used when the energy transfer between elements is performed at step 3.

Our algorithm offers only limited refinement of the hierarchy for interacting surfaces, and in contrast to the HR algorithm, an upper bound on the amount of energy transferred between initial mesh elements is not provided. The accuracy of element→element interaction is controlled only by the accuracy of form factor calculation. When the distance between elements is below a predefined threshold, we apply a closed-form solution for an arbitrary polygon (in our case triangle) and a differential element [1]. Sample points located within elements are calculated using fixed barycentric coordinates (the same for all elements). Calculations are performed for the adaptively refined density of sample points until the criterion imposed on the variance of the form factor is met. It is worth noting that this approach prevents "corner effects", i.e., shading artifacts visible when two surfaces meet, e.g., at room corners.

Our algorithm exhibits only linear memory requirements with geometric complexity of a scene, because all data structures needed for light interactions between elements and clusters are created on-the-fly (e.g., form factor calculations).

7 Results

The results of lighting simulation produced by our algorithm are used for walk-through animation and still-image generation. In the former case we use a texture mapping technique to store shading for regions where illumination is extremely complex in order to eliminate many deeply subdivided mesh elements and speed up rendering [9]. Ray tracing is used to calculate high quality images using the results of secondary lighting simulation. Primary lights are re-calculated in order to upgrade the image quality.

Fig. 2. Computer image of the measurement room

The experimental validation of our algorithm was performed comparing simulation results with measured real-world data. To our knowledge, such comparison has been done only for the conventional radiosity algorithm [8], while PR and HR algorithms have not been checked experimentally. The comparison was done for three different scenes. The main differences between the scenes are various heights of the measurement rooms and light source positions (Fig. 2). Each scene is illuminated by four light sources exhibiting various spatial distributions of candle power. The light sources are fixed to movable stands and are directed toward the ceiling so that the floor is not directly illuminated. The measurement was performed for 35 points on the floor. Simulation results (indirect light only) for the scene in Fig. 2 are summarized in Table 1 (all timings for SGI's Indigo^2). The scene was built of over 4,000 initial mesh elements. The highest simulation errors can be observed at the measurement points located near the corners and along the edges between the floor and the walls. The best results were obtained in the proximity of the center of the room. Fig. 3 presents subsequent stages

Table 1. Clustering vs. simulation error and calculation time

Avg. Cluster Size	Avg. Error	Max. Error	Time
no clusters	3.3%	5.1%	48 min.
3.2 triangles	3.8%	6.8%	11 min.
7.1 triangles	3.9%	7.8%	5 min.

of radiosity solution for the scene composed of 8,646 triangles. The initial mesh subdivision (into 59,104 elements) was done only in the regions which are illuminated by primary light sources. Time consuming subdivision due to secondary lights was not performed, while the quality of shading remains reasonable (the same strategy was applied for Figs. 4 and 5). 1,261 clusters were created and the maximal number of elements assigned to a cluster was 26. Fig. 4 presents a more complex scene used to test the performance of our algorithm. The scene is illuminated by 108 light sources. The geometric model was originally built of about 14,000 triangles. The initial mesh is built of 28,161 elements, which are further subdivided into 183,342 triangles. Cluster-based progressive radiosity took 4 hours 53 minutes, and ray tracing using results of indirect lighting simulation took 15 hours 57 minutes to generate the antialiased and textured image (at resolution 1,280×1,024). Even more complex (38,429 initial mesh elements) is the model of the unbuilt, modernist Hurva Synagogue designed by a famous american architect Louis I. Kahn (Fig. 5). Interior of the Synagogue is illuminated solely by sunlight which leaks into the building through narrow openings in the ceiling and gaps between the stone pylons. Our radiosity software required 6 hours 39 minutes to perform lighting simulation for this scene.

Fig. 3. Four stages of progressive refinement of radiosity solution

Fig. 4. An atrium of the Research Quadrangle at the University of Aizu

Fig. 5. The Hurva Synagogue

8 Conclusions

We have presented a cluster-based hierarchical approach to secondary lighting simulation within the framework of a progressive radiosity algorithm. The clusters are built automatically upon pre-meshed scene models, improving their locality and decreasing the dependency on input geometry. Spatial coherence of the resulting clusters improves the accuracy of form factor calculations and increases the number of possible high level energy transfers between clusters within the imposed error bound. The algorithm performs well for complex scenes, and significantly reduces calculation time compared to traditional PR algorithm, while progressivity and low memory requirements are not compromised. A drawback of the described algorithm is the manual setting of several control parameters, including initial mesh density and the size of clusters, which may require human experience.

9 Acknowledgements

Turbo Beam Tracing software developed by INTEGRA, Inc., was used by the authors as a testbed for implementation of cluster-based radiosity. The model of the atrium was prepared by Kouji Honma, Yuya Yaguchi, Seiji Ikuta, Toshiharu Seya and Toshitake Mashiko. The model of the Hurva Synagogue was provided by Kent Larson.

The authors would like to thank Oleg Okunev and Michael Cohen for reviewing the manuscript, as well as Koji Tsuchiya for help in collecting data describing the atrium and rendering of the Hurva Synagogue. Special thanks for helpful discussions and providing the measurement data go to Akira Fujimoto.

References

1. Daniel R. Baum, Holly E. Rushmeier, and James M. Winget. Improving radiosity solutions through the use of analytically determined form-factors. In *Computer Graphics (SIGGRAPH'89 Proceedings)*, volume 23, pages 325–334, July 1989.

2. Michael Cohen, Shenchang Eric Chen, John R. Wallace, and Donald P. Greenberg. A progressive refinement approach to fast radiosity image generation. In *Computer Graphics (SIGGRAPH'88 Proceedings)*, volume 22, pages 75–84, August 1988.

3. David W. George, Francois X. Sillion, and Donald P. Greenberg. Radiosity redistribution for dynamic environments. *IEEE CG&A*, 10(4):26–34, July 1990.

4. Pat Hanrahan, David Salzman, and Larry Aupperle. A rapid hierarchical radiosity algorithm. In *Computer Graphics (SIGGRAPH '91 Proceedings)*, volume 25, pages 197–206, July 1991.

5. Nicolas Holzschuch, Francois Sillion, and George Dretakkis. An efficient progressive refinement strategy for hierarchical radiosity. In *Fifth Eurographics Workshop on Rendering*, pages 343–357, Darmstadt, Germany, June 1994.

6. A. Kok. Grouping of patches in progressive radiosity. *Fourth Eurographics Workshop on Rendering (Paris, France)*, pages 221–232, June 1993.

7. D. Lischinski, F. Tampieri, and D. P. Greenberg. Combining hierarchical radiosity and discontinuity meshing. *Computer Graphics (SIGGRAPH'93 Proceedings)*, 27:199–208, August 1993.

8. Gary W. Meyer, Holly E. Rushmeier, Michael F. Cohen, Donald P. Greenberg, and Kenneth E. Torrance. An experimental evaluation of computer graphics imagery. *ACM Transactions on Graphics*, 5(1):30–50, January 1986.

9. Karol Myszkowski and Tosiyasu L. Kunii. Texture mapping as an alternative for meshing during walkthrough animation. In *Fifth Eurographics Workshop on Rendering*, pages 375–388, Darmstadt, Germany, June 1994.

10. Holly Rushmeier, Aravindan Veerasamy, and Charles Patterson. Geometric simplification for indirect illumination calculations. In *Proceedings of Graphics Interface '93*, pages 227–236, Toronto, Ontario, Canada, May 1993.

11. Francois Sillion. Clustering and volume scattering for hierarchical radiosity calculations. In *Fifth Eurographics Workshop on Rendering*, pages 105–117, Darmstadt, Germany, June 1994.

12. Brian Smits, James Arvo, and Donald Greenberg. A clustering algorithm for radiosity in complex environments. In *SIGGRAPH'94 Proceedings*, Computer Graphics Proceedings, Annual Conference Series, pages 435–442, July 1994.

13. Brian E. Smits, James R. Arvo, and David H. Salesin. An importance-driven radiosity algorithm. In *Computer Graphics (SIGGRAPH'92 Proceedings)*, volume 26, pages 273–282, July 1992.

14. Seth Teller, Celeste Fowler, Thomas Funkhouser, and Pat Hanrahan. Partitioning and ordering large radiosity computations. In *SIGGRAPH'94 Proceedings*, Annual Conference Series, pages 443–450, July 1994.

15. C. P. Verbeck and D. P. Greenberg. A comprehensive light-source description for computer graphics. *IEEE CG&A*, 4(7):66–75, July 1984.

A Model of Skylight and Calculation of Its Illuminance

Eihachiro Nakamae[1], Guofang Jiao[2],
Katsumi Tadamura[1], and Fujiwa Kato[3]

[1] Hiroshima Prefectural University, Shoubara 727, Japan
[2] Sanei Giken Co., Ltd, Hiroshima 730, Japan
[3] Tokyo Electric Power Company, Yokohama 230, Japan

Abstract. It has still been extremely expensive to make outdoor scenes illuminated by direct sunlight and skylight because of the limited models of these light sources and expensive algorithms of rendering. In this paper, a multi-layered parallelepiped is proposed for representing skylight and direct sunlight sources; the total energy of their light is regulated due to time and the position of a scene to be rendered. With this model, the illuminance on a calculation point is calculated. Then two methods for reducing the calculation cost, grouping and classifying obstacles, are discussed. This model makes a good trade-off between the cost and accuracy of rendering, and gives solar penumbra effects with a low cost.

Keywords: skylight, direct sunlight, spatial coherence, penumbra.

1 Introduction

It is desirable that an image created for visual environmental assessments is as realistic as possible and takes into account the effects of weather and the position of the sun. There are many discussions on the models of direct sunlight and skylight and algorithms for rendering outdoor scenes illuminated by both direct sunlight and skylight; e.g., shading models taking into account skylight were presented [2-3][5]. In [2], when the illuminance of skylight is calculated by using C.I.E. model, the skylight source, a sky dome, is divided into some band sources; the bandwidth at the center is wider than that at its both ends. The precision of illuminance near the center of each band is much lower than that close to the both ends. As the energy of skylight near the sun is much higher than that far from the sun, if the position of the sun is at the zenith, the high precision of illuminance cannot be expected unless using very narrow bands. In [5], a parallelepiped as a model of the skylight was proposed; the algorithm of rendering is simpler and the accuracy is higher, but the solar penumbra effects cast by direct sunlight are calculated separately. [1] and [6] displayed the sky and the earth considering the scattering and absorption of light in the atmosphere. The effects of specular reflection considering the spectral distributions were described in [7]. Solar penumbrae taking into account the size of the sun were depicted in [3]. The transmission effects of skylight passing through glass were proposed in [4]. The problems in every method mentioned above are still their high cost in making animation. One basic reason is that the models of direct sunlight and skylight are limited; it makes rendering algorithms complicated.

Taking into consideration the trade-offs between the physical accuracy of a lighting model and its calculation cost, we set the following assumptions.

– The light sources are restricted to direct sunlight and skylight, and only in a clear sky; direct sunlight and skylight are much stronger than the light due to interreflection, so the latter is ignored.
– The intensity of skylight arriving at one's viewing point is determined by the energy of atmospheric scattering. This energy is distributed on the surface of a hemispherical dome.

We propose a parallelepiped with multi-layered structures as a model of direct sunlight and skylight. With it, not only is the calculation cost of illuminance reduced drastically and reasonable accuracy achieved, but also the effects of diffuse and specular reflections of both the direct sunlight and skylight, and the solar penumbra effects can be easily unified into one algorithm.

2 Parallelepiped with Multi-layered Structures

In a previous paper [5], skylight was modelled by employing a parallelepiped with a uniform mesh on each face. However, the energy of skylight is, in fact, distributed non-uniformly; the energy near the sun is much stronger than that far from it. To balance the energy for each element, an additional layer surrounding the sun is added onto the center of the top face of the parallelepiped (see fig. 1(a)) and this layer is densely meshed. We call the top face the first layer and the additional layer the second layer. When the illuminance of skylight and shadow information are calculated, the top face is divided into 11×11 elements and the 3×3 elements close to the center of the top face are replaced by the second layer with 9×9 elements. The number of elements on the other faces are calculated automatically by using the optimal curve according to the solar altitude [5].

The sun has a finite size and contributes to the solar penumbrae and sharpness of specular reflection; the third layer which stands for the sun and whose inner-tangent circle has the solid angle of the sun is added onto the parallelepiped so that the effects mentioned above can be easily and quickly calculated (fig. 1(b)). The elements outside the inner-tangent circle are set as *invalid*. All of the valid elements on the third layer are used just to count the proportion of sunlight arriving at the calculation point.

According to the solar position, the top face of the parallelepiped is set towards the sun and one pair of its edges are parallel to the horizon. For every element on every face and the second layer, the energy is integrated taking into account atmospheric scattering, and contribution of skylight considering its solid angle is calculated in the same manner as [5]. The total energy in these elements is equal to that of all skylight. The energy of the direct sunlight is:

$$I_{DS}(\lambda) = I_0 e^{-t(\lambda)}, \quad \lambda = \text{the wavelengths of r, g, and b resp.,} \quad (1)$$

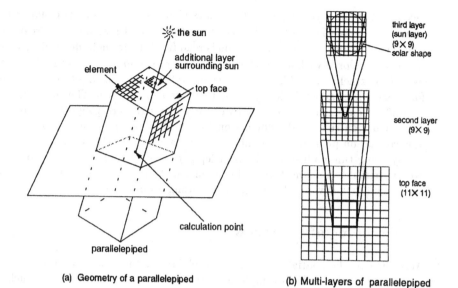

(a) Geometry of a parallelepiped

(b) Multi-layers of parallelepiped

Fig. 1. a model of skylight and direct sunlight

where I_0 is the energy of the sun at the outer surface of the atmosphere; $t(\lambda)$ is optical length of the sunlight λ passing through the atmosphere (see [5]).

According to Bouguer and Berlage formulae [8], the energy (I_{sun}) of the direct sunlight arriving at a plane perpendicular to the solar direction and the energy (I_{sky}) of skylight arriving at a horizontal plane are as follows, respectively:

$$I_{sun} = I_0 \rho^{1/sin\varphi}, \tag{2}$$

$$I_{sky} = 0.5 sin\varphi (I_0 - I_{sun})/(1.0 - 1.4 log_e \rho), \tag{3}$$

where φ is the solar altitude; ρ is the transmissivity of direct sunlight in the atmosphere. Unlike [5], each energy of skylight and direct sunlight on the parallelepiped is regulated automatically by using two proportions (S_{sky} and S_{sun});

$$S_{sun} = I_{sun}/(I_{DS}(r) + I_{DS}(g) + I_{DS}(b)), \tag{4}$$

$$S_{sky} = I_{sky}/\sum_{i=1}^{n}\{(C_i(r) + C_i(g) + C_i(b))V_{iz}\}, \tag{5}$$

where C_i is the contribution of skylight in element i on the parallelepiped and V_{iz} is z component of a vector from the center of the parallelepiped to the center of element i; n is the number of elements on every face and layer of the parallelepiped. Thus the total energy of skylight and direct sunlight is regulated by time and the place of a scene to be rendered.

The parallelepiped is used to calculate the illuminance of every point required for rendering. For every calculation point, the shadow information of all elements on the parallelepiped is checked by using graphics functions. In this case, every face or layer has a correspondant graphics viewport whose size is equal to the number of the meshes on the face or layer. After obstacles with colors are drawn into these viewports, color information is read from the framebuffer and checked; if a pixel is colored with a non-zero value, its corresponding element is shadowed by some obstacles. The diffuse and specular reflections of skylight are computed for every non-shadowed element and they are summarized. The intensities of the diffuse and specular reflections of direct sunlight are proportional to the number of non-shadowed elements on the third layer; the intensity of light at any calculation point in a penumbra is easily and accurately obtained.

By using this multi-layered parallelepiped, even if some graphics hardware are unavailable, checking the shadow information on every element also can be carried out at a low cost by using the following approaches.

3   Grouping of Obstacles

According to the spatial distribution of obstacles, they may be grouped in a hierachical structure. For example, a scene may consists of many objects such as mountains, bridges, etc.. A bridge may be composed of towers, fences, piers, etc. In general, we can create a hierachical structure as shown in fig. 2, where each node stands for a whole scene, grouped obstacles, single obstacles, or surfaces. Usually, the obstacles are grouped into one node if they are close to each other. Every node except for the leaf nodes standing for the surfaces of an obstacle has its bounding box. All of the nodes under their parent node are sorted in descending order according to their maximum z-values. The grouping is done just once before rendering the scene.

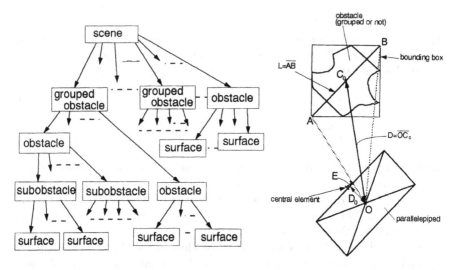

Fig. 2. hierachy of a scene   **Fig. 3.** approximation of solid angle

If such a node representing a grouped obstacle or single one only occupies a smaller angle than the solid angle of one element of the parallelepiped, only three faces of its bounding box instead of its children are drawn in a relevant viewport. The detection of a node may be approximated depending on the faces or layers of the parallelepiped as follows (see fig. 3).

$$E^2/D_0^2 >= L^2/D^2, \tag{6}$$

where E is the length of an edge of the central element on a face or layer of the parallelepiped, D_0 is the distance from the center of the parallelepiped to the center of the central element, L is the distance between two diagonal points of the bounding box, and D is the distance from the calculation point to the center of the bounding box. E, D_0 and L are calculated once; only D^2 is computed every time when the calculation point is moved.

The left side of the equation (6) stands for the maximum solid angle of the elements on the relative face or layer, while the right side approximates the solid angle of a grouped obstacle or a single one. When the equation is satisfied and the real solid angle of the obstacle is larger than the left side of the equation, the precision of the illuminance at the calculation point may be lower. A solution to decrease the occurrence of such cases is for the parallelepiped to be meshed in densely or for a ratio less than one to be multiplied to the left side of the equation. The smaller solid angle of the left side of the equation results in better precision of illuminance with increments of cost.

4 Classification of Obstacles

The classification of obstacles is based on the following facts.

- Every obstalce shadowing a calculation point is higher than that point, because the center of the sky dome is set on it (III, IV, V and VI in fig. 4(a)).
- Every obstacle shadowing the calculation point is located in the front side of the calculation plane where the calculation point is located on (see II, III, IV and V in fig. 4(a)).
- Every obstacle belongs to only some of the view volumes, viewed from the calculation point, coinciding with related faces or layers of the parallelepiped. The shadow detection should be done in the related view volume. Seven view volumes are considered for the classification of obstacles (see fig. 4(b)); one of them is for the sun layer; the other six volumes are for the parallelepiped faces. The result of the classification of obstacles in Vtop is also used for the second layer.

Before rendering, a pre-classification of all obstacles is done once for every volume. We call the planes forming each volume the classification plane. At first, the object space is uniformly divided by the directed planes which are parallel to each classification plane. For example, as shown in fig. 4(c), the planes indexed by a_i are parallel to the plane ADOFG in fig. 4(b), and planes indexed by b_j are

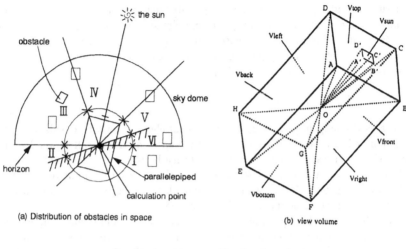

(a) Distribution of obstacles in space

(b) view volume

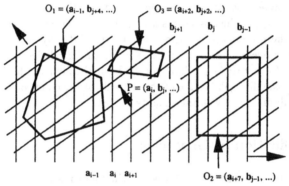

(c) division of object space

Fig. 4. classification of obstacles

parallel to the plane BCOEH. Then in fig. 2 and 3, every point on the bounding box of an obstacle or grouped ones, or vertex on a surface of each leaf is indexed due to these classification planes (e.g., $a_i, b_j, \ldots, o_n$). Every such a directed plane except for those of the Vsun is shared by two volumes, so the number of total indexes for a point is 16. For each component corresponding to a classification plane (e.g., a_i), the maximum index of points on a bounding box (or vertexes on a surface) is stored in its node, for example, the indexes of object O_1 in fig. 4(c) are $(a_{i-1}, b_{j+4}, \ldots)$ and those of O_2 are $(a_{i+7}, b_{j-1}, \ldots)$. Here $x_m = m$; $x = a, b, c, \ldots, o$.

In the rendering step, the obstacles are classified by the following steps.

At first, obstacles are classified due to a calculation plane; every node in fig. 2, whose maximum z-value is over the lowest calculation point, is traversed. If no point on a bounding box (or vertex on a surface) belongs to the front side of the calculation plane, the node together with all of its children is marked with a flag *clipped*; otherwise the node is marked *candidate*. If all of the points in a node wholly belong to the front side of the plane, its children are directly marked *candidate*; otherwise, its children are checked recursively.

Then every calculation point (e.g., P in fig. 4(c)) required for rendering on the calculation plane is indexed due to the planes parallel to each classification plane. By traversing of the hierachy of objects, every index of nodes with *candidate* and its maximum z-value over the calculation point is compared to that of the calculation point: if all of four indexes corresponding to each volume, stored in the node in the pre-classification procedure, are larger than or equal to its corresponding indexes of the calculation point, the node and/or its children (e.g., O_3 in fig. 4(c)) is selected for the detection of shadow information on the corresponding face (e.g., top face) or layer of the parallelepiped.

5 Examples and Comparison

Figure 5 and 6 are examples to illustrate the differences among three cases: (a) a denser multi-layered parallelepiped (41×41 elements for top face, 25×25 for the second layer and 19×19 for the sun layer), (b) a sparse multi-layered parallelepiped (11×11 elements for top face, 9×9 for the second layer and 9×9 for the sun layer) and (c) the same parallelepiped as (b) but without both functions of grouping and classifying the obstacles. Fig. 5(a) depicts the result of the case (a), fig. 5(b) illustrates the result of the case (b). Fig. 7 depicts the difference between fig. 5(a) and (b). Because of too small difference, it was multiplied ten times. The result of the case (c) is only discussed in table 1, because it is almost all the same as (b). The scenes in fig. 5 and fig. 6 have 27,403 and 7,470 polygons, respectively. All of the pictures in fig. 5 and fig. 6, whose sizes are 1200×645 pixels, are rendered by using the same algorithms. In fig. 7 we can recognize some differences even though it is almost impossible to observe them in fig. 5.

Table 1 lists the different calculation costs of illuminance and accuracy of rendering among the cases mentioned above. The costs were tested on IRIS Indigo 3000/Elan workstations under the same conditions and do not include the costs of the computation of the shadow volumes [2] and mirror reflection on

costs and differences scenes \ items	a dense parallelepiped (41*41, 25*25, and 19*19 for 1st, 2nd and 3rd layers resp.. (a)	a sparse parallelepiped (11*11, 9*9, and 9*9 for 1st, 2nd and 3rd layers resp.. (b)	neither grouping nor classifying functions (c)	differences between cases (a) and (b) Δn ΔN N	differences between cases (b) and (c) Δn ΔN N
a bridge (fig. 5)	36.0 minutes (36.6 min.)	24.1 minutes (24.7 min.)	529.4 min. (530 min.)	1.2388 % 3.8378 % 249,837	0.8515 % 2.0675 % 218,650
a bay (fig. 6)	6.50 minutes (8.0 min.)	3.2 minutes (4.65 min.)	33.3 minutes (34.75 min.)	0.3770 % 4.3219 % 67,522	0.1198 % 3.8144 % 24,302

Note: the costs in ( ) are total ones of rendering scenes.

Table 1. comparison of calculation costs and accuracy of illuminance

water surface. The differences between two pictures are computed by using the following equations:

$$\Delta_n = \sum_{j=1}^{n}(|v_{0j} - v_{1j}|/v_{0j})/n, \quad \Delta_N = \sum_{j=1}^{n}(|v_{0j} - v_{1j}|/v_{0j})/n, \quad (7)$$

where v_{0j} and v_{1j} are color values of two related pixels on the two pictures, respectively, n is the image size and N is total number of pairs of pixels with different values on two pictures. The first picture is a reference one here.

The table 1 indicates that a denser parallelepiped is not imperative when it is not necessary to emphasize very much the accuracy of illuminance because the extra calculation cost of 49.4% brings only 3.84% (Δ_N) higher accuracy of rendering (e.g., fig. 5). The approaches of grouping and classifying the obstacles are very effective because they considerably reduce the cost with only limited reduction of the accuracy of rendering (about 2.1%).

6 Conclusions

In this paper, we proposed a multi-layered parallelepiped as a new model for representing direct sunlight and skylight, and discussed two approaches for reducing the calculation cost drastically. A better trade-off between the cost and the accuracy of illuminance is obtained. One drawback of this paper is that only direct sunlight and skylight limited to a clear sky are considered. The overcast skylight is our theme in future.

References

1. Klassen, R. V. : Modeling the Effect of the Atmosphere on Light. ACM Trans. on Graphics **6**, 3 (1987) 215–237
2. Nishita, T. and Nakamae, E. : Continuous Tone Representation of Three Dimensional Object Illuminated by Sky Light. Computer Graphics **20**, 4 (1986) 125–132
3. Takita, S., Kaneda, K., et al: A Simple Rendering for Penumbra Caused by Sunlight. Proc. CG International '90 (1990) 187–201
4. Dobashi, Y, Kaneda, K., et al: Skylight for Interior Lighting Design. Computer Graphics forum **13**, 3 (1994) 85–96
5. Tadamura, K., Nakamae, E., et al: Modeling Skylight and Rendering of Outdoor Scenes. Computer Graphics forum **12**, 3 (1993) 189–200
6. Nishita, T., Shirai, T., et al: Display of the Earth Taking into Account Atmospheric Scattering. Computer Graphics Annual Conference Series 1993, (1993) 175–182
7. Kaneda, K., Okamoto, T., et al: Highly Realistic Visual Simulation of Outdoor Scene under Various Atmospheric Conditions. Proc. CG International '90, 117–131
8. Berlage, H.: Zur Theorie der Beleuchtung einer horizontalen Flache durch Tageslicht, Meteorologische Zeitschrift (1928, 5) 174–180

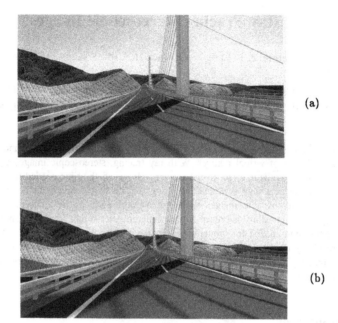

(a)

(b)

Fig. 5. a scene of a bridge

Fig. 6. a scene of a bay

Fig. 7. difference between fig. 5(a) and (b)

Ray Tracing Stereoscopic Images

Gabriel K.P. Fung   Horace H.S. Ip   Ken C.K. Law

Image Computing Group, Computer Science Department,
City University of Hong Kong. Tat Chee Ave., Kowloon, Hong Kong

Abstract. Stereoscopic images are becoming more and more in demand due to the advents of virtual reality. With ray tracing, stereoscopic images can give stunningly realistic effect to the viewer. However, the time needed to generate one raytraced image is already too long. If the time needs to be doubled, ray tracing stereoscopic images would discourage most potential users. In this paper, an algorithm is presented that generates stereo pair images in about 60% of the time needed for generating the stereo pair images separately. And the resulting images of this algorithm is effectively identical to those generated separately. We evaluate and compare the algorithm with stereoscopic images generated separately.

1. Introduction

When Whitted [11] began to work with ray tracing in 1980, this is an extremely expensive technique to use. Today, although we have much better algorithms [7][9] and computers that runs million times faster than those days, rendering with ray tracing is still difficult. One of the difficulties is the ever growing requirement. Better resolutions, more objects in one scene, and to double the hard work, stereoscopic images is required.

Stereoscopic images is a pair of images, one for the left eye and the other for the right. Since the center of projection is different for each image, rays generated for the images are totally different. However, stereoscopic images can be viewed as a temporal coherence problem, where we have a static scene and a moving view point. Temporal coherence in ray tracing has been studied by many researchers[4][5][8], and results of these works are helpful in developing an efficient solution for raytraced stereo images. In this paper, we will show that some calculations can be done once for both images and the result of one image can help us to speed up the rendering time of the second.

2. The Geometry of Stereoscopic Images

Let us first highlight the geometry of a stereoscopic viewing setup and some of its characteristics as follows: (see Figure 1)
1. The image plane lies on the x-y plane.
2. The left eye and the right eye (center of projection) are located at $(-e/2,0,-d)$ and $(e/2,0,-d)$ respectively.
3. A point $p(x_p,y_p,z_p)$ on an object, and the two projected points according to each eye, $p_l(x_l,y_l)$ & $p_r(x_r,y_r)$, lies on the same epipolar plane.
4. $y_l = y_r$, p_l & p_r lies on the same scan line / epipolar line normal viewing.

5. $x_r = x_l + z_p e / (z_p + d)$ (1)

where $z_p e / (z_p + d)$ is the disparity, notice that it only varies with z_p. For positive z_p, $z_p / (z_p + d)$ is monotonic increasing from 0 to 1, therefore, the disparity is monotonic increasing from 0 to e

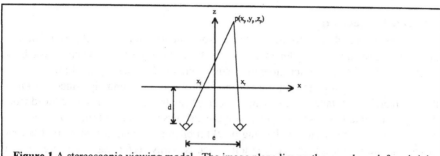

Figure 1 A stereoscopic viewing model. The image plane lies on the x-y plane, left and right eye at (-e/2,0,-d) and (e/2,0,-d) respectively.

3. Previous Work

Adelson et al. [1] investigated the extension of various popular graphics algorithms to speed up stereoscopic images rendering but ray tracing was not mentioned. Papathomas et el. [10] uses ray tracing in meteorology but they used point source data and did not account for the occlusion or the shading problem with different center of projections.

Badt [3] introduced a back projection algorithm in 1988. Back projection uses a ray traced image and back project each pixel on the image to another view point. Pixels on the new image that has not been projected by any pixel are called missing pixels. Pixels on the new image that have more than one pixel projected on it are called overlapped pixels. And pixels that have values not matching the surrounding pixels are called bad pixels. Bad pixels are found by using a box filter. Missing pixels and bad pixels are retraced as normal. In his experimental results, less than 40% of the pixels in the new images needed to be retraced.

Ezell et al. [6] adapt Badt's algorithm to speed up stereoscopic images ray tracing. They reproject the pixels in left eye image by equation (1) to the right eye image. Their tests show that about 20% to 50% of the pixels in the right images needed to be retraced.

In 1993, Adelson et al. [2] enhanced the reprojection algorithm. They observed that since a pixel on the left eye image always reprojected to the same scan line of the right eye image, rendering can be done scan line by scan line. With this algorithm, less than 10% of the pixels on the reprojected image needs to be retraced. However this algorithm contains several deficiencies. First, it eliminates the overlapping pixels problem by overwriting previously reprojected pixel with new reprojected pixels, this caused redundant work to be done. Moreover, this algorithm does not account for the backface problem. A point on an object visible to the left eye may be backface to the right eye and yet this point will be reprojected to the right eye image. Another problem is aliasing, a pixel on the left eye image will probably not projected exactly onto the center of a pixel in the right eye image. Even if the right eye also see the same object through that pixel, the intersecting point on the object will not be the same. Therefore, the specular shading or even the diffuse shading will be incorrect.

In this paper, we will show that by using our algorithm, stereoscopic images can be generated with higher speed and greatly improved image quality.

4. Back Projection

Here we choose to back project from the left image to the right image, however, the reverse can be done with exactly the same algorithm. When we use back projection, we will encounter three problems, namely, the missing pixel problem, the overlapping pixel problem and the bad pixel problem. Fortunately, since we know that the reprojection takes place on an epipolar plane, these problems are reduced from three-dimensional to two-dimensional. Figure 2 shows examples of these problems.

Let us look at the overlapping pixel problem as shown in figure 2b, it is easy to see that the rightmost pixel of the left image is always referring to a nearer object from the left eye's point of view. Therefore, reprojecting *from right to left* can eliminate this problem easily.

Bad pixel problem is harder to solve. Consider figure 2c, object 1 occlude the path from right eye to object 2, and in figure 2d, object 2 occluded the path from right eye to object 3. That means from the left image, we have no idea whether object 2 in figure 2c or object 3 in figure 3d is visible to right eye or not. We concluded that when we reproject from right to left, we have to give up the reprojected pixels which are on the right of the left most reprojected pixel on the right image. The pixels we give up are potential bad pixels.

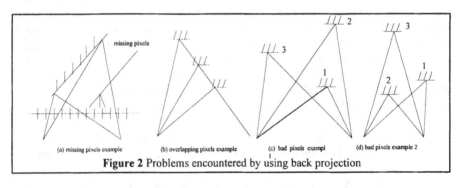

Figure 2 Problems encountered by using back projection

Figure 2a shows the missing pixel problem where consecutive pixels on the left image are reprojected to non-consecutive pixels on the right image. One simple solution is to retrace the pixels between the reprojected pixels. However, if we know that the two pixels are reprojected from the same convex object, we can safely say that the pixels between them will be ray traced to the same object so we should fire a ray directly to that object, i.e. saving the time needed to determine which object in the scene intersect with the ray. It can easily be shown that if some other object stay in front of the target object, the bad pixel problem on figure 2c will occur and change the problem to a bad pixel problem.

5. A New Algorithm

In the last section we have discussed the back projection algorithm and its problems. Now we will present our algorithm for generating stereoscopic images.

```
For each scan line
    old_obj = NULL
    last_pixel = rightmost pixel of right image
    For each pixel x₁ of the left eye image from right to left
        Raytrace thru x₁ and find curr_obj, the object being hit and its z-coordinate, zₚ
        if (curr_obj != NULL) [the ray hit curr_obj]
            calculate curr_x = x₁ + zₚe / (zₚ+d) [        where e is the distance between two
eyes and
                                                         d is the distance from the eyes to
the image plane]
                if curr_x < last_pixel (not potential bad pixel)
                    if old_obj = curr_obj
                        while last_pixel >= curr_x
                            fire a ray from last_pixel to curr_obj for intersecting point
                            calculate color for right image at last_pixel
                            last_pixel = last_pixel - 1
                        end while
                    else
                        while last_pixel >= curr_x
                            raytrace thru last_pixel for right image
                            last_pixel = last_pixel - 1
                        end while
                    end if
                end if
        end if
        old_obj = curr_obj
    end for
    while last_pixel >= 0 (retrace remaining pixels on this scan line
        raytrace thru last_pixel for right image
        last_pixel = last_pixel - 1
    end while
```

Figure 3 Pseudo code of the new reprojection algorithm

Our algorithm is also based on reprojection. However, when we do reprojection, we do not round up the results to the nearest pixel. We only fire rays from pixels between two consecutive reprojected pixels which have the same target object, similar to the solution for the missing pixel problem, instead of searching for the closest intersection in ray tracing, these rays are directed at the target object. By reprojecting pixels scan line after scan line, shading information, such as ambient and diffuse shading of an object, calculated by the left image can be used by the right image during reprojection. Figure 3 is the pseudo code of our algorithm.

Since we are not rounding up reprojected point and immediately draw on that pixel, we can get better precision on the object edge in the generated image. Since, instead of using the intersecting point from the left image, we calculate the actual intersection point for a pixel, we get more accurate lighting information to shade the pixel, resulting in better quality images (see table 1).

As discussed earlier, we only assume a target object when consecutive reprojected pixels with the latter located on the left of the former both reprojected from the same object. In this case we actually test that the target object is not backface to the right eye. (see figure 4)

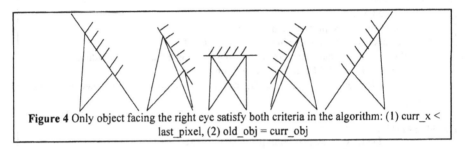

Figure 4 Only object facing the right eye satisfy both criteria in the algorithm: (1) curr_x < last_pixel, (2) old_obj = curr_obj

6. Experiment

Since coherence of stereoscopic images provide no advantage to secondary rays, we only carry out tests to reveal the performance of the algorithm on primary rays. No secondary rays are generated in the tests. All test images are rendered at 320×320. Figure 6a-6h are the resulting stereo images.

We compare our algorithm with Adelson's algorithm. Table 1 contains the results. Rays retraced is the number of rays needed to be retraced on the right image. Number of incorrect pixels are the pixels that holds different value when comparing pixel by pixel with the separately generated right image. Ray tracing time account for the total image generation time for both images. Therefore if percentage of time required = 100%, there is no savings at all in rendering the right image. If percentage of time required = 50%, there is no extra cost needed to render the right image, which is the optimal case.

The large number of retraced rays when object number is small is due to the large number of missed rays in the left image. Since missed rays are not reprojected, we must retraced rays for the right image. We can see that the percentage of retraced rays (Figure 5b) stays around 10% as the number of objects increased. This is reasonable as retraced rays usually occur on projected object edges only. And as expected, our algorithm fire slightly more (about 1%) retraced rays than Adelson's.

While the percentage of error (Figure 5c) rise to about 20% in the case of Adelson's algorithm, our algorithm has an error rate of about 0.2%. The vast difference in image quality is not surprising since we fire rays to get intersection point on the object instead of inheriting the value from those left image's pixels.

As the number of objects increase, left image has fewer missed rays. We can observed the ray tracing time (Figure 5a) has dropped to about 55% as the number of objects increase. In all cases, our algorithm is only slightly slower (about 1%) than Adelson's algorithm. Notice that we fire and traced rays from every pixel while Adelson's algorithm use approximation with reprojected pixels. Since only less than 10% of the pixels are retraced, that means our algorithm fire rays for more than 90% of the pixel. Given there is much more work to do, it is surprising that our algorithm be almost as fast as Adelson's. One reason for this is that Adelson's algorithm overwrite pixel values while we don't. Moreover, the Adelson's algorithm needs to maintain a scan line record which create extra overhead in terms of space and time complexities.

Our algorithm could in principle also be used to approximate values for shading in order to increase speed. However, we choose not to degrade the image quality since the shading of the image contains stereo cues which is important in forming a stereoscopic view. A stereo pair image with better quality is easier for the viewer to perceive relative depths between objects in the scene.

7. Conclusion

We have presented an algorithm that generate stereoscopic images in about 10% more time than that required for generating a single image. The algorithm simultaneously ray trace the left image and back project it to the right image. Since the main overhead of a ray tracer is to calculate intersection and we have avoid 90% of the intersection calculation in the right image, we have greatly reduced the ray tracing time. At the same time, we manage to maintain the image quality to 99.8%.

Stereoscopic coherence between the pair images may have other features which we can exploit for fast generation. For example, along a scan line, both images should intersect the same set of object that intersect this scan line. We are currently designing algorithm which utilizes this characteristic to speed up the retraced rays.

Fig	No. of objects in the Scene	Experimental Data	Separate generation of left & right images	Adelson's Algorithm	Our algorithm
6a	10	Rays retraced (b)	102400 (a)	87383	87684
		% of rays retraced (b)/(a)	100%	85.3%	85.6%
		No. of incorrect pixels (c)	0	3185	0
		% of incorrect pixels (c)/(a)	0%	3.1%	0%
		Ray tracing time (e)	49 (d)	36	36
		% of time required (e)/(d)	100%	73.5%	73.5%
6b	10	Rays retraced (b)	102400 (a)	84040	84150
		% of rays retraced (b)/(a)	100%	82.1%	82.1%
		No. of incorrect pixels (c)	0	3425	2
		% of incorrect pixels (c)/(a)	0%	3.3%	0.002%
		Ray tracing time (e)	43 (d)	27	28
		% of time required (e)/(d)	100%	62.8%	65.1%
6c	100	Rays retraced (b)	102400 (a)	29695	30441
		% of rays retraced (b)/(a)	100%	29.0%	29.7%
		No. of incorrect pixels (c)	0	16102	184
		% of incorrect pixels (c)/(a)	0%	15.7%	0.2%
		Ray tracing time (e)	198 (d)	127	128
		% of time required (e)/(d)	100%	64.1%	64.6%
6d	100	Rays retraced (b)	102400 (a)	28246	29118
		% of rays retraced (b)/(a)	100%	27.6%	28.4%
		No. of incorrect pixels (c)	0	16698	136
		% of incorrect pixels (c)/(a)	0%	16.3%	0.1%
		Ray tracing time (e)	187 (d)	120	121
		% of time required (e)/(d)	100%	64.2%	64.7%

6e	300	Rays retraced (b)	102400 (a)	11319	12567
		% of rays retraced (b)/(a)	100%	11.1%	12.3%
		No. of incorrect pixels (c)	0	19893	278
		% of incorrect pixels (c)/(a)	0%	19.4%	0.3%
		Ray tracing time (e)	461 (d)	263	267
		% of time required (e)/(d)	100%	57.0%	57.9%
6f	300	Rays retraced (b)	102400 (a)	9677	11204
		% of rays retraced (b)/(a)	100%	9.5%	10.9%
		No. of incorrect pixels (c)	0	20584	173
		% of incorrect pixels (c)/(a)	0%	20.1%	0.2%
		Ray tracing time (e)	460 (d)	256	261
		% of time required (e)/(d)	100%	55.7%	56.7%
6g	500	Rays retraced (b)	102400 (a)	8152	9469
		% of rays retraced (b)/(a)	100%	8.0%	9.2%
		No. of incorrect pixels (c)	0	19534	129
		% of incorrect pixels (c)/(a)	0%	19.1%	0.1%
		Ray tracing time (e)	694 (d)	381	387
		% of time required (e)/(d)	100%	54.9%	55.8%
6h	500	Rays retraced (b)	102400 (a)	6680	8426
		% of rays retraced (b)/(a)	100%	6.5%	8.2%
		No. of incorrect pixels (c)	0	20928	176
		% of incorrect pixels (c)/(a)	0%	20.4%	0.2%
		Ray tracing time (e)	687 (d)	372	380
		% of time required (e)/(d)	100%	54.1%	55.3%

Table 1 Experimental results comparing our algorithm with Adelson's algorithm

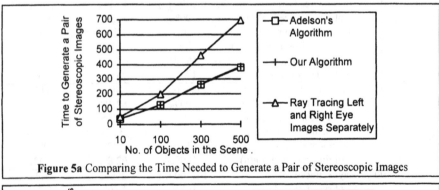

Figure 5a Comparing the Time Needed to Generate a Pair of Stereoscopic Images

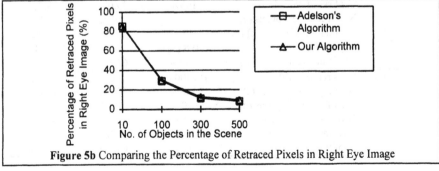

Figure 5b Comparing the Percentage of Retraced Pixels in Right Eye Image

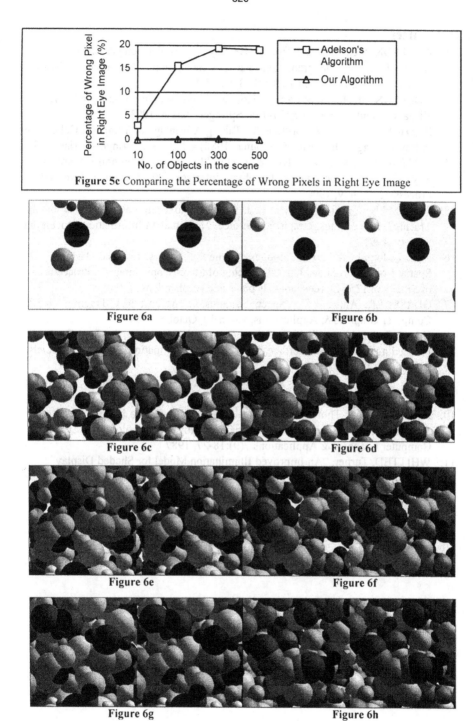

Figure 5c Comparing the Percentage of Wrong Pixels in Right Eye Image

Figure 6a

Figure 6b

Figure 6c

Figure 6d

Figure 6e

Figure 6f

Figure 6g

Figure 6h

References

1. ADELSON, Stephen J. & Jeffrey B. Bentley & In Seok Chong & Larry F. Hodges & Joseph Winograd, "Simultaneous Generation of Stereoscopic Views", Computer Graphics Forum 10(1991) 3-10, 1991

2. ADELSON, Stephen J. & Larry F. Hodges, "Stereoscopic Ray-tracing", The Visual Computer (1993) 10:127-144, Springer-Verlag, 1993

3. BADT, Sig Jr., "Two Algorithms for Taking Advantage of Temporal Coherence in Ray Tracing", The Visual Computer (1988) 4:123-132, Springer-Verlag, 1988

4. CHAPMAN, J. & T.W. Calvert & J. Dill, "Exploiting Temporal Coherence in Ray Tracing", Proceedings: Graphics Interface '90, Canadian Information Processing Society, 1990

5. CHAPMAN, J. & T.W. Calvert & J. Dill, "Spatio-Temporal Coherence in Ray Tracing", Proceedings: Graphics Interface '91, Canadian Information Processing Society, 1991

6. EZELL, John D. & Larry F. Hodges, "Some Preliminary Results on Using Spatial Locality to Speed Up Ray Tracing of Stereoscopic Images", Proceedings of SPIE Vol.1256 Stereoscopic Displays and Applications, 1990

7. GLASSNER, Andrew S., "Space Subdivision for Fast Ray Tracing", IEEE Computer Graphics & Applications, v.4, n.10, October 1984

8. JEVANS, David A., "Object Space Temporal Coherence for Ray Tracing", Proceedings: Graphics Interface '92, Canadian Information Processing Society, 1992

9. KAY, Timothy L., & James Kajiya, "Ray Tracing Complex Scenes", Computer Graphics 20(4):269-278, August 1986.

10. PAPATHOMAS, Thomas V. & James A. Schiavone & Bela Julesz, "Stereo Animation for Very Large Data Bases: Case Study - Meteorology", IEEE Computer Graphics & Applications 7(9):18-27, 1987

11. WHITTED, Turner, "An Improved Illumination Model for Shaded Display", Communications of the ACM, 23(6):343-349, June 1980.

Creating Memorable Characters with Computers

John Lasseter

Director & Animator
Vice President, Creative Development
Pixar, U.S.A.

ABSTRACT

With the latest computer animation software tools, making objects move is becoming easier and easier. But making those objects look alive, look like they are thinking, is never that easy. Computer animation software tools will never do that for you. To make characters come alive takes a knowledge of traditional animation principles and acting, regardless of the animation medium. Remember, computers don't animate...people do.

Computer Assisted Lung Cancer Diagnosis Based on Helical Images

K.Kanazawa, M.Kubo, N.Niki, H.Satoh*
H.Ohmatsu**, K.Eguchi**, N.Moriyama**

Department of Information Science, University of Tokushima, Japan
*Medical Engineering Laboratory, Toshiba Corporation, Japan
**National Cancer Center, Japan

abstract : In this paper, we describe a computer assisted automatic diagnosis system of lung cancer that detects tumor candidates in its early stage from the helical CT images. This automation of the process reduces the time complexity and increases the diagnosis confidence. Our algorithm consists of analysis part and diagnosis part. In the analysis part, we extract the lung regions and the pulmonary blood vessels regions and analyze the features of these regions using image processing technique. In the diagnosis part, we define diagnosis rules based on these features, and we detect the tumor candidates using these rules. We apply our algorithm to 224 patients data of mass screening. These results show that our algorithm detects lung cancer candidates successfully.

1 Introduction

Lung cancer is known as one of the most difficult cancer to cure, and the number of deaths that it causes is usually increasing. A detection of the lung cancer in its early stage can be helpful for medical treatment to limit the danger. One of the measures is mass screening process for lung cancer. As a conventional method for mass screening process, the chest X-ray films have been used for lung cancer diagnosis. However, the small lung cancers at early stage are difficult to detect because of the overlapping of the bone and organs shadows. One of the proposed techniques that assist the detection uses the helical CT which can make a wide range measurement of lung in a short time. We expect that the proposed technique increases the diagnostic confidence because the helical CT information have the 3D cross section images of lung. However, mass screening based on helical CT images leads considerable number of images to the diagnosis. This time-consuming fact make it difficult to be used in clinic. The automation of this process reduces the time complexity and increases the diagnostic confidence. To increase the efficiency of mass screening process, we are developing an algorithm for an automatic detection of lung cancer candidates based on the helical CT images. Our diagnostic algorithm is based on image processing techniques and medical knowledge. As input data for the automation process, we use the helical CT lung images with a specified measurement condition. We define optionally the measurement conditions of helical CT. In mass screening process, the helical CT images at a measurement condition shown on **Table 1** are used to measure all lung area at only one breath stop (about 15 seconds). For every patient we collect 35 images with the same measurement condition. **Fig.1** is an example of the collected helical CT image.

Table.1 Measurement condition

Beam wide	10.0mm
Table speed	20.0mm/sec
Tube voltage	120kV
Tube current	50mA
Reconstruction intervals	10.0mm

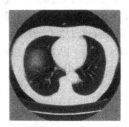

Fig.1 Helical CT image

2 Outline of Diagnostic Algorithm

In the lung area, the CT values of lung cancer are almost similar to those of pulmonary blood vessels, so it is difficult to separate them using only their CT values. So we extract the regions which are high CT values in the lung area such as the pulmonary blood vessels and the tumors, and we detect the tumor candidates from the extracted regions based on some defined diagnostic rules. Our diagnostic algorithm consists of the two following parts :

Analysis Part : We extract the necessary regions for diagnosis and analyze these regions based on image processing techniques. Firstly, we extract the lung area from the original image. Secondly, we extract the blood vessels and the tumors regions which have the high CT values in the lung area, as the candidate regions. Finally, we analyze the features of those regions for making diagnosis rules.

Diagnosis Part : We define the diagnosis rules to detect the suspicious shadows based on those features, and we detect the lung cancer using these rules.

We apply the diagnostic algorithm to each slice image, because the measurement condition for mass screening is rougher than general clinic measurement conditions and their 3D information is not confidential.

3 Analysis Part

3.1 Extraction of the Lung Area

Lung is mostly occupied by air, so its CT values are low within the lung area. The extraction process of the lung area is based on a thresholding algorithm. However, this thresholding technique excludes the lung boundary part with high CT values from the real lung area. So we follow a correction process for making up such loss parts. The procedure of this process is as follows.

(1) The original image is transformed to a binary image using the thresholding algorithm.

(2) We calculate the curvature at the boundary of such binary image, and classify each pixel into three types of concave point, convex point and smooth point.

(3) We connect between two points P1, Q1 as shown in **Fig.2**(a), where P1 and Q1 are n1 pixels away from the concave point A1 and An.

(4) We connect between A and B as shown in **Fig.2**(b) if the ray P2A or Q2A crosses the lung boundary within the distance d, where P2 and Q2 are n2 pixels away from the convex point A.

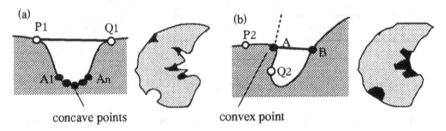

Fig.2 Correction of the lung boundary.

3.2 Extraction of Pulmonary Blood Vessels

The organ in the lung, such as blood vessels and tumors, are separately given by a segmentation process using the fuzzy clustering method [4],[5]. However, the helical CT images involve artifact values called the beam hardening effect and the partial volume effect. These artifact values affect the segmentation results and present bad segmentation results. Therefore, we cancel these artifact values as follows :

(1) We apply the smoothing method to the extracted lung images.

(2) We subtract this smoothed image from the original image in the lung area. We apply the fuzzy clustering method to the histogram of the pixel values within the lung area. We separate the lung area into two classes. One class is the air part, the other is the blood vessels and tumors.

3.3 Analysis of the Lung Area

We analyze the features of the blood vessels regions and the tumor regions for diagnosis rules. Here, we give attention to thickness and position of both blood vessels and tumors. The thickness is used as a basis to select the regions with suspicious candidates, and is given by using the gray-weighted distance transformation described in [6]. The position is determined based on the distance from the chest wall, and is given by following steps :

(1) We detect the edges of the right and left lung area, and calculate the length LR,

LL between front and rear of each lung side, and select the segmented edges as shown in **Fig. 3**.

(2) We scan the lung area pixel by pixel and calculate the distance between the current point and the segmented edges. We detect this minimum distance and consider this distance as the distance from the lung wall to the current point.

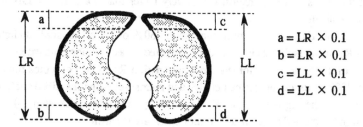

$$a = LR \times 0.1$$
$$b = LR \times 0.1$$
$$c = LL \times 0.1$$
$$d = LL \times 0.1$$

Fig.3 Exrtaction of the segment edges.

4 Diagnosis Part

Our diagnostic algorithm aims to detect not only the lung cancer but other suspicious regions as the tumor candidates. We recognize two features of tumor candidates and define the diagnosis rules based on these features to detect the tumors. Furthermore, we refer the following medical knowledge :

Knowledge 1 : The shape of the lung cancer is generally spherical, and it is seen like circle on the 2D slice image. So, the shadow like circle is a candidate for tumor.

Knowledge 2 : The thickness of the blood vessel becomes smaller as its position is near the chest wall, but the thickness of the lung cancer is generally larger than the ordinary thickness of the blood vessels at each position.

Knowledge 3 : The shadows contacting the lung wall are generally artifacts or tumors, because the periphery of the blood vessels are too small to be seen in the helical CT image and are difficult to be recognized.

In case of this diagnosis system, we classify the tumors into four types and make the diagnostic rule for each classification. We define the following rules :

[Parameter definitions]

D : the distance from the point **X** to the lung wall.

T : the thickness at the point **X**.

M : the maximum value of distance *D* on a slice image.

T_h : the threshold value of thickness *T* at the point **X**.

The threshold value T_h is varied according to distance *D* and its variation rate is higher as *M* is larger. The minimum value of T_h is setted to about 5mm.

[RULE 1] Detection of tumor candidates in case of noncontact to lung wall

(1) After applying the threshold algorithm to the distance transformed images, we eliminate the pixels lower than a threshold value t_1.

(2) We select the region which involves the point X with $T > T_h$, and apply an inverse distance transformation to this region and mark it as R_1.

(3) If the thickness T in the region R_1 is very larger than T_h, R_1 is detected as a tumor candidate.

(4) If the region R_1 occupies more than about 60% of its circumscribed circle, we decide R_1 as an isolated circle shadow and detect it as a tumor candidate.

(5) We calculate the area S_1 for the remainder region R_1 which occupies more than about 30% of its circumscribed circle, and rearrange a circumscribed circle of its area S_1 on the region R_1 as shown in **Fig.4**(a). We check step (3) for the rearranged circle and detect it as a tumor candidate if satified.

[RULE 2] Detection of tumor candidates in case of noncontact to lung wall

In RULE 1, in order to detect complicated shapes of tumors t_1 is setted low. After executing the RULE 1, some sort of region R_1 involves the blood vessels as shown **Fig.4**(b). Therefore, we set a new threshold value t_2 and repeat the same procedure from step (2) to step (5) in RULE 1.

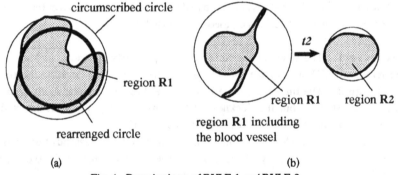

circumscribed circle

region R1

rearrenged circle

region R1

region R2

region R1 including
the blood vessel

(a)

(b)

Fig.4 Descriptions of RULE 1 and RULE 2.

[RULE 3] Detection of tumor candidates in case of contact to lung wall

(1) After applying the threshold algorithm to the distance transformed image, we eliminate the pixels lower than a threshold value t_3 ($t_3 < t_1$).

(2) We select the region which involves the point X with $T > t_3$, and apply an inverse distance transformation to this region and mark it as R_3.

(3) If the difference between the maximum value and the minimum value of distance D in the region R_3 is too small, we eliminate this region R_3.

(4) For 3 pixels dilatation area outside R_3, we count the number of pixels which are

higher than the average value of R_3 , and similarly count the number of pixels which are lower than the average value of R_3 . If the rate of these numbers is small, we consider the region R_3 as an artifact and eliminate it.

(5) If the difference between the average values of area R_3 and the inner dilatation area outside R_3 is large, we consider the region R_3 as a tumor candidate and detect it.

Fig.5 shows descriptions of RULE3.

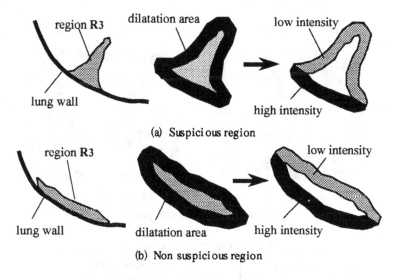

(a) Suspicious region

(b) Non suspicious region

Fig.5 Descriptions of RULE 3

5 Experimental Results

The diagnostic algorithm is applied to the helical CT images of 224 patients (total: 7,840 images) with lung cancer. **Fig.6** shows execusion results of each diagnosis process. In **Fig.6** (d), our diagnosis results show tumor candidates as red regions. All data are diagnosed by three expert doctors with the criterion as shown on **Table.2**. On the **Table.3**, we show the comparative results between our algorithm and doctors. We separate each tumor candidate into six groupgs according to the judgement and the number of the doctor who detect it. As a result, all the judgement E tumors and the judgement D tumors which are judged by three doctors (group I, II, III, IV) are detected perfectly by 100%. The tumors of group V are detected by 91% and the tumors of a group VI are detected by 82%. These results show that our algorithm is helpful in lung cancer diagnosis.

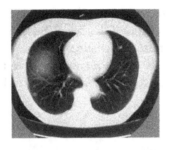
(a) Original image

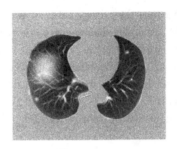
(b) Extraction of lung

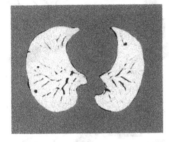
(c) Segmentation

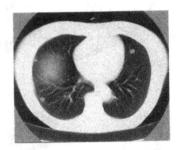
(d) Detection result

Fig.6 Results of diagnosis process.

Table.2 Criterion of judgement

Judgement E	sure malignant lesion
Judgement D	probably malignamt lesion
Judgement C	non malignant lesion
Judgement B	normal case

Table.3 Results of the diagnosis

group	Judgement	Number of doctors	Number of detection	
			Doctor	System
I		3	-	-
II	E	2	1	1
III		1	5	5
IV		3	9	9
V	D	2	22	20
VI		1	89	73

6 Conclusions

We develop a computer assisted automatic diagnosis algorithm of lung cancer using helical CT images. We applied our algorithm to 224 patients data and the results showed that our algorithm detect the suspicious shadows successfully. However, there are some false negative and false positive cases. One case of false negative is positioned outside the lung area, and the remainder of nine cases are tumor size smaller than 5mm. There are also about eleven false positive cases and they belong to mainly blood vessel shadows which are difficult to be distinguished. Currently, we are developing a high-quality diagnostic algorithm to increase the diagnostic confidence.

References

[1]T.Iinuma, Y.Tateno, T.Matsumoto, S.Yamamoto, M.Matsumoto, "Preliminary Specification of X-ray CT for Lung Cancer Screening (LSCT) and its Evaluation on Risk-Cost-Effectiveness", NIPPON ACTA RADIOLOGICA, Japan, vol.52, no.2, pp.182-190, 1992

[2]J.Hasegawa, K.Mori,J.Toriwaki, H.Anno, K.Katada, "Automated Extraction of Lung Cancer Lesions from MultiSlice Chest CT Images by Using Tree-Dimensional Image Processing", Trans.IEICE, Japan, vol.J76-D-II, no.8, pp.1587-1594, 1993

[3]M.L.Giger,K.T.Bae,H and MacMahon,"Computerized Detection of Pulmonary Nodules in computed Tomography Images",Invest Radiol,vol.29,no.4,pp.459-465,1994

[4]M.M.Trivede, J.C.Bezdek, "Low-Level segmentation of aerial images with Fuzzy clustering", IEEE Trans.Syst., Man. & Cybern., SMC-16, 4, pp.589-59, 1986

[5]N.Niki, Y.Kawata, H.Satoh, "A 3-D Display Method of Fuzzy Shapes Obtained from Medical Images", Trans.IEICE, Japan, vol.J73-D-II,no.10,pp.1707-1715, 1990

[6]J.Toriwaki, A.Fukumura, T.Maruse, "Fundamental Properties of the Gray Weighted Distance Transformation", Trans.IEICE, Japan, vol.J60-D, no.12, pp.1101-1108, 1977

[7]K.Kanazawa, Y.Kawata, N.Niki, H.Nishitani, H.Satoh, "Study of Diagnosis of Lung Cancer Using Cone-beam 3-D X-ray CT", Technical Rept., JAMIT'93, Japan, pp.62-65, 1993

[8]K.Kanazawa, N.Niki, H.Nishitani, H.Satoh, H.Omatsu, N.Moriyama, "Computer Assisted Diagnosis of Lung Cancer Using Helical X-ray CT", IEEE Workshop on Biomedical Image Analysis, Seattle, pp.261-267 ,1994

[9]K.Kanazawa, M.Kubo, N.Niki, H.Satoh, H.Omatsu, N.Moriyama, "Computer-Assisted Lung Cancer Diagnosis Based on Helical CT Images", Computer Assisted Radiology, Berlin, pp.369-374 ,1995

Computer-Aided Lung Nodule Detection in Chest Radiography

Maria J. Carreira[1], Diego Cabello[1], Manuel G. Penedo[2] and Jose M. Pardo[1]

[1]Dept. Electrónica e Computación. Fac. Física. Univ. Santiago de Compostela.
E-15706 Santiago de Compostela. SPAIN. E-mail: elmjose@usc.es
[2]Dept. Computación. Fac. Informática. Univ. A Coruña. E-15071 A Coruña. SPAIN.

Abstract. Computer-aided diagnoses programs are developed for alerting the radiologist by indicating potential sites of lesions. One of the important tasks in the development of a computational system for detecting lung nodules is to diminish the number of false positives keeping on high sensitivities. In this work we describe a system for automatic lung nodule detection. The detection is carried out in several stages. First, a knowledge-based segmentation process delimits the lung boundaries. Then, a progressive thresholding of an image in which the conspicuity of nodules has been enhanced by means of filter matching and a set of growth and circularity tests fix the areas suspicious of being nodules into region previously labelled as lungs. Finally, these suspicious regions are confirmed as nodules in a new feature (curvature) space, which gives us an important help in the task of distinguishing true and false nodules from previously extracted suspicious regions. Preliminary results are very promising, achieving high sensitivities with a little ratio of false positives.

1 Introduction

The possibilities of curing lung cancer depend on its detection in the initial stage, when the tumor is small and localized. However, this is a difficult task for the radiologist. A computational system which alerts him about the possible existence of these lesions would facilitate its early diagnose.

In the literature some computational methods are described which attach pulmonary nodule detection from several perspectives. Thus, Giger et al [1], after enhancing the original image by means of a differential technique that substracts a nodule suppresed image (through a spatial smoothing filter) from a nodule enhanced image (through a matched filter), detect areas suspicious of being nodules (suspicious nodules) in base on growth, slope and profile tests applied to regions obtained by means of a progressive thresholding operation over the enhanced image. Penedo et al. [2] look for that suspicious regions by means of a feed-forward neural network trained to recognize nodules. Nevertheless, these methods present moderate success because, although they can achieve high sensitivities in nodule detection, they do this at the expense of an excessive number of false positives. Subsequent works propose new processings in order to diminish this number. Thus, Giger et al. [3] suggest a morphological filter, Matsumoto et al. [4] make a new region growing and edge gradient analysis on the original image and Lin et al. [5] and Chiou et al. [6] apply a feed-forward neural network to distinguish true nodules from false nodules using as input vectors the proper original image or histogram features in amplitude and orientation gradient.

In this work we describe a general system for automatic detection of lung nodules which tries to keep on high sensitivities minimizing the number of false positive detections. The detection is carried out in several stages. First, a knowledge-based segmentation process delimits the lung boundaries. Then, a progressive thresholding of an image in which the conspicuity of nodules has been enhanced by means of filter matching and a set of growht and circularity tests fix the regions suspicious of being nodules into regions previously labelled as lungs. Finally, this suspicious regions are confirmed as nodules in a new feature (curvature) space, which gives us an important help in the task of distinguishing true and false nodules from previously extracted suspicious regions. Preliminary results are very promising, achieving high sensitivities with a little ratio of false positives.

2 Lung Mask Extraction

In order to extract the lung boundaries we implement a segmentation process which uses, in a progressive way, the knowledge we have about the domain [7]. Initially, an oversegmented image is obtained in base on statistical information. The next step consists in refining this segmentation using spatial information to confirm that the boundaries previously obtained are really edges. The boundaries are modified or eliminated in base on criteria that include in an implicit way a not very elaborated knowledge about the domain. This low-level algorithm, which integrates statistical and spatial information, leads to a segmentation in a reasonable number of regions, which is a good starting point for the high-level block. This first makes a split-and-merge of regions guided by knowledge about organs morphology in order to identify them. For doing this, regions are characterized by means of a set of morphometric, densitometric and relational properties and the explicit knowledge is represented by means of production rules. This process allows to extract the lungs, and to label correctly their contours (heart silhouette, aorthic node, ...).

2.1 Initial Segmentation

The initial segmentation of the image is based on the statistical information given by its histogram. For this we use a histogram division iterative algorithm based on the analysis of the local clustering centers. In a first stage, we apply this segmentation algorithm to the original image taking as a parameter the minimum percentage a cluster must have to be considered region. With this we obtain a rough segmentation of the image made up of two or three significant regions. In the second stage, we apply the algorithm to the previously obtained regions, introducing as a parameter the minimum length of the interval which must exist between two adjacent local clustering centers, controlling this way the level of detail desired for each area and leading to an oversegmentation of the image.

2.2 Elimination of no-edge boundaries

The main error observed in the segmentation provided by this clustering algorithm in chest X-ray images consists in the multiplicity of boundaries in those areas in the image with smooth transitions in grey level which basically correspond to transitions between organs. The refinement of the initial segmentation, tending to confirm, modify or eliminate the previously obtained contours, must penalize those parallel boundaries, establishing, if possible, a unique contour in the greatest contrast area. The refinement procedure consists in calculating for each boundary a merit function that integers contrast, length and surrounding information criteria and eliminating, if there are no topological restrictions which prevent it, boundaries with small merit functions [7].

2.3 Knowledge-based analysis

The elementary regions obtained from the low-level block make up a first image description which is given a clinical meaning by means of the high-level block. For doing this, these regions are described by a set of densitometric, morphometric and relational properties: area, minimum bounding rectangle (MBR), regularity, mean grey value, mass center coordinates and relational aspects (inside of, at the right of, ...).

As regards to the kind of images we're considering, we have so anatomical descriptive knowledge, represented by production rules, as heuristic knowledge, which indicates the strategy to use for analizing the regions. Thus, first a *regularization* process on elementary regions is done. Regions with *low regularity* and *large area* are splitted to obtain other more regular regions if in the contour image provided by a Canny filter there are contours strong enough to divide them. The next step in the analysis procedure consists in identifying characteristic organs (lungs), what take us to make an image plan. A later process explores the remaining regions, giving them a proper significance (hilia, heart silhouette,...) or merging them to another already identified region. The described strategy is implemented by means of a control structure which triggers the execution of region-split, organ recognition or region merge/assignation rules depending on the recognition stage. The process finishes when all regions have a label assignated.

The process of splitting some regions in the image is needed because of the irregularity of some important regions. This irregularity is caused by the loss of some important weak edges in the previous stage so, in order to restore them, the Canny image is obtained. We now compute the area and regularity of all regions in the image and look for the edges in regions large enough and with regularity lower enough. So we define the regularity of a region k as $area_k/area_{MBRk}$, where MBR represents the minimum bounding rectangle containing region k.

From the image just obtained, we compute the features of each region. Then, we look for the three largest regions in the image, which usually will correspond to right lung, left lung and mediastinum with lateral tissue. The identification of these regions will lead us to the image preliminar interpretation. For identifying lungs, the system only search for dark regions vertically centered and horizontally at right (left lung) or at left (right lung). In these rules we have injected a very simple knowledge about the position and grey level value of lungs in radiographic images. Afterwards, we look for the regions similar to right and left hilia and heart silhoutte. The reason for doing this before merging is because we only will merge no-labelled regions, and so we will not obtain erroneous merged resultant regions.

The next step is the proper merging process. We first merge regions similar to right and left hilia, then regions similar to heart silhouette and finally regions which can be associated to right or left lungs. So we allow merging regions with medium-high grey level positioned at the left of right lung (external regions) or with medium grey value and at the right or right lung (internal regions). We distinguish between internal and external regions because of the graduation in the grey level of the whole image from its center to its borders. Each time we merge a neighbor region, the properties are updated and next we try to merge another neighbor. The process finishes when there are no more regions verifying the conditions. Finally, what we obtain is a new boundary image in which we have achieved the opening of lung borders, and so we have a *cleaner* interpreted image.

3 Lung nodule detection scheme

The detection of lung nodules is carried out in two levels. The task of the first level is to detect those areas in which it is suspected the existence of a nodule. The second processing level is applied to those suspicious regions and tries to distinguish true nodules from false nodules. The first analysis is carried out over an image in which it has been enhanced the potential information about nodules in the original image; for second level we introduce a new feature space: the curvature space.

3.1 Detection of suspicious nodules

The detection of suspicious nodules is carried out from an image in which the conspicuity of nodules was enhanced by means of a filter matching. For doing this, we use a normalized statistical correlation function, taking as template a nodule gaussian model. The result is an image with enhanced nodules superimposed over a relatively uniform background. The detection process continues with a progressive thresholding of the enhanced image, the thresholds are those grey levels that contain 99%, 98%, ... of the image accumulated histogram. For each one of the regions achieved we compute its effective diameter $(d_{eff}=2(area_k/\pi)^{1/2})$ and circularity degree $(circ=(area_k \in circle)/area_k)$, where $circle$ is a circle with diameter d_{eff} centered in region mass center. We consider areas suspicious of being nodules those regions that, in this growing process, keep on certain effective diameters and circularity degrees.

3.2 Detection in a curvature space

The detection criteria employed in the latter process give a high sensitivity, even at the expense of increasing the number of false positives. For trying to decrease them, we start on a new analysis process, now in a curvature space. The basic idea is to consider the original image, in those suspicious regions, as a topographic map represented by a grey level intensity surface continuous piecewise. A patch of the intensity surface surrounding each pixel is fitted by a bivariate cubic function $f()$. From its coefficients, the curvature parameters are determined and the central pixel is assigned a peak, pit, ridge, ravine, saddle, flat or hillside (concave, convex, saddle+, saddle-, slope) label. This representation is what Haralick calls *topographic primal sketch* [8]. Besides this labelled image, we consider a new curvature image which is computed from the parameters of the original image facet model by means of eq. (1):

$$K = \frac{(-f_c \ f_r) \begin{pmatrix} f_{rr} & f_{rc} \\ f_{rc} & f_{cc} \end{pmatrix} \begin{pmatrix} -f_c \\ f_r \end{pmatrix}}{\left(f_r^2 + f_c^2\right)^{3/2}} \tag{1}$$

where $f_r = \partial f(r,c)/\partial r$, $f_c = \partial f(r,c)/\partial c$, $f_{rr} = \partial^2 f(r,c)/\partial r^2$, $f_{cc} = \partial^2 f(r,c)/\partial c^2$ and $f_{rc} = \partial^2 f(r,c)/\partial r \partial c$ in the window central point. In the topographic interpretation of the image it is expected that the nodule appears as a terrain elevation. In the label and curvature spaces, this will be reflected as an approximately circular region with a kernel of pixels labelled as hillside (concave) surrounded by pixels labelled as hillside (saddle+) and as a high curvature peak, respectively, as can be seen in Fig. 1, applying the whole process to a simulated nodule sized 51*51 pixels.

Based on label and curvature value distribution of pixels, a merit factor cf of a suspicious area of being a true nodule is defined in eq. (2):

$$cf = \frac{number \ of \ concave-hill \ pixels \in region}{region\_area} \tag{2}$$

where *region* is the area delimited as suspicious region in the first level analysis. Fig. 1.b and 1.c ilustrate its definition. The final contour of the suspicious region (darker region in Fig. 1.b) appears also superimposed over the label image. The merit factor reflects the concordance degree between the concave region obtained from the curvature analysis and the suspicious region extracted from the analysis in the original domain. This factor increase its value in $(region-area)^{-1}$ times the number of saddle+ pixels in *region* with curvature greater than a threshold K_1 and decrease it in the same quantity if curvature is less than K_2. The final confidence factor will be modified if the compactness and circularity of the regiong after the growing process are not high enough $(compact_k = 4\pi area_k/perimeter_k)$. Thus, the confidence factor will decrease in $2*(compac_{min}-compac_k)$ if the region is not compact enough and, if region is not circular enough, in $2*(circul_{min}-circul_k)$. The more the value of cf is near 1 the more will be the confidence of that suspicious structure of being a true nodule.

4 Preliminary results

The starting radiological images (postero-anterior chest radiographs) are digitalized by means of a scanner with a 2048*2048 pixel format, 256 grey levels and 130µm pixel size. Afterwards they're averaged to a 512*512 pixel matrix with .52 mm pixel size.

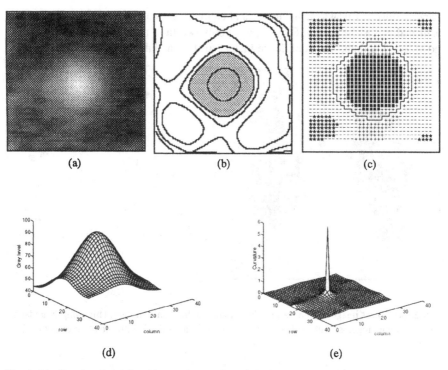

Fig. 1. (a): Simulated nodule with gaussian profile (diameter=1cm, contrast=60). **(b):** Boundary image obtained from progressive thresholding of correlation image; the region extracted as suspicious region is darker (d_{eff}=19.15 pixels=9.96mm, $circ$=0.97). **(c):** label map (■: concave pixel; ★: convex pixel; -: saddle- pixel; +: saddle+ pixel). **(d):** intensity surface (facet model for (a)). **(e):** curvature peak image. Nodule was identified with cf=0.98

To ilustrate the followed detection process we show in Fig. 2 a digitalized chest radiographic image in which a radiologist has detected the existence of 20 nodules with radii between 6 and 20mm. For the template matching process we consider as model a gaussian nodule with radium 8 mm and contrast of 60 between the gaussian central pixel and its surround. The analysis of the morphology of the regions obtained in the growing process by means of the progressive thresholding of the correlation image arised to 47 suspicious nodules; true 19 and 28 false positives. For the curvature space analysis we consider areas in the image which contain the suspicious regions. The effective diameters of the suspicious nodules fix in each case the size of the estimation window for the bicubic coefficients in each pixel surround. Fig. 3 shows the result of applying the facet model to suspicious areas pointed as '1' (true nodule, d_{eff}=25.10, $circ$=0.77) and '2' (false nodule d_{eff}=13.96, $circ$=0.89) in Fig. 2.b. The image area analyzed has size of 51*51 pixels and the kernel sizes for the estimation of the cubic were 25*25 and 13*13 respectively. The true nodule elevation in Fig. 3.a is reflected in Fig. 3.c as a high curvature peak. The confidence factor computed was 0.91. In Fig. 3.b and 3.d we have the simmetric site of Fig. 3.a and 3.c but with no nodule. As it is a bone crossing point, in the curvature peak image we can see two parallel ridges of peaks, achieving a final confidence factor of 0.56. The final results achieved, as can be seen in Fig. 2.b, were only two false positive detections, and one no detected nodule. The confidence factors for true nodules wass greater than 0.7.

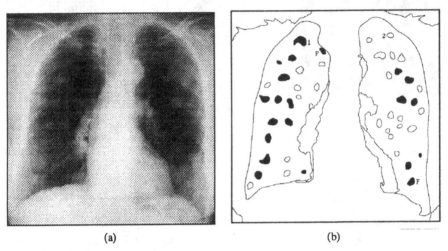

(a)   (b)

Fig. 2. (a): Chest image with a multinodular radiographic configuration. **(b):** Lung boundaries and suspicious regions. Detected nodules with cf>0.7 in dark. (F: false positive detections).

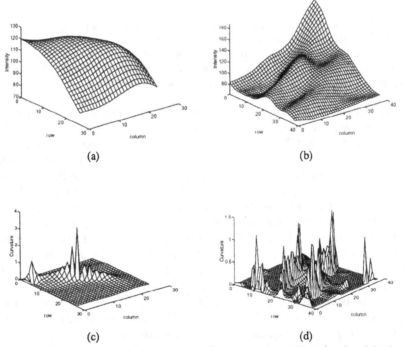

(a)   (b)

(c)   (d)

Fig. 3. Intensity surfaces and curvature images for suspected nodules pointed as 1 (a,c) and 2 (b,c) in Fig. 2.b, respectively.

We have made an initial valoration of the system with a set of 20 torax X-ray images in which expert radiologists have detected the existence of 45 nodules with diameters between 6 and 32 mm. Measures of performance has been achieved by means of accuracy $((TP+TN)/(TP+TN+FP+FN))$, sensitivity $(TP/(TP+FN))$ and specificity $(TN/(TN+FP))$, with TP=true positives, TN=true negatives, FP=false positives and FN=false negatives. With this, we have achieved a mean accuracy of 70%, sensitivity of 100% and specificity of 68%. These values are very good, because we have detected almost all nodules in images, although the variability in their size, and the number of false positives is not too high, as the specificity and accuracy show.

Acknowledgements

This work was supported by the Spanish CICyT under Grant No. TIC91/0816 and by Xunta de Galicia under Grant XUGA10501B93.
We wish to thank Dr. J.J. Vidal and Dr. M. Souto from the Dept. of Radiology of the Univ. of Santiago for images and diagnoses used in valorating the system.

References

1. M.L. Giger, K. Doi, H. MacMahon: Image Feature Analysis and Computer-Aided Diagnosis in Digital Radiography. 3. Automated Detection of Nodules in Peripheral Lung Fields. Medical Physics, 15, 2, 158-166 (1988)
2. M.G. Penedo, D. Cabello, S. Barro, M.J. Carreira, A. Mosquera: Application of a Feedforward Artificial Neural Network for Pattern Recognition in Medical Images. In: W.R. Brody, G.S. Johnston (eds.): Computers Applications to Assist Radiology. Symposia Foundation, Carlsbad, 1992, pp. 472-477
3. M.L. Giger, N. Ahn, K. Doi, H. MacMahon, C.E. Metz: Computerized Detection of Pulmonary Nodules in Digital Chest Images: Use of Morphological Filters in Reducing False-Positive Detections. Medical Physics, 17, 5, 861-865 (1990)
4. T. Matsumoto, H. Yoshimura, K. Doi, M.L. Giger, A. Kano, H. MacMahon, K. Abe, S.M. Montner. Image Feature Analysis of False-Positive Diagnoses produced by Automated Detection of Lung Nodules. Invest Radiol, 27, 18, 587-597 (1992)
5. S.J.J. Lin, P.A. Ligomenides, Y.M.F. Lure, M.T. Freedman, S.K. Mun: Applications of Neural Networks for Improvement of Lung Nodule Detection in Radiographic Images. In: W.R. Brody, G.S. Johnston (eds.): Computers Applications to Assist Radiology. Symposia Foundation, Carlsbad, 1992, pp. 108-115
6. Y.S.P. Chiou, Y.M.F. Lure, P.A. Ligomenides: Neural Network Image Analysis and Classification in Hybrid Lung Nodule Detection (HLND) System. In: Proc. of 1993 IEEE Workshop on Neural Networks for Signal Processing. Linthicum, MD, 1993
7. M.J. Carreira, D. Cabello, A. Mosquera, M.G. Penedo, J.M. Pardo: Knowledge Based Segmentation of Medical Images. In: M. Holt, C. Cowan, P. Grant, W. Sandham (eds.). Signal Processing VII: Theories and Applications. vol.2, EURASIP, Lausanne, 1994, pp. 868-871
8. R.H. Haralick and L.G. Shapiro. Computer and Robot Vision. Vol. I. New York: Addison-Wesley 1992

Neural Networks for the Segmentation

of Magnetic Resonance Images

Rachid Sammouda, Noboru Niki, and Hiromu Nishitani *

Dept. of Information Science, Univ. of Tokushima

* Medical School, Univ. of Tokushima, Japan.

Abstract : The segmentation of the images obtained from magnetic resonance imaging (MRI) is an important step in the visualization of soft tissues in the human body. In this preliminary study, we report an application of Hopfield neural network (HNN) for the multispectral unsupervised classification of head MR images. We formulate the classification problem as a minimization of an energy function constructed with two terms , the cost-term which is the sum of the squares errors, and the second term is a temporary noise added to the cost-term as an excitation to the network to escape from certain local minimums and be more close to the global minimum. We present here the segmentation result with two and three channels data obtained using the here described HNN approach. We compare these results to those corresponding to the same data obtained with the Boltzmann Machine (BM) approach.

1. Hopfield Neural Network

Hopfield network for the optimization application consists of many interconnected neuron elements. The network minimizes an energy function of the form [1]:

$$E = \sum_{j=1}^{N}\sum_{l=1}^{N} T_{jl} V_j V_l - \sum_{j=1}^{N} I_j V_j \qquad (1)$$

where N is the number of neurons, V_j is the output of the jth neuron, I_j is the bias term, and T_{jl} is the interconnection weight between jth and lth neurons. The minimization is achieved by solving a set of motion equations satisfying :

$$\partial U_j / \partial t = -\mu(t) \partial E / \partial V_j \qquad (2)$$

where U_j is the input of the jth neuron and $\mu(t)$ is a scalar positive function of time which determines the length of the step to be taken in the direction of the vector

$d = -\nabla E(V)$ in order to increase the convergence speed [2], for which a good choice allows the network to reach the local minimum in a short time. Then, if the input-output function of the neurons is monotonically increasing and the system satisfies (2), the energy function continuously reduces as a function of time and the system converges to a local minimum . The energy landscape in general has more than one local minimum due to the convex nature of the energy surface. If a problem can be cast in the form of a minimization of Hopfield energy function, a neural network can be realized to obtain a reasonably "good" solution (deep in the energy landscape).

2. Artificial Neural Network for Segmentation

2.1 Construction of the Energy Function

The segmentation problem can be seen as a partition of a set of N pixels of m features into the best L classes- best in the sense that the sum of the squares of the distances of the pixels from their respective cluster centroids is minimized. The generalized distance measure between jth pixel and the centroid of class l is defined by:

$$R_{jl} = \left\| X_j - \overline{X}_l \right\|_{A_l^{-1}} \tag{3}$$

where X_j is m-dimensional feature vector of the jth pixel, A_l is m x m positive definite weighting matrix, $\overline{X}_l$ is the m-dimensional centroid of class l, and $\|X\|_A = X^T A X$. If A_l is an identity matrix, the distance measure is Euclidean and the resulting clusters will be restricted to the hyperspherical distribution [3]. If $A_l = \Sigma_l$, the covariance matrix of class l, the distance is Mahalanobis, which allows for hyperellipsoidal cluster distributions. Then the cost-term of the energy function is given by:

$$E_c = \frac{1}{2} \sum_{j=1}^{N} \sum_{l=1}^{L} R_{jl}^2 V_{jl}^2 \tag{4}$$

Previous work [5] have reported that minimizing a similar energy function to the equation (4) for the classification of the MR images using HNN, the network converges to a local minimum and the classification results are noisy and need a post classification filtering process, which can be at the expense of losing some small structures of the image. To escape from the locals minimums and get a more clearly results, the most widely used methods for global optimization are of a stochastic nature. In these methods, random fluctuations or noise are introduced into the system in order to avoid being trapped in local minima. However, noise in Artificial neural networks (ANNs) often seems ubiquitous and apparently useless. On the other hand , by investigating neural cells of living creatures it has been found that they are essentially stochastic (random) in nature, in that responses of individual neural cells (in the isolated cortex) due to cyclically repeated identical stimuli will never result in identical responses. This means that noise plays an important role in neural networks.

Similarly, in ANNs it has been found that additive noise introduced into the network could be very useful since it increases the probability of convergence to the global minimum. However, in order to get the exact solution this additive noise should be introduced appropriately and then subsequently removed from the network as the global minimum is approached because the noise destroys valuable information[5]. In other words, during the optimization process the additive noise (perturbations) should approach zero in time so that the network itself will become deterministic prior to reaching the final solution.

Adding a noise term to the cost-term, the energy function of our system will be described as follows:

$$\tilde{E} = E_c + c(t)\sum_{j=1}^{N}\sum_{l=1}^{L} N_{jl} V_{jl} \qquad (5)$$

Where $\tilde{E}$ is called the perturbed form of the energy function, and N_{jl} is a N x L vector of independent high-frequency white noise sources, $c(t)$ is the parameter controlling the magnitude of noise which must be selected in such away that it provides zero as time t tends to "infinity". The parameter $c(t)$ is usually monotonically decreased in time. However, in some cases a more complex time schedule can be incorporated in which $c(t)$ can occasionally be increased if the network is stuck in a local minimum. To the equations (4) and (5) we applied the algorithm proposed in [5] , and the results are presented below as obtained without need to any postclassification filtering process.

3. Boltzmann Machine

In fact the idea of adding a noise term to the network to jump the local minimums , presented in the previous section is not new, but what is important here is when and how to use the noise ?

Another frequently exercised and promising approach which also use the noise to reach the global minimum is the Boltzmann Machine (BM). The BM is a kind of stochastic feedback neural network consisting of binary neurons connected mutually by symmetric weights [6,7] . In fact the BM is an energy minimization network consisting of statistical neurons which appear probabilistically in one of two states ON or OFF . The algorithm used by the BM to locate energy function minima is a simulated annealing approach [8] which is a stochastic strategy for searching the state of neurons corresponding to the global minimum of the energy function . This simulated annealing algorithm can be performed, for the classification problem with the same architecture described previously for HNN, as follows :

1/ Get an initial system configuration , for example, in each output line we assign the value one to a randomly neuron and zero to the others in order to ensure that each pixel belongs to one and only one class, and initialize all the weights to zero.

2/ Define a parameter T which represents a computational temperature, start with T at large value.

3/ Compute the energy value of the initial state using the equation (4) .

4/ Make a small random change in the output of the network .

5/ Evaluate the resulting change in the energy function .

6/ if the energy function is reduced (improved) retain the new state and increase by a constant the weights of the neurons corresponding to the modified output neurons , otherwise accept the transition to the new state with a probability $P=\exp(-\Delta E/T)$.

For this purpose select a random number Nr from a uniform distribution between zero and one. If P is greater than Nr retain the new state, otherwise return to the previous state .

7/ Repeat steps 4 through 6 until the system reaches an equilibrium , i.e. until the number of accepted transitions becomes insignificant.

8/ Update the temperature T according to an annealing schedule and repeat steps 4 through 7. (in our experience we chose the schedule $T_{new} = 0.93 \ T_{old}$) .

The algorithm stops when the temperature is small enough to consider the system to have reached a state near the ground state.

We use this algorithm for two and three channels segmentation of the MR data and the result are given in the next section.

4. Experimental Results

Figure 1. From left to right are the T1-weighted , the T2-weighted and the proton density-weighted images respectively, from a patient diagnosed with a meta-static tumor in the brain. The T2-weighted image shows an abnormal bright region in the white matter. Figure 2 shows the two dimensional data segmentation obtained by using the T2-weighted and the T1-weighted images with 7 classes based on the here described approach of HNN. The colormap shows the distribution of the pixels along their intensity values in the T2-weighted and the T1-weighted images . The tumor region is colored (red) and corresponds to high intensity in the T2-weighted image. Figure 3. shows the two dimensional data segmentation obtained by using the T1-weighted and T2-weighted images with 7 classes based on the BM . The colormap shows the distribution of the pixels along their intensity values in the T1-weighted and the T2-weighted images. Figure.4.a shows the segmentation result obtained with the T1-, T2-, and the proton density -weighted images using the HNN approach with 7 classes. Figure.4.b shows the segmentation result obtained with the T1-, T2-, and the proton density -weighted images with 7 classes using the BM approach.

4.1. HNN and BM Results Comparison

The results of the HNN and the BM presented above, look almost the same in differentiating between the different regions of the brain . However , in this case the data used present along the medical doctors diagnosis , an abnormal region composed of two kinds of tumors. Based on Figure 2 , the first tumor is an edema region colored (red) and composed with two separate parts, and the second abnormal region is the circular yellow region between the two parts of the edema and is known as a liquefied necroticportion. This region was classified in the same class with the cerebral spinal fluid (csf) colored yellow in the HNN result figure 2, and as edema (red) in the BM result Figure 4 . As a comparison tools of this two results , we first consider the energy function values at the equilibrium of the networks. We found that the energy function is more minimum and is independent of the initialization state of the network in case of HNN, however, the energy value of the BM at equilibrium and the segmentation result were found dependent on the initial value of the parameter temperature for which may be a good value can help to reach the global minimum. As a second comparison tool, the distribution of the pixels in the colormaps of the results images indicate more regular forms between the different regions in case of HNN, however in the BM result , some overlapping can be seen between the gray matter, white matter and csf regions. Furthermore , the execution time of the BM was about 7 hours but that of HNN was about 15 minutes (100 iterations) in the two channels segmentation.

In the three channels segmentation case , the HNN segmentation result presented in Figure.4.a and Figure.4.b are always like those of the two channels case with more smoothness specially in the gray matter and the edema regions. Also we realized that the network reach convergence after 70 iterations (means the time of 30 iterations faster than the two channels case convergence). However, the three channels segmentation result of the BM was a little different from its result with the two channels case, in that , the edema region was classified in the same class with the csf region. The convergence time was about 7 hours , but the energy function value was bigger than the two channels case energy. More information and details about this study are given in [9, 10] .

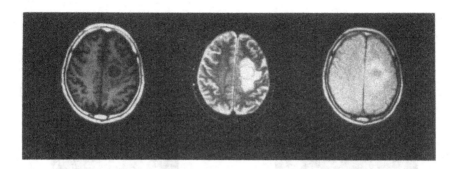

Figure 1: MR patient head images, from left to right are , the T1-weighted, the T2-weighted and the proton density weighted images.

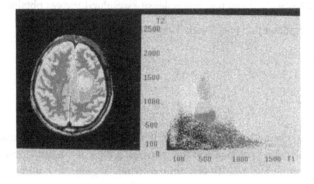

Figure 2: The two channels data segmentation result with 7 classes obtained using the T2-weighted and the T1-weighted images based on HNN.

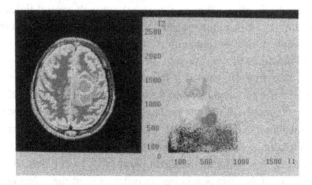

Figure 3: The two channels data segmentation result with 7 classes obtained using the T2-weighted and the T1-weighted images based on the BM.

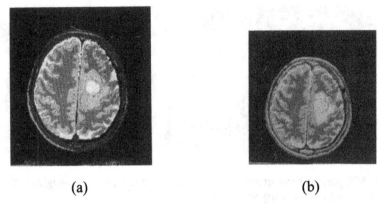

(a)   (b)

Figure 4: (a) is the three channels data segmentation result with 7 classes using the T1-weighted, the T2-weighted and the proton density weighted images obtained with HNN, and (b) is the tsegmentation result with 7 classes obtained with BM.

5. Conclusion

In this paper we presented segmentation results of MR data obtained by using the HNN and the BM approaches with two and three channels data. It was experimentally found that the two approaches results are similar when segmenting normal cases data. However, for a more complex segmentation problem, like the data presented here, with edema or cerebrospinal fluid boundary , the HNN results have been preferred over those of the BM by experts. Also, the time complexity of the HNN make it more preferable than the BM specially in clinic. We use the neural network several times for the same data in order to study the effect of the random initialization, we found that the latter does not effect the quality of the segmentation result in any sense. The performance of the network is mainly dictated by the choice of the energy function ,which provides "good" segmentation or classification when it is based on the Mahalanobis distance measure. Although, the use of the perturbation noise term in the energy function, help the network to go more fast and deeply in the energy landscape. However, we have to remember here that the clusters number was fixed by the user based on medical doctor information. An automatic determination of the clusters number during the segmentation process is necessary to make a full automatic and unsupervised segmentation. Also , a special smoothing technique of the data is required in order to limit the effect of the intensity variation of the MR data on the segmentation result.

References

1. Hopfield, J. J., "Neural networks and physical systems with emergent collective computational abilities,"in Proc. Nat. Acad. Sci., vol. 79, pp. 2554-2558, 1982
2. Jacobs, R. A., "Increased rates of convergence through learning rate adoption," Neural Networks, vol. 1, pp. 295-307, 1988
3. Duda, R. O., and Hart. P. E., "Pattern Classification and Scene Analysis," New York : Wiley, 1973
4. Geman, S., and Hwang, C. R., "Diffusions for global optimization," SIAM J. of Control and Optimization, vol. 24, no. 5, pp. 1031-1043, 1986
5. Amartur, S. C., Piraino, D., and Takefuji, Y. "Optimization Neural Networks for the Segmentation of Magnetic Resonance Images," IEEE Transactions on Medical Imaging, vol. 11, no. 2, pp. 215-220, 1992 .
6. E. Aart and J.Korst, "Simulated Annealing and Boltzmann Machines" New York : Wiley, 1989.
7. G.E. Hinton, R.J. Sejnowski and D. H. Ackley, "Boltzmann machines : Constraints satisfaction networks that learn", Tech. Rep. CMU-CS-84-119 Carnegie-Mellon Univ. Dept. of Computer Science , 1984.
8. S. Kirkpatrik, C.D. Gelatt and M.P. Vecchi, "Optimization by simulated annealing" Science, vol. 220, pp. 671-680, 1983.
9. R. Samouda, N. Niki, "Optimization Neural Networks for the Segmentation of Brain MRI Images" CAR'95, Berlin , pp. 171-176, 1995.
10. R. Sammouda, N. Niki, "Multichannel Segmentation of Magnetic Resonance Cerebral Images Based on Neural Networks", ICIP, Washington, October 1995.

Multiresolution Adaptive K-means Algorithm for Segmentation of Brain MRI*

B. C. Vemuri[1], S. Rahman[2] and J. Li[2]
[1]Department of Computer & Information Sciences
[2]Department of Electrical & Computer Engineering
University of Florida, Gainesville, FL 32611
email:vemuri@cis.ufl.edu
syed@cis.ufl.edu
li@saturn.ee.ufl.edu

Abstract

Segmentation of MR brain scans has received an enormous amount of attention in the medical imaging community over the past several years. *In this paper we propose a new and general segmentation algorithm involving 3D adaptive K-Means clustering in a multiresolution wavelet basis.* The voxel image of the brain is segmented into five classes namely, cerebro-spinal fluid, gray matter, white matter, bone and background (remaining pixels). The segmentation problem is formulated as a maximum a posteriori (MAP) estimation problem wherein, the prior is assumed to be a Markov Random Field (MRF). The MAP estimation is achieved using an iterated conditional modes technique (ICM) in wavelet basis. Performance of the segmentation algorithm is demonstrated via application to phantom images as well as MR brain scans.

1 Introduction

Magnetic Resonance Imaging has provided a very useful precision tool for information required in fields like reparative surgery, radiotherapy treatment planning, steriotactic neurosurgery, and brain anatomo-functional correlation [10]. 3-D segmentation of white matter, gray matter, cerebro-spinal fluid, bone etc. is extremely important for quantitative analysis such as volume measurements. It has already been established that volumetric analysis of different parts of the brain is useful in assessing progress or remission of various diseases like Alzheimer's disease, brain tumors, etc. "Postmortem studies of the human brain

---

*Support for the first author was partially provided by the Whitaker Foundation Award and for the second and third author from the NSF grant BCS-9396324
Manuscript submitted to the *Intl. Compu. Sci. Conf. on Image Analysis and Compu. Graphics, Hong Kong, Dec. '95*

reveal consistent age related reductions in brain size and age related increase in CSF spaces, which are accentuated in Alzheimer disease' [6].

In this paper we present a novel 3D segmentation algorithm which partitions the MR brain image into various constituent 3D structures based on their gray scale content. More specifically, we segment the MR brain scan into gray matter, white matter, cerebro-spinal fluid, bone and background (remaining pixels). A variety of approaches have been reported for brain image segmentation [10] however, none of them are fully automatic. Segmentation of isodensity regions has been reported in [4][10]. These methods require certain degree of human intervention in achieving the segmentation.

Statistical methods have become very attractive in the recent past since the work of Geman and Geman [8] who modeled images by Markov Random Fields with a superposed Gibbsian distribution and developed the theory and algorithms for maximum a posteriori estimation in image restoration applications. Since their seminal work, there has been a flurry of activity in applying their techniques to various domains including medical image analysis [2, 13, 15, 14]. In Besag [2], Lakshmannan and Derin [11], and Pappas [13], Gaussian models have been used for the probability distribution of an observed image given the uncorrupted image of a scene.

In [13], Pappas modified the K-means clustering algorithm, for image segmentation, by incorporating spatial smoothness constraints. He assumed a smooth variation of region intensity and locally estimated the means with an adaptive window. He also proposed a multigrid implementation for speeding up the MAP estimation process. An adhoc, heuristic estimate for the Gibbs Random Field (GRF) parameter β was used in his algorithm. *We propose a new segmentation algorithm which is in spirit similar to the algorithm of Pappas's but differs in some nontrivial ways namely, true 3D voxel segmentation is performed in our scheme, the MAP estimation is carried out via an ICM algorithm in a multiresolution wavelet basis and a novel and meaningful technique – analogous to the compatibility functions in relaxation labeling algorithm of Hummel et al., [9] – for defining the GRF parameter β is developed. This technique is very general and can be used with any application problem i.e., not necessarily limited to the segmentation of brain MRI, the application discussed in this paper.*

Bouman and Liu [3] proposed a multiresolution segmentation algorithm for textured images. They used a maximum likelihood type parameter estimation approach for their *a posterior* model. They state that due to the unavailability of the prior information about likely scale of regions in the image, a constant β at all resolutions was used. *In contrast, in our proposed algorithm, we determine the scaling via the usage of a wavelet-based multiresolution approach and propagate the β accordingly.*

In this paper, we present a new multiresolution 3D voxel segmentation technique which is applied to brain *Magnetic Resonance Imaging* . The algorithm has thus far been applied to several data sets yielding "visually correct" and "visually better" segmentation results. We are yet to compare the results of our segmentation with the gold standard, which is not easy to define for this application because there is minimal agreement between experts on the location of boundaries of various anatomical structures in the brain. Therefore, our future testing of the segmentation algorithm will involve a comparison of the segmentation results with that produced manually by a neuroanatomy expert.

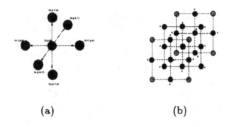

(a)   (b)

Figure 1: 3D neighborhood systems

The rest of this paper is organized as follows: Section 2 contains a description of the adaptive K-Means clustering technique applied to 2D images, its extension to 3D volume image segmentation and an embedding of the segmentation problem in to a 3D wavelet-based multiresolution framework. In Section 3, we present a novel way of computing the parameter β of the Gibbs Random Field, which has a significant influence on the segmentation. We present segmentation results on brain *Magnetic Resonance Imaging* in Section 4 and conclude in Section 5.

2 Segmentation Algorithm

In this section we will first briefly discuss the adaptive clustering for 2D images and refer the reader to [13] for details. Extension of this technique to 3D and a multiresolution embedding of the technique are discussed subsequently.

2.1 Adaptive (K-Means) Clustering in 3D

A stochastic model that includes the spatial smoothness constraint may be used to achieve the clustering-based segmentation[2, 13]. Let the observed image at location v be y_v and actual region label for that location be x_v. The a posterior probability density function can be defined as,

$$p(x_v|y_v \in V) \propto \exp\left\{-\frac{1}{2\sigma^2}[y_v - \overline{v}_v(x_v)]^2 - \sum_{c \in C} V_c(x)\right\}, \qquad (1)$$

where the subscript v is index for voxels in a volume image V which is a collection of $M \times N$ slices forming the volumetric structure of the brain scan. C defines the neighborhood system. Figure 1(a) shows a 3D neighborhood system. The simplest neighborhood system could be defined as in figure 1(a). But to get a stronger neighborhood interaction, we used an 18-point neighborhood labeled by "A" in figure 1(b). A rectangular 3D window was used in computing the local averages.

Following equation was used to define the clique energy V_c :

$$V_c(a, b_i) = -\sum_{i \in C} r(a, b_i) \qquad (2)$$

where $r(a, b_i)$ is the correlation between the classes assigned to the voxel at a and b_i. *This formulation is justified because it allows for incorporation of specific anatomical constraints in to the prior image model.* The detailed method of computing $r(a, b_i)$ is shown in a subsequent section.

2.2 Multiresolution Adaptive K-means in 3D

The 3D multi-resolution approximation using wavelet basis can be easily achieved using separable wavelets obtained from the product of one-dimensional wavelets and scaling functions [12]. For the multi-resolution approximation of volumetric data we use the tensor products of the scaling and wavelet functions. *We have built a multiresolution pyramid using wavelet transform approach to improve the speed of convergence of our segmentation algorithm.* In[13], a multigrid technique was used for improving the speed of the ICM technique applied to 2D video images. A true multigrid technique is much more complicated to implement than a multiresolution wavelet-based transform [12]. Moreover, the wavelet transform is perfectly invertible i.e., one can reconstruct the original image from the decomposition. This motivated us to achieve the energy minimization using a wavelet-based pyramid.

2.3 Problems with β computation

In MAP equation similar to the one in [13], if we drop the summation of V_c term we get the maximum likelihood estimator. Computing the clique potential using a fixed β requires the estimation of β. But the estimation of β is still adhoc [13] or time consuming [11, 3]. Derin et. al. in [7], have used a recursive algorithm that interleaves parameter estimation and segmentation of speckled images. Larger values of β lead to excessive smoothing of the regions and leaking/diffusion of the region labels into neighbouring regions, while $\beta = 0$ corresponds to the MLE approach.

To test the effect of β on the image segmentation, we created a 256×256 2D phantom image and applied our segmentation algortihm for varying β. Lowpass filtering was done to blurr the edges and Gaussian noise with mean 15 and variance 10.0 was added to it. The noisy image is shown in 2(a). Blurring was done to simulate the blending of gray and white matter as in a brain image. In our experiment, for multiresolution adaptive MAP estimation, we have observed that β has a significant impact on segmentation as shown in the figures 2(b), 2(c), and 3(a). With a fixed $\sigma = 10.0$, for (i) $\beta = 0.1$, we have achieved an MLE like segmentation, (ii) for $\beta = 0.5$, the segmentation contains some unwanted regions and (iii) with $\beta = 0.8$ the segmentation is worse.

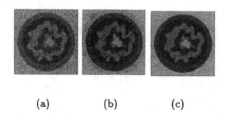

(a)　　　　(b)　　　　(c)

Figure 2: (a) Phantom with added noise (b) segmentation with $\beta = 0.1$ (c) segmentation with $\beta = 0.5$

In figure 2 (b), we depict the segmentation of the phantom image using our algorithms. Evidently, the segmentation is superior to those in the figures 2(b), 2(c), and 3(a).

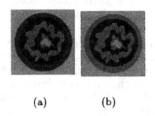

(a)   (b)

Figure 3: (a) Segmentation with $\beta = 0.8$ (b) segmentation using proposed method

3   Proposed Prior Model and β Computation

In the Gibbsian prior model β can be interpreted as a compatibility factor since, two classes which are compatible are assigned a $\beta = 1$, else $\beta = -1$. Similar definition for a compatibility factor was used by Rosenfeld et. al. [1] for scene identification using a relaxation labelling algorithm. They have shown that correlation gives the desirable properties of compatibility factor.

For our segmentation problem we used the above approach for defining the Gibbsian parameter β. The method can be illustrated by using a simple example. **Assume that the human brain contains white matter, gray matter and "other" regions.** Let us label them by A, B and C respectively. Table 4 shows the possible configurations of the three object classes. We have 11 A's, 9 B's and 10 C's out of total 30 occurrences. We have the probabilities $p(A) = \frac{11}{30}$, $p(B) = \frac{9}{30}$ and $p(C) = \frac{10}{30}$. In computing V_C, we consider the occurrence of any two classes, say, X and Y (X and Y can represent any of A, B, or C). We form Table 5 to calculate the joint and marginal probabilities, $p(X\&Y)$ and $p(X|Y)$.

Then these probabilities were used to compute the correlation coefficients using the equations $cov(X, Y) = p(X\&Y) - p(X)p(Y)$ and

$$cor(X, Y) = \frac{cov(X, Y)}{\sqrt{(p(X) - p^2(X))(p(Y) - p^2(Y))}}$$

Case	a	b	c
1	A	A	A
2	B	B	B
3	C	C	C
4	B	A	A
5	A	A	B
6	B	B	A
7	A	B	B
8	C	C	A
9	C	C	B
10	A	C	C

Figure 4: Table I

X	Y	p(X & Y)	$p(X|Y) = \frac{p(X\&Y)}{p(Y)}$
A	A	1/6	5/11
A	B	2/15	4/9
A	C	1/15	1/5
B	A	2/15	4/11
B	B	1/6	5/9
B	C	1/30	1/10
C	A	1/15	2/11
C	B	1/30	1/9
C	C	1/5	3/5

Figure 5: Table II

For our experiments with actual brain MR data we assigned the classes to the voxels based on an initial segmentation by a simple K-means algorithm. We assign the labels of components as : bones - E, gray matter - D, white matter - C, cerebrospinal fluid - B, and others - A. We have manually figured out 21 incompatible cases "BE", "EB", "BAB", "CAC", "DAD", "EAE", "BDB", "CEC", "DED", "BEB", "CBD", "CAD", "DBC", "DAC", "CBC", "DBD", "EDE", "ECE", "EBE", "AB" and "BA" out of 5! = 120 possibilities. Correlation co-efficients were then calculated based on the remaining 99 possibilities.

4 Implementation and Results

We used the hierarchical structure of [13] to implement our algorithm. A self explanatory flow chart of the algorithm is shown in Figure 6. The $K \times K$ correlation matrix for K regions was determined off-line according to the equation described in 3. The window size was gradually varied from maximum to minimum (which was set to 8 pixels in x and y direction and 2 pixels in z direction) by using the formula $(windowsize)_{max}/j$, $j = 1$ to K. Where K is $(windowsize)_{max}/8$. the z direction window size was held at 2 while the size in the x and y directions was reduced. For our experiments, the maximum window size was chosen to be 32 pixels wide in the x and y directions and 4 slices in the z direction.

The experimental result consists of the application of our segmentation algorithm to an MR data set consisting of 30 sagittal slices of a human brain scan. The data has a spatial resolution of 256×256 and a slice thickness of 1.25mm. Figure 7 depicts the result of applying our 3D segmentation algorithm to the brain MRI. The figures are organized in two columns. The first column contains arbitrarily picked slices from the original 3D MR data. The second column consists of corresponding slices from the 3D segmentation. **Gray values of 0, 12, 60, 100 and 250 were assigned in the segmented image to represent bone, gray matter, white matter, cerebro-spinal fluidand background respectively.** From our chosen gray scale mapping, bone and gray matter are indistinguishable while skin and white matter have been grouped into one class. Daubechie's 4 co-efficient orthogonal filters [5] were used for the wavelet transform. In the experiment, $\sigma = 10.00$ was used in the segmentation algorithm. The window adaptation was achieved by starting with a window size equal to the image size (in 3D) and progressively reducing the size by halving the window size. The effect of varying β on this example of segmentation has not been shown here because of the complexity of the anatomical structure and moreover, the differences are not clearly discernible in (such) images that contain very high density of detail. However, it must be noted that the importance of the β value assignment on the performance of a segmentation algorithm in the MAP estimation framework was discussed with the aid of segmentation examples in Section 2.3.

5 Conclusion

In this paper, we have presented a new 3D volume segmentation technique with application to MR brain scans. Our algorithm has three main components namely, an adaptive K-Means voxel clustering, a new way of determining the Gibbsian parameter β and finally a multiresolution 3D wavelet implementation to speed up the energy minimization. We have compared our algorithm to other algorithms that use adhoc assignment of values to β and found ours to yield better and more robust segmentation results.

Acknowledgments: The authors would like to express their gratitude to Dr. C. M. Leonard of the Neuroscience Department at the University of Florida, for providing the MRI brain scans.

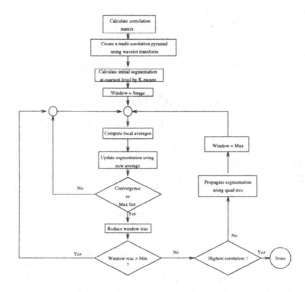

Figure 6: Flow of the segmentation algorithm

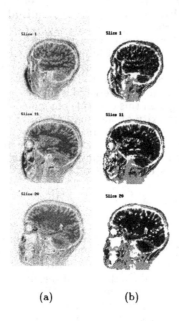

(a)   (b)

Figure 7: Results of 3D segmentation: (a) Slices of original data (b) Corresponding slices from the 3D segmented image.

354

References

[1] R. A. Hummel A. Rosenfeld and S. W. Zucker. Scene labelling by relaxation operations. *IEEE transactions on Systems, Man, and Cybernatics*, SMC-6(6):420–433, June 1976.

[2] J. Besag. On statistical analysis of dirty pictures. *Journal of Royal Statistical Society B*, 48(3):259 – 302, 1986.

[3] C. Bouman and B. Liu. Multiple resolution segmentation of textured images. *IEEE Transactions on Pattern Analysis and Machine Intelligence*, 13(2):99 –113, 1991.

[4] H. E. Cline, C. L. Doumulin, H. R. Hart, W. E. Lorensen, and S. Ludke. 3-D reconstruction of the brain from magnetic resonance images using a connectivity algorithm. *Magnetic Resonance Imaging*, 5:345–352, 1987.

[5] Ingrid Daubechies. *Ten Lectures on Wavelet*. Society for Industrial and Applied Mathematics, Philadelphia, PA, 1992.

[6] C. DeCarli, J. Moisog, D. G. M. Murphy, D. Teichberg, S. I. Rapoport, and B. Horwitz. Method of quantification of brain, ventricular, and subarachnoid csf volumes for mri images. *Journal of Computer assisted Tomography*, 16(2):274 –284, 1992.

[7] H. Derin and H. Elliott. Modelling and segmentation of noisy and textured images using Gibbs random field. *IEEE Transactions on Pattern Analysis and Machine Intelligence*, PAMI-9(1):39–55, 1987.

[8] S. Geman and D. Geman. Stochastic relaxation, Gibbs distributions, and the bayesian restoration of images. *IEEE Transactions on Pattern Analysis and Machine Intelligence*, PAMI-6(6):721 – 741, 1984.

[9] R. A. Hummel and S. W. Zucker. On the foundation of relaxation labelling process. *IEEE Transactions on Pattern Analysis and Machine Intelligence*, 5(3):267–287, May 1983.

[10] M. Joliot and B. M. Majoyer. Three dimensional segmentation and interpolation of magnetic resonance brain images. *IEEE Transactions on Medical Imaging*, 12(2):269 – 277, 1993.

[11] S. Lakshmanan and H. Derin. Simultaneous parameter estimation and segmentation of Gibbs random fields using simulated annealing. *IEEE Transactions on Pattern Analysis and Machine Intelligence*, 11:799–813, August 1989.

[12] S. G. Mallat. A theory of multiresolution signal decomposition : the wavelet representation. *IEEE Transactions on Pattern Analysis and Machine Intelligence*, PAMI-11:674 – 693, 1989.

[13] T. N. Pappas. An adaptive clustering algorithm for image segmentation. *IEEE Transactions on Signal Processing*, 40(4):901 –914, 1992.

[14] B. C. Vemuri and A. Radisavljevic. Multiresolution stochastic shape models with fractal priors. *acm Transactions on Graphics*, 13(2):177–207, 1994.

[15] B. C. Vemuri, A. Radisavljevic, and C. M. Leonard. Multiresolution stochastic 3D shape models for image segmentation. In *13th International Conference, IPMI*. Springer-Verlag, 1993.

Computer-Assisted Analysis and 3D Visualization of Blood Vessels Based on Cone-Beam CT Images

Yoshiki Kawata[1], Noboru Niki[2], and Tatsuo Kumazaki[3]

1. Department of Optical science, University of Tokushima, Japan
2. Department of Information Science, University of Tokushima, Japan
3. Department of Radiology Nippon Medical School, Japan

Abstract. In this paper, we present a method for analysis and 3D visualization of high-resolution 3D blood vessels images obtained by cone-beam CT. We are working toward an interactive system which exploits the recent 3D reconstruction approaches, computer graphics, and 3D image processing techniques to facilitate detailed anatomical measurement and visualize the complex blood vessels morphology. The key approaches of our system are a 3D reconstruction image from cone-beam projections, a quantitative analysis based on the blood vessels structure description, and a volume visualization for the inspection of blood vessels structures. From results of the application to a patient's blood vessels, we present the effectiveness of our system.

1 Introduction

X-ray angiograms have certainly aided doctors in inspection of blood vessels because of their high spatial resolution, but two-dimensional (2D) projection images have limitation for quantitative diagnosis of the blood vessel with a delicate aneurysm or stenosis. Because of that, it becomes necessary to develop a 3D imaging technique to acquit an accurate 3D blood vessels image reconstruction. In recent years, a cone-beam CT which utilizes a cone-beam x-ray source and a 2D detector has attracted much attention in the 3D blood vessels image reconstruction [1,2,3], since high-resolution 3D images can be obtained with a short data-acquisition time.

From these backgrounds, we are working toward a system for three-dimensional image analysis of blood vessels using cone-beam CT to enhance the performance of clinician in assessing anatomical information. The major feature of this work is that the analysis functions are based on two strategies for blood vessels structure description: (1) graph description of blood vessels centerlines, (2) surface representation using curvatures. First, the graph description procedure extracts the curvilinear structures from the tree-like, filamentous blood vessels image[5,6,7].

Secondly, 3D surface representation procedure extracts characteristics of concave and convex shapes on blood vessels surfaces, which are lost by the graph description procedure including 3D thinning process of blood vessels image. This paper presents the approach based on surfaces representation and examples on cone-beam CT images of a patient's blood vessels.

2 3D Reconstruction of Blood Vessels Images

The 3D reconstructed blood vessels images come from our prototype 3D image reconstruction system[2,3,4]. The prototype system takes 288 digital angiograms over 360 degrees in 4.8 seconds by an X-ray rotational angiographic system of a CT gantry equipped with a cone-beam X-ray source and an image intensifier (II)[4]. After the correction of distortions generated by II and the cone-beam geometry estimation, 3D image reconstruction is performed by a short scan cone-beam filtered backprojection algorithm due to short injection time of a contrast medium [2,3]. From full 288 projection images, 157 projection images over 180 degrees plus 16 degrees of the cone angle are selected as a data set contained blood vessels image during injecting a constant medium. The data set is approximately reconstructed into 320x320x320 voxels (a voxel size 0.5 mm).

3 Blood Vessels Structure Description

3.1 Graph Description of Blood Vessels Centerlines

The 3D reconstructed blood vessel image is processed by a succession of 3D image operations including (1)segmentation, (2)3D binary thinning procedure, (3)distance transformation of a 3D line pattern, and (4)graph description of the 3D line pattern. These operations are described as follows[6,7].

(1) Segmentation: As the region of blood vessels in a 3D reconstructed images tend to have higher contrast than other region, we use the threshold procedure and extraction of the connected components corresponding to the blood vessels regions. Hereafter, we consider 3D blood vessels images to be 3D digitized binary images in which voxel's values of the blood vessels and background are 1 and 0, respectively. In order to eliminate small halls and attachments, the 3D blood vessels images are operated by 3D fusion procedure[9].

(2) 3D binary thinning procedure : The centerlines of the 3D blood vessels image are approximately extracted by thinning the 3D object until a centerline of one voxel thickness with preservation of the geometrical structure remains. A sequential thinning algorithm for 26 connectivity case is developed based on the necessary and sufficient condition for deletability of 1-voxels in a 3D binary image derived by Toriwaki et al[10]. The thinning procedure is an iterative process, in which each iteration is divided into six sub-cycles[8,9].

(3) Distance trasformation of a 3D line pattern : The information of shape features of the centelines of the 3D blood vessels image is obtained by the 3D extension of the distance trasformation of a 2D line pattern[11].The distance trasformation operation of a 3D line pattern changes a value at each voxel in the 3D line pattern into the distance measured alng the 3D line pattern from thate voxel to the furthest end point. The value at the voxel in the 3D line pattern obtained allows us to extract the geometrical feature such as a edge point, a branch point, a loop, and a loop cluster.

(4) Graph description of the 3D line pattern : The centerlines are disassembled into line segments between the feature points and expressed as an undirected graph with vertex and edges which are obtained by using feature points and partial centerlines segmented by vertexes respectively. The graph is represented by the list representation with attributes representing the length of edge and the geometrical feature of vertex.

3.2   Surface Representation using Curvatures

The surfaces of 3D blood vessels image are considered as the interior morphology of blood vessels walls, since the 3D blood vessels image reconstructed form digital angiograms approximates the 3D image of contrast medium filled in blood vessels. The surfaces of blood vessels image are assumed to be smooth and quantified by surface curvatures which are invariant to arbitrary rotations and transformation of surfaces[12,13]. The local surface at a point P on the blood vessel surface S is represented by the augmented Darboux frame $D(p) = (P, Mp, mp, Np, \varkappa_{Mp}, \varkappa_{mp})$ [13] as shown in Fig. 1 . Np denotes the surface normal at P. $\varkappa_{Mp}$ and $\varkappa_{mp}$ are referred as the maximum and minimum principal curvatures, respectively. Mp and mp are referred to as principal directions corresponding to $\varkappa_{Mp}$ and $\varkappa_{mp}$, respectively.

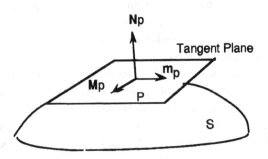

Fig. 1   The augmented Darboux frame.

The estimation of D(p) is performed by the two steps [13] : (i) local initial estimation of the D(p) from a parabolic quadric surface model fit to a local neighborhoods of an inspection point on the surface of the 3D blood vessels image, (ii) iterative refinement of the initial estimated D(P) to minimize the variation in the set of D(P) obtained from neighboring surface points of P under the constraints :

$$(Np \cdot Np) = 1, \quad (Mp \cdot Mp) = 1, \quad (Np \cdot Mp) = 0. \tag{1}$$

In order to apply the local initial estimation to a 3D binary image, we modified the calculation of the surface normal at the inspection point [14].

4   Image Analysis Functions

The image analysis functions are constructed based on the structure descriptions of the 3D blood vessels image. These functions are described as follows[6,7].

(a) 3D visualization of exterior structure and interior morphology of blood vessels: This function continuously visualize the exterior and interior morphology of the 3D blood vessels image along the blood vessel path using the centerline of blood vessel as a guideline for the trajectory of a viewpoint.

(b) Extraction of the orientation of blood vessels: This function approximates the local 3D orientation of blood vessel by calculating a local direction of the 3D centerline of blood vessel image.

(c) Measurement of the cross-sectional area : This function yields the cross-sectional area of blood vessel in the plane perpendicular to the local 3D orientation of blood vessel obtained by the extraction of the orientation of blood vessel and provides the cross-sectional shape along 3D centerline of 3D blood vessel.

(d) Measurement of the distance between two points along a 3D blood vessel path : In interventional radiology procedures, it is important to decide the adequate blood vessel path for guiding catheters without damaging blood vessels. This function automatically provides the shortest path between two selected points on the 3D blood vessels image and the distance between them is obtained by calculating the shortest path problem. The shortest path is imposed to the 3D displayed blood vessels images as the trajectory of a guide line for catheter.

(e) Measurement of the surface shapes of blood vessels: The surface representation provides the following surface characteristics : Gaussian (K) and mean (H) curvatures, surface normal direction, minimal and maximum principal directions, magnitude of curvature, and surface type using signs of K and H[12]. Using these surfaces characteristics, this function extracts the concave and convex shapes on blood vessels surfaces and visualize the shapes variation of surfaces to direct the doctor's attention to the locations of the blood vessels abnormality in the 3D blood vessels image.

(f) Evaluation of abnormal regions volumes: In surgical operation or interventional radiology procedures for aneurysms, instruments like a clip or a balloon are used. Then accurate position of the neck of an aneurysm or its volume are important information. This function allows doctors to detect an abnormal region like an aneurysm in 3D blood vessels image interactively and calculate the abnormal region's volume.

5 Experimental Results

The image analysis functions mentioned in Section 4 are applied to a patient's abdominal blood vessels with two aneurysms and a stenosis obtained by our prototype 3D image reconstruction system.

Fig. 2 shows the 3D visualization of the 3D blood vessels image by volume rendering method[15,16].The left image shows an exterior structure of the 3D blood vessels image in front of view and the right ones show composite images of exterior structures and interior morphology of the 3D blood vessels image lying viewpoints in the positions denoted by arrows.

Fig.3 shows an example of selection of a blood vessel path. After displaying 3D blood vessels image from three different views, a user interactively inputs two points on the 3D displayed blood vessels images by crosshair cursor. The shortest path between two points is automatically imposed to the 3D displayed blood vessels images and the distance between two points is presented.

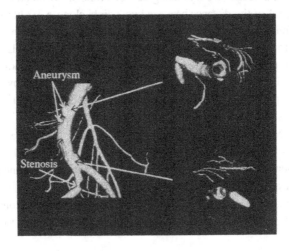

Fig. 2 3D visualization of the 3D blood vessels image.

360

Fig.4. shows the blood vessels surface shapes. The surface segmentation of the selected abnormal blood vessel is presented by the signs of K and H [12] from two different views. Peak surface is white, flat surface is orange, pit surface is green, minimal surface is yellow green, ridge surface is yellow, saddle ridge is blue, valley surface is sky blue, saddle valley is red. Since it is difficult to decide whether K and H are zero or not, the four surface types including flat surface, minimal surface, ridge surface, and valley surface are not assigned in this example. From this display, the Peak surface regions is useful to indicate the abnormal regions such as aneurysms.

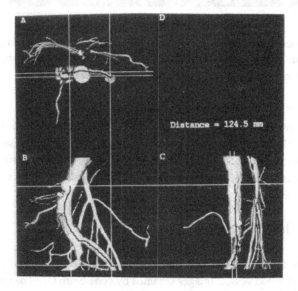

Fig. 3 Selection of a blood vessel path.

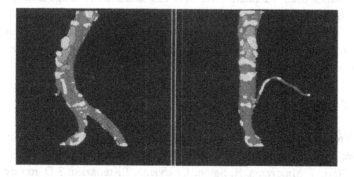

Fig.4 Segmentation of the blood vessels surface shapes.

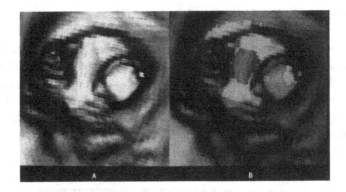

Fig.5 Surface shape analysis from inside view of the blood vessel. A is 3D display of
inside view of the blood vessel at a cross section point. B is the
segmentation of A obtained based on surface curvatures signs.

Fig. 5 shows an example of surface shape analysis from inside view of the blood
vessel. A is 3D display of inside view of the blood vessel at a cross section point. B
is the segmentation of A obtained based on surface curvatures signs. Traveling
inside the blood vessels, the concave and convex shapes on blood vessels surfaces
can be observed.

6   Conclusion

We have described a computer-assisted analysis and 3D visualization of high-
resolution 3D blood vessels images obtained by cone-beam CT. The major feature of
this work is that our method is based on two strategies for blood vessels structure
description: (1) graph description of blood vessels centerlines, (2) surface
representation using curvatures. We have demonstrated the image analysis based on
the blood vessels structure descriptions by applying the 3D image of a patient's
blood vessels. Results show that our method may be effective for providing 3D
qualitative and quantitative information of blood vessels, which are demanded for
diagnosis and therapy planning.

References

1. Y. Trousset, D. Saint-Felix, A. Rougee and C. Chardenon : Multiscale cone-
   beam X-ray reconstruction. In: Proc. of SPIE, vol. 1231, pp. 229-238,1990.
2. N. Niki, T. Mineyama, H. Satoh, C. Uyama, T.Kumazaki: 3-D reconstruction

of blood vessels using a rotational angiopraphy system. In: Med.Biol. Eng. and Comput., vol.29, part 1, p.649,1991.

3. Y. Kawata, N. Niki, H. Satoh, T. Kumazaki : Three-dimensional blood vessels reconstruction using a high-speed X-ray rotational projection system. In: Trans. IEICE, Japan, vol. J76-D-II, pp.2133-2142, 1993.

4. T. Kumazaki : Rotational stereo-digital angiography-image processing and clinical usefulness. In: Med.Image.Tech., Japan, vol. 7, pp.433-439, 1989.

5. G. Gerig, Th. Koller, G. Szekely, Ch. Brechbuhler, and O. Kubler : Symbolic description of 3-D structures applied to cerebral vessels tree obtained from MR angiography volume data. In: Proc. of IPMI'93 H.H. Barrett and A.F. Gmitro Eds., Arizona, Springer-Verlag, pp.94-111, 1993.

6 N. Niki, Y. Kawata, H. Satoh and T. Kumazaki : 3D imaging of blood vessels using X-ray rotational angiographic system. In: Conf. Record of the 1993 IEEE Nuclear Science Symp. and Medical Imaging Conf., San Fransisco, California, pp.1873-1877, 1993.

7. Y. Kawata, N. Niki, and T. Kumazaki : Three-dimensional imaging of blood vessels using cone-beam CT. In: IEEE International Conference on Image Processing, Austin, vol.2, pp.140-144, 1994.

8. Y.F. Tsao and K.S.Fu : A parallel thinning algorithm for 3-D pictures. In: Computer Graphics and Image Processing, vol.17 pp.315-331, 1981.

9. Y.F. Tsao and K.S.Fu : A 3D parallel skeletonwise thinning algorithm. In: Proc. IEEE PRIP Conf., pp.678-683, 1982.

10. J. Toriwaki and S. Yokoi : Basics of algorithms for processing three-dimensional digitized pictures. In: Trans. IECE, Japan, vol.J68-D, pp.426-433, 1985.

11. J.Toriwaki, N. Kato, and T. Fukumura : Parallel local operations for a new distance transformation of a line pattern and their applications. In: IEEE Trans. Syst., Man. & Cybern., vol. SMC-9, pp.628-643, 1979.

12. P. Besl and R. Jain : Intrinsic and extrinsic surface characteristics. In: Proc. IEEE Comp. Vision Patt. Recogn., San Francisco, pp.226-233, 1985.

13. P.T. Sander and S.W. Zucker : Inferring surface trace and differential structure from 3-D images. In: IEEE Trans. Pattern Anal. Machine Intell., vol. PAMI-12, pp.833-854, 1990.

14. N.Tayama, N.Shmizu, N.Chiba and I.Otawara : A speedy voxel-tracing method for cutting solid display of 3D images. In: Trans. IEICE, Japan, vol. J72-D-II, pp.1332-1340, 1989.

15. M.Levoy, : Volume rendering: display of surfaces from volume data. In: IEEE CG & A, vol. 8, pp.29-37, 1988.

16. N.Niki, Y.Kawata and H.Satoh : A 3-D display method of fuzzy shapes obtained from medical images. In: Trans. IEICE, Japan, vol. J73-D-II, pp.1707-1715, 1990.

An Interface for Synthesizing 3D Multibody Structures

George Baciu and Brian P. W. Lee

The Hong Kong University of Science and Technology,
Clear Water Bay, Kowloon, Hong Kong

Abstract. Specifying object interactions for virtual reality applications is an intrinsically difficult task. A script–based approach is limited due to the lack of visual feedback. Local changes in the configuration of large systems are difficult to trace unless interaction tools are provided to focus on these changes. In this article, we demonstrate a visual editing system that provides direct manipulation of objects and their spaces of interaction.

Keywords: 3D user–interfaces, kinematics, dynamics, motion, animation

1   Introduction

In this work, we focus on the construction of a general multibody system whose motion characteristics may be inspected visually. The complexity of the problem arises from the fact that it is not obvious where a consistent definition of such a system should begin. The main question that arises is: should the construction process begin with the geometry or the physical interactions? The intuitive answer seems to be geometry, but this requires many details regarding the form and shape. Our focus is, however, on the interaction characteristics of objects in a multibody system and the lack of simple and consistent tools for easily constructing such systems in a 3D environment has inspired out development.

We emphasize here *construction* rather than *manipulation*. In *the construction mode*, one may start with a completely empty environment. At each step, a new object or prossibly a relationship between two objects is added. In *the manipulation mode*, one starts with a set of objects and relationships previously defined and attempts to modify them in a meaningful way [14].

2   Related work

Mechanisms for 3D user interfaces that have been discussed in the past, range from specific virtual device paradigms, such as the Bat [13], the Virtual Sphere or Trackball [3, 5], and the Arcball [12], to spatial positioning tools [2], and general programmable widgets [15]. This progression accounts for very specific interactions, such as the Arcball for 3D scene orientation as well as for high level object

[0] Supported by the RGC grant HKUST 598/94E and the HKUST infrastructure funding.

manipulations, as in the case of the widget toolkit [15]. In each case, the user interface mechanism employed addresses object manipulation, viewing and/or placement in the 3D space, with less emphasis on constructing and manipulating *object interactions*.

Object interactions have been emphasized in the work started by Badler et al [1] in conjunction with the manipulation of articulated figures. This has been further studied by Phillips and Badler[9, 10] who implemented a system called Jack. Their system is based on an implicit hierarchy of objects that can be picked and moved around. In Jack, frames are of two types, global and local. An implicit spanning tree is generated internally based on an arbitrary choice of a *root body* allowing a complex articulated figure to be rooted at any body.

In the domain of constrained multibody systems, the choice of a spanning tree has implications in the formulation of motion equations. This influences the partition of the system of equations which in turn may affect convergence. The choice of a spanning tree should to be guided by the choice of kinematic constraints imposed within the system. Even when this choice is generated automatically, there should be some control over the joints selected in the tree.

While the choice of a spanning tree resolves the ambiguities of defining objects and linkages in a strictly hierarchical system, it does not solve the ambiguities that arise in defining closed loop systems. This is one of the main motivational points that prompted us to seek an alternate system specification and manipulation mechanism. Furthermore, in the analysis and experimentation of algorithms for computational dynamics, we need to explore the effects of different kinematic configurations and relationships between objects. This requires both local and global topological changes, which in turn, necessitates an intuitive, flexible, and yet consistent user interface that provides direct and easy manipulation of the motion spaces in the system.

The main contribution of this work is found in section 4 which describes a unified user interface mechanism, called the **Virtual Trackball-Ruler Interface** (**VTRI**). This mechanism provides a simple yet powerful and consistent manipulation of spatial objects. We illustrate the utility of an implemented system, called **FRAMES** (**FRA**me Motion Editor **S**ystem), and give some concrete examples.

3 The general framework

In the process of establishing the general framework for the user interactions, we identify a skeleton of body frames and arbitrary connections between frames. Each such connection represents an interaction between two bodies. This induces a general graph representation in which the nodes represent body frames and the edges represent the motion spaces between frames. This allows the construction of both tree–structured systems and systems with loops.

The system information is stored in a graph structure. This consists of *geometrical information* stored in the nodes of the graph and *kinematic information* stored in the edges of the graph. The geometry is generated with respect to the single frame of reference attached to the body. Hence, a node consists of at least a reference frame and, possibly, a set of points definining the center of mass and points of influence on the body. From a dynamics point of view, the reference frame is all that is necessary to extract the local information about the body.

The graph–based representation translates into the construction of a 3D skeletal structure of frames. In the process, it is necessary to have the ability to rearrange and define objects with respect to any particular frame. This implies that the system should not differentiate between local and global frames. The lack of distinction between global and local frames allows one to make a frame the reference of another independent of the current structure.

One of the difficulties involved in this construction is providing the appropriate visual feedback together with a consistent 3D user interface. This leads to the problem of specifying a point location in 3D space by only providing 2D feedback and control. The operations involved in the construction of such systems are (1) creating new frames of reference, (2) choosing a particular frame to serve as a current reference, (3) translating, (4) rotating, (5) selecting, (6) inserting, (7) deleting, (8) changing referential frames for the current objects, and (8) providing direct and immediate view of the local changes.

We propose a simple interface that encompasses these operations based on an extension of the virtual trackball which has proven very successful in scene viewing [3, 5, 12]. We call this interface the *virtual trackball–ruler* interface. The extension to the classical trackball consists of a ruler with one end anchored at the center of the sphere of orientation. The trackball–ruler interface introduces the concept of arbitrarily referenced manipulation of objects and extends the unit sphere of the manipulation space to a sphere of an arbitrary radius which measures the relative length of displacement between objects.

4 The Virtual Trackball–Ruler Interface

Three dimensional manipulations using a trackball interface have been mostly employed in scene viewing. This presumes a single instance of a trackball centered at the origin of a global frame of reference, Fig. 1. The rotation of the scene is achieved by computing an axis of rotation represented by the unit vector $\mathbf{u_s}$ whose image in the world coordinates X_w, Y_w, Z_w is $\mathbf{u_w}$. Unit vector $\mathbf{u_s}$ is the normal of the plane formed by vectors $\mathbf{a_s}$ and $\mathbf{b_s}$ whose projections onto the screen give the mouse trace endpoints A and B, respectively. Angle θ formed by vectors $\mathbf{a_s}$ and $\mathbf{b_s}$ determine the rotation about the directional unit vector $\mathbf{u_w}$. The rotation is best constructed from a quaternion of angle $\theta/2$ and unit vector $\mathbf{u_w}$ [11]:

$$\mathbf{q}(\theta, \mathbf{u}) = \left[\cos\left(\frac{\theta}{2}\right), \mathbf{u} \sin\left(\frac{\theta}{2}\right) \right] \qquad (1)$$

One of the most important perceptual feedback characteristics embedded in the analytical properties of quaternions is the elimination of hysteresis in rotation compositions [12].

A hierarchical structure of coordinate frames induces a parent–child relationship between any pair of frames, $\mathbf{F_p}$ and $\mathbf{F_q}$, represented by the relative spatial displacement transformation $\mathbf{T_q^p}$. This is composed of a rotation $\mathbf{R_q^p}$ and

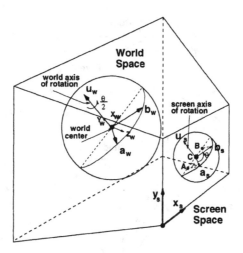

Fig. 1. Scene view manipulation

translation $\mathbf{d} = Q - P$, that takes the parent frame $\mathbf{F_p}$ into the child frame $\mathbf{F_q}$, Fig. 2. This transformation maps the coordinates of a point $\mathbf{x}$ in frame $\mathbf{F_q}$ into coordinates of $\mathbf{x}$ with respect to frame $\mathbf{F_p}$ by

$$\mathbf{x^p} = \mathbf{T_q^p}\,\mathbf{x^q} \tag{2}$$

The manipulation of the orientation of the child frame may be performed in two ways: (1) with respect to its parent, and (2) with respect to itself. The first induces a rotation of the displacement vector between the two frame origins, $\mathbf{PQ}$, resulting in the rotation of frame $\mathbf{F_q}$ fixed at the tip of vector $\mathbf{PQ}$ as $\mathbf{PQ}$ is rotated about point P. The second discards the transformation of the displacement vector $\mathbf{PQ}$. From the point of view of object manipulations both are necessary. This implies that the trackball needs to be selectively attached to either (1) the origin of frame $\mathbf{F_p}$, or (2) the origin of frame $\mathbf{F_q}$. We note, however, that both manipulate the same frame, the child frame. The addition of the *ruler interface* differentiates between the two possible orientation interactions, one that includes the displacement and orientation of frame $\mathbf{F_q}$ with respect to $\mathbf{F_p}$, and the other that restricts the operation to the orientation of $\mathbf{F_q}$ alone.

The ruler interface handles the translation between the two frame centers, P and Q, Fig. 3(a). It is based on the manipulation of two points on an infinite line, the ruler axis. One of the two points is always fixed during the translation operation. We call this point the *ruler anchor*, Fig. 3(b). The other point, the *slider*, is allowed to slide on the infinite ruler axis. This defines the head of the translation vector. In the manipulation of the two frames, P would serve as the anchor and Q is allowed to slide with the slider along the orientable axis. A trackball anchored at P, with a radius equal to the length between

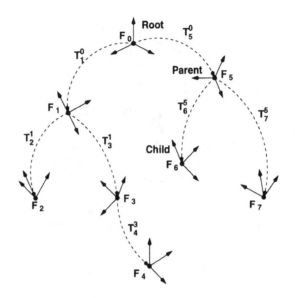

Fig. 2. Hierarchical structure of frames

P and Q, allows one to vary the orientation of the ruler axis as it rotates Q around P. Once an orientation direction is chosen, we fix the ruler axis and then perform the translation of point Q into a desired position. This operation can be constrained or unconstrained. Constrained translation can be performed by the direct specification of a length value, or by snapping onto a subdivision of the ruler.

The trackball works in conjunction with a ruler passing through the center of the virtual sphere at a specific reference point in space usually defined as the origin of another reference frame, such as a parent frame. It achieves arbitrary spatial positioning of points and the positioning and orientation of 3D objects. We have found that this paradigm not only provides a simple control for spatial positioning, but can also serve as the basis for object deformations, such as scaling.

5 Constrained manipulations

The main advantage of the virtual trackball–ruler interface is the free manipulation of objects in a 3D scene. It uses a simple unified protocol that combines rotations and translations in a natural and intuitive manner. The utility of this protocol becomes even more obvious when constrained editing of the objects in the scene is desired.

5.1 Rotation constraints

Rotations may be constrained by (1) specifying an arbitrary axis of rotation, (2) using a frame axis, such as X, Y, or Z. While the unconstrained manipulation

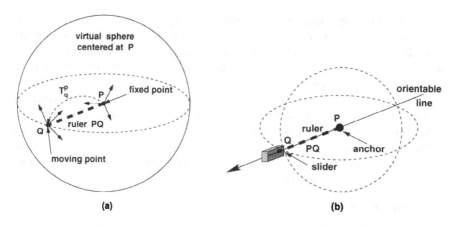

Fig. 3. Local frame manipulation

is the main mode of operation, the constrained modes are directly available via a pop-up menu. Each constrained mode has an immediate effect on the current state of the trackball–ruler interface. Some objects may require a specialization or an extension of the general trackball–ruler interface when the constrained mode is active. This is invoked in the object selection mode.

5.2 Translation constraints

Translations may be constrained by (1) explicit specification of a scale and a measure of length, (2) snapping onto the ruler subdivisions, and (3) snapping onto the subdivisions of the projection of the ruler onto an arbitrary axis. The first two have obvious implications. The third may involve multiple modes of operations depending on the projection. We may have a single projection in which case only one axis constrains the subdivisions onto which we are allowed to increment the translation length along a ruler in an arbitrary direction, or we may have up to three independent axes controlling the positioning of a point in space by simply projecting the point position onto rulers associated with the given axes, say X, Y, and Z.

6 Viewing and feedback

The viewing mechanism that we have employed provides (1) multiple viewing windows as well as stereo viewing, (2) direct view manipulation with feedback, and (3) localized view control.

The system allows as many different viewing windows as the user desires by simply creating a new viewing window while in the view mode. Each viewing window has its own view manipulation control and each maintains its own viewing status of the scene.

Badler et al [1] emphasized the problems of view manipulation without proper feedback. In order to achieve a practical mode of manipulating the view, we have treated the viewing camera just like any other object in the scene. The task is then equivalent to manipulating the eye coordinate frame with respect to another frame of reference, not necessarily the global one. However, in order to maintain a continuous view of the changes that are made to the camera position, we display the new viewing position in an auxiliary window that shows cexactly what the camera would see if it would be positioned at that location. The main window maintains the original view, but shows where the camera is being maneuvered with respect to the object in the scene. The new view shown in the auxiliary window is updated in the main window only if desired. This allows a continuous fly–by camera operation through the scene without changing the view in the main window.

7 Examples

The two examples show complex multiloop structures created with our editor. In Fig. 10, the system consists of multiple frames constrained by kinematic joints forming two loops (center and right–hand side), as well as objects in a tree formation (left).

In Fig. 11, we have constructed a mechanical hand holding a pen. The system is mostly a tree structure with one loop formed between the "thumb" the "index finger" and the pen.

8 Conclusion

Our approach to the problem of multibody system construction for motion analysis and synthesis differs from traditional CAD based systems in that we focus on the topological elements of a multibody structure rather than its geometry. This allows us to directly specify, manipulate and control the motion spaces between adjacent bodies in the system. This approach also differs from the previous work on articulated–figure animation where the frames are associated with the links in the system after the geometry of the system has been specified which makes it difficult to change or edit the motion spaces between the links.

Why is it necessary to have such refined control over the construction and manipulation of motion spaces of a multibody system? Because motion synthesis depends on the following: (1) degrees of freedom, (2) orientation of motion spaces, and (3) the structure or topology of interconnections.

The current implementation allows us to manipulate all of the above by employing a single 3D user interface protocol, the trackball–ruler interface. This provides a consistent set of a small number of operations which allows editing at all three levels of detail. The objectives targeted within this framework include both motion analysis and synthesis.

The system has been implemented as a set of classes in C++ on an SGI Indigo[2] Extreme running IRIX 5.2. Its utility is quickly expanding as we learn that it can potentially serve for easily building static scenes such as the interior room of an office space for experimental radiosity rendering projects.

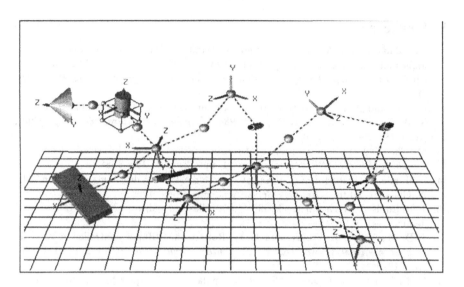

Fig. 4. A complex multi-loop system

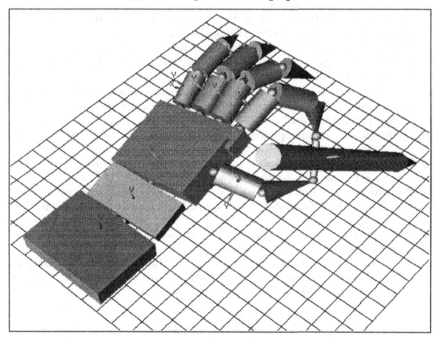

Fig 5 A mechanical hand

References

1. N.I. Badler, K.H. Manoochehri, and D. Baraff. "Multi–dimensional input techniques and articulated figure positioning by multiple constraints". In S. M. Pizer, editor, *Proceedings of 1986 Workshop on Interactive 3D graphics*, pages 151–169, Oct. 1986.

2. G. Bier and A. Eric. "Skitters and Jacks: Interactive 3–D Positioning Tools". In S. M. Pizer, editor, *Proceedings of 1986 Workshop on Interactive 3D graphics*, pages 183–196, Oct. 1986.

3. M. Chen. "A study in interactive 3d rotation using 2d control devices". *Computer Graphics (SIGGRAPH'88)*, vol. 22 no. 4, pp. 121–129, July 1988.

4. S. Houde. "Iterative design of an interface for easy 3–D direct manipulation". In A. Glassner, editor, *Graphics Gems*. Academic Press, 1990.

5. J. Hultquist. "A virtual trackball". In A. Glassner, editor, *Graphics Gems*. Academic Press, 1990.

6. J. D. Mackinlay, K. Stuart, and G. G. Robertson. "Rapid controlled movement through a virtual 3D workspace". *Computer Graphics*, vol. 24 no. 2, pp. 171–176, Aug. 1990.

7. G. Nielson and J.D. Olsen. "Direct manipulation techniques for 3d objects using 3d locator devices". In S. M. Pizer, editor, *Proceedings of 1986 Workshop on Interactive 3D graphics*, 1986.

8. J. Nielson and R. Molich. "Heuristic evaluation of user interfaces". In *CHI 90 Conference Proceedings, Seattle, Washington*, Apr. 1–5 1990.

9. B. C. Phillips and I. N. Badler. "Jack: a toolkit for manipulating articulated figures". In *Proceedings of the ACM SIGGRAPH on User Interface Software*, pages 221–229. ACM Press, Oct. 17–18 1988.

10. B. C. Phillips, N. Badler, and J. Granieri. "Automatic viewing control for 3d direct manipulation". In *Proceedings 1992 Symposium on Interactive 3D*, pages 71–74. ACM SIGGRAPH, 1992.

11. K. Shoemake. "Animating Rotations with Quaternion Curves". *Computer Graphics (SIGGRAPH'85)*, vol. 19 no. 3, pp. 245–254, July 1985.

12. K. Shoemake. "Arcball: a user interface for specifying three-dimensional orientation using a mouse". In *Graphics Interface'92*, pages 151–156, May 1992.

13. C. Ware and D. Jessome. "Using the Bat: A six-dimensional mouse for object placement". *IEEE Computer Graphics and Applications*, vol. 8 no. 6, pp. 65–70, Nov. 1988.

14. A. Witkin and M. Kass. "Spacetime Constraints". *Computer Graphics (SIGGRAPH'88)*, vol. 22 no. 4, pp. 159–168, 1988.

15. R. C. Zeleznik, K. P. Herndon, D. C. Robbins, N. Huang, T. Meyer, N. Parker, and F. J. Hughes. "An interactive 3D toolkit for constructing 3D widgets". *Computer Graphics (SIGGRAPH'93)*, vol. 26 no. 2, pp. 81–84, Aug. 1993.

Importance Ordering for Real-Time Depth of Field

Paul Fearing

Department of Computer Science,
University of British Columbia,
Vancouver, British Columbia, Canada
fearing@cs.ubc.ca

Abstract. Depth of field (DOF) is an important component of real photography. As such, it is a valuable addition to the library of techniques used in photorealistic rendering. Several methods have been proposed for implementing DOF effects. Unfortunately, all existing methods require a great deal of computation. This prohibitive cost has precluded DOF effects from being used with any great regularity. This paper introduces a new way of computing DOF that is particularly effective for sequences of related frames (animations). It computes the most noticeable DOF effects first, and works on areas of lesser importance only if there is enough time. Areas that do not change between frames are not computed. At any point, the computation can be interrupted and the results displayed. Varying the interruption point allows a smooth trade-off between image accuracy and result speed. If enough time is provided, the algorithm generates the exact solution. Practically, this algorithm avoids the continual recomputing of large numbers of unchanging pixels. This can provide order-of-magnitude speedups in many common animation situations. This increase in speed brings DOF effects into the realm of real-time graphics. [1]

1 Introduction

DOF control is a useful and important photographic technique. It draws attention to in-focus objects and areas. Changing the focus forces movement of the viewer's center of attention, allowing a cinematographer to express a change in subject importance. DOF can also be used as a general artistic tool for fade outs, fade ins and soft focus sequences. Many tiny details of the world can be omitted or approximated if the cinematographer knows they will be out of focus. This can reduce the time and effort required design scene backgrounds.

DOF provides an important contribution to the general appearance of so-called "photorealistic" images. Photorealistic rendering implies being able to simulate the entire camera and film assembly exactly, including defects and aberrations. Without these effects and defects, it is often hard to fool humans into believing a rendered image was captured by a camera. Computer generated imagery usually looks "too perfect". DOF is expected by humans in both images and our own natural vision processes.

A realistic camera model is especially important in image forgery and computed-augmented reality, where images are a blend of the real and the computer generated. DOF consistency plays an important part in the believability of the image. DOF also forms a good basis for exploring other types of focus-based lens defects, such as spherical [Cox 71] and chromatic [Boult 92] aberrations. DOF has been used experimentally for isolating areas of 3D MRI data [Wixson 90] and particle systems [vanWijk 92]. The plane of interest is rendered in focus, while other areas are drawn out-of-focus. Current techniques are far too slow to be interactive. The computer simulation of DOF is also useful in vision,

---

[1] This text has been significantly edited for length. The full text can be found at http://www.cs.ubc.ca/spider/fearing/dof

where attempts have been made to derive scene depth from focus [Pentland 87] and to sharpen out-of-focus images [Savakis 91] [Sezan 91]. Synthetic DOF images provide exact ground truth values useful in algorithm error analysis.

Even with all these proven applications, DOF is rarely used in the graphics world. The main drawback appears to be the computational cost. A single frame can take minutes to compute. Even worse, easy DOF control almost always requires a long sequence of related frames. Humans focus real cameras by trial and error: point at a subject and manually change focus until the desired effect is achieved. Slow DOF calculations preclude this sort of focus experimentation in computer generated images. The desired effect must be calculated before starting the computation, using knowledge about object depths, DOF ranges, etc. This is feasible for simple test scenes, but it becomes annoyingly time-consuming for complex scenes containing many moving objects. Often, the rendered result does not contain the exact effect desired. Try after try is required to get the precise amount of DOF. This makes it too bothersome to include DOF except in the most ambitious projects. If DOF computations were fast enough to allow near real-time computation of sequences of related frames, rendering systems could allow trial-and- error adjusting of DOF effects. This would open up DOF to many new types of applications.

2 Depth of Field

DOF has been explained in Potmesil and Chakravarty [Potmesil 81], Kingslake [Kingslake 92], and others. We will provide a brief review for clarity.

Many graphics systems use the pinhole camera model as the basis for object appearance. Light rays are scattered off objects in world space. Some of the scattered rays are bounced towards the camera. Rays originating from the same object point p_o (but travelling in different directions) hit an infinitely small pinhole lens. This lens allows only a single ray to pass through the pinhole. Rays going in other directions are ignored. Thus, when the single ray hits the imaging plane, it is always in focus.

Obviously, real lenses have a finite dimension, and let in light coming from several different directions. This can be approximated using a thin lens model. As before, rays are scattered from objects in world space. Rays originating from the same object point p_o hit the lens from a number of different directions. The incoming rays are focused by the thin lens into a point p_f. If the imaging plane is located at p_f, the image of the object will be in focus. If the imaging plane is not at p_f, the incoming cone of rays intersect the image plane to form a conic, usually approximated as a circle. This circle is called a point's "circle of confusion" (CoC). Potmesil [Potmesil 81] calculates CoC diameter for an out-of-focus point u_o as

$$C = |V_u - V_p| \left(\frac{F}{nV_u} \right) \tag{1}$$

where F is the focal length, n is the aperture number, and

$$V_u = \frac{FU}{U-F} \quad U > F \qquad\qquad V_p = \frac{FP}{P-F} \quad P > F \tag{2}$$

where V_p forms a point on the image plane. Figure 1 diagrams the various distances, including distances U and P. The CoC is used to compute how points are imaged over an area.

3 Previous Work

Existing DOF computation methods are described extremely briefly below.

3.1 Linear Postfiltering

Potmesil and Chakravarty [Potmesil 81] were the first to introduce a DOF model
to the computer graphics community. They based their approach on a two-pass
postfiltering process. The first (image rendering) pass computes an RGB image
and a corresponding Z depth map. The second (DOF filtering) pass computes
DOF effects. The CoC of each pixel is computed using Eq.1. A pixel P's intensity is then the summation of the weighted intensities of all other pixels with
CoCs that overlap P. Potmesil and Chakravarty used diffraction properties to
come up with a function that modeled intensity distribution within an individual
CoC. The authors made heavy use of lookup tables to improve processing speed.
The diffraction-based intensity distribution profile was approximated in Chen
[Chen 87], with no noticeable effect on image appearance. The vision community [Lee 90] also has a number of intensity distribution models, primarily for
depth retrieval and image restoration.

Potmesil and Chakravarty's method has the advantages of postfiltering, including simplicity and speed proportional to image size. The main disadvantage
is that the CoC is computed from a single object point. This means that filtering does not recognize objects partially blocking the CoC's effect. This partial
occlusion can cause blurry backgrounds to "leak" onto sharp foreground objects.

3.2 Distributed Ray Tracing

Cook, Porter, and Carpenter [Cook 84] implemented DOF using distributed ray
tracing. Because rays are actually traced into the environment, distributed ray-
tracing solves the partial CoC occlusion problems of linear postfiltering. It also
computes a better estimation of object color, as different parts of the lens see
the object from different angles (which implies potentially different colors). The
main disadvantage of distributed raytracing is that images are rendered much
slower than real time. As well, combining DOF with object rendering makes it
very expensive to change the DOF without changing the objects.

3.3 Accumulation Buffer

Haeberli and Akeley's [Haeberli 90] accumulation buffer was introduced to provide hardware support for antialiasing. It can also be used for DOF effects. The
accumulation buffer avoids partial CoC occlusion problems, allows a smooth
improvement in image quality with time, and can be used to simultaneously
implement antialiasing, soft shadows and motion blur. The accumulation buffer
resembles a frame-buffer implementation of distributed ray-tracing. As such,
cost is proportional to the complexity of the world scene, and the number of
viewpoint samples.

3.4 Ray Distribution Buffer

Shinya [Shinya 94] adapted the distributed ray tracing idea and converted it into
a postfiltering process. Algorithm complexity depends upon image size and RDB
size, offering an improvement over distributed ray tracing and the accumulation
buffer. However, it does not account for color changes due to variations in ray
direction.

3.5 Clustering Methods

DOF can be simulated without using a model of the synthetic camera. Scofield
[Scofield 92] groups scene objects into foreground and background planes. Each
plane is rendered separately, blurred using a low-pass filter, and then composited
together. The filter sizes are unrelated to the camera model, and are chosen ad
hoc.

4 Importance Ordering Depth of Field

All DOF methods were originally discussed as they applied to single images. This implies that all pixels must be recomputed on each and every frame, even if there is little or no change between frames. This can be especially expensive for scenes where sharp objects are moving in front of large and blurry (hence costly to compute) backgrounds. The DOF changes in only a small portion of the total number of pixels, yet the expensive background must be recomputed for each frame. There are many other examples of minimal (yet noticeable) scene changes requiring a complete image recompute. Recomputing the entire image also proves tiresome for the human viewer. Results are not available until all work has been completed. This prevents a human from previewing (and potentially interrupting) the image in-progress.

In this section we describe a fast postfiltering DOF method using *importance ordering*. The main contribution of this algorithm is to recognize that there is a great deal of consistency between sequential frames of an animation. We can use this continuity to avoid recomputing areas of the scene that do not change between frames. Pixels that do require recomputation are processed in the approximate order of their noticeable visual effect. Importance ordering DOF rendering allows substantial speedups when generating multiple frame animations. It also allows the most obvious DOF effects to be previewed at an early stage in the computation.

We have chosen a postfiltering approach for several reasons. Postfiltering requires no knowledge of world space, thus allowing a complexity dependent on image size. Postfiltering techniques can also be meshed with existing frame and Z-buffer hardware. This provides hope that fast DOF can be added to polygonal based graphics rendering engines. Adding DOF effects in after rendering allows a user to modify camera parameters without having to re-render the original image.

4.1 Algorithm

Each frame begins with the current picture, consisting of an RGB image $I_c(x, y)$, a Z-buffer $Z_c(x, y)$, and CoC values, $C_c(x, y)$. Each pixel also contains $I_l(x, y)$ and $C_l(x, y)$ elements that contain the pixel's status at the time of its last update. Individual pixels have R, G and B numerators and a single denominator to keep track of the current summation of all overlapping CoC effects, including its own.

The first pass computes $C_c(x, y)$ for every pixel P. After $C_c(P)$ is computed, a pixel P's update importance is calculated using an importance function (detailed below). This function returns an importance measure h within the range $[0..h_{max}]$. Depending on h, pixel P is placed into one of h_{max} hash buckets. Hash bucket 0 represents pixels that do not need to be recomputed this frame.

The second pass computes DOF effects for the image. A pixel P is taken from the highest non-empty hash bucket. The previous CoC effect of pixel P on its neighbors is computed using $I_l(P)$, and $C_l(P)$. The current CoC effect on P's neighbors is determined with $I_c(P)$, and $C_c(P)$. The difference of the two effects is added to all affected neighboring pixels. Once pixel P has been processed, $I_l(P)$ and $C_l(P)$ values are updated. The algorithm continues to take pixels from hash buckets until all but hash bucket 0 are empty, the user interrupts, or some preset number of pixels have been processed.

After interruption, the average intensity value of all pixels is computed. Pixels that were not updated on this pass must be included, in order to count changes due to updated neighbors. The results are immediately sent to the framebuffer for display. If another frame is required, it is loaded into $I_c(x, y)$ and $Z_c(x, y)$, and the algorithm repeats.

4.2 Intensity Distribution Function

CoC effects take the form of an intensity distribution D centered around pixel P. A neighboring pixel U is affected by the area under the intensity distribution curve D, multiplied by pixel P's color values. Intensity curves can be flat, gaussian, or as complicated as Potmesil and Chakravarty's diffraction model.

The intensity distribution function can be computed a priori, and stored as a number of tables of various sizes. Tables can be computed and interpolated between with varying degrees of precision. In order for this method to work, the intensity distribution function must be individually retrievable. That is, a pixel P must be able to determine its last contribution to its neighbors based solely on its own current and past information.

4.3 Importance Function

Every pixel is ranked in update priority by an importance function. This function attempts to link a pixel's update order to the amount of change in its appearance. Noticeable differences in a pixel occur in three cases: CoC diameter changes, Z value changes, and color changes. CoC diameters change with the camera model parameters and Z values of the target. Differing CoC diameters cause changes in the D filter size, resulting in new intensity distributions among a pixel's neighbors. Differences also occur when a pixel changes color. All of these effects will be usually present in an animation sequence.

The importance of a change in CoC for a point P is measured by $h_{coc} = |C_c(P) - C_l(P)|$. The color change effect h_{rgb} is based on a simple Euclidean color distance. The CIE LUV uniform color space can also be used to calculate color distances that are perceptually equal.

P's total importance h is a linear weighting of the CoC and color effects:

$$h = W_{coc}h_{coc} + W_{rgb}h_{rgb} \qquad (3)$$

The relative weighting between the effects can be chosen to suit a specific part of an animation. Pure color changes are most likely to occur when scene lighting moves around. Pure CoC changes are most likely to occur when changing camera parameters. Without a priori knowledge of the animation, equal weights can be used. Of course, the weighting functions need to be scaled to spread values out across h_{max} hash buckets.

Note that pixels that do not change in color or CoC are given an importance of 0, and not updated on this frame. We can also threshold very small h_{coc} or h_{rgb} to 0, if color or CoC changes are small enough not to be detectable or important. For example, CoC changes can be thresholded at $\frac{F}{1000}$, at the limit of human resolution.

Skipping a pixel P in the importance ordering algorithm means the last change to P's effect has not yet been reflected in the image. Skipping a pixel in the linear algorithm implies that pixel P's entire effect has been neglected.

4.4 DOF Interruptions

Importance ordering allows the user to interrupt the algorithm to see the most important results completed so far. The program can also interrupt the algorithm after a set percentage $M < 100\%$ of hashed pixels. This allows a gradual increase in speed with a gradual decrease in accuracy (with respect to a linear DOF method). Pixels not updated on one pass grow in importance the next pass.

If M is too small, pixels can be starved out. This can cause objectionable artifacts if starved points are part of a moving object. Reducing M is most useful for gradual zooms on static scenery, where it is harder to detect focus changes for points that lag on the update. Unchanged pixels are not hashed, allowing large speedups even when $M = 100\%$ of the hashed pixels. In this case, each frame produces the same result as the linear DOF method.

5 Experiments and Discussion

Both linear and importance ordering DOF methods were implemented as a set of library functions. These libraries read and write values directly to the framebuffer and z-buffer, allowing the addition of DOF to any framebuffer based program. Adding DOF to an existing program requires approximately 3-4 lines of new code. For simplicity, both methods used a gaussian intensity distribution function, without intensity z-scaling, or table interpolation. The distribution tables were computed to half-pixel boundaries. Filter vignetting was ignored. Because both methods use the same tables, the intensity distribution function does not affect the relative comparisons. Several experiments were carried out to test the speed of the importance ordering DOF method.

5.1 Experimental Results

Five different animations were generated, each consisting of 100 frames of size 256h by 256w. The background was raytraced offline, and was loaded into the framebuffer/z-buffer on each frame. The raytraced background allowed extremely complex scenery without a corresponding increase in rendering time. The star was rendered directly into the framebuffer/z-buffer, and thus can occlude and be occluded by the background.

In the first four experiments, the importance ordering DOF method was directly compared with the linear Potmesil DOF. The importance ordering method used $M = 100$, $w_{coc} = 0.5$, and $w_{rgb} = 0.5$. Both methods used the same code where possible, including the intensity distribution function. No particular code optimizations were implemented. Experiments were performed on a 100 mHz SGI Indy.

Table 1 shows the update speed with the cost of the first frame omitted. Note that to compute the first frame, the importance ordering method must spend as least as much time as the linear method. The longer the animation sequence, the faster the first-frame cost is ammortized across all frames.

The first experiment consisted of the focused star moving left-to- right in between an unfocussed foreground and background. The importance ordering DOF method was able to perform over 22.1× faster than the linear method, mainly because the majority of the out-of-focus area was not recomputed. Note that we could improve the importance ordering speedup even more by making the static background blurrier. The greater the cost of the unchanging area, the larger the speedup.

The second experiment involved the star zooming away from the camera. The object started in focus, and moved out-of-focus as it approached the background. Speedups were less than experiment one because the target object covered more of the total picture area over the duration of the animation.

The third experiment involved a foreground to background focus change on a stationary scene. The importance ordering DOF ran 2.4× faster, mainly because h_{coc} values less than the minimum table division were hashed to $h = 0$. There was no noticeable visual difference between the two methods. Figure 2 shows the start of the animation.

The fourth experiment consisted of a combination of experiments one, two, and three. The star moved from left-to-right, zooming away from the camera.

The final experiment approximated experiment three, except that M was varied to truncate the computation. The zoom direction was reversed to maximize blur inconsistencies. The first frame always used $M = 100\%$. Corresponding times are shown in Figure 3. Faster times mean less accuracy. In this particular experiment, a few pixels require most of the effort. Thus, large numbers of pixels can be removed without much affect on speed or visual accuracy. Figure 4 shows importance ordering with $M = 15$, on the final frame of the animation. Figure 2 shows $M = 100$ for comparison. Note the similarity of the images, even though only 15% of all changing pixels were updated each frame.

5.2 Discussion

The importance ordering DOF algorithm works extremely well for scenes with a constant focus and moving objects. This type of scene setup is very common in films and video. In experiment one, we were able to achieve a sub-second average time, even with a very blurry foreground and background. This is within our definition of achievable real-time DOF response. The main speedup comes from not having to update a large section of the image on each frame. The more expensive this unchanging area is to compute, the greater the improvement over the linear method. When objects are moving, M should be set to 100 to ensure all moving pixels are updated.

This algorithm uses frame coherence to gain considerable speedups over previous methods. Obviously, we cannot gain improvements in situations where there is little or no frame coherence, such as a scene with a moving viewpoint. If a scene changes totally, all pixels must be updated on each pass. The importance ordering method must both remove and add DOF effects, making it slower than the linear method. This is not as much of constraint as it might first seem. First, static camera shots account for a very large number of cinematographic situations. The virtual reality-like "roaming viewpoint" is not as common as the static "talking-heads" shot. In the vast majority of 30 frame/second animations with a static camera, both object motion and focus motion are slow enough to leave substantial portions of the image unchanged between frames. Secondly, we can still use importance ordering to help us set up the correct focus parameters for a moving-camera shoot, even if the algorithm does not help us during actual camera motion. Finally, we can impose frame coherence on a scene by "morphing" a few sequential frames of a moving camera sequence to a common reference frame. By imposing frame coherence, even only for limited sequences of two or three frames, we can still gain substantial speedups at the cost of a small loss in accuracy.

6 Summary

This paper describes a new method for calculating DOF based upon the notion of importance of change. Our importance ordering DOF algorithm is based upon Potmesil and Chakravarty's postfiltering process. The importance ordering DOF method avoids recomputation of large areas of unchanged pixels, concentrating only on areas of importance. In multi- frame animations, this results in large speedups over linear DOF methods without loss in accuracy. We were able to animate an in-focus object moving between an extremely blurry foreground and background with sub-second frame update rates. In addition, DOF computation can be truncated early by skipping over less important areas. This gives even faster results, and allows the user to preview progress.

Importance ordering DOF brings DOF into the feasible range of real-time applications. Real-time DOF will allow trial-and-error camera focus adjustment, as well as more realistic rendering.

References

[Boult 92]   Boult, T. and Wolberg, G. "Correcting Chromatic Aberrations Using Image Warping". In *Image Understanding Workshop*, pages 363–377. Defence Advanced Research Projects Agency, 1992.

[Chen 87]   Chen, Y. "Lens Effect on Synthetic Image Generation Based on Light Particle Theory". In *CG International 87*, pages 347–366. Computer

Graphics, 1987.

[Cook 84]   Cook, R., Porter, T., and Carpenter, L. "Distributed Ray Tracing". *Computer Graphics (Proc. SIGGRAPH)*, 18(3):137–145, July 1984.

[Cox 71]   Cox, A. *Photographic Optics*. Focal Press, New York, New York, 1971.

[Haeberli 90]   Haeberli, P. and Kurt, A. "The Accumulation Buffer: Hardware Support for High-Quality Rendering". *Computer Graphics (Proc. SIGGRAPH)*, 24(4):309–317, August 1990.

[Kingslake 92]   Kingslake, R. *Optics in Photography*. SPIE Optical Engineering Press, Bellingham, Wash., 1992.

[Lee 90]   Lee, H.-C. "Review of Image-Blur Models in a Photographic System Using the Principles of Optics". *Optical Engineering*, 5(29):405–421, May 1990.

[Pentland 87]   Pentland, A. "A New Sense for Depth of Field". *IEEE Trans. Pattern Analysis and Machine Intelligence*, 9(4):523–531, July 1987.

[Potmesil 81]   Potmesil, M. and Chakravarty, I. "A Lens and Aperture Camera Model for Synthetic Image Generation". *Computer Graphics (Proc. SIGGRAPH)*, 15(3):297–305, August 1981.

[Savakis 91]   Savakis, A. and Trussell, H. "Restorations of Real Defocused Images Using Blur Models Based on Geometrical and Diffraction Optics". In *SOUTHEASTCON 1991*, volume 2, pages 919–922. IEEE, April 1991.

[Scofield 92]   Scofield, C. $2\frac{1}{2}$ D Depth-of-Field Simulation for Computer Animation. In Kirk, D., editor, *Graphic Gems III*, pages 36–38. Academic Press Ltd, 1992.

[Sezan 91]   Sezan, I., Pavlovic, G., Tekalp, M., and Erdem, T. "On Modelling the Focus Blur in Image Restoration". In *ICASSP '91: Acoustics, Speech and Signal Processing Conference*, volume 4, pages 2485–2488. IEEE, April 1991.

[Shinya 94]   Shinya, M. "Post-filtering for Depth of Field Simulation with Ray Distribution Buffer". In *GI*, pages 59–66. Canadian Information Processing Society, 1994.

[vanWijk 92]   vanWijk, J. "Rendering Surface Particles". In *Visualization 1992*, pages 54–61. IEEE, October 1992.

[Wixson 90]   Wixson, S. "The Display of 3D MRI Data with Non-Linear Focal Depth Cues". In *Computers in Cardiology*, pages 379–380. IEEE, September 1990.

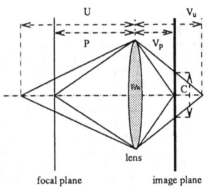

Fig. 1. Calculation of the Circle of Confusion

Table 1. Update Rate Without First Frame

Exp.#	1	2	3	4
Linear	25.7 s	11.6 s	4.8 s	5.0 s
Importance	0.9 s	0.8 s	1.9 s	1.9 s
Speed-up	28.5 x	14.5 x	2.5 x	2.6 x

Times are seconds/frame averaged over frames [2..100].

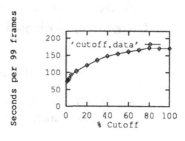

Fig. 3. Experimental Results - Running Time vs. M Cutoff

Fig. 2. Experiment 3 - Near to Far Focus Change

Fig. 4. Importance Ordering DOF, M = 15% of Changing Pixels Recomputed

A Behavioural Control Framework for Computer Animation using AI Techniques

Carlos S. N. Ho and Richard L. Grimsdale

Centre for VLSI & Computer Graphics - University of Sussex
Falmer, Brighton Sussex BN1 9QT - England

Abstract. This paper proposes a framework for controlling the behaviour of simulated robots through high-level instructions. We assume that each robot is not only capable of performing autonomous and complex movements, but also capable of interacting with each other by performing actions and reacting accordingly to the changes of the environment. These instructions are originated from the animator's scripts and may also be an autonomous response to the interactions between the animated agents. The assumption that instructions have adaptive planning of behaviours composed by sub-instructions permit us to build increasingly complex instructions to be built. The system exploits AI techniques including frame, blackboard, planning, and rules.

1   Introduction

In this work we are interested in animating multiple articulated figures, specially robots with human behaviour, where the purposeful nature of human activities and the complexity of a dynamic changing environment are simulated by computer animation. We want to provide the animator with a framework that can easily permit the simulation of patterns of behaviour in a micro-world populated with dynamic and static objects.

The animator gives the overall animation sequence as a script and supplies some knowledge about the personal aspects of the robot and its relationship with the others. With such a specification, the robots are able to develop the animation from the script and augment it with additional behavioural movements that reflect environmental changes, thus providing more realism to the animation. For example, a character could perform some activity while it has no instruction to execute, or look around when someone approaches while carrying out some task. Thus, without much effort the animator can easily explore variations in sequences by modifying a small amount of information.

We will address questions related to structured knowledge data [14], its organisation, representation, and control [3]. We will also present mechanisms, such as plans and interruptions, that permit the building of increasingly more complex interactions between the characters. For example, if the animator schedules an instruction to a figure to sit on a chair, its control system should be able to achieve this result independently of its situation or location. On its way to the chair, the figure may have to avoid collisions with other moving figures, turn down invitations, wave to somebody, etc.

2 Related Work

Task-level animation is a concept that has permitted the abstraction of the animation to evolve to a higher structured and parameterised goal specification. This approach has been one the most popular approaches to the modelling of human-like behaviour [17, 1, 2, 9]. A control layer is added to the animation system to control the motion of the limbs of a figure which makes up a behaviour. A repertoire of behaviours are created and repeatedly applied in similar contexts by the animator. This automation works well when there is only one active figure or when, in a multiple figures context, none of the figures interferes with another's control space. However, this is not always the case in a typical animation setting. In a traditional animation system, the animator must continuously control the direction and position of every object, integrating the whole environment.

In the behavioural animation, almost all the control is transferred from the animator to the individual robots. Each robot is assigned the knowledge that enables it to react to environmental stimuli or constraints [7, 11, 18]. The main aspect of behavioural animation is that it is mostly driven by relations and constraints) among the actors [13, 15, 8, 11, 16]. Many of the techniques used in robotics such as path-planning [3, 6] have been borrowed for the computer animation.

Sun [15], has discussed the problems of animating of multiple moving objects and has proposed the "relational" approach for solving the problem of specifying multiple interacting moving objects. In her example of a group of dancers, she uses a set of pre-defined relations that provide a pattern for the coordinated motional behaviour of the dancing couples in the room. She also established some structuring mechanisms to select and control the global motional behaviour of the objects.

Ridsdale makes use of an expert system for planning the motion of actors on a stage [12]. A set of staging rules guides the actors' motions relatively to the main character actions. Calvert has pointed out the problems of using an Expert System as a top layer for controlling an animation system. Simply chaining production rules does not adequately synchronise animation events to produce correct response. He has suggested the use of the *blackboard* concept [4, 5] as a way of attaining "real-time" response to asynchronous parallel events.

Mah [8] proposed a framework for creating a behavioural animation for sailing boats using *constraint logic programming*. In the first stage, a detailed plan is derived for each boat and then in the second stage, the animation is generated. This approach is intended to produce animation plans more effectively by reducing the solution space in the reasoning process. More recently, Tu [16] simulated the behaviour of different types of fishes. The perception of the environment combined with its habits and mental states (hunger, libido, and fear) trigger some of the "instinctive" behaviours of the fishes.

3 System Overview

Our system (Fig. 1) is composed of two components which interact with each other on a master/slave basis. The higher component, the reasoning system is implemented by a blackboard model. In this work we present a blackboard implementation alternative to

Calvert's proposal [4]. This model is suitable for controlling a multiple thread of tasks and allows immediate and opportunistic reactions to the environmental changes [6]. The underlying language is Flex/Prolog which provides expert system facilities to represent frames, rules, and declarative knowledge. At the lower level, the animation system converts the behaviour into a chain of library motion calls. All the functionality such as camera, display, and objects allocation of typical animation system are included.

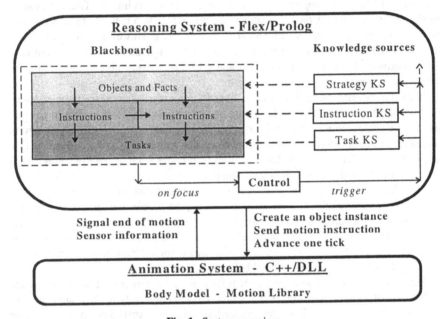

Fig. 1. System overview.

We have adopted the conceptual model of a blackboard as a problem-solving paradigm because of the dynamic nature of the behavioural animation in which tasks are created, suspended, interrupted, and completed asynchronously. For example, consider the case of a character walking to a designated place who is suddenly observed and called by another character. If the character is busy executing its original plan, then it could just wave a hand as a quick acknowledgement and carry out its given instruction. Alternatively, if it is offered an invitation it can abandon its original plan, which may not be important, and respond to the invitation. This is an example of an event that provokes the creation of a different operation from that originally planned. Another example is of a walking character that is about to collide with one that is crossing its path. Here the character has to decide to stop and wait for a while, or find another path and continue walking.

The blackboard model is analogous to a group of experts with different skills that cooperate to solve a problem. The definition of the blackboard model is quite flexible in that it permits different implementations ranging from simple to a very complex ones [5, 6]. Basically it consists of three components: knowledge sources, blackboard, and control. Each knowledge source is a specialist that solves one aspect of the problem domain. These are invoked as they are required by a process in the blackboard, and provide partial solutions that incrementally contribute to the overall execution of a task. The blackboard is a shared global data structure that is accessed by the knowledge sources (KSs). The control evaluates the blackboard context and decides which KS should be called in each step of the problem-solving. In the following sections each of these three parts are examined.

3.1 Blackboard Data Structure

The blackboard is organised into the distinct information levels of the problem solving domain. In our system, the reasoning control is partitioned into three levels of abstraction: strategy, instruction, and task (recall Fig. 1). Each level has a different view of the space solution and requires different handling by the corresponding KSs. Levels can be added or removed, as modules, as the system evolves. The blackboard consists of sets of data instances. Each instance is a separate asynchronous computing agent that encapsulates information and status of the process. However, only those instances that request KSs actions are made visible to the system control, that is, these instances are put "in focus" to invoke the corresponding KSs. An instance is put "out of focus" when it is temporarily suspended and must await another process to return it into focus.

3.2 Control

The control loop is continuously checking the blackboard for items that require responses from the KSs. That is, if any instance is turned on, or *in focus*, then the corresponding KS is invoked. The control scheme is quite simple, being restricted to instruction or task scheduling. This simplicity is partly achieved by the fact that each process instance (instruction or task) has its local control and the hierarchical structuring of the blackboard data leads to a hierarchical distribution of control.

3.2.1 The Instruction Knowledge Source

The goal of a character is to achieve a state (e.g., *John seated on the chair1*). To achieve this, we use the notion of an instruction that performs the necessary actions. The structure of an instruction is <condition>[<subject><verb><object>]. In the example in Fig. 2, the instruction is *"If John is in the room1, John sit on the chair1"*. All information associated with an instruction is conveniently stored in a frame structure called an *instruction frame*. By extending the number of slots in an instruction frame, we can encapsulate virtually all the necessary knowledge for the instruction domain, namely, initialisation functions, instruction status, plans and selection methods, links, priority, etc. The main activity of the instruction is to select a suitable plan and monitor each of its steps. Thus in Fig. 2, the instruction given above (a) is expanded into the sequence (b, c, d), (b) is an instruction which can be expanded into the tasks (e) and (f), (c) and (d) are leaves of the tree, known as *tasks*, and cannot be further expanded. The instruction is thus executed as the sequence of tasks (e), (f), (c), (d). However, some external situation may arise which makes it impossible to execute a part of the instruction, for example, if the chair1 is occupied. The instruction control is shown in Fig. 3.

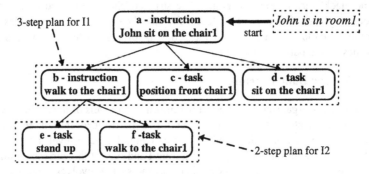

Fig. 2. Expansion of the "sit on the chair1" instruction.

Planning. There are many difficulties involved in the generation of a character's plan through a search process. For our animation purpose it is enough to assume the following conditions: (a) in any purposeful behaviour, an action is preceded and followed by a coherent one, a common sense principle; (b) a goal may be decomposable into few smaller ones which can be sub-goals or tasks, this means that sub-goals can be further expanded; (c) there are several choices of plans to match a typical situation of a goal instruction; (d) the selection of a plan for a goal is made only when it gains focus of attention; (e) there is no "backtracking" of motion, that is, if a plan fails at some point then another plan is tried, but if no suitable plan can be found then the control focus is returned to the instruction which controls it and a new solution is tried to achieve that sub-goal.

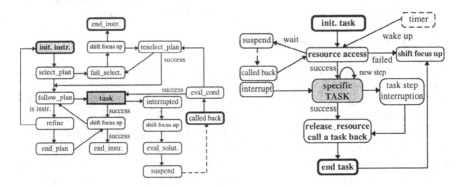

Fig. 3. Instruction control diagram.   **Fig. 4.** Task control diagram.

3.2.2 The Task Knowledge Source

The structure of a *task* is very similar to that of an instruction, except that a task is a primitive operation, with no interior planning and without the possibility of further expansion. Thus, tasks nodes are found at the bottom of a fully expanded instruction tree. A task instance contains the actual control for a specific behaviour, for example, walking. It provides a schedule of sequential movements to the animation system which are performed at tick rate. Although tasks have a uniform control structure, the detailed implementation varies considerably from task to task. Tasks have a common internal structure for information handling; resource allocation/de-allocation; starting, interruption, finalisation; and failure handling. Since each task performs a different type of operation, the number of states in its ruleset depends on its complexity. The general control of a task is shown in Fig. 4 and each of its components are described below.

Resource Access. A task gains access to perform a behaviour when all the necessary resources have been successfully allocated for its use. Firstly, a check is made to determine if any of the resources have been assigned to another task. A resource may be unallocated, allocated to a task or there is a task waiting for it to be assigned. Resource allocation is decided through a priority mechanism.

Task Specific Process. The underlying mechanism of a specific task can be implemented by procedural programs or by a ruleset describing the states of a motion. The nature of the implementation depends on the complexity of role of the task. For example, the walking task has a more complex mechanism than the task for waving a hand. The walking task is thus implemented as a finite state automaton instead of a sequence of commands. The task specific process provides the schedule of movements to the animation system which are then animated at tick rate. The Task Specific Process is the only process whose activity spans over an animation cycle because it performs the actual motion, the others are evaluated within a single cycle.

Task Control. Task control essentially is performed by both the individual actions of the *Task Specific Process* and by interruptions by events. Decisions are sent back to the co-ordinating instruction for evaluation. Task control also releases resources, suspends and reactivates the task, and handles failures.

Task Step. In order to make the behaviour of a character realistic, a task is split into short periods of time called *steps*. A *step* of motion is performed without interruption. At the end of each *step*, the constraints of the task are checked against the database and further checks are made to determine if there are requests for the allocated resources. In addition, the database is updated with the outcome of the last task step. As a consequence, a subsequent step can make an appropriate selection of the way to continue the motion based on the updated database. Examples of facts in the database are: "position is seated", "left_leg is forward", "passage is engaged", "red_chair is free".

Priorities and Interruptions. Resources are not immediately allocated to the tasks. If the current task is competing with another, the decision to allocate resources is made on a priority basis. There are three levels of ranking an action: (a) ***unimportant,*** for secondary movements, scheduled by the system to complement the motion of a character; (b) ***important,*** when the instruction is scheduled from the script or provoked by another important instruction; and (c) *urgent*, used only in exceptional occasions, when the system has to take priority action, for example, to overcome a deadlock situation.

There are two types of interruptions: internal and external. An internal interruption is when two tasks try to gain access to a resource. For example, a figure walking with arms swinging is provoked by an approaching figure to respond to it by a hand wave. Both these use the *arm* resource. Since the swinging arms task would be ranked as unimportant then it is suspended temporarily in favour of the waving instruction. An external interruption arises when two tasks in different robots dispute over the priority of action, for example, when two robots are attempting to pass through a doorway. If one has higher priority then it goes first while the other waits. With both types of interruption, the decision is straightforward when the competing tasks have different priorities. In the case of equal priority, a *common sense* solution is sought by appealing to a specific knowledge decision. For example, a figure that is carrying a load gets priority while the other awaits its turn.

Exception Handling. An *exception* is a special case of an interruption causing an instruction to suspend its activities temporarily. This can arise because constraints have been violated or because important facts which form the basis of a task have been modified. When an exception occurs, the current task is suspended. The operation of the current task at the time of the interruption is saved, and the task instance is stored in special slot. A special instruction is then scheduled to handle the problem and when the problem has been resolved the suspended task is resumed. However, before this happens an evaluation is made to check that the constraints are still satisfied.

4 Conclusion and Results

This paper has proposed the use of a blackboard approach to aid an animator in the task of generating an automatic animation with two important aspects. Firstly, the animator defines the minimum necessary script that directs the overall animation. Secondly, the characters present a degree of autonomy in performing the instructions, with the addition of secondary movements. As a system developer, the animator may wish to add new instructions and new tasks, or even extend the current instructions with new alternative plans.

The first results with a small database have produced interesting animation sequences. When the animation runs beyond the script specification the behaviours of the figures become very casual, reacting opportunistically to the environment. Future works will include more instructions and the enhancement of the knowledge source for handling more complex decisions. For example, we could define behaviours, plans, and strategies for a team playing game or simulating human jobs.

Acknowledgements

We wish to thank to the referees for the important comments, to M.D.J. McNeill and Martin White for their cooperation, and to CAPES for the funding of this work.

References

1. N.I. Badler, J.D. Korein, J.U. Korein, G.M. Radack, L.S. Brotman: Positioning and Animating Human Figures in a Task-oriented Environment. The Visual Computer 1, pp. 212-220 (1985)

2. N.I. Badler, B.L. Webber, J. Kalita, J. Esakov: Animation from Instructions. In N.I. Badler, B.A. Barsky, D. Zeltzer (eds.): Making Them Move.[O6] Morgan Kaufmann Publishers, Inc. 1991, pp. 51-93.

3. R.A. Brooks, J.H. Connell: Asynchronous Distributed Control System for a Mobile Robot. Proc. SPIE 1986 Vol. 727 Mobile Robots, pp. 77-84 (1986)

4. T.W. Calvert, R. Ovans, S. Mah: Towards the Autonomous Animation of Multiple Human Figures. Proc. of Computer Animation'94, pp. 69-75 (1994)

5. R.S. Engelmore, A.J. Morgan: Blackboard Systems. Addison-Wesley Publishers Ltd. (1988)

6. T. Lozano-Peres, M.A. Wesley: An Algorithm for Planning Collision-Free Paths Among Polyhedral Obstacles. Com. of the ACM 22(10), pp. 560-570 (1979)

7. T. Maruichi, T. Uchiki, M. Tokoro: Behavioral Simulation Based on Knowledge Objects. Proc. European Conf. on Object Oriented Programming, Special issue of BIGRE 54, pp. 257-266 (1987)

8. S. Mah, T.W. Calvert, W. Havens: NSAIL PLAN: An Experience with Constraint-Based Reasoning in Planning and Animation. Proc. of Computer Animation'94, pp. 83-92 (1994)

9. C.L. Morawetz, T.W. Calvert: Goal-Directed Human Animation of Multiple Movements. Proc. Graphics Interface'90, pp. 60-67, May (1990)

10. P. Morasso, V. Tagliasco: Human Movement Understanding. North-Holland, (1986)

11. C.W. Reynolds: Flocks, Herds, and Schools: A Distributed Behavioral Model. Computer Graphics 21(4), pp. 25-34 (1987)

12. G. Ridsdale, S. Hewitt, T.W. Calvert: The Interactive Specification of Human Animation. Proc. of Graphics Interface'86, pp. 121-130 (1986)

13. G. Ridsdale, T.W. Calvert: Animating Microworlds from Scripts and Relational Constraint. In N. Magnenat-Thalmann, D. Thalmann (eds.): Proc. of Computer Animation'90 pp. 107-117 (1990)[O8]

14. G. Ringland: Structured Object Representation - Schemata and Frames. In G.A. Ringland, D.A. Duce (eds.): Approaches to Knowledge Representation. Research Studies Press Ltd,[O9] pp. (1988)

15. H. Sun, M. Green: The Use of Relations for Motion Control in an Environment With Multiple Moving Objects. Proc. Graphics Interface'93, pp. 209-218 (1993)

16. X. Tu, D. Terzopoulos: Artificial Fishes: Physics, Locomotion, Perception, Behaviour. Proc. SIGGRAPH'94, pp. 43-50 (1994)

17. D. Zeltzer: Towards an Integrated View of 3-D Computer Animation. The Visual Computer 1, Springer-Verlag, pp. 249-259 (1985)

18. D. Zeltzer: Knowledge-based Animation. In N.I. Badler, J.K. Tsotsos (eds.): Motion: Representation and Perception. Elsevier Science Publishing Co., Inc., 1986, pp. 318-323

Time-Space Weighting for Image Sequence Quantization

Hagit Zabrodsky Hel-Or

Dept. of Psychology, Stanford University, Stanford, CA. 94305
e-mail: gigi@white.stanford.edu

Abstract. This paper introduces a method for quantization of image-sequences which takes into account the human sensitivities in both space and time. A weighted clustering approach is used for quantization which allows flexibility in the choice of weights. Assigning weights proportional to the space gradients and the time gradients is shown to produce better quantization of color image sequences.

1 Introduction

As memory costs decrease, most computers are capable of displaying images and image sequences. However, many of the color display devices are still restricted in video-memory, allowing only a limited number of colors to be displayed simultaneously. The most common color display has 8-bit video memory allowing only $2^8 = 256$ simultaneous colors. Most images, and certainly image sequences, contain more than the limited number of colors allowed on the display, therefore a scheme for representing these images with a lower color count than the original, must be used.

Color *quantization* is the process of selecting a maximally allowed set of colors (denoted the color palette or color map) and reproducing the original image with this color set. The quantization process aims at producing a quantized image which is as similar as possible to the original. The quantized image is usually represented by a color map and an assignment mapping the pixels of the original image to the entries in the color map. When dealing with color image sequences the problem of quantization is two-fold: not only is a color map to be produced for each frame, the color continuity between frames must also be maintained. Thus, the quantization process for image sequences must aim at reproducing the original as accurately as possible while reducing the flicker and unwanted color changes between frames. In this paper a method for quantization of image-sequences is introduced which takes into account the human sensitivities in both space and time. This will increase color reproduction while reducing color flicker and color inconsistencies between frames.

2 Image Sequence Quantization

When quantizing image sequences, a color map is created for every frame in the sequence with the goal of reproducing the original sequence as accurately as possible. This goal demands:

1. good *color reproduction* - colors in the quantized frame should be as similar as possible to the original.
2. good *color continuity* - objects and regions appearing in contiguous frames, should be similar in color. This reduces flickering and unwanted color drifts between frames.

As a natural extension, quantization of image-sequences is based on methods for quantization of still images which has been widely discussed. Image quantization can be improved by incorporating human sensitivity considerations. This has been shown to be successful in quantization and dithering of still images [11, 3, 10, 1]. Experimental studies have shown that human sensitivity to quantization errors increases as the spatial gradient of the image decreases. Thus two image pixels having the same color should vary in their influence on the quantization process according to the spatial gradients of the image at these pixel locations. In [11, 3, 4], human sensitivity dependent on spatial frequency was incorporated into the quantization scheme of still images by weighting the color of each pixel with a value inversely proportional to the intensity gradient at the pixel location.

In this paper a method for image-sequence quantization is presented which incorporates human spatial and temporal sensitivities. We extend the method described in [11] which incorporates human spatial sensitivities in the quantization of still images, to quantization of image-sequences using both spatial and temporal human sensitivities.

Adaptive quantization of image sequences has been previously presented [5, 12], however they do not take into consideration human sensitivities which is central to improving performance. Human models of temporal sensitivities have been incorporated in dithering and half-toning of image-sequences (see [2, 8, 7, 6]) but these schemes all assume a previously determined color map.

3 Improving Image Sequence Quantization

Throughout this paper, the quantization schemes are demonstrated on a synthesized test sequence (see Figure 3). The sequence chosen was created so as to include a large range of colors and to have stable regions and moving regions. The sequence depicts a series of color textures moving in the background with a single colored pattern serving as a stable foreground. To emphasize the quantization affects, the test sequence is always quantized to produce a color map for each frame, having only 16 entries. However, even on color displays that can display 256 simultaneous colors, the quantization affects (poor color reproduction and poor color continuity) are significant.

In quantization of image-sequences two extreme approaches can be considered:

- Every frame of the sequence is quantized separately as a still image. Figure 4 shows a sequence quantized per frame using weighted clustering [11].
- All frames are quantized *in batch* as a single image (ie a concatenated image is produced from all frames). Figure 5 shows a sequence quantized in batch using weighted clustering. The same color map is assigned to all frames.

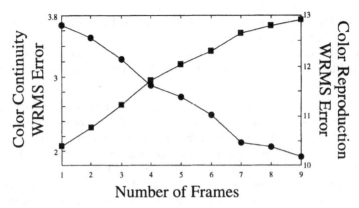

Fig. 1. Error as a function of number of frames quantized per batch. Evaluation of the color reproduction error (disks) and the color continuity error (squares).

As can be seen in Figure 4 and Figure 5[1], quantization of each frame separately produces a good reproduction of the original, however continuity of color is not maintained between frames (notice the color changes of the stable foreground patch). This loss of continuity will produce flickering and color instability when viewing these quantized frames as a time sequence. On the other hand, quantizing all frames in a single batch will produce color continuity (the foreground patch has constant color values throughout the sequence) however maintaining continuity is at the expense of reproduction quality: the quantized sequence is a poor reproduction of the original (notice the background in frame 2-3).

A natural hybrid approach to control the tradeoff of these two methods, is to create color maps by quantizing several but not all frames in batch. Thus a color map for frame i will be created by quantizing the concatenation of frames $i - m, \ldots, i, \ldots, i + m$. Figure 6 shows a sequence quantized by concatenating 3 frames in batch ($m = 1$). It can be seen that there is an improvement in color reproduction (compare with Figure 4) and in color continuity (compare with Figure 5). The tradeoff between color reproduction and color continuity is determined by the number of frames quantized per batch (the value of m). This is shown in Figure 1 where the error in color reproduction and in color continuity are presented as a function of the number of frames quantized per batch ($m * 2 + 1$). The error in color reproduction is given by a weighted root-mean-square measure (WRMS) taken over all pixels of the sequence. The error in color continuity is measured only over the pixels of the constant foreground patch. The error is given by the average of the WRMS errors measured between the contrast foreground patch of a given frame and that of the preceding frame. Note, we presume no perceptual comparison between the two error measures and present Figure 1 only to afford a qualitative evaluation of the tradeoff between color reproduction and color continuity.

---

[1] Evaluation should be performed on full color figures available at ftp://white.stanford.edu/users/gigi

4 Weighted Quantization

As mentioned in Section 2, improvement in quantization can be obtained by incorporating human sensitivity considerations. This has been shown to be successful in quantization of still images [11]. In this presentation, human sensitivity to temporal frequency is incorporated into the quantization scheme for image-sequences. Human sensitivity to contrast, chromaticity and color change is greatly reduced as temporal gradients increase [9]. In terms of quantization, objects or regions having high temporal should be assigned fewer resources in the quantization process. Accordingly, we assign a weight to every pixel in the image-sequence which is inversely proportional to the temporal gradient at that pixel location. In the scheme presented here, we combine the temporal-weights and the spatial-weights multiplicatively.

4.1 Time Dependent Weighting

Two time dependent weightings should be considered when quantizing image-sequences:

- *Time-Frame* weighting - When quantizing frames $i - m, \ldots, i, \ldots, i + m$ the pixels of the current frame (i) should be weighted more than pixels of previous and later frames. This weighting should be applied since the pixels of the current frame will be displayed using the color map obtained from the quantization process, whereas the pixels of the previous and later frames are considered only for color continuity. Increasingly smaller weight can be used for distal frames. Figure 7 shows the quantization of a sequence when three frames are quantized per batch ($m = 1$) and both spatial weighting and time frame weighting are used. The time-frame weighting are 1:2:1 for the pixels of frame $i - 1, i$ and $i + 1$, respectively (thus the weights determined from the spatial gradients are doubled for the pixels of frame i).

- *Temporal Frequency* weighting- As mentioned above, at high temporal gradients (when objects or regions are moving at high velocity in the image sequence), sensitivity to color accuracy and to color changes decreases. At low temporal gradients (specifically when regions in the image remain constant over several frames) sensitivity is maximal. Thus appropriate temporal frequency weighting is inversely proportional to the temporal gradients of the sequence. The temporal frequency weights can be evaluated by finding the temporal gradient at each pixel location for each frame of the image sequence by calculating the time-derivative between successive frames. In the synthesized sequence used in the examples, the temporal gradient is zero over the pixel of the foreground patch and is generally much larger over the background textures. Figure 8 shows the quantization of a sequence when three frames are quantized per batch ($m = 1$) and the weighting combines spatial weighting, time-frame weighting and temporal frequency weighting. The time-frame weighting are 1:2:1 for the pixels of frame $i - 1, i$ and $i + 1$, respectively and the temporal frequency weights are inversely proportional to the temporal gradient at each pixel location. The final weight for each pixels is given by the multiplication of the three assigned weightings.

Qualitative evaluation of the space-time weighting scheme for quantization of image sequences is given in the graph of Figure 2. The basic quantization scheme used in all cases is a weighted clustering scheme based on [11] (other quantization schemes such as [4] can also be used by incorporating weights). The error measures previously described for color reproduction and color continuity (Section 3) were applied to the results of quantization of the test sequence using different quantization approaches (numbers correspond to the abscissa in Figure 2):

1. Quantization of each frame separately.
2. Quantization of all frames in a single batch.
3. Every three frames are quantized per batch (variable m described in Section 1 is equal to one). In this scheme only spatial weights are used.
4. Every three frames are quantized per batch, both spatial weights and time-frame weights are used.
5. Every three frames are quantized per batch, spatial weights, time-frame weights and temporal frequency weights are used.

It can be seen that incorporating spatial and temporal weights into the quantization process, reduces both color-reproduction error and color continuity error.

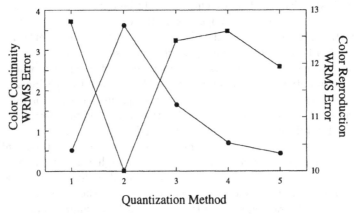

Fig. 2. Evaluation of the color reproduction error (disks) and the color continuity error (squares) for different quantization methods (see text).

5 Conclusion

In this paper, quantization of image sequences was discussed. A new approach was presented where human sensitivity in both spatial and temporal dimensions is considered in the quantization process.

The human sensitivity is incorporated into the quantization process by assigning weights to the pixels of the sequence which are then clustered using a weighted clustering scheme. The weights determine the proportion of resources allocated to each pixel in the aim of allocating fewer resources to those pixels of low human sensitivity.

The weighting scheme used for quantization can be extended to interest and target driven weighting: weights can be assigned to pixels according to the 'importance' or 'interest' of those pixels irrelevant of their spatial and temporal gradients. Some applications may prefer larger weights (and better color reproduction and continuity) to be assigned to specific objects or specific regions of space and time in the image sequence. For example, in image reproduction it is important to create a good reproduction of skin tones.

Finally, instead of considering the weight assigned to each pixel as a multiplication of distinct weights: spatial weights and temporal weights, one may approach the weight determination problem in space and time simultaneously by considering the space-time gradients of pixels in the 3D cube created by stacking the sequence frames. This would be appropriate in view of the notion that human sensitivity is not space time separable [9].

Acknowledgement: I would like to thank Prof. Brian Wandell for fruitful discussions and support.

References

1. J.P. Allebach, T.J. Flohr, P. Hilgenberg, C.B. Atkins, and C.A. Bouman. Model based halftoning via direct binary search. In *Proceedings of the IS&T*, pages 476–481, 1994.
2. C.B. Atkins, T.J. Flohr, P. Hilgenberg, C.A. Bouman, and J.P. Allebach. Model-based color image sequence quantization. In *Proceedings of the SPIE*, volume 2179, pages 310–317, San Jose, 1994.
3. R. Balasubramanian, J.P. Allebach, and C.A. Bouman. Color-image quantization with use of a fast binary splitting technique. *Journal of the Optical Society of America A*, 11(11):2777–2786, 1994.
4. R. Balasubramanian, C.A. Bouman, and J.P. Allebach. Sequential scalar quantization of color images. *Journal of Electronic Imaging*, 3:45–59, 1994.
5. J.L. Furlani, L. McMillan, and L. Westover. Adaptive colormap selection algorithm for motion sequences. In *ACM Multimedia*, pages 341–347, 1994.
6. C. Gotsman. Halftoning of image sequences. *Visual Computer*, 9(5):255–266, 1993.
7. H. Hild and M. Pins. A 3-d error diffusion dither algorithm for half-tone animation on bitmap screens. In *State-of-the-Art in Computer Animation - Proceedings of Computer Animation '89*, pages 181–189, Geneva, 1989.
8. P. Hilgenberg, T.J. Flohr, C.B. Atkins, and C.A. Bouman. Least-squares model-based video halftoning. In *Proceedings of the SPIE*, volume 2179, pages 207–117, San Jose, 1994.
9. D.H. Kelly. Visual processing of moving stimuli. *Journal of the Optical Society of America A*, 2(2):216–225, 1985.
10. J.B. Mulligan and A.J. Ahumada. Principled halftoning based on human visual models. In *Proceedings of the SPIE: Human Vision, Visual Processing, and Digital Display III*, volume 1666, pages 109–120, San Jose, 1992.
11. M.T. Orchard and C.A. Bouman. Color quantization of images. *IEEE Transaction on Signal Processing*, 39(12):2677–2690, 1991.
12. B. Pham and G. Pringle. Color correction for an image sequence. *IEEE Computer Graphics and Applications*, 15(3):38–42, 1995.

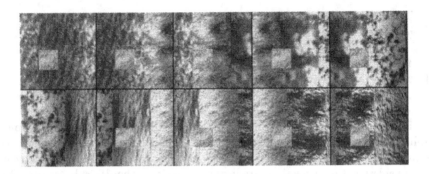

Fig. 3. A synthesized image sequence with 10 frames.[1]

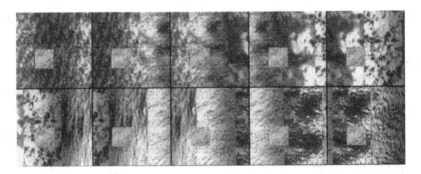

Fig. 4. Image sequence quantization by quantizing each frame separately.

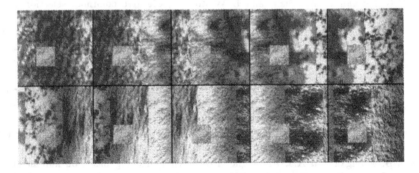

Fig. 5. Image sequence quantization by quantizing all frames in a single batch.

---

[1] Color versions of Figures 3-8 can be obtained at ftp://white.stanford.edu/users/gigi

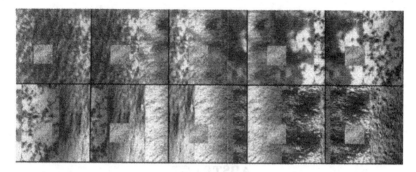

Fig. 6. Image sequence quantization by quantizing 3 frames in every batch.

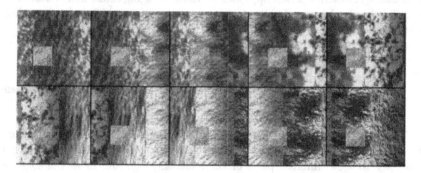

Fig. 7. Image sequence quantization by quantizing 3 frames in every batch and including both spatial weighting and time-frame weighting.

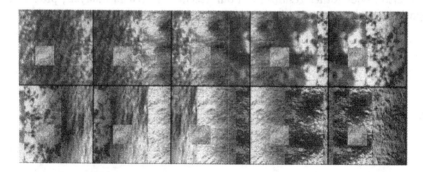

Fig. 8. Image sequence quantization by quantizing 3 frames in every batch and including spatial weighting, time-frame weighting and time-frequency weighting.

A Nonfrontal Imaging Camera

Narendra Ahuja

Beckman Institute, Coordinated Science Laboratory, and
Department of Electrical and Computer Engineering
University of Illinois at Urbana-Champaign

ABSTRACT

This talk will describe a new approach to visual imaging called nonfrontal imaging. This has lead to the design of a new type of camera which has three salient characteristics:

- It can provide panoramic images of upto 360 degree views of a scene.
- Each object is in complete focus regardless of its location.
- The camera also delivers the coordinates of each focusable, visible scene point, in addition to and registered with a sharp image.

The Nonfrontal Imaging Camera eliminates the need for mechanical adjustments required for focusing in the conventional technology. Panning, which is necessary to view different parts of the scene anyway, suffices as the sole mechanical action. This performance is achieved by exploiting a novel combination of optics and imaging geometry. The properties of the camera can be exploited in various ways to achieve novel functionalities. For example, the range estimates can be combined with the focused images to obtain stereo-viewable, focused, panoramic, 3D views of a scene using only one camera as the sensor. The talk will also review other results from our recent research in analysis, processing, synthesis and communication of video sequences.

Modifying and Controlling of Smooth Closed Surfaces

Ma Lizhuang and Peng Qunsheng

State Key Lab. of CAD&CG

Zhejiang University, Hangzhou 310027, P. R. China.

Email: cad_malz@Zunet. ihep. ac. cn

Abstract. An efficient algorithm is presented for modeling closed surfaces with bicubic Bezier patches. Starting from a control polyhedron with four-sided faces (not necessary planar), the algorithm fits the faces of the polyhedron with bicubic Bezier patches which are globally G^1 connected. Methods for controlling and modifying the smooth closed surfaces are provided by adjusting certain weight factors. The proposed method is capable of dealing with control meshes of arbitrary topology and offers a simple and convenient way for modifying the shape of smooth closed surfaces locally and interactively. Experimental results demonstrate the potential of our method.

1 Introduction

The topic of integration of surface modeling and solid modeling has received much attention [2, 16]. One approach to this integration is modeling the boundary of sculptured objects with closed surfaces [18, 19, 27, 29]. However, techniques based on the topology of rectangular mesh such as Bezier and B-spline surface method are not directly applicable in forming smooth closed or complexly connected surfaces [1, 7, 10, 13, 29]. Much work has been done on this research subject, there are, however, many problems yet to be solved [25].

There are mainly three approaches to modeling closed surfaces: recursive subdivision method, method adopting generalized types of surfaces such as generalized B-spline surfaces, Gregory patches etc., and geometric continuous patch complex method.

The method of recursive subdivision has been used extensively in surface modeling. However, the smoothness of the limit surface at extraordinary vertices presents a problem[3, 6, 24].

Generalized B-spline surfaces over n-sided patches were studied initially by Boehm and recently by Loop and Varady [2, 13, 30]. Gregory's technique was used to construct a smooth surface over a mesh of arbitrary topology ensuring the first order of geometric continuity (G^1) at edges [4]. However these methods have a disadvantage that their surface representations do not have a polynomial form, thus are difficult to be incorporated into the current surface modeling systems.

The third approach which is referred to patch complex method which represents closed surface as a union of geometrically continuous polynomial patches [9, 10, 14, 15, 17, 18, 19, 20, 21, 22, 23, 27, 28, 29]. For a control mesh of arbitrary topology, a set of bicubic patches or quartic triangular patches are constructed with G^1 continuity along their common boundary curves. Nevertheless, current methods are applicable to meshes of restricted topology only [10,11,25,27,28,29]. The method proposed by Lee and Majid [11] is valid for two classes of control polyhedron (cf. section 2. 2 in detail). Herron's method mainly treats the case that each vertex of the mesh adjoins uniformly three patches [10]. In the method given by Shirman and Sequin [28], each triangle is subdivided into three ones. The methods proposed by Loop[14,15] take an irregular control mesh as input and refine the mesh by one of the subdivision methods which are similar with the methods in [3,6]. Loop's method is powerful, howervr, it requires much more patches than our method. Although the above methods have been used successfully, only the symmetric solution of constraint equation for shape parameter is obtained in forming a G^1 closed surface (cf. eq. (2. 9)). The problem of modeling general closed surfaces has not yet been solved.

In this paper, we present a uniform method for constructing G^1 closed surface over mesh of arbitrary polyhedron by bicubic Bezier patches. Both symmetric and asymmetric solutions are obtained allowing an arbitrary number of patches to meet with G^1 continuity at a vertex. Free shape parameters with intuitive geometric meaning are available for controlling and modifying the shape of the resultant surface.

2 Closed Surface Modeling with Bezier Patches

The formulation of modeling of closed surfaces can be founded in [1,19]. Two patches $S(u,v)$ and $\bar{S}(\bar{u},\bar{v})$ defined over unit square region Ω, $[0,1]\times[0,1]$, are said to join formally, if their common boundary curve CB is the natural boundary curve of the patches, e. g., $S(0,v) = \bar{S}(0,\bar{v})$, $v=\bar{v}$. In this paper, every pair of adjacent patches is assumed to join formally and all the faces of the control polyhedral mesh are supposed to be quadrilateral.

2. 1 G^1 Conditions at A Vertex

Let $S(u,v)$ and $\bar{S}(\bar{u},\bar{v})$ be two bicubic Bezier patches

$$S(u,v) = \sum_{i=0}^{3}\sum_{j=0}^{3} B_{i3}(u)B_{j3}(v)P_{ij} \tag{2.1}$$

$$\bar{S}(\bar{u},\bar{v}) = \sum_{i=0}^{3}\sum_{j=0}^{3} B_{i3}(\bar{u})B_{j3}(\bar{v})Q_{ij} \tag{2.2}$$

Where $B_{i3}(u)$ and $B_{j3}(v)$ are Bernstein polynomials and, $\{P_{ij}\}$ and $\{Q_{ij}\}$ are sets of control points of S and $\bar{S}$ respectively. Since S and $\bar{S}$ are assumed to join formally, without loss of generality, let CB: $S(0,v) = \bar{S}(0,\bar{v})$, $v = \bar{v}$. Then the following theorem can be obtained (cf. [5,12,17])

Theorem 2. 1.   S and $\bar{S}$ meet with first order geometric continuity along CB (cf. [7, 17,19,22]), denoted by $(S,\bar{S}) \in G^1(CB)$, if there exist real numbers a ($>$ 0), b,c such that

$$T_2 = -aT_0 + bT_1 \tag{2.3}$$

$$V_2 = -aV_1 + (1 + a - \frac{2}{3}b - \frac{1}{3}c)T_1 + \frac{2}{3}b(E + \overline{T}_1) \qquad (2.4)$$

$$\overline{T}_2 = -a\overline{T}_0 + c\,\overline{T}_1 \qquad (2.5)$$

$$\overline{V}_2 = -a\overline{V}_1 + (1 + a - \frac{2}{3}c - \frac{1}{3}b)\overline{T}_1 + \frac{2}{3}c(\overline{E} + T_1) \qquad (2.6)$$

Where

$$T_0 = P_{10} - P_{00}, \quad T_1 = P_{01} - P_{00}, \quad T_2 = Q_{10} - Q_{00},$$
$$V_1 = P_{11} - P_{00}, \quad V_2 = Q_{11} - Q_{00}, \quad E = Q_{03} - Q_{00},$$

and $T_0, T_1, T_2, \overline{V}_1, \overline{V}_2, \overline{E}$ are defined similarly (see Fig. 2. 1).
T_0, T_1 and T_2 are referred to tangent vectors of S, $\overline{S}$ at $P_{00}(=Q_{00})$ respectively.
Similarly, V_1, V_2 are referred to twist vectors of S and $\overline{S}$ respectively. a, b and c are called G^1 parameters with respect to common boundary curve CB.

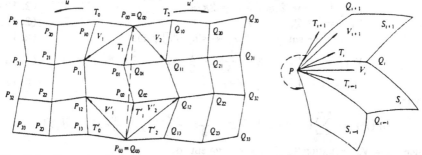

Fig. 2. 1. Control points of two adjacent Bezier patches and their corresponding twist vectors and tangent vectors

Fig. 2. 2. Tangent vectors and twist vectors at a vertex P

According to the given scheme, three real parameters can be assigned to each edges of the polyhedron. However, these parameters is interrelated: parameter a is u-niquely determined by the edge, and parameters b and c are determined by vertex P ($=P_{00}$) and $\overline{P}(=P_{03})$ respectively.

Definition Let $U = \{S_i\}_{i=0}^n (S_n = S_0)$ be a family of patches around a common vertex P of a given polyhedron with quadrilateral faces. P is called a G^1 vertex, if every pair of adjacent patches S_{i-1} and S_i join formally and meet with G^1 along their common edge e_i and, $S_i \cap S_j = P$ ($j \neq i-1, i, i+1$, $i = 1, 2, \ldots, n$). n is then called the degree of P.

Let $U = \{S_i\}_{i=0}^n$ be a family of patches around a G^1 vertex P, T_{i-1}, T_i, V_i be the tangent vectors and twist vector of S_i at P respectively, Q_i be the neighboring vertex of P. Let $E_i = Q_i - P$. By Theorem 2. 1, $(S_{i-1}, S_i) \in G^1(e_i)$, if there exist real numbers $a_i, b_i, c_i (i = 1, 2, \ldots, n)$ such that the following equations hold (Fig. 2. 2):

$$T_{i+1} = -a_i T_{i-1} + b_i T_i \qquad (2.7)$$

$$V_{i+1} = -a_i V_i + (1 + a_i - \frac{2}{3}b_i - \frac{c_i}{3})T_i + \frac{2}{3}b_i(E_i + \overline{T}_i) \qquad (2.8)$$

and similar equations holds at Q_i

$$T_{i2} = -a_i T_{i1} + c_i \overline{T}_i \qquad (2.7')$$

$$V_{i2} = - a_i V_{i1} + (1 + a_i - \frac{2}{3}c_i - \frac{b_i}{3})\overline{T}_i + \frac{2}{3}c_i(- E_i + T_i) \quad (2.\,8')$$

where two vectors T_0 and $T_1 (T_0 \times T_1 \neq 0)$ can be chosen arbitrarily and the others are uniquely determined by them. By the above definition, P is a G^1 vertex when Eqs. (2.7), (2.8), (2.7') and (2.8') hold. It is well known that G^1 parameters a_i, b_i must satisfy the following constraint equation in forming a G^1 vertex (cf. , eg. [9, 19]).

$$\begin{bmatrix} 0 & 1 \\ - a_n & b_n \end{bmatrix} \cdots \begin{bmatrix} 0 & 1 \\ - a_1 & b_1 \end{bmatrix} = \begin{bmatrix} 1 & 0 \\ 0 & 1 \end{bmatrix} \quad (2.9)$$

In practice, for the symmetry of the G^1 vertex a_i and b_i are often set to be constants for a G^1 vertex, then the symmetric solution of (2.9) is as follows (cf. , eg. , [9, 19]).

$$a = 1 , b = 2\cos\delta , \delta = 2\pi/n \quad (2.10)$$
$$T_{j+1} = - T_{j-1} + bT_j \quad (2.11)$$
$$T_j = [- \sin(j-1)\delta T_0 + \sin j\delta T_1] /\sin\delta \quad (2.12)$$
$$V_{j+1} = - V_j + (2 - \frac{2}{3}b - \frac{1}{3}c_i)T_j + \frac{2}{3}b(E_j + \overline{T}_j) \quad (2.13)$$
$$V_n = (- 1)^n V_0 + W(P) \quad (2.14)$$

where

$$W(P) = \sum_{j=0}^{n-1}(- 1)^{n-j+1}[(2 - \frac{2}{3}b - \frac{c_j}{3})T_j + \frac{2}{3}b(E_j + \overline{T}_j)]$$

Since $V_n = V_0$, equation (2.14) is equivalent to

$$\begin{cases} V_0 = W/2, & \text{when n is odd} \\ W = 0 & \text{when n is even} \end{cases} \quad (2.15)$$

Generally, when a_i and b_i are variables, the following equation can be obtained similarly [17, 19]

$$W(P) = \sum_{i=0}^{n-1}(- 1)^{n-i+1}[(1 + a_i - \frac{2}{3}b_i - \frac{c_j}{3})T_i + \frac{2}{3}b_i(Q_i - P + \overline{T}_i)]$$

$$(2.16)$$

When n is odd, twist vector V_0 is determined by Eq. (2.16), otherwise V_0 can be chosen arbitrary, however, $W(P) = 0$ must be satisfied. This condition is termed as " compatibility condition" at vertex P. In the following sections, $a \equiv 1$ for all edges. b and c are determined uniquely with the respective vertices of the control polyhedron. Since b and c can vary with vertices, it is emphasized to write $b(P)$, a real value function of vertices in stead of b and c.

2.2 Symmetric Solution of Smooth Closed Surface

In this section, a symmetric solution is presented for modeling closed surface since it is relatively simple and easy for handling a number of special cases, and then a more complicated solution is developed which is applicable for all cases.

Description of Symmetric Solution

Let Δ be a polyhedron with four-sided faces, $V(\Delta)$ be the set of vertices of Δ. If

Eqs. (2.7) and (2.8) hold for arbitrary $P \in V(\Delta)$, then it is clear that Eqs. (2. 7') and (2.8') holds true everywhere, and hence by Theorem 2.1 all vertices of the polyhedron are of G^1 vertex and the union of the corresponding patches constitute a smooth closed surfaces. In our method, Eqs. (2.7) and (2.8) are forced to hold at all vertices simultaneously in forming smooth closed surfaces. For $P \in V(\Delta)$, let $n(P)$ denote the number of edges incident to P. The symmetric solution of (2.9) is used [28,29] with

$$\begin{cases} a_i = a(P) = 1 \\ b_i = b(P) = 2\cos(2\pi/n(P)), \quad i = 0,1,\ldots,n(P) \end{cases} \tag{2.17}$$

The compatibility conditions at even vertices can be simplified as (cf. [19]):

$$W(P) = \frac{1}{3}\sum_{j=0}^{n-1}(-1)^{j+1}[-c_jT_j + 2b(Q_j + T_j)] = 0 \tag{2.18}$$

Let EQ be the set of equations of compatibility conditions, where

$$EQ = \{ W(P) = 0 \mid P \in V(\Delta) \text{ and P be an even vertex } \} \tag{2.19}$$

Thus position vectors, which are not necessary to interpolate the respective vectors, should satisfy EQ.

Discussion on the Solution

If EQ is an empty set then by Theorem 2.1 a symmetric solution of smooth closed surface can be obtained simply for this mesh [11,12,28,29]. By analyzing Eqs. (2.15) and (2.18), we can easily treat the following simple cases.

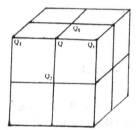
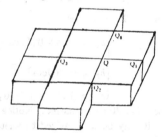

Fig. 2.3.a example of case 4   Fig. 2.3.b example of case 4

1) All vertices are of odd degree [27,28,29].
2) All vertices are of degree 4 [11,28,29].
3) Every vertex is of degree less than or equal to four and there is at most one vertex of degree 4 between each pair of odd vertices [11,27,28].
4) Every vertex is of either odd degree or degree 4. For every vertex P of degree 4 each pair of its neighboring vertices Q_0 and Q_2, Q_1 and Q_3 are of the same degree, where Q_0, Q_1, Q_2 and Q_3 are numerated around P in clockwise order as in Fig. 2. 3. (Note that other methods can not be applied to the polyhedral topology in Fig. 2.3.b).

When EQ is nonempty, it should be solved efficiently, an accelerated iterative method for solving EQ can be devised, the detailed discussion is omitted here (cf. [19]).

2.3 Asymmetric Solution

It has been pointed out that symmetric solution may fail in a number of cases (cf. [17,19]). Thus in this sections an asymmetric solution is proposed which can be applied for general cases.

Asymmetric Solution of Eq. (2.9)

When $n(v)$ is even, the symmetric condition is extended to asymmetric one. Let

$$\begin{cases} a_{2i-1} = a_1, & b_{2i-1} = b_1 \\ a_{2i} = a_2, & b_{2i} = b_2, \end{cases} \quad i = 1, 2, \ldots, n/2$$

If $n(P) \neq 4$, the following matrix equation can be obtained similarly to Eq. (2.9)

$$(G_2 G_1)^k = I, \quad k = n/2 \tag{2.20}$$

$$G_i = \begin{bmatrix} 0 & 1 \\ -a_i & b_i \end{bmatrix}, \quad i = 1, 2 \tag{2.21}$$

Especially, if $n = 4$, then G_1, G_2, G_3 and G_4 are set respectively as

$$G_1 = \begin{bmatrix} 0 & 1 \\ -1 & \lambda \end{bmatrix}, \quad G_2 = \begin{bmatrix} 0 & 1 \\ -1 & 0 \end{bmatrix},$$

$$G_3 = \begin{bmatrix} 0 & 1 \\ -1 & -\lambda \end{bmatrix}, \quad G_4 = \begin{bmatrix} 0 & 1 \\ -1 & 0 \end{bmatrix},$$

$$G_4 G_3 G_2 G_1 = I \tag{2.22}$$

When $n = 2k > 4$, let

$$\begin{cases} b_{2j} = \lambda \neq 0, 2\cos \dfrac{2\pi}{n} & j = 0, 1, 2, \ldots, k-1 \\ b_{2j-1} = (4\cos^2 \dfrac{2\pi}{n})/\lambda, & j = 1, \ldots, k \\ a_j = 1, & j = 0, 1, \ldots, 2k \end{cases} \tag{2.23}$$

then Eq. (2.20) is satisfied. Notice that n is the degree of P and λ can vary with vertex. it may be emphasized to write $\lambda(P)$, a real value function of vertex P, instead of λ.

Compatibility Condition at An Even Vertex

Let P be a vertex of the given polyhedron with degree n. From the compatibility condition, position vectors Q_1 and Q_3 must satisfy the following equation if $n=4$:

$$Q_1 - Q_3 = \frac{1}{2\lambda(P)} (10\lambda(p) - c_3 + c_1)T_1 + \overline{T}_3 - \overline{T}_1 \tag{2.24}$$

where $\lambda(P) \neq 0$. When $n = 2k > 4$, the compatibility conditions can be represented simply as

$$\sum_{i=0}^{k-1} (2b_1 Q_{2i} - 2b_2 Q_{2i+1}) = D(P) \tag{2.25}$$

where

$$D(P) = 2k(b_1 - b_2)P + \sum_{i=0}^{k-1} (c_{2i}T_{2i} - c_{2i+1}T_{2i+1} + 2b_2\overline{T}_{2i+1} - 2b_1\overline{T}_{2i})$$

Therefore, progressive refinements using iterative method can proceed in either case by replacing G^1 parameters under conditions (2.22) and (2.23)(cf. [17,19]).

3 The Computational Details of The Algorithm

In summary, we present the following procedures to form closed surface.

Step 1   Establishing the polyhedral mesh of control points which defines the connection relation of bicubic patches. Subdividing the polyhedron such that its faces are all quadrilaterals if necessary.

Step 2   Defining a pair of tangent vectors T_0 and $T_1(T_0 \times T_1 \neq 0)$ at each vertex P or by default they are determined as follows (see Fig. 3.1). Let $N(P)$ be the average normal:

$$N(P) = \sum_{i=1}^{n}(Q_i - P) \times (Q_{i+1} - P)/ \| \sum_{i=1}^{n}(Q_i - P) \times (Q_{i+1} - P) \|$$

(3.1)

The angle between T_0 and T_1 is set to be $\delta = 2\pi/n$ and

$$T_0 = w_0[Q_0 - P - (Q_0 - P) \cdot N]/ \| Q_0 - P - (Q_0 - P) \cdot N \| /3 \quad (3.2)$$
$$T_1 = w_1(\cos\delta T_0/ \| T_0 \| + \sin\delta N \times T_0/ \| N \times T_0 \|)/3 \quad (3.3)$$

Where w_0 and w_1 are length of T_0 and T_1 respectively, $Q_0, Q_1, \ldots, Q_n$ are neighboring vertices which are arranged in counter-clockwise order.

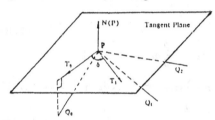 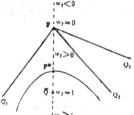

Fig. 3.1 The geometric meaning of T_0 and T_1 Fig. 3.2 Bulge controlling with w_2

Step 3   To control the bulge effect, we set for each vertex P:

$$P^* = (1 - w_2)P + w_2 \frac{1}{n}\sum_{i=1}^{n}Q_i(P) \quad (3.4)$$

where Q_i are neighboring vertices of P. (cf. Fig. 3.2 where $\bar{Q} = \sum_{i=1}^{n}Q_i(P)$).

Step 4   For each G^1 vertex P, let $U = \{ S_i \}$ be the patches around P, symmetric G^1 parameters are chosen initially as the solution of Eq. (2.9): $a_i = -1$, $b_i = b$.

Step 4.a: computing tangent vectors at all vertices

$$T_{j+1} = - T_{j-1} + bT_j, \quad j = 1, \ldots, n - 2 \quad (3.5)$$

where $b = 2\cos\delta$. If EQ is an empty set then go to step 5, otherwise,

Step 4.b: For all vertices of degree 4 related with EQ, we set asymmetric G^1 parameters satisfying condition (2.22) instead and

$$T_2 = - T_0 + \lambda T_1, \quad T_3 = - T_1$$

We can apply progressive refinements to solve EQ(cf. [17,19])

Step 4.c: For all vertices related in EQ with degree greater than four, G^1 parameters are determined with Eq. (2.23). The related tangent vectors are given with

$$
\begin{cases}
T_{2j} = - \lambda(\sin 2j\delta + \sin(2j - 2)\delta)T_0 + 4\cos^2\delta\sin 2j\delta T_1 \\
T_{2j+1} = - \lambda^2\sin 2j\delta T_0 + \lambda(\sin 2j\delta + \sin(2j + 2)\delta)T_1 \\
j = 1, 2, \ldots, \varkappa/2 - 1
\end{cases}
\tag{3.6}
$$

Progressive refinements can also be used to solve EQ.

Step 5   Computing twist vectors at each vertex .

If $n(P)$ is odd then $V_0 = W/2$ which is given by (2.15) and,

$$
V_{j+1} = - V_j + (2 - \frac{2}{3}b - \frac{1}{3}c_i)T_j + \frac{2}{3}b(E_j + \overline{T}_j), \quad j = 1, \ldots, \varkappa - 1
\tag{3.7}
$$

If $n(P)$ is even V_0 can be arbitrary, it is a good choice to set

$$
\begin{cases}
V_0 = w_3(T_{-1} + T_0) \\
w_3 \approx (2 - (b_1 + b_2)/3)/((b_1 + b_2)/2 + 2)
\end{cases}
\tag{3.8}
$$

If P is not related in EQ, the other twist vectors are determined by Eq. (3.7), otherwise from section 2.3,

$$
\begin{cases}
V_1 = - V_0 + (2 - \frac{1}{3}c_0)T_0 \\
V_2 = - V_1 + (2 - \frac{2}{3}\lambda - \frac{1}{3}c_1)T_1 + \frac{2}{3}\lambda(Q_1 - P + \overline{T}_1), \quad \text{when } \varkappa = 4 \\
V_3 = - V_2 + (2 - \frac{1}{3}c_2)T_2
\end{cases}
\tag{3.9}
$$

$$
\begin{cases}
V_{2i+1} = - V_{2i} + (2 - \frac{2}{3}b_1 - \frac{1}{3}c_{2i})T_{2i} + \frac{2}{3}b_1(Q_{2i} + \overline{T}_{2i})] \\
V_{2i+2} = - V_{2i+1} + (2 - \frac{2}{3}b_2 - \frac{1}{3}c_{2i+1})T_{2i+1} + \frac{2}{3}b_2(Q_{2i+1} + \overline{T}_{2i+1})], \\
\quad \text{when } \varkappa = 2k > 4, \quad i = 0, 1, \ldots, k - 1
\end{cases}
\tag{3.10}
$$

Step 6   Constructing the Bezier patches according to the corresponding position vectors , tangent vectors and twist vectors which are identified with steps 1 to 5.

Step 7   Displaying the results.

It is clear that every vertex becomes a G^1 vertex under the above conditions.

Theorem 2.2.   With the above seven steps, if the solution of EQ is nonempty, then a smooth closed surface can be generated which is a union of geometrically continuous bicubic Bezier patches.

Proof. The algorithm implies a proof of the theorem. Since G^1 parameters are all chosen to satisfy Eq. (2.9) and thus are well-chosen. From steps 4.a, 4.b and 4.c, tangent vectors of each pair of adjacent Bezier patches satisfy Eq. (2.3). If EQ is empty, then position vectors at all vertices of $V(\Delta)$ can be given arbitrarily. Otherwise, the related position vectors are solved to satisfy EQ. Therefore compatibility condition can be satisfied. By step 5, the twist vectors of each pair of adjacent Bezier patches satisfy Eq. (2.4). Combining Step 4 and step 5 and, noticing that the sets of tangent vectors, position vectors and twist vectors are determined in such an order:

{tangent vectors }   ⇒   {position vectors}   ⇒   {twist vectors}

From the algorithm, it is clear that the latter does not affect the former. Thus, conditions (2. 7), (2. 8) and compatibility condition can be satisfied at all vertices of V (Δ) simultaneously Therefore, by Theorem 2. 1, all vertices are of G^1 vertex and the resultant surfaces is G^1 closed.

4. Shape Controlling and Modifying

Shape modification is important in practical shape design. This section briefly summaries the shape modification of the resultant closed surface. Note that w_i (i=0,1, 2,3) are shape parameters which have intuitive geometric meanings and they can vary with G^1 vertex. If we hopes to change the shape of the resultant surface, we can simply modify the shape parameters w_i(i=0,1,2,3) interactively until a desired smooth surface is obtained . The following table gives a list of shape parameters and distinguishes which parameters are free or not.

degree \ shape parameter	w_0	w_1	w_2	w_3	λ
n is odd	Yes	Yes	Yes	No	No
n = 4	Yes	Yes	Yes	Yes	Yes
n = 2k > 4	Yes	Yes	Yes	Yes	Yes

Table 1.

a) w_0 and w_1 are the lengths of tangent vectors T_0 and T_1 at vertex P respectively. They affect the flatness of the closed surfaces near the vertex P. When the values of w_0 and w_1 are increased/decreased the closed surfaces becomes flatter/ sharper near vertex P , cf. Fig. 5. 1. With our experience, w_0 and w_1 should satisfy the following constraint so that a well-shaped surface can be obtained :
$$0. 5 < w_0, w_1 < 1. 5$$

b) w_2 control the bulge of the surface at vertex P. When the value of w_2 is increased/decreased , the bulge of closed surface at P will be changed accordingly, If we want to interpolate position vector at P , we set w_2= 0(cf. Figs. 3. 2 and 5. 2)

c) λ determine the angles between tangent vectors T_0 and T_1 and therefore control the "twist degree" of the adjacent patches at vertex P. Since the angle between T_0 and T_1 is in a domain (-π, π), it is recommended that λ should satisfy the following condition :
$$- 2 < \lambda < 2$$

d) w_3 determine the length of the twist vector at P. It should be mentioned that with the proposed algorithm tangent vectors T_0 and T_1 can be chosen arbitrarily within the tangent plane given at each G^1 vertex, and the position vector can be given arbitrarily if it is not related with EQ, otherwise it is determined by other quantities. The recommend value of w_3 is given by Eq. (3. 8).

5 Conclusions

A unified approach to forming smooth closed surface over a control polyhedron with four-sided faces using the bicubic Bezier patches has been presented. The proposed method are consistent with the ones given by other authors [11,14,15,27,28,29]. When a symmetric solution exists for the control polyhedron given, the proposed method obtains certainly this solution , otherwise asymmetric solution will be given according to the selected shape parameters as in table 1. The proposed method is useful since the resultant surface is represented by the popular bicubic Bezier patches which are commonly used in current CAD systems. The corresponding algorithm has been coded in the C Programming Language and implemented on Sun Sparc and HP work stations. Examples are illustrated with color pictures for the controling of smooth closed surfaces (cf. Figs. 5. 1~5. 5). In these examples, w_{0i}, w_{1i}, and w_{2i} denote the corresponding values of w_0, w_1 and w_2 at the i-th G^1 vertex and $\lambda \equiv 0$. 5 for all even degree vertices which are related in EQ.

Acknowledgements

This project is supported by National Natural Science Foundation of China and HUO Ying-Dong Foundation for Excellent Young Teachers. We are grateful to the members of State Key Lab. of CAD & CG at Zhejiang University for their helps. Special thanks due to Ms Xu Xiaoyan, Mr. Yin Jiangguo and Ms Hu Ming for their helps in preparing this paper.

References

1. Barnhill,R. E. , Surfaces in CAGD: A survey with new results, CAGD 2, 1— 17 (1985)
2. Boehm,W. , Farin,G. and Kahmann,J. , A survey of curve and surface method in CAGD 1(1), 1—60 (1984)
3. Catmull,E. E. and Clark,J. , Recursively generated B—spline surfaces on arbitrary topological meshes, CAD 10, 350—355 (1978)
4. Chiyokura,H. and Kimura,F. , Design of solids with free form surfaces, Computer Graphics 17(3), 289—298,SIGGRAPH'83
5. DeRose,T. D. ,Necessary and sufficient conditions for tangent plane continuity of Bezier surfaces, CAGD 7, 165—177 (1990)
6. Doo,D. , A subdivision algorithm for smoothing down irregular shaped polyhedra, Proc, Conf. Interactive Technique in CAD, 156 — 165, IEEE Computer Society 78, CH1289—86(1978)
7. Farin,G. , Bezier polynomials over triangles and the construction of piecewise C^1 polynomials, Department of Mathematics TR/91, Brunel University , Uxbridge, England(1980)
8. Forrest, A. R. , Freeform surfaces and solid modeling, SIGGRAPH Freeform curves and surfaces tutorial notes, SIGGRAPH'84
9. Hahn,M. J. , Geometric continuous patch complexes, CAGD 6,55—67 (1989)

10. Herron G. J. , Smooth closed surfaces with discrete triangular interpolators, CAGD 2, 297—306 (1985)

11. Lee,S. L. and Majid,A. A. , Closed smooth piecewise bicubic surfaces, ACM Transactions on Graphics 10(4), 342—365(1991)

12. Liang,Youdong, Ye,Xiuzi and Fang,Xiaofen, G^1 smoothing solid objects by bicubic Bezier patches, Eurographics' 88, 343—355 (1988)

13. Loop, C. and DeRose,T. , Generalized B—spline surfaces of arbitrary topology, Computer Graphics 24(4), SIGGRAPH'90

14. Loop, C. , A G^1 triangular spline surface of arbitrary topological type, CAGD 11, 303—330 (1993)

15. Loop, C. , Smooth closed surfaces over irregular meshes, SIGGRAPH'94, 303 —510 (1994)

16. Ma Lizhuang, Dong Jingxiang and He Zhijun, Advanced curve and surface design in a CAD system using STEP, IEEE TENCON'93, Beijing (1993)

17. Ma,Lizhuang, Theory of Geometric Continuity and Its Applications, Zhejiang University, Ph. D. Thesis(1991)

18. Ma Lizhuang, Peng Qunsheng and He Zhijun, Conditions of G^n continuity between surfaces, Science in China 37(3), 365—378 (1994)

19. Ma Lizhuang & Peng Qunsheng, Modeling of smooth closed surfaces with Bezier patches, Progress in Natural Science 3(3),253—269 (1993).

20. Ma Lizhuang, Liang Youdong and Peng Qunsheng, Equidistant smoothing of polyhedra with arbitrary topologies, EUROGRAPHICS'92, England (1992)

21. Ma Lizhuang, Peng Qunsheng, Smoothing of free-form surfaces with Bezier patches, CAGD 12, 231—249 (1995)

22. Ma Lizhuang, Peng Qunsheng, Recursive G^k transformations between adjacent Bezier surfaces, CAGD 12 (1995)

23. Ma Lizhuang, Explicit G^n transformations and G^n conditions between Bezier surfaces, Journal of Physics Science, Baltzer Publisher (1995)

24. Nasri,A. H. , Polyhedral subdivision methods for free-form surfaces, ACM Transaction on Graphics 6(1), 28—73 (1987)

25. Peters,J. , Local smooth surfaces interpolation; A classification, CAGD 7,191 —195 (1990)

26. Preparata,F. P. and Shamos,M. I. , Computational Geometry—An Introduction, Springer-Verlag (1985)

27. Sarraga,R. F. , G^1 interpolation of generally unrestricted bicubic Bezier curves, CAGD 4,pp23—29 (1987)

28. Shirman,L. A. and Sequin,C. H. , Local surface interpolation with Bezier patches, CAGD 4, 279—295 (1987)

29. Van Wijk,J. J. , Bicubic patches for approximating non-rectangular control-point meshes, CAGD 3(1), 1—13 (1986)

30. Varady,T. , Overlap patches : a new scheme for interpolating curve networks with n-sides regions, CAGD 8, 7—27 (1991)

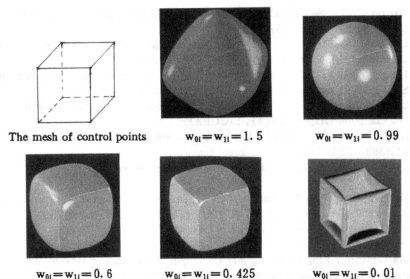

The mesh of control points $w_{0i}=w_{1i}=1.5$ $w_{0i}=w_{1i}=0.99$

$w_{0i}=w_{1i}=0.6$ $w_{0i}=w_{1i}=0.425$ $w_{0i}=w_{1i}=0.01$

Fig. 5.1 The mesh of control points and shaded pictures with respect to different values of shape parameters w_0 and w_1. The other shape parameters are: $w_{2i}=0.1$, $0 \leqslant i < 8$. As the lengths of the tangent vectors at corners decrease in an order of 1. 5, 0. 99, 0. 6, 0. 425, 0. 01, the closed surface becomes sharper and sharper near corners.

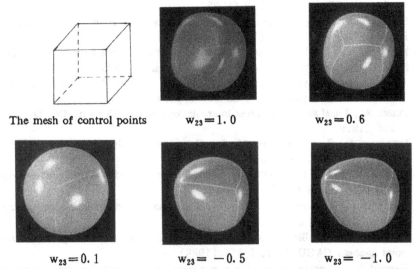

The mesh of control points $w_{23}=1.0$ $w_{23}=0.6$

$w_{23}=0.1$ $w_{23}=-0.5$ $w_{23}=-1.0$

Fig. 5.2 The mesh of control points and shaded pictures with respect to different values of shape parameters w_2. The other shape parameters are: $w_{0i}=w_{1i}=0.99$, $0 \leqslant i < 8$; $w_{2i}=0.1, i \neq 3, 0 \leqslant i < 8$. As the shape parameter w_2 at corners P_2 decreases in an order of 1. 0, 0. 6, 0. 1, $-0.5, -1.0$, the shape of the closed surface at P_2 varies from concave to convex.

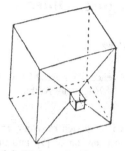

Fig. 5. 3 (a) The mesh of control points.   (b) Shaded pictures
Shape parameters: $w_{0i} = w_{1i} = 1. 0$, $w_{2i} = 0. 2$, $0 \leqslant i < 16$

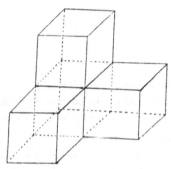
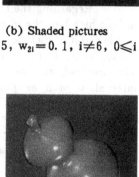

Fig. 5. 4 (a) The mesh of control points.   (b) Shaded pictures
Shape parameters: $w_{0i} = w_{1i} = 0. 9$, $0 \leqslant i < 20$; $w_{26} = 0. 5$, $w_{2i} = 0. 1$, $i \neq 6$, $0 \leqslant i < 20$

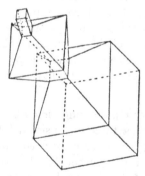
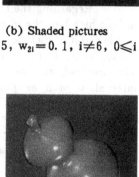

Fig. 5. 5 (a) The mesh of control points.   (b) Shaded pictures
Shape parameters: $w_{0i} = w_{1i} = 1. 0$, $0 \leqslant i < 24$; $w_{2i} = 0. 2$, $0 \leqslant i < 8$ $w_{2i} = 0. 1$, $8 \leqslant i < 24$

Designing of 3D Rectangular Objects

Muhammad Sarfraz

Department of Information and Computer Science, King Fahd University
of Petroleum and Minerals, Dhahran 31261, Saudi Arabia.

Abstract. This paper reviews the curve method [6] which recovers, as special cases, the two spline methods: one with interval tension in [5]: and the other with point tension in [4]. This curve scheme has been generalized for the designing of surfaces i.e. 3D objects (open or closed) can be captured, together with the facility of local as well as global point and interval shape controls, with any rectangular domain.

1 Introduction

Interactively designing the curves and surfaces is a hot topic of Computer Graphics. Particularly, in the area of Computer Aided Design (CAD), many authors have worked in the last decade and still a lot is needed to be done. For the details, the reader is referred to ([1]-[7]).

Regarding the curve designing, one interpolatory scheme was described in [5] which had the interval tension control facility in its description. Later on another spline method was introduced in [4] which had the facility of point tension control. The two methods were merged into another new method [6]. This method, reviewed here in Section 2, provides not only the facility of interval as well as point tension in one rational spline presentation, but recovers the above mentioned two spline methods as its special cases. This new rational spline method covers all the features of the weighted ν-spline method [3]. On top of that, it gives comparatively better controlled shape effects both locally and globally as well as a higher C^2 continuity is achieved in comparison with GC^2.

The solution to the problem of representing smooth rectangular surfaces, for the designing purposes of distinct three dimensional (3D) objects, has been considered, in Section 3, utilizing the above mentioned curve scheme. Similar to that in the previous paper of the author [4], the objective of designing the 3D objects with the facility of shape control, in a desired region, has been obtained by generalizing the blending-function method of Gordon [7]. The shape control achieved here is in a much more well controlled and broader sense than it was in [1] and [2]. A practical method that attempts to compute this surface method is presented. This method does not exactly compute the required C^2 theoretical formulation and so there is a slight loss of C^2 continuity which is not that important for the practical point of view. The shape effects of the shape parameters are demonstrated in Subsection 3.4 by pictorial examples.

2 Review of Curve Scheme

This section reviews the curve method in [6] with point and interval tension, for the designing of curves in interpolatory form, to provide a basis for the designing of 3D rectangular objects with local shape control. This curve method is such that the interpolatory methods studied independently in [4] and [5] can be recovered as special cases. Following subsection introduces the piecewise C^1 rational cubic interpolant, makes its analysis, and discusses its geometreic behaviour. These pieces of rational cubics are then stitched together with an amount of C^2 continuity to produce a smooth spline.

2.1 The Rational Spline Interpolation

Let $F_i \in \mathbb{R}^N$, $i = 0 , \dots , n$ be a given set of data points, $t_0 < t_1 < \dots < t_n$ be the knot spacing, $D_i \in \mathbb{R}^N$ denote the first derivative values defined at the knots and $\theta(t) \equiv (t - t_i)/h_i$ where $h_i = t_{i+1} - t_i$. We consider the C^1 piecewise rational cubic Hermite function defined by:

(2.1) $\qquad P\big|_{[t_i,\ t_{i+1}]}(t) = N(\theta)/D(\theta)$

where

$$N(\theta) = (1-\theta)^3 \alpha_{i+1} F_i + \theta(1-\theta)^2 (1+\gamma_i \alpha_i)\alpha_{i+1} V_i +$$
$$\theta^2(1-\theta)\alpha_i(1+\gamma_i \alpha_{i+1}) W_i + \theta^3 \alpha_i F_{i+1}$$

$$D(\theta) = (1-\theta)^2 \alpha_{i+1} + \gamma_i \alpha_i \alpha_{i+1}\theta(1-\theta) + \theta^2 \alpha_i,$$

(2.2) $\qquad V_i = F_i + \dfrac{1}{1 + \gamma_i \alpha_i} h_i D_i\ , \quad W_i = F_{i+1} - \dfrac{1}{1 + \gamma_i \alpha_{i+1}} h_i D_{i+1}$

We shall use this to generate interpolatory parametric curves which control the shape at the data points. It can be noted that $P(t)$ interpolates the points F_i and the tangent vectors D_i at the knots t_i.

The scalar weights in the numerator of (2.1) are those given by degree raising the denominator to cubic form, since

(2.3) $\qquad (1-\theta)^2 \alpha_{i+1} + \gamma_i \alpha_i \alpha_{i+1}\theta(1-\theta) + \theta^2 \alpha_i$

$$= (1-\theta)^3 \alpha_{i+1} + \theta(1-\theta)^2(1+\gamma_i\alpha_i)\alpha_{i+1} + \theta^2(1-\theta)\alpha_i(1+\gamma_i\alpha_{i+1}) + \theta^3 \alpha_i$$

It follows that if

(2.4) $\qquad \alpha_i , \alpha_{i+1} \geq 0$ and $\gamma_i \geq \alpha_i , \alpha_{i+1}$,

then, from the Bernstein-Bézier theory, the rational curve segment $P\big|_{[t_i,t_{i+1}]}$ lies in the convex hull of the control points $\{F_i, V_i, W_i, F_{i+1}\}$ and its variation diminishing property holds with respect to the *control polygon* joining these points. The following cases can easily be seen:
(a)   The case

(2.5) $\alpha_i = 1 = \alpha_{i+1}$ and $\gamma_i = 2$

recovers the standard cubic interpolant.

(b)   The case

(2.6) $\alpha_i = 1 = \alpha_{i+1}$ and $\gamma_i = r_i$ - 1

recovers the rational cubic interpolant with interval tension in [5].

(c)   The case

(4.7) $\gamma_i = 2$

recovers the rational cubic interpolant spline with point tension in [4].

Let us now describe a parametric C^2 rational cubic spline representation which has interval and point tension weights to control the shape of the curve. The introduction of weights in the description of rational functions gives a powerful tool for manipulating the shape of the curve within one simple representation.

Let $\Delta_i = (F_{i+1} - F_i)/h_i$, then the C^2 constraints:

(2.8) $P^{(2)}(t_{i+}) = P^{(2)}(t_{i-})$, $\quad i = 1, \ldots, n-1,$

give the triagonal system of *consistency equations*:

(2.9) $\dfrac{h_i}{\alpha_{i-1}} D_{i-1} + \left(h_i \gamma_{i-1} + h_{i-1} \gamma_i \right) D_i + \dfrac{h_{i-1}}{\alpha_{i+1}} D_{i+1}$

$$= h_i(\gamma_{i-1} + 1/\alpha_{i-1}) \, \Delta_{i-1} + h_{i-1}(\gamma_i + 1/\alpha_{i+1}) \, \Delta_i, \quad i = 0, \ldots, n-1.$$

Suppose that

(2.10) $\gamma_i > 1/\alpha_i, 1/\alpha_{i+1}, \quad i = 1, \ldots, n-1,$

and assume that the end conditions D_0 and D_n are also given (the well known end conditions, for example the periodic end conditions in case of parametric closed curve, can be applied). Then (2.9) defines a diagonally dominant tridiagonal system of linear equations in the unknowns D_i, $i = 1, \ldots, n-1$. Thus (2.10) provides a sufficient condition for the existence of a unique, easily computable solution.

There is no need to develop a separate shape control analysis for this new curve method as the interval and point tension properties from [4] and [5] follow straightaway. The shape behaviour of the rational cubic spline interpolant is illustrated by the simple examples for a data set in $\mathbf{R}^2$ in Figure 1. The first curve (from left to right) is the cubic spline curve (default spline curve). Second and third curves show the point and interval shape effects when $\alpha_i = 50$ and $\gamma_i = 50$ in the effected areas of the curves respectively.

2.2   Algorithm for Curve Manipulation

For practical purposes, the choice of α_i's and γ_i's will be considered as $0 \leq \alpha_i \leq 1$ and $1 < \gamma_i < \infty$. The choice of parameters $\alpha_i = 1$, $\gamma_i = 2$, $\forall i$, will be considered as default choice. This choice reduces the rational cubic into the cubic polynomial form.

To display the graph of the curve method efficiently, it should be noted that in the ith interval, the curve presentation can be simplified as follows:

(2.11) $P(t) = F_i(1 - \theta) + F_{i+1}\theta$
$$+ [(1 - \theta)(D_i - \Delta_i)\alpha_i + \theta(\Delta_i - D_{i+1})\alpha_{i+1}]h_i\theta(1 - \theta)/D_i(\theta)$$

This form is much more economical computationally. This form of rational cubic also reduces to the linear form:

(2.12) $P(t) = F_i(1 - \theta) + F_{i+1}\theta$,

when either $(\alpha_i, \alpha_{i+1}) \rightarrow (\infty, \infty)$ or $\gamma_i \rightarrow \infty$.

In case of point tension, a user can note that the rational part in (2.11) reduces to a rational quadratic with quadratic numerator and linear denominator. This is very useful to economize further calculations.

The evaluations of the derivative parameters, constrained in system of equations (2.9), is suggested through *LU-decomposition* algorithm.

3   Rectangular Surfaces with Shape Control

Firstly, we describe surface representation that uses rational spline curves and this is the tensor product representation which is mentioned for the sake of notation and background, as it is not very useful regarding shape control. Secondly, we shall generalize the idea of blending-function method of bicubic spline surfaces of Gordon [7].

3.1   Tensor Product Surfaces

This subsection reviews the tensor product rational spline surfaces to make the basis of the theory constructed in the next subsection. We can represent tensor product surface as

(3.1) $P(\tilde{t}, t) = \sum\limits_{i=0}^{m} \sum\limits_{j=0}^{n} F_{i,j} \tilde{A}_i(\tilde{t}) A_j(t), \quad \tilde{t}_0 \leq \tilde{t} \leq \tilde{t}_m, \quad t_0 \leq t \leq t_n$,

which presents the rational bicubic interpolating spline with shape parameters

(3.2) $\tilde{\gamma}_i \geq 2, \ i = 0,...,m-1, \ \tilde{\alpha}_i > 0, \ i = 0,...,m; \ \gamma_j \geq 2, \ j = 0,...,n-1,$
$\alpha_j > 0, \ j = 0,...,n.$

Here

(3.3) $F_{i,j} \in \mathbb{R}^3, \quad i = 0,...,m, \quad j = 0,...,n,$

are the data points and $\tilde{A}_i, \ i = 0,...,m$ and $A_j, \ j = 0,...,n$ are the cardinal splines for the rational cubic splines of Section 2. In particular

(3.4) $\tilde{A}_j(\tilde{t}_i) = \delta_{i,j}, \ i,j = 0,...,m, \quad A_i(t_j) = \delta_{i,j}, \ i,j = 0,...,n.$

This tensor product is such that, for a fixed value of one of the parameters, say t, the trace curves, as functions of $\tilde{t}$, are geometric rational cubic splines. In particular, let $f_j(\tilde{t})$ denote the rational cubic spline at $t = t_j$. In C^1 Hermite form, $\tilde{t} \in [\tilde{t}_i, \tilde{t}_{i+1}), \quad i = 0,...,m-1$, it can be represented as:

(3.5) $P(\tilde{t}, t_j) = f_j(\tilde{t})$,

which is the rational cubic of the form (2.1) in parameter $\tilde{t}$ with shape parameters $\tilde{\gamma}_i$, $\tilde{\alpha}_i$, $\tilde{\alpha}_{i+1}$ and the derivative parameters $F_{i,j}^{\tilde{t}}$ which are computed by the algorithm in Subsection 2.5. Similarly, if $\bar{f}_j(\tilde{t})$ denotes the rational cubic spline at $\tilde{t} = \tilde{t}_i$, then it can be represented, for $t \in [t_j, t_{j+1})$, $j = 0,...,n-1$, as:

(3.6) $P(\tilde{t}_i, t) = \bar{f}_j(t)$,

which is again the rational cubic of the form (2.1) in parameter t with shape parameters γ_j, α_i, α_{i+1} and the tangent vectors $F_{i,j}^t$, $j = 0,...,n$, are determined by algorithm in Section 5. The C^t Hermite interpolants (3.5) and (3.6) can be expressed respectively as:

(3.7)
$$
\begin{cases}
\tilde{a}_0(\tilde{t}) F_{i,j} + \tilde{a}_1(\tilde{t}) F_{i+1,j} + \tilde{a}_2(\tilde{t}) F_{i,j}^{\tilde{t}} + \tilde{a}_3(\tilde{t}) F_{i+1,j}^{\tilde{t}}, \text{ and} \\
a_0(t) F_{i,j} + a_1(t) F_{i,j+1} + a_2(t) F_{i,j}^t + a_3(t) F_{ij+1}^t ,
\end{cases}
$$

where $\tilde{a}_i$, a_j, $i,j = 0,...,3$ are Hermite basis functions.

It should be noted that, over any subrectangle $[\tilde{t}_i, \tilde{t}_{i+1}] \times [t_j, t_{j+1}]$, the tensor product surface is a rational bicubic patch. The Hermite representation of the surface is

(3.8) $P(\tilde{t}, t) = P_{i,j}(\tilde{t}, t) = \tilde{A}(\tilde{t}) \, F(i,j) \, A^{\mathrm{T}}(t)$,

where

$$\tilde{A}(\tilde{t}) = \begin{bmatrix} \tilde{a}_0(\tilde{t}) & \tilde{a}_1(\tilde{t}) & \tilde{a}_2(\tilde{t}) & \tilde{a}_3(\tilde{t}) \end{bmatrix},$$
$$A(t) = \begin{bmatrix} a_0(t) & a_1(t) & a_2(t) & a_3(t) \end{bmatrix},$$

and

(3.9)
$$
F(i,j) = \begin{bmatrix}
F_{i,j} & F_{i,j+1} & F_{i,j}^t & F_{i,j+1}^t \\
F_{i+1,j} & F_{i+1,j+1} & F_{i+1,j}^t & F_{i+1,j+1}^t \\
F_{i,j}^{\tilde{t}} & F_{i,j+1}^{\tilde{t}} & F_{i,j}^{\tilde{t}t} & F_{i,j+1}^{\tilde{t}t} \\
F_{i+1,j}^{\tilde{t}} & F_{i+1,j+1}^{\tilde{t}} & F_{i+1,j}^{\tilde{t}t} & F_{i+1,j+1}^{\tilde{t}t}
\end{bmatrix}
$$

To construct the rational bicubic spline surface, all that required to know is the values of the vectors in (3.9) $\forall$ i,j. $F_{i,j}$ are known as they are interpolatory points; the tangent vectors $F_{i,j}^{\tilde{t}}$ and $F_{i,j}^t$ can be computed, respectively, by $n+1$ and $m+1$ applications of the algorithm in Subsection 2.5; the twist vectors $F_{i,j}^{\tilde{t}t}$ are theoretically given by

$$(3.10) \qquad P^{\tilde{t}t}(\tilde{t}_i, t_j) = \sum_{k=0}^{m} \sum_{l=0}^{n} F_{k,l} \tilde{A}_k^{\tilde{t}}(\tilde{t}_i) A_l^t(t_j)$$

using the cardinal basis functions. In practice, the twist vectors are computed by using the fact that each partial derivative curve $P^t(\tilde{t}_i, t)$ (repectively $P^{\tilde{t}}(\tilde{t}, t_i)$) is also a rational cubic spline and thus again use the algorithm in Subsection 2.2 to solve for these values.

Unfortunately, these tensor product surfaces are not that useful in connection with interactive surface design as any one of the shape parameters will apply to an entire network of curves. Thus there is no local control on the surface.

3.2 Surfaces with local control

Suppose that we are given points (3.3) and knot sequences along t and $\tilde{t}$ directions. We concentrate, in this subsection, on the construction of a parametric rational cubic spline surface method which, in addition to interpolating the points (3.3), also controls the shape of the surface with shape parameters simlar to those used for rational spline curves in both $\tilde{t}$ and t directions but with local control. The approach taken here is equivalent to forming a rational bicubic spline surface $P(\tilde{t}, t)$ such that $P(\tilde{t}, t_j) = f_j(\tilde{t})$ is a geometric rational cubic spline curve in $\tilde{t}$ for each $j = 0,...,n$; and $P(\tilde{t}_i, t) = \tilde{f}_i(t)$ is a geometric rational cubic spline in t for each $i = 0,...,m$, and $f_j(\tilde{t}_i) = \tilde{f}_i(t_j) = F_{i,j}$.

Given shape parameters

$$(3.11) \qquad \tilde{\gamma}_{i,j}, \gamma_{i,j} > 2, \quad i = 0,...,m\text{-}1, \ j = 0,...,n\text{-}1, \ \tilde{\alpha}_{i,j}, \alpha_{i,j} \geq 0,$$
$$i = 0,...,m, \ j = 0,...,n,$$

we define the rational bicubic spline surface as:

$$(3.12) \qquad P(\tilde{t}, t) = \sum_{i=0}^{m} \tilde{C}_i(\tilde{t}) B_i(t) + \sum_{j=0}^{n} \tilde{B}_j(\tilde{t}) C_j(t) - \sum_{i=0}^{m} \sum_{j=0}^{n} F_{i,j} \tilde{C}_i(\tilde{t}) C_j(t),$$
$$\tilde{t}_0 \leq \tilde{t} \leq \tilde{t}_m, \ t_0 \leq t \leq t_n,$$

where $\tilde{C}_i$, $i = 0,...,m$ and C_j, $j = 0,...,n$ are cardinal cubic splines in $\tilde{t}$ and t directions respectively, and $\tilde{B}_i$, $i = 0,...,m$ and B_j, $j = 0,...,n$ are rational cubic splines in $\tilde{t}$ and t directions with shape parameters $\{\tilde{\gamma}_{i,j}, \ j = 0,...,n\text{-}1, \ \tilde{\alpha}_{i,j}, \ j = 0,...,n\}$ and $\{\gamma_{i,j}, \ i = 0,...,m\text{-}1, \ \alpha_{i,j}, \ i = 0,...,m\}$ respectively.

Now, for the computational purposes, we seek a Hermite approximant of the form (3.8) to the rational bicubic spline surface (3.12), i.e. we seek an approximation

$$(3.13) \qquad P(\tilde{t}, t) = \tilde{A}(\tilde{t}) \ F(i,j) \ A^{\mathsf{T}}(t),$$

The tangent vectors in $\tilde{t}$ and t directions can be computed by algorithm in Subsection 2.5 and then the twist vectors can be computed by:

$$(3.14) \qquad P^{\tilde{t}t}(\tilde{t}_i, t_j) = \sum_{r=0}^{m} \tilde{C}_r^{\tilde{t}}(\tilde{t}_i) P^t(\tilde{t}_r, t_j) + \sum_{s=0}^{n} P^{\tilde{t}}(\tilde{t}_i, t_s) C_s^t(t_j)$$
$$- \sum_{r=0}^{m} \sum_{s=0}^{n} F_{r,s} \tilde{C}_r^{\tilde{t}}(\tilde{t}_i) C_s^t(t_j),$$

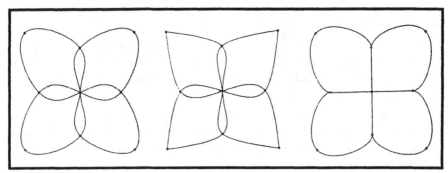

Figure 1

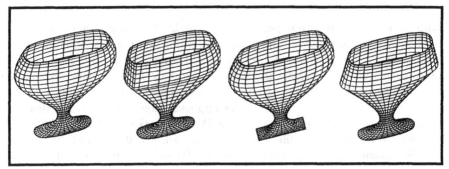

Figure 2

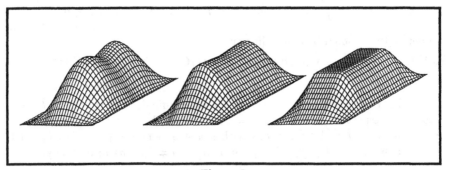

Figure 3

Some computational savings can be made as follows:

(a)   The uniform parametrization can be used i.e. one can assume equispaced data in which case $\tilde{h}_i = 1 = h_j$, $\forall i,j$. This will save some calculations and storage.

(b)   Zero twist vectors may be considered as mentioned in [4] to simplify the surface evaluation somewhat. However, zero twists may cause *pseudo-flats*.

(c)   Like the algorithm for curve manipulation, in Subsection 2.5, the surface representation (3.14) can also be simplified for specific range of shape parameters. This will reduce a lot of arithmetic calculation cost.

Suppose that for each i and j, $\tilde{\gamma}_{i,j} = \tilde{\gamma}_i$, $\tilde{\alpha}_{i,j} = \tilde{\alpha}_i$, $\gamma_{i,j} = \gamma_j$ and $\alpha_{i,j} = \alpha_j$, then the surface (3.14) takes the form of a tensor product surface. In this case, the shape parameters control entire rows or columns of the surface. The special case $\tilde{\gamma}_{i,j} = \gamma_{i,j} = \tilde{\alpha}_{i,j} = \alpha_{i,j} = 3$, $\forall\ i,j$ corresponds to the interpolatory bicubic spline surface.

3.3 Surfaces Demonstration

There are a number of ways to achieve the shape control on these kind of surfaces. Let us consider two different data sets in $\mathbf{R}^3$ and implement our scheme on these datas. First surface (from left to right) in each of the Figures 2 and 3 corresponds to the global values $\tilde{\gamma} = \gamma = 2$ and $\tilde{\alpha} = \alpha = 1$ (the bicubic spline surfaces). In Figure 2, second surface is an example of the effect of increasing shape parameters α's in both directions on a corresponding point, third surface demonstrates the tension behaviour along a network curve and causing the whole curve to tend to a polygon by increasing shape parameters $\tilde{\gamma}_{i,j}$ or $\gamma_{i,j}$, fourth surface is achieved by applying tension accross a curve and thereby creates a crease in the surface: this effect is achieved by increasing point tension parameters. Second and third surfaces in Figure 3 are demonstrating the interval tension effects in one direction and both directions, respectively, on two consecutive patches. It should be noted that where ever the tension is applied, the values of γ's or α's are taken 50 and otherwise default values i.e. 2 and 1 are considered respectively.

Acknowledgement. The author acknowledges the support of King Fahd University of Petroleum and Minerals. The author also likes to thank the referees for some useful comments in the improvement of the paper.

References

1. M. Sarfraz: Designing of curves and surfaces using rational cubics. Computers and Graphics 17, 529-538 (1993)
2. G. M. Nielson: Rectangular ν-splines. IEEE Computer Graphics and Applics. 6, 35-40 (1986)
3. T. A. Foley, H. S. Ely: Surface interpolation with tension controls using cardinal bases. Computer Aided Geometric Design 6, 97-109 (1989)
4. M. Sarfraz: Curves and surfaces for CAD using C^2 rational cubic splines. Engineering with Computers 11, (1994)
5. J. A. Gregory, M. Sarfraz: A rational spline with tension. Computer Aided Geometric Design. 7, 1-13 (1990)
6. M. Sarfraz: Curves and surfaces for computer aided geometric design, Academic press, New York
7. W. J. Gordon: Blending function methods of bivariate and multivariate interpolation and approximation. SIAM J. Num. Anal. 8,158-177 (1971)

Classification Algorithm for Multi-Echo Magnetic Resonance Image Using Gibbs Distributions

Junchul Chun[1]   and Ian R. Greenshields[2]

[1]Department of Computer Science, Kyonggi University,
Suwon, Korea
[2]Department of Computer Science, University of Connecticut,
Storrs CT., U.S.A

Abstract. This paper describes a new three dimensional image (volumetric image) classification technique which is based on the Markov Random Field (MRF)–Gibbs Random Field (GRF) model together with a stochastic relaxation algorithm.   For the classification of Multi-Echo (multispectral) Magnetic Resonance Images (MRI), a Bayesian context decision rule is adopted and an MRF–GRF stochastic model is introduced for the original image. To obtain the maximum a posterior probability (MAP) classification a new multivariate image context-dependent classification based on relaxation and annealing is developed. Conventionally, a digital image is considered as a two-dimensional random field defined over rectangular lattice structure and the domain of image classification is the plane. However, in the volumetric image classification, we use volumetric images, i.e., three dimensional image data sets.

1 Introduction

For the visualization or quantitative analysis of normal or abnormal soft tissues in biomedical images, proper classification of soft tissues is needed. However, there are a few reasons which make classification difficult in Magnetic Resonance Images (MRI). In MRI the intensity-level distributions between different soft tissues are not widely distributed and moreover the complexity of tissue boundaries cause many pixels to contain mixtures of tissues (this type of pixel is called mixel[2]).

Meanwhile, the use of statistical models and methods in image processing has increased considerably in recent years.   Many of theses studies involve the use of Markov Random Fields (MRF) models and the processing techniques associated with these models[3,4,5]. The inherrent difficulties in the characterization and processing of MRF images[5] such are alleviated by charactering MRF through the GD. Numerous applications of Gibbs distributions have been found in texture modeling and analysis, image segmentation, and image enhancement[6,7,8,9,10].

This paper presents a computationally inexpensive, novel approach for the classification of MRI. This paper also describes a statistical volumetric image model based on the Markov Random Field and Gibbs Random Field (MRF-GRF) model and an algorithm for the classification of such images.

2 Related Background

2.1 The Aspects of Multi-Echo MR Image Model

Let S be a set of sites over which an MR image is defined. In Multi-Echo MR images, at each location $s \in S$, the three channel observation (gray level) $y_s = (y_s^1, y_s^2, y_s^3)$ can be constructed. Each component of y_s, $y_s^1 = SD$, $y_s^2 = T1$, and $y_s^3 = T2$, is called spin density (proton density), spin-lattice relaxation time and spin-spin relaxation time, respectively. Usually it is not possible to acquire all three of these signatures simultaneously. However, it is possible, using specific sequences of RF pulses, to acquire approximations to some of the signatures from the same slice almost simultaneously. One such imaging methodology is called the Spin-Echo protocol. The imaging protocol results, in our case, in images which are predominatly SD and T2. These multisignature images are referred to as Multi-Echo images. From the same anatomical section of the Multi-Echo image, SD-weighted and T2-weighted images can be obtained[1].

2.2 Volumetric Image Model

The conventional structure of digital image we have dealt with to date is a two-dimensional random field defined over a rectangular lattice structure,and the domain of image classification is thus the two-dimensional plane E^2. However, the domain of volumetric image classification becomes E^3 and we call volume data elements voxels whose intensity represents the average physiologic signal over the volume. Thus a voxel is the three dimensional analog of a pixel[13].

Suppose that an object Γ has been scaled to fit the unit cube V in E^3, we divide this into subcubes V_{ijk} of size of $h_x \times h_y \times h_z$ where $h_i = 1/n_i, i = x, y, z$. When a three dimensional data set I is defined as

$$I = \{(i, j, k) : 1 \le i, j, k \le n\}$$

Then the subcube V_{ijk} is referred to as a voxel and it is represented by

$$V_{ijk}[(i-1)h_x, ih_x] \times [(j-1)h_y, jh_y] \times [(k-1)h_z, kh_z]$$

3 MRF-GRF Model

In stochastic representation, the Markov Random Field model is able to explain the characteristics of the image properly by using the conditional distribution of the random field. However, because of some restriction on characterizing and processing MRF images, an alternative approach is needed. The alternative is Gibbs Random Field (GRF).

3.1 Markov Random Field (MRF)

The Markov Random Field (MRF) is a multidimensional generalization of Markov chains defined by conditional probabilities associated with spatial neighborhoods. The brightness level associated with each pixel in the image is viewed as a random variable X_{ij} that takes one of M values in the state space $\Lambda = \{0,1,\ldots,g\}$. Thus, the collection of random variables defined over the lattice S is expressed as follows:-

Definition 1: Let $X = \{X_{(ij)}, (i,j) \in S\}$ be a family of random variables indexed by with Λ and $\Omega = \{\omega = x_{(ij)_{i,j=i}} : x_{ij} \in \Lambda\}$ denote the configuration space. X defined over the lattics S is a MRF with respect to the neighborhood system, $\{\eta_{ij}(i,j) \in S\}$ if $P(X_{ij} = x_{ij} | \{X_{kl} = X_{kl}(k,l) \neq (i,j)\}) = P(X_{ij} = x_{ij} | \{X_{kl} = x_{kl}(k,l) \in \eta_{ij}\}$ and $P(X = \omega) > 0$ for all $\omega \in \Omega$.

In MRF, it is not trivial to verify the consistency of a given family of conditional probabilities. However, there is an equivalent characterization of MRF's satisfying $P(X = \omega) > 0$ for all ω, through their joint distributions, which are Gibbs distributed.

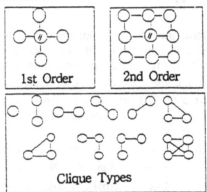

Fig. 1. Neighborhood Systems and Their Associated Clique Type

3.2 Gibbs Random Field (GRF)

Let $C(S, \eta)$ be the set of all cliques of (S, η). The clique types associated with first-order and second-order neighborhood systems are illustrated in Figure 1. Now we can define a GRF as follows:-

Definition 2: A random field $X=\{X_{ij}\}$ defined on S is a GRF with respect to the neighborhood system η if and only if its joint probability distribution of X is

$$P(X=\omega) = \exp^{-U(\omega)/T}/Z$$

where T is the temperature of the model, $Z = \sum_\omega \exp^{-U(\omega)}$ is the partition function and $U(\omega) = \sum V_c(\omega)$ is called energy function. Each clique potential $V_c(\omega)$ depends on the clique type and pixel values in the clique c but not on the position of the clique in the lattice S. The MRF–GRF equivalence provides a simple, though indirect, way of specifying a probability distribution whose conditional probabilities are Markovian, and resolves limitations of the MRF model.

4 Unsupervised Clustering Analysis

The task of clustering analysis is to uncover a reasonable categorization of the data set. We adopt agglomerative algorithm which is based on the unsupervised segmentation technique performed by Perkins et. al[12] for the clustering analysis of MR images. The idea behind the agglomerative clustering algorithm is as follows. First, the MR image is subdivided into $n \times n$ square in the case of two dimensional image or $n \times n \times n$ cubic neighborhoods in the case of three dimensional image. For each neighborhood, the mean vectors and covariance matrices are computed. Then initial clusters are chosen from spatial neighborhoods which occur in homogeneous regions of the image. When an arbitrary number of clusters are found, then they are merged to provide a number of final clusters. The criteria we use to merge the classes are the class seperability measures such as Euclidean distance and Bhattacharyya distance. Then the estimation of the mean vectors (M_m) and covariance matrices (C_m) for the merged clusters is required and expressed by the following formulas provided the clusters being merged are Gaussian:-

$$M_m = \frac{n_p M_p + n_q M_q}{n_p + n_q}$$

$$C_m = \frac{n_p(C_p + M_p M_p^T) + n_q(C_q + M_q M_q^T)}{n_p + n_q} - M_m M_m^T$$

where C_p and C_q are the predecessor covariance matrices. The clustering process is continued until some predetermined number of classes are found or the smallest distance between clusters is greater than a threshold value.

5 Spatial Stochastic Model : MRF–GRF Classifier

The MRF–GRF classifier is a discrete optimizting classifier which assigns the image location x with observed image intensity f(x) to the class

ω_i by estimating the *Maximum A Posteriori* (MAP) estimate of the class distribution of the image. For a given image G and its corresponding intensity fileld F, the spatial stochastic model defines the neighbors such that the site j is a neighborhood of site i if and only if the functional form of $P(g_i|g_1,\ldots,g_{i-1},g_{i+1},\ldots,g_n)$ is dependent on the variable g_i. Since the scene realization x cannot be obtained deterministically from any given realization g, the objective is to find an estimation rule which yields the $\hat{x}$ that maximizes the a posteriori distribution $P(X=\omega|G=g)$. By using Bayes' rule[12], the posterior distribution for all possible configuration ω, for each g, can be determined. Maximizing the posterior distribution $P(X=\omega, G=g)$ is equivalent to maximizing $\log P(G=g|X=\omega) + \log P(X=\omega)$ since $P(G=g)$ is just a normalizing factor which can be optimized, and log is a monotonic increasing function. The calss conditional probabilities $P(G=g|X=\omega)$ are assumed to be multivariate normal. Then $P(X=\omega|G=g)$ is a Gibbs distribution over $\{S, \eta\}$ for each g with energy function

$$U(F) = \frac{1}{z} \exp^{-U(\omega)/T} + \log(G=g|X=\omega)$$

Maximization of the posterior distribution for a fixed g is determined by minimizing the energy function $U(F)$.

Consequently, the best decision in the Markov model is to assign category lable $\hat{\omega}$ to intensity field F_{ij} which yield the maximum condition

$$P(\hat{\omega}) \prod_{(lm)\in\eta_o} P(f_{lm}|\hat{\omega}) \geq P(\hat{\omega}) \prod_{(lm)\in\eta_o} P(f_{ij}|\omega_{lm})$$

for all $\omega \in \Omega$. In the Markov–Gibbs Bayes Model, $P(F_{ij}, \omega)$ is defined as a Gibbs distribution

$$P(F_{ij}, \omega) = P(\omega) \prod_{(lm)\in\eta_o} P(f_{lm}|\omega_{lm}) = \frac{1}{z} \exp^{-U(F_{ij}\omega)/T}.$$

6 Simulated Annealing: Stochastic Relaxation Algorithm

Simulated annealing is a stochastic optimization procedure that attempts to find an optimization configuration $\hat{\omega}$ from the configuration space Ω[11]. The simulated annealing algorithm can be stated as follows. For each configuration space ω_i of a model Ω a random perturbation is made based on the current values of intensity in the neighborhood system. Let U_c and U_t denote the energy level of current and trial configurations, respectively. The change in energy, $U^d = U_t - U_c$ is computed. If $U^d < 0$ then a lower energy level has been reached, and the trial configuration replaces the current configuration. On the other hand, if $U^d \geq 0$ then conditional acceptance is made based on a uniformly distributed random number $R(0 < R < 1)$ i.e., the trial configuration is accepted as the current configuration with the probability $P(U^d) = \exp(-U^d/T)$ if $P(U^d) > R$; otherwise the change is rejected. The process continues until a transition to a configuration of higher energy level is not necessarily rejected. A system obeying this rule eventually reaches thermal equilibrium, where the probability of a configuration approaches the Gibbs distribution.

7 Experimental Results

The MRF–GRF classification results for two dimensional MRI and volumetric MRI are illustrated in figure 3 and 5 respectively. Figure 2 and 4 are two dimensional MRI and the reconstructed volumetric image.

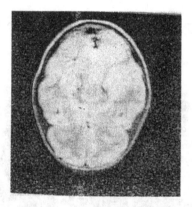

Fig. 2. A Multi-Echo Magnetic Resonance Image.

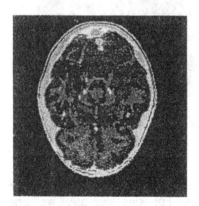 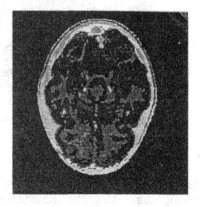

Fig. 3. Classification results Using Euclidian Distance Clustering with Maximum likelihood Classification and 1st-Order MRF-GRF Classification.

Fig. 4. Volumetric Magnetic Resonance Image

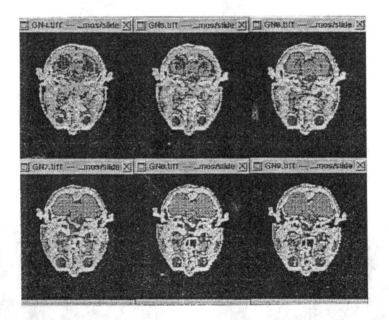

Fig. 5. Class Maps for Volumetric Image Based on Gibbs Classification.

8 Conclusion

The goal of this paper was to develop a MRF–GRF classifier for volumetric multisignature Magnetic Resonance images. For this purpose, we first expanded the domain of image classification from conventional two dimensional plane to three dimensional space. A three dimensional Bayesian model is constructed based on the MRF–GRF stochastic model. Finally, a relaxation and annealing algorithm was used to obtain three dimensional MAP estimates of the volumetric multisignature images. In evaluating the relative performance of the classifier, we have used the subjective analysis of professional clinical scientist. The calssification results will provide the clinically important data to analyze the abnormal tissue in the human brain.

References

1. S. C. Bushong: Magnetic Resonance Imaging-Physical and Biological Principles, The C. V. Mosby Company, 1988.
2. H. S. Choi, D. R. Haynor, and Y. Kim: Partial Volume Tissue Classification of Multichannel Magnetic Resonance Images-A Mixel Model, *IEEE Trans. on Medical Imaging*, Vol. 10, No. 3, pp. 395-407, September. 1991.
3. E. J. Wegman and D. J. Depriest: Statistical Image Processing and Graphics, Marcel Dekker, Inc., 1986.
4. J. W. Woods: Two-Dimensional Discrete Markovian Fields, *IEEE Trans. Inform. Theory*, Vol. 18, pp. 232-240, March 1972.
5. J. E. Besag: Spatial Interaction and Statistical Analysis of Lattice Systems, *J. Roy. Stat. Soc.*, Vol. 36, Series B, pp. 192-236, 1974.
6. S. Geman and D. Geman: Stochastic Relaxation, Gibbs Distributions, and the Bayesian Restoration of Images, *IEEE Trans. Pattern Anal. Machine Intell.*, Vol. PAMI-6, No. 6, pp. 721-741, Nov. 1984.
7. W. Qian and D. N. Titterington: Multidimensional Markov Chain Models for Image Textures, *J. R. Stat. Soc.* Vol. 53 Series B, No. 3. pp. 661-674, 1991.
8. C. O. Acuna: Texture modeling using Gibbs distribution, *CVGIP: Graphical Models and Image Processing*, Vol. 54, No. 3, pp. 661-674, 1991.
9. H. Derin and H. Elliott: Modeling and Segmentation of Noisy and Textured Image Using Gibbs Random Fields, *IEEE Trans. Pattern Anal. Machine Intell.*, PAMI-9, No. 1, pp. 39-55, January 1987.
10. H. Derin and W. S. Cole: Segmentation of Textured Images Using Gibbs Random Fields, *Computer Vision, Graphics, and Processing*, Vol. 35, pp. 72-98, 1986.
11. S. Z. Selim and K. Alsultan: A Simulated Annealing Algorithm for the Clustering Problem, *Pattern Recognition*, Vol. 24, No. 10, pp. 1003-1008, 1991.
12. J. B. Perkins, I. R. Greenshields, F. Dimario, and G. Ramsby: Unsupervised Classification of Multi-Echo Magnetic Resonance Images of the Pediatric Brain with Implicit Spatial and Statistical Hypotheses Validation, in *Proc. SPIE, Medical Imaging.*, Vol. 1692, CA. 1993.
13. M. R. Stytz, G. Frierder and O. Frieder: Three-Dimensional Medical Imaging: Algorithms and Computer Systems, *ACM Computing Surveys*, Vol. 23, No. 4, pp. 421-499, December 1991.

Parameter Estimation for SAR Image by a Model Based Approach

Fang Luo[1], Liu Lu[2], and Z.Houkes[2]

1: PB 162, P.O.Box 6, 7500AA, Enschede,
International Institute for Aerospace Survey and Earth Science, the Netherlands
2: Vision Lab., Dept. of Electrical Engineering,
7500AE, Enschede, University of Twente, the Netherlands

Abstract. In this paper, a model-based method is presented for the analysis of SAR images. The problem of image analysis is formulated as the task of cost minimization. Firstly, in the presence of imperfect SAR data, a cost function is defined which combines both of radiometric and geometric properties of objects. Secondly, the estimation procedure is modeled with Markov process, which leads to the use of a globally converged algorithm i.e. the simulated annealing algorithm. Thirdly, the convergence of the algorithm is studied and the order of Markov process is suggested to be used for speeding up the convergence. At last, the experimental data both on testing and real SAR images are provided for evaluating the proposed method.

1. Introduction

In remotely sensed applications, there are a huge number of objects that need to be processed. We, therefore, do not attempt to find a generic solution but limit our attention to the application of land inventory, where agricultural fields are the objects of interest. In the application, the task of image analysis can be simplified to answer two questions:(1) what is the type or class of the vegetation of the object? (2)what is the size, position, and shape of the object? The questions concern actually two aspects of an object: radiometric and geometric. Object model can be used to contain these information and the model parameters characterizing objects can be estimated by solving an model inverse problem, where an objective function is required to denote the goodness of fitting between the model and measurement.

Analyzing synthetic aperture radar(SAR) images is part of the automation of land inventory by using remote sense. SAR return signals represent the backscattered power that is detected, and usually cross section $\sigma°$ is used to denote the power per unit area. Relevant literature of radar remote sensing is referred to [6]. A SAR image is composed of a large number of cells. In each resolution cell, the reflected or backscattered signals return from an ensemble of independent scatters and often may cause a complex speckle phenomenon (fading characteristics). The phenomenon shows up clearly, even for systems with a high signal-to-noise ratio.

From the point of view of image analysis, it is difficult to extract object parameters from SAR image because of these random fluctuations. In addition, one pixel in an image can be just considered as a backscattered sample which contains very limited information about objects. Traditional bottom-up approaches which follow a series of subroutines such as image filtering, edge detection, and segmentation etc, had shown their weakness in handling backscattering noisy images. Although some region-based methods can perform better, most methods still rely on local features while available knowledge about objects is ignored.

2. Object Models

The attractive characteristic of model based methods is that it effectively utilizes problem-related knowledge and leads to processing in a top-down way. In the presence of imperfect SAR data, more specific information should be added into object model. Geometric model contains the geometric information of objects on rotation, translation, and scale. It can be specified with a parameter vector α, for instance, $\alpha = (\theta, xt, yt, xs, ys)$ for a rigid object with rectangular shape, where θ indicates the rotation, xt, yt are the translation in x,y direction, and xs, ys are the scale in x,y direction.

A radiometric model of SAR always relates to many parameters of imaging system, objects, and atmosphere. In practice, it is seldom necessary to actually know the effect of all factors involved [3]. In this research, often only crop type related variables are of interest. The SAR backscattering model for a homogenous area can be related to a conditional probability density function(pdf) [1]:

$$p(I|C_i) = \frac{1}{(\sigma^o/N)(N-1)!}(\frac{I}{\sigma^o/N})^{N-1}e^{(-\frac{I}{\sigma^o/N})} \qquad (2.1)$$

where C_i denotes object type, N is the number of independent samples of intensity, averaged to form I. σ^o is the radar cross section.

3. A Definition of the Cost Function

The Maximum Likelihood(ML) classifier plays an important role in image analysis for remote sensing. The conditional pdf $p(I|C_i)$ denotes the probability that a spectral feature I will occur, given that the feature vector belongs to an object class C_i. It enable us to compute the conditional probability that a certain class will occur, given a spectral vector, represented as $p(C_i|I)$ and called a posterior probability. Bayesian formula provides us following calculation:

$$p(C_i|I) = \frac{p(I|C_i)p(C_i)}{p(I)} \qquad (3.1)$$

where $p(C_i|I)$ is a posteriori probability, $p(C_i)$ is a priori probability for the occurrence of the class C_i, $p(I)$ is a normalization factor which quantifies a posteriori probabilities to a unit measure. Its practical calculation may be substituted by:

$$p(I) = \sum_{i=1}^{m} p(I|C_i) * p(C_i) \qquad (3.2)$$

where m is the number of object classes.

For the discrimination purpose, a spectral feature vector always is assigned to its most likely object class. The ML classier makes decision on each feature vector with following rule:

if $p(I|C_i) \cdot p(C_i) \geq p(I|C_j) \cdot p(C_j)$, $j \in [1,m]$ and $j \neq i$, then the spectral feature vector I belongs to the class C_i.

Techniques based on the ML classifier has been widely applied to a variety of problems of image analysis. However it is noted that a priori probability $p(C_i)$, which is not precisely acquired in practice, has most effect on classification accuracy. In addition, a severe problem with such a classifier is its inability to distinguish those pixel which have the same spectral properties but come from different land-use classes. Mis-classification is unavoidable and the result usually is produced in a snow-like map which is not consistent with the assumed object. The reason for such a deficiency is that the ML classifier assumes explicitly that the spectral property of a pixel is completely independent of that of all of the others and that discrimination function takes into account only the Mahalanobis distances from the mean values.

Pixel in the land-use objects often appears in the form of distinct parcels, and all pixel in a specific parcel are assumed to be from a single object class. This property must be of great importance and should be taken into account in cost function. Before a cost function is defined, an image formation model is introduced which is used to contain both of radiometric and geometric information. For simplicity, we consider a two-class problem, i.e. an image containing two distinct objects. Let C_1 and C_2 denote the background and foreground object respectively. Their density functions of pixel value are denoted as $d_1(x,y)$ and $d_2(x,y)$ and have the distributions in a gamma form, described in equation 2.1 fora SAR application. Over C_1 and C_2, two two-valued functions can be defined in following forms, called hypothesis functions[2] and represented as $H_1(x,y)$, $H_2(x,y)$.

$$H_i(x,y) = \begin{cases} 1 & (x,y) \in C_i \\ 0 & (x,y) \notin C_i \end{cases} \qquad i=1,2. \qquad (3.3)$$

An image can thus be described by its density functions and hypothesis functions, i.e.
$$I(x,y) = \{ ((x,y), i(x,y)) \mid (x,y) \in N_x \times N_y \}$$
$$\text{and } i(x,y) = H_1(x,y) \cdot d_1(x,y) + H_2(x,y) \cdot d_2(x,y) \qquad (3.4)$$

The same concept can be extended to multi-object case. Actually the function $H(x,y)$ determines a configuration in 2D lattice, and directly is related to geometric parameters of object model. Usually an image can be viewed as a constant for once processing so that a cost function C is defined as the function of the model parameters that determine a series of $H_i(\cdot)$, given measurement $I(x,y)$. Let $H_i(\cdot)$ be the hypothesis function of the i-th object. $I(x,y)$ denotes the measured image. A cost function can be defined by introducing an evidence function $e_i(x,y)$ of the i-th object. The cost function has the following form:

$$C(h_i) = \sum_{i=1}^{m} \sum_{(x,y) \in \mathbf{R}} [h_i(x,y) + (-1)^{h_i} * e_i(x,y)] \qquad (3.5)$$

where $e_i(\cdot)$ may be any one function in a range [0,1], which has following form in this application.

$$e_k(x,y) = \frac{p(I|C_k) * p(C_k)}{\sum_{k=1}^{m} p(I|C_k) * p(C_k)} \qquad (3.6)$$

where $p(I|C_j)$ can be described with equation (2.1). H_i is determined by the parameters of the geometric model.

4. Parameter Estimation by Cost Minimization

The simulated annealing algorithm is an analogy of a physical system presented in [5]. This algorithm draws a lot of attention since the global optimum can be achieved with probability 1. Rather different from other algorithms, it accepts the increase of function evaluation with a limited way. A continuous version of simulated annealing is similar in spirit to the random direction method. Having arrived at some point X, the method will generate a random neighbouring points X^* and accepted it if $\Delta C = C(X^*) - C(X) \leq 0$ or with probability $\exp(-\Delta C / k \cdot T)$ if $\Delta C > 0$. On theory [5], the global state is ensured if an appropriate cooling schedule is followed in which T has decrement rate in the order of $1/\log(n)$. Long computational time may be taken during this procedure, and usually only asymptotic results are obtained in practice. In following discussion, we focus on the study on speeding up the convergence of the algorithm.

Let a state X denote a configuration of 2D lattice. Its hypothesis functions are specified by shape parameters, represented $X(\alpha)$ and radiometric one by a radiometric model. The estimation procedure must scale, translate and rotate a rigid shape model to fit the optimal position. Each modification is based on the cost of the last estimation. As a result a sequence of states will be generated, and this process can be modeled with a Markov process with respect to a neighbourhood set.

Definition 1: Let Ω be a finite state set. A neighbour set Z of X on Ω is defined as
$$Z = \{ \eta_X \subset \Omega : X \in \Omega \}$$
such that for any $X \in \Omega$, $X \notin \eta_X$ and $X' \in \eta_X$ iff $X \in \eta_{X'}$.

The order m of Markov process indicates the size of the local neighbourhood area Z that is considered.

Definition 2: The state set $\{ X(\alpha) \}$ is said to be the m-th order Markov process with respect to a neighbourhood set Z, where α is a w-dimensional vector, i.e, $\alpha^T = [x_1, x_2, ,,, x_w]$, if $p (X(\alpha) | $ all $X(s)$, $s \neq \alpha) = p (X(\alpha) | $ all $X(\alpha+r)$, $X(\alpha+r) \in Z)$

In a Markov process, a transition matrix can be set up where the conditional probability p_{ij} indicates the probability of a transition from state i to state j. p_{ij} is called the transition probability.

The transition probability from state i to state j ($i \neq j$) is the multiplication of g_{ij} and a_{ij}, i.e. $\quad p_{ij} = g_{ij} * a_{ij} \qquad (4.1)$
where g_{ij} is the generation probability from state i to state j, and a_{ij} is the acceptance probability of accepting state j, once it has been generated from i. The neighbourhood

set of $X(\alpha_i)$ is represented as $Z^m_{\alpha i}$, and let $|Z^m_{\alpha i}|$ denote the number of vectors contained. When the order of Markov process and the neighbourhood configuration are fixed, the neighbourhood set can be specified, represented in default as Z_α and $|Z_\alpha|$ can be calculated as:

$$|Z^m_{\alpha_i}| = \prod_{k=1}^{w} V_k \qquad (4.2)$$

where V_k denotes the range of the k-th parameter in vector α_i, $k \leq w$. Since the generation probability actually is a uniform distribution over the neighbourhood area Z defined, it can be computed as:

$$g_{ij} = |Z^m_{\alpha i}|^{-1} \qquad (4.3)$$

With respect to the acceptance probability in simulated annealing, the transition probability p_{ij} can be rewritten as:

$$p_{ij} = \begin{cases} \exp((-\Delta_{ij}/T) \cdot (\prod_{k=1}^{w} V_k^m)^{-1} & \Delta C_{ij} > 0 \\ 1 & \Delta C_{ij} \leq 0 \end{cases} \qquad (4.4)$$

When the temperature T is close to T_0 (initial phase), suppose that the state transition from $X(\alpha_i)$ to $X(\alpha_j)$ requires s steps, the transition probability can be thus written as

$$\begin{aligned} p^{(s)}_{ij} &= p_{i,k} \cdot p_{k,k+1} \cdots p_{k+s-1,j} \\ &= a_{i,k} \cdot g_{i,k} \cdot a_{k,k+1} \cdot g_{k,k+1} \cdots a_{k+s-1,j} \cdot g_{k+s-1,j} \\ &= [|Z_\alpha|^s]^{-1} \cdot a_{i,k} \cdot a_{k,k+1} \cdots a_{k+s-1,j} \qquad (4.5) \end{aligned}$$

In the initial phase, temperature T is usually large enough so that state transition is rather easy to be accepted, i.e. $a_{ij} \approx 1$. The transition probability is approximately determined by the generation probability, i.e.

$$p^{(s)}_{ij} \approx [|Z_\alpha|^s]^{-1} \qquad (4.6)$$

If the order is small so that few elements are contained in the corresponding neighbourhood set Z_α, it may result in reaching to $X(\alpha_j)$ by many steps. Thus the transition probability may be decreased rapidly with the increase of s. If the order becomes large so that many elements are contained in the corresponding neighbourhood set, it may result in reaching the state $X(\alpha_j)$ by few steps to increase the transition probability. When $|Z_\alpha|$ becomes too large, the transition probability becomes small again since it is proportional to $1/|Z_\alpha|^s$. Hence to gain a large transition probability, an suitable order is required.

The algorithm starts at a high initial temperature T_0. In this case, nearly 100% of the tested states are accepted even for those transitions with cost increase . As the temperature is gradually decreased, those transitions with cost increase become less likely accepted. When the temperature is decreased so low that those transitions are essentially impossible to be accepted. In most cases, the algorithm may get stuck in a local minimum so that if the order is small, few states are included in the neighbourhood set Z_α and the transition probability is mainly determined by the acceptance probability, i.e.

$$p^{(s)}_{ij} = e^{(-\Delta C_{i,k}/T_r)} \cdot e^{(-\Delta C_{k,k+1}/T_{r+1})} \cdots e^{(-\Delta C_{k+s}/T_{r+s})} \cdot [|Z_\alpha|^s]^{-1} \qquad (4.7)$$

In this situation, escaping from the local minimum is very difficult because the acceptance probability a_{ij} is near to zero. Therefore the small value of the order does not benefit escaping from the local minimum. In contrast, when the value of the order is increased, the set Z_{α} is enlarged so that more states are included and the escaping from the local minimum becomes more likely. In this case, the transition probability becomes large and is mainly determined by the generation probability. However, if the order m is increased to too large, the transition probability becomes small again since the transition probability is approximately an exponential function of the order, i.e. tm_{ij} $\approx (\prod V^m_k)^{-1}$. However if the order becomes extremely large, e.g. $Z_{\alpha} \rightarrow \mathbf{R}^w$ where all the states are included, the algorithm thus is nearly "blind" algorithm with which the optimal state is found with the probability of $|\mathbf{R}^w|^{-1}$. Therefore, considering the practical availability of the algorithm, an appropriate value of the order is necessary to be experimentally specified.

5. Experiments

Testing images (256x256) are used in which only one assumed object with a rectangular shape is put. For the purpose of comparison, the overlap degree, represented as Ψ, is defined as follows:

$$\Psi(C_1,C_2) = \frac{2 - \sum_I |p\ (I|C_1) - p\ (I|C_2)|}{2} \qquad (5.1)$$

where $p(I|C_1)$ and $p(I|C_2)$ represent the pdf of two objects C_1 and C_2 in an image $I(x,y)$. In this experiment, $p(I|C_1)$ and $p(I|C_2)$ are assigned to pdf's in a gamma form. Table 1 gives the comparison of different initializations with which the simulated annealing algorithm starts. With the increase of Ψ, the algorithm needs more iterations to reach the global minimum, and the optimal parameters are obtained with higher cost value for lower Ψ. Figure 1 shows the convergence rate of the algorithm, starting with two different points. The stability of the algorithm is guaranteed by spending more computational time.

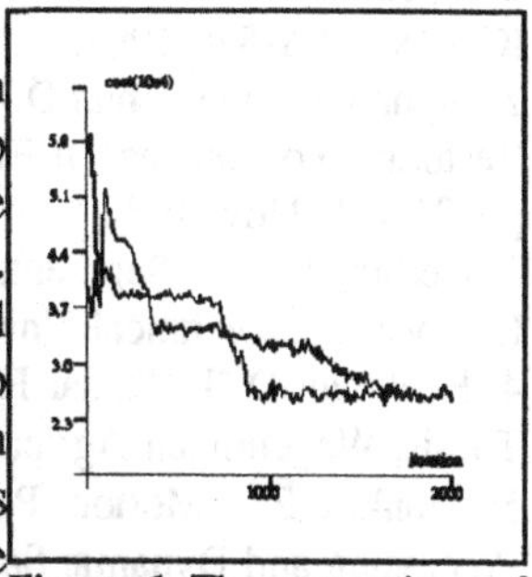

Different order values of the Markov model are set in the second experiment. For comparison, m is assigned to 2,4,and 8 respectively. It shows that in the finite time, the algorithm can reach the minimum cost with a limited way. For the cases where the value of the order is too small (typically m=2, and 3), it may require infinite time to converge. Figure 2 is a convergence comparison with different m values. In figure 3, the vertical axis denotes the number of function evaluations required, and the horizontal one denotes the value of m. It shows that the appropriate value of m can benefit the convergence of the

Figure 1 The comparison of initializations.

algorithm. In this experiment, the optimal value is in the range [3,5].

At last, the proposed method is applied to a real SAR image. Figure 4 is a SAR image(C-band and VV polarization) from the 1991 NASA/JPL multi-band, multi-temporal polarimetric SAR campaign. The SAR image is overlapped with the geometric parameter result estimated by the proposed method. Figure 5 gives the index of the objects and the experimental data is provided in the table 2.

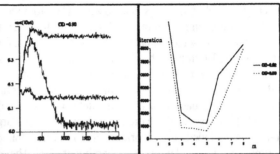

5. Conclusion

We have described a model based method which leads to an accurate and the minimum cost parameter estimation. From the experimental results, the method can be concluded that (1) the method can produce the rather good

Figure 2 The comparison of different m value.

Figure 3 The comparison of different Ψ.

parameter estimation of objects from the imagery since the global feature of objects is considered in the cost function and the explicit feature extraction algorithms are not needed; (2) because of the use of the explicit shape model, the results produced can be quit consistent with object model; (3) comparing with other methods, the proposed method does not depend on the initialization even in the situation with very high overlap degree; (4) the method is not attracted by the insignificant local minima by using a globally converged algorithm so that the optimal solution can be obtained constantly; (5) since the stochastic mechanism is used, the optimal result is obtained at the expense of computational time. The trade-off solution between the accuracy and computational time can be achieved by setting an appropriate value of the order of Markov process.

References:

1. Frost V.S., Shanmugan K.S. and Holtzman J.C. "An Information Theory Characterization of Radar Images and a New Definition for Radiometric Resolution", IGARSS, TA-5.4, 1993.

2. Geman S. and Geman D. "Stochastic Relaxation, Gibbs Distributions and Bayesian Restoration of Images" IEEE Trans. Pattern Anal. Machine Intell., vol.PAMI-6, No.6, pp721-741, Nov. 1984

3. Gerbrands J.J. "Segmentation of Noisy Images", Ph.D Thesis, Dept. of Electrical Engineering, Technical University of Delft, Netherlands, 1988.

4. Hoekman D.H. "Radar Remote Sensing Data for Applications in Forestry", Ph.D. Thesis, Wageningen Agricultural University, The Netherlands, 1990

5. Houkes Z. "Motion Parameter Estimation in TV-Pictures", Image Sequence Processing and Dynamic Scene Analysis, Springs-Verlag Berlin Heidelderg, ISBN 3-540-11997-3,pp249-263,1983.

6. Kirkpatrick S. et al, "Optimization by Simulated Annealing", Science, Vol.220, No.4598, pp.671-680.1984.

7. Ulaby F.T. et al, "Microwave Remote Sensing, Active and Passive", Vol III, Addison-Wesley Publishing Company, ISBN 0-201-10760,1986.

Table 1. The comparison of initialization, initial parameter:(0,50,50,20,20),cost=45901 with Ψ=0.32, cost=57705 with Ψ=0.62, cost=63201 with Ψ=0.80, the truth value parameter:(36,110,135,98,158).

Ψ	(θ,xt,yt,xs,ys)	cost (x 10^4)	No. of function evaluation
0.80	(36,110,135,96,157)	6.1151	6002
0.62	(36,110,135,96,158)	4.9918	5446
0.32	(36,110,135,97,158)	2.8627	4013

Table 2. The experimental data for SAR image.

#	type	σ°(DB)	initial	final
1	wheat	-10.08	(45,140,64,30,30)	(60,154,64,22,37)
2	sugar beet	-3.42	(55,135,80,20,35)	(60,141,87,23,38)
3	wheat	-9.85	(55,112,130,25,30)	(60,112,136,24,35)
4	potato	-5.63	(61,100,150,25,25)	(60,100,160,23,35)
5	wheat	-10.24	(55,160,120,15,30)	(60,167,127,14,35)
6	sugar beet	-3.82	(62,140,160,10,30)	(60,142,168,10,34)
7	potato	-5.74	(61,128,180,10,30)	(60,127,186,10,31)
8	barley	-7.58	(65,180,150,100,50)	(60,196,151,135,35)

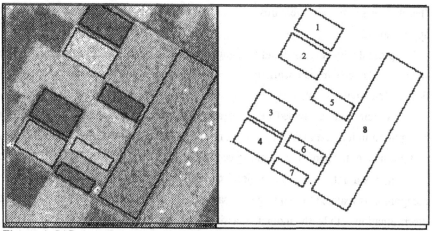

Figure 4 SAR image, overlapped with the result. **Figure 5** The edge map of the objects.

A Synthesized Computer Recognition System for Human Hands

Chuanxue WANG   HanQing LU   SongDe MA

National Lab. of Pattern Recognition, Institute of Automation
Chinese Academy of Sciences, Beijing, 100080, P. R. China

Abstract. A computer recognition system for human hands is presented in this paper. The system is based on infrared images. A multi-grid normalization technique is developed to normalize the position of the hand and fingers. Sets of geometric features, Zernike moment features and algebraic features are used in a two-stage recognition scheme. The system works very well on 300 hand samples of 30 persons with a 97% discrimination rate.

1 Introduction

One of the fascinating powers of human vision is its ability to recognize human faces. Because the detection of face features is quite sensitive to personal state and facial expressions, face recognition is still a difficult task for computer vision system. We are developing a hand recognition system for identification and we argue that "hand" has some stable features and are very convenient to be used in practical applications[1,2].

We present a system for hand recognition in this paper. We use infrared image such that the system can work in bad weather conditions, in nights or in badly-illuminated environment.

Our system can be divided into 4 parts: a preprocessing unit, a training unit, a recognition unit and a database. After an infrared image is taken, we first process it and normalize it. Then we extract the geometric features(lengths of fingers), Zernike moment invariant, subspace projective features from the training set. The recognition is realized in two stage: a coarse match by geometric classifier and a fine discrimination both by the moment classifier and subspace classifier.

2 Preprocessing and normalization of the hand images

An HR-2 type infrared camera was used to capture the hand image represented by a 256*256 pixel array, 8 bits for each pixel.

2.1 Preprocessing

To get a clear hand image for recognition, first we do a geometric deformity removing by a polynomial approximation method. Then we smooth he image by weighted averaging operation. The hand image is then segmented from the background using a traditional method by he histogram of the image. Figure 1 shows this process.

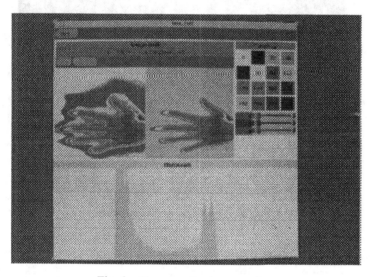

Fig. 1   Preprocessing demonstration

2.2 Normalization

Hand is s deformable object, the non-fixed fingers position causes a great difficulty for stable feature extraction. So we developed a normalization scheme:
  (1) Calculate the centroid and do contour tracing to obtain sequential boundary points from the binary image of hand;

(2) Calculate the boundary-centroid distance function. the feature points of hand is considered to be the local maximum of the distance function;

(3) Based on these feature points, we can easily cut the fingers respectively and rotate them to a predefined position relative to the central finger;

(4) Calculate the angle between the central finger and the horizontal line, then rotate it to make the one of he central finger locating in the direction of horizontal axis. Translate the whole hand to make the centroid of the hand locating on the center of the image.

This normalization process is shown in figure 2.

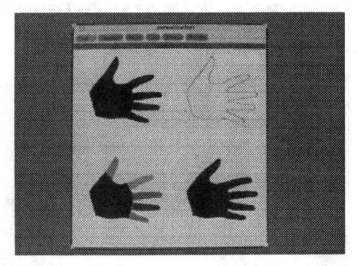

Fig. 2   Normalization demonstration

3   Feature extraction

3.1 Geometric features extraction

We calculate the lengths of the five fingers as geometric features $L = \{l_1, l_2, l_3, l_4, l_5\}$. They have the advantage of simplicity and can be used in the first stage matching. Figure 3 shows these feature.

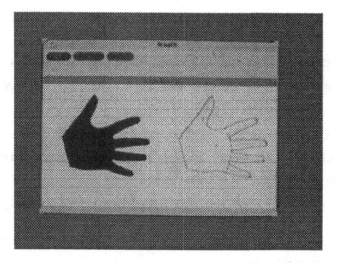

Fig. 3   Feature points and fingers' lengths

3.2 Zernike moment invariant

Moment invariant has very attractive properties. It is scale, translation, rotation and reflection invariant. We choose a new form of Zernike moment invariant for use, which have a reduced dynamic range[3,4].

The Zernike moment is defined as:

$$A_{nL} = \frac{n+1}{\pi} \int_0^{2\pi} \int_0^{\infty} f(r\cos\phi, r\sin\phi) R_{nL}(r) e^{-J\phi_r} dr d\phi \tag{1}$$

Where:

$n = 0,1,2,\cdots,\infty$, n-L is an even number, and $n \geq L \geq 0$. R_{nL} represents a real-value set of Zernike polynomials orthogonal inside the unit circle.

We construct 2-5th order Zernike moments ant according to the following theory[3]:

$$(ZM\ I)_{n0} = A_{n0} \tag{2}$$

$$(ZM\ I)_{nL} = |A_{nL}| \tag{3}$$

$$(ZM\ I)_{n,n+z} = \left[A_{mh}^* (A_{nL})^p \right]_-^+ \left[A_{mh}^* (A_{nL})^p \right]^* \tag{4}$$

Where $h \leq L, m \leq n, p = h/L, 0 \leq p \leq 1$ and $z = L/h$.

3.3 Algebraic features using algebraic subspace method

An image can be considered as a vector, which is a point φ^i in a very high dimensional space. Putting all the training image vectors φ^i (i=1,2, $\cdots$,N) together, we have a matrix A={$\varphi^1, \varphi^2, \cdots, \varphi^N$}.

We use K-L transformation to get the principal eigenvector μ_j(j=0,1, $\cdots$,k) of the scatter matrix $\Phi = A A^T$, which consists of a subspace called "Eigenhand space"[2].

Project every image into the eigenhand space:

$$U: \quad \phi^n = \omega_1^n \mu_1 + \omega_2^n \mu_2 + \cdots + \omega_k^n \mu_k = \sum_{i=1}^{n} \omega_i^n \mu_i \quad (n = 1,2,\cdots, N)$$

The projective coefficient set W={$\omega_1^n, \omega_2^n, \cdots, \omega_k^n$} (n=1,2, $\cdots$,N) can be used as algebraic features of hands.

4. System description and performance evaluation

The block diagram of the whole system is shown in Figure 4

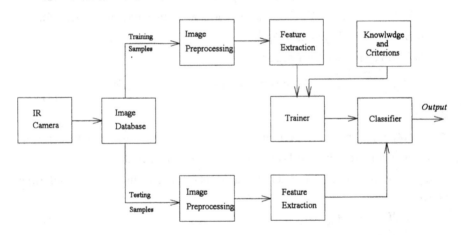

Fig. 4   Block diagram of the hands recognition system

4.1 Samples for experiments

300 hand infrared images were taken from 30 persons(10 images/a person) to form an image database. The 10 images of the same person differ from each other because of the environment temperature or hand posture and orientation. 4 of them were used as training samples, the other 6 as testing ones. Figure 5 shows some hand image samples of different persons.

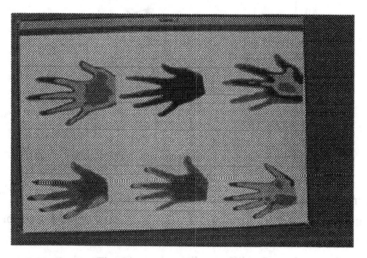

Fig. 5   Hands of different persons

4.2 Experiments of each kind of feature

We extract three kinds of feature as described in the previous sections for the training sample set.

By employing the nearest or K-nearest neighbor rules, we construct a K-nearest neighbor distance geometric classifier, a weighting Zernike moment classifier and a nearest distance classifier for subspace method.

Performance of the geometric classifier under different discrimination threshold is presented in figure 6. It shows that the information of these features is not enough for recognition.

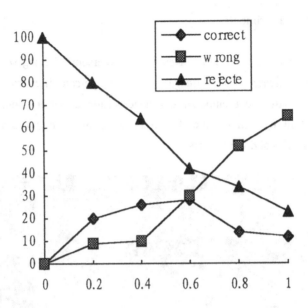

Fig. 6   The performance of the geometric classifier on 300 samples

Experiment results for the moment classifier based on 2-5 ordered Zernike moments are presented in figure 7.   4 order moments can work well for hands recognition.

Recognition results under different dimensions of eigenhands space are shown in figure 8.   7 eigenhands are informative enough to contain 91 percent of the total image energy.

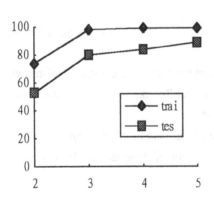

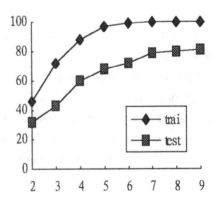

Fig. 7 The recognition results for Zernike moments of different order, when N=30

Fig. 8 The recognition rate and the number of eigenhands, when N=30

4.3 Integrated recognition system

The geometric features can not work well, but because their computation is very simple, which can greatly speed up our recognition, we use them for the first step hand matching. Choosing the discrimination threshold $\theta = 0.2$ can make sure all recognized samples belong to the correct class with a rejected rate of 75%.

Once a sample is rejected by the first match, the second discriminator will continue to work to make the final decision. From figure 7 and 8, we know the 4 order moment classifier or the subspace classifier is not good enough if hey are used separately, so we developed a fine discriminator by integrating them together using a weighted decision rule.

Using our integrated system, we arrived at a 97% recognition rate for all the 300 hand samples of 30 persons.

5 Summary

The success of our integrated hand recognition system demonstrates the application potential for human identification. Improved schemes and hardware structure need to be investigated to realize the real-time application.

Reference

1. M. Turk and A. Pentland: Eigenfaces for recognition. Journal of Cognitive Neuroscience, March 1991.
2. J.H. Ma, R.L. Zhao and S.D. Ma: Infrared eigenhands for human recognition. In Proceeding of The 1st Asian Conference on Computer Vision, Osaka, Japan, 1993.
3. M.R. Teague: Image analysis via the general theory of moments. J. Opt. Soc. Am., Vol.70, No.8, August 1980.
4. B.C. Li and J. Shen: Fast computation of moment invariant. Pattern Recognition 24, 1991.

Independent Hand Gesture Recognition in HandTalker

Wen Gao and Shuanglin Wang

Department of Computer Science, Harbin Institute Technology
and
Department of Computer Science, City University of Hong Kong

Abstract: HandTalker is a system we designed for enhanced user interface which allows user to communicate with computers or through computer network with others by hand gesture. One of the application cases of HandTalker is to help deaf people to "see" everyday news and to talk with other people. HandTalker consists of three parts: learner, recognizer, and synthesizer. In the recognizer, NN is applied for independent element recognition and HMM is applied for continuous gesture flow recognition. This paper describes our works on design and implementation for the part of independent hand gesture recognition in HandTalker.

1. Introduction

In this research, we are working on a general approach of automatically hand gesture recognition and (Chinese) sign language synthesis. The prototype system for proving the proposed approach is called HandTalker, which consists of three parts: a learner, a recognizer, and a synthesizer. The synthesizer is based on the animation of sign language sequence, facial expression and lip movement, driven by given text. The recognizer is based on image processing and pattern recognition techniques, in which NN is applied for independent gesture element recognition and HMM is applied for continuous hand gesture flow recognition. In this paper, we focus on looking for the basic solution of independent hand gesture element recognition for HandTalker, i.e., we aim at solving the issue of independent hand gesture recognition in a random background. Here, the independent hand gesture means that every target gesture is meaningful and not depended on any of others. In other words, only the basic elements of hand gesture are processed, no hand gesture flow or sequence is considered in this stage, even a gesture in the flow is actually more easy to understand than that of independent ones from the perceptual point of view.

In related work of HandTalker, Hauptmann, McAvinney and Shepard developed a gesture classification scheme for graphics manipulation which allows people to use gesture and/or speech to describe the computer task they wanted to accomplish without hints or prompting[4]. Rubine developed a gesture·classifier that is trained by examples[6]. Darrell and Pentland designed a system for learning and recognizing dynamic hand gesture[2]. Cui and Weng use learned decision boundaries to recognize sequences of vector-quantized images of hands[1]. Starner and Pentland extract the position and dominant orientation of both hands for the recognition of simple American Sign Language[7]. Rehg and Kanade implemented a model-based hand tracking system named DigitEyes using kinematics and geometric hand models[5].

For the task of hand gesture recognition, two procedures are necessary: gesture capturing and interpreting. Currently the technology for capturing gestures is expensive and difficult, for that implementation either a vision system or a dataglove system is needed. The dataglove provides easier access to highly accurate information, but it is a relatively intrusive technology, requiring the user to wear the special dataglove. Another input device is video camera, it is more difficult than the first one because information its provided is always incomplete, inaccurate and redundant. It needs image processing technique to segment the useful information and understanding it from a sequence of images, but computer vision is a far mature technique for real environments. The technology for interpreting hand gesture in real time is more difficult than capturing, it is extremely dependent of the quality of the captured gestures.

A complete gesture is composed of three part information: posture, orientation and motion (speed and orbit). In order to recognize a gesture, we must know these information of gestures. So it should first recognize the hand posture (gesture element), and then decide its state of motion, and at last combining these information to interpret the meanings of the gestures.

As the first step of continuous hand gesture understanding by computer, we have set up a sub-goal on the elements of hand gesture recognition using video camera. For our requirement, a hand target must be detected from an image sequence of any random background in real time. The background may be target person's cloth, indoor wall, or other things. Assuming the background is still (in a relative short period), it is not a problem to measure the target by frame difference even if the background is random and complex. On hand gesture recognition, the precondition of a high performance recognition system is to use good features and good classification model. After some experiments, we found that a set of edge features with the difference contour chain-code is quite good. For the recognition procedure, we use the well-known neural network: BP network, to build up the system kernel.

2. Prototype System of HandTalker

The system structure of HandTalker in blocks is given in Fig.1. The knowledge of hand gestures, which will be used for either hand gesture interpreting or hand gesture synthesizing, is stored into four databases: rule database, for human found rules on single hand gesture and hand gesture sequence; flow database, for machine found rules on continuous hand gestures, described by HMM parameters; hand database, for machine found rules on single still hand gesture described by weight parameter of neural network; and parameter database, for human and machine made parameter on 3D hand graphics generating.

The prototype of HandTalker consists of three parts: learner, recognizer, and synthesizer. Most modules are same in both learner and recognizer, except the parameter modifying module on NN weight matrix and HMM weight matrix.

In this paper, we will discuss only the algorithms and implementation for the part of single still hand gesture recognition.

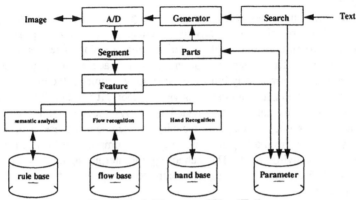

Fig.1 Block Diagram of HandTalker

3. Capturing Hand Target

In current stage, we use following constraints to avoid any expensive preprocessing in recognition:

- camera is mounted in a position where the target person should be faced to,
- intensity of hand image is clearly different with background image(say at least over 20 gray levels), so does color,
- background is relatively still.

For capturing the hand, we use motion analysis to detect a stable hand. The analysis is based on a comparison decision algorithm which is described in below.

Let G_B indicate the background image, G_x indicate the current image. Using G_d to indicate the difference image between G_B and G_x,

$$G_d = \left[G_{d_{ij}} \right] = |G_B - G_x| = |\left[G_{B_{ij}} - G_{x_{ij}} \right]| \tag{1}$$

Now to generate a set dG by G_d: dG={ $G_{d_{ij}}$ |0<i<W,0<j<H}. If no target hand on the current image, the mean of dG should be zero, otherwise it should be greater than zero. In order to resist the noise effect from any possible resources, also in order to obtain the possible target hand allocated area in the current image, a binary image G_b is generated on a threshold T_b,

$$G_B = (G_{Bij}) \tag{2}$$

$$G_{bij} = \begin{cases} 1 & G_{B_{ij}} > T_b \\ 0 & G_{B_{ij}} \leq T_b \end{cases} \tag{3}$$

where T_b is a variable determined by a function of, $T_b = g(G_d)$.

Moreover, in order to get rid of two classes of explicit non-hand noise: the small object target which size less than possible hand target, and the large object target which size greater than possible hand target, we use a N decision. Let R,

$$R = \sum_{i=0}^{W-1} \sum_{j=0}^{H-1} G_{Bij} \Big/ W * H \qquad (4)$$

(1) there is no hand in G when R less than the lower bound R_{lt},

(2) there is no hand in G when R greater than the upper bound R_{ut},

where $R_{lt}, R_{ut} \in (0,1)$, R_{lt} and R_{ut} are the parameters determined by a learning procedure. This decision works well even in the case when only a part of hand appeared in current image.

It believes that a hand gesture is meaningful if and only if it could be seen clearly by others. This means that a meaningful hand gesture must be still for at least several milliseconds. On this knowledge, we use a S decision to find the stable target image:

(1) given G_x and G_y in time period s, calculate G'_B

$$G'_B = G_{B_x} - G_{B_y} \qquad (5)$$

(2) given Q_t,

$$Q = \sum_{i=0}^{W-1} \sum_{j=0}^{H-1} G'_{Dij} \Big/ W * H < Q_t \qquad (6)$$

where parameters s and Q_t are also the parameters determined by a learning procedure which related to camera features and hand gesture samples.

If an image passed both the N decision and the S decision, then the closed region of all "1" on G_B is a possible hand target, we denote this closed region as Ph (possible hand target candidate) region.

4. Feature Extraction

After the procedure of hand target detection, a Ph region might be found. In next step, we generate a Ph window which is the smallest square which included Ph region. From now, all processing are taken place on the Ph window of original image G.

4.1 Edge Based Feature

In the processing of feature extraction, the first thing is to obtain the edge of a hand. On edge detection, an edge following algorithm is applied. For getting a smoother and more continuous edge, we apply the Sobel operator to sharpen the edge of the hand in the Ph window. After the Sobel operation, some preprocessing are done for thinning and smoothing edge to improve the edge into unit width and continuous curve. In current stage, for a real time limitation we overlap the sharpening result on the binary image G_b and follow the edge on G_b starting from a seed point, and then generate the Freeman chain code of the target edge from G_b.

On the other hand, because the direction and 'depth' of the hand gesture in the scene is variable, we have to capture the exact hand region from image, instead of a rich region of possible targets for recognition processing. So we should locate the position of the wrist to get rid of the useless data, i.e., we only pay attention to the parts of hand image from fingers to wrist. The rule applied is the minimal distance method to do so. Let A and B are two point sets of two side of the arm near the boundary of the scene respectively, to search for two points a and b that satisfy the following equation:

$$|ab| = \min(A, B) \tag{7}$$

Where a and b, the line ab is considered as the approximate position of the wrist.

After motion analysis, segmentation, binary operation, filtering by non-hand rule, left and/or right hand judgment, and wrist point judgment, a contour of target is obtained. We then use the CC code to represent this contour in this research[3], by which a two dimensional image is able to be mapped into an one dimensional signal sequence that is more easily to recognize by neural network. An example of hand gesture edge and difference chain code Df(n) is given in Fig.2. In where an edge of hand gesture of digital number 8 is shown in Fig.2(a), its Df(n) code is shown in Fig.2(b), and its CC code is shown in Fig.2(c).

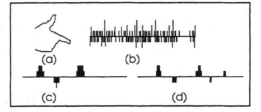

Fig.2 Difference chain code and low-pass filter

To get rid of the noise in Df(n) code sequence as shown in Fig.2(b), a good filter will be helpful for finding the robust fingers state in a played gesture. In fact, the filter design is one of the most important jobs in our implemented system. Let $D(i)$ denote the difference code string i, Wc denote channel width, the filter parameter can be described as,

$$Sum = \sum_{j=0}^{Wc-1} D(j) \tag{8}$$

$$R(i) = \begin{cases} Sum & Sum \geq Tf \\ 0 & Sum < Tf \end{cases} \tag{9}$$

where Tf indicates the threshold which usually choice as Tf=1,2,3, or other value based on the historical data and experiment. Different Tf stands for different shape of area. The relationship between the value Tf and the shape of area is shown in Fig.3. In fact, we can prove that the filtering result on a given difference code string is only dependent on the

T=1	T=2	T=3	T=4

Fig.3 Relationship between Tf and Shape

width of channel, and independent on the detail value of the difference code in current window. That is,

$$F(a) = \Phi(f(a) - f(a + Wc))\tag{10}$$

Sometimes, there are still a few sharp signal (usually 2 or 3 units in width) reminded even after low-pass filtering, as two examples of point a and b shown in Fig.4. These independent points are also the noise effect in difference code string. For smoothing this kind of noise, we simply erase all signals which width less than 3.

Fig.4 Independent points a and b in difference code string

After above processing, we finally obtain the feature set of hand gesture element representation, which is denoted as *FD(n)*.

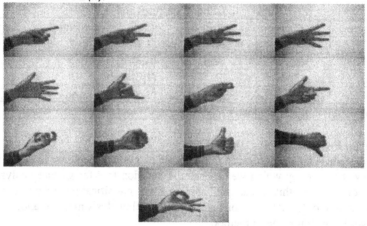

(a) gestures {1,2,3,4,5,6,7,8,9,10,good,bad,okay} by left hand

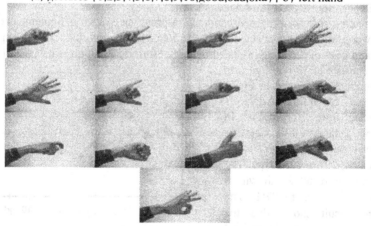

(b) gestures {1,2,3,4,5,6,7,8,9,10,good,bad,okay} by right hand

Fig.5 Samples of 13 gesture elements

5. Recognition Experiments and Analysis

From the pattern recognition point of view, the hand gesture element recognition problem is a pattern classification problem. For classifying the 13 types of gesture pattern given in Fig.5, we can simply use (f,v) to indicate a hang gesture, where f is the number of convex in $FD(i)$ which stands for the number of extended finger, v is the number of concave in $FD(i)$ which stands for the number of appeared finger valley. The relation of (f,v) and hand gesture elements is given in Table.1. Under this simple representation, we can intuitively classify the 13 elements into {{{0,7}, {1,gd,bd}}, {{2,9}, {8}}, {{3}, {6}, {ok}}, {4}, {5}}. This is a nested set in hierarchy structure, so that it is reasonable to build up the neural network in the hierarchy architecture.

Table.1 Relation of gestures and (f,v)

gesture	(f,v)	gesture	(f,v)	gesture	(f,v)
0	(1,0)	1	(1,1)	2	(2,1)
3	(3,2)	4	(4,3)	5	(5,4)
6	(3,1)	7	(1,0)	8	(2,2)
9	(2,1)	gd	(1,1)	bd	(1,1)
ok	(3,3)				

5.1 Hierarchy Analysis

It is quite convenient to consider that the set of gesture elements is classified by hierarchy structure, by which we can use the decision tree for gesture analysis and recognition. Under this idea, we applied two classification schemes in our implementation of HandTalker: one is the multilevel analysis method, another is the multilayer BP neural network method.

5.2 Experiment Results and Analysis

For making sure the proposed approach, a prototype system is implemented on PC and workstation that connected in a local area network environment. An experiment on hand gesture detection in real time and gesture recognition is designed in which data consists of 13 types gesture elements as mentioned in Fig.5. The set of training data is collected from 10 persons. In testing stage, 130 gesture samples, out of training data, are presented, 10 for each type. The recognition result is shown in Fig.6, from 88% to 97%. The testing result shows that the implemented system works well on most selected classes of hand gesture elements. However, it is not satisfying on classes of '7'

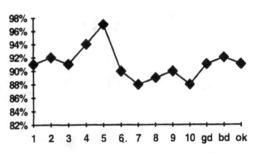

Fig.6 The recognized rate of 13 types of gestures (1,2,...,10, gd, bd and ok stand for gestures 1,2,...,10, good, bad and okay respectively)

and '10'. It might understandable if taking a look at the classification set of Table.1 again, in which '7' and '10' are with a same (f,v) touple so that it is difficult to classify them.

6. Conclusion and Future Works

A first stage result on independent hand gesture detection and recognition for HandTalker is reported in this paper. In the part of hand target detection, a scale judged method is presented for detecting hand target from image sequence in a random still background. The completeness and existence of a hand gesture are measured by a difference operation on background image and target image, and the stability of the target is measured on comparison of two successive target images. In the recognition part, a feature vector which is based on edge and shape information is defined. A decision tree is designed to recognize hand gesture from coarse to fine, and a BP neural network is applied to realize the decision tree.

The experimental result demonstrates that our proposed approach is efficient and acceptable. The prototype system can catch a target hand in real time, and can recognize it almost correctly.

Now we are working on following problems. Firstly, we are making use of the color information for catching more useful features from hand gesture elements. We are enlarging the set of gesture elements from 13 types to all types using in real sign language. In the same time, we will try to use a method of vision learning to improve the decision tree design. Secondly, we will integrate our approach to the continuous hand gesture recognition. Finally, pushing the real application of HandTalker.

References

[1] Y.Cui and J.Weng, "learning-based hand sign recognition", In Proc. of the Intl. Workshop on Automatic Face and Gesture Recognition, Zurich, 1995

[2] T.J. Darrell and Alex P. Pentland, "Recognition of space-time gestures using a distributed representation," Vision and Modeling Group Technical Report No.197, M.I.T. 1994

[3] W.Gao, "Enhanced user interface by using hand gesture recognition", in Proc. ICYCS'95 workshop on software computing, Beijing, 1995

[4] A.G.Hauptmann, P.McAvinney and S.R.Shepard, "Gesture Analysis for Graphic Manipulation," Technical Report CMU-CS-88-198, Department of Computer Science, Carnegie Mellon University, 1988

[5] J.M.Rehg and T. Kanade, "Digiteyes: Vision-Based Human Hand Tracking," Technical Report CMU-CS-93-220, Carnegie Mellon University, 1993

[6] D.H.Rubine, The automatic recognition of gesture, Ph.D. Dissertation, Department of Computer Science, Carnegie Mellon University, 1991

[7] T.E.Starner and A.Pentland, "Visual recognition of American Sign Language using hidden Markov models", In Proc. of the Intl. Workshop on Automatic Face and Gesture Recognition, Zurich, 1995

An Adaptive Estimation and Segmentation Technique for Determination of Major Maceral Groups in Coal

J. Dehmeshki, M. F. Daemi, B. P. Atkin and N. J. Miles*

Recognition Engineering Group
Department of Computer Science
*Department of Mineral Resources Engineering
University of Nottingham
University Park
Nottingham NG7 2RD, UK.
Tel +44 115 9514207
Fax +44 115 9514255
mfd@cs.nott.ac.uk

Abstract

This paper describes the development of an automated image based system for the classification of macerals in polished coal blocks. Coal petrology, and especially the estimation of the maceral content of a coal, has traditionally been considered to be a highly skilled and time consuming operation. However the recent upsurge in interest in this subject, driven by environmental legislation related to the utilisation of coal, has necessitated the development of a reliable automated system for maceral analysis. Manual maceral analysis is time consuming and its accuracy is largely dependent upon the skill of the operator. The major drawbacks to manual maceral analysis are related to time and operator fatigue, which can develop after the analysis of only one or two polished blocks. The reproducibility of the results from manual maceral analysis is also dependent upon the experience of the operator.

In this paper, a cooperative, iterative approach to segmentation and model parameter estimation is defined which is a stochastic variant of the Expectation Maximization (EM) algorithm. Because of the high resolution of these images under study, the pixel size is significantly smaller than the size of most of the different regions of interest. Consequently adjacent pixels are likely to have similar labels. In our Stochastic Expectation Maximization (SEM) method the idea that neighboring pixels are similar to one another is expressed by using Gibbs distribution for the priori distribution of regions (labels). We also present a suitable statistical model for distribution of pixel values within each maceral groups. This paper illustrate the power of the SEM method for the segmentation of macerals types.

Key Words: Macerals, Coal, Segmentation, Expectation maximization, Gibbs distribution, Stochastic Model.

1. Introduction

Coal petrology, and especially the estimation of the maceral content of a coal, has traditionally been considered to be a highly skilled and time consuming operation. However the recent upsurge in interest in this subject, driven by environmental legislation related to the utilisation of coal, has necessitated the development of a reliable automated system for maceral analysis. At least five hundred data points have to be investigated, and the maceral identified, on each block of coal examined. This is time-consuming and tiring for the analyst with operator fatigue often developing after the analysis of only one or two polished blocks. The accuracy and reproducibility of the results from manual maceral analysis are largely dependent upon the experience of the operator. The degree of subjectivity inherent in the analysis is also a cause for concern. For example, British Standard 6127 (British Standard 1981) discusses the repeatability and reproducibility of point counting using 500 points. For 95% significance the repeatability is $(2\sqrt{2})S$, where S is the standard deviation. This means that for a maceral group recorded at 50% the result could lie between about 47% and 53%, assuming that the operator makes negligible errors in identification. For reproducibility between operators from different laboratories S is replaces by S_0, the observed standard deviation which has been found to vary from 1.5 to 2 times the theoretical value due to operator errors in identifying macerals. Thus, at 50% the result could lie between about 44% and 56%. Table 1 is a good example of the variability of the method where six different workers in this and associated laboratories carried out on analysis on a single block of UK coal (Lester. et. al. 1994). The results show a reproducibility of about ± 5%.

One way of potentially overcoming these problems mentioned above is to apply Automated Image Analysis (Pratt, 1989). This paper describes a new method, namely SEM, which is a stochastic variant of the Expectation Maximization (EM) algorithm. Use of the SEM algorithm leads to a technique that allows for more accurate segmentation of macerals types in comparison with the other statistical technique such as EM or Maximum Likelihood classification

The number and type of maceral classes is a major variable between different coals and therefore between images. However, the following classes can be expected to occur in most coal samples studied:

- Simplex rapid mounting media,
- Holes
- Liptinite (including Miospore, Megaspore, Evtinite)
- Vitrinite (including type A and B)
- Inertinite (include Semifusinite, Fusinite, Macrinite)
- Pyrite

Of these classes liptinite and vitrinite are generally dominant with inertinite and pyrite generally occurring in lesser amounts. The presence of holes in the polished surface and the amount of mounting media visible is a function of the preparation of the sample but have to be correctly identified in a full maceral analysis.

	Major	Maceral	Groups		
	Vitrinite (%Vol)	Liptinite (%Vol)	Inertinite (%Vol)	Mineral (%Vol)	Pyrite (%Vol)
Operator 1	72.0	13.0	12.8	2.0	0.2
Operator 2	81.8	4.2	10.0	3.4	0.6
Operator 3	78.0	8.2	10.2	3.6	0.0
Operator 4	75.8	8.8	12.2	2.8	0.4
Operator 5	77.4	5.6	14.8	1.8	0.4
Operator 6	82.2	6.6	9.8	1.2	0.2

Table 1 Maceral group analysis on single block of UK Coal by six operators from different laboratories

Notation:

Let $I \subset \overline{Z}^d$ denote a set which indexes a finite rectangular region in a d-dimensional lattice system. For a two-dimensional lattice system, the index set can be denoted as

$$I = \left\{ k = (i,j) \mid 0 \le i < N, 0 \le j < N \right\}$$

At each location $k \in I$, suppose we have an observation, y_k, and an non-observation, z_k, which is intensity value and label of image respectively in the location k. We suppose there are L different classes. Therefore z_k can take any values of set of $\overline{L} = \{1, 2, \ldots, L\}$.

2. The Images Segmentation Problem

The aim of image segmentation is to assign a class or label to each pixel in an image Y. In our approach we infer the labels using a stochastic variant of the Expectation Maximization (EM) algorithm. In the following subsection the method will be outlined.

2.1. Modeling Posterior density of pixel values

The objective in this section is to present a suitable statistical model for distribution of pixel values. We assume a mixture model with L normal component.

$$p(y_k | \theta) = \sum_{l \in \overline{L}} \alpha_l p_l(y_k | \phi_l), \quad k \in I \tag{2-1}$$

Where, for each k,

$$p_l(y_k|\phi_l) = \frac{1}{\sqrt{2\pi\sigma_l}} e^{-(y-\mu_l)/2\sigma_l^2} \qquad \text{is Gaussian distribution with}$$

$$\phi_l = (\mu_l, \sigma_l^2)^T \in R^2$$

and

$$\theta = (\alpha_1, ..., \alpha_L, \phi_1, ..., \phi_L)$$

This model seems well suited for images under study since the difference maceral usually follow normally distribution. In order to characterize the image model (expression 2-1), the parameters need to be estimated which result in the segmentation of image. Although there are many general iterative procedure which are suitable for estimation of the parameters, such as Newton's method and conjugate gradient methods, EM method has been found in most instances to have the advantage of reliable global convergence, low cost per iteration, economy of storage and ease of programming (Pichard and Redner 1984). In sections 2.2 and 2.3 we review basic terminology related to the EM algorithm and present a novel segmentation technique base on EM.

2.2. The EM Method

The EM algorithm is an iterative method for the computation of the maximize of the posterior density. EM algorithm interprets the mixture density estimation problem as an incomplete data problem. As in the previous section, let Y=y be the observed incomplete data (i.e., a given image); let Z be the unobserved incomplete data (i.e. the labeling of image which is to be estimated); and let X=(Y,Z) be unobserved complete data. It is assumed that, given both y and z, it is straightforward to calculate and maximize the expectation of log-posterior $\log(p(\theta|y,z))$. To obtain the maximizer of the observed posterior $p(\theta|y)$, One first computes the expectation of $\log(p(\theta|y,z))$ with respect to the conditional predictive distribution $p(z|y,\theta^m)$, where θ^m is the current approximation to the mode of the observed posterior. This is Known as the E step. In the M step, one obtains the maximizer of this conditional expectation. The conditional predictive distribution is then updated by the new maximizer and the algorithm is iterated (Render and Walker 1984, Dempster et al. 1977). More formally, The EM algorithm consists of two steps:

E step: form $Q(\theta'|\theta) = E_\theta(l_X(\theta')|y)$

M step: maximize $Q(.|\theta)$

$E_\theta(.|y)$ denote the conditional expectation given Y=y, where θ is the true parameter and $l_X(\theta')$ is the log-likelihood of X. Capital letters are used for random variables and corresponding small letters for observed values. According to the model (2-1) for a given $\phi_l^m = (\mu_l^m, \sigma_l^{2\,m})$, the unique solution $\phi_l^{m+1} = (\mu_l^{m+1}, \sigma_l^{2(m+1)})$ of M-step is given by (Redner and Walker 1984)

$$\mu_l^{m+1} = \frac{\left\{ \sum_{k\in I} y_k \dfrac{\alpha_l^m p(y_k|\phi_l^m)}{p(y_k|\theta^m)} \right\}}{\left\{ \sum_{k\in I} \dfrac{\alpha_l^m p(y_k|\phi_l^m)}{p(y_k|\theta^m)} \right\}} \qquad (2\text{-}2\text{-}a)$$

$$\sigma_l^{2(m+1)} = \frac{\left\{ \sum_{k\in I} (y_k - \mu_l^{m+1})^2 \dfrac{\alpha_l^m p(y_k|\phi_{li}^m)}{p(y_k|\theta^m)} \right\}}{\left\{ \sum_{k\in I} \dfrac{\alpha_l^m p(y_k|\phi_l^m)}{p(y_k|\theta^m)} \right\}} \qquad (2\text{-}2\text{-}b)$$

$$\alpha_l^{m+1} = \frac{1}{N} \sum_{k\in I} \frac{\alpha_l^m p(y_k|\phi_l^m)}{p(y_k|\theta^m)} \qquad (2\text{-}2\text{-}c)$$

It should be pointed out that $\dfrac{\alpha_l^m p(y_k|\phi_l^m)}{p(y_k|\theta^m)}$ is the posterior probability that y_k originated in the lth class, given the current approximate maximum-likelihood estimate θ^m. We can denote this with z_{kl} and consider it as criteria for labeling pixels as follows:

After enough iteration we terminate process by labeling each pixel by assigning that member of $\overline{L}$ which maximise z_{kl} that is

$$z_k^* = \arg\max_{l\in K} z_{kl} \qquad (2\text{-}3)$$

The above algorithm in each iteration not only estimate (modify) parameters of models but it also classifies pixels of each group. For this reason we can call it an adaptive estimation and segmentation technique. Figure 4(d) shows the results of segmentation using this algorithm which applied for image of Figure 4(a).

From (2-3) It can be remarked that the above approach from segmentation point of view is a local maximise approach which can tend to noisy results as the Figure 4(d) shows that. This is mainly due to the fact that in the above method we implicitly assumed the independency of pixel labeling which is not desirable in some cases such as our applications. Therefore smoothing is necessary.

The adjacent labels are likely to belong to the same pattern and the boundaries between the segments tend to be smooth. MRF or GRF (there are one-to-one corresponding between MRF's and GRF's which known as the Hammersley-Clifford theorem, Besag, 1974) are appropriate for prior distribution of the pixel labeling Z in the absence of the observed data Y because they can specify the local properties of regions. We do not give fully details about MRF since these stochastic processes are now very popular (Dehmeshki 1995(a) and (b), Geman, 1984, Laskshmanan & Derin, 1989). In the following section we will modify the above EM algorithm by applying an appropriate Gibbs distribution. We call this technique, Stochastic Expectation Maximization technique (SEM).

2.3. Gibbs distribution and SEM method.

Before proceeding to describe the SEM algorithm, we review basic terminology related to the Gibbs distribution .

Definition : A random field $X = \{X(i,j), (i,j) \in \Omega\}$ is a GRF with respect to a given neighborhood system D if and only if its joint probability distribution function is of the following form:

$$p(Z = z) = S^{-1} \exp[-\beta u(z)] \tag{2-4}$$

where,

$$u(z) = \sum_{c \in C} v_c(z) \quad \text{energy function}$$

$v_c(z)$ = potential associated with clique c and it depend only the points in clique c.

β is a fixed non-negative parameters,

$S = \sum \exp[-\beta u(z)]$ is a normalising constant called partition function to make a valid probability distribution.

In above definition, it can implicitly be seen, by clique associated with neighborhood system D and, consequently, by the potential functions defined for these cliques, we can have a wide variety of GD.

One typical neighborhood system configuration is illustrated in Figure 1. As indicated there, a neighborhood system can be classified as first-order, second-order, and so on; according to number of neighbors a lattice point has. The clique type associated with the first-order and second-order neighborhood systems are illustrated in Figure 2.

To avoid boundary problem (due to the finite lattice used), a toroidal lattice structure is assumed. Under this assumption, the neighborhood of pixels on the boundaries are the same as those of inside.

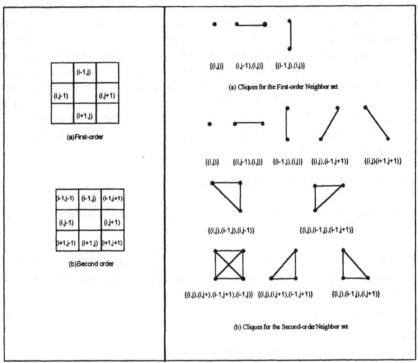

Figure 1. The Neighborhood System

Figure 2. The Clique type

As mentioned earlier, the characteristics of the model GRF is determined by the clique type and the potential function. Here we will consider second-order neighborhood system and pairwise interaction clique between neighbors. With this in mind, we define a potential function $v_c(z_k)$ associated with clique c as follow:

$$v_c(z_k) = \xi_s z_{sl}$$

Where, $s \in c$ and $k \in I$

$$
\text{Where } \begin{cases} \xi_s = 1 & \text{if } \{k,s\} \text{ are horizantal and vertical cliques} \\ \xi_s = \dfrac{1}{\sqrt{2}} & \text{otherwise} \end{cases}
$$

(2.5)

Recall that $z_{sl} = \dfrac{\alpha_l \, p(y_s|\phi_l)}{p(y_s|\theta)}$.

The conditional probability can be derived in what follows from the MRF-GRF equivalence.

$$p(z_k|z_{sk}, s \in D_k) = \frac{\exp[-\sum v_c(z_k)]}{\displaystyle\sum_{z_k \in \bar{L}} \exp[-\sum v_c(z_k)]} \tag{2-6}$$

Where $v_c(.)$ is the potential function defined in (2-5), and the summation $v_c(z_k)$ are over all pairwise interaction cliques contain k.

Now, with considering all aforementioned material, we are ready to modify the previous mixture model (expression 2.1) as follow

$$p(y_k|\theta) = \sum_{l \in \bar{L}} \alpha_l(k) p_l(y_k|\phi_l), \qquad k \in I \tag{2-7}$$

Note at the above expression we have replaced α_l by $\alpha_l(k)$ to show the dependency α_l to location k (and its neighborhood). As result of this modification, the expression of 2.2 will be changed as follow:

According to the new model (2-7) for a given $\phi_l{}^m = (\mu_l{}^m, \sigma_l^{2\,m})$, the unique solution $\phi_l{}^{m+1} = (\mu_l{}^{m+1}, \sigma_l^{2(m+1)})$ of M -step will be given by:

$$\mu_l{}^{m+1} = \frac{\left\{ \displaystyle\sum_{k \in I} y_k \frac{\alpha_l{}^m(k) p(y_k|\phi_l{}^m)}{p(y_k|\theta^m)} \right\}}{\left\{ \displaystyle\sum_{k \in I} \frac{\alpha_l{}^m(k) p(y_k|\phi_l{}^m)}{p(y_k|\theta^m)} \right\}} \tag{2-8}$$

$$\sigma_l^{2(m+1)} = \frac{\left\{ \displaystyle\sum_{k \in I} (y_k - \mu_l^{m+1})^2 \frac{\alpha_l{}^m(k) p(y_k|\phi_{li}{}^m)}{p(y_k|\theta^m)} \right\}}{\left\{ \displaystyle\sum_{k \in I} \frac{\alpha_l{}^m(k) p(y_k|\phi_l{}^m)}{p(y_k|\theta^m)} \right\}}$$

where $\alpha_l{}^m$ in each step can be approximately calculated by assuming

$$\alpha_l^m(k) \approx p(l \mid z_{sk}, s \in D_k) = \frac{\exp[-\sum v_c(l)]}{\sum_{z_k \in \bar{L}} \exp[-\sum v_c(z_k)]} \qquad (2\text{-}9)$$

The above algorithm is summarized below

The SEM Algorithm

1. Start with the initial parameters μ_l^0, σ_l^0 and $\alpha_l^0 = \dfrac{1}{L}$,set m= 0.

2. Find $z_{kl} = \dfrac{\alpha_l\, p(y_k|\phi_l)}{p(y_k|\theta)}$ for $k \in I$ and $l \in \bar{L}$.

3. Increment m and re-estimate μ_l^m, σ_l^m, and $\alpha_l^m(k)$ according to (2-8) and

   (2-9)
4. Repeat steps 2 and 3 for a predefined number of iterations.
5. Find $z_k^* = \arg\max_{l \in \bar{L}} z_{kl}$ for $k \in I$.

The initial parameters of the model can be estimated by using a K-means clustering or ISODATA, in the case of unsupervised segmentation. These parameters are then modified in each iteration of SEM. In the case of supervised segmentation, the initial parameters can be obtained from a classifier training data set and then re-estimated in the SEM method. The reason for this re-estimation is that a set of classification parameters obtained from a classifier training data set may not produce satisfactory results on images which were not used to train the classifier. Therefore the above SEM algorithm provides estimation of parameters of model as well as segmentation of images.

3. Experimental results and discussion

In order to verify the ability of the SEM technique to segment images of under study, we first apply the SEM on a synthetic image composed of two different region generated by Gaussian model (Figure 3(a)). In obtaining this realisation, we have used (85,30) and (40,30) as parameters of the distribution. The original region boundaries that were used to assemble Figure 3(a) are shown in Figure 3(b) for visual comparison. As illustrated in Figures 3(c), 3(d) and 3(e), the segmentation obtained with the SEM method is much better than the one obtained with either the ML (given the parameters of the model) and the EM methods. The performance of our SEM is further illustrated in Figure 3(f) which shows the error between the SEM result and the Real segmentation. This result is in agreement with our idea that adjacent pixels are likely to have similar labels. Parameter estimates obtained are shown in Table 2.

Figure 4 shows a comparison of the experimental results using three methods for segmentation of a microscopic image of the coal. Figure 4(a) shows a typical subregion of microscopic image of coal. For this experiment we consider five classes, namely of Vitrinite, Fusinite, Liptinite, Semifusinite and resins. Figure 4(b) shows the segmentation result using Maximum Likelihood segmentation technique (with assumption of Gaussian distribution for the intensity value within each class). The parameters of different classes were obtained using the training data set. Figure 4(c) show segmentation result using the EM method. The parameters of the mixture model were re-estimated in each iterations of the segmentation process. The reason for this re-estimation is that a set of classification parameters obtained from a classifier training data set may not produce satisfactory results on image which was not used to train the classifier. Although EM technique improves the segmentation result, it still leads to a noisy segmentation result. This problem is due to the fact that the EM method is non-contextual, i.e. it does not take into account the local interactions of adjacent pixels resulting in noisy segmentation. Figure 4(d) shows the segmentation result using SEM method. This clearly shows the advantage of this technique over the others because of its Contextual nature.

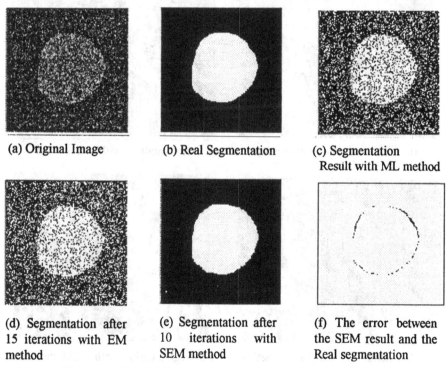

(a) Original Image

(b) Real Segmentation

(c) Segmentation Result with ML method

(d) Segmentation after 15 iterations with EM method

(e) Segmentation after 10 iterations with SEM method

(f) The error between the SEM result and the Real segmentation

Figure 3. Segmentation Results using synthetic Images

Method	Number of iterations	Initial parameters	Estimated parameters	Real parameters
EM	5	(30,21) (95,15)	(34.350,22.503) (82.998,25.683)	(40,30) (85,30)
EM	15	(30,21) (95,15)	(34.460,23.091) (86.423,27.408)	(40,30) (85,30)
SEM	5	(30,21) (95,15)	(41.082,27.536) (85.143,29.975)	(40,30) (85,30)
SEM	10	(30,21) (95,15)	(41.052,27.580) (84.863,30.206)	(40,30) (85,30)

Table 2. Comparison of the performance of different techniques

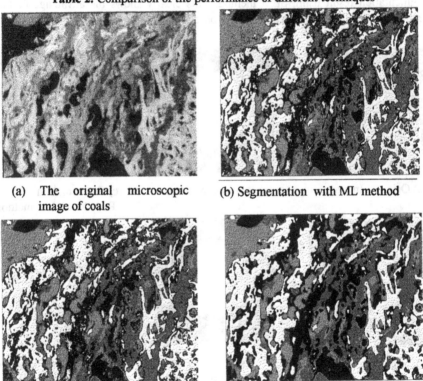

(a) The original microscopic image of coals

(b) Segmentation with ML method

(c) Segmentation with EM method after 10 iterations

(d) Segmentation with SEM method after 5 iterations

Figure 4. The segmentation results for a typical coal image.

4. Conclusions

The SEM method presented in this paper has been tested on both synthetic and real microscopic images of coals. The results indicate that the proposed SEM segmentation method is superior to non-contextual classifiers, such as EM and ML. However the SEM method is iterative in its nature. Consequently, its convergence behavior, which is only scarcely known, should be studied in detail.

REFERENCES

- Besag, J. (1974)., " Statistical Interaction and the Statistical Analysis of Lattice Systems." Journal of The Royal Statistical Society", Series B, Vol. 36, pp. 192-239.
- British Standard, 6127 (1981), British Standards Institute, Milton Keynes, UK.
- Dehmeshki, J., Daemi, M. F. and Marston, R. E. (1995 - a), "Unsupervised Segmentation of Textured Images using Binomial Markov Random Fields", Accepted for presentation at the Iranian Conference on Electrical Engineering (ICEE'95), May 1995, Tehran, Iran.
- Dehmeshki, J., Daemi, M. F., Miles, N.J., Atkin, B.P. and Marston, R. E. (1995 - b), " Classification of Coal Images by a Multi-Scale Segmentation Technique", Presented at the IEEE Symposium on Computer Vision, Coral Gables, Florida, November 1995.
- Dempster, Laird, Rubin. (1977), "Maximum Likelihood from Incomplete Data via the EM Algorithm " J. Royal Stat. Soc., Series B, Vol. 39, pp. 1-38
- Derin, H. and Elliott, H. (1987), "Modeling and of Noisy and Textured Images using Gibbs Random Fields". IEEE Trans. Pattern Anal. Machine Intell. Vol. PAMI-9, pp. 39-55.
- Geman, S. and Geman, D. (1984), "Stochastic Relaxation, Gibbs Distributions, and the Bayesian Restoration of Images", IEEE Trans. Pattern Anal. Machine Intell. Vol. PAMI_6, pp. 721-741.
- Lakshmanan, S. and Derin, H. (1989), "Simultaneous Parameter Estimation and Segmentation of Gibbs Random Fields using Simulated Annealing", IEEE Trans. Pattern Anal. Machine Intell., Vol. 11, pp. 799-813.
- Lester, E. Allen, M. Clock, M. and Miles, M. J. (1994), "An Automated Image Analysis System for Major Maceral Group Analysis in Coals". Fuel Vol. 73, pp. 1729-1734.
- Pratt, K. C. (1989), In 'Contribution to Canadian Coal Geoscience', Geological Survey of Canada, Canadian Government Publishing Center, Ottawa, pp. 146-148.
- Render, R. A. and Walker, H. F. (1984), "Mixture Densities, Maximum Likelihood, and the EM Algorithm," SIAM Review, Vol. 26, No. 2, pp. 195-239.

Expression and Motion Control of Hair using Fast Collision Detection Methods

Makoto Ando   Shigeo Morishima

Faculty of Engineering, Seikei University
Tokyo, Japan

Abstract. A trial to generate the object in the natural world by computer graphics is now actively done. Normally, huge computing power and storage capacity are necessary to make real and natural movement of the human's hair. In this paper, a technique to synthesize human's hair with short processing time and little storage capacity is discussed. A new *Space Curve Model* and *Rigid Segment Model* are proposed. And also high speed collision detection with the human's body is discussed.

1   Introduction

The image of the human's head by using computer graphics, is now used in various fields. For instance, in the field of entertainment, including the amusement and the movie etc., requested more realistic image of a character. Moreover, the technology of the computer graphics is taken to the research in the field of the information communications, to achieve a more flexible interface. In the image of these human's head, the hair is visually one of the most important elements. However, the hair is formed by lot of the objects which shape is extremely thin and long, and was one of the difficult objects in the computer graphics. Therefore, the hair is often substituted partially of texture. If the highlight of the hair moves while changing position of the light source, or the shape of the hair is transformed by external force such as wind or movement of the head, it is clear that the image of the hair becomes more real. However, a definite technique excelled in all points such as computing time, necessary storage capacity, reality and simplicity of modeling, has not existed yet. The mapping technology such as alpha-blending technique[1], anisotropic reflection model[2], or Texel[3] put high result with quality of the hair. On the other hand, when the animation of the hair is considered, it is general to use method which control the movement each of hair. These typical techniques include technique which modeled each hair with a triangular pillar[4] or other geometrical primitive[5]. Moreover, the technique which obtain the movement of the hair using probability model based on the measurement value, are proposed. In addition, the technique so called *Projection Equation Method* which solved to get the behavior of a minute segment, and rendered by anisotropic reflection model, is proposed[6][7]. The problem of these techniques are an increase calculation load and huge amount of the storage capacity, causes a huge number of the hair. In this paper, we discuss about modeling of the hair using space curve, and collision detection between human's body, to process motion of hair at high speed and reduce the storage capacity of computer. The space curve can describe the hair with mighty little data. Moreover, it is very suitable also for the control of the movement. The Rigid segment model and the control method are described too. In addition, we explain about the introduction of modeling tool which facilitates modeling of the hair, and about the settings of the external force field for get movement more really.

2 Modeling of Hair

As already described, it is necessary to control the movement of each hair one by one, to express the motion of the hair which waves delicately by the wind. So, it is necessary to model each hair. But the polygon increases extremely, when all minutely structre of hair was approximated by polygon. Therefore, a huge amount of storage capacity is needed, to model the entire hair. By the way, width of the hair which expressed by the computer graphics is narrow enough compared with each pixel on the screen. In our approach, it is not so important to solve the local structure of each hair, but to describe the shape of the curve. So, shape of the hair is approximated by the space curve and only the shape control points were stored as the data to describe this curve. However, it is impossible to perform rendering on the space curve, because a normal vector of an arbitrary point on these space curve cannot be decided because the curve does not have structure as three dimension. But by assuming the space curve as a very thin cylindrical pipe, then it is possible to perform the rendering by the reflection model without using the actual structure of the hair.

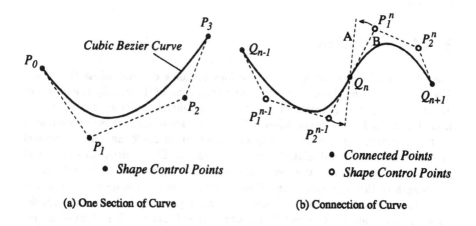

(a) One Section of Curve   (b) Connection of Curve

Fig. 1. Cubic Bezier Curve

Cubic Bezier curve is selected for the space curve, because it is easy to control the shape of curve, and function is comparatively easy. To generate each section of cubic Bezier function as shown in Fig.1(a), four shape control points, is needed to realize the curve interpolation. Because each section of the curve is independent, it's not sure whether end of a certain section will connect smoothly with the begining of the another section. So, it is neccessary to determine the connected point Q_n and two control points of the curve P_2^{n-1}, P_1^n so that these will come on the same line B and generate a smooth curve as one, as shown in Fig.1(b). In case of hair modeling, only by providing the shape control points which correspond to the connecting points of each section and by calculating the rest points automatically, smooth and continous curve can be defined. In addition, the wavy hair such as curl, can be easily modeled by changing an angle between straight line A and tangential line B in connected point as shown in Fig.1(b). The simplest way to provide these shape control points to a computer is to give the 3-D coordinate values to the each hair. But it is clear that this methods is not the clever way to create the whole hair. So more simplified way for hair modeling is proposed. First, the user selects one hair generating area on the head displayed by the polygon in the screen. This hair generating area is one of the divided scalp which generate the hair, including front, rear, left side, right side, top, and back of the head. Next, a typical hair is made in the selected area. The curve is gradually displayed, while pointing in a three-dimensional space by using mouse device. A supplementary axis is displayed for each direction of x, y, z, to manifest current point. When the shape of one curve decides, it is reproduced by all polygons in the selected hair generating area which number are 10 on the average. Because the curves of the hair in the generating area have the same shapes with the others, fine adjustment is needed to change the shape of each hair. Finally, the whole hair is formed by duplicating the hair from about 200 to 400 on each polygon depending on the given density. The parameters including density, disorderliness and color of the hair can be changed at every polygon.

3   Motion Control

Now the method to determine the positions of shape control points of curve is discussed. In this method, contraction and expansion of the hair by the influence of external force are disregarded, and the shape control points are mutually connected with the Rod as *Rigid segment*. So, the motion of the hair is approximated by the movement of this linked segment as shown in Fig.2, and the movement of each segment can calculate by using geostatics. The position of each Rigid segment is represented in the spherical coordinates expressions as (r, ϕ, θ). Here, r is length of the segment, ϕ and θ are directions of the segment in the space. The shape control point which becomes starting point of the segment link, defined as fixed node P_0. Oppositely, the other side of segment link, defined as free node P_n. Each segment is rotatable in all directions around the adjacent node of fixed end side. That is, the position vector of all nodes is decided with Rigid

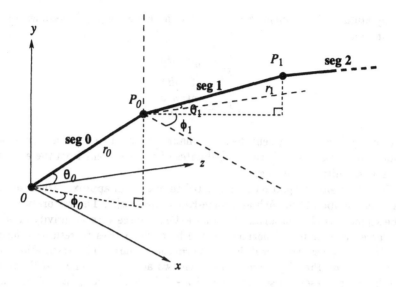

Fig. 2. Linked Segment

segment, and the shape of space curve is clarified uniquely. In this case, the degree of freedom of the movement is two. Therefore, if the link composed from n segment, the freedom degree of the movement becomes $2n$, and the motion equation of this model becomes a coalition partial differential equation with the variable of $2n$. It is important to model a physical phenomenon faithfully, but solving this equation of motion is a complex, nonlinear problem, and is unuseful. If the external force are not so large, and the object moves in the constant fluid, it can simplify the model that each segment moves independently and be not influenced by other segments in minute time. On the strength of this simplification, the motion of the segment can be described as the motion of Rod which have mass.

The motion equation of the Rod which rotate around arbitrary axis O is expressed as follows.

$$N = I_O \frac{d\omega}{dt} \tag{1}$$

Where N is moment of Rod, I_O is an inertia moment around axis O, and ω is an angular velocity of the Rod. Inertia moment I_O were decided as $I_O = ml^2/3$, where l and m is length and mass of the Rod respectively. The motion of each segment N is described as $N = F \times r$, where r is the position vector of gravity center, F is the total active force of segment. So, expression 1 become as follows.

$$F \times r = \frac{ml^2}{3} \frac{d\omega}{dt} \tag{2}$$

The equation of component ϕ and θ from the expression (2) becomes to the following form.

$$\frac{1}{2}F_\theta = \frac{ml^2}{3}\frac{d^2\theta}{dt^2}$$
$$\frac{1}{2}F_\phi = \frac{ml^2}{3}\frac{d^2\phi}{dt^2} \tag{3}$$

Because the length of segment does not change, component F_r is not necessary. Actually, to obtain the spherical coordinates of each segment from the equation (3), first the initial value is given.

Then the motion equation is calculated to obtain an approximation solution by a numeric operation, such as Runge-Kutta method[8]. The restoration force of the segment is also important, besides external force such as gravity or wind. This force arise from transforming of the hair which tries to return to former shape, and becomes stronger if the transformation is large. This restoration force depends only on the displacement between two adjacent segment. If the initial angle between these two segment i and $i - 1$ is defined as ξ, and ξ' as angle after transforming, the restoration force is assumed that become proportional to $\xi' - \xi$. The direction of this force correspond to the direction which returns the segment to the origin position.

4 Collision Avoidance

There are two previous works, to handle collision detection between hair and human's body. One is using *Pseudoexternal Force Area* which surounds the whole head so that the hair will not slip inside the head by the effect of this pseudoexternal force. The other method prepare a surface in cylindrical coordinate system as buffer which stored the distance between center and surface of head, to detect collision with simple comparison[7]. In the former technique, a special collision processing is not necessary, and the calculation time is sped up. However, strict collision avoidance is not executed, and the user should set pseudoexternal force so that the hair does not slip into the head. The latter technique requires slight time for the detection, but it is necessary to prepare the buffer for each object to detect the collision. In addition, it is necessary to transform the coordinate for all of the individual objects. Here collision detection methods using rectangular coordinate system where the hair movement is actually calculated is proposed. In this method, there is no need to transform the coordinate for collision detection, and the collision detection is done at high speed only with a simple comparison. In this method, first of all, a virtual surface is set in rectangular coordinate system as shown in Fig.3, so that all objects concerned with the collision are possible to project parallely on this surface and no intersection is occured with any objects. Next, the corresponding two dimensional array of virtual surface is prepared. In the element $[x_p, z_p]$ of the array stored y value of the point which intersects the perpendicular from point (x_p, z_p) with

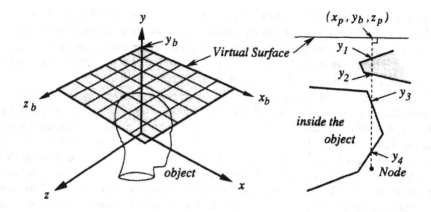

Fig. 3. Virtual Surface

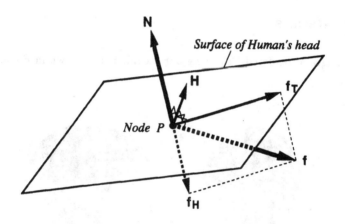

Fig. 4. Preventing the Node from Slipping

each object, such as $y_1, y_2, y_3, \ldots$ in Fig.3, in order of intersection. While detecting the collision, the nearest element form x_p and z_p is refered, where x_p and z_p are the coordinate of shape control point. This element kept y value of intersection point with the polygon on same x_p, z_p as $y_1, y_2, y_3, \ldots$. If all objects are closed, the control point which exist its y value within the range of $y_p > y_1, y_2 > y_p > y_3, y_{2n} > y_p > y_{2n+1}$ $(n = 1, 2, 3, \ldots)$, is always outside of all objects. Here, the calculation of collision detection is only comparison with array. The result is decided immediately that the object does not exist, when coordinate of the control point exceed the range of the array.

The problem is that it is not possible to detect collision correctly, in the environment that another object slips into the inside of the object, or existing the object which does not closed completely. Moreover uselessness is caused easily in the array, because the array is on rectangular coordinate system. The latter problem can solve by controlling the mesh of virtual surface adaptively, instead of delimiting simply. This will be our future work.

The avoidance is necessary by controlling the movement of the hair when the collision is detected. The colliding hair behaves for a while as flowing along the surface of the head. To achieve this, the following collision processings were done. The speed and the acceleration of node P on the surface of the object can be divided into the element of normal direction and tangent direction on the surface, as shown in Fig.4. The element in the tangent direction is an irrelevant component that the hair goes into the head. Then, only the tangent direction component f_T of the acceleration and the speeds of this node is preserved, and the normal direction component f_H is adjusted to zero. Thus, we prevented the node from going inside object.

5   Test Results

Several images of rendered hair using our technique are shown in Fig.5. In this

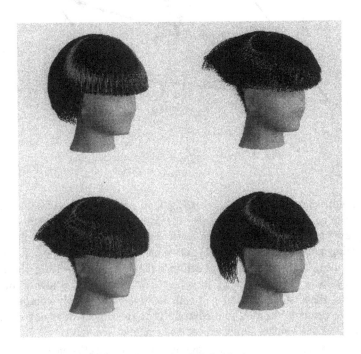

Fig. 5. Example of Hair Motion

animation, the wind is going front to rear of head, besides gravity. The entire hair contains about 15,000 piece, and each hair consist from 8-12 shape control points of the space curve. It takes about 20 seconds to render the image of 512x512, using a graphics workstation with the CPU ability of 85 MIPS. The motion is sampled every 1/400 seconds, to get the position of all segments, and it takes about 40 seconds for the processing of collision avoidance. This result is about 2.6 times faster than our old method which examine intersection with all polygons.

6 Conclusions

As for a thin, soft object like a hair, the approximation with the space curve seems to be excellence. The storage capacity for the calculation was reduced by a large margin with space curve. In addition, a real rendering of the hair was realized by assuming the space curve to be a thin pipe, though there was no actual structure of the hair. Moreover, by the Rigid segment model, it becomes easier to control the space curve, and it is more faithful to a actual physical model. As the future work, in respect of rendering, the shadow from the hair has to be considered. And the high-speed algorithm has to be designed, to reduce the calculating time. Computing time has been considerably shortened by our collision detection method. However, the array for the collision detection should be more uselessness.

References

1. A. LeBlanc, R. Turner, D. Thalmann, "Rendering Hair using Pixel Blending and Shadow Buffers", The Journal of Visualization and Computer Animation 2, 3, pp. 92-97, 1991b
2. W. T. Reeves, "Particle Systems - A Technique for Modeling a Class of Fuzzy Objects", Computer Graphics, 17(3), pp. 359-376, 1983
3. J. T. Kajiya and T. L. Kay, "Rendering Fur with Three Dimensional Textures", Computer Graphics(Proc. SIGGRAPH89), Vol. 23, No. 3, pp. 271-280, Jul. 1989
4. Y. Watanabe and Y. Suenaga, "Drawing Human Hair using Wisp Model", Proc. CG International '89, pp. 691-700, 1989
5. R. E. Rosenblum, W. E. Carlson, E. Tripp III, "Simulating the Structure and Dynamics of Human Hair: Modelling, Rendering and Animation", The Journal of Visualization and Computer Animation, Vol. 2, No. 4, pp. 141-148, 1991
6. K. Anjyo, Y. Usami, T. Kurihara, "A Simple Method for Extracting the Natural Beauty of Hair", Computer Graphics, Vol. 26, No. 2, pp. 111-120, 1992
7. T. Kurihara, K. Anjyo, D. Thalmann, "Hair Animation with Collision Detection", In: Models and Techniques in Computer Animation, Springer-Verlag, Tokyo, pp. 128-138, 1993
8. D. F. Rogers and J. A. Adams, "Mathematical Elements for Computer Graphics", McGraw-Hill, 1976

3-D Emotion Space for Interactive Communication

Fumio KAWAKAMI[a]   Motohiro OHKURA[a]   Hiroshi YAMADA[b]

Hiroshi HARASHIMA[c] Shigeo MORISHIMA[a]

[a]Faculty of Engineering [b]Lab. of Psychology [c]Faculty of Engineering
Seikei University   Kawamura College   University of Tokyo
Tokyo, Japan   Tokyo, Japan   Tokyo, Japan

Abstract. In this paper, the methods for modeling facial expression and emotion are proposed. This Emotion Model, called *3-D Emotion Space* can represent both human and computer emotion conditions appearing on the face as a coordinate in the 3-D Space.

For the construction of this 3-D Emotion Space, 5-layer neural network which is superior in non-linear mapping performance is applied. After the network training with backpropagation to realize Identity Mapping, both mapping from facial expression parameters to the 3-D Emotion Space and inverse mapping from the Emotion Space to the expression parameters were realized.

As a result a system which can analyze and synthesize the facial expression were constructed simultaneously.

Moreover, this inverse mapping to the facial expression is evaluated by the subjective evaluation using the synthesized expressions as test images. This evaluation result proved the high performance to describe natural facial expression and emotion condition with this model.

1 Introduction

The goal of research is to develop a very natural human-machine communication environment by giving a face and emotion to a computer terminal or communication system itself. To achieve this goal the computer have to recognize one's emotion condition appearing on the face, and synthesize the reasonable and suitable facial image sequence against the human's condition. For this purpose, the human's and computer's emotion condition should be described quantitatively based on facial expressions. If the emotion condition of operator and computer can be spatially represented in the space, 3-D space for example, both emotion condition of the operator and computer can be displayed visually as the coordinates in the 3-D space.

Moreover, for facial expression analysis and synthesis this 3-D space should realize both mapping from the expression to this space and inverse mapping from points of space to the expressions.

In our system, by supposing the 5-layered neural network's middle-layer as 3-D Emotion Space, these both mapping and inverse mapping can be realized by the non-linear mapping performance of the network via the Emotion Space.

Further more, generalization performance of neural network enable the system to analyze and synthesize the facial expression other than the basic expressions.

Inverse mapping performance of 3-D Emotion Space is also checked by the subjective evaluation using synthesized facial expression determined by the 3-D coordinate of the Space. This subjective evaluation is performed by 76 psychological students by passing the photographs of synthesized expression one by one which are determined by the coordinates in the 3D space and getting the answer of one of the 6 categories. Very interesting result from this subjective evaluation is obtained which make sure the continuity of emotion impression in this 3D Emotion Space.

Further, by deforming 3 kinds of personal model from the same facial parameters which are determined by the point in the 3-D space, expression of 3 persons can be synthesized.

2 Modeling of Expression

For description of human's facial expression, Facial Action Coding System(FACS) proposed by Ekman[1] is introduced. FACS divides the movement of facial muscle action movement appears on the face into 44 standard units. Each standard unit is AU(Action Unit). And it's possible to describe any face by combining these AUs. Of the 44 Action Units in FACS, 17 units shown in Table 1 were selected because they give strong influence to emotion expression.

Further more, the intensity which is from 0 to 100% is given to each AU , but to extradite to the input-layer of neural network, its intensity of each AU parameter is normalized to [0, 1] value. Table 2. shows the AU parameters' combinations and intensities for each basic expression. The number in the parenthesis indicates the intensity of each AU parameter.

Table 1 Action Unit Selection

AUNo	FACS Name	AUNo	FACS Name
AU1	Inner brow raiser	AU14	Dimpler
AU2	Outer brow raiser	AU15	Lip corner depressor
AU4	Brow lower	AU16	Lower lip depressor
AU5	Upper lid raiser	AU17	Chin raiser
AU6	Cheek raiser	AU20	Lip stretcher
AU7	Lid tighter	AU23	Lip tighter
AU9	Nose wrinkler	AU25	Lip part
AU10	Upper lid raiser	AU26	Jaw drops
AU12	Lid corner puller		

Table 2 Action Unit for Basic Expressions

Basic Expression	Combination of AU parameters
Surprise	AU1-(40), 2-(30), 5-(60), 15-(20), 16-(25), 20-(10), 26-(60)
Fear	AU1-(50), 2-(10), 4-(80), 5-(60), 15-(30), 20-(10), 26-(30)
Disgust	AU2-(60), 4-(40), 9-(20), 15-(60), 17-(30)
Anger	AU2-(30), 4-(60), 7-(50). 9-(20), 10-(10), 20-(15), 26-(30)
Happiness	AU1-(65), 6-(70), 12-(10), 14-(10)
Sadness	AU1-(40), 4-(50), 15-(40), 23-(20)

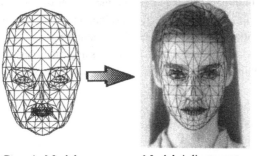

Generic Model   Model Adjustment   Synthesized Expression
                                                  (AU1 +AU6 + AU12 +AU14)

Fig.1 Personal Model Construction and an Example of Expression Synthesis

For facial expression synthesis, a 3-D generic model, as shown in Fig.1, which can approximately represent a human face is used. This model is composed of about 600 polygonal elements and it was constructed by measuring mannequin's head with markers using stereo cameras. As shown in Fig.1, generic model is 3-D affine-transformed to harmonize several of its feature point positions with those of a given 2-D full face image captured by a 2D camera. This point adjustment is done by using our interactive tool to generate a personal model with the generic model

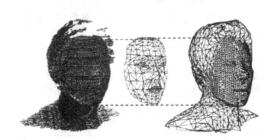

Cyberware Data   Generic Model   Reconstructed Model
(24000 mesh)   (600 mesh)   (2000 mesh)
Fig.2 Personal Model from Cyberware Data

The personal model can be also got by Cyberware 3D range scanner(Fig.2). But it has too many polygons to realize high speed processing and there is no explicit data about the feature points on the face. So the number of polygons is reduced to 2000 by Delaunay net and lack of data is also reconstructed. To synthesize expressions, the rules for generic model modification are used to hierarchically control the 3D range data employed for mesh construction.

3   Construction of 3-D Emotion Space

3.1   Network for Emotion Space

When the same data is given to both the input and output layer of a neural network (hereinafter referred to as Identity Mapping training), various internal representations in the given data can be acquired in the network.

Some experiments concerning with the sandglass type network's structural specificity, concluded that only by the 3-layered network, non-linear performance is not so effective and also concluded that to realize a mapping which takes advantage of non-linear performance effectively, at least 5-layered structure is needed[2].

From the experiments mentioned above, neural network has the ability of getting internal representations which are included in the training data. Then, especially when input and output units are given the same training sequence the Identity Mapping can be realized even if the number of units in the middle layer is small. It was considered that by linking the input and middle-layer, the features of the training data could be extracted. Following this, the data would be regenerated by the linking the middle-layer and output-layer. So it's expected that a facial expression space can be constructed in the middle-layer by applying this model exactly to the analysis and synthesis of the facial expressions. So, a 5-layered feed-forward network which is superior in non-linear performance is good for modeling the feature of facial expressions. This network structure is shown in Fig. 3.

This network has 17 units in the input layer and output layer corresponding to the number of Action Units we actually use. The hidden-layer has 19 units and middle-layer has 3. Unit functions of the 1st, 3rd and 5th layers are linear functions to maintain a wide dynamic range of the parameter space. Those of 2nd and 4th layers are sigmoid functions for non-linear mapping. Regarding the facial expression space constructed in the middle-layer as an Emotion Space, a system is simultaneously constructed to recognize and synthesize human faces.

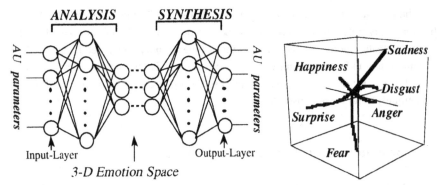

Fig.3 Network for Emotion Space   **Fig.4** 3-D Emotion Space

3.2 Training Process

For the training process 6 basic expressions described by the Action Unit parameters are given to the both input and output layer of the NN to perform Identity Mapping training. Then this training is performed repeatedly by backpropagation algorithm until network satisfies the convergence conditions.

As a result, 3-D Emotion space shown in Fig.4 was constructed in the middle layer.By giving the intensity of emotion degree from 0 to 100%, decided by the parameter level, continuously to the input-layer and regarding the middle-layer's 3 outputs as x, y, and z, the locus of each basic expression can be plotted in the 3-D space. The basic emotion locations in the middle-layer are extended and distributed in all directions like the spokes of a wheel in the 3-D space. Therefore, many routes of emotional changes between basic emotions can be described without crossing any locus of others, and more delicate expressions can be synthesized by the interpolation or combination of 6 basic expressions with the generalization effect of the network. A specific expression is described only by a 3D coordinate value in the Emotion Space.

4   Evaluation of Emotion Space

4.1 Test Image Synthesis

All expressions described by AU parameters are transformed to the 3D coordinates by mapping from the input layer to the middle layer of network. On the other hand, all points in the Emotion Space have a specific facial expressions by inverse mapping from the middle layer to output layer. The experiments mentioned in the previous chapter were mainly concerned with the mapping from expression to Emotion Space. This chapter describes the evaluation of inverse mapping. To evaluate this inverse mapping performance, an expression image determined by a 3D coordinate is synthesized and printed as a picture as shown in Fig.5. As the synthesis process are mentioned in chapter 2, facial expression test images for this evaluation are synthesized from the AU parameter combination gotten from the NN's output layer.

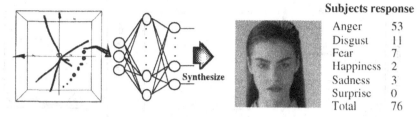

Subjects response

Anger	53
Disgust	11
Fear	7
Happiness	2
Sadness	3
Surprise	0
Total	76

Fig.5 Test Image Synthesis Process & Example of Response

In this experiment, when the test images were synthesized from the AU parameter combinations, these parameters were given to 3 kinds of personal model. This means that facial expression of 3 persons are synthesized from the same AU parameter combinations. Fig.6 shows the examples of test image which are synthesized from the same AU parameter combinations to examine personal difference of each facial expression. Focusing on a certain emotion change between 2 emotion in the 3-D Space , the interval of this couple is divided into 9 points. Then this process are done to the whole couples of the emotion changes. As a result, the number of test images amounted to 141 images for each model.

Fig.6 Expression Synthesis from same parameters

4.2　Response of the Subjects

76 subjects of psychology students categorized the test images into 6 groups that is 6 basic expressions. The expression test image were passed through one by one to the subject and it took 15 seconds to categorize the given image. As a result, the subjects' response for each test image was obtained. Fig.5 also shows a example of subjects' response for a certain test image. This Figure shows that there are 53 people who answered "Anger", 11 people who answered "Disgust" and so on as the subjective evaluation for this test image.

One example of the experimenalt result is shown in Fig.7. The line between Sadness and Surprise is divided into 11 points on the 3D Emotion Space. Expression images were synthesized with these 11 (x,y,z) coordinates and evaluated.

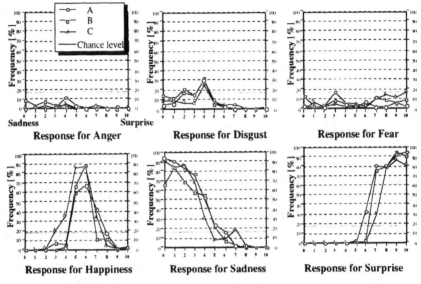

Fig.7 Subjects' Response

In Fig.7, the horizontal axis from left to right means the change of emotion from Sadness to Surprise and the vertical axis is the number of supporters. The 6 graphs correspond to the 6 basic expressions.

According to the change from left to right on the horizontal axis in Fig.7, one can see that the support for "Sadness" are gradually reduced, a few "Disgust" appears for a moment, and then support for "Surprise" gradually increases. This result confirms the interpolation effect of the 5-layered network. Therefore, all of the expressions in this Emotion Space are continuously located at an impression level. Moreover, from Fig.7, the response for each person (person A, person B, person C) which was synthesized by the same combination of AU parameter, has the similar response. From this point of view, it seems that the personality of facial expressions absorbed and the impressions of them remained. This indicates the possibility that can apply this 3-D Emotion Space to any other person.

5 Discussion

In this paper, methods for modeling facial expression and emotion is discussed. Many delicate faces can be expressed using FACS and compressed into the 3-D Emotion Space. By the evaluation result of the Emotion Space, the interpolation effect and continuous feature were confirmed. So it satisfied some of the condition for the criteria of recognition, synthesis and compression of face image

However the previous chapter is about the evaluation of inverse mapping performance of the network. Namely, network's synthesis side has evaluated.

The Emotion Space has to be able to represent both human and computer emotion

478

condition appearing on the face compactly as a coordinate. To capture and represent human's emotion condition, the Action Unit have to be extracted from real image. We are now engaging in automatical extraction of Action Unit by using 3-layered neural network.

This is shown in Fig.8. Input Vector corresponds to the feature points displacements and data for the output-layer are the AU parameters of these expressions. By this mapping from feature points displacements to the Action Units human's facial expression from the real image can be translated to a point in our Emotion Space.

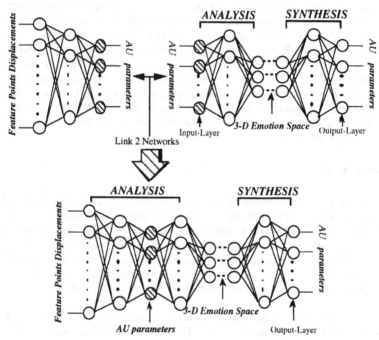

Fig.8 System for expression analysis and synthesis

References

[1] P.Ekman and W.Friesen:"Facial Action Coding System", Consulting Psychologists Press, 1977.

[2] Y.Katayama and K.Ohyama:"Some Characteristics of Self Organizing Back Propagation Neural Networks", Spring National Convention Record, IEICE-J, SD-1-14, p.7-309, 1989.

Iterative Human Facial Expression Modeling

Antai Peng and Monson H. Hayes

School of Electrical and Computer Engineering
Georgia Tech, Atlanta, GA 30332-0250

Abstract. Human facial expression modeling and synthesis have recently become a very active area of research. This is partially due to its potential application in model-based image coding, as well as the possibility of using it to enhance human-computer interactions. The majority of the research that has been done in this area has focused on facial expression analysis, modeling and synthesis. Although good results have been obtained in analysis and synthesis, not much effort has been spent on attempting to synthesize facial images that are natural looking. In this paper, we describe our research on facial expression modeling and synthesis. We propose an iterative framework that uses a genetic algorithm to synthesize natural looking facial images. Facial expression representation and distortion measures will also be discussed. Preliminary results are presented.

1 Introduction

Modeling of human facial expressions has recently become a very active area of research. The interest in this research can be attributed to the fact that face-to-face communication is still the most effective and straight-forward manner for human interactions. Videoconferencing, for example, has become fashionable because people are no longer satisfied with voice only two-way communication. As another example, human-computer interaction which used to be solely based on text display and text entry via keyboard, now varies widely from graphics display, mouse input, voice input and output and, eventually, image input and output.

Research in facial expression modeling and animation includes the pioneering work by F. Parke on parameterized facial animation modeling [7, 8], facial animation based on the Abstract Muscle Action (AMA) model [10], facial image analysis and synthesis using physical and anatomical models [11], knowledge-based facial expressions analysis and synthesis [13], and many others. In addition, a facial image synthesis system driven by speech and text has been presented in [12], and problems related to facial expression have been discussed in [9] by drawing parallels between speech synthesis and facial expression synthesis. More recent work includes analysis-based facial expression synthesis [14] in which a 3-D wire-frame is deformed based on the results from analysis, and animation based on examples using neural network [5, 14]. Research on facial image analysis and synthesis has also been carried out within the context of model-based image coding. Good results have been reported in [6] where an iterative analysis method was proposed to extract facial expression parameters as well as the parameters for head motion. Facial images have been synthesized using deformation rules based on Action Units defined in [1]. In [5], a similar approach has been taken to synthesize an image based on the parameters extracted from image analysis.

Table I. Action Units Used in the Expression Synthesis System

Action Unit Groups	AU	Description
Vertical AUs	AU 10	Upper Lip Raise
	AU 15	Depress Lip Corner
	AU 25	Mouth Apart
	AU 26	Mouth Open
	AU 27	Mouth Wide Open
Horizontal AUs	AU 20	Lip Horizontal Stretch
Oblique AUs	AU 18	Lip Pucker
	AU22	Lip Funneler
Orbital AUs	AU 12	Lip Corner Puller
Misc. AUs	AU 29	Jaw Thrust
	AU 32	Bite

The facial expressions that we are mainly interested in are those related to speech. Using the Facial Action Coding System (FACS) developed by P. Ekman and W. Friesen [1] as our modeling foundation, we have identified a basic set of Action Units that are associated with speech and have proposed a method that allows us to represent an expression as a vector in the AU space [3]. Thus, each facial expression associated with speech is decomposed into a combination of Action Units. At the early stage of our research, the expression vectors were empirically obtained through trial and err. More recently, however, we have developed an iterative modeling method based on a genetic algorithm which allows us to automatically determine the expression vectors.

The organization of this paper is as follows. First we introduce the facial expression representation that we have developed. Then we will describe our iterative modeling framework, including the genetic algorithm, facial image synthesis, and distortion measurement. Finally we present some experimental results and discuss future work.

2 Facial Expression Representation

The facial expressions that we are primarily interested in are those that are generated by speech. Using the FACS system, our goal is to find a mapping between speech phonemes and realistic facial expressions. We have identified a subset of Action Units as shown in Table I, and used them as a basis for the expression vectors in our system. These basis vectors, [AU10, AU12, AU15,..., AU32], form an AU space. If we let vector v_1 represent AU10, v_2 represent AU12 and so on, then the basis may be represented as follows:

$$V = [v_1, v_2, v_3, ..., v_{11}]^T \qquad (1)$$

Since each Facial Action Unit can be specified either as a translation along the x, y or z axis, or as a rotation about some point, we can represent each AU as the following: $u = [dx, dy, dz]^T$. For example, a Vertical Action Unit is basically a translation in the z-direction whereas an Oblique Action Unit consists of translations along the y-axis and z-axis.

With this representation for each Action Unit, our AU space may now be represented as:

$$V = \begin{bmatrix} dx_1 & dx_2 & ... & dx_{11} \\ dy_1 & dy_2 & ... & dy_{11} \\ dz_1 & dz_2 & ... & dz_{11} \end{bmatrix}$$

We have made the assumption that each phonemic facial expression of interest may be constructed from an appropriate linear combination of AUs,

$$f = w_1v_1 + w_2v_2 + ... + w_{11}v_{11} = V^Tw$$

where w is a vector of expression weights that must be determined. Once we have this representation, constructing the facial expression is narrowed down to adjusting the expression weight vector. For instance, to model the upper lip raising, we set the weight associated with AU10, w_1, equal to 1 and $w_i = 0$ for $i = 2, 3, ..., 11$. To model the mouth opening, we can set the weight associated with AU26, w_4, equal to 1 and the rest of the weights to zero. The expression weight vector is then used as the input parameter for the synthesizer to generate a synthetic facial image.

3 Iterative Facial Expression Modeling

In this section, we describe our iterative facial expression modeling framework which uses a genetic algorithm to automatically obtain the expression weight vectors. Genetic algorithms have been used in a wide variety of applications to solve nonlinear optimization problems. Although the use of a genetic algorithm to synthesize facial expression is exploratory, computer graphics algorithms based on evolutionary procedures have achieved very encouraging and interesting results [2]. Before we describe the details of the algorithm, we will first rephrase our objective in terms of an optimization problem. What we want to achieve is the synthesis of a facial image that possesses an expression that is as close as possible to one contained in a given image. Using the facial expression representation described in Section 2, we can state the problem as follows: Let M{} be an expression quantifier that can be applied on face image. Given a target image with an expression that we want to synthesize, let M{target} be the quantification of the target expression. Let D(M1, M2) be a function that measures the distortion between two expressions quantified as M1 and M2. Also let S[w] be a function which takes an expression weight vector w and generates a synthetic facial image. The problem is then to find a $\tilde{w}$, such that the D(M{target image}, M{S[$\tilde{w}$]}) is minimized. In the following sections, we will describe the genetic algorithm, the quantification of an expression, and the distortion measurement function.

3.1 Genetic Algorithm

A genetic algorithm is characterized by a set of "chromosomes", an "initial population" that defines the first generation, or initial solution, a set of operators that allow each generation to evolve and mutate, and a fitness function that may be applied to the gene pool. In the following paragraphs, we describe how these are defined in our facial expression synthesis algorithm.

A. Representation
The chromosome that is used in our genetic algorithm is the expression weight vector $w=(w_1, w_2, ..., w_{11})$. Each w_j is a real-valued number in the range of [0, 1]. Since the AU space we are currently experimenting with has 11 Action Units, each chromosome consists of 11 floating point numbers.

B. Initial Population
The initial population has an expression weight vector of all zeros, which corresponds a synthetic face image with a neutral expression (mouth closed).

C. Operators for Generating New Population

Both the crossover and mutation operators are maintained but modified to suit our need. For the mutation operator, we have adopted the approach suggested in [4]. Two basic mutation operators, uniform mutation and non-uniform mutation, are implemented. Specifically, let $v = (v_1\ v_2\ ...\ v_s\ ...\ v_{11})^T$ be the chromosome to be mutated. A uniform mutation generates a new chromosome $\tilde{v}$:

$$\tilde{v} = (v_1\ v_2\ ...\ \tilde{v}_s\ ...\ v_{11})^T$$

where s is between 1 and 11 and $\tilde{v}_s$ is a random number that is uniformly distributed over the interval [0, 1]. The uniform mutation is used primarily at the early stage of the iterations so that a wide range of values can be evaluated. A non-uniform mutation is used mainly for fine-tuning within a smaller search area. Using the representation above, with a non-uniform mutation, $\tilde{v}_s = v_s + \Delta$ where Δ is a random number that is non-uniformly distributed between 0 and 1.

Besides the two fundamental mutation operators, we have also developed a special mutation operator which we call it complement mutation operator. In our system, we keep track of the convergence rate. If, after a certain number of iterations, no improvements are achieved, the complement mutation operator is applied. After this operation, $\tilde{v}_s = (1.0 - v_s)$, where s is a random number between 1 and 11.

Four types of crossover operators are utilized in our system: simple crossover, arithmetic crossover, single crossover and heuristic crossover. With $v_1 = (v_{11}\ v_{12}\ ...\ v_{1,11})^T$ and $v_2 = (v_{21}\ v_{22}\ ...\ v_{2,11})^T$ as two chromosomes that are to be crossed, these crossover operators are as follows:

a) Simple Crossover
The new chromosomes are $\tilde{v}_1 = (v_{11}\ v_{12}\ ...\ v_{2m}\ ...\ v_{2,11})^T$ and $\tilde{v}_2 = (v_{21}\ v_{22}\ ...\ v_{1m}\ ...\ v_{1,11})^T$ where m is a random number between 1 and 11.

b) Arithmetic Crossover
The new chromosomes are defined as $\tilde{v}_1 = (v_{11}\ v_{12}\ ...\ \alpha v_{2m} + (1-\alpha)\ v_{1m}\ ...\ \alpha v_{2,11} + (1-\alpha)v_{1,11})^T$ and $\tilde{v}_2 = (v_{21}\ v_{22}\ ...\ (1-\alpha)v_{2m} + \alpha\ v_{1m}\ ...\ (1-\alpha)v_{2,11} + \alpha v_{1,11})^T$ where m is a random number between 1 and 11, and α is a real number between 0 and 1.

c) Single Crossover
Like simple crossover, a random number m between 0 and 1 is generated. The new chromosomes are $\tilde{v}_1 = (v_{11}\ v_{12}\ ...\ v_{2m}\ v_{1m+1}\ ...\ v_{1,11})^T$ and $\tilde{v}_2 = (v_{21}\ v_{22}\ ...\ v_{1m}\ v_{2m+1}\ ...\ v_{2,11})^T$.

d) Heuristic Crossover
This is a special crossover operator. We call it heuristic because it uses domain specific knowledge. In our application, each chromosome represents an expression weight vector $w=(w_1, w_2, ..., w_{11})$ to be used to synthesize a facial image. Since each weight component is associated with a specific AU, given an image to be modeled, it is possible to pose some constrains on the range of the weight component. For example, if the facial image has a wide open mouth, as would be the case in saying the word 'far', we know that AU 26 or AU 27 must be dominant. Using this kind of knowledge, the performance can be improved by reducing the parameter search space.

Both the mutation and crossover operations may generate expression weights that do not correspond to any meaningful phonemic expressions. For instance, weights associated with

AU27 (mouth open) and AU32 (lip bite) should not be approaching 1 at the same time since one cannot bite the lips when the mouth is open. Similar constraints are posed on other weights so that non-realistic synthetic images are not generated. We have found that by incorporating these constraints the search process is accelerated significantly.

D. System Parameters

There are three probabilities related to the crossover operators: the single crossover probability *Psnc*, the arithmetic crossover probability *Pac*, and the simple crossover probability *Psic*. The system parameter set also includes two non-constant probabilities, one for the uniform mutation *Pum* and another one for the non-uniform mutation *Pnm*. At the beginning of the iteration, *Pum* is significantly greater than *Pnm*. Each time a better solution is found, *Pum* is decreased while *Pnm* is increased. The idea is to first look "loosely and evenly" in the search space. Once a potential solution is detected, the non-uniform mutation is applied more frequently than the uniform mutation. However, if no improvements are made after a certain number of iterations, the complement mutation is applied. This resets the uniform mutation probability as well as the non-uniform probability to their initial values.

E. Fitness Function

The fitness function is closely tied to the optimization problem to be solved. In our case, the fitness function evaluates the similarity of the synthesized image to the target image. A detailed description of the distortion measurement is covered in the next section.

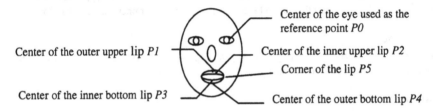

Figure 1. Lip Locations for Quantifying Phonemic Facial Expression

3.2 Distortion Measurement

A. Expression Quantification

Developing a measure that will quantify the similarity between two facial expressions is very difficult due to the almost infinite variations of facial expressions. Since we are mainly interested in speech related expressions, our efforts to measure the similarity of facial expressions have concentrated on the lips. Our method does not require the target image and synthetic image be from the same individual. Therefore, our method allows us to synthesize facial images of person A with an expression that is close to the target image which may belong to person B. To accomplish this goal, expression quantification must be normalized so that expressions from different individuals can be compared. It is assumed in our normalization process that the neutral (closed mouth) face image of the target is available. In our preliminary experiments, the following lip control locations are used for expression quantification purpose: lip corner, center of the outer upper lip, center of the inner upper lip, center of the inner bottom lip and center of the outer bottom lip. The center of the eye is used as a reference point. These control points are shown in Figure 1.

Using these lip locations, the following distances can be calculated:

      $d(1)$ = distance between center of the eye and center of the outer upper lip

      $d(2)$ = distance between center of the eye and center of the inner upper lip

      $d(3)$ = distance between center of the eye and center of the inner bottom lip

      $d(4)$ = distance between center of the eye and center of the outer bottom lip

      $d(5)$ = distance between center of the eye and corner of the lip

Instead of using geometric distance, we separate the horizontal component from the vertical component. For instance, $d(1)$ is actually a vector of two components, a horizontal measurement $d(1)_h$ and a vertical measurement $d(1)_v$:

$$(d(1)_h, d(1)_v) = (\| P1_x - P0_x \|, \| P1_y - P0_y \|)$$

Here P_x and P_y are notations representing the x and y components of a point. This definition allows us to quantitatively measure the expression surrounding the lips. For example, the value of $d(5)_h$ for a lip that has been stretched should be smaller than the value for a neutral face (no stretch).

The distances defined above must be normalized before being used in a distortion measure. To do this, we first calculate the distances for the neutral face image $(d_n(1), d_n(2), d_n(3), d_n(4), d_n(5))$ and the distances for the target face image $(d_t(1), d_t(2), d_t(3), d_t(4), d_t(5))$. Then we compute the *expression ratios* of corresponding components between the neutral face and the target image { $R_h(1), R_v(1), R_h(2), R_v(2), ... , R_h(5), R_v(5)$} = {$d_n(1)_h/d_t(1)_h, d_n(1)_v/d_t(1)_v, d_n(2)_h/d_t(2)_h, d_n(2)_v/d_t(2)_v, ... , d_n(5)_h/d_t(5)_h, d_n(5)_v/d_t(5)_v$}. Obviously, when the ratio is 1, there is no difference between the target image and the neutral face image at that location. When the ratio is not equal to one, then the target image has either "shrunk" or "stretched" at the particular location compared to the neutral image. For example, if $R_v(5)$ is greater than 1, the bottom lip deviates from the neutral position (closed mouth) which will occur when the target image contains an open mouth expression. Note that not all of the ratios may be useful in modeling ordinary people's speech expressions. For instance, the horizontal distances between the eye and the lip locations may not change at all due to the lip movement. Those ratios, therefore, will remain close to 1 most of the time.

B. Distortion Measurement

To measure the expression distortion between a synthesized image and the target image, the procedure described above is applied to the synthesized image to obtain its expression ratios. The distortion is computed as a weighted sum of the difference between the corresponding ratio components as follows:

$$D(\text{synthesized expression, target expression}) = \sum_1^5 w(i) [(Rs_h(i) - Rt_h(i)) + (Rs_v(i) - Rt_v(i))]$$

Here Rs_h and Rs_v are the horizontal and vertical expression ratios from the synthesized image and Rt_h and Rt_v are the horizontal and vertical expression ratios from the target image. This distortion function is used in the genetic algorithm as the fitness evaluation function.

4 Experiments and Discussion

To evaluate the system described above, we have implemented a prototype system on a Window's NT platform using OpenGL and C. Both the neutral face image and the target image (with an expression to be modeled) are displayed. The lip control locations are specified interactively via a mouse input. The quantitative expression is then generated using the distance definitions presented in Section 3.2. The iterative modeling process is invoked after the user specifies a maximum iteration number. During the iterative process, each meaningful expression weight vector is passed as parameters to the synthesizer. The synthesized facial image is updated on the screen in real-time. To increase the realism, we have also applied texture mapping on the wire-frame face model.

4.1 Experimental Results

In our experiments, we have used target images that portray primarily phonemic expressions. Figure 2 shows a target image and two synthesized images generated after 20 and 60 iterations. In Figure 3, a different target image and the synthesized images after 20 and 60 iterations are shown. Notice that the current implementation assumes the left and right side of the face are symmetric. Even though in both target images, the shape of Miss America's mouth is not symmetric (right side opens wider than the left side), our synthesized images do not portray this asymmetry (in our experiment, the expression measurement is based on the right side of the face). This is one of the areas for future research.

It can be seen that our iterative modeling method generates good quality synthetic facial images after a small number of iterations. Unlike other optimization problems, where the "optimal" or "best" solutions is required, one unique aspect of the use of genetic algorithm in our application is that, because of the relative insensitivity of the human eyes to fine detail, it is not necessary to find the optimal solution. In other words, although additional iterations may further reduce the distortion between the synthesized image and the target image, and although a larger number of control points may improve the quality of the synthesized image, the difference may not be noticeable to the human eyes, particularly in a real-time video sequence with speech. From our preliminary experiments we have found that, on average, 60 iterations will generally produce a synthesized facial image that looks close to the target image.

Figure 2(a). Target image

Figure 2(b). Synthesized image after 20 iterations

Figure 2(c). Synthesized image after 60 iterations

4.2 Discussion and Conclusion

In this paper, we have presented an iterative facial expression modeling method that allows us to generate realistic phonemic expressions. Although phonemic expressions are our main concern, the method can be easily extended to model other expressions such as eye and eyebrow movements. To do this, all that is required is to expand the vector space to include Action Units that are associated with the eye and eyebrow movements. Once this is done, same iterative procedure can be applied.

Because of the relatively low number of iterations required to generate a synthetic image that looks similar to the target image, it is possible to incorporate this method in real-time applications. It is also possible to apply this method to image coding in applications such as videoconferencing. When combined with a Text-To-Speech system, our iterative modeling process can generate good quality talking head image sequences. We are currently conducting research in this area.

Some additional areas of research that are currently being investigated are the following. The lip control locations are currently interactively obtained via mouse input. A fully automatic lip control points locator is necessary. Also, to further improve the realism of the synthesized facial images, facial textures such as furrows and wrinkles need to be added. In addition, in order to model expressions at a finer level of details, more sophisticated quantification method needs to be developed.

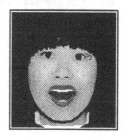

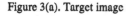

| Figure 3(a). Target image | Figure 3(b). Synthesized image after 20 iterations | Figure 3(c). Synthesized image after 60 iterations |

References

1. P. Ekman and W.V. Friesen, "Facial Action Coding System", Consulting Psychologists Press, 1977
2. A. Watt and M. Watt, "Advanced Animation and Rendering Techniques ", Addison-Wesley, 1992
3. A. Peng and M. Hayes, "Modeling Human Facial Expressions at Multiple Resolutions ", ICASSP95, pp. 2627-2629
4. Z. Michalewicz, "Genetic Algorithms+Data Structures = Evolution Programs", Springer-Verlag, 1994
5. S. Curinga, A. Grattarola and F. Lavagetto, "Synthesis and Animation of Human Faces: Artificial Reality in Interpersonal Video Communication", pp. 397-40
6. C.S. Choi, K. Aizawa, H. Harashima and T. Takebe, "Analysis and Synthesis of Facial Image Sequences in Model-Based Image Coding", IEEE-Trans. on Circuits and Systems for Video Tech., Vol. 4, No. 3, June, 1994, pp. 257 - 274
7. F.I. Parke, "A model for human faces that allows speech synchronized animation", Computer Graphics, Vol. 1, pp. 3-4 (1975)
8. F.I. Parke, Parameterized models for facial animation", IEEE Computer Graphics Applications, Vol. 2, no. 9, pp. 61-68 (1982)
9. D. Hill, A. Pearce, and B. Wyvill, "Animating speech: A automated approach using speech synthesized by rules", Visual Computer, Vol. 3, pp. 277-287 (1988)
10. N.Magnenat-Thalmann, E. Primeau, and D. Thalmann, "Abstract muscle action procedures for face animation", Visual Computer, Vol. 3, pp. 290-297(1988)
11. D.Terzopoulous, K. Waters, "Analysis and synthesis of facial image sequences using physical and anatomical models", IEEE Trans-PAMI, Vol. 15, No. 6, pp. 69-579 (1993)
12. S. Morishima, K. Aizawa, and H. Harashima, "A real-time facial action image synthesis system driven by speech and text", SPIE Vol. 1360 Visual Comm. Image Proc., pp. 1151-1158(1990)
13. S. Morishima, K. Aizawa, and H. Harashima, "An intelligent facial image coding driven by speech and phoneme", IEEE ICASSP89, Pres. No.M8.7, pp. 1795-1798 (1989)
14. L. Tang and T.S. Huang, "Analysis-Based Facial Expression Synthesis ", pp. 98- 102, ICIP94

Shape from Shading Using Near Point Light Sources*

Sheng-Liang Kao and Chiou-Shann Fuh
Department of Computer Science and Information Engineering
National Taiwan University
Taipei, Taiwan

1 The *Approximate Solution Curve Tracing* (*ASCT*) Method

1.1 The *correct solution space* (*CSS*)

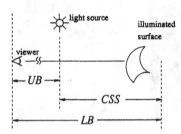

Figure 1: The *CSS* represents the *correct solution space* which all of the depth values on the illuminated object are included in. *LB* is the lower bound of the *CSS*. All of the depth values on the illuminated object will be not "deeper" than it. *UB* is the upper bound of the *CSS*. All of the depth values on the illuminated object are always "deeper" than it.

Before recovering the depth map of the illuminated object, we can assume that there exists a range to include all of the depth values of the points on the surface, as shown in Figure 1.

1.2 The *approximate solution difference* (*ASD*)

Now suppose we have two images I_1, I_2, the corresponding point light sources are (S_{x1}, S_{y1}, S_{z1}) and (S_{x2}, S_{y2}, S_{z2}), the illuminated point is (x, y, z), and the normal vector is $(p, q, -1)$. Then,

$$I_1(x,y) = k \cdot \frac{(S_{x1} - x)\,p + (S_{y1} - y)\,q - (S_{z1} - z)}{[(S_{x1} - x)^2 + (S_{y1} - y)^2 + (S_{z1} - z)^2]^{\frac{3}{2}}(p^2 + q^2 + 1)^{\frac{1}{2}}} \tag{1}$$

$$I_2(x,y) = k \cdot \frac{(S_{x2} - x)\,p + (S_{y2} - y)\,q - (S_{z2} - z)}{[(S_{x2} - x)^2 + (S_{y2} - y)^2 + (S_{z2} - z)^2]^{\frac{3}{2}}(p^2 + q^2 + 1)^{\frac{1}{2}}} \tag{2}$$

Substitute a value in the *CSS*, called z_{css}, for the unknown variable z in the denominator of both equations and divide Equation (1) by Equation (2). After simplifying the coefficients, a linear equation (Equation (3)) with three unknowns is obtained. These unknown values are p, q, and z.

$$A\,p + B\,q + C\,z = D \tag{3}$$

where

$$A = (S_{x1} - x) - \alpha(S_{x2} - x)$$
$$B = (S_{y1} - y) - \alpha(S_{y2} - y)$$
$$C = 1 - \alpha$$
$$D = S_{z1} - \alpha S_{z2}$$
$$\alpha = \frac{I_1 \cdot [(S_{x1} - x)^2 + (S_{y1} - y)^2 + (S_{z1} - z_{css})^2]^{\frac{3}{2}}}{I_2 \cdot [(S_{x2} - x)^2 + (S_{y2} - y)^2 + (S_{z2} - z_{css})^2]^{\frac{3}{2}}}$$
$$z_{css} = \text{a value in the } CSS$$

*This research work was supported by National Science Council of Taiwan, ROC, under NSC Grants NSC 83-0422-E-002-010, NSC 84-2212-E-002-046, and NSC 85-2212-E-002-077 , and by Cho-Chang Tsung Foundation of Education under Grant 84-S-26.

take four images as I_1, I_2, I_3, and I_4 and pair these images (e.g. I_1/I_2, I_2/I_3, and I_3/I_4). There will be a system of linear equations generated.

$$\begin{cases} A_1 p + B_1 q + C_1 z = D_1 \\ A_2 p + B_2 q + C_2 z = D_2 \\ A_3 p + B_3 q + C_3 z = D_3 \end{cases} \tag{4}$$

where A_i, B_i, C_i, and D_i ($i = \{1, 2, 3\}$) are similarly derived from the ith pair of images by the procedure to derive Equation (3). Thus we can obtain a solution for the z value in the system of equations.

$$z_{app} = \frac{\begin{vmatrix} A_1 & B_1 & D_1 \\ A_2 & B_2 & D_2 \\ A_3 & B_3 & D_3 \end{vmatrix}}{\begin{vmatrix} A_1 & B_1 & C_1 \\ A_2 & B_2 & C_2 \\ A_3 & B_3 & C_3 \end{vmatrix}} \tag{5}$$

We call the solution, z_{app}, the *approximate solution (AS)* and the difference function

$$\Delta Z(z_{css}) = z_{app} - z_{css} \tag{6}$$

is called the *approximate solution difference (ASD)*.

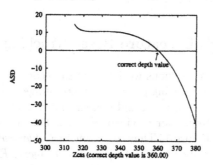

Figure 2: *Approximate solution curve:* in this example, there is a z_{css} which makes the ASD approximate zero. This z_{css} is also the correct depth value of the illuminated point. It is pointed by an arrow.

We call the curve in Figure 2 the *approximate solution curve (ASC)*.

Therefore, If the range of the CSS is properly chosen, the correct depth value of the illuminated point can be found by tracing the ASC in the range of CSS. The way to find out the depth value is called the *approximate solution curve tracing* method.

Feature Replenishment for Long-Term Visual Motion Tracking *

Tak Keung Cheng, Les Kitchen and Zhi-Qiang Liu

Computer Vision and Machine Intelligence Laboratory, Computer Science Department, The University of Melbourne, Parkville, Victoria 3052, AUSTRALIA

Abstract. This paper presents the feature replenishment technique used by our 3D Feature Based Tracker (3DFBT). The 3DFBT is a distributed, agent-based system for real-time 3D visual motion tracking using stereo. Feature replenishment means that the system can find new trackable features to replace those lost to noise and occlusion, and on new objects entering the scene, or revealed by dis-occlusion. This allows tracking to be continued over longer periods.

1 Overview of 3D Feature Based Tracking System

The 3D-FBT builds on previous work in real-time edge detection, region tracking [2], and 2D feature tracking [1]. It is the largest agent-based system we have built to date. Its goal is to track and segment moving 3D objects in real time, using input from a stereo pair of video cameras. The system is made up of six agents, as shown in Figure 1. They are *Camera Calibration Agent, Converting Agent, Stereo Feature Agent, 3D Motion Cluster Agent, Replenishment Agent, Display Agent*. The Replenishment Agent is described in Section 2. Detailed description of experiment results for the system and the functions of the other agents can be found in [3].

2 Replenishment Agent

During the continuous tracking state, some new feature points may appear in the scene because there are new objects entering the scene, or because previously occluded features are revealed by object movement. Or features on still visible objects may be lost through noise, and need replacing. In any case, we need a agent to handle rescanning some part of the scene to discover new feature points. The Replenishment Agent is designed for such purpose. The other major reason for setting up this agent is to make the system more robust for long-term tracking.

Whenever we need to add a set of new features into the database, we need to stop taking any new frames until the Replenishment Agent finishes its processing. So if we analyse the whole image in every frame time or some specified period of

---

* The work reported here is supported in part by the Australian Research Council, Large Grants Scheme. First author's email address is derek@cs.mu.oz.au.

time, this would slow down the running of the whole system too much. Our aim for this system is real-time performance, so we cannot afford to use this strategy. In the current setup, we split up the whole scene into a number of blocks as in Figure 2.

The agent enforces that there is at least one feature point in each block. If a block does not contain any features for five successive frames, then the agent will rescan that part of image. If new features are detected, then it will try to match the corresponding position in the other view of the scene to determine parallax and depth. (That is, if the feature is detected in the right image, then the agent will try to find the corresponding feature in the left image or vice versa.)

3 Closing Remarks

We have presented the feature replenishment technique recently introduced into the 3D Feature Based Tracker. This enables the system to replace features lost because of noise and occlusion, and to find new features on objects entering the scene or revealed by dis-occlusion by other moving objects. The replenishment technique is designed so that it causes minimum disruption of the tracking, while still providing a usable distribution of trackable features over the visible scene. Introducing feature replenishment also required automating the stereo correspondence process.

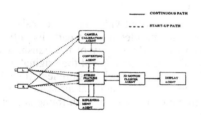

Fig. 1. 3D-FBT System.

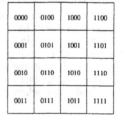

Fig. 2. 16 Blocks with labels.

References

1. Cooper, J., Kitchen, L.: Multi-Agent Motion Segmentation for Real-Time Task Directed Vision. Australian Joint Conference on A. I., Perth, Australia (1990)
2. Cooper, J., Kitchen, L.: A Region Based Object Tracker. Third National Conference on Robotics, Melbourne, Australia (1990)
3. Cheng, T. K., Kitchen, L., Liu, Z. Q., Cooper, J.: Multi-Agent 3D Motion Tracking and Segmentation Using Binocular Stereo. Proceedings of the 1995 National Conference of the Australian Robot Association, Australia (1995), pp. 272-287

An Imprecise Real-Time Video Transmission Algorithm

Albert Mo Kim Cheng and Xiaofen Huang

Real-Time Systems Laboratory
Department of Computer Science
University of Houston--University Park
Houston, TX 77204-3475

Abstract. Multimedia systems are becoming increasingly popular. One major requirement in these systems is the efficient transmission of multimedia information over a communication or computer network. Current image and video transmission techniques work well if sufficient processing power, network bandwidth, and transmission time are available, but do not adapt properly to a reduction in one or more of these resources. This paper proposes an imprecise image/video transmission algorithm which yields a balanced tradeoff between the quality of the image/video transmitted and the available time for transmission. Our experimental results show that the proposed approach has better performance than conventional precise algorithms and some progressive transmission algorithms. It also compares favorably with commercially available systems such as InPerson made by Silicon Graphics Inc.

1 Introduction

Limitations in time and bandwidth often make the transmission of high definition images or video difficult. For instance, to display video, we normally need to show at least 24 frames per second in order to see continuous movement. When a video is displayed remotely, the transmission of one frame must be completed within 1/24 second (assuming that the video is taken at the rate of 24 frames/second). Failing to do so would distort the rendering of the original motion.

The real-time video transmission problem is to transmit video in a hard real-time environment with stringent timing constraints. This problem can be partially solved by the technique proposed in this paper which trades the quality of the transmitted video with the amount of available time. Instead of an exact copy of the original one, a lower-quality version of the original video can be sent when sufficient time is unavailable. This ensures that the receiver is able to display frames at the same rate as that of the original video when it was taken, though the image in each frame is more fuzzy.

2 Imprecise Video Transmission

Many algorithms are currently being used to reorganize image data, transmit them progressively, and then reconstruct a single image by incrementally increasing its resolution at the destination. A general technique proposed in [1] constructs a hierarchical structure of images with increasing resolution from top to bottom. It is adopted and further extended in [2] to reorganize the image data and transmit the details of the image in a non-increasing order of their significance. A video consists of a sequence of images. To transmit a video, we perform motion estimation and temporal interpolation of skipped frames [3,4]. By dividing the entire video into several frame pieces, carefully scheduling the progressive data transmission, and reconstructing frames by motion prediction, the video can be gradually recovered. The commercial product InPerson running on Silicon Graphics workstations provides tools for teleconferencing between two or more parties. It takes a live video and transmits it to the other

*This material is based upon work supported in part by the National Science Foundation under Award No. CCR-9111563, the Texas Advanced Research Program under Grant No. 3652270, and a grant from the University of Houston Institute of Space Systems Operations.

party; at the same time it receives and displays the video sent from the other party. If the network traffic becomes heavy, the images from the remote site(s) become fuzzy. If the rate of motion of the video increases, the continuity as well as the quality of the transmitted video decrease. This software implements the video progressive transmission techniques in a practical product. However, it does not perform any time-quality trade-off to enforce the continuity of the video.

Since progressive transmission results in partially transmitted images, it can be modeled by the imprecise computation framework first proposed in [5]. The purpose of the imprecise computation is to utilize the partial results in case of insufficient execution time. Thus real-time video transmission may apply this idea and automatically adjust the accuracy of the transmitted video according to the processing time available. Two imprecise approaches have been proposed in [5] to utilize partial results in case of insufficient resources. Both approaches can be adopted in one algorithm. When the computation takes the form of progressive refinement of the final results, it can be divided into a sequence of sieve functions. The milestone approach is used to save intermediate results after distinct stages of the computation.

General Imprecise Video Transmission

```
ImpreciseVideo () {
    Initialization ();
    while the execution is not completed and there is available time do {
        Setup ();
        AdjustWCRatio ();
        activate the sieve function with highest w/c rate;
        while the sieve function is not completed do {
            inquire system time;
            if the deadline is approaching
                then terminate the sieve function and break the loop;
            if some environmental factors have changed so that the costs of
                sieve functions should be adjusted
                then interrupt the sieve function, save its current status
                            and break the loop;
                else wait a short period; }
        End-handling (); }
}
```

References

1. P. J. Burt and E. H. Adelson, "The Laplacian Pyramid As a Compact Image Code," *IEEE Transactions on Communications*, vol. 31, pp. 532-540, April 1983.

2. G. Mongatti, L. Alparone, G. Benelli, S. Baronti, F. Lotti and A. Casini, "Progressive Image Transmission By Content Driven Laplacian Pyramid Encoding," *IEEE Proceedings-I*, vol. 139, No. 5, Oct. 1992.

3. Ehud Weiner and David Malah, "Interpolation of Skipped Images for Image Sequence Coding," *17th Convention of Electrical and Electronics Engineers in Israel, Proceedings 91*.

4. T. Naveen and J. W. Woods, "Motion Compensated Multiresolution Transmission of High Definition Video," *IEEE Transactions on Circuits and Systems for Video Technology*, vol. 4, pp. 29-40, Feb. 1994.

5. Kwei-Jay Lin, Swaminathan Natarajan and Jane W. S. Liu, "Imprecise Results: Utilizing Partial Computations in Real-Time Systems," *Proc. 8th IEEE Real-Time Systems Symposium*, pp. 210-217, Dec. 1987.

Mechanisms for Automatic Extraction of Primary Features for Video Indexing

Donald A. Adjeroh and M.C. Lee

Department of Computer Science, The Chinese University of Hong Kong
Shatin N.T., Hong Kong

Abstract. Automatic video indexing has mainly involved the partitioning of video into separate scenes and the manual selection of a key frame to represent each scene. We present some techniques for automatic selection of key frames after video partitioning. The first uses the statistical distribution of pixels in the frames, and the other makes a spatio-temporal consideration of the primary features in the scene using a relevance and persistence criteria.

Introduction

The major approaches to video indexing can be grouped as either automatic or manual. Manual indexing usually involves the use of metadata [3] which records information about the video, such as the producers, cast, text description of contents, etc. This is usually very laborious, and the results are often subjective. Automatic video indexing involves automatic detection of scene changes in the video, effectively partitioning the video into separate scenes [2, 4]. Automatic video indexing should not stop at just video partitioning, but should also provide key frames for the scenes. Apart from query and search, the key frame also plays a role in video storage, transmission, on-demand applications, etc.

Abstractions for Partitioned Video

After video partitioning, we still need some abstractions for the representation of the video contents. An arbitrary selection of the first or last frame as is currently practised cannot guarantee the selection of the most effective representative frame. We propose some techniques to approach this problem.

Statistical Techniques. Assuming a Gaussian probability distribution for the frame histogram differences, we can choose a representative frame by finding a frame pair whose histogram difference is closest to the average difference within the scene. However, this does not take the spatial distribution of pixels into account. To capture some spatial relationship among pixels, we use a technique based on the generalized co-occurrence matrix GCM[1]. This facilitates the use of some spatial constraint predicates in defining arbitrarily complex relationships between pixels. To select the key frame, we divide each frame into subframes and for each subframe, the GCM is used to compute normalized values for the statistical features, such as entropy, uniformity, contrast, moments, etc.

Spatio-Temporal Techniques. For a true representation of the scene, and to support within-frame query and search, the key frame should contain as many of the relevant features in the scene as possible. We use the notion of tokens to describe the objects in a frame together with their respective features, and use the relevance and persistence of the objects to select the key frame.

Relevance of a Token. The relevance of a token is determined using the reliability and significance of the token. The *reliability* indicates the likelihood that a token corresponds to a physical object in the frame as opposed to segmentation artefact; and is computed using some features or attributes of the token, such as contrast, size, regularity, etc. The reliability of a token α, is defined as: $\psi(\alpha) = \sum_{i=1}^{N} R_i(\alpha)$, where: N =no. of reliability attributes; $R_i(\alpha)$=normalized value for the ith reliability attribute. The *significance* of a token indicates the token's distinctiveness, and if it is likely to be a major object of interest in the frame. The significance criteria is based on measures such as area, location, sharpness, etc. The significance, of a token α is defined as: $\xi(\alpha) = \sum_{i=1}^{M} S_i(\alpha)$, where: M =no. of significance attributes, $S_i(\alpha)$=normalized value for the ith significance attribute. The relevance is then computed as: $\zeta(\alpha) = \psi(\alpha).\xi(\alpha)$. Tokens are then ranked using their relevance, and only those that pass a *relevance threshold* are further checked for temporal persistence across the frames.

Persistence of a Token. We define the persistence as the probability that a token appears in all the frames in a scene, i.e. persistence of token α, $\wp(\alpha) = N_F(\alpha)/N_T$ where: $N_F(\alpha)$ =no. of frames containing α; N_T=total no. of frames.

Selection of Representative Frame. By ranking the frames according to the relevance and persistence of their primary features, we determine the frames that will provide the most appropriate representation of what happens in the scene. Thus, for each relevant token α in a frame k, we compute: $\aleph_k(\alpha) = \zeta(\alpha).\wp(\alpha)$, and the overall ranking of the frame: $\Re_k = \sum_{i=1}^{n} \aleph_k(\alpha_i)$ where: $\alpha_i = i^{th}$ token;n=total no. of relevant and persistent tokens in frame k. Where the maximum ranking is recorded by two or more frames, we select the frame k where the frame difference $D = min(|\Re_k - \Re_{k-1}| + |\Re_k - \Re_{k-1}|)$.

Concluding Remarks

Some mechanisms for selecting appropriate representative frames based on the statistical distribution of pixels in the frame and on the spatio-temporal aspects of the objects in the video sequence have been proposed. The spatio-temporal technique uses object relevance and persistence to determine the primary features and thus the key frames in the video. This approach is more robust and more effective, but requires more complicated image analysis techniques.

References

1. L. Davis, S. Johns, J.K. Aggarwal: Texture analysis using generalized cooccurrence matrices. Proc. IEEE Conf. Pattern Recogn. & Image Processing, Chicago, 1978.
2. A. Nagasaka, Y. Tanaka: Automatic video indexing and full-video search for object appearances. In: E. Knuth, and L.M Wegner (eds.), Visual Database Systems II, Elsevier Science Publishers, 113-127, 1992.
3. L.A. Rowe, J.S. Boreczky, C.A. Eads: Indexes for User Access to Large Video Databases, IS&T/SPIE Symp. Electronic Imaging Sc. & Tech., California, 1994.
4. H-J. Zhang, A. Kankanhilli, S.W. Smoliar S.W: Automatic partitioning of full-motion video. Multimedia Sys. 1, 10-28, 1993

An Estimation of Low Bound for Two-Dimensional Image Compression Coding

Huijuan Li[*][+]   Qingdong Yao[**]   Jae-Ho Choi[*] and Hoon-Sung Kwak[*]

 * Department of Computer Engineering, Chonbuk National University, Chonju, R. Korea
** Information and Electronic Engineering Department, Zhejiang University, P. R. China

Abstract. Based on Shannon information and random field theories, a low bound estimation is developed in this paper for the transmitting bit rate in image compression coding. Taking the correlation coefficients between the adjacent pixels as parameters, a relation between the signal-to-noise ratio and the estimated low bound of image transmitting bit rate is obtained. As examples, several experiment results are utilized to verify the rationality of the presented results by applying some conventional compression coding methods to two standard pictures.

1 Introduction

It is known that in compression coding processes there exists a low bound which, for a given reconstruction image quality, is the theoretically accessible limit of image compression coding approaches. To optimize a compression coding process one needs to know the low bound so as to avoid to make efforts in vain. This paper presents an approximately analytical 2-D relation between the signal-to-noise ratio and the low bound of image transmitting bit rate based on the two-dimensional power spectrum model of the wide sense stationary image and the rate distortion function. Further reduction of the bit rate is carried out by considering the human visual effects providing the same subjective image quality. Calculations are performed to verify the model through some examples.

2 Two-Dimensional Low Bound Model

Let R(D) denote the low bound of the transmitting bit rate, which can be obtained by compression coding subject to an average distortion not larger than a given distortion D. Then in two-dimensional case for the two signal power spectrum models proposed in [1], if assuming that the bandwidths of signals are F_{c1} and F_{c2}, and the power spectrum of a quantization is uniform, through an analog of the one-dimensional approach proposed in [2], we can finally have:

$$R_1(D) = \frac{4}{25}[\frac{\overline{P}_{m1}}{\overline{N}_m}]_{db} - \frac{1}{2}\log_2\{\frac{f_{01}\,f_{02}}{F_{c1}\,F_{c2}}\tan^{-1}(\frac{F_{c1}}{f_{01}})\tan^{-1}(\frac{F_{c2}}{f_{02}})\}$$

[+] On leave as a young exchange scholar from Zhejiang University, Zhejiang, CHINA

$$+\log_2 f_{01} - \frac{1}{2}\log_2(F_{c1}^2 + F_{c2}^2) + \frac{1}{\ln 2} - \frac{f_{01}}{F_{c1}\ln 2}\tan^{-1}(\frac{F_{c1}}{f_{01}})$$

$$+\log_2 f_{02} - \frac{1}{2}\log_2(F_{c1}^2 + F_{c2}^2) + \frac{1}{\ln 2} - \frac{f_{02}}{F_{c2}\ln 2}\tan^{-1}(\frac{F_{c2}}{f_{02}}) \tag{1}$$

and

$$R_2(D) = \frac{4}{25}[\frac{\overline{P}_{m2}}{\overline{N}_m}]_{dB} - \frac{1}{2}\log_2[\frac{1}{4F_{c1}F_{c2}}\int_{-F_{c1}}^{+F_{c1}}\int_{-F_{c2}}^{+F_{c2}}\frac{1}{1+f_1^2 f_{01}^{-2} + f_2^2 f_{02}^{-2}}df_1\,df_2]$$

$$-\frac{1}{8F_{c1}F_{c2}}\log_2[\frac{1}{4F_{c1}F_{c2}}\int_{-F_{c1}}^{+F_{c1}}\int_{-F_{c2}}^{+F_{c2}}\log_2\frac{1}{1+f_1^2 f_{01}^{-2} + f_2^2 f_{02}^{-2}}df_1\,df_2] \tag{2}$$

for separable and inseparable models, respectively. Here, $\overline{P}_{mi}$, $(i = 1,2)$ denotes the average power and $\overline{N}_m$ indicates the average noise power; $f_{01} = -(2\pi)^{-1}f_s\ln\rho_1$ and $f_{02} = -(2\pi)^{-1}f_s\ln\rho_2$ while f_s is the sampling frequency of the video image and, in normal case, $f_s = 10$ MHz.

From the above results, it can be seen that for a given signal-to-noise ratio, the low bounds of the transmitting bit rates of the images obtained are associated to the correlation coefficients between the adjacent pixels.

Human visual effect on image compression coding is studied in terms of the weighted computation of the subjective visual perception distortion D. From the analysis we conduct it is shown that with the same subjective image reconstruction quality one can demonstrate that the image compression coding bit rate is reduced by around 0.832 bit/pel compared with that without considering the human effect.

3 Note

The obtained low bound estimation provides a theoretical basis, though approximately, for practical compression coding problems. It indicates that in practices one is able to find a coding method which best approximates the low bound of the compression coding. And, on the other hand, it also predicts that at a given image reconstruction quality level, there always exists a low bound for the image compression rate, under which no available compression coding methods can reach.

References

[1] W. K. Pratt, Digital Image Processing, John Wiley & Sons, Inc. 1978
[2] L. E. Franks: A model for the random video process. Bell System Technical Journal, 45(4), 609-630 (1966)

Texture Comparison Based on Selected Texture Primitives

David K.Y. Chiu and David A. Gadishev

Dept. Computing & Information Science, University of Guelph, Canada

Abstract. The texton theory proposed by Julesz defines textons as hypothetical basic elements for texture images. In this research, we propose an operational interpretation of textons and show experimentally that they can be used in a similarity measure for texture discrimination and characterization. The method is based on evaluation of the complete set of primitives to obtain a smaller set for texture analysis. We call these texture primitives. Similarity between pairs of textured images is defined as a sum of the similarities of the individual selected texture primitives in both images. Extensive experimentation in texture characterization and discrimination using prototype texture images were performed. The results show that the method achieves a large amount of representation reduction (>90%) and yet the proposed similarity obtains impressive results in texture characterization and discrimination.

1. Generation of Feature Primitive Image

We use a relational database to store the complete set of primitives and extract primitives that have demonstrable properties consistent of textons. First, observations are performed on the gray levels of a 3x3 window for each positions in a texture image. The primitives are defined in terms of the gray level differences between the neighboring pixels and the center pixel, represented as 8-vectors $\overline{d} = (d_1, d_2, ..., d_8)$. We call these the *difference primitives*. To label the difference primitives into different types, we perform an approximation process by discretizing each component of gray level difference into 3 levels using a method known as maximum entropy discretization. This discretization process minimizes the information loss by maximizing the Shannon's entropy function. The estimated probability distribution is based on the frequency histogram of the difference primitives observed in the image. After discretization, the 8-vector is denoted as $\overline{z}$ such that each component is represented by either -1, 0 or 1. The value -1 reflects a sufficient decrement in gray level, the value 1, a sufficient increment in gray level and the value 0, no sufficient change in gray level. We call these *feature primitives*. Since there are 3 possible values for each of the 8 components, there are altogether $3^8 = 6561$ types of feature primitives. The number of levels reflects the degree of approximation in their gray level difference that is acceptable for the subsequent analysis.

2. Selection of Texture Primitives and Calculating Texture Similarity

After the set of feature primitives is identified, the texture image is divided into equal non-overlapping small regions. Each region defines the area where a feature primitive is observed or not, analogous to observing an image at a certain resolution. A larger region is analogous to a lower resolution observation, whereas a smaller region is analogous to a higher resolution observation.

a) Selection of Texture Primitives Based on Repetitive Periodicity

We design the criterion to identify repetitive periodicity as follows. A primitive is repetitive with certain periodicity if it is observed in sufficiently large proportion of regions, or larger than a predefined threshold.

b) Selection of Texture Primitives Based on High Line and Gradient characteristics

We use a new criterion in defining high line and high gradient characteristics. Texture characterization and discrimination is then based on high gradient or line primitives only.

c) Differentiating Common and Unique Primitives

Given two texture images for comparison, and feature primitives are selected satisfying the above properties, the resulting set of primitives will either be observed in one image only (*unique primitives*) or in both images (*common primitives*).

d) Labeling Common Primitives Based on Differences in Repetitive Periodicity

The common primitives are high line or gradient primitives which satisfy the repetitive periodic criterion, and are observed in both images in texture comparison. To calculate the similarity due to this type of primitives, we use a statistical method to evaluate the differences in their repetitive periodicity of occurrence in each image, and determine whether their characteristics between the two images are: 1) significantly different, 2) significantly the same or 3) in between. The common primitives can then be defined according to the value of the statistic D and their level of confidence using piecewise linear interpolation.

Interpreting these selected primitives as the basic elements, texture similarity is calculated as follows: Given two texture images A and B, and a set of selected feature primitives having high gradient or line characteristics and is repetitive periodic, denoted as $\{\bar{t}\} \subset \{\bar{z}\}$ from the original feature primitives, a measure of texture similarity is defined as the summation of the similarity of the individual primitives, or $\Delta(A,B) = \sum_{\bar{t}} \delta_{\bar{t}}(A,B)$ where $\delta_{\bar{t}}(A,B)$ measure the similarity between a selected feature primitive $\bar{t}$. We call $\bar{t}$ the *texture primitive*, a basic element for texture characterization and discrimination. In the experiments, we used prototype images from Brodatz's album. The reason prototype texture images are used is to extract the more representative texture primitives. The resulting texture primitives, identified as only 10% of the complete set, performs very well for texture characterization and discrimination. In other words, the experimental results support that only a small number of basic elements is sufficient for texture comparison as described by the texton theory.

Texture Analysis of Ultrasonic Images Using Backpropagation Neural Networks

*Jo Ann Parikh**, John DaPonte**, Meledath Damodaran**

*Corresponding Author

University of Houston - Victoria, 2506 E. Red River, Victoria, Texas 77901, USA

e-mail: damodaran@vicvx1.vic.uh.edu

**Southern Connecticut State University, New Haven, Connecticut 06515, USA

Abstract. Backpropagation neural networks are applied to the problem of characterization of ultrasonic image texture to detect abnormalities in tissue texture which are indicative of liver disease. Twenty-one texture features were extracted from regions of interest in digitized ultrasonic images. A feature subset, identified by a stepwise selection process, formed the sample input to the networks together with the physician-supplied diagnosis. The classification performance of the backpropagation network is evaluated using a jackknife testing procedure. The performance of the networks is compared with results obtained from linear discriminant analysis and logistic regression techniques.

1 Introduction

Computer-assisted diagnostic systems may incorporate a variety of methods for recognition of disease patterns. Two of these methods are statistical pattern recognition techniques and neural networks.

In this paper we investigate backpropagation neural networks for ultrasonic image texture analysis and evaluate their classification ability using jackknife testing. We also compare error rates with the performance obtained using more conventional statistical techniques. In the final section we summarize our conclusions and indicate future research directions.

2 Texture Feature Extraction

A total of 134 cases were obtained. Twenty-one features were extracted from each. A subset of these features, identified by applying a stepwise selection procedure to the entire feature set, was used for training the statistical and the neural network classifiers.

3 Network Architecture

Backpropagation learning algorithm, which is well-known, is described in [1]. We used a network with one hidden layer of eight nodes, an input layer of five nodes, and an output layer of one node. The five features were scaled between values of -1 and +1 to form the inputs to the networks. Weights were randomly initialized to values between -0.3 and +0.3. In addition, a bias node was added to the input and the hidden layers. A proof that networks with a single hidden layer (with perhaps a very large number of nodes) can approximate arbitrarily complex decision regions was given by Cybenko [2]. Training was terminated when the network had correctly classified 129 of the 133 training cases.

4 Comparison with Statistical Techniques

Three pattern recognition algorithms - stepwise selection, linear discriminant analy.
and logistic regression - were used to differentiate abnormal from normal tissue textu
First, stepwise selection was applied to the entire set of twenty-one features to identi
a feature subset that optimizes classifier performance; features were added to or delet
from the feature subset based on Wilk's Lambda Likelihood Ratio Criterion [3].

5 Results and Conclusion

We used a very exhaustive type of testing, which is the jackknife testing: in a data set
consisting of N samples training is done on N - 1 samples and testing on 1 sample. This
"leave-one-out" procedure is repeated N times allowing each case to be tested against
the other N - 1 cases of training data.

The classification performance of backpropagation classifiers proved superior to that
of linear discriminant analysis and logistic regression for our application. See Table 1

Table 1: Comparative Performance of Classifiers

Procedure	Lin. Discr. Analysis	Lin. Discr. Analysis	Logistic Regression	Backprop. Neural Net	Backprop. Neural Net
Testing procedure	Jackknife	Train & Test all data	Train & Test all data	Jackknife	Train & Test all dat
Agreement	83%	84%	83	87%	99%

Areas which remain to be explored are the performance characteristics of alternative
architectures such as the radial basis function networks, and alternative feature
dimension reduction methods such as subspace projection by principal component
analysis. The latter method is promising since the features chosen may be correlated.

6 References

1. D.E. Rumelhart and J. McClelland: Parallel Distributed Processing, MIT Press, 1986

2. G. Cybenko: Approximations by Superpositions of a Sigmoidal Function,
Mathematics of Control, Signals, and Systems, 2, No. 4

3. W.R. Klecka: Discriminant Analysis, Sage University Paper on Quantitative
Applications in the Social Sciences, Series No. 07-019, Beverly Hills, CA, 1980

B-Spline Based Multiscale Signal Derivative Filtering

Ge Cong   SongDe Ma

National Lab. of Pattern Recognition , PO.Box 2728, Beijing 100080,
P.R.China, e-mail congge@prlsun1.ia.ac.cn

Abstract We first generalize the multiscale filter proposed by Li and Ma[1] and then we use the method and B-spline as its kernel to construct multiscale derivative filters, we show that the filter can be recursively implemented.

1 Introduction

Must of the work in computer vision needs derivative filters to extract features such as edges, corners, etc., so far, Gaussian filter is the most widely used filter because it is the optimal filter according to Canny[2], But Gaussian is extensively computation expensive, to many research concentrated on finding recursive filters. Recently, Li and Ma[1]presented a new way to design derivative filter, the filter is the weighted sum of several kernels with the same form but applied to different scales. In this paper, we show that in the method, we can use B-spline to construct the derivative filters and they can be easily recursively implemented.

2 A generalized multiscale derivative filter

In their method, Li and Ma[1] proved that a (2k)th order derivative filter can be constructed as the weighted sum of (k+1) even functions, every such function had the same kernel but different scales; and a (2k+1)th order derivative filter can be designed as the weighted sum of (k+1) odd functions. One difficulty in using their filter is that the different order derivative filters are constructed separately, there could be no relationship between different order filters, so the (n+1)th order derivative filter may not be the derivative of the nth order derivative filter. In this paper, we change the filter to:

$$h_n(x) = \sum_{i=0}^{k} a_{n,i} \frac{1}{\sigma_i} g_n(\frac{x}{\sigma_i}) \qquad 0 \le n \le 2k+1 \qquad g_{n+1} = \frac{dg_n}{dx} \text{ and } a_{n-1,i} = a_{n,i}\sigma_i \qquad (1)$$

3 B-spleen based Same Order Multiscale Filtering(SOMF)

As in (1), we begin at a given even order 2n to construct any order derivative filter using B-spline $N_m(x)$, a mth order B-spline based 2nth order derivative filter $h_{2n}^{(m)}(x)$ can be obtained from (1):

$$h_{2n}^{(m)}(x) = \sum_{i=0}^{k} a_{n,i}^{(m)} \frac{1}{\sigma_i} N_m(\frac{x}{\sigma_i}) \qquad 0 \le n \le 2k+1 \qquad (2)$$

the $a_{n,i}$ are obtained by moment conditions[1]. The signal convoluted with $h_{2n}^{(m)}(x)$ can be obtained as:

$$h_{2n}^{(m)}(x)*f = \sum_{i=0}^{k} a_{n,i}^{(m)} \frac{1}{\sigma_i} \int_{-\frac{\sigma_i}{2}}^{\frac{\sigma_i}{2}} \cdots \int_{-\frac{\sigma_i}{2}}^{\frac{\sigma_i}{2}} f(x-t_m-t_{m-1}\bullet\bullet\bullet-t_1-t_0)dt_0 dt_1 \bullet\bullet\bullet dt_{m-1} dt_m \quad (3)$$

In digital case, the integral can be implemented by add operation, so we have:

$$h_{2n}^{(m)}(k)*f(k) = \sum_{i=0}^{k} a_{n,i}^{(m)} \frac{1}{\sigma_i} \sum_{r_0=-\sigma_i/2}^{\sigma_i/2} \sum_{r_1=-\sigma_i/2}^{\sigma_i/2} \cdots \sum_{r_m=-\sigma_i/2}^{\sigma_i/2} f(k-r_m-\cdots-r_1-r_0) = \sum_{i=0}^{k} a_{n,i}^{(m)} SUM(k,\sigma_i) \quad (4)$$

we can get $SUM(k,\sigma_i)$ from $SUM(k-1,\sigma_i)$ and $SUM(k,\sigma_{i-1})$ without multiply operation, so the filtering can be recursively implemented. Since the derivative and the integral of $N_m(x)$ are also B-spline, the derivative filters of other orders can also be recursively implemented.

4 B-spline based Different Order Multiscale Filtering(DOMF)

The filter constructed by different order B-spline can be represented as follow:

$$h_{2n}(x) = \sum_{i=0}^{k} a_{n,i} \frac{1}{\sigma} N_{m_i}\left(\frac{x}{\sigma}\right) \qquad 0 \le n \le 2k+1 \qquad (5)$$

Since it have a different form from (1), it should be proved that (5) is a 2nth order derivative filter and get the $a_{n,i}$. We use the moments conditions presented in [1] to prove it is a 2nth order derivative filter. Its implementation is very like that of the previous section.

5 Extension to two dimensional case and experiment results

Since the two dimensional B-spline is separable so the two dimensional derivative filters constructed by our method can also be recursively implemented. We use SOMF and DOMF to one dimension signal and two dimensional signal edge detection, the results show the soundness and robustness of our method. The criteria proposed in[3]shows our filter is comparable with Gaussian filter in optimal smoothing considerations.

6 Conclusion

We generalize the filter proposed by Li and Ma and use same order and different order B-spline to construct multiscale derivative filter, they can be recursively implemented.

Reference

[1]B.C.Li and S.D.Ma, Multiscale-Filtering Based Computation of High Order Derivatives, *SPIE. on Visual Commu. and Image Processing*, Chicago, USA, 1994.

[2]J.Canny, A Computational Approach to Edge Detection, *IEEE Trans. on Pattern Analysis and Machine Intelligence*, vol.8, no.6, pp679-698,1986.

[3]S.Sarkar and K.L.Boyer, Optimal Infinite Impulse Response Zero Crossing Based Edge Detection, CVGIP:Image Understanding, vol.54, No.2,1991.

[4]T.Poggio, H.Voorhees and A.Yuille, A regularized solution to edge detection, M.I.T. AI Lab.   A.I.Memo 833,May,1985.

Contour Decomposition
Using Dominant points and Moment Difference Method

P C Yuen, *S D Ma, J Liu and Y S Yeung

Department of Computing Studies
Hong Kong Baptist University

*National Pattern Recognition Laboratory
Institute of Automation
Chinese Academy of Sciences

A novel scheme for constructing a robust contour description has been developed and presented in this paper and its block diagram is shown as follows.

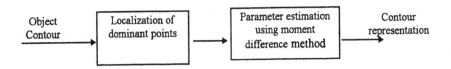

Dominant points [1] which are the characteristics of an object shape are first extracted. Corners and terminals of arcs like segments of the boundary are taken as the dominant points. Figure 1 shows the detected dominant points on a scissors boundary. The boundary is then partitioned into contiguous segments with detected dominant points. They are the inherent structural nodes of an object shape, and are invariant to its orientation and insensitive to its size. The parameters of each segment are then calculated using moment difference method [2]. It is also proven that moment difference method is an unbiased and consistent estimator. The estimated parameters of each segment are tabulated in Table 1.

A sequence $S = \{E_1, E_2, ...E_i,...E_n\}$ is then constructed for representing the object shape with each of its element describing the geometrical specifications of the approximated segment, where $E_i = (\theta_i, \rho_i)$, θ_i and ρ_i are the angular change and the curvature of the circular arc segment i, respectively.

$$S= \{ \quad (0.9085, 0.0228), (0.0906, 0.0021), (0.0692, 0.0014), (0.6093, 0.0173),$$
$$(3.8188, 0.0396), (0.0965, 0.0023), (0.6762, 0.0195), (0.0786, 0.0024),$$
$$(0.2783, 0.0028), (0.0019, 0.0000), (0.0593, 0.0007), (0.3527, 0.0036),$$
$$(0.2034, 0.0068), (0.8759, 0.0187), (0.1947, 0.0061), (4.0895, 0.0407)\}$$

(x,y) represents (angular change, radius of curvature) of an arc segment.

Segment bounded by dominant points	(center x, center y)	Interior angle	curvature
(1,2)	(47,124)	0.908583	0.022851
(2,3)	(361,-276)	0.090611	0.002149
(3,4)	(511,719)	0.069201	0.001385
(4,5)	(44,96)	0.609355	0.017316
(5,6)	(38,180)	3.818832	0.039588
(6,7)	(-325,-11)	0.096518	0.002319
(7,8)	(115,184)	0.676197	0.019535
(8,9)	(-46,-260)	0.078653	0.002368
(9,10)	(275,-195)	0.278343	0.002839
(10,11)	(-16961,-26917)	0.001899	0.000024
(11,12)	(728,1316)	0.059318	0.000750
(12,13)	(251,355)	0.352739	0.003624
(13,14)	(61,241)	0.203441	0.006780
(14,15)	(115,47)	0.875835	0.018732
(15,16)	(-85,129)	0.194692	0.006113
(16,1)	(36,53)	4.089518	0.040731

Table 1: Estimated parameters of the pair of scissors shown in Figure 1

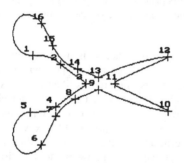

Figure 1: A scissors contour

References

[1]   W M Tsang, P C Yuen and F K Lam, "Localization of dominant point on an object boundary: A discontinuity approach", *Image and Vision Computing*, Vol. 12, No. 9, pp.547-557, 1994.

[2]   B Li and S D Ma, 'Moment difference method for the parameter estimation of a quadratic curve", *Proceeding of 12th IAPR International Conference on Pattern Recognition*, Vol. 1, pp.169-173, 1994.

An Inherent Probabilistic Aspect of the Hough Transform*

Zhanyi. Hu and Songde. Ma

National Laboratory of Pattern Recognition P. O. Box, 2728, Beijing 100080,
P. R. China, E-mail: hu@prlsun5.ia.ac.cn

Abstract: In this paper, we clarify the probabilistic nature of the Hough transform embedded in the transformation process from image space to parameter space, and demonstrate that such probabilistic aspect of the Hough transform is independent of the input image, and will strongly influence its performance.

1 Introduction

Since its discovery, although the Hough transform[1] has been widely used in computer vision and pattern recognition, its properties, especially its probabilistic characteristics, are still far from being well understood. In the literature, concerning the probabilistic characteristics of the Hough transform, the majority of the works are concentrated either on the probabilistic nature of the input image [2] [3][5] or on the randomness of the feature points combinations [4] [6]. In this paper, we show that there exists an inherent probabilistic aspect of the Hough transform during the transformation from image space to parameter space, and that this probabilistic aspect is independent of the input image and will strongly influence the performance of the Hough transform.

2 Basic principles

For the traditional Hough transform, when it is used to detect a pattern which is parameterized by $F(A, x,y)=0$, where $A=[a_1,a_2, ... ,a_n]$ is a parameter vector, the mostly used implementation procedure in the literature is like the following one:

Each feature point (x_i,y_i) maps to those parameter points which lie on the curve (or surface if n>2) $F(A, x_i,y_i)=0$ in the $(a_1,a_2, ... ,a_n)$ space. It is noted that each parameter point $(a_1', a_2', ..., a_n')$ being on the curve(surface) $F(A, x_i,y_i)=0$ will parameterize a particular instance of the pattern, and this instance will go through point (x_i,y_i). Since in practice, given a feature point, we do not know, without a priori knowledge, which instances (instance) really pass(es) through this feature point, the parameters $(a_1,a_2, ... ,a_n)$ can be considered as random variables. Since the parameters $(a_1,a_2, ... ,a_n)$ are constrained on the curve (surface) $F(A,x_i y_i)=0$, thus we can use curve (surface) density function to specify the probabilities with which different instances of the pattern go through a given feature point.

The above discussions are somewhat abstract. Let us take straight line detection as an example to illustrate the basic principles mentioned above.

A straight line can be parameterized by two parameters. For a given parameterization (P_1,P_2), under the standard Hough transform, a feature point (x_i,y_i) maps to a curve $C(x_i,y_i,P_1,P_2)=0$ in the (P_1, P_2) space, and each point lying on the curve $C(x_i,y_i,P_1,P_2)=0$ will parameterize a line passing through this feature point. For a given feature point, since we do not know which lines (line) really pass(es) through this feature point during the transformation, the parameters (p_1,p_2) of a line (Note:(p_1,p_2) is a pair of specific values of (P_1,P_2)) can be considered as random variables. Since (P_1,P_2) are constrained on a curve $C(x_i,y_i,P_1,P_2)=0$, then the two parameters P_1 and P_2 are not

* This work was supported by the Chinese National foundation of Sciences and the National High Technology Program

independent. Thus we can use density function $f(P_1)(f(P_2))$ of parameter $P_1(P_2)$ to specify the probabilities with which different lines pass through a given feature point. We define such a density function as curve density because the parameters (P_1, P_2) are constrained on a curve $C(x_i, y_i, P_1, P_2) = 0$ in the (P_1, P_2) space. In fact, for any real implementation, a curve density function must be provided. In the previous works in the literature, a curve density was provided implicitly rather than explicitly. For example, under the normal (ρ, θ) parameterization, a straight line is defined as $\rho = x\cos\theta + y\sin\theta$ $\theta \in [0, \pi)$, and each feature point (x_i, y_i) maps to a sinusoidal curve $\rho = x_i\cos\theta + y_i\sin\theta$ $\theta \in [0, \pi)$ in the (ρ, θ) space. Since this sinusoidal curve is almost always implemented by equidistantly discretizing θ in practice, then the curve density in this case is implicitly assumed being $f(\theta) = 1/\pi$. i.e., θ has the uniform distribution within the interval $[0, \pi)$. However, under the slope-intercept (a, b) parameterization, a straight line is defined as $y = ax + b$, and each feature point (x_i, y_i) maps to a straight line $b = y_i - ax_i$ in the (a, b) space. In the most cases in the literature, the line $b = y_i - ax_i$ in the (a, b) space is implemented by equidistantly discretizing parameter a, as a result, the curve density was implicitly assumed to be $f(a) = Const$. In what follows, we show that these two curve densities are fundamentally different, and that each one of them implies a different assumption of a priori knowledge associated with feature points.

Under the normal (ρ, θ) parameterization, $f(\theta) = Const.$ means that for a given feature point, every straight line has equal chance to pass through this feature point. If the number of the straight lines passing through this feature point is limited, then $f(\theta) = Const.$ means that any two consecutive lines has a constant intersection angle, which is quite consistent with the intuition. However, under the slope-intercept (a, b) parameterization, $f(a) = Const.$ means that a straight line which has a large intersection angle with the x-axis has more chance to go through a given feature point than a straight line with a small intersection angle. It is clearly contrary to the intuition as well as to the spirit of the Hough transform since one of the fundamental point of the Hough transform is that before the transformation, which lines (line) have (has) more chance to go through a given feature point is unknown.

In summary, it was shown that during the transformation from image space to parameter space, the Hough transform possesses some inherent probabilistic features, and an appropriate curve (surface) density function must be provided to eliminate the uncertainties coming from such probabilistic features. In addition, the inadequacy of widely used uniform sampling was exposed.

References

[1]: P. V. C. Hough (1962), A method and means for recognizing complex patterns, U.S. Patent 3,069,654.

[2] M. Cohen and G. T. Toussaint (1977), On the detection of structures in noisy pictures, Pattern Recognition 9, pp.95-98.

[3] H. Maitre (1986), Contribution to the prediction of performances of the Hough transform, IEEE T-PAMI 8, pp.669-674.

[4] V. F. Leavers (1990), The Dynamic generalized Hough transform, in Proceedings, First European Conference on Computer Vision, pp.592-594.

[5] Z. Hu and J. Destiné (1993), Parameter probability density analysis for the Hough transform, Signal Processing, Vol. 33, No. 2, pp.159-168.

[6] L. Xu and E.Oja (1993), Randomized Hough Transform: Basic Mechanisms, Algorithms, and Computational Complexities, CVGIP:Image Understanding, Vol. 57, No.2, pp.131-154.

A Fuzzy Structural Approach to Handwritten Word Recognition*

Richard Buse [†] and Zhi-Qiang Liu [‡]

Computer Vision and Machine Intelligence Lab, Department of Computer Science
The University of Melbourne, Parkville, Victoria, Australia 3052
[†] richgb@cs.mu.oz.au   [‡] zliu@cs.mu.oz.au

Abstract. In this paper, we present a new off-line word recognition system that is able to recognise unconstrained handwritten words from their grey-scale images, and is based on structural information in the handwritten word. We use Gabor filters to extract oriented features from the words. A 2D fuzzy word classification system has been developed where the spatial location and shape of the membership functions is derived from the training words. The Gabor filter parameters are estimated from the grey-scale word images enabling the Gabor filter to be automatically tuned to the word image. Our experiments show that the proposed method achieves high recognition rates compared to standard classification methods.

1 Introduction

Essentially, characters or words can be considered as a construction of parts or segments at different orientations, lengths, and positions A method for extracting such oriented parts from a grey level image is required. Gabor filters offer a solution to this problem. They are a frequency and orientation selective filter which have the property of minimising the uncertainty simultaneously in the spatial and frequency domains. As the Gabor filter is orientation selective, a bank of n Gabor filters oriented at different angles can be used to extract the oriented parts from words. The Gabor filter is defined in the spatial domain as: $g(x, y) = \exp\left\{-\pi\left(\frac{x'^2}{\sigma_x^2} + \frac{y'^2}{\sigma_y^2}\right)\right\} \times \exp\left\{j2\pi\left(u_0 x + v_0 y\right)\right\}$, where $x' = x\cos\phi + y\sin\phi$, $y' = -x\sin\phi + y\cos\phi$, $u' = u\cos\phi + v\sin\phi$, $v' = -u\sin\phi + v\cos\phi$, $u_0' = u_0\cos\phi + v_0\sin\phi$, $v_0' = -u_0\sin\phi + v_0\cos\phi$, $u_0 = f\cos\theta$, $v_0 = f\sin\theta$, and $j = \sqrt{-1}$.

Due to huge variations in writing styles, a word can be written in a variety of ways by different writers, thus the position, size, and orientation of these extracted parts will vary. Traditional methods extract features which are mostly invariant to the writing styles and generate a set of rules to characterise the words. The major problem with this approach is that with a test word whose features fall outside those of the training set will be rejected or misclassified. The fuzzy pattern recognition approach was chosen in order to deal with the huge variation in writing styles.

---

* This work is supported in part by an Australian Research Council (ARC) large grant.

Our method uses a 2D fuzzy pattern recognition system to describe and classify words. Fuzzy positional information, for instance, a *t* stroke will probably appear at a certain position within the structure of the word, is used to distinguish one word from another assuming that the structure of the word will be consistent between different writers. In this way, a word whose features are outside of the trained words, will possess a *degree* of match to each trained word, and thus the word class which has the closest match will be selected. These fuzzy structural properties of the word can be learnt by combining the structural features extracted by the Gabor filters from many training words.

The procedures to extract the oriented parts from the word and then classify the word are outlined below, and detailed descriptions can be found in [1, 2].

- Slope and tilt correction is performed to reduce the amount of variations in writing styles.
- The Gabor filters parameters $\Delta\phi$, θ, f, σ_x, σ_y are determined [1]. The correct selection of these parameters is essential as the the words vary in size and thickness of the writing.
- The power of the output of the Gabor filters is calculated.
- Each of the word parts in a class are roughly aligned then summed.
- The summed parts are clustered in regions.
- The 2D fuzzy membership functions (two oriented rectangles in a twisted trapezoid form) are now fitted to the oriented regions.
- A test word is classified as belonging to one of the trained word classes by calculating a degree of match to each of the trained words and the decision made using the fuzzy decision theory we developed [2]. The measure of match is determined by finding to what degree each point in the test word belongs to each of the trained membership functions.

2 Results

To test our system, a set of words was extracted from [3]. These words consisted of USA city names which had a sufficient number of samples and were similar in size and structure. Both printed and cursive writing samples were used. A total of 14 words were used for the experiments with 215 samples being selected - 103 randomly chosen samples were used for training, and the remaining 112 samples used for testing. Table 1 shows the initial results of our system. These results are significantly higher those recently published, though our system achieved this with only 7.4 samples per word class for training.

References

1. R. Buse, Z.Q. Liu, T. Caelli, "A Structural and Relational Approach to Hand-Written Word Recognition", *IEEE Trans. on Systems Man and Cybernetics*, in submission.
2. R. Buse, Z.Q. Liu, "On the Recognition of Cursive Handwritten Words Using 2D Fuzzy Measures", *IEEE Trans. on Fuzzy Systems*, in submission.
3. CEDAR CDROM 1, *USPS Office of Advanced Technology*, CEDAR, SUNY at Buffalo, 1992.

Word	Classification Percentages					Word	Classification Percentages				
	1	2	3	4	5		1	2	3	4	5
Baton	66.7	83.3	83.3	83.3	83.3	Moines	85.7	85.7	85.7	100.0	100.0
Boise	75.0	75.0	100.0	100.0	100.0	North	83.3	100.0	100.0	100.0	100.0
Dallas	77.8	88.9	100.0	100.0	100.0	Salem	85.7	100.0	100.0	100.0	100.0
Falls	85.7	92.9	100.0	100.0	100.0	Sioux	91.7	91.7	91.7	100.0	100.0
Haute	100.0	100.0	100.0	100.0	100.0	South	60.0	100.0	100.0	100.0	100.0
Little	83.3	100.0	100.0	100.0	100.0	Terre	25.0	75.0	100.0	100.0	100.0
Louis	58.3	66.7	75.0	75.0	83.3	Tulsa	33.3	50.0	66.7	66.7	83.3

Table 1. Word classification results. The five columns indicate the classification percentages of the word being placed within the top n positions. (Results are specified as percentages).

An Arabic OCR Using Neural Network Classifiers

Hazem Raafat and Gasser Auda

[1] Department of Mathematics and Computer Science,
Kuwait University, Kuwait - hazem@mcc.sci.kuniv.edu.kw

[2] PAMI Research Group, Systems Design Engineering Department,
University of Waterloo, Canada - gasser@watnow.uwaterloo.ca

Abstract. A typewritten Arabic OCR (Optical Character Recognition system) is introduced. The system automatically predicts the size of the font, and uses it in separating lines, words and subwords. Then, it scans the text in a way similar to what the Arabic readers do to recognize and segment the different characters. A set of nine Neural Network modules is used for this process guided by a novel algorithm. The whole text is, then, rebuilt using the recognized characters and some error correction loops are applied. Using Neural Network classifiers allows an efficient hardware implementation and good "generalization" abilities.

1 Introduction

The language of the text to be recognized affects the text recognition system design. For example, Kanji, Japanese, and Indian text recognition problems are more difficult than the English text problems due to the nature of the line segments forming the characters. These segments are oriented in different directions and are having complex relations between them. Thus, the feature selection is the critical part of the system. Moreover, the Japanese text has some unique features, such as its up-to-down reading direction, and the existence of many characters which are composed of more than one of the other simpler characters [1, 6]. The large number of characters of the Chinese alphabet (5000 characters) puts a constraint on the size of the recognition system. The practical way of dealing with this large number of categories is to recognize (segment) simple shapes (primitives) rather than recognizing individual characters [8].

The Arabic text has also some special features which should be considered in the design of its text recognition systems [1, 3, 6, 7]. For example:

- An Arabic word may consist of two or more separated sub-words.

- There are several groups of characters which are similar in shape except for the place of one or more dots.

- Some characters allow vertical overlapping with near characters.

- Each character has up to four shapes according to its place in the word.

- There are unique shapes of combining some pairs of characters which cannot be segmented into the original shapes.

- Finally, there are hundreds of Arabic fonts.

In this paper, a typewritten Arabic OCR is proposed for the most famous font (Naskh font). It "slices" lines, words, and subwords using a moving window before applying a set of Neural Network classifiers.

2 Identifying Sub-words

Horizontal and vertical projection profiles [2] are used in this system (Figure 1):

$horiz - prof(i) = \sum_j P(i,j)$, and $vert - prof(j) = \sum_i P(i,j)$.

where $P(i,j)$ is a pixel value (0 or 1), and i and j are the horizontal and vertical coordinates of the pixel on the image grid.

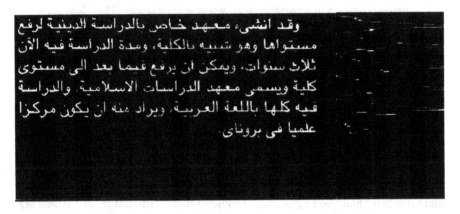

Fig. 1. Horizontal projection profile for a sample text.

In many samples, a small overlap between successive lines appears in the horizontal profile as non-zero values in the regions separating the lines. Moreover, there are more "minima" than the number of interline spaces due to random occurrence of dots and large characters (Figure 1). Low-pass-filtering the profile solved this problem, and the line slices are defined according to the resultant local minima. There are some tiny undesirable segments appearing after cutting lines. However, after character segmentation, these segments are considered noise, and they are successfully filtered out by the applied robust Neural Network (NN) classifiers.

The average height of the detected lines implies the size of the font used and hence, the number of pixels separating words and sub-words. These numbers are used with the vertical profile zero regions in slicing words and sub-words.

Arabic Character Recognition Based on MCR

A. ZIDOURI, S. CHINVEERAPHAN and M. SATO

Abstract. In this paper we propose an off-line recognition system for machine printed Arabic characters based on the Minimum Covering Run expression method (MCR). The recognition is achieved by matching to reference prototypes. We report a recognition rate of 97.5% and possibility of generalising the system to other symbols and characters.

1 Introduction

The MCR[1] expression and its modified version [2] offer structural information that could be useful to several tasks in document image understanding. Since the early work by Amin[3], reasonable interest was devoted to Arabic. This is one application of modified MCR to partition Arabic printed cursive text into strokes, used to build the ORAN System (Off-line Recognition of Arabic a New System).

2 MCR Expression

The MCR expresses binary document images by a minimum number of selected horizontal and vertical runs. it has been shown that horizontal and vertical runs of binary image can be thought of as *partite* sets of a *bipartite* graph. From this correspondence between the binary image and the bipartite graph, where type of runs correspond to partite sets and edges of the graph correspond to pixels in the image, finding the MCR expression amounts to constructing a minimum covering or a maximum matching in the corresponding bipartite graph.

3 Baseline Detection

Most Arabic characters have their horizontal part written on a baseline. We detect it by looking for the line with the largest number of horizontal strokes and label it as baseline. This is used to divide the text line into four horizontal zones where the zone zero is that which contain the baseline. The three others are a lower zone below, and a middle and upper zones above the baseline.

4 Feature Extraction

The strokes are divided into overlapping and non-overlapping parts. The non-overlapping parts of a pattern are labeled and ordered with respect to their absolute position in the document image. Fig.1 shows a 5 character Arabic word

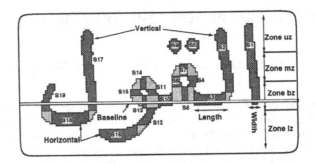

Fig. 1. A word and its parts showing the features used

and the features used. From these features we were able to construct a description of characters in forms of strokes (parts) connections. We designed prototypes for every character shape of Arabic. Then the recognition was performed by matching.

5 Matching and Recognition

The recognition is based on the matching of a candidate character with a reference prototype. The features selection proved to be effective. With simple right to left analysis, we match a candidate character $\mathbf{C}$ to a prototype $\mathbf{P}$ having the same number of strokes. If for a prototype $\mathbf{P} = (S_1, S_2, \ldots, S_k)$ there is a candidate character $\mathbf{C} = (s_1, s_2, \ldots, s_k)$ such that:

$\forall S_j \in P \;\exists s_j \in C, \;\; j = \{1, 2, \ldots, k\}, \;\; S_j = (f_{1_j}, f_{2_j}, \ldots, f_{m_j}, connection\_rule)$

$s_j = (\{ln_j\}, \{wd_j\}, \{tp_j\}, \{ld_j\}, \{rd_j\}, \{ps_j\}, \{con_j\}, \{rgn_j\}, \;\; connection\_rule)$

$if : \forall f_{p_j} \in S_j \quad \exists f'_{c_j} \in s_j$ where f_{p_j} is a relationship to, or a value of one of the 8 features, $p = \{1, 2, \ldots, m\}, \quad m \leq 8, \quad c = \{1, 2, \ldots, 8\}$ such that $f_{p_j} \supseteq f'_{c_j}) \;\land\; (Connection\_Rule\_True)$ then the candidate character shape $\mathbf{C}$ is matched to the prototype $\mathbf{P}$.

The overall recognition rate for the test documents is 97.5% for a data set of more than 6800 characters.

References

1. Chinveeraphan, S., Douniwa, K., and Sato, M., *"Minimum Covering Run Expression of Document Images Based on Matching of Bipartite Graph."* IEICE *Trans. Inf. & Syst.*, vol.E76-D, no.4, pp.462–469, Apr. 1993.
2. S. Chinveeraphan, A. Zidouri, and M. Sato, *"Modified Minimum Covering Run Expression of Binary Document Images,"* IEICE *Trans. Inf. & Syst.*, vol.E78-D, no.4, pp.503–507, Apr. 1995.
3. A. Amin, and G. Masini, *"Machine Recognition of Multi-fonts Printed Arabic Text,"* Proc. 8th Inter. Conf. on PR, (Paris), pp. 392–395, Oct. 1986.

Geographic Map Understanding.
Algorithms for Hydrographic Network Reconstruction.

R. Mariani+, M.P. Deseilligny+, J. Labiche*, Y. Lecourtier* and R. Mullot*.

+ IGN DT/SR, 2, av. Pasteur 94160 Saint-Mandé, France. Email mariani@ign.fr.
* La3i-LACIS, Université de Rouen, UFR Sc & Tech, 76821 Mont Saint Aignan.

Abstract. This paper describes a high-level reconstruction method of the hydrographic "linear" network graph, represented in a french geographic map, with dashed lines and interrupted solid lines. The process takes into account drawing rules used by cartographers and properties of the natural network graph, in order to provide a geometrically and topologically correct graph. Working with a graph, obtained by vectorization, we have a good matching between the data and the natural graph concept and so, we apply directly the rules defined on the real network for reconstructing the cartographic network.

1. Introduction.

This paper describes a high-level method for automated linear network reconstruction of hydrographic network graphs. This work is included in a larger one [3] and the global issue is "map understanding for GIS data capture". The hydrographic linear network is represented with dashed lines and interrupted solid lines. The method is general and can be used for other linear networks reconstruction problems. The aim is to provide a geometrically and topologically correct graph.

We proceed in three steps: 1) the map is simplified by extracting objects which trouble the reconstruction process; 2) the remaining image is vectorized by skeletonization and polygonal approximation [3]; we obtain then the interrupted network; 3) the reconstruction is computed.

2. Features of the Hydrographic Network.

The purpose of this section is to exhibit rules concerning the hydrographic network. There are two kinds of knowledges: those relative to real hydrographic network, and those relative to its graphic representation on the map. At the end, we give the consequences for the reconstruction process.

2.1 Properties of the Real Hydrographic Network.

The graph of the natural hydrographic network is planary and contains few connected components and very few cycles (as much as islands). In fact, in a theoretical point a view, it can be roughly assimilated to a forest, say a tree list. There are few connected components in front of the size of the network and so the number of trees is limited. This graph would verify a global connectivity property.

2.2 Exceptions.

But practically, there are two major exceptions to those rules: 1) channels frequently create cycles; 2) because of map windowing, we study only the part of the real network limited to the rectangle (or window) of the map. Windowing will cause the most frequent disconnexions and so will create a lot of connected components.

Because of these exceptions, we cannot use directly the predefined strong topologic rules on the real network. In fact, cartographic network verifies " fuzzy topologic properties ": a planary graph with " not a lot of " connected components and " not a lot of " cycles.

2.3 Features of Graphic Representation.

There are two drawing rules for dashed lines: 1) distance between two dashes is quite regular; 2) there is not a strong curvature between two dashes.

For the interrupted solid lines, there are four drawing rules: 1) interruptions, caused by the presence at the same place of other objects on the map, (for instance, a string can partially cover a river) have a maximum size, determined by the objects which create occlusion; 2) curvatures, which are important in a geographic map, are largely represented; 3) a connexion between two solid lines is often the continuation of one of them; 4) the shortest connexion may not be the best one.

2.4 Consequences for the Reconstruction Process.

Cartographic objects are frequently interrupted (dashed lines, occlusion made by other objects ...). So, an important step of the reconstruction task will be, after vectorization of the linear network, to add to the graph the likely edges, in order to obtain a coherent network according to the a priori topologic knowledges (§ 2.2).

Cartographic rules used to represent dashed and solid lines are different. In order to take into account those drawing rules, we have decomposed the reconstruction process in two steps: 1) transforming dashed lines into solid lines; 2) reconstructing interrupted solid lines.

3. Map Simplification.

The simplication process is able to recognize and delete objects which do not belong to the linear network. These objects are conserved and will be used later for the global map understanding. Here, the aim is to provide an image which contains only lines.

At the end of the simplification, the remaining image (fig 1) is vectorized. We then obtain the interrupted network.

Fig. 1: initial and simplified image.

Automatic Analyzing of a Weaving Design with the Spatial Frequency Components

Ken'ichi Ohta, Yoshito Nonaka, Fujio Miyawaki

Himeji Institute of Technology, Himeji-shi, Japan

Abstract In the textile design process, textile samples are often copied for reference. In these cases, weaving information is required to produce copies of that textile. This information includes the thread placement of the stripe patterns, the weaving design that shows the intersecting and twisting conditions, and the textile's density. In the past, these tasks replied on manual labor, which took a long time and was the source of error. Therefore, a method for extracting information on a weaving design from the patterns on the textile's surface with the objective of automating a part of the textile design process is proposed.

1 Introduction

Textile designs are made with pattern on the textile's surface by the placement of variously colored warp and weft threads. Consequently, the features of warp and weft threads are consistent in the warp and weft directions. Moreover, they are repetitive patterns that have periodicity and are exhibit features in the spatial frequency components. Therefore, a method for extracting a weaving design with the use of the Fourier transform is discussed.

2 The way to extract a weaving design

As a weaving design is extracted by distinguishing warp and weft threads, intersections which show the current positions of warp or weft threads and the current positions appearing on the textile's surface because of the threads weaving by using the Fourier transform and bandpass filters, limited in the lengthwise or widthwise direction in the spatial frequency domain must be obtained.

2.1 The two-dimensional discrete Fourier transforms

The sample image of the textile's surface used as a textile design was scanned by an image scanner and the Fourier transform which is used to determine the spatial frequency components is performed by the two-dimensional discrete Fourier transform that corresponds to the optical Fourier transform. Furthermore, by applying a bandpass filter in the spatial frequency domain to the spectrum obtained by performing a Fourier transform, then performing a two-dimensional inverse Fourier transform, a bandpass image with any spatial frequency range can be obtained.

2.2 Rectangular and ring type bandpass filters

Because the spatial frequency components related to the thread direction are sought, the center of the filter's distribution is focused on the origin of the lengthwise and widthwise axes and the rectangular type bandpass filters and the ring type bandpass filters limited in the warp or the weft threads direction are produced. Figure 1 shows a rectangular type bandpass filter limited in the weft threads direction and figure 2 shows a ring type bandpass filter limited in the warp threads direction. The passband of these filters are 1.0 and the stopband is 0.0. The black shaded part indicates the passband in figures 1 and 2. The current positions of warp and weft threads are obtained by using rectangular type bandpass filters. The current positions appearing on the textile's surface because of the weft threads weaving are obtained by using a bandpass filter shown in figure 2.

2.3 Producing a weaving design

The intersections and the current positions appearing on the textile's surface because of the threads weaving are extracted when the binarization process is applied to the bandpass filtered images. Figure 3 shows a binarization image obtained by using the bandpass filter shown in figure 2. As shown in figure 3, we can verify that the current positions appearing on the textile's surface because of the weft threads weaving were extracted. The warp and weft threads are distinguished by using these intersections and figure 3. The black shaded part indicates information on the weft threads and the white shaded part indicates information on the warp threads in figure 4. As shown in figure 4, warp and weft threads are almost distinguished except outside the image. Since this method is not concerned with individual colors and features of each thread, but is concerned with the use of two types of bandpass filters considered features of a weaving design, it is simpler and more efficient than earlier methods.

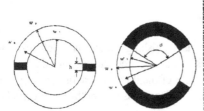 

Fig.1 Rectangular type   Fig.2 Ring type band-   Fig.3 Binarization image   Fig.4 Figure of a weaving
   bandpass filter   pass filter   that shows weft threads   design

References

1. Y. Koshimizu. Development of a Simple Image Processing System and Its Application to Industry. Computer Vision, **30**, 4,pp. 1-8 (1984).
2. K. Ohta, K. Sakaue, and K.Saeki. Research on Pattern Recognition of Textile Surface (Threads Directionality).T.M.S.of Japan,**41**,8,pp.424-432 (1988).
3. N. Ohtu. An Automatic Threshold Selection Method Based on Discriminate and Least Squares Criteria. Trans.I.E.I.C.E.(D), **J63-D**, pp.349-356 (1980).

Visual Inspection of Watermeters Used for Automatic Calibration

Robert Sablatnig

Technical University Vienna, Dept. of Pattern Recognition & Image Processing, Treitlstr. 3/183-2, A-1040 Vienna, Austria, e-mail: sab@prip.tuwien.ac.at

Abstract. To be acceptable in industry, automatic visual inspection systems must be inexpensive, very accurate and should be flexible enough to accommodate changes in products. This flexibility can be reached if a modular concept that allows a quick and inexpensive adaption of the inspection process to any changes is used. This paper presents a concept where the detection of primitives is separated from the model-based analysis process. Existing pattern recognition software is re-used in the detection stage, allowing any detection algorithm to be tested and used without changing the analysis process. The visual inspection of analog watermeters serves for a demonstration of this concept.

1 Introduction

An industrial visual inspection system should be based on an architecture that encourages portability, giving systems that are easy to install, modify and support [3]. These requirements can be reached by separating the application independent primitive detection process from the application dependent analysis and inspection process. The Top-Down approach starts with the definition of the problem space in which the specific problem is embedded. The primitives of the object form the vocabulary of a "Description language", relations among the primitives "hold" the information about the specific application. The visual inspection of analog watermeters serves for a demonstration of the proposed separation. These instruments have to be calibrated after the manufacturing process. An automated visual inspection of analog instruments provides faster execution and quality control. Three primitives describe watermeters: pointers, scales and lettering elements. A **pointer** can have any symmetric shape with an easy detectable medial axis. The shape of a **scale** depends on the motion of the pointer. The shape of the scale for a rotating pointer is a **circle** or a **circular arc**. Pointers moving straight usually have rectangular scales. There are other layout elements of a measuring unit that carry information about the measurement and the global orientation, classified as **lettering**.

2 Image Analysis Process and Results

The kind of primitives to be detected to inspect watermeters are circles, rectangles and pointers. To detect circular, arc-shaped scales in the intensity image, we used a circular arc detection method based on the Hough transformation [2]. Rectangular scale detection is based on the grouping of 4 straight lines, which we can detect by using an approach by Burns [1]. Pointers in the intensity image are detected using gray level profiles along circles in the image plane [5]. Water meters have a special feature: coupled pointers, which means that the previous pointer defines the position of the following pointer. Lettering elements are taken to check and verify the type and orientation of the measuring instrument by computing the correlation coefficient between the window in the intensity image, and the bitmap of the lettering element. All of the algorithms were used because the source code of the programs already existed and they where passing our laboratory tests with a recognition rate close to 99%. Following the pattern recognition software testing stage, the analysis process to perform the reading has to be carried out, using the model of the watermeter described in generic parameters and relations between primitives in the description language [4].

In a laboratory test series (200 frames), the positions of **all scales and pointers** were determined in the **requested time**, with the requested **accuracy** and **reliability**. Fig.1 shows the intensity image of the measuring instrument and the detected scales and pointers. Note that the coupled pointer computation method is used, therefore pointers which

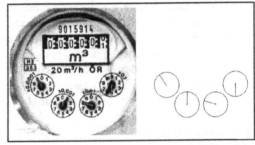

Fig. 1. Detected scales and pointers (0.5809 units)

have not passed a value on a scale completely are considered to display the previous value. To find out if the laboratory results can also be achieved in the final application, a industrial test series (300 frames) was conducted, detecting two problems: unstable illumination conditions and air bubbles next to pointers. The reliability of the reading process was 97%, borders of the air bubbles effected the determination of the pointer position producing the errors. As a result of this test series the illumination device for the final application was reconstructed and the pointer detection algorithm was displaced by a new algorithm using matched filters for pointerdetection. A second industrial test series (600 frames) was conducted, resulting in a reliability of 100%.

References

1. J.B. Burns, A.R. Hanson, E.M. Riseman, "Extracting Straight Lines", *IEEE PAMI*, Vol.8, No.4, pp.425-455, 1986.
2. P. Kierkegaard, "A Method for Detection of Circular Arcs Based on the Hough Transform", *Machine Vision and Applications*, Vol.5, pp.249-263, 1992.
3. T.S. Newman, A.K. Jain, "A Survey of Automated Visual Inspection", *CVGIP*, Vol.61, No.2, pp.231-262, 1995.
4. R. Sablatnig, W.G. Kropatsch, "Automatic Reading of Analog Display Instruments", Proc. of the 12th *ICPR94*, Jerusalem, Israel, October 9-13, pp.794-797, 1994.
5. R. Sablatnig, W.G. Kropatsch, "Application Constraints in the Design of an Automatic Reading Device for Analog Display Instruments", Proc. of the 2nd *IEEE Workshop on Applications of Computer Vision*, pp.205-212, Sarasota, 1994.

Computer Aided Diagnosis in Radiology

S.Vitulano, C.Di Ruberto, M.Nappi

Istituto di Medicina Interna - Clinica Medica "M.Aresu"
Università di Cagliari - Via S.Giorgio, 12- 09124, Cagliari (ITALY)
Fax +38-70-663651, E-Mail vitulano@facmed.unica.it

Abstract. The most important roles of our model of human perceptive process are played by the evaluation function (e.f) and the control strategy. The e.f. is related to the ratio between the entropy of one region or zone of the picture and the entropy of the entire picture. The control strategy determines the optimal path in the search tree so that the nodes of the optimal path have the less as possible entropy.

1 Introduction

Typically segmentation describes the process, both human and automatic, that individuates in a pictorial scene zones or regions showing some characteristics with respect to a certain e.f.. The e.f. plays a very important role in the entire process of segmentation. In fact for a same pictorial scene it's possible to obtain different segmentations in relation to the e.f. adopted. So, for example, it is possible to choose as e.f. a very simple measure, the gray tone, and according to this choice the pixels of the scene with a same gray tone belong to the same region. The e.f. is the result of a measure computable on a picture. The more used measures are: the gray tone, the color, the texture, the application of a local operator (gradient, laplacian, average), filter and so on.

We consider as regions all those zones of the picture whose entropy is negligible (reversible states) and for which it is possible to determine a statistical function or mathematical structure describing them. On the contrary for those regions (catastrophes) that present a high value of entropy (irreversible states) it is not possible to determine a statistical function or a mathematical structure but, perhaps, a catastrophe. We say that the zones of the picture where entropy is high correspond to the contour or the silhouette of the object.

The purpose of the split phase is to divide each region, individuated by the merge phase, in subregions which can be described by means of different mathematical structures; for these subregions the entropy changes are infinitesimal.

2 The proposed method

The proposed technique divides the whole segmentation problem into two subproblems: the merge and the split.

The task of the merge phase is to obtain some information about the different regions of the picture: the number of existing regions, their areas and topological positions in the domain, their features and their contours. The goal we intend to realize in this phase is to highlight, inside the pictorial scene, those areas whose entropy is equal to zero or however does not present sudden variations. In other words, the zones extracted as regions are those ones whose evaluation function is stable or gradually decreasing.

The aim of the splitting phase is to distinguish the structures associated with each region whatever is their statistics. The merging phase divides an image into regions whose elements satisfy a predicate of uniformity and it associates with each region the dimensions of the partition element and its evaluation function. In a region two elements can satisfy the same uniformity predicate but this does not imply that they have the same texture or structure. For structure associated with an element, we intend a description of the mutual relations among the pixels contained in the partition element.

Therefore the basic task of the split phase is to associate a structure with the region under investigation or, if the elements haven't the same shape, to split the region in more regions.

3 Concluding remarks

The model has been widely experimented on different kinds of pictures: natural scenes, CT, MR and mammographies images.

During the period of collaboration with several hospitals we have observed that the perceptive model proposed in this paper could be very useful for the doctor in the diagnostic iter; in fact, we think that such a model makes much more evident the information contained in the images.

We'll now explain what the computer model and the human operator have to do in the whole process. The model puts in evidence the different regions of the pictorial scene according to their structure. The human operator has to understand the presence of a certain structure in the image and according to this understanding to realize the diagnosis.

During all the segmentation process the human operator doesn't intervene, only the control strategy guides the whole process.

References

1. R.M.Haralick, Statistical and Structural Approaches to Textures, Proc. IEEE 67, pp.786- 804, 1979
2. J.M.Keller, S.Chen, R.M. Crownover, Texture Description through Fractal Geometry, C.V.G.I.P., v.45, pp.150-166, 1989.
3. H.Samet, The Quadtree and Related Hierarchical Data Structures, ACM Computers Surveys 1984.
4. B.Julecz, Foundation of Ciclopean Perception, University of Chicago Press, Chicago and London 1971.
5. R.M.Haralick, L.Shapiro, "Survey: Image Segmentation Techniques", Computer Vision Graphics and Image Processing, 29, pp. 100-132, 1985.
6. A.Rosenfeld, A.C.Kak, Digital Signal Processing, New York, 1982.
7. P.J.Burt, T.Hong, A.Rosenfeld, "Segmentation and Estimation of Image Region Properties Through Cooperative Hierarchical Computation", IEEE Trans. on System, Man and Cybernetics, v.11, n.12, 1981.
8. C.Di Ruberto, N.Di Ruocco, S.Vitulano "A Segmentation Algorithm based on AI Techniques", Pattern Recognition in Practice IV, 1994, ED. E.S. Gelsema and L.N. Kanal, Elsevier Science Publishers .

Image Analysis for Dating of Old Manuscripts

Emanuel Wenger[1], Viktor N. Karnaukhov[2], Alois Haidinger[3], and Nikolai S. Merzlyakov[2]

[1] Austrian Academy of Sciences, Institute of Information Processing,
Sonnenfelsgasse 19/2, A-1010 Vienna, Austria,
[2] Russian Academy of Sciences, Institute for Information Transmission Problems,
19 Bolshoij Karetny Str., GSP-4, 101447 Moscow, Russia,
[3] Austrian Academy of Sciences, Kommission für Schrift- und Buchwesen des
Mittelalters, Postgasse 7-9/4/3, A-1010 Vienna, Austria

Abstract. This paper presents an application of digital image processing to historical sciences. A major tool for dating old undated documents are watermarks found in the paper. Hardcopies of the watermarks are scanned, preprocessed, improved and contrast enhanced by adaptive digital filtering methods for printing, storing in an image database, and extracting the watermark as a set of strokes from the image. For extraction, a semiautomatical procedure is suggested. The extraction result is a short sequence of cubic spline curves representing the watermark fully and allowing to select identical or similar watermarks from the existing database.

1 Motivation

A major tool for dating an undated medieval manuscript, written on paper, is the analysis of the watermarks found in the paper. In the case of identity of an undated watermark with a dated one, it is possible to determine rather precisely the time of production of the paper. However, the large number of similar watermarks, the additional necessity to include into the investigation also the sieve marks in the paper, plus the low contrasts of the watermarks and the big quantity of artefacts make an analysis and a comparison of watermarks a tedious task. Digital image processing tools, database systems and computer graphics are applied to support handling and identification of watermarks.

2 Input and Preprocessing

All paper marks including watermarks are small deviations in the thickness of paper. Prior to inputting the watermark, a hardcopy by X-rays or betaradiography has to be produced. These hardcopies have very low contrast except some very bright or very dark spots and areas caused by holes in the paper or special color ink (see Fig. 1a). The scanning can be done by a drum scanner or a sensitive flatbed scanner with a transparency extension.

The first digital image processing step aims at the suppression of impulse noise inherent in all images. Two thresholds for the detection of down-directed

Fig. 1. a) original image, b) enhanced image, c) image plus watermark

and up-directed noise outburst respectively are calculated using the cumulative histogram. A locally-adaptive rank algorithm [1] appeared to be the best choice for the estimation of the correct values of the distorted pixels.

3   Image Enhancement

The very low contrast between watermarks and background makes it necessary to enhance the local contrast. For this aim the nonsharp masking algorithm [2] is applied which enhances the local contrast but reduces spatially slow variations of the background (see Fig. 1b).

4   Extraction

The major step in our watermark processing procedure is the extraction of the watermark as skeleton from the image. It appeared that an automatic procedure does not work properly in most cases due to the quality of the images. Hence, a semi-automatic procedure was chosen. For each motif, a short sequence of special control points are marked manually. These control points result in a cubic spline representation which describes the watermarks completely (see Fig. 1c). This representation allows the search for existing identical or similar watermarks in the database and yields also a very comprehensive coding.

References

1. Yaroslavsky, L. P.: Linear and Rank Adaptive Filters for Picture Processing. In: E. Wenger, L. Dimitrov (eds.): Digital Image Processing and Computer Graphics. Wien: Oldenbourg 1991, pp. 327–372
2. Pratt, W. K.: Digital Image Processing. John Wiley & Sons, New York, 2nd edition, 1991

Document Layout Analysis Using Pattern Classification Method

Masaki Yamaoka and Osamu Iwaki

Laboratory for Information Technology,
NTT Data Communications Systems Corporation, Japan
E-mail:yamaoka@lit.rd.nttdata.jp

Abstract. This paper presents a bottom-up approach for segmenting document images and labeling the segmented regions with logical names. Our method uses image features in terms of the characteristics of text lines, such as margin and character size, then our method can analyze an unstable document image that has floating elements such as figures and tables. Experimental application of this method to images of technical journals written in Japanese yielded classification rates of 98.6 % for the front pages and 90.0 % for the final pages that have floating elements.

1 Introduction

The big task in developing document information systems is media exchange, which converts existing paper-based documents into the retrievable form in computers. This task requires not only character recognition but also extraction of logical structures from documents. Layout analysis is one approach to segmenting document images and labeling them with logical names. The dominant method uses top-down strategies, which divide images into some portions by using projection profiles, recursively. Dengel[1] proposed a geometric tree for analyzing single-sided letter images. It is difficult, however, to analyze an unstable document image because top-down strategies use a spatial relationship of components. Technical journals, for example, have figures or tables that are called floating elements, and for which a geometric tree can't be defined. In this paper we propose a new layout analysis method without a spatial relationship.

2 Proposed Method

First black-and-white document images are captured by scanning the papers. After skew correction and noise reduction, connected components are extracted by using horizontal and vertical projection profiles. A basic rectangle is extracted by merging connected components horizontally[2]. Most of the basic rectangles form regions of text line. A feature vector including eleven features is calculated for each basic rectangle. There are four coordinate values that present upper-left and bottom-right corners, and three features concerned with text line (line height, line spacing above and below). The remaining features are the number of connected components in the basic rectangle, the width-to-height ratio of the basic rectangle and the ratio of the sum of connected components' area to the area of the basic rectangle. In the next step, the basic rectangles are labeled with logical names. In case of a technical journal, for example, with names like "Title" and "Author." Discriminant analysis and the minimum distance classification method are used. Reference vectors are created in advance for each category by using a canonical correlation analysis. A reference vector is defined as the vector that has the mean values for each feature. After the feature vector is extracted from an unlabeled basic rectangle, the

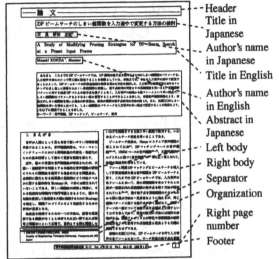

This image is from Document Image Database JEIDA'93, published by the Japan Electronic Industry Development Association.

Figure 1 : Logical elements regions of an IEICE front page.

Euclid distances from each reference vector to the feature vector are calculated. Then the component that gives the minimum distance is selected and the basic rectangle is labeled with the name of that components.

3   Experimental Results

We evaluated the proposed method experimentally, using the transactions of the IEICE (Institute of Electronics, Information and Communication Engineers) D-II written in Japanese. We used 110 front pages as an example of a stable document image and 86 final pages as an example of an unstable document image. A front page and a final page include the twelve and eight logical components respectively (Figure 1). The results were evaluated by calculating the classification rate R that is defined as $R = N_c/N_b$ where N_b is the number of basic rectangles and N_c is the number of rectangles with correct labels. The classification rates were 98.6% for the front pages and 90.0% for the final pages when we used the leaving-one-out method.

4   Conclusion

The proposed method can analyze images that have floating elements by using image features. The future research is to construct a logical structured map; for example, linking the author's name to the author's affiliation.

References

1. A.Dengel, "ANASTASIL : A System for Low-Level and High-Level Geometric Analysis of Printed Documents," Structured Document Image Analysis, pp. 70-98, Springer-Verlag, 1992.
2. K.Iwane, M.Yamaoka and O.Iwaki, "A Functional Classification Approach to Layout Analysis of Document Images," Proceedings of the Second International Conference on Document Analysis and Recognition, pp. 778-781, 1993.

Recognition of Engineering Drawings Based on Frame Structure Theory

Xu Yaodong   Ying Daoning

State Key Laboratory of CAD & CG, Zhejiang University
Hangzhou 310027, P.R.China

Abstract: Engineering drawings' recognition is a processing to interpret an image of line drawings into vector format appropriate for computer-aided draughting system. This paper proposes a new method which is based on Frame Structure Theory. At first, Frame structure is defined, and then, Frame Structure Theory is introduced. Finally, method of recognition of engineering drawings based on Frame Structure Theory is also described . The result of recognition is seems as a contribution to the solution of the problem of engineering drawings' recognition.

1 Introduction

Physical model of ED(Engineering drawings) has well structural feature, therefore, it can be formed with many source patterns by defined product rules, source pattern is one of basic elements for pattern recognition.

In ED recognition, selection of source pattern determines the method of recognition, nowadays, most of recognition methods take skeleton as source pattern[1], this kind of method includes binary image thinning processing, but this processing brings many difficult problems and more time consuming[2].

In this paper, according to especial feature of ED, Internal & External Frame Structure of ED are taken as source pattern, and then, the Frame structure which based cyclic tree is also set up.

Definition: Frame structure is an enclosed structure which is the border between drawing and background image in ED, where, frame bordering external boundary is defined as external frame, and internal boundary is defined as internal frame,(see fig.1).

External frame is a set of pixel whose value is 2. internal frame is a set of pixel whose value is 3.

```
000000000000000000000000
022222222222222222222220
021111111111111111111120
021133333333333333331120
021130000000000000031120
021130000000000000031120
021133333333333333331120
022222222222222222222220
000000000000000000000000
```

fig. 1

2 Frame structure theory

In order to obtain powerful algorithms for matching and expressing, many researchers have studied verify typical schemes in pattern recognition for many years, the three basic schemes are string, tree and graph, some schemes extended on the three basic schemes are applied to make them more efficient, however, these schemes usually lead to exponential time complexity.

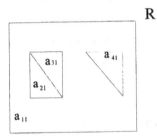

$\$$

R

a_{11}

a_{21}

a_{31}

a_{41}

fig.2 description of ED by the frame structure cyclic tree representation scheme

In this paper, we proposes a representation scheme which is suitable for representing ED, and lead to describe ED through its inner cycles whatever they are. Fig.2 shows the description ED by the proposed representation scheme.

Frame structure cyclic tree is a structure which allows to describe ED by means of a tree which branches and nodes are cyclic. indeed the frame structure cyclic tree is not a tree, is a graph which is structured as a tree in order to allow doing partial operations in the same way that are done in a tree.

In the frame structure cyclic tree. moreover there is information concerning coordinates, area of frame structure, etc., fig.3 shows the structure of frame structure cyclic tree, where a_{ij} is a frame structure,(x1,y1,x2,y2) is coordinate value which enclose frame structure, BS is frame area, $a_{ai},...a_{af}$ is frame structure belong to a_{ij}, SI are the relative frame structures of a_{ij}.

FERSA: Lip–Synchronous Animation

Patricia A. Griffin, Han Noot

Department of Interactive Systems, Centre for Mathematics and
Computer Science, Amsterdam, The Netherlands

The goal of the FERSA project[1] (Facial Expression Recognition for lip–Synchronous Animation) is to automate the production of lip–synchronous animations, specifically for use in a television post–production environment. Computer Vision techniques are employed to automatically process and analyze video images of a narrator and to identify the necessary mouth position needed to reconstruct a lip–synchronous animation using the narrator's original voice track.

The creation of lip–synchronous facial animations has been time consuming, costly and non–automatic. Approaches to automate this work has been: synthetic speech to image synthesis (text–to–speech)[2], audio speech recognition to image synthesis and visual speech recognition to image synthesis[3]. Our approach could be referred to as visual shape recognition to image synthesis or performer driven animation [4].

Previous research [5,6] shows that only a small set of mouth shapes are needed to reconstruct a 'convincing' lip–synchronous speech animation. For French and English this number is on the order of 20 mouth shapes. However, this holds for the reconstruction of animations at unequal intervals. Since we sample at equal intervals of 25/sec we need to accommodate for 'in–between' mouth positions.

We employ Computer Vision techniques to recognize mouth shape parameters from each input video frame. Thus, there is no speech recognition involved. We create an animation using these mouth shape identifiers to access frames, creating an animation by means of two simple methods: a 'flip–book' method or a 3D key–frame animation method. The original voice track is recombined with the reconstructed images for full lip–synchronization.

The FERSA system is composed of two main modules. Module I processes the video images, extracts features and classifies the mouth shapes of the narrator. Module II uses the recognition results of the classifier to access the proper animation frame or identify the proper key frame to form the animation.

Module I is first 'trained'. The narrator reads a phonetically rich text in front of the camera. The script can take less than one minute to read. The images are analyzed and the narrator's characteristics are extracted for later classification of any general video input of the narrator. With proper choice of the training script the system can be trained for any language.

The software of Module I tracks the nostrils of the speaker, thus finding the region of interest, i.e., the mouth and surrounding area. Measurements, pertaining to the mouth and mouth area, are taken from the thresholded input images. From these measurements we derive 13 relevant features. Using standard statistical methods, the degree of statistical independence between features can easily be determined. In our experiments we reduced the feature space to two and three dimensions. Considering our statistical analysis, however, we believe that optimum results would be achieved on a five dimensional space.

From the training data set we design a classifier by partitioning our feature space into 15 to 30 classes. The type of animation determines the number of classes needed. Due to the nature of our data we can not simply apply statistical methods for determining the classes. These methods have the tendency to dismiss outlying or 'strange' data points. These 'strange' data point could very well be a smile, smirk or some other gesture of the mouth that may add expression. We do not want to exclude any possible 'expression' points. Given the features used we know the type of data cloud to be expected and can divide it accordingly, leaving room for possible 'expression points'. The training software also allows the experimenter the possibility of viewing any of the outlying points for error checking.

After the training session the narrator can now speak any text into the camera. The images are processed and classified to the mouth centers of the partitions by means of a simple euclidean distance.

For our experiments we constructed animations using a simple 'flip book' animation method. The animation frames were created by an artist. The number of animations frames can be less than or equal to the number of classes. The mapping between mouth shape class and animation frame is also determined by the artist. The animation frames can be drawings, photo stills or rendered key frames. Module II receives the results of the classifier and accesses the corresponding animation frame. Images are displayed to screen synchronous with the original voice track to form the completed lip–synchronous animation. In a television post–production studio we produced off–line animations using a more sophisticated 3D Graphics package for the animations. The system could easily be used for parameter driven facial models.

Performance could be improved by the use of principle component analysis and a larger dimensional feature space.

1. P. Griffin, H. Noot: The FERSA project for lip–sync animatin. In Proceedings Image'Com 93, pages 111–116, Bordeaux, France

2. K. Waters, T.M. Levergood: DECface: An Automatic Lip–Synchronization Algorithm for Synthetic Faces Digital Equipment Corporation, Technical Report Series Cambridge Research Lab; CRL 93/4 September 23, 1993

3. J. Lewis: Automated Lip–sync: Background and Techniques, The Journal of Visualization and Computer Animation, vol. 2, pp. 118–122, 1991

4. L. Williams: Performance–Driven facial animation. ACM SIGGRAPH'90, 24(4): 235–243

5. C. Benoit and T. Lallouche: Nineteen (+–19) French Visemes for visual speech synthesis. In Proceedings of the ESCA workshop on Speech Synthesis, September 1990.

6. S. Brennan: Master's Thesis, School of Architecture and Planing, Architecture Machine Group, MIT, Cambridge, M.A. 1982

Author Index

Lecture Notes in Computer Science

For information about Vols. 1–945

please contact your bookseller or Springer-Verlag

Vol. 981: I. Wachsmuth, C.-R. Rollinger, W. Brauer (Eds.), KI-95: Advances in Artificial Intelligence. Proceedings, 1995. XII, 269 pages. (Subseries LNAI).

Vol. 982: S. Doaitse Swierstra, M. Hermenegildo (Eds.), Programming Languages: Implementations, Logics and Programs. Proceedings, 1995. XI, 467 pages. 1995.

Vol. 983: A. Mycroft (Ed.), Static Analysis. Proceedings, 1995. VIII, 423 pages. 1995.

Vol. 984: J.-M. Haton, M. Keane, M. Manago (Eds.), Advances in Case-Based Reasoning. Proceedings, 1994. VIII, 307 pages. 1995.

Vol. 985: T. Sellis (Ed.), Rules in Database Systems. Proceedings, 1995. VIII, 373 pages. 1995.

Vol. 986: Henry G. Baker (Ed.), Memory Management. Proceedings, 1995. XII, 417 pages. 1995.

Vol. 987: P.E. Camurati, H. Eveking (Eds.), Correct Hardware Design and Verification Methods. Proceedings, 1995. VIII, 342 pages. 1995.

Vol. 988: A.U. Frank, W. Kuhn (Eds.), Spatial Information Theory. Proceedings, 1995. XIII, 571 pages. 1995.

Vol. 989: W. Schäfer, P. Botella (Eds.), Software Engineering — ESEC '95. Proceedings, 1995. XII, 519 pages. 1995.

Vol. 990: C. Pinto-Ferreira, N.J. Mamede (Eds.), Progress in Artificial Intelligence. Proceedings, 1995. XIV, 487 pages. 1995. (Subseries LNAI).

Vol. 991: J. Wainer, A. Carvalho (Eds.), Advances in Artificial Intelligence. Proceedings, 1995. XII, 342 pages. 1995. (Subseries LNAI).

Vol. 992: M. Gori, G. Soda (Eds.), Topics in Artificial Intelligence. Proceedings, 1995. XII, 451 pages. 1995. (Subseries LNAI).

Vol. 993: T.C. Fogarty (Ed.), Evolutionary Computing. Proceedings, 1995. VIII, 264 pages. 1995.

Vol. 994: M. Hebert, J. Ponce, T. Boult, A. Gross (Eds.), Object Representation in Computer Vision. Proceedings, 1994. VIII, 359 pages. 1995.

Vol. 995: S.M. Müller, W.J. Paul, The Complexity of Simple Computer Architectures. XII, 270 pages. 1995.

Vol. 996: P. Dybjer, B. Nordström, J. Smith (Eds.), Types for Proofs and Programs. Proceedings, 1994. X, 202 pages. 1995.

Vol. 997: K.P. Jantke, T. Shinohara, T. Zeugmann (Eds.), Algorithmic Learning Theory. Proceedings, 1995. XV, 319 pages. 1995.

Vol. 998: A. Clarke, M. Campolargo, N. Karatzas (Eds.), Bringing Telecommunication Services to the People – IS&N '95. Proceedings, 1995. XII, 510 pages. 1995.

Vol. 999: P. Antsaklis, W. Kohn, A. Nerode, S. Sastry (Eds.), Hybrid Systems II. VIII, 569 pages. 1995.

Vol. 1000: J. van Leeuwen (Ed.), Computer Science Today. XIV, 643 pages. 1995.

Vol. 1002: J.J. Kistler, Disconnected Operation in a Distributed File System. XIX, 249 pages. 1995.

Vol. 1004: J. Staples, P. Eades, N. Katoh, A. Moffat (Eds.), Algorithms and Computation. Proceedings, 1995. XV, 440 pages. 1995.

Vol. 1005: J. Estublier (Ed.), Software Configuration Management. Proceedings, 1995. IX, 311 pages. 1995.

Vol. 1006: S. Bhalla (Ed.), Information Systems and Data Management. Proceedings, 1995. IX, 321 pages. 1995.

Vol. 1007: A. Bosselaers, B. Preneel (Eds.), Integrity Primitives for Secure Information Systems. VII, 239 pages. 1995.

Vol. 1008: B. Preneel (Ed.), Fast Software Encryption. Proceedings, 1994. VIII, 367 pages. 1995.

Vol. 1009: M. Broy, S. Jähnichen (Eds.), KORSO: Methods, Languages, and Tools for the Construction of Correct Software. X, 449 pages. 1995. Vol.

Vol. 1010: M. Veloso, A. Aamodt (Eds.), Case-Based Reasoning Research and Development. Proceedings, 1995. X, 576 pages. 1995. (Subseries LNAI).

Vol. 1011: T. Furuhashi (Ed.), Advances in Fuzzy Logic, Neural Networks and Genetic Algorithms. Proceedings, 1994. (Subseries LNAI).

Vol. 1012: M. Bartos˘ek, J. Staudek, J. Wiedermann (Eds.), SOFSEM '95: Theory and Practice of Informatics. Proceedings, 1995. XI, 499 pages. 1995.

Vol. 1013: T.W. Ling, A.O. Mendelzon, L. Vieille (Eds.), Deductive and Object-Oriented Databases. Proceedings, 1995. XIV, 557 pages. 1995.

Vol. 1014: A.P. del Pobil, M.A. Serna, Spatial Representation and Motion Planning. XII, 242 pages. 1995.

Vol. 1015: B. Blumenthal, J. Gornostaev, C. Unger (Eds.), Human-Computer Interaction. Proceedings, 1995. VIII, 203 pages. 1995.

Vol. 1017: M. Nagl (Ed.), Graph-Theoretic Concepts in Computer Science. Proceedings, 1995. XI, 406 pages. 1995.

Vol. 1018: T.D.C. Little, R. Gusella (Eds.), Network and Operating Systems Support for Digital Audio and Video. Proceedings, 1995. XI, 357 pages. 1995.

Vol. 1019: E. Brinksma, W.R. Cleaveland, K.G. Larsen, T. Margaria, B. Steffen (Eds.), Tools and Algorithms for the Construction and Analysis of Systems. Selected Papers, 1995. VII, 291 pages. 1995.

Vol. 1020: I.D. Watson (Ed.), Progress in Case-Based Reasoning. Proceedings, 1995. VIII, 209 pages. 1995. (Subseries LNAI).

Vol. 1021: M.P. Papazoglou (Ed.), OOER '95: Object-Oriented and Entity-Relationship Modeling. Proceedings, 1995. XVII, 451 pages. 1995.

Vol. 1022: P.H. Hartel, R. Plasmeijer (Eds.), Functional Programming Languages in Education. Proceedings, 1995. X, 309 pages. 1995.

Vol. 1023: K. Kanchanasut, J.-J. Lévy (Eds.), Algorithms, Concurrency and Knowlwdge. Proceedings, 1995. X, 410 pages. 1995.

Vol. 1024: R.T. Chin, H.H.S. Ip, A.C. Naiman, T.-C. Pong (Eds.), Image Analysis Applications and Computer Graphics. Proceedings, 1995. XVI, 533 pages. 1995.

Vol. 1025: C. Boyd (Ed.), Cryptography and Coding. Proceedings, 1995. IX, 291 pages. 1995.